The Book of Carlaverock
Volume 1

·The·Book·of·Carlaverock·

R M

I·BID·YE·FAIR

·Edinburgh: MDCCCLXXIII·

The Book of Carlaverock

Memoirs of the Maxwells,
Earls of Nithsdale
Lords Maxwell & Herries
(1873)

by
William Fraser

Volume 1
Memoirs

The Grimsay Press

The Grimsay Press
an imprint of
Zeticula Ltd
The Roan
Kilkerran
KA19 8LS
Scotland.

http://www.thegrimsaypress.co.uk
admin@thegrimsaypress.co.uk

First printed for private circulation in 1873
in a limited edition of 150 copies.

This edition first published in 2013.

This edition © Zeticula 2013

ISBN 978-1-84530-140-8

The Book of Carlaverock

Memoirs of the Maxwells,
Earls of Nithsdale Lords Maxwell & Herries

By William Fraser.

Vol. I. Memoirs.

Edinburgh · MDCCCLXXIII

THE BOOK OF CARLAVEROCK.

PRIVATELY PRINTED FOR

William Lord Herries,

IN FULFILMENT OF THE WISHES

OF HIS LATE BROTHER THE HONOURABLE

Marmaduke Constable Maxwell
of
Terregles.

IMPRESSION ONE HUNDRED AND FIFTY COPIES.

N.º

CAERLAVEROCK CASTLE.

FRONT VIEW.

Contents.

ILLUSTRATIONS IN VOLUME FIRST.

PORTRAITS, LITHOGRAPHED.

ARMORIAL SEALS AND SIGNATURES, &c. *Woodcut of—*

CONTENTS OF VOLUME FIRST.

THE FOLLOWING ILLUSTRATIONS ARE LITHOGRAPHED:—

PREFACE

 QUARTER of a century has now elapsed since I was first engaged in professional investigations connected with the historical Houses of Maxwell and Herries. These inquiries related chiefly to the constitution and descent of the ancient Barony of Herries of Terregles, which was originally conferred by King James the Fourth on Herbert Herries of Terregles, and afterwards continued by Queen Mary to Sir John Maxwell of Terregles, who, as Lord Herries, appears prominent as the trusted friend and defender of his unfortunate sovereign. A long-disputed question, as to whether the heir-female or the heir-male of the Maxwell family had right to the title of Lord Herries, was definitely raised in the year 1847. In that competition it was my lot to take an active part on behalf of the heir-male; and after a protracted discussion the question was finally settled by the House of Lords in favour of the heir-female, in the year 1858, when I thought that my labours connected with the noble Houses of Maxwell and Herries had closed. Scarcely, however, had the Herries Peerage Case been finally decided, when the late Sir John Maxwell of Pollok, Baronet, desired me to undertake the task of writing the history of his family, the oldest of the numerous branches of the House of Maxwell. In the course of a few years, under the auspices of Sir John, I was enabled to complete " Memoirs of the Maxwells of Pollok."[1]

---

[1] Two large quarto volumes, fully illustrated, printed in 1863 for Sir John Maxwell of Pollok, Baronet.

VOL. I.   *b*

In concluding my Preface to that work, I stated that " my long labours in various forms on the history of the distinguished House of Maxwell are now terminated." These expressions were used at the time quite sincerely, as I really believed that I had done all for the Maxwell family that I should ever be required to do. But it has turned out otherwise. Soon after the issue of the Pollok Book I was asked on behalf of the present Lord Herries, and his brother, the late Honourable Marmaduke Constable Maxwell of Terregles, to edit the printing of inventories of their muniments, preserved at Terregles. In compliance with this request, I completed, in the year 1865, "Inventories of the Muniments of the Families of Maxwell, Herries, and Nithsdale, in the Charter-Room at Terregles."[1] Before that volume was completed, the late Mr. Marmaduke Maxwell of Terregles arranged that I should undertake a history of the families of Maxwell and Herries, and also edit the printing of their charters and correspondence. The result of other eight years' labour upon a subject which had previously so long engaged my attention now appears in the present work, under the general title of " The BOOK OF CARLAVEROCK ; " a title sufficiently appropriate for a Record of the House of Maxwell, as the castle of that name, so celebrated in history for its memorable sieges, is now the oldest inheritance of the Family.

This work consists of two volumes. The first embraces Memoirs of the various representatives of the House of Maxwell, from Undwin and Maccus, 1070-1150, the earliest of the family whose names appear in any record down to the present time, though after the biographies of William, fifth Earl of Nithsdale, who joined in the insurrection of 1715, and of his intrepid Countess, who effected his escape from the Tower of London, the account of their descendants is brief. The representatives of the House of Maxwell having been frequently employed in State affairs, their lives are, for the most part, of

[1] One volume quarto, pp. 360, and Preface, pp. viii., of which the impression was limited to twenty copies. From the valuable nature of that work, the very limited impression is now regretted.

great historical interest. The first of the family raised to the rank of nobility was Sir Herbert Maxwell of Carlaverock, who was created Lord Maxwell about the year 1440. His descendant, John, eighth Lord Maxwell, was created Earl of Morton soon after the forfeiture of the famous Regent, Douglas Earl of Morton. John Maxwell Earl of Morton appears conspicuous in Border history; and he lost his life, while yet a young man, in one of the Border battles. After the restoration of the Morton title to the Douglas family, the title of Earl of Nithsdale was conferred, in 1620, on Robert, the tenth Lord Maxwell.

The Second Volume is composed of letters,—royal, family and domestic, —and of ancient charters. The letters and the memoirs reflect light on each other, and impart, the one to the other, additional interest. Charters are important contemporary authorities in archæological research, which often confirm or correct statements resting on less certain authority, and restore interesting facts in family history which had fallen into oblivion.[1] Among the charters and other writs are included a considerable number of bonds of manrent, which were granted by the principal Border families to the Lords Maxwell, chiefly to Robert, the fifth Lord. These singular bonds, so characteristic of former times, not only illustrate the history of the families by whom and to whom they were granted, but they also throw much light on the manners and customs of Scotland at periods in which they were so different from those of the present day. The bonds of manrent granted to the Family of Maxwell are believed to be more numerous than those obtained by any other Border family, not excepting even the great House of Douglas. Many important Maxwell documents have been destroyed amidst the ravages of the Border raids, for-

[1] In a letter from Mr. William Maxwell, advocate, of Springkell, dated 10th September 1668, and addressed to John, third Earl of Nithsdale, the writer refers to the evidents to be produced and recorded in " your lordships register, which I have at Edinburgh to delyver to your lordship, and coast me near 40 pound, the tyme of your Cousein the last Earle, wherein are registrat all the charters his lordship past be my advyce, bot he did enter many more without my knowledge."—[Original Letter.] The Register of Charters here referred to is not now known to exist.

merly so fierce and prevalent.[1] But the collection still preserved is both extensive and interesting. It contains many writs referring to the historical position of the Maxwell family, as proprietors of extensive territories, as wardens of the Marches, and as keepers of the principal strongholds on the Borders. One of these strongholds was the Castle of Carlaverock, which endured the memorable siege by King Edward the First, as early as the year 1300, and was also invested by the Covenanters in the seventeenth century. The Castles of Lochmaben, Dumfries, and Threave, all notable in Border history, were also at various times in the hands of the Lords of Maxwell.

The Abstracts of the Memoirs in the First Volume, and of the Letters and Charters in the Second Volume, with a copious General Index to both volumes, will facilitate reference to the several sections of this voluminous work.

During the progress of the work through the press, a lamentable event occurred in the unexpected death of its munificent projector, the Honourable Marmaduke Constable Maxwell. From the great interest which he took in its progress, it would be ungrateful not to pay a tribute to his worth. It would afford me a melancholy pleasure to be able to perform this duty in a fitting manner. But my offering, however unworthy, may be accepted, not as what can adorn the tomb of the departed, but as a small token of respect for his memory.

Mr. Marmaduke Maxwell was the second son of Marmaduke Constable Maxwell of Nithsdale and Everingham Park, in the county of York. He was born at Everingham, on the 1st of January 1806. His father, writing from Everingham on that date, says, " It is with much satisfaction I inform you that this morning my dear wife presented me, as a New Year's gift, another son, who both continue to do well." [2]

---

[1] When the Castle of Carlaverock was besieged in 1640, it contained, as appears from the Inventory printed in Volume Second, No. 123, " Pictures " of Robert, first Earl of Nithsdale, and Elizabeth Beaumont, his Countess. But no trace of these " Pictures " has since been found.

[2] Original Letter at Carruchan.

I am Very sincerely Yours

Thos C Maxwell

As shewn in the notice of his father, that gentleman, by a deed of entail, executed in 1814, divided his estates in Scotland into two portions, the one including Carlaverock, or the Nithsdale estates, which he entailed on his eldest son, William, now Lord Herries ; and the other Terregles, or the Herries estates, which he entailed on his second son, Marmaduke.

When the succession to the Terregles estates opened to Mr. Marmaduke Maxwell, by the death of his father in the year 1819, he was in his thirteenth year. He was educated at Stonyhurst College, Lancashire, and during his minority the management of the estates was intrusted to Mr. Middleton of Stockeld Park, Yorkshire, his father's nephew, till Mr. Maxwell attained his majority, in the year 1827, when he entered upon the superintendence of them himself.

On the 1st of January that year, the birthday and majority of Mr. Marmaduke Maxwell were celebrated with the rejoicings usual on such occasions, by his tenantry at Terregles, Kirkgunzeon, and Lochrutton.[1]

In personal appearance Mr. Marmaduke Maxwell answered the description given of his grandfather when he came from Everingham to Terregles to woo the little heiress of Nithsdale—he was very tall and of great size.

For upwards of half a century, from 1819 to 1872, he possessed the ancient estates of the Lords Herries, which comprehended the baronies of Terregles, Kirkgunzeon, and Urr, in the stewartry of Kirkcudbright. In so far as related to territory, he thus occupied the position of the ancient Lords of Herries. He was a constant resident on his property ; and as his brother, Lord Herries, resided on his estate of Everingham, with the exception of occasional visits to his brother at Terregles, chiefly in the autumn, Mr. Marmaduke Maxwell might also be said, as regarded personal residence, to have been the representative of the family of Nithsdale.

His mansion-house of Terregles, situated in the stewartry of Kirkcud-

---

[1] A full account of these rejoicings was given in the Dumfries and Galloway Courier of 9th January 1827.

bright, is within a few miles of the town of Dumfries. As a large landed proprietor, and one of the representatives of an ancient race, he was placed in a prominent position for more than half a century. For such a position he was admirably qualified by his inherent qualities, as was testified by the whole course of his life. In the capacity of landlord he was just and liberal towards his tenants, by whom he was much esteemed; and in that of a country gentleman, while never courting prominence, he yet came forward on all important occasions, and performed with ability his full proportion of the general business of the county. He personally superintended his own estates, and made extensive improvements. His success as an agricultural improver is manifest in many portions of his property, where large tracts of barren land have been converted into fruitful fields. His farm-buildings were also carefully repaired or rebuilt, and many of the new steadings were designed by himself.

In the year 1841, Mr. Maxwell publicly proposed the late Mr. Murray of Broughton as the Liberal candidate for the representation of the stewartry of Kirkcudbright in Parliament. Mr. Murray was elected; and on his death, in the year 1845, Mr. Maxwell himself was brought forward by the leaders of the Whig party as a fit and proper person to succeed Mr. Murray as representative in the stewartry. His address to the electors is here subjoined, as indicating his political opinions :—

To THE FREE AND INDEPENDENT ELECTORS OF THE STEWARTRY OF KIRKCUDBRIGHT.

GENTLEMEN,—The much to be lamented death of Mr. Murray having occasioned a vacancy in the representation of the Stewartry of Kirkcudbright, I, at the request of a numerous body of Electors, now presume to offer myself as a Candidate for the high and distinguished honour of representing you in the House of Commons.

As my political opinions, in most particulars, coincided with those held by your late Representative, I cheerfully proposed him at the last Election as a fit person to represent your interests in Parliament. Should you, Gentlemen, do me the honour to place me in the proud position of your Representative, I shall, on every occasion, advocate and support Civil and Religious Liberty, without regard to country or sect. I shall endeavour to promote all

TERREGLES HOUSE,

THE RESIDENCE OF THE LATE HONOURABLE MARMADUKE CONSTABLE MAXWELL.

THE GARDENS, TERREGLES.

such ameliorations in our laws and institutions as may be considered advantageous for the public, without, however, consenting to such alterations as have merely change to recommend them. I am a firm advocate for the strictest economy in every department of the State, and for the reduction of Taxation, in so far as is consistent with the maintenance of public credit.

Being well aware of the many advantages of Free Trade, I shall willingly advocate the removal of all Duties vexatious to Commerce, in so far as it can be done with safety and justice to the general interests of the community ; but, in the present circumstances of the country, I am opposed to the total and immediate abolition of the Protective Duty on corn.

As regards Ireland, I consider that the repeal of the Union would be attended with the most fatal consequences to the Empire at large, and shall therefore, on all occasions, strenuously oppose any proposal that may be advanced for that purpose. I fervently trust that, by just, mild, and conciliatory measures, the evils which at present afflict that distracted and unfortunate country may be removed, and shall in consequence give my willing support to any measures that may tend to this desirable object ; and, whilst claiming that liberty of conscience for myself in matters of religion, which I readily concede to all others, I shall deem it my duty decidedly to oppose any State Endowment for the Roman Catholic Church.

Electors of the Stewartry, I have now shortly laid before you the principles on which I solicit your support, and trust that they are such as may meet with your approval, and entitle me to the high and distinguished honour of representing you in the House of Commons.

Should you, Gentlemen, so far honour me as to return me to Parliament, I shall devote my time to your service, and earnestly endeavour to promote your interests, and those of the country.

In hopes of meriting your confidence, permit me to trust, however unworthy you may consider the individual who now addresses you, that you will vindicate the independence of the Stewartry, and favour me with your support.—I am, Gentlemen, your most obedient humble servant,   MARMADUKE CONSTABLE MAXWELL.

Terregles, July 31st, 1845.[1]

Opposition having been offered to Mr. Maxwell, on the ground of his religion, he retired in favour of Mr. Thomas Maitland, afterwards Lord Dundrennan. The following is his letter to the Electors of the Stewartry of Kirkcudbright, by which he withdrew from the Parliamentary contest :—

To the Electors of the Stewartry of Kirkcudbright.

Terregles, 11th August 1845.

GENTLEMEN,—I have thought it right to retire from any contest for the honour of representing the Stewartry in Parliament ; and the result of which, I grieve to find, would, in my case, turn far more upon *religious* than *political* feelings. Could I have anticipated this, nothing would have induced me to come forward at the risk of creating any division in the

[1] Dumfries and Galloway Courier of 9th August 1845.

Liberal party, which, in so far as it exists at this moment, will, I trust, be at once healed by my retirement. I owe you much gratitude for the kindness and urbanity with which I have been everywhere received, even by those who conscientiously consider my religion to be an objection to me as a Candidate.

With the most anxious wishes for the success of the Liberal party, in the person of another candidate, I beg to subscribe myself, your very obedient servant,

MARMADUKE C. MAXWELL.[1]

Mr. Maitland was successful in the contest with Colonel M'Dowall of Logan.

Mr. Maxwell was a consistent member of the Catholic Church. In a letter, dated 25th December 1871, he wrote,—" I have always been proud to think that no head of the Maxwell family ever at any period gave up his religion."[2] But for the circumstance of his religion being different from that of the majority of the constituents, he would probably have become the representative in Parliament of either of the two counties with which he was closely connected.

In his mansion of Terregles, Mr. Maxwell, with his amiable and accomplished lady, as a fitting helpmate, dispensed a generous hospitality, keeping up even in the " spare days " enjoined by his Church, something like the old baronial style. He also exercised a discriminating charity, and treated his dependants with uniform kindness and consideration.

Mr. Maxwell was a liberal supporter of St. Andrew's Catholic congregation at Dumfries. For many years it chiefly depended upon him. Only recently, at great expense, he extended and beautified the church. The design, which was by Mr. Goldie, architect in London, provided a new and enlarged chancel, beginning where the old one ended, and a vault for the interment of the Terregles family. The mason work of this addition is of the most substantial description, and the interior is remarkable for its massive magnificence. It was unfinished at the time of Mr. Maxwell's death. It has since been completed by Lord Herries, his executor, and the chapel was

[1] Dumfries and Galloway Courier of 11th August 1845.   [2] Letter to Mr. Fraser.

formally re-opened on Thursday, the 24th of October 1872, having been consecrated by Bishop Strain on the preceding day. Monsignore Capel preached
on the occasion, and feelingly alluded to the hand and the heart that gave
that spot to the Lord, and made it worthy of Him.

The late Charles, eighth Earl of Traquair, who died in the year 1861, and
Mr. Marmaduke Maxwell, were both descended from Maxwell ancestors. The
Earl of Traquair having no children, and no brothers, made a disposition in
favour of his only sister, Lady Louisa Stuart, of the Traquair estates, to trustees, to be held for her benefit during her lifetime ; and on her death, they
were to be entailed on Mr. Marmaduke Maxwell, whom failing, on his brother
Mr. Henry Maxwell, who is now the heir-apparent of the Traquair estates. At
the time of the death of the late Earl of Traquair, his sister had reached the
advanced age of eighty-five years, and Mr. Maxwell was aged fifty-five. It
might have been anticipated that Mr. Maxwell, from his strength and difference
in years, would be the survivor, yet the elder and weaker of the two has
survived the younger and stronger, her faculties remaining wonderfully entire
in her ninety-sixth year. For his cousin Lady Louisa, Mr. Maxwell ever
entertained an affectionate regard. In July 1867, he wrote that she was then
on a visit to him at Terregles, that she was in her ninety-second year, and
as well as possible.[1]

In the present work Mr. Maxwell took much interest. The letters which
form the second volume were chiefly selected by himself, and transcribed
under his superintendence, with the intention of being printed and edited by
himself in one volume. The notes of his proposed preface to that contemplated
work have been preserved, and will best explain his own views :

Family history and domestic details are often of a character so uninteresting to the
general reader, that it is not without a certain degree of diffidence and reluctance that I venture to lay the following pages before him. Lest my motives for doing so may be miscon-

[1] Letter to Mr. Fraser.

strued, it will be necessary to make a few introductory remarks, and thus explain my reasons and the object I had in view.

A spirit of inquiry into the records of the past has been strongly manifested of late years by many amongst the old families of the kingdom ; charter-chests that had been for generations a prey to dust, damp, and decay, unopened and uncared for, have been searched and examined, and thus many curious and historical documents, valuable and interesting letters, closely connected with the history of families as well as of the country, have been brought to light.   Many of these have, either by the liberality of individuals, or the praiseworthy exertions of different learned and antiquarian societies and clubs, been printed, and thus saved from destruction, and preserved for the study and use of the future historian.   The good example of those alluded to above is one that no one can be found fault with for imitating ; and though an inexperienced person may, perhaps, in compiling and publishing a series of letters, insert many that may in his eyes be valuable and interesting when viewed from a family point of view, may incur censure from many who differ from him in this estimate of their worth.   Still he may console himself with the thought, that trifling details of domestic life, the mode and style of living, the means and method of travelling, cost of labour, materials, or food, etc., all tend to illustrate the history of a country, and if not read with or considered of much interest now, may a century or two hence be read by posterity, with the same relish as we read now of the domestic details of the times of the Edwards and Henrys.

In 1855 the late Sir Henry Bedingfield, on examining the papers left by his mother, the lately deceased Dowager Lady Bedingfield, found amongst them the original letter of Winifred Countess of Nithsdale to her sister, the Lady Lucy Herbert, superioress of the English convent at Bruges, in which she describes the escape, by her means, of her husband, the Earl of Nithsdale, from the Tower of London, on the eve of the day appointed for his execution. This interesting letter is entirely in the handwriting of Lady Nithsdale, and quite perfect, with the exception of the signature, which has been neatly cut off.   On comparing, however, the writing, as well as the paper on which it is written, with other original letters recently discovered of hers at Traquair and Terregles, any doubt that might have been raised as to the authenticity of the letter is placed beyond question.   On the back of the letter the late Dowager[1] Lady Bedingfield has written,—" This letter or account was addressed to Lady Nithsdale's sister, Lady Lucy Herbert, superioress of the English nuns at Bruges, and given to me by those ladies, 1820." (Signed)   " C. B."

The late Sir Henry Bedingfield presented the letter to the Honourable Mrs. Charles Clifford, who gave it to her brother, William Constable Maxwell of Nithsdale, now Lord Herries, in whose possession it now is.

This, what may be called, most valuable and interesting letter has often been printed, but evidently only from a copy, not very accurately, taken at some time or other from the original, which, though supposed to have been lost, its recent recovery now enables me to give the letter taken word for word from the original document.

Of the antiquity and descent of the families of Maxwell Earls of Nithsdale, and Stuart

---

[1] Sir Richard Bedingfield married, June 1795, Charlotte Georgiana, daughter of Sir William Jerningham, Baronet, and sister of George, late Lord Stafford of Cossey, Norfolk. She died 1854.

Earls of Traquair, it is far beyond the purpose of this volume to treat. To trace them from the earliest times of Scottish history, to show their rise to rank, wealth, influence, and importance, their services to their King and country, this is not the object of these pages.

Should some future antiquarian or lover of family history undertake the task, this volume may then be of service in shewing the later times of these families, when having sacrificed almost everything but their loyalty and their faith, in their devotedness to their monarch, they were at the period immediately preceding the revolution of 1688 in an all but destitute condition, and reduced to the state of suppliants to the Crown for means to support and educate their families. From the intimate friendship and very near relationship existing between the families of Nithsdale and Traquair at the close of the seventeenth century, it would be difficult to enter upon the family details of the one without embracing more or less those of the other. The two families were second to none in Scotland, in their steadfast adherence to the cause of their legitimate kings, and in their sufferings for their loyalty, and superior nearly to all, in their firm and undeviating attachment to the Catholic religion, the faith of their ancestors.

Before the printing of the volume of Correspondence commenced, Mr. Maxwell purposed to include, with the letters, the ancient charters of the families of Maxwell and Herries; and instead of trusting to " some future antiquarian or lover of family history," as he originally intended, he also resolved on having an exhaustive history of these two distinguished Houses. This arduous task he was pleased to intrust to me; and as I then was occupied with several similar works, I undertook it, not without diffidence, although I knew that I could rely on the cordial assistance of Mr. Maxwell himself, and of many other friends. My satisfaction at the completion of this Work would have been greater had Mr. Maxwell survived to see it, as a whole, after the great interest which he took in its progress.

In the Memoirs of the Nithsdale family, as contained in this First Volume, Mr. Maxwell took a lively interest. The proof-sheets were submitted to him as the work proceeded, and he uniformly approved of them, making, though in rare instances, such suggestions as occurred to him from their perusal.

The Second Volume, so far as it contains the Correspondence, was completed long before the death of Mr. Maxwell.

His correspondence with myself in reference to both volumes, evinces the hold which the subject had taken of his mind, and the pleasure which he took in searching out biographical materials. In a letter, dated 26th May, he says, "In looking over old factory accounts, etc., in my Charter-room yesterday, I found the enclosed documents, viz., Lord Nithsdale's bond to C. Evans, and C. Evans's assignation to Mrs. Lindsay, maid to Lady Bellew. I think these documents most interesting, and do think they should be added, by way of Appendix, to the volume of Letters. They shew who Mrs. Evans was, evince the sense Lord and Lady Nithsdale had of her devotedness to them, and her gratitude and attachment to the family. Mrs. Evans seems to have been as heroic and firm a character as Lady Nithsdale herself, and the signature, a clear and beautiful one, the best I have seen of hers." In another letter, dated 1st June 1868, he writes : "Since I wrote last, I have been carrying on my searches amongst the factory accounts, and found more interesting documents, which I now send you. There are many orders and receipts from Rome, signed *William Brown*,—surely this signature must have been an assumed one by Lord Nithsdale.[1] . . . I believe the letter signed Alexander Smith is from the Reverend A. Smith, who was made Vicar Apostolic of the Lowland district of Scotland in 1766."

The courtesy and consideration which uniformly characterized Mr. Maxwell's intercourse with me, whether in personal interviews in Edinburgh or at Terregles, or by epistolary correspondence, during the years in which this work and the printed Inventories of the Maxwell and Herries Muniments were in hand, I cannot here omit gratefully to acknowledge. Always friendly and encouraging, his letters, even when of a business description, almost invariably, from the natural affability and frankness of his character, close with some friendly allusion to the family at Terregles, or to the public events of the day.

When, in the year 1865, he resolved to have a Family Book arranged,

[1] In this supposition Mr. Maxwell is quite correct.

to include full Memoirs of the Lords Maxwell and Herries and Earls of Nithsdale, as well as their ancient charters and correspondence, he wrote to me on the 29th of April that he "should wish it to be got up and executed in the best style." Part of that and the following year was occupied in arranging and transcribing the Maxwell and Herries Muniments for the press. No man took more interest in this work than the late Mr. Francis Maxwell of Breoch, who was factor on the Nithsdale and Terregles estates; but while it was in progress, he was removed from the scene of his earthly labours, in the year 1867. Mr. Marmaduke Maxwell intimated his death to me with much feeling: "It is with much pain I have to inform you of the death of poor Breoch, this morning, about eight o'clock. I have lost in him a valuable friend and factor, and he will be much regretted by his numerous acquaintances." He also alluded to the loss which would be sustained in the compilation of the Family History, with the arrangement of which Mr. Maxwell of Breoch was so familiar.

By the beginning of the year 1868 considerable progress had been made in printing the Correspondence, Mr. Maxwell, in a letter of date 21st January, writes, "I am glad you seem to be getting on so prosperously. The letters will make an interesting volume."

It was not till the commencement of the year 1871 that the History of the Maxwell Family, contained in the First Volume, was first sent to press. In March of that year, Mr. Maxwell, having examined several sheets of the early history, wrote, "I think that you are making out the early history of the Maxwells very satisfactorily and clearly."

In April he remarked in reference to several of the succeeding proof-sheets, "Aymer Maxwell must have given you considerable trouble. I think, however, you have worked him out very satisfactorily."

The last letter received by me from Mr. Maxwell referred to the memoir

of John, eighth Lord Maxwell, who was beheaded in 1613, for the slaughter
of the Laird of Johnston. In this brief notice of Mr. Maxwell, I have a
melancholy satisfaction in quoting that letter :—

Crawley's Hotel, Albemarle Street, 23d April 1872.

MY DEAR SIR,—The Memoir of John Lord Maxwell was forwarded to me here. It is
interesting. . . . He certainly had plenty of courage and pluck. I was not aware before
that he was buried at Newbattle. The volume will be of large dimensions, as there is much
to be written yet.

My brother, Lord Herries, is employing men to clear out the moat at Carlaverock. So
far nothing of consequence has been found, except a lot of cannon balls, one of iron, 3 lbs.
weight, and 21 inches in girth. I trust some curiosities will be found. I have for some time
back been more or less laid up with pain and weakness in my knee, which I think is rheuma-
tism ; I hope not gout. We are thinking of going, in two or three weeks' time, to the
Continent for a short time. If so, I am not likely to be at Terregles till July. Town is
beginning to fill fast now, but at present there is not much going on in the gay world.—
Believe me, very truly yours,   MAR. C. MAXWELL.

William Fraser, Esq.

The expectation of Mr. Maxwell's returning with invigorated health to
Terregles was not to be realized. In the very month to which he looked forward for returning home, after he had commenced his homeward journey, and
in sight of the very channel which he longed so much to cross, he was seized
with a fatal malady—paralysis of the spine,—and within eight hours after
the attack he calmly departed this life at Calais, on 16th July 1872, at the
age of sixty-six. He was accompanied by the Honourable Mrs. Maxwell and
his two nieces. He had left Hamburg apparently in good health, but was
taken ill at Mayence, his anxiety to reach home having caused him to overtask
his strength, and continue his journey when quite unfit to travel.

His remains were brought from Calais to Dumfries, where they arrived
on Friday, 19th July, and they were immediately removed to Terregles House,
in order to their interment in the burial vault, which he had formed for the
Terregles family, in St. Andrew's Catholic Church, Dumfries, which he was
himself the first to occupy before the building was completed.

The funeral was at ten o'clock on Monday morning, 22d July, and it was attended by a large number of gentlemen of Dumfriesshire and the stewartry of Kirkcudbright, the tenantry of Terregles estate, and others from Dumfries and the surrounding district. The procession was headed by a carriage drawn by two horses, in which were the Right Rev. Bishop Strain, and other clergymen who had conducted a short service at Terregles House. Next came the hearse, drawn by four bay horses, followed by four mourning coaches containing the chief mourners, viz., the Right Honourable Lord Herries and his two sons, Marmaduke Master of Herries, and the Honourable William Maxwell, the Honourable Henry Maxwell, brother of the deceased, and his son, Arthur Maxwell, Mr. William Langdale, Mr. Henry Clifford, and Mr. Maxwell of Breoch. Next to these appeared the family omnibus, drawn by two horses, containing servants, and others employed on the Terregles estate. Then followed a number of gentlemen of the county in their carriages, and the tenantry on the Terregles and Kirkgunzeon estates. Several of the principal shops in the town of Dumfries were closed, and the bells of the middle steeple tolled as the procession moved slowly along in the presence of a large concourse of spectators.

The coffin having been borne into the church, mass was celebrated, after which the Rev. Father Gallway delivered the funeral oration.

" It was," he said, " a mournful arrangement of God's providence that on this day, when the congregation of St. Andrew's came back for the first time to take possession of their church, they had in their midst the coffin of him whose last effort it was to render this church a more befitting home for our Lord Jesus Christ and His poor. He was quite sure they would not expect him to speak to them of the social position which Mr. Maxwell held, the extent of his domains, and the story of his ancient family. Those topics would, to them who knew him, be quite unprofitable, and to the dead, could

he now hear the words spoken, utterly distasteful. But a very short while
had elapsed, according to our way of thinking, since the spirit of their friend
was called out of his body. Yet to him was that time short? During that
short interval there had been time enough, and more than enough, to revolu-
tionize all his ideas in regard to this world. What cared he now for what was
called the business, the politics, the important matters of this poor world?
The one thing that made him happy now, the one thought that could give
real consolation to those that stood around his grave, was this, that he was
wise enough during the few years that he passed on earth, to foresee the everlasting life that was coming hereafter. He spoke of the 'few years that he
had passed on this earth.' Some might remind him that their friend was
already stricken with years. He was aware that, according to our way of
reckoning, many long years had gone by since the body now lying there was
first brought in front of the altar to be washed in the waters of baptism, and
that many things had happened that we called important. But he would ask
the dead what the longest life on earth now seemed to them? It was but as
the dream of one night—the passage of the swiftest arrow that pierced the
air, and left no trace of its flight—the course of a ship that sailed across the
waters, and left no mark behind it. Ah! when we went into eternity, then we
saw that our real life was there; and melancholy beyond conception was the
deathbed of that man who, from one cause or another, had not been wise
enough while upon the earth to foresee the long hereafter; and sad must be
the hearts of survivors who loved him if, bewitched and fooled with the
vanities around him here, he had neglected to lay up a store for the everlasting life that was to be spent in one or other of the great homes of eternity."

The oration being concluded, the coffin was moved out of the chapel and
carried to the outside, where the vault of the Terregles family is situated,
immediately beneath the apse, where the high altar stands. The choir, the

priests, and the mourners went with the coffin into the vault, which contains compartments for twenty-four bodies. An altar which is erected there was draped with black, and had candles burning. Bishop Strain read the church service, and the body was consigned to its resting-place in the second compartment in the upper row to the left of the altar.

Mr. Maxwell married, in the year 1836, Mary, only daughter of the Reverend Anthony Marsden of Hornby Castle, Lancashire, a most amiable helpmate for the Lord of the Manor of Terregles. Mrs. Maxwell survives her husband. As they had no children, the Terregles estates, as entailed by Mr. Maxwell's father, devolved upon the nephew, Frederick, eldest son of his late brother, Peter Constable Maxwell, Esquire, who is now Frederick Constable Maxwell of Terregles, Esquire.

Mr. Maxwell conveyed his heritable estates, so far as unentailed, including Kinharvey, in the parish of New-Abbey, and also his moveable property, to his brother, Lord Herries, who has undertaken the completion of this work, in fulfilment of the wishes of his late brother.

Although this work does not profess to be a history of the Borders, it probably contains more history, or more materials for a history of these interesting territories, than any other work of recent times. In addition to the records of the Houses of Maxwell and Herries, the private records of many other Border houses, and the National Records, both of Scotland and England, have been examined for information bearing on the subject. The State Paper Office, London, and particularly the Records of the Privy Council of Scotland, have yielded much important matter on the Borders, as may be seen from the memoirs of John Lord Herries and his nephew, John Earl of Morton, Lord Maxwell, both of whom held the office of Warden of the West Marches.

In case of omitting names, I am almost afraid to enumerate the noblemen and gentlemen who have generously afforded me the freest access to their Charter Muniments in connexion with this work. His Grace the Duke of Buccleuch and Queensberry, K.G., has, on this as on many other occasions, allowed me to use his great collections, which bear so directly on the history of the Borders, with which both sides of his House, the Scott and Douglas, have been prominently identified.

By favour of his Grace the Duke of Argyll, K.T., I have been enabled to quote, in the memoirs of John Lord Herries, the commission from Queen Mary, which invested the Duke's ancestor, Archibald, fifth Earl of Argyll, with the office of Lieutenant-General of all her forces, on the morning of the day of the fatal field of Langside, where Lord Herries and other Maxwells supported the cause of the Queen, and from which, after her defeat, they escorted her to Terregles.[1]

The Marquis of Tweeddale and the Earl of Airlie have been pleased to allow me to print two charters of William the Lion, one at Yester and the other at Cortachy, both bearing on the early history of the Maxwells and their possessions. To Lord Airlie I am also indebted for permission to make special search at Cortachy for the correspondence between his ancestor, Lord Ogilvy, and the first Earl of Nithsdale regarding the expedition to Denmark, in the reign of King Charles the First.

To the ready access afforded me by Mr. Hope Johnstone of Annandale to his charter muniments at Raehills, I owe much valuable information

---

[1] It is much to be regretted that the correspondence of Queen Mary with John Lord Herries has not been preserved. In addition to the articles mentioned in the Memoir of John Lord Herries, p. 523, *infra*, as having belonged to Queen Mary, and now in the possession of the present Lord Herries, there is also in his Lordship's possession a crucifix of gold which belonged to the Queen. One of the notices of this crucifix is contained in a letter from John Hebrune to William Maxwell, son of the Earl of Nithsdale, dated 26th January 1669, in which it is described as " a littill crucifix of gold, which was Queene Mareys."—[Original Letter.] This crucifix is about three inches in length.

contained in the memoir of those members of the Maxwell family who were in deadly feud with members of his own clan. These feuds raged so long and so fiercely that at one time they seemed interminable. But many incidents have since shewn that the two families of Maxwell and Johnston have happily now become as fast friends as they were previously furious foes. Many years ago, the late Mr. Alexander Maxwell of the Grove was on a visit at Raehills to his friend, the present Mr. Hope Johnstone. The late Reverend Dr. John Jameson, author of the Dictionary of the Scottish Language, was then on a similar visit at Raehills. When introduced to Mr. Maxwell by Mr. Hope Johnstone, the learned doctor knowing well from history the old feud, could not help expressing his surprise at meeting a Maxwell as an honoured guest of a Johnston. As I explained to Mr. Maxwell, when he mentioned to me the circumstance, he might have increased the surprise of the Doctor by informing him that he, Mr. Maxwell, comprehended in his own person the two apparently antagonistic natures of Maxwell and Johnston, for although bearing the name of Maxwell, he was in the male descent a Johnston. His father, Mr. Wellwood Johnston, of the family of Johnston of Clauchrie, a cadet of Johnston of that Ilk, changed the surname of Johnston to that of Maxwell on receiving from his maternal uncle, James Maxwell, the estate of Barncleuch. It is gratifying to record these tokens of amity and friendship now existing between two families who were formerly at deadly feud.

I have also been favoured in the most liberal manner by Mr. Wellwood Herries Maxwell of Munches and Terraughty, M.P., with access to his charter repositories. Being the nephew of Mr. Alexander Maxwell above mentioned, he is another marked instance of the union of the Maxwell and Johnston Houses in one and the same person. His estates of Munches, Terraughty, and Barncleuch have long been possessed by the Maxwells, and have descended to him, although a Johnston, through several alliances. The late Mr. John Herries Maxwell of Munches, father of the present proprietor, made extensive investigations into the history and descent of many of the families of Maxwell. From his great care, accuracy, and sound judgment, his notes are very valuable, and from them I have derived much assistance.

After this work was nearly completed, several papers were received from Mr. Maxwell of Munches, three of which may here be noted as of general interest.

The first, which is a letter of invitation by a master to the marriage of his servant, is in these terms :—

SIR,—The favour of your Presence to celebrate the nuptials of David Marshall, my servant, on Tuesday next, the 10th instant, at twelve o'clock forenoon, at the Head of Burnet's Closs, immediately above Bell's Wynd, where the Bridegroom will attend and conduct you to the Place. And altho' this is not a Peny Wedding, yet you are intreated not to neglect to have an Half-Dollar about you (or if your affairs will not allow of your Presence, to send it by the Bearer), for defraying the necessary charges, etc. In so doing you will very much oblige, —Sir, Your most humble Servant,

JA. WATSON.

Edinburgh, March 7, 1702.

The original letter is addressed to the Laird of Elshiesheills, who was a Johnston. It is printed in italics, with an ornamental woodcut at the commencement ; and the cost of printing these letters of invitation would probably form part of the necessary charges upon the half-dollars, which were more earnestly entreated than the personal presence of the contributors themselves.

The second paper referred to is " Proof of the Genealogy of the Family of Maxwells of Barncleugh, taken by John Maxwell of Terraughtie, at the request of Major Bourk, to ascertain that he was of noble descent; copied from an original copy very much defaced, 18th January 1816." The copy made at that date is holograph of the late John Herries Maxwell of Munches.

The proofs of the descent of the Maxwells of Barncleuch were taken in the year 1764, in presence of Ebenezer Hepburn, Provost and Chief Magistrate of the town of Dumfries.

Mr. John Mackenzie, notary public and conjunct town-clerk of the burgh of Dumfries, attested the authenticity of the subscription of the witnesses, and also that the office of Provost of the royal burgh of Dumfries, "in point of rank, power, and dignity, may be compared to the office of Lord Mayor of London." Mr. Mackenzie probably thought that it would be a foolish modesty to hesitate in placing the Provost of Dumfries on a footing of equality with the Lord Mayor of London.

The third paper referred to is a Pedigree of the Maxwells of Breconside, written by the late John Herries Maxwell in the year 1826. In the Pedigree John Maxwell, the second laird of Breconside, is said to have been brother-uterine to the first and second Lords Kenmure, who were sons of Sir Robert Gordon of Lochinvar. John Maxwell died unmarried at Buittle, in the beginning of the year 1719. He was buried in the kirk of Buittle, but was afterwards raised by the Whigs of Urr, who carried the corpse to a knoll in a moss in the lands of Meikleknox, where they set the coffin on one end, and let it fall to the ground, with all its weight. From that place he was carried by his friends to the church of Terregles, and buried there.

Sir William Stirling Maxwell of Keir and Pollok, Baronet, a recent addition to the ranks of the Maxwells, of whom they may well be proud, has allowed me the readiest use of his Maxwell Muniments, so rich in charters and correspondence bearing directly on the Maxwell family. To his advice I have been indebted for several valuable suggestions, in connexion with the illustrations.

Sir William Maxwell of Monreith, Baronet, not only allowed me to use his charter muniments, but also furnished an account of his own House of

Monreith, specially written by himself for this work. I much regret that want of space has prevented me from including a document so interesting, and has admitted a place only for the Pedigree, which gives a succinct deduction of the line of Tinwald and Monreith from Herbert the first Lord Maxwell. In the Monreith line there have been members of great distinction in the army and navy. Mr. Herbert Eustace Maxwell, younger of Monreith, has kindly given me several beautiful designs connected with the heraldry of the Maxwells, with which, as well as with the rules of the "Noble Science of Heraldry" in general, he is intimately acquainted.

Mr. and Mrs. Maxwell Witham of Kirkconnell have also furnished me with several valuable charters, and documents bearing upon their ancient branch of the House of Maxwell, which has also produced many learned members, including James Maxwell, author of the Account of the Insurrection in Scotland in 1745. The large armorial seal of John Earl of Morton, Lord Maxwell, on page 299 of his Memoir, is engraved from the original at Kirkconnell. It is a beautiful specimen of seal engraving of the sixteenth century.

Mrs. Maxwell of Carruchan has also kindly placed at my disposal the Carruchan papers; and to many of these I have referred in the course of the Memoirs. One of them, which I have not elsewhere mentioned, refers to the destruction of the ruins of the College of Lincluden, which is part of the Terregles estate. In a memorandum, dated at Terregles 5th May 1801, it is said that the neighbouring heritors at the College, and others, are carrying away the stones from that building, and are pulling down the walls. To prevent this destruction from going on, it is proposed to build walls along the east side of the road leading to Clouden Water, adjacent to the College.[1]

[1] Original Memorandum at Carruchan. Lincluden College was within the regality of Robert Earl of Nithsdale, as appears from a case before the Privy Council on 3d August 1663. The case was singular:—James Gilkers, indweller in the College of Lincluden, and Roger Safely, indweller in

In the Carruchan charter-chest are two characteristic letters from Lady Catharine Stuart, wife of William Lord Maxwell, written from Paris, in 1764, where they were then resident, to the factor at Terregles. Lady Catharine writes to the factor with great confidence on the affairs of the family. She alludes to her husband's having kept household accounts since her indisposition ; and she regrets his doing so, as, although more extravagant, she was not so easily cheated.

Mr. Maxwell of Broomholm has recently favoured me with a copy of the judicial proceedings against his ancestor, John Maxwell of Broomholm, as judge and bailie of the first Earl of Nithsdale, within the lordship of Esk-dale, for the drowning in the water of Ew, near Langholm, of two persons who had been convicted of theft. The proceedings are referred to in pp. 360-363 of Volume First. It now appears that on the 10th of June 1641, King Charles the First addressed a letter to Sir Thomas Hope, Lord Advocate, in which he alludes to the hazard in which the defender was, of being con-victed of wilful murder, by reason of the mere informality of not having stated that the thieves were caught red hand, which ought not to be " balanced with the life of ane subject executing the laws ;" and therefore he desires the Lord Advocate to desist from the further prosecution of the case.

While these and many other Maxwells have contributed materials to me so liberally, I must next acknowledge the ready assistance which I have re-ceived in moulding the numerous documents into their present permanent form.

the Knockans (now called Terregles Banks), in the regality of Terregles, belonging to John Lord Her-ries, being together, Roger Safely in " merriment " desired James Gilkers to " wish him to a wyfe : " the said James jestingly "answered that provyding he could be quatt of his wyfe he should be content, he might have her for a groat, and he having merrily declared that he was content to accept her upon the pryce, without any real intent." The Commissary-depute of Dumfries having heard of this pretended sale of a wife, obtained a conviction against the seller and purchaser for £100 and 100 merks re-spectively, and they were also ordained " to stand in the jogges " for one hour on the market day. The delinquents brought their case before the Privy Council, and they complained that the Commissary acted through deadly enmity and mere malice. The Privy Council absolved the delinquents from the sentence and fines.—[Register of Secret Council, Decreta, 3 August 1663, fol. 391.]

The late Mr. Francis Maxwell of Breoch knew more of the history of his ancestors, the Maxwell and Herries families, than any other person, either in or out of his clan. To great natural capacity, he added careful study of the history of Scotland and the Scottish families, more particularly those of the Borders. Allusion has been made already to the loss caused by his death, in the year 1867. It is gratifying to find that his mantle has descended upon his son, the present Mr. Robert Maxwell of Breoch, who now occupies a similar position to that which was held by his father. It is only justice to acknowledge that Mr. Robert Maxwell has co-operated with me in this work with an untiring assiduity beyond all praise.

While writing the Memoirs in this work, I have been often reminded of how many Maxwells, who were alive and flourishing when my connexion with them commenced, have disappeared from this living world. The latest loss, in the honourable owner of Terregles, has been specially noticed. To his lamented death may be added the deaths of the genial and very genealogical Lord Farnham, in circumstances so melancholy; the knightly Sir John of Pollok, and the amiable Lady Matilda; the chivalrous Carruchan and his learned cadet of Breoch; Wellwood and Alexander, the good men of the Grove; young Wellwood of Glenlee, and many more, all swept away, but all leaving pleasant Maxwell memories. When can I forget these modern members of an eminently loyal house, the history of which, for upwards of seven centuries, I have here endeavoured faithfully to record.

WILLIAM FRASER.

EDINBURGH, 32 CASTLE STREET,
    1st May 1873.

ABSTRACT OF THE MEMOIRS OF THE MAXWELLS
EARLS OF NITHSDALE AND LORDS MAXWELL AND HERRIES.

to have kept the Castle of Carlaverock in the interest of that Monarch—Ranked himself soon after 1312 among the supporters of Bruce, and in retaliation the English laid siege to the Castle of Carlaverock, which, however, Sir Eustace successfully defended against them—Obtained from Bruce for this devotion to his interests a Charter of the lands of Westerraw, Pedynan and Park, etc.—Was a member of the Parliament held at Arbroath in April 1320—Joined with the King, the barons and freeholders, in framing a letter to the Pope, who had excommunicated Bruce, and laid the kingdom of Scotland under interdict, exhibiting the grounds of quarrel between Scotland and England, and praying his Holiness to admonish Edward the Second to allow the Scots to remain in undisturbed possession of their rights and liberties—Accused in the year 1320 of having been implicated with William de Soulis and others in a conspiracy against the life of King Robert the Bruce, for which he was tried with others by the Parliament held at Scone in August of that year, but was acquitted, though several were convicted and punished—Sir Eustace, after the death of King Robert the Bruce in 1329, when the right to the crown was contested by Edward Baliol, embraced the cause of the latter, and co-operated with King Edward the Third in supporting his claims—Acted a prominent part on the side of Baliol during the blockade of Perth in 1332 by the Earl of March, and was present at the coronation of Baliol at Scone in September of the same year—Was subsequently appointed a commissioner by Edward the Third to ascertain the valuation of the county and town of Berwick-upon-Tweed—Incurred the censure of the English King—Was appointed in October 1335 one of the conservators of the truce between King Edward and the Regent of Scotland —Abandoned about 1337 the cause of Baliol and the English interest—In the year 1339, again made his submission to King Edward, and obtained a pardon for his former defection— Married Helen Maxwell of Pollok—Died at Carlaverock, on 3d March 1342—Left no issue, and was succeeded by his brother John . . . .

VII.—2. SIR JOHN OF MAXWELL, KNIGHT, EIGHTH LORD OF MAXWELL, AND SIXTH OF CARLAVEROCK, 1342-1347.

Succeeded his elder brother, Sir Eustace—Acted a less conspicuous part in the public transactions of his time—Near the close of his life, appears as a supporter of King David the Second —Was present with that Monarch when he stormed the Castle of Liddell, and plundered the Abbey of Lanercost, and the Priory of Hexham—Was engaged in the battle of Nevil's Cross, fought between the Scots, under the command of King David, and the English, including numerous Scots under the command of Baliol, when King David was defeated, with a loss of 15,000 men, including many earls and barons, Randolph Earl of Moray being among the slain—The King himself and Sir John of Maxwell taken prisoners—The prisoners conducted to London by the High Sheriff of Yorkshire, with an army of 20,000 men, and lodged in the Tower—Sir John did not live long after his imprisonment, but the circumstances attending his death are unknown—Supposed to have had two sons and a daughter

VIII.—1. HERBERT OF MAXWELL, NINTH LORD OF MAXWELL, AND SEVENTH OF CARLAVEROCK, 1347-1354.

Was probably the eldest son of Sir John, and succeeded him in the Maxwell estates— Little known of his history—Does not seem to have lived long after his succession to the family inheritance—Like many others of rank, submitted to the authority of King Edward the Third—Negotiating in London shortly after with the Earl of Northampton, he engaged to deliver to that Earl certain hostages at the Castle of Carlaverock—Obtained from King Edward in return letters of protection for himself, his men, and his Castle of Carlaverock, dated at Gloucester, 5th September 1347—Was punished for his rebellion by King David the Second—His lands of Pedynane granted to others—Died before 1st April 1354, at which date the Maxwell estates were in possession of Sir John Maxwell . . . . .

Governor of Scotland, a Charter of the lands of Carnsalloch and of Dursquen in the barony of Dalswinton—Was served heir to his father in the lands of Meikle Drippis on 16th October 1421 —Appears to have continued a loyal subject of King James the First during his protracted captivity in England—Proceeded to Durham to meet the King when he acquired his liberty in 1424, for which journey he obtained a safe conduct from Henry the Sixth of England—Was present at the coronation of King James and Joanna Beaufort, his queen, at Scone, in April that year, on which occasion he received from his Majesty the honour of knighthood—Soon after fell under the suspicion of the King, but while the Duke of Albany, who was similarly suspected, was arrested, imprisoned in the Castle of Carlaverock, and carried to Stirling and executed, Sir Herbert was received into the royal favour upon promise of loyalty in time to come—Was frequently a member of Parliament during the reign of King James the First, and distinguished himself by his valour in the field of battle—Was the first of the House of Maxwell who was raised to the dignity of the peerage, with the title of Lord Maxwell—Was one of the conservators appointed for preserving the five years' truce, from 1431-1436, between England and Scotland, and one of the wardens of the marches of Scotland—Held similar positions, under the designation of "Herbert Lord Carlaverock," in a subsequent truce for nine years, from May 1438 to May 1447—Obtained from King James the Second, in 1440, a confirmation of the office of steward of Annandale, originally conferred by Archibald Earl of Douglas—Built the Castle of Mearns, for which he received a license from King James the Second, dated 15th March 1449—This Castle the occasional residence of the Lords Maxwell for two centuries after its erection—It was sold about the year 1650, along with the barony of Mearns, to Sir George Maxwell of Pollok, and is now the property of Sir Michael Shaw Stewart, Baronet—Herbert Lord Maxwell was one of the commanders of the Scottish army at the battle of Sark in 1448, in which the English were defeated—His marriages and children   125-139

XII.—ROBERT, SECOND LORD MAXWELL, 1453-1485.

Eldest son of Sir Herbert—Succeeded his father in 1453, being served heir to him on 14th February of that year in the barony of Carlaverock, etc., and in May following in the lands of Mearns and Nether Pollok—Previous to the death of his father, had been infefted in the lands of Libberton, in the barony of Carnwath—During the repeated rebellions of James, ninth Earl of Douglas, against King James the Second, Robert Lord Maxwell supported the royal authority —Was a member of the Parliament held in June 1455, in which the Douglases were forfeited, and his Lordship's seal was appended to the instrument of the proceedings against them—In the truce between England and Scotland, in 1457, was appointed one of its conservators, and one of the admirals of the seas and one of the wardens of the marches of Scotland—Was closely allied in political affairs with the powerful house of the Boyds during the minority of King James the Third, but is not mentioned as having been personally concerned with Lord Boyd in seizing the young King's person at Linlithgow on 10th July 1466—Was a member of the Parliaments held at Edinburgh in 1467 and 1469—In September 1474 was infefted in the lands and Castle of Crawfordmuir—In 1476 assumed into his own hands the lands of the barony of Maxwell until the tenants should take new leases thereof—Soon after resigned the baronies of Maxwell and Carlaverock, and the lands of the Mearns, in favour of John Maxwell, his eldest son, reserving to himself the liferent of Carlaverock and Mearns, and a terce thereof to Janet his spouse—On 9th May 1483, granted a Charter of four acres of land for the support of a chaplain in the Kirk of Carlaverock—In the following month infefted Master David Tyndinge, chaplain of Carlaverock, therein—Married Janet Forstar—His death   .   140-151

XIII.—JOHN MAXWELL, MASTER OF MAXWELL, COMMONLY CALLED THIRD LORD MAXWELL, 1454-1484.

Was the eldest son of Robert, second Lord—Predeceased his father—Having been put in possession of the barony of Maxwell, was occasionally styled Lord Maxwell—Married Janet Crichton, daughter of George Earl of Caithness, and with her obtained from her father the lands and barony of Tybberis, which, in the event of the lady's death, were to return to the granter— The lands of Barnton, in the county of Edinburgh, granted to her by her father, and subsequently resigned by her in favour of her son, George Maxwell—In February 1477 John Maxwell, Master of Maxwell, obtained from King James the Third, on his father's resignation, a Charter of the baronies of Maxwell and Carlaverock and the lands of Mearns, under reservation of his father's liferent thereof, and a terce to his mother—Was subsequently knighted— Held the office of steward of Annandale, which was hereditary in his family from the year 1409—Was killed by a Scotsman of the name of Gask, after a battle fought near Kirtle Water, on St. Magdalene's day, in 1484, between the Scots and 500 English horsemen, under the Duke of Albany and the Earl of Douglas—His family   152-156

XIV.—JOHN MAXWELL, FOURTH LORD MAXWELL, 1485-1513.

Was the eldest son of John, third Lord—Was one of the commissioners appointed for publishing the truce concluded at Nottingham in 1484, between King James the Third of Scotland and King Richard the Third of England—Was infefted, on 8th May 1485, as heir of his grandfather, Robert, second Lord Maxwell, in the lands of Carnsalloch, and two days after in the lands of Grenan—On 29th April 1486, was retoured heir of his father, John Lord Maxwell, in the £40 lands of the barony of Maxwell, and on the 10th of May following was infefted as heir of his grandfather in the superiority of the lands of Nether Pollok—In 1486 was appointed, along with Archibald Earl of Angus, Warden of the Middle and Western Marches of Scotland —Strengthened himself as Warden by entering into bonds with other families for mutual protection and assistance—Feud between the Maxwells and the Murrays—Is believed to have been involved in the conspiracy formed by a faction of barons against King James the Third— Was a member of the Parliament held at Edinburgh after the imprisonment of the King— Battle at Sauchie Burn, on 11th June 1488, between King James the Third and his barons, when the royal forces were routed and the King slain—Lord Maxwell was a member of the first Parliament of King James the Fourth, by which an act of indemnity was passed in favour of the barons involved in the late war—On 13th May 1495, his Lordship, and Robert and Herbert, his sons, were constituted bailies of all the barony of the Abbey of Holywood for nineteen years, a grant subsequently renewed in favour of Robert and Herbert Maxwell in liferent—Received from King James the Fourth numerous lands in the stewartry of Annandale and the shire of Dumfries, which were held of the Crown, including Langreggis, Denby and Hoddom, Greskin, Malinqschaw, Rontausyde, and others—Assigned these lands to Robert, his son and heir, who obtained a Crown Charter thereof on 15th November 1510 —Was among the slain at the battle of Flodden, 9th September 1513—Married Agnes Stewart of Garlies—Had five sons and four daughters   157-172

XV.—ROBERT, FIFTH LORD MAXWELL, 1513-1546.

Was eldest son of the fourth Lord—Was distinguished as a statesman, a Warden of the Marches, a general, and an admiral—Enjoyed for many years the favour of his Sovereign—Was early employed in the public service—Was admiral of a fleet on its way to France at the time of Flodden Field, and driven back by a tempest—On hearing of the slaughter of the King and of his own father, he seized upon the Castles of Thrieve and Lochmaben, with the assistance of the captains of the fleet—Soon after was appointed by Margaret, the Queen-Dowager, captain and keeper of the Castle of Thrieve and steward of Kirkcudbright—Appointed by the Duke of Albany, in 1515, Warden of the West Marches—Acted as bailie and justice-general over the lands, baronies, and regalities which belonged to the abbeys of Dundrennan, Tungland, Sweetheart, Holywood, the Provostry of Lincluden, and the Preceptory of Trailtrow—Was appointed captain of a guard of 200 men, to whom the care of the person of the young King, James the

Fifth, was intrusted, when, on the departure of the Regent Albany, in 1524, the King was invested with the supreme power—Was one of the Privy Council appointed by the Parliament in 1526 to assist the Earl of Angus as guardian of the King's person—His great influence as a courtier—Was present at the Parliament held at Edinburgh in July 1525, which condemned the "heretik Luther"—Accompanied the King from Stirling to Edinburgh in 1528—Took active measures against the Earl of Angus, when King James became wholly alienated from that nobleman—Was a member of the Parliament which, in 1528, resolved to attaint the Earl of Angus, and was one of a jury of eleven persons who returned a verdict of forfeiture against him and his two brothers—Received as his share of the forfeited estates of Angus the lordships of Crawfurd-Douglas and Drumsiar—Warded in Edinburgh Castle 1529—Reconciled to the King, and appointed by him an extraordinary Lord of Session—Was one of the Lords of Regency named by the King previous to his setting out for France, in 1536, to visit his affianced bride, Marie de Bourbon ; a journey which, however, resulted in his marrying Magdalene de Valois—Prevented by Archbishop Beton from being appointed to accompany, as Lord Admiral of Scotland, a fleet intended for reducing to submission the Isles and northern portions of the kingdom—As Warden of the West Marches was written to by the King upon the subject of raising a new army to invade England upon the west coast, and chiefly by his exertions an army of 10,000 men was raised on the Borders—Ought, as Warden, to have been appointed Commander-in-chief of the army, instead of Oliver Sinclair, who, to the great dissatisfaction of the nobility, was put in that post—Panic of the Scottish army, who, at Solway Moss, fled without offering resistance—Lord Maxwell and a thousand men were made prisoners—The King himself died of a broken heart within three weeks after the fatal event— Lord Maxwell and twenty-four other prisoners carried to London and committed to the Tower —Design of King Henry of England, after the death of the King of Scots, to marry his son, Edward Prince of Wales, to the infant Princess Mary, and to subdue Scotland—Lord Maxwell and his fellow prisoners subscribed a humiliating bond to Henry—They were set at liberty, on condition of their leaving their eldest sons or nearest relatives as hostages for their fidelity, and of their engaging to return to their prisons in England if they failed to accomplish Henry's designs—In addition to this Lord Maxwell was to pay 1000 merks as his ransom— Was a principal agent of the Earl of Angus in conducting the intrigues for furthering Henry's projects against the independence of Scotland—In 1543 was imprisoned in the Castle of Edinburgh—In the following year, being in the Castle of Glasgow when surrendered by the Earl of Lennox to the Governor, Cardinal Beton, and others, was brought to Hamilton, and there again imprisoned—Was soon set at liberty, and received another commission as Warden of the West Marches—His conduct exciting the suspicions of the English Government, and he not fulfilling his engagements to them, he was recalled to England and once more lodged in the Tower—Not long after allowed by the English Government to go to Carlisle, with the view of conferring with the Earl of Angus—Whilst his Lordship remained a prisoner at Carlisle, the Scottish Government made Robert Master of Maxwell engage to keep the Castles of Carlaverock, Lochmaben, and Thrieve for the Queen against the English—Efforts of the Earls of Cassillis and Lennox for the liberation of Lord Maxwell long unsuccessful—Was in danger of being sent back to the Tower of London, as his son, the Master of Maxwell, refused to go to Carlisle to remain in pledge for him—Was ordered by King Henry to be sent to Pomfret Castle—His son, the Master of Maxwell, being soon after taken prisoner, the English were in great hopes that the castles above mentioned would be surrendered to them—The Castle of Carlaverock not surrendered till October 1545, when Lord Maxwell was allowed to return to Scotland—The Castles of Lochmaben and Thrieve, held by Lord Maxwell's sons, were besieged by the Scottish Lords, and were surrendered— Lord Maxwell taken prisoner and carried to Dumfries as a traitor—Soon received a remission from Queen Mary and the Regent Arran, and was appointed Chief-Justice of Annandale, Kirkcudbright, Wigtown, and Dumfries, and Warden of the West Marches—Built the Castle

warlike manner against him—Litigation between him and John Johnston of that Ilk—They are induced by the Privy Council to subscribe a mutual assurance—Lord Maxwell restored to the office of Warden of the West Marches—Grant made to him in 1581, on the execution of James Earl of Morton, by King James the Sixth, of the earldom of Morton—Created Earl of Morton—In close confederation with Esme, first Duke of Lennox—Summoned to appear before the Council, and to present his men, servants and their accomplices, for scenes of plunder committed on the Borders in 1582—Deprived of the Wardenship of the West Marches, which was conferred on the Laird of Johnston—Persecuted by Stewart Earl of Arran in 1584 —Ordered to be imprisoned in Blackness Castle in 1585—His raid on the barony of Johnston—Involved in a plot formed by the Master of Gray for the destruction of Arran—Accessory to a new plot against Arran—Assisted in the capture of Stirling, 1585—Caused mass to be openly celebrated in the College of Lincluden—Was not deprived of the title of Earl of Morton when Regent Morton's forfeiture was rescinded in 1585, nor by any other Act of Parliament —A prisoner in the Castle of Edinburgh—Required by the Privy Council to appear before the General Assembly to satisfy the Kirk for hearing mass—Again appointed Warden of the West Marches in 1586—Consulted by King James the Sixth on his receiving intelligence of the death of his mother—His license from the King to go abroad, 1587—Went to Spain—In close communication with the Spanish Court in the preparations made for the invasion of England— Landed at Kirkcudbright from Spain about the end of April 1588—Intercommuned—Put to the horn—Fortified his castles, and levied some companies of foot and horse against the Government—Arrested by Sir William Stewart—Encouraged Philip the Second, King of Spain, even after the defeat of the Armada, to renew the enterprise—His letter to that King in 1589— Eulogized by Mr. Robert Bruce, a Jesuit—Liberated from the Castle of Edinburgh on 12th September 1589—Bond subscribed by him on his liberation—Commanded by the King to co-operate with other Lords in maintaining tranquillity on the Borders during the King's absence in Norway on the occasion of his marriage with Princess Anne of Denmark—Continued feud between him and the Johnstons—Received, on 28th July 1592, a commission as Warden of the West Marches—Subscribed the Confession of Faith as Earl of Morton—A special commission granted to him by the King to execute justice on the Johnstons for their depredations and slaughters—His death at the battle of Dryfe Sands, 6th December 1593—His children   223-299

XVIII.—JOHN, NINTH LORD MAXWELL, SECOND EARL OF MORTON, 1593-1613.

Was born about the year 1586—In March 1596-7 was served heir to his father in the lordship of Maxwell, and afterwards in the office of bailie of the Provostry of Lincluden, in the office of heritable Keeper of the Castle of Lochmaben, in the lands of Duncow, Keir, Tinwald, Broomholm, etc., the offices of Steward of Kirkcudbright, Keeper of Thrieve Castle, and Bailie of Sweetheart and Drundrennan, etc.—While still in his minority he married Lady Margaret Hamilton, only daughter of John Marquis of Hamilton—Was a member of the Convention of the Estates held at Holyroodhouse in 1599, in which it was ordained that Sir James Johnston of Dunskellie, who had been Warden of the West Marches, should be warded— Sir James was liberated in 1600, and restored to his offices of Warden and Justiciar, which aggravated the ill-feeling between the Maxwells and the Johnstons—Lord Maxwell a steadfast adherent of the Roman Catholic religion—Was declared rebel, and put to the horn for violating the laws against attending mass, etc.—In March 1601, for favouring Popery, was imprisoned in Edinburgh Castle, from which he made his escape in January 1602—Was prevailed upon by the Lords of Privy Council to execute " letters of Slannis " in favour of Sir James Johnston, whereby he forgave the latter, his kin, friends, and servants, for the slaughter of John Lord Maxwell, his father, and all other slaughters that followed thereupon—On 28th September 1605, a remission was granted, under the Great Seal, to Sir James and his friends, for the burning of the Kirk of Lochmaben and for the slaughter of John Lord Maxwell—By asserting his claim to the title of Earl of Morton, Lord Maxwell was involved in disputes with William Douglas of Lochleven, who became Earl of Morton in 1588—Having refused to dismiss his forces when ordered by the Privy Council, and having challenged the Earl of Morton to determine the controversy between them by single combat, was again imprisoned in the Castle of Edinburgh, by order of Parliament—Made his escape after an imprisonment of eight weeks—Openly travelled through the country, accompanied by not fewer than twenty horse, in defiance of His Majesty's authority, although the Privy Council issued proclamations for his apprehension—One of his retreats in the parish of Kirkgunzeon is still called Lord Maxwell's cave—To effect reconciliation between Lord Maxwell and the Laird of Johnston, an interview between them was arranged by Sir Robert Maxwell of Spottis, Lord Maxwell's cousin and Johnston's brother-in-law—Lord Maxwell was attended by Charles Maxwell, who fixed a quarrel upon William Johnston, the friend and attendant of the Laird of Johnston—Burst from the grasp of Sir Robert Maxwell, and, hastening towards the Laird of Johnston, fired a pistol after him, which inflicted a fatal wound—Granted, on 6th April 1608, the very day on which this tragic scene occurred, at Lincluden, to the said Charles Maxwell and his heirs, without reversion, a charter of the £5 land of Numbellie, in the parish of Kirkbean and stewartry of Kirkcudbright—By his violence, had made many enemies, who united with the relatives and friends of the deceased Laird of Johnston in loudly demanding the punishment of the murderer of their chief—Great efforts made to capture him and bring him to justice, but he eluded his pursuers, and escaped to France, where he remained for several years—A poem entitled "Lord Maxwell's Good-night"—A summons of treason executed against him, on 27th January 1609, at the Market-Cross of Edinburgh, on the 28th of the same month at the pier and shore of Leith, and on the 4th and 5th February thereafter at the Castles of Carlaverock, Langholm, and Dumfries—On 17th June following, when the case was taken up by Parliament, did not compear—Sentence of forfeiture pronounced against him on the 24th of the same month—Ventured to return to Scotland in March 1612, without the King's licence, but was obliged to lead the life of a hunted fugitive—Was dissuaded by his relative, George Sinclair, fifth Earl of Caithness, from executing his design of escaping to Sweden—Was betrayed to the Government by the Earl of Caithness, who promised him secrecy and shelter in Castle Sinclair—By orders of the Privy Council was warded in the jail of Edinburgh—The execution of justice upon him demanded by the Johnstons—Endeavours made by his friends to effect a reconciliation between him and the relatives of the deceased Laird of Johnston—Offers in writing presented to them in his name, which were not entertained—On 18th May 1613, a warrant was issued by the Privy Council to the Provost and Bailies of Edinburgh to behead him at the Market-Cross, on the 21st of that month—The sentence carried into effect—His body interred in the Abbey of Newbottle, belonging to Mark Ker, Earl of Lothian, whose Countess, Margaret Maxwell, was the daughter of Lord Herries, Lord Maxwell's granduncle 300-324

XIX.—ROBERT, FIRST EARL OF NITHSDALE, 1613-1646.

Was the younger brother of the preceding—Did not for some time obtain a restoration of the titles and possessions of his ancestors, owing to the forfeiture of the ninth Lord Maxwell—In August 1615 was infefted, on a Crown precept, in the barony of Carlaverock and others, as heir to John Lord Maxwell, his father—By patent dated 29th August 1620, was honoured with the title of Earl of Nithsdale in exchange for that of Earl of Morton, granted to his father in 1581, with the precedency due to the last-mentioned title—The precedency thus conferred opposed by those noblemen who had been elevated to the peerage subsequently to 1581, among whom were the Earls of Wintoun, Linlithgow, Perth, Wigtoun, and others —This opposition withdrawn—The Earl of Nithsdale, who, unlike his brother, was peaceably disposed, successfully exerted himself to extinguish the feud that existed between the Max-

XX.—1. ROBERT, SECOND EARL OF NITHSDALE, "THE PHILOSOPHER," 1646-1667.

Succeeded his father, the first Earl, in 1646—Was a steadfast supporter of King Charles the
First—Made prisoner at Newcastle by General Leslie—Brought to Edinburgh and imprisoned
in the Tolbooth—Found it necessary, from the losses sustained by himself and his father,
to sell part of the family inheritance—Repaired his house in Dumfries in 1659—Advised by
his friends to go to Court after the restoration of Charles the Second—His petition to that

WINIFRED COUNTESS OF WILLIAM, FIFTH EARL OF NITHSDALE, 1699-1749.

DESCENDANTS OF THE LAST EARL OF NITHSDALE, 1744-1873.

SIR JOHN MAXWELL, FOURTH LORD HERRIES OF TERREGLES, 1512-1582.

His birth about the year 1512—Educated in Sweet Heart Abbey—Tutor to two of his nephews —When Master of Maxwell married, in 1547, Agnes Herries, eldest daughter of William, third Lord Herries—Tragic circumstances connected with his marriage—Large extent of the Herries estates—Gifts of them by Queen Mary and the Regent Arran in favour of the second son of the latter, John Hamilton, Commendator of Arbroath—Papal dispensation for the marriage of John Master of Maxwell and Agnes Herries—Appointed Warden of the West Marches after the death of his brother, Robert, sixth Lord Maxwell, in September 1552 —Demitted the office, which was conferred on Sir James Douglas of Drumlanrig, knight— Brought intelligence to the Lords of the Congregation at Glasgow of Queen Elizabeth's resolution to interpose in behalf of the Scottish Protestants—Subscribed with other Com- missioners the Treaty between England and Scotland, at Berwick, 27th February 1559-60 —As Warden of the West Marches of Scotland complained against Lord Dacre, Warden of the West Marches of England opposite—Was invested, in September 1561, with the office of Warden of the West Marches in presence of Queen Mary—Difficulties in discharging his duties, as Warden 1564—Incurred the resentment of Queen Mary by associating himself with the Lords opposed to her—Submitted to her at Dumfries in 1565, and obtained from her remission—Declaration of confidence in him by the Queen, 1566—Special Charter in his favour—Queen Elizabeth's testimony to his efficiency as Warden of the West Marches—Became Lord Herries in the end of the year 1566—Patent of his armorial bearings, 1567—Was one of the Assize on the trial of Bothwell before the Court of Justiciary, 12th April 1567—Is said to have besought Queen Mary not to marry Bothwell—Defeat of Queen Mary's troops, and her surrender at Carberry Hill—Her imprisonment in Lochleven Castle—Lord Herries's correspondence with Sir Nicholas Throkmorton, with the view of obtaining the liberty of his sovereign—His character by Throkmorton—Would not permit the Proclamation of Murray as Regent by a herald at Glasgow—Was reconciled to the Regent—His speech in Parliament acknowledging Murray as Regent, and the King's authority—Entered into a bond for the liberation of Queen Mary in 1567—Repaired to Hamilton to her after her escape from Lochleven —Commanded her horse at the battle of Langside, 13th May 1568—Escorted her from the field after the defeat of her troops, and conducted her to Terregles—Articles supposed to have been left by her at this time at Terregles, or given to Lord Herries—Lord Herries was much opposed to her resolution to retire into England, and throw herself on the protection of Queen Elizabeth—Accompanied her to Carlisle—Was sent by her to London, carrying letters from her to Queen Elizabeth—Unsuccessful in his mission—Requested leave from the English Court to return to Carlisle—Intended to visit France, and a passport was requested for him by Queen Mary from Queen Elizabeth in 1568—Does not appear to have made this journey— His house of Terregles saved by the Regent Murray for a curious reason—Deprived by the Regent of the Wardenship of the West Marches—Queen Mary carried from Carlisle to Bolton Castle—Lord Herries left the English Court for Bolton Castle to see Queen Mary—His report of his embassy at the English Court—Queen Mary and the English Common Prayer-book—Lord Herries's departure from Bolton Castle—Regent Murray's Parliament on 16th August 1568, in which sentence of forfeiture was passed upon the chief of Queen Mary's adherents—The sentence delayed in regard to Lord Herries—Pressed Queen Elizabeth to bring the question between Queen Mary and her rebellious subjects to a speedy decision—His statement of the promises which Queen Elizabeth made to him of supporting his Sovereign—Was one of the Commissioners appointed by Queen Mary to state her case before Queen Elizabeth's Commissioners at York—Queen Mary's instructions to her Commissioners—The proceedings opened at York—Her Letter of Credence to the Bishop of Ross and Lord Herries, dated Bolton, 22d October 1568, addressed to Queen Elizabeth—Unprinted Letter from Queen Mary, dated at "Bowtoun," 24th October 1568—Lord Herries and the Bishop of Ross appeared before Queen Elizabeth and some of her nobility at Hampton Court in the cause of their Queen—Conference at Westminster—Murray and his party now accused Queen Mary as having been privy to and devised the murder of Darnley, an accusation which they had previously suppressed—Lord Herries's speech in defence of Queen Mary—Presented, along with Mary's other Commissioners, a Petition to Elizabeth, praying that their Sovereign might have access to the presence of Elizabeth, etc., for the declaration of her innocence, which was unfavourably answered—Was challenged by Patrick Lord Lindsay of the Byres —His answer—His Letter to the Earl of Leicester, who had desired him to come to the Court—Received new instructions from Queen Mary, dated Bolton, 1568, authorizing her Commissioners to charge the Earl of Murray and his adherents with being the authors, and some of them the proper executors, of the murder of Darnley—Communicated with his fellow-Commissioners these instructions to Queen Elizabeth and her Council, at Hampton Court, on 7th January 1568-9—Close of the Conferences—Queen Mary's removal from Bolton Castle to the Castle of Tutbury—Ratification by her of the proceedings of her Commissioners—Lord Herries supported the claims of the Duke of Chatelherault to the Regency in opposition to the Regent Murray—An agreement between the Duke of Chatelherault, as representing Queen Mary's party and the Regent—Lord Herries imprisoned in Edinburgh Castle in 1569

MEMOIRS OF THE MAXWELLS,
EARLS OF NITHSDALE.

MACCUS, THE SON OF UNDWIN, A.D. 1100–1150.

THE family of Maxwell, which for centuries held the titles of Lord Maxwell and Earl of Nithsdale, is of Saxon origin, and can be traced as far back as the middle of the eleventh century, when Undwin and his son Maccus, on the conquest of England by William of Normandy, took refuge in Scotland. Maccus was the founder of the surname and family of Maxwell.

Nothing certain is known of the ancestors of Undwin. In the history of England the name of Maccus, son of Anlaf, King of Northumbria, occurs in the tenth century. On the expulsion of King Anlaf, Eric, son of the Danish King Harold, was placed on the Northumbrian throne. But Eric, his son Henry, and his brother Regnald, were slain in the wilds of Stanmore by the hand of Maccus, the son of Anlaf.[1]

Maccus of Man and of the Hebrides was one of the eight sub-kings who, in the year 973, attended King Edgar of England on the Dee at Chester, when that king made his annual voyage along his coasts. Kenneth, King of Scotland, was another of the sub-kings who attended Edgar on that occasion.[2]

In the Chronicle of Melrose mention is made of Maccus, "plurimarum rex Insularum," as present with Kenneth, King of the Scots, and Malcolm, King of Cumbria. This great Sea King is also dignified with the somewhat equivocal title of the "Prince of Pirates," a title of which, however, he appears to have

[1] Lappenberg's History of England under the Anglo-Saxon Kings. Thorpe's translation, vol. ii. p. 125. London, 1845.   [2] *Ibid.* p. 143.

been proud, as, in attesting as a witness a charter of Edgar, King of England, he boldly subscribes himself—

Ego Mascusius Archipirata confortavi.

His signature is appended immediately after the subscriptions of "Kinadius rex Albanie," and of the royal family, and before all the bishops, high as was the rank which they then held. This was in the year 971.[1]

Between this Royal Maccus and Maccus the founder of the Maxwell family probably three or four generations of persons existed. None of these generations are known, and it is now impossible to show the connexion between them and Undwin, the father of the latter. But looking at the important position which the second Maccus at once took in Scotland, and at the identity of the names, it is possible that he may have been a descendant of the Royal Archpirate.

From Doomsday Book we learn that before the subjugation of England by the Norman William, a baron whose name was Maks or Max, of which the Latin form is Maccus, was in possession of several manors in England. Some places in England have names of which this is a prefix, such as Maxborough in Yorkshire, and Maxtoke in Warwickshire. Maxtoke is said to have been the property of Almundus or Ailwynd, which, without any straining, may be regarded as identical with Undeweyn. This would lead to the inference that some of Undwyn's ancestors had borne the name of Maccus, from which the designation of their property was taken.

Maccus, the son of Undwin, was an active and distinguished person in the reigns of Alexander the First and David the First of Scotland. With the latter, he was especially associated; and he frequently appears among those who attended his Court. He was witness to an inquest which David, then Prince of Cumbria, ordered to be made concerning the lands and churches belonging to the Church of Glasgow, in sundry provinces of Cumbria, when that diocese was restored by the Prince.[2] After narrating the traditions then current respecting the first foundation of the Church of Glasgow—the Episcopal seat of the region of Cumbria, and its subsequent history down to the time of the investigation, the inquest records that Prince David, deploring the misery of the profane multitude so long destitute of pastoral

---

[1] Chronica de Mailros, p. 34. *Vide* also Roger of Wendover, p. 263. William of Malmesbury, p. 147. Dugdale's Monasticon, vol. i. p. 17.   [2] Registrum Episcopatus Glasguensis, tom. i. p. 7.

care, chose for Bishop, by the counsel and assistance of his learned clerks, John, a certain religious man, who had fervently devoted his life to God; that this ecclesiastic, though, from knowing the barbarity and multiplicity of the vices of the unhappy people, at first somewhat reluctant, was consecrated bishop by Pope Paschal the Second; and that being welcomed by the Prince and the nobles of the kingdom, he joyfully, and to the gratification of the people, diffused the preaching of the gospel through the region of Cumbria. Among the other witnesses to this inquest, besides Maccus, were Matilda, Countess, who, on her part, made the grant, and William, grandson of that Princess.

The date of this inquest is omitted, but it must have been about the time of the consecration of Bishop John, as mentioned in the document, by Pope Paschal the Second, which Bishop Keith assigns to the year 1115, although without giving his authority. Father Innes is probably not far wrong in referring the date of the instrument to the year 1116.

Maccus, son of Undwin, also witnessed a charter granted by King David the First to God, Saint Mary of Melrose, and the Monks of the Cistercian order there serving God, of the lands of Melrose, Eldune, and Dernewic, the pasture, wood, pasturing of cattle for the use of the monks in the granter's land and forest of Selkirk and Traquair, and fishing in the waters of the Tweed, and besides, in augmentation of their revenues, Galtuneshalech and the whole land and wood of Galtunesside, as the King and Henry his son, and Richard, abbot of that monastery, perambulated the same on the Friday after the ascension of the Lord, in the second year of the capture of Stephen, King of England.[1] Among the other witnesses to this charter, besides Maccus, were Henry, King David's son; John, Bishop; William, King David's grandson; William, Chancellor; Maddach, Earl; Robert de Humphramville; Hugo de Moreville; Walter, son of Alan; Osbert de Ardene. After these names, and those of other witnesses, are recorded, it is added, "besides men of the same land," whose names are then given, among whom is that of Maccus, from which it is clear that he had possessions or resided in the district. This charter is dated at Ercheldon in June, the year being omitted; but, from internal evidence, an approximation may be made to the year. Stephen,

---

[1] Liber Sancte Marie de Melros, tom. i. p. 4; tom. ii. p. 666.

King of England, was made prisoner in 1141, and Prince Henry died in 1152, from which it is evident that the charter must have been granted between 1143 and 1152.

Maccus was witness to another charter, granted in 1113 by David, for founding a monastery at Selkirk, in favour of certain monks of the order of the Tyronenses, who derived their name from their first abbey, called Tyronium (Tiron), in the diocese of Chartres, and who were admitted into their order only after being instructed in some branch of science or art, and thus were of a more useful character than many of the other orders. The monastery was dedicated to God, the Virgin Mary, and Saint John the Evangelist, for the welfare of the soul of the founder, and of the souls of his father and mother, his brothers and sisters, and all his ancestors. It was endowed by Prince David with extensive possessions in Scotland, and also with lands in the southern earldom of Huntingdon. Among the witnesses to this charter, besides Maccus, were John, Bishop of Glasgow; Matilda, Countess; Henry, son of the Earl; Osbert, Chaplain; Alwyn, Chaplain; William, grandson of the Earl; Robert of Bruce; Robert of Umframville; Odard, Viscount of Babenburch; Lyulf, son of Uchtred; Adam, Chamberlain.[1] The charter is without date; but in a contemporary chronicle it is asserted that the Tyronese monks came into this country in the year 1113.[2]

The situation of the Abbey of Selkirk on the banks of the Ettrick river was not altogether satisfactory to the French monks, who pronounced it a place unsuitable for an abbey; and in 1126, after David's accession to the Scottish throne, John, Bishop of Glasgow, who had been his tutor, and who during life continued his counsellor in all matters ecclesiastical, procured the removal of the monastery from Selkirk to the Church of the Virgin Mary,[3] upon the banks of the river Tweed, at Kelso, then called Calkow, which, besides being a situation more beautiful and attractive, was much nearer the Royal Castle of Roxburgh. That castle, which stood on an eminence in the vicinity of the present town of that name, had been, during the reign of Alexander the First, the favourite residence of David, when Prince of Cumberland and of a large district in the south of Scotland, and upon his elevation to the throne, he made it one of his royal residences, where courts, councils, and parliaments were held,

[1] Liber S. Marie de Calchou, tom. i. p. 3.   [2] Chronica de Mailros, p. 64.   [3] Fordoun, v. 36.

and ambassadors and papal legates received. The King would be well pleased to have a body of cultivated men living in the neighbourhood of his favourite residence. The new site of the Abbey was quite close to the territory of Maccuswell, which was acquired by Maccus about the same time from King David the First.[1]

From the position which the name of Maccus occupies amongst the witnesses to the deeds above referred to, it may be fairly concluded that he occupied a high place in the estimation of King David, and, like him, was a warm supporter of all institutions intended for the advancement of religion.

THE BARONY OF MAXWELL.

The lands which Maccus, as already mentioned, obtained in Roxburgh-shire, from King David the First, were on the south side of the river Teviot, and opposite the Castle of Roxburgh.

The original charter, granting to Maccus the lands which were afterwards formed into the barony of Maxwell, has not been preserved, and the exact extent of these lands cannot now be determined. The early charters of the barony of Maxwell were probably lost in some of those Border raids in which the mansion on it was destroyed, and it is impossible to ascertain the exact date of the erection of the barony from any other documents. It appears, however, from charters to be subsequently quoted, that Maxwell was a barony before the year 1373. The lands which had been granted to Maccus soon came to be known as the lands of Maccuswell, afterwards contracted to Maxwell ; and, as subsequently described in the charters of his descendants, they are known to have included the town of Maxwell, Maxwell-heugh, the Mains, Springwood Park, Pinnaclehill, the Woddens Easter and Wester, the Softlaws Easter and Wester, Chapel, the Kirklands, etc. The barony of Maxwell was estimated as a forty-pound land of old extent, which gives some idea of the value of the lands.

The lands of Maxwell were probably a part of the royal domains. One of the parks immediately opposite the Castle of Roxburgh is called the King's Haugh. The lands may have been bestowed upon Maccus by King David the

[1] Liber S. Marie de Calchou, tom. i. p. 5.

First, in token of his special friendship for Maccus. Being opposite Roxburgh Castle, and coming close to it, it is certain that they would not have been granted by the King to any subject but one who held a special place in his favour.

It may perhaps be presumed that Maccus, about the same time, was appointed Sheriff of Roxburghshire, though we have no distinct information to that effect. The office of Sheriff of that county was instituted previous to the reign of King David the First, and was held for many years by Herbert of Maxwell, the son of Maccus, and also by John of Maxwell, the grandson of Maccus. The office of Sheriff was frequently made hereditary, and may therefore have been transmitted to them from the original founder of their family.

Here we may subjoin the following notices of the barony of Maxwell, so long as it continued the property of the Maxwell family.

John of Maxwell, lord of that Ilk, granted to the Monastery of Kilwinning the patronage of the Church of Libberton, and that grant was confirmed by King David the Second [A.D. 1367].[1] The same John of Maxwell, then become a knight, obtained from King Robert the Second a charter, dated 11th November 1373, of the lands of Softlaw, in the barony of Maxwell, forfeited by William Steuart from his having rendered allegiance to the King of England.[2]

On the 14th of May 1476, Robert Maxwell, bailie of the barony of Maxwell, specially constituted by the lord thereof, in a court of that barony, gave public warning, in the name and on the part of Lord Maxwell, that whoever had any lands in tack, in any way, in any part of that barony, should be wholly denuded of their lands and tacks after the Feast of Pentecost, and should not have them until they received them anew from the foresaid lord and his bailie.[3]

Robert, second Lord Maxwell, on 10th February 1477, resigned into the hands of King James the Third, in the royal chapel in the Monastery of Holyrood of Edinburgh, the lands of his barony of Maxwell, in the shire of Roxburgh, the lands of his barony of Carlaverock, in the shire of Dumfries, and his lands of the Mearns, in the shire of Renfrew.[4]

[1] Reg. Mag. Sig., 1814, fol. printed volume, p. 33, No. 86.
[2] Ibid. p. 103, No. 42.
[3] Original Instrument at Terregles.
[4] Original Resignation, ibid.

Four days after this resignation, namely, on the 14th of February 1477, a charter was granted by King James the Third to John de Maxwell, eldest son and heir-apparent of Robert Lord Maxwell, of the lands and barony of Maxwell, in the shire of Roxburgh, and of the lands and baronies of Carlaverock and Mearns, in the shires of Dumfries and Renfrew, to be held by the foresaid John and his heirs of the king and his heirs, in feu and heritage for ever, as the said Robert or his predecessors held them before his resignation, of the king and his predecessors, for rendering the rights and services due and wont therefrom ; the free possession of the lands of the barony of Carlaverock, and of the lands of Mearns, being reserved to the said Robert Lord Maxwell during his lifetime, and a third part of the lands of the barony of Carlaverock, and of the lands of Mearns, being reserved to Janet, spouse of the same Robert, during her lifetime.[1]

At Jedburgh, on 29th April 1486, John, fourth Lord Maxwell, was served heir of his father, John, third Lord Maxwell, in the barony of Maxwell, which in the retour is described as a forty-pound land of old extent, and which was then valued at twenty pounds Scots per annum, and was held in chief of the King for payment of a rose, if asked, upon the ground of the principal messuage of the said lands.[2] On a Crown precept following on the retour, Lord Maxwell was infefted in the barony of Maxwell on the 12th of May that year.[3]

On 28th July 1534 Robert Lord Maxwell obtained from King James the Fifth a charter of the forty-pound lands of the barony of Maxwell, and of many other lands and baronies, which were thereby erected into the free lordship and barony of Maxwell, and the Castle of Carlaverock was ordained to be the principal messuage thereof.[4] Sasine was given in terms of this charter on 19th August 1534.[5] The charter was confirmed by another by King James the Fifth in favour of Robert Lord Maxwell, dated 19th July 1537.[6]

Having rendered great services to King James the Fifth, as Warden of the West Marches, Robert Lord Maxwell received from that King another

---

[1] Original Charter at Terregles.
[2] Original Retour, *ibid.*
[3] Original Sasine, *ibid.*

[4] Original Charter at Terregles.
[5] Original Sasine, *ibid.*
[6] Original Charter, *ibid.*

charter of the forty-pound lands of old extent of the barony of Maxwell, in the shire of Roxburgh, and of many other lands and baronies, which were all united into a free barony, to be called the barony of Maxwell, and the Castle of Carlaverock was ordained to be the principal messuage thereof.[1]   In terms of this charter Lord Maxwell was infefted in the barony of Maxwell on 19th June 1540.[2]

In the Parliament of King James the Sixth, held on 29th November 1581, John Earl of Mortoun, the grandson of that Lord Maxwell, appeared personally, and protested that albeit the King granted to Sir Thomas Ker of Farniehirst, and others, the benefit of the pacification made at Perth on 23d February 1572, and thereby rehabilitated the said persons to their lands, this should not prejudice the Earl in regard to his right and possession of the lands of Pendiclehill, Wester Wooden, Saint Thomas's Chapel, the half of the Haugh, and the half mill of Maxwell, all within the barony and lordship of Maxwell, pertaining to the said Earl heritably.   It was admitted by the King and Parliament that this protest was well founded.[3]

The barony of Maxwell continued the property of the Lords Maxwell after their creation as Earls of Nithsdale.   But after being in the uninterrupted possession of the descendants of Maccus for about five centuries, the barony was acquired from Robert, first Earl of Nithsdale, in 1631, partly by the Earl of Roxburghe, and partly by Sir Andrew Ker of Greenhead, who changed the name of Maxwell to Brigend, from the situation of the house, which was built in the haugh near to the old ford in the Teviot.

The portion of Maxwell which became the property of the Earl of Roxburghe has descended to the present Duke of Roxburghe; while the larger portion, of which Sir Andrew Ker became the owner, was afterwards purchased by Sir James Douglas, second son of George Douglas of Friarshaw, a branch of Cavers, and ancestor of the present Sir George Henry Scott Douglas, Baronet.   Sir James Douglas changed the name of Maxwell to Springwood Park.

---

[1] Original Charter at Pollok-Maxwell.
[2] Original Sasine at Terregles.

[3] The Acts of the Parliaments of Scotland, vol. iii. p. 282.

THE CASTLE OF MAXWELL.

On the fair domains which Maccus had acquired he built a residence for himself, in the style of the baronial mansions of those times, and around his castle was gradually formed a town or village, occupied by his retainers. Of this castle no part of the building now remains, and even its site is not certainly known. It is supposed to have stood on a field between Pinnacle Hill and the present village of Maxwellheugh, where are still indications of the former existence of buildings of considerable dimensions. The elevated position of Maxwellheugh would render it, in remote times, a very eligible site for a castle, as from its summit the surrounding country could at all times be observed, and timely warning of the approach of danger could be given; and the supposition is further confirmed by the Motehill, which is adjacent, and is believed to have been the seat of the baronial courts held by Maccus for the administration of justice. This Motehill, which is now enclosed, and forms part of the garden grounds of Pinnacle Hill, is of considerable elevation, being thirty-five feet high, and the slope of the sides is thirty-five yards.

To Maxwell, as the head mansion of the Lord of Maxwell, special reference is made, in a grant in the year 1354 of the lands of Wester Softlaw, which formerly belonged to Herbert of Maxwell, lord of the same.[1] That Herbert was probably the seventh Lord of Maxwell.

As a Border fortress, the castle of Maxwell was liable to suffer from the hostile raids of the English. Among the places destroyed by the Earl of Hertford, in his ravages in Scotland in the year 1545, were Maxwellheugh, Brigend, St. Thomas's Chapel, East and West Wooden and Harden, all in or connected with the barony of Maxwell.[2] The mansion-house of Maxwell, although then destroyed by Hertford, was afterwards repaired or rebuilt, as appears from its having been used subsequently to that date by the Lords Maxwell as one of their Border residences.

The town of Maxwellheugh,[3] in the neighbourhood of which the castle of Maxwell stood, is mentioned by King James the Fifth, in a letter to James

[1] Liber de Calchou, p. 3¶2.
[2] Morton's Monastic Annals of Teviotdale, p. 116, and MSS. Harl. 289, fol. 179, there quoted.

[3] Original Letter, formerly in possession of the late Rev. William Robertson of Monzievaird.

Leirmonth of Darsay, his ambassador to King Henry the Eighth, dated 2d September 1542.

In public documents, Maxwellheugh is frequently referred to as a place of rendezvous for royal armies. When the Earl of Murray, on being appointed Regent after Queen Mary had resigned the Crown of Scotland in favour of her son, King James the Sixth, raised an army to enforce his own authority, and to subdue the adherents of the Queen, a rendezvous of this army took place at Maxwellheugh in the month of October 1567.[1]

In the end of the sixteenth century, John Earl of Morton, Lord Maxwell, who was the representative of the main line of the family of which Maccus was the progenitor, had a house at Maxwellheugh, which is included in a list of the houses of the noblemen of Scotland, prepared for Queen Elizabeth. But whether this was the old castle, or whether the old castle formed a part of it, cannot now be determined.

The celebrated Castle of Carlaverock, as we shall presently see, was acquired at an early date by the Maxwells; and, being the key to the south of Scotland, on the shores of the Solway, it required the utmost energies of its owners to maintain it against the frequent attacks of the English. Under these circumstances, it was necessary that their residence at the Castle of Carlaverock should be constant, and the consequence was that they naturally paid less attention to their original mansion at Maxwell. This readily accounts for the entire disappearance and the meagre historical notices of the Castle of Maccus on the Tweed.

Although they ceased to reside at the Castle of Maxwell thus early, the Maxwell family long retained the barony of Maxwell, as has been just now shown, and continued to take their territorial designation from it; and from it the first title of honour conferred on the descendants of Maccus was derived.

---

[1] The Chiefs of Colquhoun, by William Fraser, 1869, vol. i. p. 129. Maxwellheugh appears to have been favourable to the growth of trees. A poplar there grew to a great size. In 1825, the late Harriet Lady Polwarth noted that this tree was then supposed to be about 140 years old; and in 1859 the girth of the tree was 32 feet 6 inches, its height 92 feet, and it contained 700 cubic feet of timber.

THE PARISH OF MAXWELL.

On the estate of Maxwell, besides a castle, Maccus built a church for the accommodation of himself and his dependants. It was dedicated to Saint Michael, and was in the archdeanery of Teviotdale and diocese of Glasgow.

The parish of Maxwell, which was afterwards formed, was only about two miles in length and one mile in breadth. It was probably of the same extent with the original barony of Maxwell, though that barony was afterwards much more extensive. After the Reformation the parish of Maxwell was united to that of Kelso. Maxwell appears to have comprehended that part of the united parishes which lies to the west and south of the Tweed as far as the parish of Roxburgh, which was the boundary of Maxwell on the west. The church of Maxwell was erected in the haugh now called Brigend Park, near the junction of the rivers Tweed and Teviot : this was the centre of the parish, and therefore conveniently situated for the attendance of the parishioners on divine service.

In the year 1159 the Church of Maxwell was gifted by Herbert of Maccuswell, Sheriff of Teviotdale, and son of Maccus, to the monks of Kelso—a grant which was confirmed in that year by King Malcolm the Fourth ; in 1180 by Jocelin, Bishop of Glasgow ; between 1195 and 1199 by King William the Lion ; and in 1232 by Walter, Bishop of Glasgow.[1]

To this church was granted, previous to the year 1180, by Herbert, son of Maccus, an oratory which had been founded in the territory of Maccuswell, in honour of St. Thomas the Martyr, with a toft which he had given to that oratory. The grant of this oratory, which appears to have been called the Chapel of St. Thomas of Harlawe, was confirmed to the monks of Kelso by Jocelin, Bishop of Glasgow.[2]

A confirmation was made of this church and chapel to the monks of Kelso by King William the Lion.[3] Walter, Bishop of Glasgow, also confirmed, 19th May 1232, to the monks of Kelso, among other churches, the church of Maxwell and the chapel of Harlawe, as had been agreed between these monks and

---

[1] Liber de Calchou, pp. 229, 316, 319.   [2] *Ibid.* pp. 319, 325.   [3] *Ibid.* p. 316.

the lepers of the chapel of the foresaid place.[1]   They were confirmed to the monks of the same Abbey by Pope Innocent the Fourth between the years 1243 and 1254.[2]

The church of Maxwell appears to have been served by a vicar.   Sir John Robsoun, perpetual vicar of Maxwell, was one of the witnesses to a resignation, in the Monastery of Kelso, 20th April 1489, by John Kerr of Cavertoun, of three husband lands in Hownum, into the hands of Walter Ker of Cessfurd, the superior.[3]

Subsequent to the Reformation, Paul Knox, a nephew of John Knox, was minister of Kelso and Maxwell in the year 1574 ; and, in 1576, John Howie or Howieson had the spiritual charge of Sprowstoun, Maxwell, and Lempetlaw. William Balfour, minister of Kelso in 1585, was translated to Maxwell in 1589, but returned to Kelso in 1591.   He was presented to the vicarage of Maxwell by King James the Sixth, 2d February and 4th May 1604.   James Knox, probably grand-nephew of John Knox, was presented to the vicarage of Maxwell by King James the Sixth on 15th November 1605.   As vicar of Maxwell and Kelso, he was allowed certain old vaults in the Abbey of Kelso, which he used as a manse ; one of these was a hall and kitchen, and another was used as a bed-chamber and closet, though both were much under the level of the surrounding ground.

Robert Knox, eldest son of James Knox, succeeded his father as vicar of Maxwell and Kelso in 1633.   To the accommodations occupied by his father as a manse he received in addition two galleries, or to-falls, one to walk and study in, the other as a bed-chamber.[4]

In an information concerning the kirks of the Abbey of Kelso, prepared about the year 1620, it is stated that the kirk of Maxwell is " ane litle kirk,

---

[1] Liber de Calchou, pp. 229, 332.

[2] *Ibid.* p. 350.

[3] Original Instrument of Resignation in Roxburghe Charter-chest.

[4] Scott's Fasti Ecclesiæ Scoticanæ, part ii. pp. 453, 455, 456.   In that work is recorded an anecdote of a later minister of Kelso and Maxwell, James Ramsay, who was admitted in 1707. He also officiated for a short time as chaplain to a regiment from Yorkshire.   Some troops of cavalry being quartered in Kelso, he applied to one of the officers for a horse to carry him to a meeting of Synod in a distant town.   He rode to the place of meeting, but the animal being high spirited, and beyond his control, he was unable to dismount.   He took his brethren to witness that if he had failed in his duty, in not attending the Synod, it was through no fault of his, and then returned home.   On his arrival, the corps were being drawn out on parade when the animal quietly took its place, with the minister still mounted, to the discomfiture of himself, and the amusement of the assembled troops.

and the cure thereof servit be the minister of Kelso." In another paper, entitled " Form of the setting downe the teyndis for obedience of the commission
be Mr. James Knox in Kelso," 26th April 1627, it is said with respect to the
barony of Maxwell :—

" 1. Imprimis, the nvmber of the communicants, being examinit according to the buikis of the
examination going befoir the last communion, ar fund to be fourteen hunder four scoir threteene, of
the quhilk number, twa hunder threttie three did appertaine to that pairt of the parishe quhilk is
callit Maxwell.

" 2. This part of the parische, quhilk is callit Maxwell past memorie of man, hes bene servit
be ministeris of the kirk of Kelso, and was vnited thereto be the late erection, being ane kirk of
the same Abbacie.

" 3. The length of the parische is about tua myll. The breid ane myll. The kirk standethe
directlie in the middis."

Then follows an account of the stipend of the minister of Kelso out of
the teinds of various lands. " The haill teindis of Maxwell parochin are thocht
to be worth, *communibus annis*, sex hundred merk." [1]

Until a date comparatively recent, the walls of the church of Maxwell
were standing, but from the united effects of time and neglect, or from the
mal-appropriation of the stones by some covetous contractor, they have now
entirely disappeared. It may, however, be doubted whether these walls formed
a part of the church which was built by Maccus. Only a few tombstones
around the site of the church are now to be seen, and these are of very
modern date ; the plough having encroached upon the ancient burying-
ground.

THE MILL OF MAXWELL.

Besides his castle and church, Maccus, it is probable, erected a mill for
the convenience of his dependants ; a valuable establishment in the olden
times, from the rights and privileges attached to it.

The Mill of Maxwell is not, however, mentioned in charters relating to
the barony of Maxwell till the middle of the fourteenth century. About the
year 1354, Robert Sadler of Wester Softlaw granted to Rodger of Auldtoun

[1] Original Information in Roxburghe Charter-chest.

his land and tenement of Wester Softlaw, as they had been held by Herbert of Maxwell, formerly Lord of Wester Softlaw, with the privilege of grinding corn, "roum fre," at the Mill of Maxwell, on condition of his giving annually, at the Feast of Saint John the Baptist, at Maxwell, the head mansion of the lord of the fee, a pair of gold spurs, or twelve pence sterling.[1] This charter is without date. It was confirmed by Sir John Maxwell, Knight, Lord of Maxwell, who also remitted to Roger of Auldtoun the annual rent of a pair of gold spurs or twelve pence sterling for the lands of Wester Softlaw, which were held of him ; a remission which was confirmed by King David the Second at Inverkeithing, 1st April 1354.[2] The want of earlier notices of the Mill of Maxwell may be accounted for from the loss of the early charters of the family.

A mill still stands on the low grounds of the barony of Maxwell.

MAXTON OR MACCUSTOUN.

Among the territorial acquisitions made by Maccus on his establishment in Scotland was the territory known by the name of Maxton, which is only a short form of expressing the name of Maccustown or Makistown, that is, the town or manor of Maccus. It is situated in Roxburghshire, on the south side of the Tweed, and was probably co-extensive with the parish of that name, which is nearly four miles in length, and three in breadth.

The parish church of Maxton, which was dedicated to Saint Cuthbert, was probably built and endowed by Maccus.

This church derived tithes and revenues from certain lands which belonged to the Monastery of Melrose. An amicable agreement was afterwards made between that Monastery and the Baptismal Church of Mackestun, about the year 1227, with the assent of the abbot and monks of Melrose, of Leon, parson of Mackestun, of Walter, Lord Bishop of Glasgow, and of Sir John of Normanville, patron of that church, in regard to all the tithes and revenues from the whole land which the said monks possessed. By this agreement, beginning with that year, the monks of Melrose were to pay annually within

---

[1] Liber de Calchou, p. 382.   [2] Ibid. pp. 383-385.

the boundaries of the parish of Mackestun, at Pentecost, to the Church of Mackestun, four merks of silver *pro bono pacis;* and for the payment of this sum these monks were to be wholly free for ever in regard to that church and its rectors from all exaction of tithes, and all other revenues from the said land.[1]

Maxton soon passed out of the family of Maxwell, by marriage, to the Berkeleys; and from them again, by marriage, to the Normanvilles. At the close of the twelfth century the Manor of Maxton was the property of Robert de Berkeley and his wife Cecilia, daughter of Liulf, son of Maccus. Robert de Berkeley and Cecilia, his spouse, granted, in the reign of King William the Lion, to the Monastery of Melrose, a carucate of land in the territory of Mackistun, the tithes of the Church of St. Cuthbert being reserved; and this donation was confirmed by King William.[2]

In the reign of King William the Lion, the estate of Maxton was in the possession of the family of Normanville, who acquired it through intermarriage with the Berkeleys.[3] Hugo de Normanville and his wife Alina granted to the Monastery of Melrose the land of Keluesete and Faulawe by the boundaries therein described, in excambion for the land in the territory of Mackestun, which Robert de Berkeley and Cecilia his wife had given to that monastery.[4] John de Normanville, Lord of Makeston, for the souls of all the kings of Scotland, and of all his ancestors, and for the welfare of his sovereign, Alexander King of Scotland, and for his own welfare and that of his wife and children and parents, granted to the monks of Melrose, in free and perpetual alms, a portion of land in the territory of Makeston, as therein described.[5] Among the witnesses to this charter was John de Makeswel, evidently the grandson of Maccus. It is undated, but it was confirmed by Alexander the Second at Selkirk, on 22d July 1226.[6]

John, son of Philip of Mackustun, in a renunciation in favour of the monks of Melrose, of all right of pasture in a certain part of his land, on receiving an equivalent in the territory of Newton, mentions that John of Normanville, who had given them the territory in which that portion of his land was situated, was his superior.[7]

[1] Liber Sancte Marie de Melros, tom. i. p. 220.
[2] *Ibid.* tom. i. pp. 77, 78.
[3] *Ibid.* tom. i. p. 20.
[4] *Ibid.* p. 79.
[5] Liber Sancte Marie de Melros, tom. i. p. 219.
[6] *Ibid.* tom. i. p. 220.
[7] *Ibid.* tom. i. pp. 226, 227.

Many early grants in connexion with the Church of Maxton were made by the Normanvilles. But the patronage of that church was afterwards granted by King Robert the Bruce to Walter, Lord High Steward, who gifted it to the Monastery of Dryburgh, by which it was retained till the Reformation of the sixteenth century.

ETYMOLOGY OF THE NAME OF MAXWELL.

Different opinions have been expressed by several learned authorities as to the etymology of the name of Maxwell. Mr. George Chalmers, author of " Caledonia," Mr. John Riddell, advocate, in his History of the Maxwells of Pollok, and Mr. Innes in the " Origines Parochiales Scotiæ," have stated that the original name was " Maccusville"—the ville or town of Maccus, and that " Maccuswell" and " Maxwell" are corruptions of the former name. But if this view were correct, some instances should be adducible from early charters in support of the theory. No such charter, however, has yet been found containing the name of Maccusville. In the heading of the account of the parish in the " Origines," the editor while giving twelve different modes of spelling the name of Maxwell, from early charters, does not quote a single instance of Maccusville.[1]

The name is always written with the termination "well" or "wele," and there is an incongruity in the Norman "ville" being affixed to the Saxon Maccus, which has lead us to endeavour to find a derivation more in harmony with the original spelling.

Not far from Maxwell, as we have just shown, there is situated another barony, which was in the possession of Maccus and his immediate descendants, and was probably the earliest residence of Maccus in Roxburghshire: it was therefore called Maccustun or Maxton. When Maccus acquired the more important property near Roxburgh and took up his residence there, the natural name for his new castle was already appropriated, and to make a distinction between it and the old castle, some feature of the surrounding country would be sought.

Near Maxwellheugh there is a salmon-cast, well known to anglers as Maxwheel (*wele, well,* or *weil* being the Saxon for an eddy), the well of

---

[1] Origines Parochiales Scotiæ, vol. i. pp. 297, 445.

Maccus. This eddy wheeled in Tweed before that river had a name ; and the character of the rock which produces it must have made it a noted spot before Saxon set foot on Scottish ground. Maccus having fixed his residence on the heights above this eddy, what more natural than that it should be called the wele of Maccus ; that his descendants should be spoken of as those who came from the neighbourhood of Maccus wele—de Maccus wele ? If they once were so designated, their name would soon assume the form of Maxwell.

This derivation is not offered without hesitation ; but it appears at least as good as one which requires a flagrant violation of the ordinary rules of etymology, and assumes that the scribe who could spell the names of Morville, Umfraville, and Somerville correctly, was completely at a loss when he came to the name of Maccusville.[1] But whether the name be Maccusville or Maccuswell, the descendants of Maccus do not need to avail themselves of Norman or Saxon derivatives to give lustre to the now Scottish name of Maxwell.

THE PERSONAL HISTORY AND CHILDREN OF MACCUS.

Judging from the few memorials extant connected with the name of Maccus, we may infer that he came much in contact with the ecclesiastics of the shire of Roxburgh. That shire was one of the most distinguished in Scotland for its monastic establishments, including the Abbeys of Jedburgh, Melrose, and Kelso, which were conspicuous for the architectural grandeur of their buildings, and for the wealth with which they were endowed ; and as the ecclesiastics were at that time the only learned men in Scotland, a great part of whom had come from other countries, Maccus would thus mingle with the most refined society of his age.

The name of the wife of Maccus has not been ascertained. But there is evidence that he had four sons, whose names frequently occur in the writs of the period. The order of the birth of each is not exactly known. We can only state the order which is most probable.

1. Herbert was probably the eldest son, as he succeeded his father, Maccus, in the lands of Maxwell, etc., as will be afterwards shown.

[1] Liber Sancte Marie de Melros, tom. i. p. 4.

2. Liulphus. As Liulphus inherited from his father the lands of Maccus-toun, it has been inferred that he was the eldest son of Maccus. But he is never designated "of Maccustoun" or "of Maccuswell," as might have been expected if he had held that position. He frequently appears as a witness to charters. "Liolphus, son of Maccus," was a witness to a charter by Malcolm the Fourth in favour of the Abbey of Saltreia in Huntingdon,[1] and to a charter by that King in favour of Walter, Lord High Steward, son of Alan, in 1158.[2] He was also a witness to a charter by Malcolm the Fourth, granted at Roxburgh, in the year 1159, confirming to the Abbey of Kelso the lands, mills, fishings, pastures, tithes, churches, and all the rights and privileges which that Abbey possessed from the liberality of his grandfather, his father Earl Henry, and himself.[3]

Under the designation of "son of Maccus," Liulphus was a witness to a charter of confirmation, without date, by Robert of Landeles and Muriel, his spouse, to the Church of St. Mary of Kelso, and to the monks there serving God, of six oxgangs of land in the territory of Brockesmuth, which William of Moreville, and "I, Muriel, his spouse," had formerly granted in free and perpetual alms in the time of King Malcolm.[4]

Liulphus, son of Maccus, was witness to a charter, without date, but granted in the reign of King William the Lion, by Walter, Lord High Steward, son of Alan, to the monks of Melrose, of the lands of Mauhelin in Kyle, as described in the charter, the whole pasture of the granter's forest, to the marches of Doueglas, Lesmagu, and Glengeuel, on the north side of the river Ayr, but five merks of silver were to be paid to the granter and his heirs annually, while he reserved his forest only for beasts and birds.[5] He was also witness to a charter by Alan, son of the said Walter, making the same grants to the Monastery of Melrose.[6]

Under the same designation "Liulfus, son of Macchus," was witness to a charter by Philip de Valoniis, the King's Chamberlain, to the Monastery of Melrose, of the lands of Ringwude, for redemption of the soul of King David and his son Henry, and for the soul of King Malcolm, and for the welfare of

[1] Dugdale's Monasticon Angl., vol. i. p. 850.

[2] The Acts of the Parliaments of Scotland, vol. i. p. 83.

[3] Liber de Calchou, tom. i. p. vii.

[4] Liber de Calchou, tom. i. p. 259.

[5] Liber Sancte Marie de Melros, tom. i. p. 56.

[6] *Ibid.* tom. i. p. 57.

King William and his brother.[1] The charter is without date; but as one of the witnesses was Philip de Valoniis, the King's Chamberlain, who did not hold that office in 1171, when Walter de Berkeley, Lord of Reidcastle, under the designation of "Camerarius," was witness to a grant by William the Lion of the church of Egilsgreg to the canons-regular of the Priory of St. Andrews, and as Osbert, Abbot of Jedburgh, another of the witnesses, died in the year 1174, it must have been granted between the years 1171 and 1174.[2]

Liulphus, as being probably the second son of Maccus, inherited the lands of Maccustoun. He had a daughter, *Cecilia*, who married Robert de Berkeley; and, as if she had been her father's only surviving child, the lands of Maccustoun descended to her. As before stated, Robert de Berkeley and Cecilia, daughter of Liulf, his spouse, made a grant from these lands to the Monastery of Melrose; and by intermarriage with the Berkeleys, the family of Normanville inherited the lands of Maccustoun.[3]

3. Edmund. "Edmund of Macheswel," who, it is probable, was the son of Maccus, was one of the witnesses of a charter by Uchtred, son of Liulphus, granting to the Abbey of Kelso the church of Molle and the contiguous land. The charter is undated, but it was probably granted about the year 1152.[4]

4. Robert. As son of Maccus, Robert was witness to charters by Walter son of Alan, and Alan son of Walter, mentioned under the notice of Liulphus. He was also a witness to a charter by Roger Burnard, granting to the Monastery of Melrose, for the welfare of the souls of King David, King Malcolm, and King William, etc., a certain part of the granter's peat moss in Faringdun, for a free and perpetual alms. The charter is without date, but appears to have been granted in the reign of King William the Lion.[5]

"Robert, son of Maccus," was also witness to a charter by Hugh of Normanville, and Alina, his wife, granting to the Monastery of Melrose, for the souls of David and Malcolm, Kings of Scotland, and of Earl Henry, and for the welfare of our lord, William King of Scotland, and Alexander his son, and Earl David, the King's brother, the lands of Keluesete and Fawlawe, for a free and perpetual alms. This charter is undated; but, as appears from internal evidence, it was granted in the reign of King William.[6]

[1] Liber Sancte Marie de Melros, tom. i. p. 141.
[2] Chronica de Mailros, p. 86.
[3] *Vide* p. 15.
[4] Liber de Calchou, tom. i. p. 144.
[5] Liber Sancte Marie de Melros, tom. i. p. 76.
[6] *Ibid.* tom. i. p. 81.

Robert, the son of Machus, was again a witness in the chapel of the Castle of Roxburgh, on the day of the Holy Innocents (28th December) 1221, to an amicable agreement which took place between Walter, Bishop of Glasgow, on the one side, and the Abbot and Convent of Kelso on the other, in regard to a controversy between them as to the Church of Campsy, in presence of William de Bosco, the King's Chamberlain, Sir Hugh Mortimer, Dean of Glasgow, Sir Robert and Sir Thomas, canons of Glasgow, and several other magnates of the King's Court. The agreement was to the effect that the Abbot and Convent of Kelso quitclaimed to Walter, Bishop of Glasgow, and to his successors, and to the Church of Glasgow in perpetuity, all right which they had to the Church of Campsy; that whoever should hold that church by the gift of the said Bishop, or his successors, was to pay annually to the house of Kelso ten merks of silver, free from all burdens, and to swear fidelity to the said house; and, should payment cease to be made at any term, the Bishop or Chapter of Glasgow was to compel him who held the said church, by ecclesiastical censure, without right of appeal, to make payment of the foresaid ten merks to the said church.[1]

A charter was granted by King William the Lion to Robert, son of Maccus, of a carucate of land in the territory of Lesedwin. Of that charter the following is a translation :—

William, by the grace of God, King of the Scots, to all upright men of his whole land, clerical and lay, Health. Let all present and future know, that I have given and granted, and by this my charter have confirmed to Robert, son of Maccus, one carucate of land in the territory of Lesedwin, namely, that which Herbert de Maccuswell, my sheriff, and Galfrid, clerk, by my precept delivered to him : To be held by him and his heirs of me and my heirs in feu and heritage ; for rendering thence annually twenty shillings, namely, ten shillings at the feast of Saint Martin, and ten at Pentecost ; and performing all the services which pertain to that land and which that land has been accustomed to render, except ploughing and reaping. Witnesses, William, Elect of Glasgow, my Chancellor ; Richard de Prebenda, my clerk ; Philip de Valoniis, my Chamberlain ; William Cumin ; William of Hay ; William de Muntfort ; Alexander, Sheriff of Stirling ; Richard, son of Hugo ; Alexander of Sintun. At Forfar, the 28th day of December [1200].[2]

Maccus died about the year 1150, and was succeeded in the barony of Maxwell by his eldest son.

[1] Registrum Episcopatus Glasguensis, tom. i. p. 100.
[2] Original Charter at Pollok Maxwell. Printed and lithographed in Memoirs of the Maxwells of Pollok, vol. i. p. 121.

III. HERBERT DE MACCUSWELL OF MACCUSWELL
AND SHERIFF OF TEVIOTDALE, 1150-1200.

Herbert de Maccuswell, the eldest son and successor of Maccus in his lands of Maxwell, lived during the reigns of Malcolm the Fourth, who succeeded to the Crown of Scotland in the year 1153, and of William the Lion, who succeeded Malcolm in the year 1165, and died in the year 1214. The name of Herbert of Maccuswell does not appear in the records of either private or public affairs during the short reign of King Malcolm the Fourth. But he seems to have attended the Court of King William the Lion. He was a witness to many charters and public transactions, the most of which related to the property and privileges of the religious houses during the reign of that sovereign. In giving a summary of these charters, we can, of course, from such materials, give only a part of his history, but still they throw much light on many leading events of his life, and also on the history, particularly the ecclesiastical, of the times in which he lived, and in which he took a special concern, often presenting curious and valuable information respecting the rights and privileges of the Church, and the condition of the occupants of the soil when they lived under its shelter. These charters also show the class of persons with whom he was in the habit of associating, who were the chief of the ecclesiastics and the principal courtiers.

Herbert, like his father, appears to have been devotedly attached to the church. Under the designation of "Herbert of Macuswel," he made a donation, in or before the year 1159, to the Church of the Virgin Mary of Kelso, and to the monks there serving God, of the Church of Maccuswel or Maxwell.[1] In that year this donation, along with numerous lands and churches, was confirmed to that Abbey by Malcolm the Fourth, at Roxburgh. It was afterwards confirmed, in 1180, by Jocelin, Bishop of Glasgow; by King William the Lion, at Jedburgh, 4th July, between the years 1195 and 1199, along with many other churches; and, on 19th May 1232, by Walter, Bishop of Glasgow.[2]

The Church of Maxwell was dedicated to Saint Michael, and it was in

---

[1] Liber de Calchou, tom. i. pp. vi., 14.　　[2] *Ibid.* tom. i. p. 229, and ii. pp. 316, 319.

the diocese of Glasgow.   To it was granted, as already observed, before the year 1180, an oratory, which was founded in the territory of Maccuswell, in honour of Saint Thomas the Martyr, with one toft which he had given to it for a free and perpetual alms.   This grant was confirmed by Jocelin, Bishop of Glasgow, so that the monks of Kelso, from their possessing the Church of Maccuswell, might also possess that oratory.

The confirmation is in the following terms :—

" Jocelin, by the grace of God, Bishop of Glasgow, to all the sons, as well future as present, of Holy Mother, health in Christ,—Know that we have granted, and by the present writing have confirmed to the Church of St. Michael of Maccuswel a certain oratory, which *ex novo* is situated in the territory of Maccuswel, in honour of St. Thomas the Martyr, with a toft, which Herbert, lord of the same feu, gave to that oratory for a free and perpetual alms ; so that the monks of Kelchou, to whom belongs the before-mentioned Church of Maccuswel, may have and possess the above-written oratory as a member of the foresaid church, as freely and quietly for ever as they have and possess their other donations, under reservation of episcopal right and usage ; the witnesses being Simon, Archdeacon of Glasgow ; Richard de Theuidale, dean ; Richard, monk, the Bishop's chaplain, and others." [1]

This oratory was called the Chapel of Saint Thomas of Harlawe.

Herbert of Maccuswell was witness to a charter granted by King William the Lion to Saint Kentigern and the Church of Glasgow, and Jocelin, Bishop of Glasgow and his successors, bishops thereof, for augmentation of the bishoprick of Glasgow, of the lands of Badlayn, to be held for free and perpetual alms. Among the witnesses, besides Herbert, were the granter's brother David ; Walter of Bidun, Chancellor ; John, Abbot of Kelso ; Richard of Morville, Constable ; and Robert of Bruce.   The charter is dated at Linlithgow, the year not given ; but it appears to have been granted soon after Jocelin became Bishop of Glasgow, a dignity to which he was elected at Perth, 23d May 1174, and to which he was consecrated at Clairvaux, 1st June 1175.[2]   In the charter King William asserts that he was led to grant it on account of the bereavements suffered by him and his after the decease of Engelramus, Bishop of Glasgow.[3] That bishop died 2d February 1174.   After this King William was taken prisoner by the English in his camp near Alnwick, on 13th July 1174, imprisoned in the Castle of Richmond, and, on 8th August, taken by the English King into Normandy, but was set at liberty on 15th February 1175-6, having

[1] Liber de Calchou, tom. ii. p. 325.
[2] Chronica de Mailros, pp. 86, 87.
[3] Registrum Episcopatus Glasguensis, tom. i. p. 36.

given his oath of fidelity to the English King as his liege lord, and submitted to other conditions, for the observance of which he delivered to him the castles of Roxburgh, Berwick, Jedburgh, Castrum Puellarum (the Castle of Edinburgh), and Stirling, and a number of hostages.[1] The above charter must have been granted after the liberation of King William. King William's bereavements, to which reference is made in the charter, were caused by an inundation of the Tay, which overflowed and destroyed the palace and the greater part of the town of Perth. By this calamitous event, from which the King himself narrowly escaped with his life, his son and his nurse, fourteen of the royal domestics, and many of the inhabitants of Perth, perished.

Herbert of Maccuswell was also a witness to a charter of confirmation, by the same King, confirming to God and Saint John's Church of the Castle of Roxburgh, that carucate of the dominical land of Roxburgh which King David, the granter's grandfather, gave to that church, and a full toft and a residence in the castle, together with the whole oblations of those who resided in the castle, a [fourth] part of the granter's oblation when he or his family should be in it, a tenth of his grove, and a tenth of the tallow of what was slaughtered for him in Teviotdale. The charter is dated at Roxburgh, the year being omitted, but it must have been between the years 1189 and 1199, as Hugh, the King's Chancellor, who was a witness to the charter, was made Chancellor in the former of these years, and died 10th July 1199.[2]

If Herbert of Maccuswell did not inherit from his father the office of Sheriff of Teviotdale, he was, from his position, and from the estimation in which he was held by King William and by the community, appointed by the King to that office.

In a charter by Bernard of Hauden, granting to the Abbey of Kelso the mill and mill-pond of Reuedene, Herbert's son John, who was a witness, is styled " John de Maccuswell, son of Herbert, Sheriff."[3]

Under the designation of " Sheriff of Theuydale" [Teviotdale] Herbert of Maccuswell was witness to the amicable settlement of a dispute that had arisen between the Abbot and monks of Kelso, on the one side, and Henry

[1] Palgrave's Documents and Records illustrating the History of Scotland, p. 63.

[2] Registrum Episcopatus Glasguensis, tom. i. p. 66.
[3] Liber de Calchou, tom. i. p. 176.

of Molle and his wife Eschina, on the other, concerning the pasture which the former claimed in the territory of the latter's land of Molle by right of the church, and in name of the parson. The agreement was to the effect that the said Henry and his wife Eschina granted and confirmed a right in perpetuity in the territory of their land of Molle to the Abbot and monks of Kelso of pasture for 700 sheep and 120 animals, which they claimed as aforesaid ; and besides, that the vicar appointed by the monks, and their men dwelling on the land of the church, should have common pasture with Henry of Molle's men of that land. The witnesses, besides Herbert, were Robert, Archdeacon of Glasgow ; John, Dean of Roxburgh ; Hugh, Chaplain ; Elias, parson of Old Roxburgh ; and Edward of Lyntun.[1] The document is without date, but it probably belongs to the year 1190.

Herbert of Maccuswell was also witness to a charter by Roland of Inverwic and Helewis his wife, granting in feu-farm for ever, to the Abbot and monks of Kelso the granters' land, grove and pasture, in the territory of Inverwic, which was opposite the land of the Monastery of Kelso, situated as described in the charter. This charter also granted to them various rights and privileges which at that time were commonly enjoyed by the religious houses. They were to have liberty to erect, and to inhabit, and otherwise to use for their advantage, dwellings or huts for themselves, or for their men or animals, where- ever they chose, within the boundaries described, nor was it to be allowed to any except these monks to place huts, or to build houses, within these boundaries. The monks themselves and their men were to receive from the grove as much firewood or wood for building purposes as they desired, both for the town of Sperdeldun and for the land which they held of the granters ; but they were not to be permitted to sell any of the wood, though they might sell the brush- wood. The monks were to put in defence a part of the grove for their own convenience, and to place a forester, if they pleased, for keeping it, that none might receive anything therefrom without their permission.[2] This charter is without date, but it was probably granted about the year 1190.

The name of Herbert of Maccuswell again appears among the witnesses to a charter by King William the Lion, granting to the Abbey of Kelso three carucates of land in the territory of Edenham, as therein described, and the

---

[1] Liber de Calchou, tom. i. p. 136.   [2] Ibid. tom. i. p. 208.

fishing in the Tweed which belonged to Edenham, extending from the marches of Kelso to those of Brigham. These three carucates of land, and the fishing in the Tweed, King William gave to the monks of Kelso in exchange for twenty chalders of corn and meal of the standard measure of the time of his grandfather, King David, which they used to have in the King's mill of Roxburgh, and in exchange for two chalders of malt, which they were wont to have in his mill of Edenham, by the gift of his grandfather, King David. He granted also to them, should their mill of Kelso, either by inundations of water or by reason of ice, be prevented from grinding, or be broken by accident, liberty to grind at his mill of Edenham the corn which grew upon the forementioned land of Edenham for their food freely, without multure, immediately after that which was already in the hopper, unless it was corn from his dominical land. This charter is dated at Roxburgh, the year being omitted, but as "Hugo the King's Chancellor," who was one of the witnesses, was made Chancellor in the year 1189,[1] and as Arkenbald, Abbot of Dunfermline, another of them, died in 1198,[2] it must have been granted between the years 1189 and 1198. Others of the witnesses were Henry, Abbot of Aberbrothoc; Guido, Abbot of Lundores; Hugh, the King's chaplain, clerk; and William of Lindsay, justiciar.[3]

In a confirmation by King William the Lion to Saint Kentigern and to William, Bishop of Glasgow, and his successors, of the whole right which William Cumin said and believed he had in the land of Muncrath, lying between Badlayn and Kirkentulaht, Herbert de Maccuswell again appears as a witness. Among the other witnesses were Osbert, Abbot of Kelso; Robert de Lundon; William de Lindesay; and Thomas de Colleuill.[4] The charter is dated at Roxburgh, 1st March, the year not given, but as William, Bishop of Glasgow, to whom it was granted, was consecrated Bishop of Glasgow in 1200,[5] and as Osbert, Abbot of Kelso, who was one of the witnesses, died in 1203,[6] it must have been granted between these years.

The last transaction in which the writs of the period that have been preserved present Herbert of Maxwell as having been engaged, was his granting,

[1] Crawfurd's Officers of State, p. 10.
[2] Chronica de Mailros, p. 103.
[3] Liber de Calchou, tom. ii. p. 304.
[4] Registrum Episcopatus Glasguensis, tom. i. p. 79.
[5] Crawfurd's Officers of State, p. 11.
[6] Chronica de Mailros, p. 105.

as Sheriff, to Robert, son of Maccus, possession of a carucate of land in the territory of Lesedwin, to which King William the Lion granted a charter of confirmation in favour of the said Robert on 28th December 1200. It is probable that he died soon after this date.

Herbert of Maxwell left three sons—

1. John, who succeeded him.

2. Robert.

3. Aymer, who succeeded his eldest brother John in Maxwell and Carlaverock.

Robert, son of Herbert of Maccuswell, was witness to a charter by Richard of Lincolnia, and Matilda, daughter and heiress of Anselm of Molle, his wife, granting to the monks of Kelso sufficient pasture for seven hundred sheep and one hundred cattle in the pasturage of the granter's feu of Molle, and annually from the grove of the foresaid feu what may be necessary for constructing sheep-cots, and quitclaiming for ever to the monks their multures of Molle, as they had remitted to Anselm and his heirs the tithe of his mill of Molle for ever. Among the other witnesses were Hugh, the King's chaplain, clerk ; Galfrid of Lempedlawe, King's clerk ; Adam, Chaplain of Kelso ; Bernard of Hauden ; Nigel of Heriz ; and Malcolm of Keth.[1] The charter is without date, but from the reference made in it to Osbert, Abbot of Kelso, who held that place from 1182 to 1203, it must have been granted between these years.

Robert, brother of John of Maccuswell, son of Herbert, Sheriff, was witness to a charter by Bernard of Hauden, granting to the monks of Kelso whatever right they claimed to the mill of Reuedene or to the pond of that mill, or to that piece of Meadow, which lay on the north side of the half carucate of these monks, to the ditch made between that half carucate of land and the granter's land, even to the rivulet which anciently was the boundary between Hauden and Reuedene.[2] The charter is without date, but was granted probably about the year 1210. Robert does not appear to have left any children.

[1] Liber de Calchou, tom. i. p. 128.   [2] *Ibid.* tom. i. p. 176.

IV. SIR JOHN DE MACCUSWELL, SHERIFF OF TEVIOTDALE AND FIRST OF CARLAVEROCK. A.D. 1200-1241.

Sir John succeeded his father, Herbert, in the territory of Maccuswell not long after the year 1200.

During his father's lifetime, "John de Maccuswell," designated "son of Herbert, Sheriff," was witness to a grant, without date, made by Bernard de Hauden to the monks of Kelso, of whatever right they claimed to the mill and mill-pond of Reuedene. To this charter his brother Robert was also, as we have seen before, a witness.[1]

Whether John de Maccuswell inherited the office of Sheriff of Roxburgh from his father, or whether he obtained it by a new grant from King William the Lion, is uncertain; but he held the office in the reign of that King. Under the designation of "Sheriff" he was witness to an agreement between R. Abbot and the Convent of Kelso, and Sir Eustace de Vescy, without date, whereby, at the King's request, the former granted to the latter and to his spouse, the King's daughter, and to his heirs born of her, a chapel in his Court at Sprouston, in which they might observe divine service when they were at that place.[2] "The King's daughter," whom Eustace de Vescy married, was Margaret, daughter of King William. The Abbot of the Convent of Kelso, referred to in the charter, was clearly Ricardus de Cane, who was chosen to that dignity 29th March 1206, and who died in the year 1208. This, then, limits the date of the charter within these years.

Under the designation of "Sheriff," John de Maccuswell was also a witness to a charter by Eustace de Vescy, to the Church of Saint Mary of Kelso, and to the monks there serving God, of twenty shillings annually in the mill of Sprouston;[3] and to a charter by Margaret de Vescy, daughter of the King of Scotland, granting to the monks of Kelso, in free and perpetual alms, twenty shillings of silver annually in her mill of Sprouston, to be received from him who should hold that mill.[4]

Under the designation of "Sheriff of Roxburgh," he was, along with

---

[1] Liber de Calchou, tom. i. p. 176.
[2] *Ibid.* tom. i. p. 172.

[3] Liber de Calchou, tom. i. p. 173.
[4] *Ibid.* tom. i. p. 174.

John, dean of Fogghou, Hugh, the King's chaplain, Ingelramus, the King's clerk, and others, a witness to a charter by William de Veteri-Ponte (Vyerpunt), undated, but belonging to the reign of King William the Lion, as appears from its being made for the welfare of King William and the Queen, and of their son Alexander, granting to the Abbey of Kelso the Church of Langtone, with the lands, tithes, and all the ecclesiastical rights belonging thereto, as his father had done before him, and the Church of Horuerdene.[1]

Under the designation of "Sheriff of Teviotdale," which is equivalent with Roxburgh, he was again a witness, in the reign of King William the Lion, to a charter, without date, by Patrick de Withichun, granting to the Church of Saint Mary of Melrose and the monks there serving God, in free and perpetual alms, a certain portion of his land in the territory of Spot, namely, Lochaneshalech, as therein described.[2]

In the reign of the same King he and his brother Ailmer and others were witnesses to a charter, without date, by Roger Burnard, granting to the monks of Melrose thirteen acres of his lands and one particate in the territory of Faringdun.[3]

At an early period he acquired the esteem of King William the Lion, though he was much younger than that monarch. From various charters, in which his name occurs as a witness, it is evident that he was a frequent attendant at the Court during the reign of King William.

He appears with that King and his Court at Selkirk, where was a castle in which the Kings of Scotland in ancient times occasionally resided, though little is now known of its history, nor can its exact site be pointed out; and here he was present at an amicable composition made in the presence of King William, in full Court, between Earl Patrick of Dunbar, Patrick, his son and heir, consenting, on the one part, and the House of Melrose on the other, in regard to a dispute that had arisen between them concerning a pasture towards the west from the Ledoe. Among the others who were present were Bricius, Bishop of Moray; Radulph, Bishop of Dunblane; William and Oliver, the King's chaplains; Robert de London, the King's son; David de Lindesay; Gervasius Auenel, Justiciar; William de Bosco and Hugh, the King's clerks; and all of them were witnesses to a confirma-

---

[1] Liber de Calchou, tom. i. 109.   [2] Liber S. Marie de Melros, tom. i. p. 47.   [3] Ibid. tom. i. p. 75.

tion by King William of that agreement, dated at Selkirk, 6th November, the year not given, but it must have been in or before the year 1211.[1]

Some time after, John de Maccuswell was with the Court of King William at Selkirk Castle. Among other affairs which then occupied the attention of the Court, was the Abbey of Aberbrothoc, which that monarch had founded in the year 1178, in honour of Thomas à Becket, Archbishop of Canterbury, who was assassinated at the altar of his own church of Canterbury, 29th December 1170. Many years had now elapsed since its foundation; and, besides the lands and churches with which its founder had endowed it, it had by this time been greatly enriched by benefactions in land, churches, and tithes, bestowed by the barons of the north. King William accordingly now granted to that Abbey a charter of the numerous lands and churches which it had acquired. Among the witnesses were John de Maccuswell, and others at the Court, including Alexander, the King's son; Henry, Abbot of Kelso; William de Bosco, Chancellor; and Philip de Valoniis, Chamberlain.[2] The charter is dated at Selkirk, 25th February, the year not given; but as William de Bosco, Chancellor, one of the witnesses, was made Chancellor in 1211, and King William died in 1214, it must have been granted between these years.

John de Maccuswell was also with King William and his Court at Traquair, 19th January, year not given, but between 1211-1214, when the King granted to the Abbey of Aberbrothoc the churches of Inuirbondin and Banef, with their lands, tithes, and oblations for a free and perpetual alms. Among the witnesses were William de Bosco, the King's Chancellor, and Philip de Valoniis, the King's Chamberlain.[3]

On the death of King William, who died on 4th December 1214, in the seventy-second year of his age and the forty-ninth of his reign, his son Alexander, who was born 24th August 1198,[4] succeeded to the throne.[5]

John de Maccuswell continued to hold the same high place in the counsels of Alexander the Second which he had attained in those of King William the Lion. He was a witness to a charter by Alexander the Second, confirming

[1] Liber Sancte Marie de Melros, tom. i. p. 93.

[2] Liber S. Thome de Aberbrothoc, tom. i. p. 8.

[3] *Ibid*. tom. i. p. 21.

[4] Chronica de Mailros, p. 103.

[5] Palgrave's Documents and Records, vol. i. pp. 73, 74.

to the Monastery of Melrose numerous lands which had been granted to it by different parties. The charter is dated at Edinburgh, 3d April, year not given, but probably soon after Alexander's accession to the throne. Among the other witnesses were William de Bosco, the King's Chancellor ; Seiher de Quinci, Earl ; Malcolm, Earl of Fife ; Philip de Valoniis, the King's Chamberlain ; William de Valoniis, his son ; and Robert, the King's chaplain.[1]

John de Maccuswell was soon after employed by his Sovereign in affairs of greater importance, a proof of the distinction which he had acquired as an able and an accomplished statesman. By King Alexander, he and the Bishop of St. Andrews, Philip de Mubray, Robert de St. Germain, Walter de Lindesay, and Ingelramus de Baliol,[2] were despatched as ambassadors to John, King of England, by a letter from the former King to the latter, dated 7th July 1215, for transacting certain business of the Scottish monarch with the King of England.

After this we find John de Maccuswell attending his Sovereign and the Court at Forfar, where was a castle situated on an eminence to the north of the town, and occasionally the residence of royalty. Among other things transacted at that time at the Court was the granting of a charter by that monarch " for the love of God, and for the welfare of the soul of his father, King William, and for the welfare of his own soul, and of the souls of his ancestors and successors," confirming to the Monastery of Aberbrothoc, which his father, King William, had founded in honour of Saint Thomas, Archbishop and Martyr, numerous lands and churches. To this charter John de Maccuswell was a witness, and among others who were present with the Court on that occasion, and who also witnessed the charter, were Hugh, Bishop of Brechin ; Robert, Elect of Ross ; Gwydon, Abbot of Lindores ; William de Bosco, the King's Chancellor ; Malcolm, Earl of Fife ; and Robert, the King's Chaplain.[3] The names of the ecclesiastical dignitaries occur first, and they ranked among, and even took precedence of, the highest of the lay nobility. This charter is dated 17th February, year not given, but it must have been between the 4th December 1214, when Alexander came to the throne, and 1218, when Hugh, Bishop of Brechin, one of the witnesses, died.

[1] Liber Sancte Marie de Melros, tom. i. p. 161.
[2] Rymer's Fœdera, tom. i. p. 203. Lond. 1704.
[3] Liber S. Thome de Aberbrothoc, tom. i. p. 74.

At another time, John de Maccuswell was a witness to a confirmation by Alexander the Second, at Forfar, 8th June, to the monks of Aberbrothoc of that donation which William, son of Bernard, made to them of two oxgangs of land in the territory of Caterin.[1]

John de Maccuswell was also with King Alexander and his Court at Perth, which anciently was deemed the first town in Scotland, where the sovereigns frequently resided, and where great national councils were held. Here many public transactions took place, as appears from numerous charters which were granted by King William the Lion, Alexander the Second, and succeeding kings of Scotland. At Perth John de Maccuswell, with William de Bosco, Chancellor, William Cumyn, Earl of Buchan, and Robert de London, son of King William, was witness to a charter by his Sovereign, 18th April, year not given, granting to the Abbey of Arbroath one full toft without his Majesty's burgh of Perth, as was perambulated to them within the two ports.[2]

In the year 1220, John de Maccuswell was again sent as ambassador, along with the Bishops of Glasgow and St. Andrews, William de Bosco, Chancellor, Walter Cumin, and others, to negotiate a marriage between his sovereign, Alexander, and the Princess Johanna, daughter of the late John, King of England, and sister of Henry the Third, who then occupied the English throne, to which he had been elevated in the year 1216.

This mission was successful. Henry the Third, King of England, engaged by letters, dated at York 15th June 1220, in the presence of Lord Pandulff, Elect of Norwich, Lord Chamberlain of the Pope and Legate of the Apostolic Seat, addressed to Archbishops, Bishops, Abbots, Earls, Barons, Knights, and to all his faithful subjects, to give his eldest sister Johanna to wife to Alexander, King of Scotland, at the Feast of Saint Michael, in the year 1220, if he could obtain possession of her person, for which he and his Council would labour faithfully, and if he could not obtain her, to give him to wife his younger sister, Isabella (who afterwards married the Emperor Frederick the Third), within fifteen days after the foresaid term.[3]

John de Maccuswell came under obligations, along with various bishops,

[1] Liber S. Thome de Aberbrothoc, tom. i. p. 90.
[2] Ibid. tom. i. p. 78.   [3] Rymer's Foedera, tom. i. p. 240.

nobles, and others, that he would do what he could for the completion of this marriage. The following is a translation of the deed by which Alexander on his part formally agreed to the treaty :—

"Alexander, by the grace of God, King of the Scots, to all the faithful of Christ who shall see or hear the present writing, Health,—Know ye all that we have sworn on our soul, without fraud and evil intention, that we will marry Johanna, eldest sister of Lord Henry, King of England, at the Feast of Saint Michael, in the year of the Lord one thousand two hundred and twentieth, if the same Lord King of England can obtain possession of her person, and shall give her to us ; or before, if it can be done : and if perchance he cannot obtain her, we swear that we will marry Isabella, younger sister of the said Lord Henry, King of England, within fifteen days thereafter, or before, if it can be done : and that in the meantime we will not marry, nor enter into treaty for marrying any other. Concerning this, we have caused this our charter to be made to the foresaid Lord King of England ; and the Bishops of St. Andrews and Glasgow, and William de Bosco, our Chancellor, have promised, *in verbo veritatis*, that they will faithfully labour that these things may be completed in good faith ; as to which they have given their charter. And the Earl of Buchan and Alan of Galweya, Constabularius, and others, our barons, namely, Philip de Mobray and Walter Elifend, and Dunecan of Carric, and Henry de Baliol, and Thomas, hostiarius, and John of Maccuswell, and David [Mar]escallus, and Walter Cumin, and Randulph de Bor——yl [Bernevylle], and Heruic Marescallus, have sworn that they will observe in good faith this same, which the foresaid bishops have promised *in verbo veritatis*, and have made their charter thereupon. Done at York, in the presence of Lord Pandulph, Elect of Norwich, Lord Chamberlain of the Pope and Legate of the Apostolic Seat, on the 15th day of June, in the year of our reign the sixth."[1]

Johanna, daughter of King John, father of Henry, King of England, had been given by her father, when formerly in the parts of Pictavia, for marriage to Hugh of Lezignan, son of the Earl of March. But Hugh, although he accepted her from the hands of her father, and swore to take her to wife, yet not observing his oath, and despising Johanna, formed a marital union with

---

[1] Rymer's Fœdera, tom. i. p. 241.

the Queen, mother[1] of Henry, King of England, and refused to restore Johanna, whom he detained, contrary to the King's mandate, attempting to force from the King a price for her redemption. Henry accordingly sent letters to the Pope, dated at Nottingham, 20th June 1220, supplicating that he would be pleased to write to the Lord Bishop of Saintes, and to the Lord Bishop of Limoges, and to the Dean of Bordeaux, that the said Hugh, if, after being warned, he should refuse to restore to Henry his sister, should be compelled to do so by the spiritual sword.[2] A letter was also sent by King Henry to the cardinals of the Roman Church, dated from the same place, on the same day, asking them to inform the same bishops and dean, by letter, that unless, after warning, he restored the King's sister, he should be compelled to do so by ecclesiastical censure.[3]

King Henry, in a letter to Hugh, Earl of March, dated at Winton, 16th September 1220, says :— " We have commanded you, at another time, as you value our honour, to send to us our beloved sister whom you have in keeping, and to restore her into the hand of the venerable father, Bishop of Saintes, in our town of Rupel. But now we command you, in the confidence of your obedience, and as you value our perpetual honour (unless you have restored her into the hand of the foresaid Bishop), to deliver her without further delay to our beloved and faithful Philip de Uletot, to whom we have committed the keeping of our land of Pictavia and Wasconia, and to the Dean of Pictavia in our town of Rupel." [4]

Johanna, having been restored to her brother, Henry, King of England, the marriage between her and Alexander, King of Scotland, was celebrated.

John de Maccuswell was one of the witnesses to letters-patent by the Scottish monarch, dated at York, 18th June 1221, granting to Johanna, sister of the King of England, and his beloved spouse, for dowry, various lands, of the estimated value of a thousand pounds, including Jeddewurth, Lessedwin, and Kymgor. The other witnesses were William, Bishop of St. Andrews ; Walter, Bishop of Glasgow ; William de Bosco, Chancellor ; Thomas, Prior of Cesdiugh ; Earl Patrick ; William Cumin, Earl of Buchan, Justiciar of Scotland ;

[1] Isabella, daughter and heiress to Ailmer, Earl of Angoulesme, the third wife of John, King of England, and the mother of Johanna, as well as of Henry the Third, King of England.

[2] Rymer's Fœdera, tom. i. p. 242.
[3] *Ibid.* tom. i. p. 242.
[4] *Ibid.* tom. i. p. 248.

Robert de London ; Walter, the Steward, son of Alan ; Robert de Brus ; Walter Olifard, Justiciar of Lothian ; Engelramus de Baliol ; Philip de Mobray ; and Henry de Baliol.[1]

For the success of his mission in negotiating the marriage between King Alexander and the Princess Johanna, John de Maccuswell, it would appear, had conferred upon him the honour of knighthood.

Under the designation of " Dominus" he was witness to an amicable agreement, made in the Castle of Roxburgh, 28th December 1221, between Lord Walter, Bishop of Glasgow, and the Abbot and Convent of Kelso, in regard to the Church of Campsy, whereby the Abbot and Convent of Kelso quitclaimed to the said Bishop and his successors, and to the Church of Glasgow, all right which they had in the Church of Campsy.[2]

Under the same designation he was witness to a charter, without date, by Walter, the King's Steward, son of Alan, granting to the Monastery of Melrose the territory of Mauchelin and the Church of Saint Michael, situated therein, and remitting to the said Monastery for ever the payment of five merks, payable annually for the said land by it to him and his heirs.[3]

Between the years 1220 and 1231, Sir John appears to have been in constant attendance at the Court. During that period we can trace, from contemporary charters, his presence with the King and the Court at the principal places in Scotland which they were accustomed to visit.

These notices not only show the consideration in which he was held, and supply the names of those who with him were most about the person of the Sovereign, and who assisted him in the administration of public affairs, but also indicate the character of the transactions which occupied Sir John's attention and that of the King and the Court, relating largely to the legal security of property acquired by the monastic establishments—the monasteries of Melrose, Kelso, Aberbrothoc, and Paisley, which in the time of Sir John possessed vast and constantly increasing wealth.

In the spring of the year 1222, John de Mackeswell was with King Alexander and his Court at the Castle of Roxburgh, which had been the residence of David the First, both before and after his succession to the Scottish throne,

[1] Rymer's Fœdera, tom. i. p. 252.

[2] Registrum Episcopatus Glasguensis, tom. i. p. 101.

[3] Liber Sancte Marie de Melros, tom. i. p. 65.

and which continued to be a royal castle during the reigns of several of his successors. Whilst with the Court at this celebrated castle, he and William de Boscho, Chancellor, Walter Olifard, Justiciar of Lothian, Bernard de Hauden, and others, were witnesses to a charter by the King, dated 20th April that year, granting to the Church of St. Mary of Kelso, and to Herbert, its Abbot, the same liberties and customs which the abbots, his predecessors, had formerly possessed ; and wherever that abbot should find natives and fugitives, his men, beyond his Majesty's dominions in his whole land, he was to have them restored to him without delay, and all were prohibited, under pain of forfeiture, from unjustly detaining them, or his cattle, from him, or unjustly molesting him or his servants on this account.[1]

In the summer of the year 1223, John de Maccuswell was with the King and his Court at Ayr, a royal burgh, erected by King William the Lion, where was anciently a fortlet, at which some of the kings of Scotland occasionally made a temporary stay. At this town King Alexander, by a charter, dated 8th May that year, granted to the Church of Glasgow forty shillings from the rents of the royal burgh of Rutherglen for light to that church ;[2] and also, by a charter of the same date, those six merks which King William, his father, had given to the Church of Glasgow from the rents of the burgh of Rutherglen for behoof of a dean and sub-dean, that, according to the Statutes of the Church of Glasgow, they might walk decently and elegantly attired, with surplices and black caps, like other vicars. To both these charters John de Maccuswell was a witness. The other courtiers who were witnesses to the last-mentioned charter were Walter, the Steward, son of Alan ; Walter Olifard, Justiciar of Lothian; Radulf, Chaplain ; Ingelram de Baliol ; Henry de Baliol, Chamberlain ; and Henry of Stirling, son of Earl David.[3]

In the summer of the year 1225 Sir John accompanied his Sovereign and the Court to Glasgow. At this town, which was then of small importance, he, along with Thomas of Stirling, Archdean of Glasgow, Radulph, the King's Chaplain, and others, witnessed a charter by the King, dated 9th May that year, confirming that donation, which Robert of London, the King's brother,

---

[1] Liber de Calchou, tom. i. p. 9.

[2] Registrum Episcopatus Glasguensis, tom. i. p. 102.

[3] Registrum Episcopatus Glasguensis, tom. i. p. 103.

had made to Saint Kentigern and the Church of Glasgow, of one stone of wax for light.[1]

Between two and three months after, the King and the Court were at Selkirk, and here again Sir John was with them. At this place, he, and other courtiers, among whom were Thomas of Stirling, Chancellor, Walter Olifard, Justiciar of Lothian, Henry de Baliol, Chamberlain, John de Vallibus, William de Veteri Ponte, and Bernard de Hauden, were witnesses to a confirmation by the King, dated 22d July 1225, of that donation of a portion of land in the territory of Makestown which John de Normanville had made to the Abbey of Melrose.[2]

Towards the close of the year 1225, Sir John appears with the King and his Court at Cadihou or Cadzow, now Hamilton, where the Kings of Scotland had a family seat, and the barony and castle of that name continued in the possession of the Crown till the time of Robert Bruce, when they were bestowed by that monarch on Sir Walter de Hambleton for his faithful services, and came to be called Hamilton, after the name of their new proprietor. Whilst here, Sir John, under the designation of " Sheriff of Roxburgh," along with Walter Olifard, Justiciar of Lothian, Henry of Baliol, Chamberlain, and William de Hertesheued, Sheriff of Lanark, and others of the Court, witnessed a renunciation by his Majesty, dated 12th November that year, to Walter, Bishop of Glasgow, and his successors, bishops, of whatever right the King had in Gillemichel, son of Bowein, and Gillemor his son, and Buzer and Gillys, son of Eldred, whom Adam, son of Gilbert, had quitclaimed to the foresaid Bishop and his successors, bishops of Glasgow.[3]

He was also witness to a charter by Alexander the Second, dated at Cadihou, 22d November 1225, confirming to Saint Kentigern and Walter, Bishop of Glasgow, and to the bishops, his successors, their right to have a burgh at Glasgow, with a market on Thursday, as the charter made by that King's father to Jocelyn, formerly Bishop of Glasgow, testified.[4]

In November, same year, Sir John was present with the King and the Court, at Lanark, which is said to have been a royal burgh in the time of Alexander the First, but which was certainly so in the reign of Malcolm the

[1] Registrum Episcopatus Glasguensis, tom. i. p. 115.   [3] Registrum Episcopatus Glasguensis, tom. i.
[2] Liber Sancte Marie de Melros, tom. i. p. 220.   p. 111.   [4] Ibid. tom. i. p. 113.

Fourth (1153-65), who, in granting a toft in the place, called it "my·burgh;" and at which was a castle, which was a royal residence, situated, it is said, on an eminence south from the town, and now forming a bowling-green. At this place King Alexander the Second issued letters dated 19th November that year to the justiciars, sheriffs, provosts, ministers, and all upright men of the Episcopal See of Glasgow, commanding them to yield reverence and obedience to their bishop, archdean, and ministers, and to pay fully and without reluctance their tithes and other ecclesiastical rights to their churches. To these letters "John de Maccuswell, Sheriff of Roxburgh," Henry de Baliol, Chamberlain, William de Coleuill, Heruicus Marscallus, Walter Biset, and William Biset were witnesses.[1]

In the autumn of the following year Sir John was with his Sovereign and the Court at Jedewurth [Jedburgh], where was, perhaps, the strongest and largest castle on the borders. Here he and others of the Court, including Thomas de Stirling, Chancellor, Henry de Baliol, Chamberlain, Roger de Quenci, David Marscallus, Henry Mar, and Walter Biset, were witnesses to a charter by King Alexander, dated 29th October 1226, securing to the Church of Saint Kentigern of Glasgow, and to Walter, its Bishop, and his successors, bishops, that neither his Majesty's provosts, nor bailies, nor servants of Rutherglen should receive toll or custom in the town of Glasgow.[2]

In the spring of the year 1226, he attended the King and his Court at Stirling, which anciently was one of the principal seats of royalty. While in this town he took part in effecting an amicable agreement between William, Bishop of St. Andrews, on the one side, and the Abbot Randulph and the Convent of Aberbrothoc on the other, with regard to the lands and rents of Fyvyn, Tarueys, Inverbondyn, Munbre, Gameryn, Inverugyn, and Munedin, about which a dispute had arisen, the Bishop of St. Andrews having now quitclaimed for himself and his successors these lands to the Abbot and Convent of Aberbrothoc. Under the designation of "Sheriff of Roxburgh," he was witness to a confirmation of that agreement by Alexander the Second, dated at Stirling, 30th March 1226. Among the other witnesses were Andrew, Bishop of Moray ; Robert, Bishop of Ross ; Thomas Stirling, Chancellor ;

[1] Registrum Episcopatus Glasguensis, tom. i. p. 116.   [2] *Ibid.* tom. i. p. 114.

Malcolm, Earl of Fife ; Patrick, Earl of Dunbar ; Walter, son of Alan Steward ; and Walter Olifard, Justiciar of Lothian.[1]

In the year 1228, Sir John sojourned with King Alexander and his Court at Musselburgh.   Here the King granted a confirmation dated 16th April that year, of that donation which Maldouen, Earl of Lennox, made to Robert Hertford, clerk, of the half of the fishing of a yare in the Leven, on the east side of that river ; and also a confirmation of the donation of the land of Dollenlenrach which Dungallus, son of Alwyn, Earl of Lennox, made to Robert Hertford, clerk.   To both these confirmations " John Maxswell" was a witness.[2]

In the autumn of the year 1228, Sir John again with the King and the Court visited Stirling.   At this place he and others of the Court, including Mathew, Chancellor ; William Cumin, Earl of Buchan ; Olifard, Justiciar of Lothian ; Walter the Steward, son of Alan ; and Peter de Valoniis ; were witnesses to a charter by King Alexander, dated 22d October that year, confirming that donation of the Church of Kilpatrick which Maldouen, Earl of Lennox, made to the Abbey of Paisley.[3]

John of Maxwell sat in the Parliament of Alexander the Second, held in October 1230, as appears from the following Act :—

" In the year of grace 1230, the Sunday next before the Feast of St. Luke the Evangelist, in presence of the magnates of his kingdom, [W.] Bishop of St. Andrews ; Malcolm, Earl of Fife ; William Comyn, Earl of Buchan and Justiciar of Scotland ; Thomas, Prior of Coldinghame ; Walter Olifard, Justiciar of Lothian ; Walter, Steward of Scotland, the son of Alan ; John of Maxwell, and many others, King Alexander ordained at Stirling, by the counsel and assent of the same magnates, and of his whole community, that no bishop, abbot, or clerk, earl, baron, or knight, or any other of the kingdom of Scotland, from henceforth, shall borrow any man as his man, nor seek to borrow any one who has been charged with any misdeed or crime, unless the same person be his liegeman or born bondman, or dwelling on his land or of his family. But if, perhaps, it is known by lawful men of the country that it is not so, but that he who borrows the same wishes to borrow him that is accused for his

---

[1] Liber S. Thome de Aberbrothoc, tom. i. p. 120.   [2] Registrum Monasterii de Passelet, pp. 214, 215.   [3] *Ibid.* p. 172.

fine, as the magnates were hitherto wont to do, by taking of the malefactor wax, pepper, cumyn, or any other annual, the lord that borrows him is at the King's mercy, because he has forbidden such gifts."[1]

In the year 1230, Henry de Baliol, Lord of Reidcastle (son of Ingelram de Baliol, Lord of Bernard Castle), having resigned the office of Chamberlain, which he had held in the reign of Alexander the Second for several years, Sir John was appointed his successor.[2]

Under the designation of " Chamberlain," he was a witness to a precept by Alexander the Second, dated at Melrose, 19th March 1230, to the Sheriffs of his whole kingdom, commanding them vigorously to assist in prosecuting certain evildoers, who had stolen the cattle or money of the monks of Melrose.[3] In the year 1231, under the designation of *"Dominus* Maccuswell, King's Chamberlain," he witnessed a charter by Henry de Beletun, granting to the monks of Melrose his lands of Kingisset.[4]

As " Chamberlain," he was witness to a charter by King Alexander, dated at Traquair, 4th February 1232, confirming the donation of a certain part of his land in the territory of Makestoun, which John de Normanville made to the Abbey of Melrose ;[5] to a charter by the same King, dated at Selkirk, 7th June 1233, granting to the monks of Kelso, for the perpetual maintenance of the bridge of Ettrick, the land which Richard, son of Edwin, had held on each side of the water of Ettrick, and which he had quitclaimed to the granter ;[6] and to another royal charter, dated at Forfar 3d July 1233, granting to the Abbey of Aberbrothoc the whole of his land of Nig, reserving to himself the fishings which he was wont to have in that land.[7]

Soon after, Sir John appears to have resigned his office of Chamberlain, but for what reason we are not informed, and was succeeded by Philip de Valoniis. Without any designation he was a witness to two charters by King Alexander, dated at Edinburgh 3d April, the year not given, along with Philip de Valoniis, who is designed by the King, "my Chamberlain," the one confirming to the Abbey of Melrose all its lands, and the other confirming to the same

[1] The Acts of the Parliaments of Scotland, Statuta Alexandri II., p. 69.

[2] Crawfurd's Lives of the Officers of the Crown and State, pp. 260, 261.

[3] Liber Sancte Marie de Melros, tom. i. p. 162.

[4] Liber Sancte Marie de Melros, tom. i. p. 195.

[5] *Ibid.* tom. i. p. 222.

[6] Liber de Calchou, tom. ii. p. 309.

[7] Liber S. Thome de Aberbrothoc, tom. i. p. 75.

Abbey the whole fishing of Old Roxburgh in the Tweed to Brockestream, which King David his great-grandfather had given to it.[1] From his still remaining at the Court and taking part in its business, it may be concluded that he did not resign his office of Chamberlain from any misunderstanding between him and his royal master. There is abundant evidence that, during the remainder of his days, he continued as much about the King as formerly.

He was witness to a charter by Thomas Alnot, Knight, granting to the Abbey of Melrose the lands of Brunsceth, Hauthyncref, and Dergauel, dated 1237.[2]

The last instance in which his name occurs as a witness, is in a charter by Alexander to Earl Maldouen, of the Earldom of Levenax, on the 28th of July 1238.[3]

Sir John died in the year 1241, a year notable as that in which Gregory IX. died, and in which the eldest son of Alexander the Second (afterwards Alexander the Third) was born. He was interred in Melrose Abbey, as we learn from a contemporary chronicle. "A.D. 1241. Johannes de Macheswel apud Melros sepelitur."[4] He was succeeded by his brother Aymer.

Upon the authority of the earlier writers on the family of Maxwell, Sir John acquired the barony of Carlaverock and other extensive additions to the barony of Maccuswell. No positive proof in support of this statement has been discovered. But Carlaverock must have been acquired by the Maxwells at a very early period, and from the constancy of the tradition and the numerous opportunities which Sir John, as appears from the preceding notices of his history, must have had of obtaining grants from the Crown, we may accept it as a fact that he did acquire the barony of Carlaverock. The early charters of Carlaverock have been lost, like those of the barony of Maccuswell, having pro-bably been destroyed in the many sieges which the castle sustained, and this explains how the dates of the erection of the barony of Carlaverock, and of the first of the Maxwells who acquired it in property, have not been ascertained. In a history of the family of Maxwell, written about the end of the sixteenth century, it is stated that Carlaverock Castle was the chief seat of the family

[1] Liber Sancte Marie de Melros, tom. i. pp. 159, 228.   [3] Cartularium de Levenax, p. 2.
[2] Ibid. tom. i. p. 187.   [4] Chronica de Mailros, p. 154.

of Maxwell in the days of King Malcolm Canmore, when Eugin or Ewin Maxwell of Carlaverock was at the siege of Alnwick with the King, in the twentieth year of his reign, A.D. 1097. It is further said in that history that Eugin or Ewin Maxwell was succeeded by Uthred Maxwell, who was at the battle of Allartown in 1134; and that Uthred was succeeded by Eugin, who died on 27th December 1199.[1] But these statements, although unusually explicit as to day and date, are quite inaccurate. In the Memoirs of Maccus, who is entirely omitted in the history now quoted, it has been shown that he was the first of the family who gave rise to the surname of Maxwell.

If the first of the family who acquired the barony and Castle of Carlaverock[2] was the grandson of Maccus, John de Maccuswell, Lord Chamberlain of Scotland, about the year 1200, it is uncertain whether he obtained it as a direct feudal grant in property or as official Castellan. But whether as actual owners or official castellans the Castle was acquired by the Maxwells before the celebrated siege in the year 1300; and having continued, with the exception of a few short intervals, chiefly in the wars of succession, to be the property of the Maxwell family, it may be considered as one of the oldest hereditary castles of Scotland.

The Castle of Carlaverock, which Sir John is believed to have acquired, is entitled to special notice in a work on the history of the family of Maxwell. Its connexion with various events in the lives of particular representatives of the family will be narrated in the progress of these biographies. But the Castle has a history of its own, and to collect into a connected narrative the scattered notices to be found concerning it ought to have a special interest to the enlightened reader of Scottish history. In this place we shall bring together these various notices, though necessarily carrying the history downwards many centuries after the time of its supposed original acquirer.

---

[1] Original MS. in a volume in possession of Lord Herries, printed in Minutes of Evidence in Herries Peerage Case, 20th May 1851, p. 294.

[2] The exact date of the erection of the barony is unknown. But it was before the year 1324. After Christian Bruce, sister of King Robert the Bruce, had founded a chapel at Dumfries, on the fatal spot of the execution of her husband, Sir Christopher Seton, the King granted, in December 1324, a hundred shillings yearly, out of the barony of Carlaverock, to a chaplain, for performing prayers within the chapel for the soul of Sir Christopher, who had been killed in his service.—(Sir Lewis Stewart's MS. Collection.)

THE CASTLE OF CARLAVEROCK.

The boundaries of the ancient barony of Carlaverock are almost identical with those of the parish of the same name in the county of Dumfries, which is about six miles in length and two in breadth, sloping gradually from the north, where it is bounded by the parish of Dumfries, to the flat ground on the Solway Firth, which bounds it on the south. The higher ground also slopes towards the rivers Nith and Lochar, which bound the parish on the west and east, and with the sea on the south form it into a sort of peninsula. Upon the flat ground is a considerable extent of wood, apparently of natural growth, in the midst of which the towers and chimneys of the ruined Castle of Carlaverock present a conspicuous object from all parts of the surrounding country, being visible even from the opposite shores of England upon a clear day. Although the country immediately surrounding the Castle is somewhat tame, the views from it are in the highest degree striking. On the west is the Firth, here widened out into a broad bay, bordered by the noble woods of Arbigland, Kirkconnel, and New Abbey, above which tower the massive heights of Criffel hill. On the south may be seen the broad Solway, stretching to the coast of Cumberland, backed by the lofty mountains of the Lake Country, while to the the east is Lochar Moss, with its vast expanse of wild and irreclaimable moorland.

Venerable as these ruins are, they may be said to be modern when compared with those of the more ancient castle, whose foundations can still be clearly traced in the Bowhouse wood, about 300 yards to the south of the present ruins and on a somewhat lower level.[1] These are the remains of what was probably the original Castle of Carlaverock, which must have been of great antiquity, although no record of its history is now known to exist. Camden and other writers endeavour to identify it with the Carbantorigum of Ptolemy, but other places in the same county are identified with the same place on equally sufficient or insufficient grounds. Tradition assigns the reign of King Arthur, in the sixth century, as the date of the erection of the original Castle of

[1] From the appearance of the ground surrounding these more ancient remains it is probable that the walls of the original castle were at one time washed by the waters of the Solway.

CAERLAVEROCK CASTLE.

MURDOCH'S TOWER & INTERIOR.

Carlaverock, while Grose fixes upon Lewarch Ogg, son of Lewarch Hen, a cele-brated British bard, as the founder of it, and derives its name from him. But as there are several other places in Scotland of the same name with which Lewarch Ogg could have had no connexion, this etymology is not of much value.

The importance of the position of Carlaverock, as being the key of a great part of the south-west of Scotland, must have been very early discovered; and the Maxwells, when they acquired the barony of Carlaverock, if no stronghold previously existed there, must speedily have erected one, had it been only to enhance their own influence as the holders of one of the most important defences of their country against their English neighbours. It is, however, certain that the Castle of Carlaverock, soon after the Maxwell family acquired it, became their chief residence, and that it continued to be so for several centuries, completely eclipsing their original manor of Maxwell, of which the notices to be found even in family records are very scanty.

From its position, as well as from the skill with which it was built, the Castle of Carlaverock was a place of great strength; for though it did not stand on the banks of a rapid river, or the summit of a precipitous rock, yet the approaches to it were protected on one side by the waters of the Solway, and on another by the impassable moss of Lochar.

In this castle Sir William Wallace, after he had captured Enoch, Tibbers, and other strong places in Nithsdale, and routed a party of English in Dalswinton wood, lodged one night with Sir Herbert Maxwell, its owner, with whom he was on terms of friendship.[1] In the war between Scotland and England in the reign of Edward the First, King of England, it held out against that monarch after he had made himself master of the prin-cipal strongholds of Scotland, such as Edinburgh, Stirling, Dunbar, Dun-dee, Brechin, Dunnottar, and others. The continued resistance which it offered to Edward, after he had captured so many other castles in Scot-land, roused his wrath, and he determined to besiege it in person. The Castle, against which the power and chivalry of England were thus to be brought, its favourable situation, and its excellent means of defence at that

[1] Blind Harry.

time, are thus graphically described in a contemporary metrical history of the siege :[1]—

"Carlaverock was so strong a castle that it did not fear a siege ; therefore the King came himself, because it would not consent to surrender. But it was always furnished for its defence, whenever it was required, with men, engines, and provisions. Its shape was like that of a shield [triangular], for it had only three sides all round, with a tower on each angle ; but one of them was a double one, so high, so long, and so large, that under it was the gate, with a drawbridge, well made and strong, and a sufficiency of other defences. It had good walls and good ditches, filled to the edge with water ; and I believe there never was seen a castle more beautifully situated, for at once could be seen the Irish Sea towards the west, and, to the north, a fine country surrounded by an arm of the sea, so that no creature born could approach it on two sides without putting himself in danger of the sea. Towards the south it was not easy, because there were numerous dangerous defiles of wood and marshes and ditches, where the sea is on each side of it, and where the river reaches it ; and therefore it was necessary for the host to approach toward the east, where the hill slopes."[2]

Such were the Castle of Carlaverock and its fortifications at the time when Edward the First resolved on besieging it.

By an order, dated 29th December 1299, all who owed King Edward the First military service were summoned to attend him at Carlisle, on the Feast of the Nativity of John the Baptist next to come, 24th June 1300, to serve against the Scots. On that day the whole host assembled at the place of rendezvous, with their commanders, consisting of the Prince of Wales, the King's eldest son (afterwards Edward the Second), and the most illustrious barons and knights of the realm, to the number of eighty-seven, ranked under their respective banners; and they filled the road to the castle. They and the King left Carlisle about the 1st of July, and marched to the Castle of Carlaverock. They "set forward against the Scots," says the author of the metrical narrative, "not in coats and surcoats, but on powerful and costly chargers ; and that they might not be taken by surprise they were well and securely armed. There

[1] This metrical history, entitled " The Siege of Carlaverock," written in Norman French, is preserved in the British Museum. Pennant, in his account of Carlaverock Castle, in his Tour in Scotland in 1772, had the use of a copy of this work, from which he makes several extracts. In the year 1828 it was published, with a translation, by Sir Harris Nicolas, who attributes its authorship to Walter of Exeter, a Franciscan friar, the author of the history of Guy of Warwick, which he wrote in the year 1292. Whoever was the author, it is certain that he was present with the English army at the siege, for he informs us in the poem that he was so. The description of the siege of this ancient Castle suggested to Sir Walter Scott the idea of the siege of the castle of Front de Bœuf in " Ivanhoe."

[2] The Siege of Carlaverock, translated by Sir Harris Nicolas, pp. 61, 63.

were many rich caparisons embroidered on silks and satins ; many a beautiful pennon fixed to a lance, and many a banner displayed. And afar off was the noise heard of the neighing of horses : hills and valleys were everywhere covered with sumpter horses and waggons with provisions, and sacks of tents and pavilions. And the days were long and fine. They proceeded by easy journeys, arranged in four squadrons."[1]

The poet then gives the names of the barons and knights who accompanied the English monarch, eulogizes the personal merits of each, and describes especially their banners, and the arms with which they were emblazoned, affording evidence of the importance then attached to heraldry, and, as Sir Harris Nicolas observes, of its perfect state as a science at that early period.

Take the following as specimens :—

" Henry, the good Earl of Lincoln, burning with valour, and which is the chief feeling of his heart, leading the first squadron, had a banner of yellow silk with a purple lion rampant.

" With him Robert de Fitz Walter, who well knew the use of arms, and so used them when required. In a yellow banner he had a fess between two red chevrons.

" The Earl's companion was the Constable, who was Earl of Hereford, a rich and elegant young man. He had a banner of deep blue silk, with a white bend between two cotises of fine gold, on the outside of which he had six lioncels rampant.

" With him was Nicholas de Segrave, whom nature had adorned in body and enriched in heart. He had a valiant father, who . . . had by his wife five sons, who were valiant, bold, and courageous knights. The banner of the eldest, whom the Earl Marshal had sent to execute his duties because he could not come, was sable, with a silver lion rampant, crowned with fine gold.

" John, the good Earl of Warren, held the reins to regulate and govern the second squadron, as he who well knew how to lead noble and honourable men. His banner was handsomely chequered with gold and azure.

" Edward, King of England and Scotland, Lord of Ireland, Prince of Wales, and Duke of Aquitaine, conducted the third squadron at a little distance, and brought up the rear so closely and ably that none of the others were left behind. In his banner were three leopards courant, of fine gold, set on red, fierce, haughty, and cruel ; thus placed to signify that, like them, the King is dreadful, fierce, and proud to his enemies, for his bite is slight to none who inflame his anger ; not but his kindness is soon rekindled towards such as seek his friendship or submit to his power. Such a prince was well suited to be the chieftain of noble personages.

" I must next mention his nephew, John of Brittany, because he is nearest to him ; and this preference he has well deserved, having assiduously served his uncle from his infancy, and left his father and other relations to dwell in his household when the King had occasion for his followers. He was handsome and amiable, and had a beautiful and ornamented banner, chequered with gold and azure, with a red border and yellow leopards, and a quarter of ermine.

[1] The Siege of Carlaverock, translated by Sir Harris Nicolas, pp. 3, 5.

" Robert, the Lord of Clifford, to whom reason gives consolation, who always remembers to overcome his enemies.   He may call Scotland to bear witness of his noble lineage, that originated well and nobly, as he is of the race of the noble Marshal who at Constantinople fought with an unicorn, and struck him dead beneath him ; from whom he is descended through his mother.   The good Roger, his father's father, was considered equal to him, but he had no merit which does not appear to be revived in his grandson ; for I well know there is no degree of praise of which he is not worthy, as he exhibits as many proofs of wisdom and prudence as any of those who accompany his good lord the King.   His much honoured banner was chequered with gold and azure, with a vermilion fess.   If I were a young maiden I would give him my heart and person, so great is his fame.

" The fourth squadron, with its train, was led by Edward, the King's son, a youth of seventeen years of age, and bearing arms for the first time.   He was of a well-proportioned and handsome person, of a courteous disposition, and intelligent ; and desirous of finding an occasion to display his prowess.   He managed his steed wonderfully well, and bore, with a blue label, the arms of the good King, his father." [1]

As has been observed before, it was necessary for Edward to approach the castle towards the east, where the hill slopes ; and there, by his command, the host was formed into three battalions, as they were to be quartered, and then were the banners arranged, there being 3000 men-at-arms.   " Those of the castle," says the author whom we have already quoted, " on seeing us arrive, might, as I well believe, deem that they were in greater peril than they could ever before remember." [2]   For their accommodation the soldiers immediately began to erect huts.   " As soon as we were thus drawn up, we were quartered by the marshal, and then might be seen houses built without carpenters or masons, of many different fashions, and many a cord stretched, with white and coloured cloth, with many pins driven into the ground, many a large tree cut down to make huts ; and leaves, herbs, and flowers, gathered in the woods, which were strewed within ; and then our people took up their quarters." [3]

The castle was formally summoned to surrender, and, not complying, it was regularly invested on the 10th July 1300.   Little or no improvement had been made in the construction of military engines since the days of the Romans, but the English lost no time in bringing up such as they had, for doing which they had the advantage of a commanding fleet on the Solway. Battering-rams were landed ; so were robinets, springalds or espringalls, the

[1] The Siege of Carlaverock, pp. 5, 11, 13, 15, 23, 25, 27, 29, 43.

[2] The Siege of Carlaverock, p. 63.
[3] *Ibid.* p. 65.

catapultæ or *balistæ* of the Romans; the machine called the sow, moving on wheels, and resembling the Roman *testudo*, covered over with raw hides, under the protection of which the besiegers of a town were enabled to get close to the walls.

Carpenters, smiths, and other workmen had been employed for the construction of these engines, and they accompanied the English army to Carlaverock, apparently for the purpose of keeping the engines in repair. Engines were also brought to the siege from Carlisle, Lochmaben, the Castle of Roxburgh, the Castle of Jedburgh, and Skynburness. These and other facts relating to the siege we learn from the " Liber Quotidianus Garderobæ," which contains numerous entries in regard to the payments made to artificers for work connected with the siege. Some of these entries, translated into English, may be here extracted, as throwing some light on the preparations made by the King of England for the siege :—

" To Mr. Richard de Abyndon [for the vintage of wine, etc., and] for the wages of divers workmen, smiths and carpenters, sent from Carlisle to Carlaverock, for the King's engines, by the hands of Sir Henry of Sandwic, chaplain of Sir John of Drokenesford, delivered in pence to the same at Carlisle, in the month of July, ij *li.* iiii *s.* xj *d.*[1]

" To Mr. Richard de Abyndon, clerk, for the wages of carpenters, smiths, and divers other workmen, retained at the King's pay, by a precept of the King, by a letter of the Treasurer of the Exchequer, for constructing a cat, one *multo* or engine for throwing stones, one *berfrarium*, and other engines, under the inspection and by the orders of Sir John de la Dolive, Knight, for making an assault on the Castle of Carlaverock on the coming of the King and his army there in the present year, and for taking them with the King in the same war to divers places of Scotland, between the 20th day of November in the foresaid year, beginning at the 24th day of July in the same year, together with divers carriages brought for carrying timber and sundry other things necessary for the . foresaid matters to divers places, within the same account, as appears from the foresaid account, xlvj *li.* xiij *s.* j *d. ob.*[2]

" To Sir John de la Dolyve, Constable of the Castle of Dumfries, for the expenses of certain men thereabout for obtaining victuals, for the fortifying of the said castle, for the expenses of certain messengers carrying letters by turns, for cups, wood, tables, and platters for meat, bought by the said Sir John, for the shoeing of certain cross-bowmen dwelling in the foresaid fort, and for their expenses, and those of certain men, going by command of the King, in order to obtain engines from Carlisle to Carlaverock, for the taking of the same castle, within the time foresaid [from the 9th day of March, in the present year, to the 30th day of July in the same year] iij *li.* xix *s.* ix *d. ob.*[3]

" To Mr. Adam Glasham, carpenter, retained in the same way, at the King's pay, for an engine

---

[1] Liber Quotidianus Garderobæ, p. 259.   [2] *Ibid.* p. 140.   [3] *Ibid.* p. 153.

coming from Loghmaban to the siege of the Castle of Carlaverock, for his wages, and those of seven of his fellow carpenters, from the 10th day of July to the 20th day of the same month, in each account for eleven days, to the said Adam, per day, vj *d.*, and to each of the other carpenters iiij *d.* per day, j *li.* xj *s.* ij *d.*[1]

"To Robert de Wodehous for money paid by him to Peter de Preston and nine of his companions, with horses covered, for their wages; 660 foot, bearing arrows, in coming to Carlisle from the county of Lancaster, for two days; in coming from Carlisle to Carlaverock to the King on the 8th day of July, for the first account, xij *li.* xj *s.*; to the same for the payment of two balistae and forty-two arrows from the fortification of the Castle of Roxburgh, of one balista and eleven foot-bearing arrows from the fortification of the Castle of Geddeworth [Jedburgh], for the same two days, in coming in the same way to the King, j *li.* ij *s.* viij *d.*; to the same, for the wages of five light horsemen, from the fortification of Roxburgh, for the same time, in so coming, 5*s.*; to the same, for the wages of four carpenters and five trench-diggers for one day, namely, the 8th day of July, in coming as above, ij *s.* ij *d.* Summa, xiv *li.* x *d.*[2]

"To Stephen Banyng, master of a ship, . . . and to his ten companions, crew of the same ship, carrying in his foresaid ship a certain engine from Skynburnesse to Carlaverock, for their wages, for two days, on the 10th day of July, for the first account, the master receiving per day vj *d.*, and each of the crew iij *d.*, vj *s.*"[3]

The operations of the siege are minutely and graphically described in the metrical history of the siege, before quoted, and they illustrate the way as well as the kind of weapons and engines by which military enterprises of this kind were conducted at that period.

When the first attack was made, which was by the foot, so effectually did the besieged return it that in the course of an hour many of the foot were killed and wounded. When the men-at-arms saw that such heavy losses had been sustained by the footmen who had begun the attack, they made the utmost haste to renew the assault. "Then might there be seen such kind of stones thrown as if they would beat hats and helmets to powder, and break shields and targets in pieces; for to kill and wound was the game at which they played. Great shouts arose among them when they perceived that any mischief occurred."[4] "The first body was composed of Bretons, and the second were of Lorrain, of which none found the other tardy, so that they afforded encouragement and emulation to others to resemble them."[5]

The intrepidity and enterprise of some of the barons are specially commemorated. The followers of "Thomas of Richmont passed quite to the bridge

[1] Liber Quotidianus Garderobæ, p. 258.   [4] Siege of Carlaverock, p. 67.

[2] *Ibid.* p. 259.   [3] *Ibid.* p. 272.   [5] *Ibid.* p. 67.

and demanded entry; they were answered with ponderous stones and cornues. Robert de Willoughby in his advances received a stone in the middle of his breast, which ought to have been protected by his shield, if he had deigned to use it. John Fitz-Marmaduke had undertaken to endure as much in that affair as the others could bear, for he was like a post; but his banner received many stains, and many a rent difficult to mend. Robert de Hamsart bore himself so nobly that from his shield fragments might often be seen to fly in the air. . . . Those led by Graham did not escape, for there were not above two who returned unhurt, or brought back their shields entire. Then you might hear the tumult begin. With them were intermixed a great body of the King's followers, all of whose names, if I were to repeat, and recount their brave actions, the labour would be too heavy, so many were there and so well did they behave. Nor would this suffice without those of the retinue of the King's son, great numbers of whom came there in noble array; for many a shield newly painted and splendidly adorned, many a helmet and many a burnished hat, many a rich gambezon garnished with silk, tow, and cotton, were there to be seen, of divers forms and fashions. There I saw Ralph de Gorges, a newly dubbed knight, fall more than once to the ground from stones and the crowd, for he was of so haughty a spirit that he would not deign to retire. He had all his banners and attire mascally of gold and azure. Those who were on the wall Robert de Tony severely harassed; for he had in his company the good Richard de Rokeley, who so well plied those within that he frequently obliged them to retreat. He had his shield painted mascally of red and ermine. Adame de la Forde mined the walls as well as he could, for his stones flew in and out as thick as rain, by which many were disabled. The good Baron of Wigtoun received such blows that it was the astonishment of all that he was not stunned, for, without excepting any lord present, none showed a more resolute or unembarrassed countenance. Many a heavy and crushing stone did he of Kirkbride receive, but he placed before him a white shield with a green cross engrailed. So stoutly was the gate of the castle assailed by him, that never did smith with his hammer strike his iron as he and his did there." . . . "John de Cromwell, the brave and handsome, who went gliding between the stones, bore on blue a white lion rampant, double-tailed, and crowned with gold; but think not that he brought it away, or that it was not bruised, so much was it battered and defaced by stones before he retreated." . . . "Then the followers of my lord of Brittany recommenced the assault, fierce and daring as lions of the mountains, and every day improving in both the practice and use of arms. Their party soon covered the entrance of the castle, for none could have attacked it more furiously."[1]

The chronicler does equal justice to the gallantry of the besieged, and to the vigour with which they repelled the assailants. "There were showered upon the besiegers such huge stones, quarrels, and arrows, that with wounds and bruises they were so hurt and exhausted that it was with very great difficulty they were able to retire."[2] "Those within continually relieved one another, for always as one became fatigued another returned fresh and stout; and notwithstanding such assaults were made upon them, they would not surrender, but so defended themselves that they resisted those who attacked all that day and night, and the next day until tierce"[3] [about nine o'clock in the morning].

The last efforts of the besieged are thus told : "Their courage was considerably depressed during the attack by the brother Robert, who sent numerous stones from the robinet, without cessation, from the dawn of the preceding day until the evening. Moreover, on the other side he was erecting three other engines, very large, of great power, and very destructive, which cut down and cleave whatever they strike. Fortified town, citadel nor barrier—nothing is protected from their strokes. Yet those within did not flinch until some of them were slain, but then each began to repent of his obstinacy, and to be dismayed. The pieces fell in such manner, wherever the stones entered, that when they struck either of them, neither iron cap nor wooden target could save him from a wound."[4]

This furious assault led to the surrender of the garrison, who, according to our author, "when they saw that they could not hold out any longer, or endure more, begged for peace, and put out a pennon, but he that displayed it was shot with an arrow by some archer through the hand into the face. Then he begged that they would do no more to him, for they will

[1] Siege of Carlaverock, pp. 71, 73, 75, 77, 79, 81.   [3] Siege of Carlaverock, p. 83.
[2] Ibid. p. 77.   [4] Ibid. pp. 83, 85.

give up the castle to the King, and throw themselves upon his mercy. And the Marshal and Constable, who always remained on the spot, at that notice forbade the assault, and these surrendered the castle to them. Then was the whole host rejoiced at the news of the conquest of the castle, which was so noble a prize."[1]

When the garrison, after a gallant defence of the fortress for nearly two days, surrendered, the English were greatly surprised to find that it consisted of only sixty men.

It would be gratifying if we could accept as true the account of the treatment which the gallant little band received at the hands of their conquerors, as given in the poetical narrative of the siege. According to it, the King commanded that life and limb should be spared to the garrison, and that each of them should receive a new garment.[2] But the Chronicle of Lanercost Abbey gives a different and probably a more correct version of the treatment of the prisoners, less creditable to the generosity and truer to the character of Edward. " Many," it says, " that were found within the castle were hanged by the orders of the King."[3]

On the 12th of July Edward offered an oblation of seven shillings at the altar in his own chapel at Carlaverock, in honour of St. Thomas.[4]

The Castle of Carlaverock having thus fallen into the hands of Edward, he commanded his banner, and that of Saint George, Saint Edmund, and Saint Edward, together with the banners of Sir John Segrave, who had performed the duties of Marshal during the siege, of Humphrey, Earl of Hereford, Constable of England, and of Lord Clifford, apparently because he was appointed governor of the castle, to be displayed on its battlements.[5]

Upon the surrender of the castle, and after he had appointed Lord Clifford its keeper, the English King went into Galloway, visiting Kirkcudbright, Twynham, Flete, and other places. On the 29th of August he returned to Carlaverock, where he found Robert Winchelsey, Archbishop of Canterbury, who, in obedience to the express command of Pope Boniface the Eighth, had come with a bull from his Holiness to the King, urging him to make peace with the Scots.

[1] Siege of Carlaverock, pp. 85, 87. [2] *Ibid.* p. 87.
[3] MS. quoted by Sir Harris Nicolas in his Preface to the Siege of Carlaverock, p. xiv. The notice in the Chronicle of Lanercost Abbey, and a single line in the Metrical Chronicle of Peter de Langtoft, with several entries in the Liber Quotidianus Garderobæ, are the only accounts, besides the poem so often quoted, which we have of this siege.
[4] Liber Quotidianus Garderobæ, p. 41.
[5] Siege of Carlaverock, p. 87.

Edward followed this pacific advice, and after concluding a truce finally left the castle about the 10th of November, and on the 11th arrived at Carlisle.

The castle remained in the hands of the English for a number of years, and during this time all that we know concerning it is gathered from occasional notices of the provisions and men sent to it from England.

On the 12th of May 1309, being the second year of the reign of King Edward the Second, orders were given to the Sheriffs of Somerset and Dorset to send to Skinburness 150 quarters of corn and an equal quantity of malt for the Castles of Dumfries and Carlaverock. On the 15th of December, in the same year, Robert Lord Clifford was similarly ordered to provide the Castle of Carlaverock, and other castles, with men and provisions, and whatever was necessary for their defence, and the constables of these castles were commanded to defend them against the King's rebels and enemies. In the year 1312 the Castle of Carlaverock was still in the possession of the English, with Sir Eustace Maxwell as its keeper, in their interest. This we learn from a remission granted to him by Edward the Second on 30th April 1312, of twenty-two pounds, which he owed to his Majesty's Exchequer of Berwick, to enable him the more securely to keep the castle against the stratagems of the Scots, his Majesty's enemies.[1] Soon after this date Sir Eustace declared himself a supporter of Robert Bruce. His former friends forthwith laid siege to his castle, but not in such force as on the previous occasion, and after carrying on their operations in a feeble manner for several weeks they were obliged to retire. Sir Eustace, notwithstanding this failure on the part of the English, was doubtful of the capability of the castle to hold out against a more determined attack, and he accordingly demolished, or at least partially dismantled, the fortifications, so that, should it be taken, it might be of less advantage to the enemy. For this patriotic sacrifice Bruce granted him a charter of an annual rent, and released him from various payments due to the Crown for his lands, amounting to £32 sterling.[2] Herbert of Maxwell of Carlaverock, son of Sir John, Eustace's brother, who possessed the estates of Maxwell between the years 1347 and 1354, made submission to Edward the Third of England as his liege lord, and in security delivered hostages at the castle to

[1] Rot. Scot. tom. i. p. 110.

[2] Robertson's Index of Missing Charters, p. 15.

In the grant the words occur, " for demolishing the Castle of Carlaverock."

William de Bohun, Earl of Northampton. He received in return letters of protection, dated 5th September 1347, to himself and his men, and to the said castle, with its armour, victuals, and other goods and cattle that were in it.[1] The fortifications of the castle had been restored, it is probable, by Sir Eustace, or by his brother, Sir John, who succeeded him ; and in the year 1355, it was taken by Roger Kirkpatrick of Closeburn, a true patriot, who never swore fealty to the King of England, and who by his own efforts reduced the whole territory of Nithsdale into submission to the Crown of Scotland.[2] The character of Kirkpatrick is thus given by Wyntoun in his Chronicle :—

> " Hoge of Kyrk-Patryke Nyddysdale
> Held at ye Scottis Fay all hale,
> Fra ye Castelle of Dalswyntown
> Wes takyn, and syne dwyn down.
> Syne Karlaverok tane had he.
> He wes a man of gret bownte,
> Honorabil, wys, and rycht worthy :
> He couth rycht mekil of cumpany." [3]

Not long after the castle fell into the hands of Kirkpatrick, it was the scene of a dreadful tragedy, which was at the time interpreted as a judgment upon Kirkpatrick for the share he had taken in the murder of the Red Comyn. When Bruce, after stabbing Comyn in the Dominican or Grey Friars Church at Dumfries, rushed out of the church in great excitement, with his poniard covered with blood, he exclaimed to two of his attendant barons, Kirkpatrick and Lindsay, " I doubt I have slain the Red Comyn !" " Doubt it !" cried Kirkpatrick, " I's mak sicker !" and, hastening into the church, he inflicted additional wounds on Comyn. The monks, scandalized at the desecration of their altar, asserted that at midnight, when those who were assisting at the religious services performed on the occasion had all fallen fast asleep, with the exception of one aged father, a supernatural voice, resembling the cry of an infant, was heard to utter the words, " How long, O Lord, shall vengeance be deferred ?" to which another voice replied, " Endure with patience till the anniversary of this day shall return for the fifty-second

[1] Rot. Scot. tom. i. p. 704 b.

[2] Major's Historia Britanniæ, p. 248.

[3] The Orygynale Cronykil of Scotland, by Androw of Wyntown, edited by David Macpherson, 2 vols. 8vo, London, 1795, vol. ii. p. 277.

time." The murder of Comyn was committed in the year 1305 : in the year 1357 the Castle of Carlaverock was inhabited by Roger Kirkpatrick, the son of Bruce's friend, and he was entertaining as a guest Sir James of Lindsay, a descendant from the other participator in the slaughter of Comyn. Sir James, from what motive it is not now known, but, according to tradition, because a beautiful lady, of whom he was much enamoured, had become the wife of Kirkpatrick, stole to Kirkpatrick's bedside in the dead of night, and stabbed him to the heart as he lay asleep.[1] The murderer hurried from the castle and mounted his horse, which was ready saddled, and rode hard until daybreak ; but in his confusion he lost his way, and in the early morning he was arrested by Kirkpatrick's men, not far from the castle. He was brought to trial, and, notwithstanding the entreaties of his wife, Egidia Stewart,[2] a niece of the King, he was executed in June 1357. The story is narrated by Wyntoun in the following lines :—

> " Dat ilk yhere in oure Kynryk
> Hoge wes slayne of Kilpatrik
> Be Schyr Jakkis ye Lyndyssay
> In-til Karlaverok ; and away
> For til have bene wyth all his mycht
> Dis Lyndyssay pressyt all a nycht
> Furth on hors rycht fast rydand.
> Nevyryeless yhit yai hym fand,
> Noucht thre myle fra yat ilk place.
> Dare tane, and broucht agayne he was
> Til Karlaverok be ya men,
> Dat frendis war til Kilpatrik yen :
> Dare wes he kepyd rycht straytly.
> His wyf passyd til ye Kyng Dawy,
> And prayid hym of his Realte,
> Of Lauche yat sho mycht serwyd be.
> De Kyng Dawy yan alsa fast
> Til Drwmfres wyth his Curt he past,
> As Lawche wald.   Qwhat was yare mare ?
> Dis Lyndyssay to Dede he gert do yare."[3]

[1] The murder of Kirkpatrick has been made the subject of a ballad by Charles Kirkpatrick Sharpe, published in the Minstrelsy of the Scottish Border. To quote from it would not however illuminate our history, as it simply expresses the fancy of its author.

[2] Egidia Stewart, half-sister of Robert the Second, afterwards married Sir Hugh Eglinton, Justiciar of Scotland.

[3] The Orygynale Cronykil of Scotland, by Androw of Wyntown, vol. ii. p. 287.

Tradition relates that the body of Lindsay was buried on the rampart of the Castle of Carlaverock, nearly opposite the round tower, which was formerly in the south-east angle of the castle. In apparent confirmation of this, a few years ago, on digging at this spot, there was found the entire skeleton of a tall and powerfully built man, in a wonderful state of preservation, though it partly crumbled to ashes on exposure to the atmosphere. But if the new Castle of Carlaverock afterwards built was on a different site from the old, this skeleton could not have been the body of Lindsay.

After the execution of Lindsay, the original Castle of Carlaverock appears to have been levelled with the ground, and a new castle was built by Sir Robert Maxwell of Maxwell and Carlaverock, who became head and representative of the Maxwell family in 1373, and died between the years 1407 and 1413. A question has been raised whether this new castle was built on the site of the present more conspicuous ruins, or on that of the former castle, which is nearer to the sea, and of which, as already stated, the foundations may still be traced. It is probable that the castle built by Sir Robert Maxwell was entirely new, though the materials of the old castle may have been used in its construction, and that it was erected on the site of the present ruins. This opinion is confirmed by the great antiquity of some portions of the castle still standing,—more ancient apparently than is often found in the baronial residences of Scotland. In recent years, there was discovered in the inner fosse a strong sluice, formed of oak and bound with iron, by which the waters of the Solway at high tide could be admitted. It is also to be noted that the ruins exhibit the same form and other peculiarities as well as a site analogous to that indicated by the chronicler of the Siege of Carlaverock before quoted. From this, Pennant thinks that a new castle on a new site was not built, but only the old one repaired, and " that it was never so entirely destroyed, but that some of the old towers yet remain." Another antiquary, Francis Grose, was of a different opinion. Grose states that when he wrote, in the year 1789, the site and foundations of the ancient castle were very conspicuous, and easily traceable in a wood about 300 yards to the south-east of the present building. From these foundations it appears to have been of somewhat less extent than the present castle, but of a similar figure, and to have been surrounded by a double ditch.[1] It is highly probable that the architect, in building a new castle, would adopt the plan of the old one, which had been so successful in withstanding sieges.

After the return of King James the First from his protracted captivity in England, Murdoch, Duke of Albany, while under a charge of high treason, for which he was afterwards executed, was confined in the new Castle of Carlaverock, which was probably selected as the place of his incarceration in consequence of its distance from his retainers in Perthshire, and the nobles with whom he was in alliance. The ground storey—which is about eleven feet in diameter—of the round tower on the south-western angle is still pointed out as the place in which he was confined; and the tower itself is called "Murdoch's Tower."

Robert, second Lord Maxwell, who succeeded his father, Herbert the first Lord, about the year 1452, "completed the bartizan of Carlaverock."[2]

In the year 1542, King James the Fifth, two years after he granted the new charter of the barony of Maxwell, with Carlaverock as the chief messuage, stopped at the castle for a short time previous to the disastrous battle at Solway Moss, on 27th November, where his army was completely routed, and many taken prisoners, among whom was Robert, fifth Lord Maxwell, who obtained his liberty only on payment of 1000 merks sterling.[3]

Henry the Eighth of England, fully appreciating the value of the Border strongholds in his military operations against Scotland, instructed his ambassadors, Lord Wharton and Sir Robert Bowes, in April 1544, to send a trustworthy person, under colour of some other purpose, to view the castles of Lochmaben, Threave, Carlaverock and Langholme, which were in the custody of Robert Lord Maxwell, as the King wished to know their strength and situation, whether any or all of them were in such a condition that, were they in his possession, they might be successfully held against his enemies; and should it be found that any of them were so, his ambassadors were " ernestly to travail with Robert Maxwell for the delyverie of the same into his Majestie's hands, if with money and rewarde, or other large offers, the same may be

[1] Grose's Antiquities of Scotland. London, 1789, vol. i. p. 160. The wood referred to is Bowhouse, on the farm of Bowhouse of Carlaverock.

[2] History of the Maxwells, in Herries Peerage Minutes, 1851, p. 296.

[3] Rymer's Fœdera, tom. xiv. p. 796, old edition.

obtayned." They were further instructed to endeavour to learn the mind of Maxwell on these points.[1] Lord Maxwell yielded. On 24th October 1545, he surrendered Carlaverock to the English. But the English were not allowed to remain in possession of it undisturbed. Carlaverock and Lord Maxwell's other castles, Lochmaben and Thrieve, were immediately after besieged by the Governor of Scotland and Cardinal Beaton.[2]

John, eighth Lord Maxwell, having joined the ranks of the Lords who supported Queen Mary, and having in 1570, when only seventeen years of age, resisted with a considerable body of men Lord Scrope, who was sent by Queen Elizabeth to lay waste in Dumfriesshire the lands of such as were attached to Queen Mary, the Castle of Carlaverock, as Camden informs us, again sustained, in that year, a siege by the Earl of Sussex, who acted nominally in the interests of James the Sixth,[3] and by him its fortifications were so dismantled that it ceased to be a place of strength. He "took and cast down the castles of Carlaverock, Hoddam, Dumfries, Tinwald, Cowhill, and sundry other gentlemen's houses, dependers on the house of Maxwell." By the same author, in his Britannia, written about the year 1607, Carlaverock is called "a weak house of the Barons of Maxwell."

The castle was again repaired and fortified, in the year 1638, by Robert, first Earl of Nithsdale, and to that date the more modern part of the building is to be attributed.

The castle, thus rebuilt, was ornamented by numerous heraldic decorations similar in style to the ancient portions of Winton Castle in East Lothian, which was built by George, third Earl of Winton, whose second Countess was Elizabeth Maxwell, aunt of the third Earl of Nithsdale. Over the arch of the gate of Carlaverock Castle is placed a large stone containing, in the centre, the crest of the Earls of Nithsdale. This is a stag attired proper, lodged before a holly-bush, with a shield resting on his fore-legs, bearing the Maxwell saltire, with the motto below, "I bid ye fair." The four corners of this stone contain armorial bearings. In the dexter chief corner are the Royal Arms of Scotland surmounted by a crown, and in the sinister chief corner a double-headed displayed eagle, also surmounted by a crown, supposed to represent the imperial arms of Germany. The double-headed eagle was first adopted by John, eighth

[1] Hayne's Burleigh Papers, pp. 27, 28.   [2] Diurnal of Occurrents, 1833, p. 41.   [3] Camden's Annals.

Lord Maxwell, afterwards Earl of Morton, from his having fought for the Emperor. In the dexter corner of the base are the arms of Maxwell impaled with those of Mar, being a bend between six crosslets. In the sinister corner of the base are the arms of Stewart of Dalswinton, whose daughter was married to Sir Herbert Maxwell, father of the first Lord Maxwell.

In the entrance gateway there is lying a large armorial stone, partly broken. It contains a shield with a double-headed eagle displayed, surmounted with an escutcheon bearing a saltire. On the sinister side is part of a stag as a supporter. The dexter side is broken off. Part of a scroll at the foot containing these words— . . . D · THE · FAIR · " I bid the fair," has reference to the hospitality of the hall. On another old carved stone, also lying in the gateway, is this motto :—" QVAM · GRAVE · SERVITIUM · EST · QUOD . . . . LEVIS . ESCA · PARIT." This stone is semicircular, and had probably been placed above one of the windows, now demolished, on the east side of the court.

The castleyard, which is entered by this gateway, is triangular. The building on the east side of the triangle is three stories high, besides the attics. The ground story is all arched, and is supposed to have been the kitchen apartments. In one of these is a draw-well, now filled up, in which

on being cleared out some years ago, a silver cup was found. The remaining portion of this east court wall is 55 feet in length. The masonry of this part of the building is finer than any other part of it now remaining, and it appears to have been cased or veneered on the original rougher building. The doors and windows of the east wall of the court are all handsomely sculptured. The carving above the first court door is nearly destroyed. Fragments now only remain which indicate that it had originally contained a large eagle and a rose on each side of the shield at the base. The annexed woodcut shows the initials of Elizabeth, Countess of Nithsdale, as engraved on the pediment above the second remaining door of the first story.

Above the first staircase window is a heart-shaped shield, with the plain Maxwell saltire.

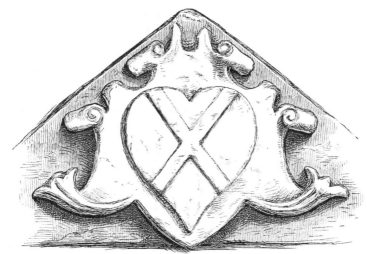

Above the staircase window, on the second story, is a shield supported by two cherubs, bearing a double-headed eagle, charged with a shield and

saltire surmounted with an earl's coronet. Under the shield is a human head, with two paws of an animal drawing the jaws apart in a grotesque manner. Above the third staircase window is a stone with the Beaumont arms, being semé of fleur-de-lis, a lion rampant,—all surmounted by an earl's coronet. At the sides of this stone are grotesque figures, like a dolphin. Above the fourth staircase window are the Maxwell arms repeated.

Above the second window on the ground story is a shield with the double-headed eagle, charged with the Maxwell saltire and surmounted with an earl's coronet.

Above the second window of the second story, on the dexter side, is a tree, from a branch of which is suspended a small shield bearing the Maxwell saltire. From the same branch an earl's coronet is suspended. Below the coronet and shield are the initials R ^{E} N, evidently for Robert Earl of Nithsdale. On the sinister side of the same window is suspended, from a branch of another tree, a shield bearing a fleur-de-lis. Another coronet is suspended from a separate branch, and below are the initials E ^{C} N, for Elizabeth (Beaumont) Countess of Nithsdale. From another branch of the tree, on the same side, is suspended a lover's knot. Above the third window of the second story are three figures, with the letters R. N., evidently for Robert, first Earl of Nithsdale, the restorer of this part of the castle. Over two of the remaining windows of the second story, and also over three of those of the third story, are carvings of subjects taken from Ovid's *Metamorphoses*.

The opposite or west side of the court is plain building, probably reconstructed by John Earl of Morton.

A handsome doorway on the south side of the court leads to the great banqueting hall, which was flanked by the two towers at the base of the triangle, and is 104 feet long by 26 broad.

In the year 1640, Carlaverock was besieged by the Covenanters. The garrison, under Robert, first Earl of Nithsdale, successfully defended it for thirteen weeks. King Charles the First repeatedly promised to send assistance to the Earl, but, unable to do so, at last advised him to shift for himself. The correspondence of the King on that occasion, in which he particularly refers to a breach between him and his " covenanting rebels," and regrets that the Earl has been so long beleaguered in his Castle of Carlaverock, is printed in the second volume of this work.[1] The Castle was surrendered only after receipt

---

[1] Vol. ii. pp. 15-17.

of letters from the King, authorizing the Earl to deliver up it and the Castle of Thrieve, upon the best conditions he could obtain. Carlaverock, after its prolonged defence, was surrendered to Lieutenant-Colonel Home. By the articles of capitulation agreed upon between the Earl of Niths-dale and that Colonel, 26th September 1640, the castle, with the cannon, surplus of ammunition, and other provisions, was to be delivered up to the Lieutenant-Colonel betwixt that date and the 29th of that month ; and the Earl, his friends, followers, and soldiers, each with his arms and shot, with all their bag and baggage, trunks, household stuff belonging, on their honour and credit, to his Lordship and them, were to have safe-conduct to Lang-holm, or any other place within Nithsdale.

The conquerors afterwards seized upon the furniture within the castle, and demolished the building. Upon this complaints were made that the articles of capitulation had been violated. " A note of the household stuff intromitted with by Lieutenant-Colonel Home at Carlaverock " has been preserved, afford-ing an illustration of the magnificent hospitality of the baronial House of Nithsdale in the seventeenth century. Among other articles with which he had intromitted, may be mentioned, as an evidence of this, eighty-five beds. Of these beds were five, two of silk and three of cloth, consisting each of five coverings, with massy silk fringes of half a quarter deep, and a counterpane of the same stuff, all laid with braid silk lace, and a small fringe about, with feather-bed and bolster, blankets, etc., every bed estimated at £110 sterling. Ten lesser beds were each estimated at £15 sterling ; and seventy other beds for servants, consisting of feather-bed, bolster, rug, blankets, were each estimated at £7. Colonel Home had also intromitted with a library of books, which cost the Earl of Nithsdale £200 sterling. The drawing-room, with the furniture of which he had intromitted, was hung with cloth of silver, and the chairs and stools in it were covered with red velvet, with fringes of crimson silk and gilt nails.[1]

Besides the comfortable beds, the occupants of the castle had in the wine cellars four barrels of sack and three hogsheads of French wine.

Against the charge of having broken the articles of capitulation Colonel Home defended himself by affirming that he acted according to the instructions

[1] Original Papers at Terregles.

of the Committee of Estates, by whom he had been ordered to demolish the
castle, on their being informed that the Earl's officers and soldiers had broken
their parole, and were then actually in arms.

From this time this venerable and once magnificent structure, which had
been so frequently taken and re-taken, demolished and restored, ceased to be
a place of residence. It has remained ever since a massive and picturesque
ruin, attracting the curiosity of the antiquarian and the tourist, and the pencil
of the artist, as one of the finest specimens of the old baronial residences
of Scotland. In form it is triangular, and it was surrounded by a double
moat; and, still further to obstruct the efforts of an assailant to capture it,
there were three portcullises, each after the other, which are still to be seen.
There is also to be traced an apparatus for discharging a torrent of molten
lead on the besiegers, illustrating the mode of warfare and the methods
of defence which were formerly adopted.

Opposite to the Castle of Carlaverock, on the north side, is the Hill of
Wardlaw, or the Beacon Hill. Anciently that hill had been the site of British
and Roman camps, of which traces yet remain. Being contiguous to Carla-
verlock, and convenient for the gathering of hosts, Wardlaw became the place
of rendezvous of the family of Maxwell, and their slogan or war-cry was
A Wardlaw, upon the hearing of which the clan assembled there for attack or
defence. On Wardlaw hill, also, the Barons of Carlaverock executed justice,
for in feudal times a gibbet stood on Wardlaw.[1]

John Maxwell, Lord Herries, succeeded his cousin, Robert, second Earl of
Nithsdale, as third Earl in the year 1667. His residence was at the Herries
mansion-house of Terregles, in the stewartry of Kirkcudbright. The estate
of Carlaverock is now the property of his lineal heir, William Lord Herries,
who carefully preserves the ruins of the castle.

In his "Tour in Scotland" in 1772, Thomas Pennant has an engraving
of the principal entrance and the three remaining round towers of the castle.[2]

Grose, in his "Antiquities of Scotland," has done honour to the Castle
of Carlaverock, by giving three engravings of the ruins, of which one is the
frontispiece to the first volume. The views from which these engravings were

[1] Maxwell History in Herries Peerage Minutes, 1851, p. 297. Pennant's Tour, vol. i. p. 99.
[2] Pennant's Tour in Scotland, published at Chester in 1774, 4to, vol. ii. p. 100.

made were drawn in the year 1789. The first shows the ruins of the south-west portion; the second exhibits the east side; and the third was taken a little more to the eastward than the first.[1]

In the " Baronial Antiquities of Scotland" are three engravings of Carlaverock, consisting of a general view, the entrance gateway and flanking towers, and the courtyard, besides woodcuts of the interior of the entrance tower, and the portcullis room.[2]

In the "Memoirs of the Maxwells of Pollok" a representation of the Castle of Carlaverock is given; and in the present work is another view of the castle.

[1] Antiquities of Scotland, by Francis Grose, London, 1789, vol. i. pp. 159-168.

[2] The Baronial Antiquities of Scotland, by Robert William Billings, 1845-52, 4to, vol. i.

 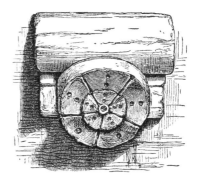

Two corbel stones in the Hall on the west side of the Courtyard of Carlaverock Castle.

IV.—2. AYMER DE MAXWELL,[1] FOURTH LORD OF MAXWELL, SECOND OF CARLAVEROCK, AND FIRST OF MEARNS, CHAMBERLAIN OF SCOTLAND, SHERIFF OF DUMFRIES AND JUSTICIAR OF GALLOWAY, 1241-1266.

MARY OF MEARNS, HIS WIFE.

The name of Aymer de Maxwell, who succeeded his brother, John Maccuswell, in the year 1241, occurs in various deeds previous to that period. Under the designation of " brother to John de Mackuswel," he was witness to a charter by Roger Burnard, granting to the monks of Melrose thirteen acres of his land and one particate in the territory of Farningdun.[2] This charter is without date, but from a confirmation of it by King Alexander the Second, which also is without date, it was probably granted during his reign, and its date must therefore have been after the year 1214.[3]

During the lifetime of his brother John, Aymer de Maxwell was a frequent attendant at the Court of Alexander the Second, and was often a witness to royal charters. He was witness to a charter granted by that monarch in favour of the monks of Coldingham, dated at Berwick, 16th May 1232 ;[4] to a confirmation by the same King, dated at Traquair, 4th February 1232-3, of that donation of land in the territory of Mackestoun which John de Normanville made to the Church of St. Mary of Melrose, and to the monks there serving God ;[5] to a charter by King Alexander the Second, dated at Stirling, 16th March, in the nineteenth year of his reign (1232-3), granting to Patrick, son of William, the son of Orm, the lands of Glengeych, Ardauch, and others ; and to a charter by King Alexander, dated at Selkirk, 21st February 1235, granting to the same Monastery of Melrose his waste land of Ettrick, as therein described. His brother John was also a witness to this

---

[1] Aymer is the first of the family whose name receives in contemporary records the modern spelling of Maxwell. It so occurs in an Act of Parliament, to be afterwards quoted (vide p. 65), and this spelling we now adopt, though in the Memoir of Aymer, and in the memoirs of some of his successors, the orthography of the original writs is generally followed.

[2] Liber Sancte Marie de Melros, tom. i. p. 75.

[3] Ibid. tom. i. p. 216.

[4] Raine's History of North Durham, in which it is printed.

[5] Liber Sancte Marie de Melros, tom. i. p. 222.

last-mentioned charter, and among the other witnesses were William, Bishop of Glasgow, Chancellor; Walter, Abbot of Dryburgh; Robert, the King's Chaplain; Mr. David de Bernham, Chamberlain; and Mr. William de Lindesay, Dean of Glasgow.[1]

Aymer de Mackiswell, along with Malcolm Earl of Fife, Malcolm, son of the Earl of Lennox, Thomas Croc, Galfrid Marscall, and others, was witness to a charter by Walter, Steward of the King of Scotland, son of Alan, granting to St. James and St. Mirin of Paisley, and the monks there serving God, the churches of Dundonald, Senechar, and Achinlec. The charter is without date, but it has been assigned to the year 1239.[2] In that year, on the Sabbath immediately after the Nativity of the blessed Virgin Mary, it was confirmed by William, Bishop of Glasgow, with the assent of his chapter.[3]

After the death of his brother John, in the year 1241, and his succession to the baronies of Maxwell and Carlaverock, Aymer was still an attendant at the Court of Alexander the Second, though he does not appear to have held any office in the State during the reign of that monarch. He was witness to a confirmation by King Alexander, dated at Roxburgh, 7th February 1244, granting to William, Bishop of Glasgow, the land of Mosplat, in the bailiary of Lanark, to be held by him and his successors, bishops of Glasgow.[4] Aymer of Maxwell is especially mentioned as one of the members of the Parliament of Alexander the Second, which met on Monday next after the Feast of St. Scolastick, 1244.[5]

He was a witness to a charter by Walter, the King's Steward, son of Alan, confirming to St. Mirin of Paisley, and to the monks there serving God, all the rents in the lands, mills, pastures, fishings, and other goods which he had formerly conferred on the canons and monks of Simpringham, and which they, of their own free will, afterwards resigned, to be held for a pure and perpetual alms, for rendering to the foresaid canons and monks forty merks annually in the house of Dryburgh.[6] This charter is without date, but it has been assigned to the year 1246.

Alexander the Second having died at Kerrera, an island in the Sound

---

[1] Liber Sancte Marie de Melros, tom. ii. p. 667.

[2] Registrum Monasterii de Passelet, p. 19.

[3] Ibid. p. 225.

[4] Registrum Episcopatus Glasguensis, tom. i. p. 151.

[5] The Acts of the Parliaments of Scotland, Statuta Regis Alexander II., vol. i. p. 73.

[6] Registrum Monasterii de Passelet, p. 24.

of Mull, in the year 1249, in the fifty-first year of his age and thirty-fifth of his reign, he was succeeded by his son Alexander the Third, who was then a child of only eight years of age.

During the minority of Alexander the Third the administration of public affairs was successively in the hands of two conflicting factions. The one was headed by Alan Durward (Hostiarius), Lord Justiciary of Scotland, who had married Alexander's natural sister, Marjory. At the head of the other were Walter Comyn, Earl of Menteith, Alexander Comyn Earl of Buchan, and William Earl of Mar, the chiefs of what has been called "the national or Scottish party."[1] Walter Comyn, Earl of Menteith, had given proof of his fidelity by demanding the coronation of Alexander the Third immediately after his succession, when Alan Durward, under various pretexts, strenuously pressed its delay ; and in this Comyn was supported by many of the chief of the nobility, and also by the most influential of the dignitaries of the Church. To this party Aymer de Maxwell belonged. With them he steadily acted, and, his fortunes corresponding with theirs, he lost political power when they lost it, and attained to offices of dignity in the State when they acquired the ascendency. As he was a prominent actor in the most stirring public transactions that took place in the early part of the reign of Alexander the Third, or was mixed up with them, it is necessary, in order to render intelligible what is known of his life, to relate—which, however, shall be done as briefly as possible—some of the leading facts of our national history during this period.

Towards the end of the year 1251, two years after his succession to the Crown, Alexander went to York, attended by a large retinue, to be united in marriage with Margaret, daughter of Henry the Third of England. On Christmas day (25th December) that year, he was invested with the honour of knighthood by the hands of Henry, and on the following day his marriage with Margaret was celebrated with much splendour and festivity. By the marriage-settlement Henry came under various obligations, and Alexander bound himself to follow the counsels of Henry in the administration of the affairs of his kingdom.[2] At that time Alexander's chief counsellor was Alan Durward. But from that position he was speedily dismissed for alleged treasonable practices, which appear to have had some foundation in

[1] Robertson's Scotland under her Early Kings, vol. ii. p. 55.   [2] Wyntown's Cronykil, vol. i. p. 384.

truth. While the festivities of the Scottish King's marriage were going on at York, this intriguing statesman was accused by Walter Comyn, Earl of Menteith, and William Earl of Mar, of sending messengers with presents to the Pope, to obtain, if possible, from his Holiness letters of legitimation in favour of his daughters, who had been born to him of his marriage with the King's natural sister, that, should the King die without heirs of his own body, they, or their issue, might succeed to the Crown ; an attempt in which he was supported, among others, by Robert, Abbot of Dunfermline, the Chancellor, who is said to have moved in the Council that a legitimation under the Great Seal of the kingdom should be granted in favour of Durward's daughters. For this alleged treasonable plot, Durward and others suspected of being implicated were, by the advice of Henry King of England, deprived of their places as guardians of the Scottish King, and others deemed it prudent to return to Scotland.[1]

Walter Comyn, Earl of Menteith, and the principal men of his party were the new guardians of the young King, appointed by Henry, whose resentment was excited against Durward for his plot to open to his own children the succession to the Crown of Scotland, upon which the English King himself had fixed a covetous eye. Aymer of Maccuswell was one of the new guardians, and with these statesmen he was constantly associated in the discharge of the duties with which they were jointly intrusted. Accordingly his name, along with theirs, frequently occurs among the witnesses to charters granted by Alexander the Third. He was witness to a confirmation by that King, dated at Roxburgh, 30th April 1251, of that donation which Maldouen Earl of Lennox made to Malcolm, son of Duncan and Eve, sister of the Earl of Lennox, of the lands of Glaskhel and Brengoenis, and of the Church of Moniabrocd ;[2] and to a confirmation by the same King, dated at Newbottle, 8th June 1252, of that sale which Richard Burnard of Farningdun, Knight, made to the Abbot and Convent of Melrose of the meadow of Farningdun, which is called East Meadow. Among the witnesses to this last-mentioned confirmation were Alexander Cumyn, Earl of Buchan ; William, Earl of Mar, Chamberlain ; and Robert de Ross.[3]

[1] Wyntown's Cronykil, vol. i. pp. 383, 384 ; Chronica de Mailros, p. 179.

[2] Memoirs of the Maxwells of Pollok, vol. i. p. 123.

[3] Liber Sancte Marie de Melros, tom. i. p. 300.

Aymer de Maxwell was again a witness to a confirmation by Alexander the Third, dated at Roxburgh, 12th November 1253, of that donation which Isabella de Valoniis, Lady of Killebrick, made to Saint Kentigern and to the Church of Glasgow of fifteen pounds of land in the feu of Kirkpatrick, being her whole forest, which was called Dalkarn. The other witnesses were Matthew, Abbot of Melrose; William, Earl of Mar, Chamberlain; Robert de Ros; Walter de Moravia; and Richard de Mariscall.[1]

Under the designation of "dominus," Aymer was witness to a charter by John Auenel, son of Geruasius Auenel, granting to God and St. Mary, and the port of Melrose, for the use of the poor coming there, that half carucate of land in the territory of Torthorald, which William, son of Glay, gave to the granter for homage and service.[2]

In the year 1255, Aymer de Maxwell was deprived of his place as one of the guardians of the King along with the others with whom he had been conjoined in that trust for several years. The circumstances which led to and attended this deprivation may be briefly narrated.

Alan Durward having, in the year 1253, accompanied the King of England, who had gone to Guienne to defend his transmarine possessions, regained, by his valour and address, the friendship of Henry. Taking advantage of this favourable turn in his fortunes, he retaliated upon his former accusers and their accomplices by criminating them in turn before the English King. Queen Margaret had brought with her to Scotland many English persons of rank and consideration as her attendants. Between these persons and the Scottish nobles, who were extremely jealous of their rights and privileges, differences and irritations arose. The Queen was chagrined on finding that the less refined Court of Scotland had not the attractions of the English Court, in which she had been brought up. She complained that she was in a manner kept a prisoner in the Castle of Edinburgh; that her English attendants were not allowed to wait upon her person, and that she was excluded from the society of her husband. Of these grievances, which were much exaggerated, Aymer de Mackeswell and his co-guardians of the King were accused of being the authors, and a representation of them was made to the Court of England. It was even reported that by the same party the Queen's physician had been

[1] Registrum Episcopatus Glasguensis, tom. i. p. 161.   [2] Liber Sancte Marie de Melrose, tom. i. p. 186.

poisoned because he remonstrated against the hard treatment of the Queen. Durward availed himself of these complaints, on which he expatiated to the King in highly coloured terms.   The effect upon Henry's mind was that he resolved on removing from their places, as the Scottish King's guardians and counsellors, the Earls of Menteith, Buchan, and Mar, Aymer of Maccuswell, and others, the more especially as their zeal for the honour and independence of their country led them to oppose the designs of the English King to subject it to England. He according despatched the Earl of Gloucester and Maunsell, his chief secretary, accompanied by the Earl of Hereford, William de Fortibus, Earl of Albemarle, and R. Walerand, Seneschal, to the Court of Scotland, for the purpose of dismissing them.   In his commission to these ambassadors Henry pledged himself that he would do nothing against the person of King Alexander, or in the way of disinheriting him, or breaking the marriage-settlement; engagements which suggest that he had been suspected or accused of meditating the overthrow of the independence of Scotland by bringing that kingdom into vassalage to the Crown of England.

In the year 1255, when a meeting was held at Edinburgh, composed of the *natu majores* of Scotland on the one side, and of Alan Durward and his favourers, who had greatly increased in number, on the other, there was some prospect of a reconciliation between the two factions.   But these hopes were speedily disappointed.   It was agreed upon that the two parties should meet again within a few days at Stirling, with a view to their coming to some amicable agreement, and that the King's councillors, with other magnates, should go thither to make the necessary preparations for the approaching meeting.   But in the meantime Patrick Earl of Dunbar and others of the Durward faction suddenly entered the Castle of Edinburgh, armed, and having ejected those who were of the royal family, took the King and the Queen, whom they professed to deliver from their real or pretended captivity, and conducted them to the bridal chamber, though the King was scarcely fourteen years of age, while they fortified the Castle with their men, commanding others of their associates to be in readiness to assist them in conveying the King whither they pleased.   If the Durward party ever really had any intention of composing the differences between them and their opponents, it is certain that they abandoned that intention ; and this invasion of the Castle of Edinburgh, and seizure of the person of the King, perpetrated by the counsel of the Earl of Gloucester, and the English statesmen who had accompanied him to Scotland, which was regarded by Aymer de Makeswell and the other legal guardians of the King as a treasonable action, completely destroyed all hopes of reconciliation between the two factions. Henry, with his Queen, followed the Earl of Gloucester to Scotland, attended by a numerous body of military tenants, and though it was believed that his purpose was the subjugation of Scotland, he disclaimed, in a declaration from Newcastle, dated 25th August 1255, all intention, in this progress to visit his son-in-law, of doing anything to the prejudice of the King of the Scots, or of the liberties of his kingdom.[1]

Intelligence of the seizure of the King by Patrick Earl of Dunbar, and his faction, soon reached the ears of the Earl of Menteith, Buchan, and Mar, Aymer of Maxwell, and the other counsellors and tutors of the King. Affected equally with surprise and resentment, they collected their forces. But their antagonists, with a powerful body, conducted the King and his Queen to the Castle of Roxburgh. King Alexander and his Queen met Henry at Werk Castle, upon the Borders, and after some friendly intercourse between them the King of Scots departed on the same day for Scotland, leaving his Queen in that place with her mother. Henry entered Roxburgh Castle on the day of the Assumption of the blessed Mary (15th August), and was met and welcomed by his son-in-law, Alexander, who conducted him, with a large imposing procession, into the Abbey of Kelso. On the occasion of this visit, Henry personally expressed his purpose that the Earls of Menteith, Buchan, and Mar, Aymer of Maxwell, and others, should be dismissed from their posts as guardians of the King of Scots, and that Durward and the principal of his partisans should be appointed in their place. Having commended his son-in-law to the Earl of Dunbar, one of the chief of the Durward faction, and having partaken of a royal refreshment, he returned to England, much offended with the Bishop of Glasgow, the Elect of St. Andrews, Walter Comyn, Earl of Menteith, and other magnates of the kingdom, with whom Aymer of Maxwell was closely connected in political opinion and action, because they would not place their seals to a certain writing, described as most nefarious, which Durward and his party had made and confirmed by their seals, containing, it was said, many things

[1] Rymer's Fœdera, new edition, tom. i. pp. 560, 561.

which would imperil or destroy the rights and liberties of the King and kingdom of Scotland.[1]

In the Parliament which met at Roxburgh on 20th September 1255, effect was given to the wishes of King Henry. Aymer of Maccuswell, and the other guardians and counsellors of the King, were removed from their places of trust "as they deserved," to use the words of the Act. It may not be unimportant to give the names of all the persons to whom this Act of exclusion extended,[2] as showing the persons with whom Aymer de Makeswell was accustomed to act. The Act specially mentions that this exclusion was made by King Alexander at the instance of Henry King of England, whom he styles "our dearest father," who, "for our honour and advantage, and for the honour and advantage of our kingdom, had by his favour personally come to the borders of the kingdoms of England and Scotland ; and by the counsel of his magnates." The names of the magnates by whom this counsel was given may also be quoted entire from the Act,[3] as this also serves to illustrate the then state of parties.

After excluding the persons named from the King's counsels, the Act proceeds : "And we will not admit them or their complices or favourers to our counsels, and to manage the affairs of our kingdom, or any one to our favour or friendship, till they shall have made amends in full, by agreement or judgment, to the foresaid King, and to us, for the delinquencies committed by them : to do which in all the ways in which it shall be just we will compel them, should it be necessary. It is also agreed and conceded on both

---

[1] Chronica de Mailros, pp. 180, 181.

[2] The names of the guardians removed were :— William, Bishop of Glasgow ; Clement, Bishop of Dunblane ; Gamelin, Elect of St. Andrews ; Walter Comyn, Earl of Menteith ; Alexander Comyn, Earl of Buchan ; William Earl of Mar ; John de Bayllol ; Robert de Ros ; Aymer de Makeswell, and Mary his wife ; John Comyn ; Nicholas de Sules ; Thomas de Normanvyle ; Alexander Vinet ; John de Dundemor ; David de Graham ; John le Blund ; Thomas, son of Ranulf ; Hugh Gurle, and William his brother ; William Whischard, Archdeacon of St. Andrews ; brother Richard, Elemosinar of the Order of the Knights Templar ; David de Louchor ; John Whyschard ; William de Cadyhou ; and William, formerly the King's chaplain.

[3] These were—William, Bishop of Glasgow ; Richard de Inverkeithing, Bishop of Dunkeld ; Peter de Ramsay, Bishop of Aberdeen ; and Gamelin, Elect of St. Andrews ; the Abbots of Dunfermline, Kelso, Jedburgh, and Newbottle ; Malcolm Earl of Fife ; Patrick Earl of Dunbar ; Neil Earl of Carrick ; Malise Earl of Strathern ; Alexander, Steward of Scotland ; Robert of Bruce ; Alan Durward (Hostiarius) ; Walter de Morrevia ; David de Lindesay ; William de Brechyn ; Hugh Giffard ; Roger de Mumbray ; Gilbert de Hay ; Robert de Meyners ; William de Duueglas ; John de Vallibus ; William de Rammesay ; and many others the King's barons.

sides that should any foreign prince invade or attack the kingdom of Scotland, it shall be lawful for us to admit and to call in the foresaid magnates, now removed from our Council, and others whomsoever to our assistance." The new guardians of the King are next named, as ordained "by the counsel of the foresaid King, and of our said magnates." They are "the venerable fathers Richard and Peter, Bishops of Dunkeld and Aberdeen, Malcolm Earl of Fife, Patrick Earl of Dunbar, Malise Earl of Strathern, Neil Earl of Carrick, Alexander, Steward of Scotland, Robert of Bruce, Alan Durward (Hostiarius), Walter of Morrevia, David of Lindesay, William of Brechin, Robert of Meyners, Gilbert of Hay, and Hugh Giffard;" and it is ordained that, "being appointed for our councils and the government of our kingdom and the guardianship of our person and of our royal spouse, for the term of seven years complete, beginning at the Feast of the Translation of St. Cuthbert (4th September), in the year of the Lord 1255, or a shorter term, on which the said King or his heirs, and we in common, shall think it proper to agree, they shall not be removed unless they manifestly deserve it, by taking less interest in our councils and in the affairs of our kingdom than they ought."[1]

Thus early did the King of England, taking advantage of the circumstances that the Scottish King was a minor, and his son-in-law, interfere with the affairs of the kingdom of Scotland, and seek to reduce it to the power of England; a scheme which afterwards formed the principal policy of Edward the First, during his long reign, and of succeeding English monarchs.

To these sinister designs of Henry the Third against the honour and independence of Scotland Aymer de Maxwell was a conspicuous and strenuous opponent.

Aymer de Maxwell and his friends did not quietly submit to their exclusion from the guardianship and councils of the King, and they gradually regained their former ascendency. The Comyns were formidable, there being then in Scotland thirty-two knights and three earls of that name.[2] They could thus assemble numerous vassals, and they were supported by many of the nobility. The old guardians of the King, after Durward and his friends had established their authority, were summoned by the latter to give an

[1] The Acts of the Parliament of Scotland, reign of Alexander the Third, vol. i. p. 77.
[2] Fordun, vol. ii. p. 92.

account of their administration, but this they refused to do, and circumstances arose which greatly increased their power. Gamelin, the Bishop Elect of St. Andrews, who was deprived of the Chancellorship by the new guardians, had been named to the Chapter of St. Andrews by their predecessors, as a fit person to occupy the Episcopal seat of that place, which was then vacant ; and he was consecrated, on the 26th of December 1255, to that bishopric by William, Bishop of Glasgow, notwithstanding a prohibition by the new counsellors of the King, by whom he was also outlawed, and who seized upon the revenues of his bishopric. The case was brought before the Papal Court at Rome ; and the Pope, having heard both sides, pronounced in judgment that the Bishop was free from all the crimes laid to his charge, and was worthy of his bishopric, while he excommunicated the Bishop's accusers, and the dilapidators or invaders of the episcopate, commanding the Bishop of Dunblane and the Abbots of Melrose and Jedburgh to publish the sentence pronounced by him against the King's counsellors, at first without expressly naming them, and then by name should they prove contumacious. A general sentence was published against them at Stirling, and repeated, " with book, bell, and candle," in every church and chapel of the kingdom ; and disregarding this they were excommunicated by name, as contumacious offenders, in the Abbey Church of Cambuskenneth.[1]

The judgment of the Pope in favour of Gamelin, and the fulmination of the Papal sentence of excommunication against Gamelin's enemies, greatly strengthened the friends of Aymer de Maxwell, who could now wield against their enemies the weapon—a very formidable one in those days—that the King was in the hands of excommunicated persons, and that unless he was wrested from their power, the whole kingdom would speedily be laid under a Papal interdict—a sentence still more terrible. Aymer's friends also gained something by the accession of Mary de Couci, the widow of Alexander the Second, who, with John de Brienne, her husband, passed at that time through England into Scotland, to visit the Court of her son, and whose influence was exerted on their side.[2] Emboldened by these favourable circumstances, they invaded, during the night of the 28th of October 1257, the chamber of the King, who was with his Court at Kinross, seized upon his person when he was in bed, and, having

[1] Chronica de Mailros, pp. 181, 182.   [2] Rymer's Fœdera, tom. i. p. 625.

gained possession of the Great Seal of the kingdom, carried him and his queen to Stirling Castle, where he was again surrounded by his former guardians. Alan Durward hastily fled to England, and his faction was dispersed. The result was that the principal power fell anew into the hands of the old guardians of the King, four of the other faction having, for the object of conciliation, been united with them.[1]

Under the new administration, Aymer, in the year 1257 or 1258, was made Lord Chamberlain of Scotland in the room of Sir David Lindsay, Lord of Crawfurd, who had been appointed to that office in 1256, but who was deprived of it when his party was driven from power, and who afterwards lost his life in one of the Crusades.

Still further to strengthen themselves, Aymer and his friends entered into a treaty of mutual confederation and friendship with Llewellyn, Prince of Wales, and other magnates of that kingdom, which was then at war with England, dated 18th March 1258, engaging that they would not make peace or a truce with the King of England, or with such of the magnates of the kingdoms of England and Scotland as were then enemies or rebels to the Prince and grandees of Wales, and Aymer's friends, without the consent of the foresaid Prince and grandees ; and that they would not permit any power, such as an army of horse or foot, to leave Scotland, nor would they succour or favour in any thing the foresaid King of England against them. They also thereby granted liberty to the merchants of Wales to come to Scotland, to sell their wares there to the best advantage under their protection, and to depart without molestation whenever they pleased ; and engaged that they would endeavour to persuade the merchants of Scotland to go to Wales with their merchandise ; a proof of the enlightened interest which Aymer and his friends took in matters of commerce. In this treaty Aymer is designated " Camerarius Scotiæ." [2]

How long Aymer held the office of Chamberlain is uncertain. He appears under the designation of " Chamberlain," in witnessing a letter by King Alexander the Third, dated at Inverness, 18th August 1260, to the

[1] Chronica de Mailros, p. 183 ; Wyntown's Cronykil, vol. i. p. 386 ; Robertson's Scotland under her Early Kings, vol. ii. pp. 72, 73 ; Rymer's Fœdera, vol. i. p. 670 ; Tytler's History of Scotland, vol. i. pp. 30-33.

[2] Rymer's Fœdera, tom. i. p. 653, last edition.

provosts and bailies of the north of Scotland, concerning the accommodation and entertainment rightfully or reasonably due, in burghs and in the King's manors, to the Bishop of Aberdeen.[1] This is the last instance in which his name occurs as bearing this designation. In that office he was succeeded by Gilbert de Lempedlar, who is designed "the King's Chamberlain," in a charter of mortification by Richard de Lincoln and Matilda, his wife, daughter and heiress of Anselm de Molle, whereby they gave to the Abbey of Kelso the whole land, meadow and grove, in the territory of Molle. The deed is undated, but Crawfurd, by the exactest computation which he could make, assigns it to the year 1260 or thereabout.[2]

A brief was addressed by Alexander the Third to Eymer de Mackiswell, as Sheriff of Peebles, commanding him to cause inquiry to be made, by upright and faithful men, into a dispute between Robert de Cruik and the burgesses of Peebles, dated at Lanark 7th October 1262.[3]

In the reign of King Alexander the Third, Aymer Maxwell was Justiciar of Galloway. Under this designation he was witness to a charter by that King, dated at Selkirk, 9th December 1264, whereby, following in the footsteps of his dearest father, from his special favour for the Monastery of Melrose, he confirmed to the Abbot and Convent of that Monastery all the charters, confirmations, liberties, and rights granted to them by his predecessors, Kings of Scotland. The other witnesses were Hugh de Berkeley, Justiciar of Lothian ; Nicholas de Corbeith ; Guydon de Baliol ; and John de Lamberton.[4]

About the same time, Aymer appears as Sheriff of Dumfriesshire. As holding this office, he rendered an account, of which an extract, as printed from extracts from a roll of accounts in the reign of King Alexander the Third, 1263-1266, is as follows :—

From the account of Eymer de Maccuswell, Sheriff of Dumfries, etc., rendered by him . . . between Kollyn and Dumfries, answering to the Feast of St. Martin, for the whole year, xxxv *li.* vj *s.* iiij *d.* ; also by the decease of Matilda of Kirkeblan, namely, for the third part of Kirkeblan, x *s.* ; the sum of the annual rents, etc., and of the debt of John of Genilstun of his fine, xv *li.* ; also by ale sold, viij *li.* iij *d.* namely, by eleven chalders and fifteen bolls of malt malted and sold ; also by the gains of the sheriff in the Bishoprick of Glasgow, besides the eighth

[1] Reg. Epis. Aberd., tom. i. p. 27.

[2] Crawfurd's Officers of State, tom. i. pp. 262, 263.

[3] The Acts of the Parliaments of Scotland, Formulæ Agendi, vol. i. p. 90.

[4] Liber Sancte Marie de Melros, tom. i. p. 274.

of the Bishop, which is xxxiii *s.* iij *d. ob.*, viii *lib.* xxij *d.* ; also by the gains of the Sheriff in Galloway xx *s.*, of which an eighth is not given ; also by the gains of the Justiciar in Galloway, besides an eighth of the Bishop of Glasgow, which is xxvij *s.* j *d.*, ix *lib.* ix *s.* vij *d.* ; also by the goods of two men beheaded at Senewar in the time of Stephen of Fleming, Justiciar, besides the eighth of the Bishop of Glasgow, which is xij *s.* vi *d.*, iiii *lib.* vii *s.* vi *d.* ; also by pennies delivered to him of the gain of the Justiciar of Lothian for the work of the Castle of Dumfries xx *lib.* ; also in furnishing necessaries to the Lesser Friars, iiij *lib.* ; also for expenses of seven hostages of Mann, cij *s.* iiij *d.* ; also for expenses of the Preaching Friars going into Mann, viij *s.* ; also for the office of Justiciar with the maintenance of the imprisoned, xli *s.* ix *d.*

Receipt of the same in cows by the gains of the Justiciar of Galloway and of the Sheriff, acquired in the Bishoprick of Glasgow—besides the eighth of the Bishop, which is viii cows—forty-four cows.[1]

In an account of Hugh of Abernethy, Sheriff of Roxburgh, are entered twenty chalders of barley, which were taken from the lordship of Aymer de Maccuswell for the Castle of Roxburgh ;[2] and in the account of W. of Saint Clair, Sheriff of Haddington, under the head of expenses, are entered—*Item*, for the charge for four prayers for mercy remitted to Aymer of Maccuswell by a letter of the King, besides the tithe of the Abbot of the Holy Cross, lxiiij *s.* x *d.*[3]

Aymer is said, in the genealogical history of the family of Maxwell, to have been killed at the battle of Largs. But as this battle took place in October 1263, and as he was certainly alive at the close of the year 1264, this must be a mistake. He probably died soon after the last-mentioned year. The year 1266 may be stated as an approximation to the time of his death.

Aymer de Makeswell married Mary, the heiress of Mearns, before the year 1255, and with her he acquired the lands and barony of Mearns in Renfrewshire.

The Mearns, which Aymer de Makeswell acquired by this marriage, lies in the south-eastern portion of the shire of Renfrew. It is an inland territory, and was, in remote times, chiefly remarkable for the pasturage of cattle and its dairy produce. Though not of a mountainous character, it is diversified by the undulating or swelling nature of the ground. Its surface gradually rises from the eastern extremity to the west or upper part of the barony, in which is the muir or commonty of Mearns, forming an extensive

---

[1] Accounts of the Great Chamberlains of Scotland, vol. i. p. 26*.

[2] Accounts of the Great Chamberlains of Scotland, vol. i. pp. 45*, 46*.   [3] *Ibid.* vol. i. p. 50*.

tract of pasture land, in which in ancient times numerous proprietors and vassals had the right of pasturing their cattle, but which at last was portioned out among the respective claimants or heritors. It is not distinguished by any large river, but there are several lochs in the muir, the most extensive of which are the Brother Loch, which is about three miles in circumference, and the Little Loch, the Black Loch, and the White Loch, all of which are nearly as large, and abound in trout and other fish.

The affiliation of Mary of Mearns has not been established by documentary evidence. But it is presumed that she became heiress of the family of that name, and that with her Aymer acquired the barony of Mearns, which continued in possession of the family of Maxwell for about 400 years. Such is the account which Crawfurd gives of the acquisition of the Mearns by the Maxwells.[1] In a MS. history of the Maxwells in the British Museum, the addition of the barony of the Mearns to the family inheritance of the Maxwells is similarly explained.

" Homer [Aymer], Lord Maxwell of Carlaverock and Mernes," it is said, " [is] recorded to have been present in Parliament, holden by King Alexander the Second, in the twenty-first year of his reigne, anno 1244, and so to have been a Lord of Parliament," [and to have] "married Marie Makgaghan, heretrix of the Mernes." This MS. is incorrect in various of its statements concerning the family of Maxwell; but the particulars, now quoted, taken in connexion with what we know from other circumstances, there is reason to accept as in the main correct.

The records of the period enable us to trace what we understand to be the ancestry of Mary of Mearns, the wife of Aymer. Rothland or Roland of Mernes, the first whom we have found mentioned under the designation of Mearnes, was witness to a charter by Eschina, wife of Walter, High Steward of Scotland, son of Alan, to the Church of St. James, St. Mirin, and St. Milburga of Paisley, and the Prior of that place, of a carucate of land in Molle, undated, but which must have been granted before the year 1177, when her husband, who was one of the witnesses, died.[2] Rodlannus de Merness was also witness to a charter, about the year 1200, by Nicholas de Constentin, granting

---

[1] Crawfurd's Officers of State, vol. i. p. 263.
[2] Registrum Monasterii de Passelet, p. 74 ; Chronica de Mailros, p. 88.

to the monks of the Abbey of Paisley a portion of his land of Innerwick;[1] and, about 1204, he was a witness to a confirmation by Alan, son of Walter, and High Steward of Scotland, confirming to the monks of Paisley that donation which Henry of St. Martin had made to them by his counsel of his whole land between Kert and Grif.[2]   Roland was succeeded by his son, Nicholas de Mernes.   Nicholas, son of Roland, John de Mundegumery, and four others, granted to the Abbey of Melrose certain lands in the territory of Innerwick. The charter is without date, but it was probably granted about the year 1170. The seal of Nicholas de Mernis is still appended to this charter.   It is of an oval shape, charged with a *fleur de lis*, not on a shield.[3]   The seal of John de Mundegumery, which is also appended, bears in like manner a *fleur de lis*. The next who appears on record as Baron of Mearns was Robert de Mearns, probably the grandson of Roland.   Robert de Merness was witness to a license granted by King Alexander the Third, dated at Edinburgh, 1st June 1250, to the Abbot and Convent of Paisley, to rebuild and repair the fishing-pond which they were wont to have upon the water of the Leven, near Dumbarton.[4]   Richard of Mernes, who in 1262 was witness to a charter by Cecilia, late spouse of John of Perthec, granting to the Abbot and Convent of Paisley the whole right which belonged to her in some land which lay in the town of Rutherglen, may be supposed to have been a younger brother of Robert.[5] Mary of Mearns, with whom Aymer acquired the barony of Mearns, was, it is probable, the daughter of Robert of Mearns, and succeeded to the property on the death of her brother Richard without heirs.

The Mearns was early formed into a parish.   The Church of Mearns is mentioned as attached to the Abbey of Paisley even in the time of Roland of Mearns.   That church, with its lands and teinds, was granted to the abbey by Helyas, clerk, son of Fulbert, and canon of Glasgow;[6] and between the years 1189 and 1199 that grant was confirmed by Peter of Polloc, Helyas's brother.[7] It was also confirmed by King William the Lion; by Jocelin, Bishop of

[1] Registrum Monasterii de Passelet, p. 116.
[2] *Ibid.* p. 15.
[3] Liber Sancte Marie de Melros, tom. i. p. 50. Memorials of the Montgomeries, Earls of Eglinton, vol. ii. p. 1; and Memoirs of the Maxwells of Pollok, vol. i. p. xxxv.

[4] Registrum Monasterii de Passelet, p. 215.
[5] *Ibid.* p. 377.
[6] *Ibid.* pp. 100, 101, 234.
[7] *Ibid.* p. 98.

MEARNS CASTLE

RENFREW.

Glasgow, in whose diocese it was ;[1] and on 2d June 1219 by Pope Honorius the Third, in the third year of his pontificate.[2] The name of the Maxwells is not, however, associated with that church in such of the family writs of the House of Maxwell as have been preserved, or in others which have come under our notice, till about the year 1300, when various gifts were made to it by Herbert of Maxwell, Knight, as will be particularly mentioned under the Memoir of Herbert.

The ancient Castle of Mearns, of the time of Roland of Mearns and of Aymer, does not now exist. It probably stood on a commanding rocky eminence about a mile to the south-east of the village of Newton, on which was erected a new castle by Herbert, first Lord Maxwell, in whose time the original castle had fallen into a decayed condition. The new castle, which was built by Lord Maxwell, will be afterwards particularly described. From the top of the castle could be obtained an extensive and magnificent prospect of the surrounding country, very different indeed from what it now is in respect of cultivation and population, the grand outlines, however, being exactly the same. Southward were the bleak moors of Eaglesham, gradually ascending to Ballygeich, and supplying pasture to the sheep and cattle of the territory. Towards the west, the eye ranged over large tracts of undulating ground, and extensive plantations of wood, and was attracted by the old parish church, and the hamlet of Newton, which was even then a village. Northward and eastward appeared the extensive valley of the Clyde, in all its primitive simplicity, beauty, and grandeur, and in the distance were to be seen the hills of Renfrewshire, Kilpatrick, and Campsy, while beyond them rose the loftier mountains which separate the Highlands from the Lowlands.

In the Act of Parliament of King Alexander the Third, which was passed on 20th September 1255, and which excluded Aymer of Maxwell and others from the guardianship of the King, as already explained, the name of Mary, the wife of Aymer, is included, being the only lady named, from which it would appear that she occupied a place of special dignity among the guardians of the minor King.

---

[1] Registrum Monasterii de Passelet, pp. 100, 101.   [2] The Maxwells of Pollok, vol. i. p. 121.

By his wife, Mary of Mearns, Aymer de Makeswell had four sons, who survived him :

1. Herbert, who succeeded to Maxwell, Carlaverock, and Mearns.

2. Edward. The name of Edward of Maxwell appears among other magnates before whom King Alexander the Second enacted in May 1248, at Stirling, that henceforth none should be on an assize of life and limb in the trial of a man, whether a landholder or gerysman, except leal men, of good report, and freeholders by charter.[1]

In the genealogical history of the family of Maxwell in the British Museum, already referred to, it is said that Edward de Maxwell, with others of his countrymen, joined Louis King of France in one of the Crusades. Dugdale, in his *Monasticon Anglicanum*, after mentioning certain Scottish noblemen who went with that King to the Holy Land, says, "Edward Maxwell, Baron of Carlaverock, the progenitor of the barons and earls of the Maxwell family, namely, of Robert Earl of Nithsdale, etc., joined them." Dugdale's authority is a historian of the Cistercian order, who, it is probable, derived his information from tradition, or from monastic records, or from both. He is incorrect in calling Edward Maxwell " Baron of Carlaverock : " it is certain that he never was so, for during his lifetime the barons of Carlaverock were John and Aymer ; but otherwise the account may be founded in truth.

3. Sir John, the founder of the Pollok branch of the Maxwell family. This branch has formed the subject of two volumes, under the title of " Memoirs of the Maxwells of Pollok," by the author of the present work, printed for the late Sir John Maxwell of Pollok, Baronet, with numerous illustrations : Edinburgh, 1863.

4. Alexander. He and his brother John were witnesses to a charter by their brother Sir Herbert, to the Church of St. James and St. Mirin of Paisley, of eight acres and a half and of twenty-eight particates of land in the new town [Newton] of Mearns.[2]

[1] The Acts of the Parliaments of Scotland, Statuta Regis Alexandri II., vol. i. p. 74.

[2] Memoirs of the Maxwells of Pollok, vol. i. p. 125.

V. SIR HERBERT OF MAXWELL, KNIGHT, FIFTH LORD OF MAX WELL, THIRD OF CARLAVEROCK, SECOND OF MEARNS, AND FIRST OF PENCAITLAND.

1266-c. 1298.

During his father's lifetime, Herbert, under the designation of son and heir of Sir Aymer of Maxwell, obtained from William of Coninburcht a charter of one carucate of land in Langeholme, as therein described, in name of feu-farm, and a half carucate of land in Brakanwra, to be held for rendering to the granter and his heirs, in name of feu-farm, twelve pennies for every secular service, exaction and demand.[1] The charter is undated; but as it was granted in the lifetime of Sir Aymer of Maxwell, the father of Herbert, its date must have been in or before the year 1266.

For a number of years after he came into possession of the family inheritance Sir Herbert's name does not appear in contemporary memorials in connexion with any transaction, private or public.

He was the first of the house of Maxwell who acquired the lands of Pencaitland, in the constabulary of Haddington and county of Edinburgh. They became his property about ten years after his father's death. On the 18th of May, being the Monday following the Ascension, 1276, resignation was made by John of Pencaitland in favour of Herbert of Mackeswell, and his heirs, of the land of Pencaitland on the west side of the water of Tyne, with the patronage of the Church of Pencaitland, before Sir Hugh of Berkelay, Justiciar of Lothian, in full court, at the Castle of Edinburgh (Castrum puellarum). Of these lands William of Douglas, John of Lambertoun, and Richard of Bigirton, knights, had ascertained the extent for the King, with the exception of the copse of Suth, the copse that Sir Alan of Ormiston held of the resigner, and also the Ruthirkroc. Among the witnesses were John Cumyn, son, John of Lyndesay, Richard Fraser, John of Lamberton, Walter of Lyndesay, lord of Periston, knights, William of Lyndesay, Ralph of Eyclyn and others. To this resignation were appended the seals of the

[1] Memoirs of the Maxwells of Pollok, vol. i. p. 124.

granter, of Sir Hugh of Berkelay, Justiciar of Lothian, and of Sir Symon Fraser; but they are now wanting.[1]

About eight and a half years after, Herbert, under the designation of "dominus Herbert de Maxwel," was witness to an agreement between the Abbot and Convent of Paisley on the one side, and John of Aldhus, son of Roger of Aldhus, on the other. By this agreement, John of Aldhus, at Glasgow, on the Tuesday immediately before the Feast of St. Nicholas, bishop, (December 5th,) in the year 1284, in presence of William of Soulys, then Justiciar of Lothian, and other magnates, in full court, renounced in favour of the Abbot and Convent of Paisley his whole right in the land of Aldhus; and the foresaid Abbot and Convent, with the consent of their chapter, granted in farm to the foresaid John that portion of land in the territory of Aldhus which Patrick, son of Neuyn, formerly held in farm of the monks of Paisley.[2]

Herbert of Maxwell, like his father, acted a prominent part in the political transactions of the kingdom. In the reign of King Alexander the Third, and in the calamitous times which followed on the death of that monarch and on the death of his grand-daughter, Margaret of Norway, he appears as sharing constantly in the administration of public affairs.

He sat in a Parliament of the Estates of the kingdom, held at Scone, on the 5th of February 1283-4, consisting of thirteen earls, eleven bishops, and twenty-five barons, who bound themselves to acknowledge, maintain and defend Margaret, Princess of Norway (commonly called the Maiden of Norway), born of Alexander's daughter Margaret by her marriage with Eric, King of Norway, as heiress of the kingdom of Scotland, the Isle of Man, the Hebrides, Tynedale and Penrith, should King Alexander die without lawful children, male or female, of his own body, or should no child of the body of the deceased Prince Alexander be born by his widowed Princess.[3]   This Parliament was assembled within a week after the death of Prince Alexander, and when it was uncertain whether his Princess Margaret of Flanders, a daughter of Count Guy de Dampierre, to whom he was married on 12th November 1281,[4] would have offspring by him.   It was rendered necessary

---

[1] Original Resignation at Terregles.   A facsimile of this Resignation in lithograph has been made for this Work.

[2] Registrum Monasterii de Passelet, p. 66.

[3] The Acts of the Parliaments of Scotland, Alexander III., p. 82.

[4] Wyntown's Cronykil, vol. i. p. 395.

for the settlement of the succession to the Crown, as King Alexander the Third had become childless by a rapid series of domestic calamities. His youngest son, David, died, aged only ten years, in the year 1280 ; and his daughter Margaret, Queen of Norway, having also died, there remained only of his issue the infant Princess Margaret, the daughter of that queen. The King also was a widower, his queen, Margaret, having died in 1275.

Alexander the Third met with an accidental death. On the 16th of March 1285, the night being dark, he left Inverkeithing on horseback for Kinghorn. The road at some points passed dangerous cliffs overhanging the sea, and over one of these the King was thrown, and killed on the spot, owing to a false step made by his horse. He was succeeded by his granddaughter Margaret, Princess of Norway.

Herbert of Maxwell united with other prelates, nobles and barons in promoting the proposed marriage of Margaret with Henry, eldest son of Edward the First, King of England ; a measure which promised greatly to contribute to the tranquillity and prosperity of the kingdoms, both of Scotland and England. As a member of the Estates of the kingdom of Scotland which met at Brigham, a village on the Tweed, in the county of Berwick, Herbert of Maxwell signed a letter, dated 17th March 1289-90, which was despatched by that Parliament to Edward the First of England, relating to that proposal. The letter expressed the joy of the Estates at the news in common circulation, that a Papal dispensation had been granted for the marriage of his son, Prince Edward, with Margaret Queen of Scotland, their dearest lady. It also desired that he would be pleased to send them direct intelligence regarding a measure so closely connected with the well-being of both kingdoms. It further assured him of their cordial approval of the alliance, upon certain reasonable conditions, for the settlement of which they would send delegates to him, and to his Parliament, which was to meet at London at Easter.[1] This letter is signed by the Bishops of St. Andrews and Glasgow; by John Comyn and James the Stewart of Scotland, guardians of the kingdom of Scotland ; and by twelve bishops, twelve earls, twenty-three abbots, eleven priors and forty-eighty barons.[2]

---

[1] The Acts of the Parliaments of Scotland, Queen Margaret, vol. i. p. 85 ; Rymer's Fœdera, tom. ii. p. 471.

[2] The Acts of the Parliaments of Scotland, Queen Margaret, vol. i. p. 86.

On the same day, Sir Herbert of Maxwell joined with the Estates in sending a letter to Eric King of Norway on the same topic. They informed him that, with the assent of the whole kingdom of Scotland, they had, sensible of the great advantage which would thereby accrue to both kingdoms, agreed to the marriage of Queen Margaret with the Prince of England. They requested him to send his daughter into England before the Feast of All Saints. In conclusion, they warned him that should he fail to do this, it would be necessary for them to follow the best counsel which God might give them for the welfare of the kingdom. The tone of the letter testifies to the great anxiety of the Scottish nobility for the arrival of their Queen. Their solicitude in this respect did not exceed that of Edward. He, however, did not trust to simple entreaty to gain his object. As a more effectual means of persuasion, he despatched to Norway one of his principal counsellors to distribute money, under the name of presents, to the King's ministers.[1]

Queen Margaret, attended by a suitable escort, left the shores of Norway for Scotland; but she unhappily died on her passage, near Orkney, in September 1290, an event which, though she was a child of only eight years of age, was most calamitous for Scotland, and the melancholy tidings of which spread gloom and sorrow over the whole kingdom. As she was the last of the descendants of Alexander the Third, her death gave rise to disputes about the succession, which, heightened and embittered by the interference of Edward the First, King of England, who availed himself of an opportunity so favourable for attempting the subjugation of Scotland to the power of England, involved the kingdom in confusion and misery for many years.

Twelve competitors for the crown came forward. It is sufficient here to mention only two, by whom the contest was maintained, Robert de Bruce, who was the son of Isabella, second daughter of David Earl of Huntingdon, brother of King William the Lion, by her husband, Robert Bruce, Lord of Annandale; and John de Baliol, who was the grandson of Margaret, the eldest daughter of the same earl. The former rested his claims on his being the grandson of the Earl of Huntingdon, by which, though born of a younger daughter, he was a degree nearer than his competitor; and the latter laid claim to the succession because, though a degree more remote than Bruce, he was a descendant of the eldest daughter.

[1] Rymer's Fœdera, vol. ii. p. 472; Tytler's History of Scotland, vol. i. p. 77.

The decision of the claims of the competitors was referred to Edward King of England; but before he would undertake the office of umpire, he required from them, and from the nobility, what he had not much difficulty in obtaining, an acknowledgment of his prerogative as Lord Superior of the kingdom of Scotland.

Herbert of Maxwell supported the claims of Baliol; and when auditors, amounting to one hundred and four, were appointed, eighty from Scotland by Bruce and Baliol, and twenty-four from England by King Edward, to hear the petitions and arguments of the competitors, and to prepare the case for the final decision of King Edward,[1] Herbert of Maxwell was one of the auditors who were named by John de Baliol.

On the 12th of August 1291, in the court of the Castle of Berwick, the petitions of the claimants of the Crown of Scotland were read in the presence of King Edward, before the auditors, and before the bishops, earls, barons and other great men of the kingdom of Scotland. This was followed by the pleadings of the parties. At the close Edward, with the consent of the foresaid prelates, earls, etc., appointed that they should meet on the morrow of the Holy Trinity, namely, on the 2d of June 1292, in the same place, for further proceedings.[2] On the 2d of June, at Berwick, the auditors were charged to determine the rights as between Bruce and Baliol. On 18th June, the Wednesday after the Feast of St. Botolph, at Berwick, Bruce replied to the exceptions taken by Baliol,[3] and on the following day Baliol delivered his last objections.[4]

Sir Herbert of Maxwell, as one of the auditors, attended these meetings, and heard the lengthened pleadings of Bruce and Baliol in support of their respective claims.

On the 21st of June, the Saturday before the Nativity of St. John the Baptist, at Berwick-upon-Tweed, Sir Herbert joined with the other auditors in delivering their letters-testimonial, in which they declared that the arguments adduced by the two competitors and their counsel before them, and finally given in writing, were all that needed to be said to enable the King of England

[1] Palgrave's Documents and Records, illustrating the History of Scotland, p. 50.
[2] *Ibid.* p. 35.
[3] Palgrave's Documents and Records, illustrating the History of Scotland, pp. 36-50.
[4] *Ibid.* pp. 50-52.

to proceed to give judgment between the two parties. Herbert of Maxwell was one of the one hundred and four auditors who appended their seals to that letter.[1]

His seal, with the saltire on a shield, which is appended to one of the documents connected with the case of these competitors, is the earliest known heraldic cognisance of the family, and it is said to have been first assumed by an ancestor who had been in the Crusades.

At a meeting of a Parliament of England held at Berwick on the 14th of October 1292, Herbert of Maxwell again attended as one of the auditors. On this occasion, Bruce and Baliol being present, Edward, as Lord Superior of the kingdom of Scotland, submitted two questions to the nobility and bishops of both kingdoms and the auditors, for decision. The one was, By what laws or customs he was to proceed to give judgment? or, if the laws or customs of the kingdoms of England and Scotland were different as to the question in dispute, how he was to proceed in pronouncing judgment? The second was, Whether the succession to the Crown of Scotland was to be decided according to the principle by which the succession to earldoms and baronies was regulated? They unanimously replied that he was to judge in this case by the laws and customs of the kingdom of Scotland; that if such did not exist, he was, in respect of his regal dignity, with the counsel of the nobles, prelates, and great men of his kingdom, to make a new law; and that the succession to the Crown of Scotland was to be determined on the same principle as the succession to earldoms, baronies and other indivisible inheritances.

Bruce and Baliol, on being interrogated by the King, having expressed their desire to be permitted to make additional statements in support of their claims, Herbert of Maxwell, along with the other auditors, at the King's command, withdrew to the church of the Preaching Friars to hear what the competitors had further to adduce. Bruce argued that the claim was to be judged by the law of nations; and Baliol that it was to be determined by the law of ordinary succession. Having heard both parties, the auditors reported to the King the substance of what had been said. The King then asked the bishops, earls, barons, magnates and his whole counsel and the auditors, which of the two competitors they would, on the consideration of the arguments advanced on

---

[1] Palgrave's Documents and Records, illustrating the History of Scotland, pp. 52-55.

both sides, prefer as successor to the sovereign power of the kingdom of Scotland ? and whether a competitor lineally descended from the eldest daughter of the deceased rightful heir, though more remote by one degree in the succession, ought, according to the laws and customs of both kingdoms, to exclude one descended from the second eldest daughter of the deceased rightful heir, though one degree nearer in the succession ; or *vice versa ?* The nobles, prelates, auditors and others of both kingdoms unanimously answered that of these two competitors the one descended from the eldest daughter ought to be preferred.[1]

On the 17th of November, King Edward, in presence of his Council and the Parliament of England assembled in the Castle of Berwick, with the nobility of both kingdoms, gave judgment in favour of John Baliol, as being entitled to the crown of Scotland.

Herbert of Maxwell was a member of a Parliament held at Dunfermline on 23d February 1295-6, which ratified a treaty for the marriage of Edward, Baliol's eldest son and heir-apparent, with a niece of Philip King of France, and for a league offensive and defensive between the Scots and the French. To this treaty Herbert's seal, and the seals of certain bishops, earls, and barons were appended.[2] Baliol and the nobles and barons of Scotland had been impelled to take this step by the arrogance with which Edward maintained his assumed prerogative of Lord Paramount of Scotland, to which Baliol, Bruce, and the nobility of Scotland had only too tamely submitted. War having broken out between England and France, Edward demanded that the Scots, according to their oath of fealty, should assist him against the French. Philip, the French monarch, on the other hand, requested that the Scots would renew the ancient league between France and Scotland. Baliol

[1] Palgrave's Documents and Records, illustrating the History of Scotland, pp. 52-55. Illustrations, pp. xvii.-xxvii.

[2] The Acts of the Parliaments of Scotland, Acta Regis Johannis, tom. i. p. 95*-97*.

Those whose seals were appended to the treaty were the following :—William, Bishop of St. Andrews ; Robert, Bishop of Glasgow ; Mathew, Bishop of Dunkeld ; Henry, Bishop of Aberdeen ; the abbots of the monasteries of Abyrbrothoc, Dunfermline, Holy Rood of Edinburgh, Kelso and St. Andrews ; John Comyn, Earl of Buchan ; Douenald Earl of Mar ; Malise Earl of Strathern ; John Earl of Athole ; John Comyn ; James, Seneschal of Scotland ; Alexander of Balliol ; Gaufrid of Mubray ; Richard Syward ; Herbert of Makyswell ; Patrick of Graham ; Nicholas of Hay ; Nicholas of Graham; Alexander Comyn of Buchan ; Alexander of Bonekill, Barons ; the communities of the towns of Aberdeen, Perth, Stirling, Edinburgh, Roxburgh, and Berwick, in token of their consent and approbation.

and the national council, who felt the humiliation of having given their oaths of fidelity to the English king, ready to avail themselves of the first opportunity that promised to deliver them from their degraded position, refused to give Edward the assistance which he required.   At the same time, by letters-procuratory, dated at Stirling, 5th July 1295, they despatched ambassadors to France, to negotiate the treaty above mentioned, which was entered into at Paris on the 23d of October.

Irritated at this league between the Scots and the French, the English monarch hastened to invade Scotland with a powerful army.   His object was the complete prostration of that kingdom to the power of England.   It was necessary for Baliol to take up arms.   Herbert of Maxwell, along with others, joined in supporting him and in defending his country against the English king.   But Edward proved victorious.   At the battle of Dunbar he defeated, with great slaughter, the Scots, of whom ten thousand were killed, and many, including the principal of the Scottish nobility, were made prisoners.   He made himself master of the castles of Berwick, Dunbar, Roxburgh, Dumbarton, Edinburgh, and Stirling, and many of the Scottish nobility submitted to the conqueror.   Baliol resigned his kingdom into the hands of Edward as his liege lord, in the Castle of Brechin, on 10th July 1296 ;[1] and, after being confined at Hertford from 20th November 1296 to 6th August in the following year, he was transferred to the Tower of London, where he remained until the end of May 1299.   Proceeding to Montrose, Aberdeen, and Elgin, in Moray, Edward met with no opposition, and received in his progress the submissions of most of the Scottish barons who had not fallen in battle or been made prisoners.

On the same day on which Baliol resigned his crown into the hands of Edward, the chief of his supporters were required unconditionally to submit, like their master, to the English king at Montrose, to renounce the recent treaty entered into between Scotland and France, and to swear homage and fealty to him, namely, John Comyn, Earl of Buchan ; Douenald Earl of Mar ; Sir Alexander of Baliol ; Sir John Comyn of Badenach, elder, knight ; Sir Herbert of Makeswell, and Sir John of Murray, knights.   Each gave in a separate document his oath of homage.[2]

Sir Herbert of Makeswell, knight, on the same day, in the presence of

---

[1] The Ragman Rolls, p. 84.   [2] The Ragman Rolls, pp. 85-87.

King Edward, the venerable father in Christ the Bishop of Durham, John of Warenn, Roger of Norfolk, Humphrey of Hereford, William of Warwick, Patrick of Dunbar, and Gilbert of Angus, earls and a notary, made his submission. He wholly renounced the confederations and treaties, under whatever name, if any such ever existed in his name, entered into with the King of France against the King of England, with every advantage which could from thence accrue to him. Touching the sacred Scriptures and kissing the Gospels of God, he made faith to the King of England by his letters-patent, which are in French, and which, translated into English, are as follows:[1]—

" To all those who shall see or hear these letters, Herbert of Makeswell, chevalier, Health : As I have come to the faith and to the will of the most noble Lord Edward, by the grace of God King of England, Lord of Ireland, and Duke of Aquitaine, I promise, for myself and for my heirs,[2] under pain of body, according to our ability, that we shall serve him well and loyally against all people now or hereafter living, expressly against John of Baliol, who was King of Scotland, and against all his helpers and favourers in the kingdom of Scotland, and that we shall have all the fidelity which shall be required of us by our Lord the King of England beforesaid, or by his heirs, and that we shall not know of any injury to be done them which we will not prevent to the utmost of our power, and cause them to know it. To observe these things I bind myself and my heirs, and all my goods ; and, besides, I have sworn upon the holy Gospels. In testimony of which thing I have caused these letters-patent to be sealed with my seal. Given at Monros, the 10th day of July, in the 24th year of the reign of our Lord the King of England"[3] (1296.)

On what occasion the dignity of knighthood was conferred upon Herbert of Maxwell we have not discovered. He is designated as Knight in the Ragman Rolls, when, at this time, he swore fealty to the King of England.

A Parliament was held at Berwick-upon-Tweed, on the 28th of August 1296, by King Edward of England. To this Parliament, to which the nobles, prelates, barons, and esquires of the kingdom of Scotland flocked in great numbers to do homage to the English king, Sir Herbert of Maxwell also

---

[1] The Ragman Rolls, pp. 85-87.

[2] The conclusion is defaced, but what follows is supplied from other letters, as it evidently runs in the same terms.

[3] Palgrave's Documents and Records, illustrating the History of Scotland, p. 169.

hastened for the same purpose.   Like them he renewed the oath of fidelity to Edward which he had formerly sworn, did homage to him for the lands which he possessed in the kingdom of Scotland, and engaged to be loyal to him and to his heirs, to protect their persons and their honour against all whomsoever, and never to bear arms nor to give counsel or assistance against them in any case whatever.   The name of Sir Herbert of Makeswelle stands at the head of one of the many lists containing numerous names of persons who thus swore allegiance to the King of England ; and, like the others, he ordered the letters-patent in which he thus swore allegiance to be sealed with his seal.[1]

Having now subjugated Scotland, Edward pursued in some respects a prudent and equitable policy.   He ordered that the forfeited lands of the clergy should be restored to them, and that the sub-tenants of Baliol, formerly King of Scotland, and of other lords, should also have their lands restored to them, on condition of their rendering fealty to the crown of England. Orders to that effect were sent to the Sheriffs of the different counties in Scotland.

In October 1296 orders were given by Edward to the Sheriff of Lanark, that Herbert of Makeswell, who held certain lands in Lanarkshire of Thomas of Somerville, should have his lands restored to him.   Similar precepts were at the same time issued to the Sheriffs of Roxburgh and Edinburgh in favour of John of Makeswell, who held of Herbert of Makeswell lands in both these counties.[2]

At a later period Sir Herbert of Maxwell is said to have entertained one night, in the castle of Carlaverock, his friend Sir William Wallace, after he had taken various strongholds in Nithsdale, and vanquished a party of English troops in Dalswinton wood.[3]

Under the designation of knight he granted to the Church of St. James and St. Mirin of Paisley, and to the monks there serving God, for a free and perpetual alms, and exempt from every secular service and demand, eight and a half acres and twenty-eight particates of land in the new town [Newtown] of Mearns, which he had caused to be measured, and which was bounded as therein described.   The charter was sealed with the granter's seal and with the seal of Robert, Bishop of Glasgow.   Among the witnesses were John and

---

[1] The Ragman Rolls, pp. 113, 114, 162.   [2] Rot. Scot. tom. i. p. 27.   [3] *Vide* p. 43.

Alexander, the granter's brothers, Sir William and Bricius, chaplains of Paisley.[1] The charter is without date.

Herbert of Maxwell, Knight, made provision for the sustentation of a chaplain, who should yearly, in perpetuity, celebrate divine service in honour of the blessed Virgin Mary, in the parish church of Mearns, for the living and the dead. This he did for the welfare of his soul, and of the souls of his ancestors and successors. The money appropriated for this object was six silver merks of annual rent from the profits of his mills of Mearns in the Aldton, and from the profits of his other mills of Mearns, to be held in pure and perpetual alms. He also ordained that as often as the chaplain who should be appointed to execute that office should leave it vacant by death or otherwise, he and his heirs should have the power of appointing another chaplain in his place. Among the witnesses was John of Maxwell, Lord of Nether Pollock.[2] This charter is also without date.

About the same time, Sir Herbert granted an obligation to the Abbot and Convent of Paisley, binding himself and his heirs to find a chaplain to celebrate divine service *in perpetuum*, in honour of the blessed Virgin Mary, for the granter, his predecessors, and successors, in the church of Mearns, according to the tenor of a letter made thereupon by the granter, which was to remain in the hands of the Abbot and Convent of Paisley.[3]

In the genealogical history of the family of Maxwell in the British Museum, Sir Herbert of Makeswell is said to have been killed at the battle of Falkirk, in the year 1298. But this genealogical history, as has been observed before, is not one of the best authorities. The exact date of the death of Sir Herbert must therefore be left uncertain.

Sir Herbert had a son, John. Whether John succeeded his father, or predeceased him, we are unable to determine, though there is some reason to think that the latter is the fact.

---

[1] Memoirs of the Maxwells of Pollok, vol. i. p. 125 ; Registrum Monasterii de Passelet, p. 101, and again printed, p. 379.

[2] Memoirs of the Maxwells of Pollok, vol. i. p. 127 ; Registrum Monasterii de Passelet, p. 103.

[3] Memoirs of the Maxwells of Pollok, vol. i. p. 127 ; Regis. Monas. de Passelet, p. 104.

VI. JOHN OF MAXWELL, SIXTH LORD OF MAXWELL, FOURTH OF CARLAVEROCK, THIRD OF MEARNS, AND SECOND OF PENCAITLAND.

Of the subject of this memoir little can be said. Like his father, Sir Herbert, he submitted to the triumphant arms of Edward King of England. On 17th July 1296, at Aberdeen, "John, son of Herbert of Makeswell," gave his oath of homage and fidelity to that king. He is so styled in a general enumeration of those who, at that place on that day, thus gave their oaths ; and, in his letters of submission and fealty, he is designated "John of Makeswelle, Chevalier, the son of Sir Herbert of Makeswelle." On the same day and at the same place, a person of the same name, who is probably identical, though represented in the English accounts as a different person, "Johannes dominus de Makeswelle," so called in the enumeration of names referred to, and in his letters of submission, "John de Makeswelle, Chevalier," gave his oath of homage and fidelity to Edward King of England.[1]

John of Maxwell obtained from his father, Sir Herbert, a grant of certain lands in the shire of Edinburgh, probably those of Pencaitland, and part, if not the whole, of Maxwell in the shire of Roxburgh, which he held of him. This suggests that Sir Herbert may have granted to his son John the fee of the family estates, reserving to himself the liferent.

In 1297, John of Maxwell, "son and heir of Herbert of Maxwell," gave a charter, "Domino Ade de Gordon," of lands in Glenkenns, in the stewartry of Kirkcudbright.[2]

In the preceding memoir we have brought down the history of the family of Maxwell to nearly the close of the year 1296. From that time to the spring of the year 1312, when Sir Eustace was Lord of Maxwell, there is almost a blank in the history of the family.

These blank years were a very unsettled and disastrous period in the history of Scotland. Edward the First, King of England, had overrun the

[1] The Ragman Rolls, pp. 95, 96.

[2] This Charter is entered in the Inventory Book of the Muniments of Kenmure estate, of which Glenkenns is a part. But the original charter itself cannot now be found at Kenmure. A copy of the charter is referred to as in the collections of Macfarlane, the antiquary. But the copy is not in the collections deposited in the Advocates' Library at Edinburgh.

kingdom, and the most of the nobles of Scotland had been reluctantly constrained to submit to his overwhelming power. It seemed as if the conquest of Scotland was complete. In this melancholy state of affairs, a champion appeared in the person of Sir William Wallace, who, from his success against the English, was chosen Governor of Scotland, and who, after a brief and noble struggle for the liberty and independence of his country, fell into the hands of Edward, and was executed at London, with ruthless barbarity, on 23d August 1305. Only a few months after the death of Wallace, a new deliverer arose in Robert Bruce, Earl of Carrick, grandson of the competitor for the throne ; and he was crowned King of Scotland on 27th March 1306.

During the period between 1296 and 1312, Sir Herbert and his son John certainly died ; but the exact date of the death of either of them is unknown. This John, we presume, is the "John Maxwell of Pencateland" who granted to the Abbey of Dryburgh the patronage of the Church of Pencateland and the chapel of Payston.[1] The Abbey of Dryburgh, with which the name of John of Maxwell was thus associated, has been generally considered as founded between 1150 and 1152, by King David the First, who in his charter in its favour describes it as "the church of St. Mary of Dryburgh, which I have founded."[2] In the Chronicle of Melrose, its founder is said to have been Hugh of Morville, Constable of Scotland in the reign of King David the Second.[3] But these conflicting statements may perhaps be reconciled by supposing that Morville, if not the founder, was the earliest benefactor of the abbey. It is said to have been erected on the site of a druidical temple. Its striking and picturesque ruins, standing on a plain at a bend of the Tweed, and surrounded by the lofty trees that cover its banks, are objects of special attraction to the antiquary, the historian, and the tourist.

John of Maxwell, who, in a charter by his son John, afterwards given at length, is designated "Dominus Johannes de Maxwell de Pencateland," had two sons, Eustace, who was in possession of the estates of Maxwell in the year 1312, and John, who succeeded his brother Eustace.[4]

[1] Liber S. Marie de Dryburgh, p. 272.
[2] *Ibid.* Preface, p. lxix.
[3] Chronica de Mailros, p. 78.
[4] *Vide infra,* pp. 106, 107.

VII.—1. SIR EUSTACE OF MAXWELL, SEVENTH LORD OF MAX-WELL, AND FIFTH OF CARLAVEROCK, AND SHERIFF OF DUM-FRIES, 1312-1342.

The exact time when Sir Eustace succeeded to the family possessions is uncertain. It is not till the spring of the year 1312 that he first appears in authentic history. Whether he or his grandfather Herbert was the chief of the house of Maxwell at the period of the siege of the Castle of Carlaverock in the year 1300 by Edward the First, King of England, is not quite certain. At the time of that siege the proprietor of the castle was opposed to the English ; but Sir Eustace, when we meet with notices of him in 1312, was on the side of Edward the Second,[1] in opposition to King Robert the Bruce. On the 30th of March in that year he obtained from Edward a remission of £22 to enable him the more effectually to keep the Castle of Carlaverock. The King's letter in reference thereto, translated from the original Latin, is as follows :—

The King to his well-beloved clerk, William de Bevercotes, his Chancellor of Scotland, greeting —That our well-beloved Eustace of Maxwelle may put a better and more secure guard in his Castle of Carlaverock for us against the stratagems of the Scots our enemies, we have granted to him that twenty and two pounds annually which he owes every year to us, at our Exchequer of Berwick, of blench farm for the keeping of his foresaid castle, for his assistance in the effectual performance of that duty, at our will : And therefore we command you that you cause the same Eustace to obtain without delay our letters sufficient to him thereupon : Whereof the King was witness at Newcastle-upon-Tyne, 30th day of April [1312].[2]

Not long after, Sir Eustace emancipated himself from the English yoke, and ranked himself among the supporters of King Robert the Bruce. During the first years of the contest, in which he struggled for existence, Bruce stood rather on the defensive, but gradually he assumed the offensive, and his arms against the English were crowned with a succession of victories. His efforts were specially directed to recover the strongholds of Scotland out of the hands of the English garrisons or of the Scottish barons who held them for the English. In 1312 he took from the English the castles of Bute, Dumfries, and Dalswinton, and the town of Perth. In the following year, Roxburgh was captured for him by Sir James Douglas, and the Castle of Edinburgh by Thomas

---

[1] Edward the Second succeeded his father 8th July 1307.   [2] Rot. Scot. vol. i. p. 110.

Randolph, lately created Earl of Moray. In the summer of the year 1313 all the strongholds of Scotland held by the English were reduced by Bruce. From Bruce's success many of the Scottish barons in the English interest were gained over to his support.

In retaliation for Sir Eustace Maxwell having adhered to Bruce, the English laid siege to the Castle of Carlaverock. But the force which they brought against it was much less formidable than that which attacked it in the year 1300, and after feebly conducting the siege for several weeks, they found it necessary to abandon the enterprise.

Notwithstanding this successful defence, Sir Eustace, doubtful whether the Castle could sustain a more formidable assault, demolished, or partially demolished, the fortifications, that, should it be afterwards reduced, it might not be of much service to the captors. This devotion to his interests was acknowledged by Bruce, who granted Sir Eustace a charter of an annualrent, and relieved him from the payment of various sums to which the Crown was entitled from his lands, amounting to £32 sterling.[1]

From Bruce Sir Eustace of Maxwell also received a charter of the lands of Westerraw, Pedynan, and the lands of Park, which John, son of Valdevus, had forfeited, having died against the faith of the king.[2]

Sir Eustace of Maxwell appears to have remained faithful to the interests of King Robert the Bruce to the death of that monarch. He was a member of the Parliament held at Aberbrothoc on 6th April 1320; and persuaded, like the King, barons and freeholders then assembled, that their cause had been much misrepresented by the English ambassadors at the Court of Rome to Pope John the Twenty-Second, who, gained over to the King of England's interest, had excommunicated Robert the Bruce and all his accomplices, and laid the kingdom of Scotland under interdict, Sir Eustace united with them in sending a letter to that Pope, exhibiting the grounds of the quarrel between Scotland and England, asserting the independence of Scotland, and praying his Holiness to admonish the English king to allow the Scots to remain in the undisturbed possession of their rights and liberties.

The first name in the body of this famous letter is that of Duncan Earl of Fife, and the second is that of Thomas Randolph Earl of Moray. Among the

---

[1] Robertson's Index of Records and Charters, p. 12, No. 75, and p. 15, No. 13.   [2] *Ibid.* p. 11, No. 49.

barons prominently appears "Eustachius de Maxwelle." The letter was signed by eight earls and thirty-one barons.

It begins with referring to the origin of the nation of the Scots according to the traditions then current; to their conversion to the Christian faith by St. Andrew, the brother of St. Peter; and to the uninterrupted succession of 113 kings in the royal line (many of them doubtless fabulous), who, it is affirmed, reigned over them without the intervention of an alien.

The letter then dwells upon the liberty and independence which they had enjoyed till the kingdom was invaded by Edward the First, King of England, and upon the intolerable oppressions to which by his tyranny it had been subjected. "Considering these things, with anxious mind, most holy fathers, and your predecessors, did, with many great and singular favours and privileges, fortify this kingdom and people, as the peculiar charge of the brother of St. Peter, so that our nation, under their protection, continued in freedom and quietness, until that mighty King of the English, Edward, father of him who now is, did, under the semblance of a friend and confederate, hostilely invade our kingdom, when without a head, and our people, suspecting no evil or deceit, and who were then unaccustomed to wars or attacks. The injuries, slaughters, and deeds of violence, the depredations and burnings, the imprisonments of prelates, the firing of monasteries, the spoliations and murders of religious men, and also other enormities, which that king perpetrated on the said people, without sparing any sex or age, religion or order of men whatsoever, it would be impossible for any one who had not learned it from experience to describe or fully understand."

The letter next expatiates on the merit and valour of their deliverer, Robert the Bruce, to whom it was their purpose loyally to adhere. "But from these innumerable evils, by the help of Him who heals the wounds that have been inflicted and restores to health, we have been delivered by our most valiant Prince, King, and Lord, our Lord Robert, who, that he might rescue his people and his heritage from the hands of enemies, did, like a second Maccabæus or Joshua, endure with a cheerful mind all manner of toil and fatigue, hunger and dangers; whom, also, divine Providence and the right of succession, according to our laws and customs, which we will defend to the death, and the due consent and assent of us all, have made our Prince and

King. To him, as being the saviour of our people and the defender of our liberty, we are bound and resolved to adhere in all things, both on account of his right and of his merits."

Their loyalty to Bruce was not, however, to be a blind devotion. It was only as the hero of the independence of the kingdom that they were to follow even him. This they express in these resolute terms :—" But should this prince desist from what he has so nobly begun, wishing to subject us or our kingdom to the king or the people of England, we would immediately do our utmost to expel him as our enemy, and as the subverter of his own and our right, and would make another king who should be able to defend us ; for so long as a hundred of us are left alive we will never in any degree be subjected to the dominion of the English. It is not for glory, riches, or honours that we fight, but for liberty alone, which no good man loses but with his life."

Then comes the practical point in the letter, which is to beseech the Pope to tender his paternal counsel to the King of England to be content with his own dominions and to refrain from disturbing his neighbours. " For these reasons, reverend father and lord, we, with all the earnestness of entreaty, and on the bended knees of our hearts, beseech your Holiness, that, sincerely and devoutly reflecting that with Him, whose vicegerent you are, there is no respect of persons, nor distinction of Jew or Greek, Scot or English, and looking with paternal eyes on the tribulations and straits brought upon us and the Church of God by the English, you would vouchsafe to admonish and ex-hort the King of the English, to whom, that which he possesses, ought to suffice, since England of old used to be sufficient for seven or more kings, to leave in peace us Scots, who dwell in the narrow spot of Scotland, the extreme boundaries of the habitable globe, and who desire nothing but our own." Referring to the Crusades for the recovery of the Holy Land from the infidels, in which, inspired by religious zeal and a thirst for glory, so many kings and princes had embarked, the barons beseech his Holiness to procure the peace of Christendom, that the obstructions to this sacred enterprise might be removed, declaring the alacrity with which they and their King would lend their assistance if the King of England would allow them to remain in peace.

The conclusion of the letter is remarkable for the freedom of its tone. " If your Holiness, too credulous of the misrepresentations of the English, do not give firm credit to what we have said, nor cease to favour them to our confusion, all the destruction of life, ruin of souls, and other calamities which they shall inflict on us and we on them, will, we believe, be laid to your charge by the Most High."

The original of this letter, or a duplicate, is now in Her Majesty's General Register House, Edinburgh. An excellent engraving of it was made about fifty years ago by Mr. Lizars as an illustration for the Acts of the Parliaments of Scotland.[1] The letter has recently been photozincographed both from the original and also from the engraving for the National Manuscripts of Scotland.[2] The learned editor of that work says that the letter " is surely the noblest burst of patriotic feeling, the finest declaration of independence that real history has to show, and that has been preserved in the language in which it was uttered. We can forgive the Scotch schoolmaster who used this letter as an exercise for his boys in Latin, holding that its patriotism covered any defects of Latinity."[3]

This famous letter was preserved nearly entire for five centuries; it was all but entire when the engraving referred to was taken, as appears from the engraving itself; but a part of it is now decayed.

With this letter Sir Edward Mabuisson and Sir Adam de Gordon were despatched to the Pope at Avignon. The letter was only partially successful. The Pope earnestly recommended a peace between the two kingdoms; but Bruce and Edward could not agree about the conditions.

In the year 1320, Sir Eustace Maxwell was accused of having been impli-

---

[1] The Acts of the Parliaments of Scotland, reign of Robert the First, vol. i. p. 114.

[2] National Manuscripts of Scotland, Part ii. No. xxiv.

[3] Preface to National Manuscripts, Part II. p. viii., and Photograph of the Original in that Work, No. xxiv. The late Professor James Y. Simpson, in an address on Archæology to the Society of Antiquaries, on 28th January 1861, referred to this letter to the Pope as having been discovered by a late Scottish nobleman in the fireplace of his drawing-room at the moment that the housemaid was about to apply a match to kindle a fire, and that the letter thus narrowly escaped being sent up the chimney in a blaze. The nobleman referred to was Thomas Earl of Haddington, who found the letter to the Pope not in the fireplace in his drawing-room, but in his charter-room at Tyninghame, without any risk of fire such as is described in the lecture. When there, on one occasion, the author of this work was told by his Lordship of the discovery. His Lordship at the same time pointed to the exact spot where the letter was found. Professor Simpson, on these facts having been communicated to him by the author, after his address, modified his statements in the print of it which was issued.— (Proceedings of the Society of Antiquaries, vol. iv. part i. pp. 43, 44.)

cated in a conspiracy against the Crown and life of King Robert the Bruce. The object of the conspirators was to put to death King Robert, in order to place on the throne Sir William Soulis, High Steward, grandson of Nicholas de Soulis, who had been one of the competitors for the Crown on the death of Margaret of Norway, and whose claim rested on his grandmother, Marjory, the wife of Alan de Durward, who was a natural daughter of Alexander the Second, and consequently the sister of Alexander the Third ; a claim which, but for the illegitimacy of his grandmother, would have been superior to the claims of either Bruce or Baliol.   The others, besides Sir Eustace, who were accused of complicity in this conspiracy, were William de Soulis, the Steward ; Sir David de Brechin, the King's nephew ; Sir Gilbert de Malherbe ; Sir John Logie ; Sir Walter de Berklay, Sheriff of Aberdeen ; and Sir Patrick de Graham ; with Richard Brown, Hameline de Troupe, and Eustace de Rattray, Esquires.   The plot was discovered by the confessions of the Countess of Strathern, who was in the secret.

Sir Eustace Maxwell and the others accused were brought to trial at a Parliament held at Scone in the beginning of August in the year 1320.[1]   Soulis and the Countess of Strathern were convicted, and were sentenced to perpetual imprisonment.[2]   Soulis, when he was arrested, was at Berwick with 360 esquires who attended him, and he was imprisoned in the Castle of Dumbarton, but he died soon after.   Sir David de Brechin, Malherbe, Logie, and Brown were cruelly put to death, being drawn by horses and beheaded, because, though they knew of the conspiracy, they did not reveal it, having sworn to secrecy.   Sir Eustace Maxwell, Sir Walter de Berklay, Sir Patrick de Graham, Hameline de Troupe, and Eustace de Rattray were acquitted.

Atrocious as were the crimes of plotting the death and dethronement of the King, the execution of the principal conspirators with circumstances of such barbarity excited general commiseration and was condemned as unnecessarily severe ; especially the fate of Sir David Brechin, who—though he had been a pensioned emissary of the Court of England, which however was not generally known—was popular from the valour he had displayed in his expedition to the Holy Land.   As a proof of the unpopularity of these judicial pro-

[1] The records of the trial, which would doubtless have thrown much light on the conspiracy, have not been preserved.   [2] Fordun, vol. ii. p. 274.

ceedings, it may be mentioned that the Parliament by which the conspirators were tried and condemned was long called the Black Parliament.[1]

King Robert the Bruce died at Cardross on the 7th of June 1329, and was succeeded by his son, David the Second, who was then a boy not much more than five years of age. The kingdom therefore, in an age in which the vigour of the administration depended much on the capacity of the monarch who occupied the throne, suffered all the evils incident to a protracted minority. Its liberties were assailed by Edward the Third, a prince of great political and military abilities, whose policy, like that of his father and grandfather, was the subjugation of Scotland to the power of England. Torn by factions, and feeble in resources compared with England, Scotland, though never permanently subdued, was yet unequal to the contest; and the most powerful of the Scottish nobility were often found in the ranks of the English during the reign of King David the Second and his successors.

Though Sir Eustace Maxwell had continued loyal to King Robert the Bruce from the time he espoused the interest of that monarch to his death, yet his hereditary feelings were in favour of the Baliol family; and when, on the death of Bruce, and the succession of his son David to the throne, the right to the crown was contested by Edward, the eldest son of John Baliol, who died in the year 1314, Sir Eustace Maxwell embraced the interest of the new aspirant to the throne, and co-operated with Edward the Third of England in supporting his claims. Among others with whom he was now politically associated were Henry Viscount Beaumont, who, in right of his wife, claimed the earldom of Buchan; the young David Strabolgie, Earl of Athole; Gilbert Umfraville, Earl of Angus; Sir John Mowbray; Sir Alexander Mowbray; and Sir Richard Talbot, who were supporters of Edward Baliol.

When, on the 31st of July 1332, Edward Baliol, at the head of English lords and Scottish refugees, with about 6000 soldiers, according to Buchanan, but according to the English historians only 2500, arrived before Kinghorn, in Fife, to assert his right to the crown of Scotland, Sir Eustace Maxwell was ready to support him. In that year Edward Baliol, with his small army, defeated the Scots at Duplin, with great slaughter; and after the battle he took possession of Perth, which he fortified, for successfully sustaining what he expected—an

[1] Extracta ex Cronicis Scocie, printed for the Abbotsford Club, p. 150.

assault from the army of the Scots, which amounted to 30,000 men, under the command of the Earl of March. The Earl advanced against the town, but in place of assaulting it he subjected it to a blockade, which was understood as a sign that he was favourable to Baliol. Amidst these exciting events, Sir Eustace of Maxwell acted a prominent part on the side of Baliol. He was in the field with his Galloway men,[1] and in diversion of the siege he invaded the lands of the besiegers. By this means, and from other circumstances favourable to the besieged, the blockade ended in the withdrawal of the army of the Scots and their complete dispersion, while the Earl of March not long after went over to the English.

Sir Eustace was present at the coronation of Baliol at Scone, on 24th September same year. After the coronation he accompanied him in his march towards the south, a journey undertaken with a view to maintain communication with England; and in less than a month he was in the Castle of Roxburgh, which submitted to Baliol's authority on his first approach. Sir Eustace's name occurs, under the designation of " Knight," as witness to a charter granted by Edward [of Baliol] King of the Scots, dated at Roxburgh, 20th October, in the first year of the reign of the granter, in favour of Thomas Ughtreth, knight, of the manor of Bonchill or Bonkil, with all and sundry other lands and tenements which belonged to John Steward, knight, within the kingdom of Scotland, under whatever right or title, and which fell into the hands of the granter by the forfeiture of the said John. The other witnesses were Henry Beaumont, Earl of Buchan ; David Strabolgie, Earl of Atholl ; Duncan Earl of Fife ; Gilbert Umfraville, Earl of Angus; Richard Talbot, Henry of Ferrariis, Alexander Mowbray, knights, and many others whose names are not given.[2] The charter was confirmed by Edward King of England, at Newcastle-upon-Tyne, 19th June 1334.

While at Roxburgh Castle Edward Baliol acknowledged Edward the Third as his feudal lord. Great as was the success which had hitherto attended his enterprise, he was soon compelled to escape, which he did with great difficulty, on horseback, without bridle or saddle, to Carlisle. But, supported by the English, his party continued to triumph. At the battle of Halidon Hill, fought on 20th July 1333, between the English and the Scots, the latter were com-

[1] Chronicon de Lanercost, p. 269.   [2] Rot. Scot. tom. i. p. 274 a ; Rymer's Fœdera, edit. 1704, tom. v. p. 177.

pletely routed, many of the nobility and barons of Scotland and 14,000 soldiers being killed. Upon this, Berwick, to which Edward King of England laid siege with a powerful army, surrendered, and Baliol became master of almost the whole kingdom, though some important fortresses still remained in possession of the adherents of David the Second.

Whilst these scenes were enacting, Sir Eustace of Maxwell, it may be presumed, was not inactive. Upon the surrender of Berwick he was appointed, along with seven others, Alexander of Seton, Thomas Brown, Eustace of Lorreyne, Roger of Mauduyt, Adam of Bowes, Ambrose of Newburgh, and Robert of Tughale, by Edward the Third and his Council, 15th December 1333, to ascertain the annual value of the castle, county, and town of Berwick-upon-Tweed, in all their revenues, and was commanded to cause an inquest to be made, under oath, by upright and leal men of the county and town, by whom the truth of the matter might be better known.[1]

Sir Eustace, as we shall afterwards see, incurred the censure of King Edward by his negligence in the execution of this commission.

In the truce, which, by the persuasion of the King of France and the Pope, was entered into between Edward the Third and Sir Andrew of Moray, knight, who had been created Regent of the kingdom of Scotland[2] in the room of Randolph Earl of Moray, then a prisoner in England, Sir Eustace of Maxwell had a special part assigned him to act.

On 29th October 1335, King Edward, by letters to all and sundry his sheriffs, bailies, and others, his faithful subjects, both in England and Scotland, commanded them to see to the observance of the truce, which was to continue to the Lord's-day on the morrow of St. Martin in winter next to come (11th November). The truce was from time to time prolonged, and while it lasted several fruitless attempts were made to effect a peace.[3] When after repeated prolongations the truce was, on 26th January 1335-6, continued from a date formerly fixed to the Lord's-day on the *quindena* of Easter next to come (14th April), Godefrid de Ros and Eustace of Makeswell were on that day appointed by Edward the Third conservators of the truce. The commission, translated from the original Latin into English, is in the following terms :—

[1] Rot. Scot. tom. i. p. 260 *b*.

[2] He was married to Christian, sister of King Robert the Bruce.

[3] Rot. Scot. tom. i. pp. 385, 387, 388, 391, 395.

The King to his beloved and faithful Godefrid of Ross and Eustace of Makeswell, Greeting : Know that since, from reverence for the sovereign lord Pontiff, and at the request of Lord Philip, King of France, our dearest cousin, and of their ambassadors, sent over to the parts of our kingdom about the affairs of Scotland, and from other causes, we have granted to the men of Scotland, nobles, and commons, not being at our peace and faith, a truce, to last to the Lord's-day on the *quindena* of Easter next to come, that Lord's-day included, as in our letters-patent made thereupon is more fully contained : We, willing that the foresaid truce, as far as it belongs to us, may be observed, and confident of your fidelity and circumspection, have appointed you, conjunctly and severally, to preserve, and cause to be preserved beyond the Forth for us and in our name, that truce which we send to you under our seal, in all and sundry its articles : Giving to you, and to each of you, by the tenor of these presents, the power of repressing and punishing all those who shall offend or attempt anything against the form of the foresaid truce, or any article thereof, and to execute justice on all and sundry brought before you, or one of you, in regard to the injuries and molestations done by them against the tenor of the same truce, or any article of it, and to do all other and sundry things which shall be necessary, or even advantageous, even as justly and reasonably to do, for the preservation of that truce, and as has hitherto been wont to be done : And, therefore, we command you, and each of you, firmly enjoining you to do and to fulfil all and sundry the premises in the form foresaid : For we have commanded archbishops, bishops, abbots, priors, earls, barons, knights, our sheriffs, bailies, servants and faithful subjects, as well within as without the liberties, to be diligent in assisting you, and each of you, in all things which pertain to the conservation of the foresaid truce, as often as and when they shall be required, or even forewarned. In testimony of which thing, etc., to continue as long as it shall be our pleasure ; the King being witness, at Berwick-upon-Tweed, 26th day of January [1335-6]. By the King himself.[1]

The truce, which was protracted still further, finally expired about the middle of May 1336, upon which hostilities between Scotland and England were renewed. The Scots, encouraged by the considerable supplies, which by this time they had received, of men, money and ammunition from France, and by the assurances of still more effective support which Philip King of France had given them, resolved to make themselves masters of some strong places, before the main army of Edward King of England could be brought together. They besieged and captured the castles of St. Andrews and Bothwell. Under the command of the Earls of March and William Lord of Douglas, they also laid siege to Stirling Castle, which, in those days, was almost impregnable, and on the arrival of King Edward on a new expedition into Scotland, they assaulted it with great fury ; but they were successfully repulsed, and found it necessary to raise the siege and to retreat. The war was conducted with varied fortune on both sides. The English King overran large parts of Scotland, but he entirely

---

[1] Rot. Scot. tom. i. p. 397.

failed of accomplishing what he aimed at in his expeditions into that kingdom, namely, its complete conquest; and the strongholds which he took and the advantages which he gained at one time were recovered by the Scots at another.

Sir Eustace was not always so zealous in promoting the English interest as Edward desired. He had, as we have seen, been, along with others, appointed to give in to his Majesty's Exchequer at Berwick an account of the annual revenue of the castle, town, and shire of Berwick. But he had been neglectful of the execution of that trust. In the year 1336, whilst some of the King of England's sheriffs in Scotland were blamed by Edward for remissness in rendering their accounts, complaints of this kind were made against Eustace of Maxwell, and a letter to that effect was sent to him by the King, commanding him speedily to render the account referred to. The letter translated from the original Latin is as follows :—

The King to his beloved and faithful Eustace of Maxwell, our Sheriff of Dumfries in Scotland, Greeting : Since we have intrusted you with the keeping of our foresaid county and the pertinents thereof, so that you may answer concerning the revenues accruing to us at our Exchequer of Berwick, as in our letters-patent made thereupon is more fully contained, and have learned that the account which we hold you to be bound to render to us of your receipts of the said revenues from the time when you had the said charge, as yet remains to be rendered, at which we are much surprised : We therefore command you, firmly enjoining that, whenever you are forewarned by our beloved Thomas de Burgh, our Chamberlain of Berwick, to render your said account at the foresaid Exchequer, you, without making any excuse whatever, go and there render that account, as is customary, and according to the tenor of your commission above said : And this you are by no means to omit : For we have commanded the foresaid chamberlain to hear that account and to do further what the nature of the account requires in this part :

The King being witness, at the town of St. Johnston, 13th day of August [1336]. By the King himself.[1]

About the year 1337 the patriotism of Sir Eustace de Maxwell revived. He abandoned the cause of Baliol and the English interest. Kept down as the barons in the south of Scotland were by the English king, they were probably only too glad of opportunities to throw off the yoke. In that year war broke out between England and France, Edward having laid claim to the throne of the last-named kingdom ; and, in July 1338, he made a hostile expedition into France. Before setting out he appointed Richard Earl of

---

[1] Rot. Scot. tom. i. p. 441 a.

Arundel, General, and Gilbert of Umfraville, Earl of Angus, Lieutenant-General of the army intended to act in Scotland in support of Baliol and of the English interest. But, partly from his absence and partly from the diversion made by the war in a distant quarter, important advantages were obtained over the English by the Scots, who regarded this as a favourable opportunity for even attempting to expel the English from Scotland.

Whether the change of Sir Eustace Maxwell from English to Scottish interests was owing to the circumstances now referred to, or to other causes, it may be difficult to determine. But he incited the men of Galloway on this side of the Cree to take up arms against King Edward. This he did although he had immediately before received from the English King, for the keeping of the Castle of Carlaverock, money out of the English Exchequer, arms, and warlike engines and all kinds of provisions. All these he greatly needed, even as they were needed by and granted to other fortresses in Scotland owning the authority of Baliol or of King Edward, in consequence of the desolate condition of the country, which, having been so often overrun and wasted by friends and enemies, lay in a great measure uncultivated.[1] The castles of Dumbarton and Carlaverock are said to have been the only fortified places which were then held by the Scots.[2]

In the year 1339 Sir Eustace again returned to his submission to King Edward, and obtained a pardon from him. On 20th August that year letters from the King were addressed to his bailies and faithful subjects, informing them that he had admitted Eustace of Makeswell, lately adhering to certain of that King's enemies in Scotland to the King's faith, peace, and goodwill, and had pardoned him and his adherents for the homicides, felonies, robberies, larcenies, and offences whatsoever perpetrated by them in Edward's kingdom of England as well as in Scotland, against that King's peace. Two others, Duncan Makduel and Michael Mageth, both of Scotland, were at the same time admitted to the peace of King Edward.[3]

Sir Eustace married Helen Maxwell of Pollok, by whom he had no children. On his death at Carlaverock, on 3d March 1342,[4] he was succeeded by his brother John.

[1] Chron. de Lanercost, p. 290.
[2] *Ibid.* p. 296.
[3] Rot. Scot. vol. i. p. 571 *b.*
[4] History of Maxwell Family.

VII.—2. SIR JOHN OF MAXWELL, KNIGHT, EIGHTH LORD OF MAXWELL, AND SIXTH OF CARLAVEROCK.

1342-1347.

JOHN OF MAXWELL, son of Sir John of Maxwell of Pencaitland, succeeded his brother Eustace in the barony of Maxwell. He is described as John of Maxwell, son of the deceased Sir John of Maxwell of Pencaitland, knight, in a charter in which he granted to the Abbey of Dryburgh the patronage of the Church of Pencaitland, with the Chapel of Payston. The charter, which is undated, but probably granted about the year 1340, is in Latin, and translated, is in the following terms :—

To all the sons of holy Mother Church who shall see or hear this writing, John of Maxwell, son of the deceased Sir John of Maxwell of Pencaitland, knight, everlasting salvation in the Lord : Know all of you that I, from motives of piety, have given, granted, and by this my present charter have confirmed to God and the Church of St. Mary of Dryburgh and to the abbot and canons of the Order of Præmonstratenses of the diocese of St. Andrews, that there serve God, and that will hereafter serve Him, in perpetuity, the right of the patronage of the Church of Pencaitland, to be held and had for free, pure, and perpetual alms, with the Chapel of Payston, by them and their successors, for the welfare of my soul and that of my wife, and for the welfare of the souls of my father and my mother, and of all my ancestors and successors, with the church land of the same and of the said chapel, and for augmentation of the church land, ten acres of land near the south side, and with all other easements and liberties belonging, or that in any way at any time shall belong to the same church and the said chapel, as freely, quietly, and fully as any patron in the kingdom of Scotland can confer any right of patronage on any church or religious men. But I, the said John, and my heirs and assignees, shall warrant, acquit and defend for ever my foresaid donation to the foresaid abbot and canons of Dryburgh against all men and women. And that this my donation, grant, will and confirmation may have the force of perpetual firmness, I have strengthened my present charter by the appending of my seal. And for the greater security I have procured the seal of the venerable father Lord William of St. Andrews, by the grace of God then Abbot of Melrose, to be placed to my present charter : Witnesses, Lord William, then Abbot of Kelso ; Lord Bartholomew, then Abbot of Holyrood, of Edinburgh ; Lord Patrick, Earl of March ; Sir Robert of Keth, lord of the same ; Sir Alexander of Sethon, lord of the same ; Sir William de Abyrnythyn, knights ; Robert Maitland, lord of Thyrlstane ; Alan of Trebrone, lord of the same ; Ingeramus of Wynton, Lord of Fenton ; Hugh of Wynton ; Thomas de Leys de Sawlton, and many others.[1]

At the date of this charter John of Maxwell had not received the dignity of knighthood. But when his name next appears he is designated knight, even

---

[1] Original Charter in the Earl of Lauderdale's Charter-chest. Liber S. Marie de Dryburgh, p. 271.

before he had succeeded his brother Sir Eustace. In another charter, which he granted soon after to the Abbey of Dryburgh, of the right of the patronage of the Church of Pencaitland, with the Chapel of Payston, and the land of the said church and chapel, he is described as " Sir John of Maxwell, knight, son of the deceased Sir John of Maxwell, and heir of Sir Eustace of Maxwell, his brother." The witnesses to this charter were Robert, Steward of Scotland; Patrick Earl of March; Sir Maurice de Moravia; Sir William of Levynston; Sir Robert of Erskyn; Sir William Vallibus, knights; Herbert of Maxwell, etc. This charter is also undated.

In a confirmation of these grants to the Abbey of Dryburgh by William, Prior of St. Andrews, and the chapter thereof, they are said to have been made by " John of Maxwell of Pencaitland and Sir John Maxwell, knight, Lord of Maxwell," from which we learn that these grants had originally been made by the father of Sir John. The witnesses included William, then Prior of St. Andrews; Mr. Robert of Den, then the granter's steward; Patrick of Louer, rector of Tyningham; Sir William of Abernethy; and Sir Robert of Irskyn, knights. This confirmation is dated on Friday, on the morrow of the blessed martyr Vincentius, [January] 1343-4.[1]

A confirmation of the same charter was granted by King David the Second, dated 14th April 1346. The witnesses were Thomas de Carnotto (Charteris), the King's Chancellor; William and Adam, Bishops of St. Andrews and Brechin.[2]

Sir John Maxwell acted a less conspicuous part in the public transactions of his time than his brother Sir Eustace. It is only at the close of his life that his name appears in the history of the period. He is then on the side of King David the Second. He was in the army of that King, probably at the head of a body of his retainers, when his Majesty, who had imprudently resolved on invading England, entered, with a strong force, on 6th October 1346, into that kingdom. The King then invested and stormed the Castle of Liddel on the borders, putting all the garrison to the sword. After this, marching to Lanercost, he despoiled the abbey of that name of its wealth. Then passing from Cumberland into Northumberland, he desolated everything in his course with

[1] Original Charter in the Earl of Lauderdale's Charter-chest. Liber S. Marie de Dryburgh, p. 272.
[2] *Ibid.* p. 272.

fire and sword, till he came to the Priory of Hexham, which he pillaged and sacked ; and, intending to go to York, he carried, as he advanced, his devastations to the very gates of the city of Durham.

Sir John of Maxwell was with King David's army when encamped within three leagues of the city of Durham, adjacent to the wood of Bear Park and not far from Nevil's Cross, and was engaged in the battle which was fought there between the Scots, under the command of King David, and the English, including numerous Scots, under the command of Baliol, who had the Earl of Angus and the Lords Moubray and Ross among his principal officers. The fight, which took place 17th October 1346, continued at least three hours, that is, from nine o'clock in the morning till noon.   King David, as is admitted by all historians, conducted himself with great bravery on this occasion ; but the fortune of battle went against him : he was defeated with great slaughter.   Fifteen thousand of his men, including many earls and barons, fell on the field of battle, and many of the Scots army were taken prisoners.[1] Among the slain was John Randolph, Earl of Moray.   John of Maxwell was one of the prisoners, and besides him were taken King David himself, the Bishops of St. Andrews and Aberdeen, the Earls of Fife, Sutherland, Douglas, Menteith, Carrick, and Wigton, and many others, barons and knights.   The captor of the King was John Copeland, a gentleman of Northumberland, who carried him without delay to the Castle of Ogle, about twenty miles distant, where, having secured him against personal violence, he kept him till he received orders from his sovereign as to the disposal of the royal prisoner.

Orders were given by King Edward, on 8th December 1346, that the prisoners should be conducted to the Tower of London, and detained there until further orders concerning them.   From the Castle of Ogle King David was conducted to the borders of Yorkshire, with an army of twenty thousand men. He was delivered on the 20th of December to Sir Thomas Rokesby, high sheriff of the county, by whom he was conducted to London with the same army.   On entering the English metropolis, mounted on a noble black courser, he was received by the Lord Mayor, aldermen, and citizens with great pomp, the various companies of the city attending the cavalcade in its progress from street to street, whilst vast multitudes followed, and every window and

[1] Rymer's Fœdera, 1704, tom. v. pp. 533, 534, 545.

balcony was crowded with spectators who were anxious to behold the person of the captive Scottish sovereign. He entered the Tower on the 2d of January 1347. Adam de Kendale was commanded to conduct John of Makeswell and Fergo of Craweford, prisoners, to the Tower.[1] On being lodged in the Tower, Sir John, like the King and the other prisoners, had to maintain himself at his own expense.

After the battle of Durham, Baliol followed the shattered army of the Scots across the borders, took the castles of Hermitage and Roxburgh, and reduced, without any considerable opposition, the districts of Annandale, Teviotdale, Tweeddale, the Merse, and Ettrick Forest, by which the English dominions were enlarged to Cockburn's Path and Soutra Edge.

Having laid waste Nithsdale, Galloway, and Carrick, Baliol got possession of the Castle of Carlaverock, which Sir John of Maxwell had held for King David; and in this favourable turn in his affairs, he now flattered himself that the sovereign power in Scotland was for ever wrested from the Bruces. In that castle he took up his residence for some time, having been reinforced by a considerable body of men from Galloway.[2]

Sir John did not live long after his imprisonment in the Tower of London, but the precise time and circumstances of his death have not been recorded.

He had, it may be presumed, two sons, Herbert and John, though their filiation is not distinctly verified, who successively inherited the estates of the house of Maxwell. Sir John of Maxwell had also a daughter Agnes, who married Sir Robert Pollok of that Ilk, in the county of Renfrew. John Pollok, son and heir of Robert Pollok of that Ilk and of Agnes Maxwell, daughter of Sir John Maxwell, obtained a charter of his lands of Pollok from Sir John Maxwell, dated at Carlaverock 1372.[3] The first Sir John Maxwell mentioned in this charter is the subject of this notice. The second, as is evident from the date, is his second son, Sir John, the tenth baron of Maxwell. Sir Robert, the son and successor of this last Sir John, was consequently the nephew of the said Agnes and "the cousin" of the said John Pollok; even as he so designates him in a charter granted in his favour afterwards quoted.[4]

---

[1] Rotuli Scotiæ, vol. i. p. 678.

[2] Knighton, quoted in Tytler's History, vol. i. p. 452.

[3] Crawfurd's History of the Shire of Renfrew, p. 209.

[4] *Vide* p. 119.

VIII.—1. HERBERT OF MAXWELL, NINTH LORD OF MAXWELL, AND SEVENTH OF CARLAVEROCK.

1347-1354.

HERBERT OF MAXWELL, who was probably the son—the eldest son of Sir John, succeeded to the estates of the house of Maxwell in the year 1347. Little is known of his history, and he does not seem to have lived long after coming into possession of the family inheritance.

Scotland was then in a very depressed condition. King David was a prisoner in the Tower of London, and Herbert's father had died shortly after his imprisonment in the Tower. Baliol, after his victory at Durham, had reduced the greater part of the south of Scotland to his obedience ; and Robert, Lord High Steward of Scotland (afterwards Robert the Second, King of Scotland), now made a second time guardian of the kingdom, could not, at this juncture of affairs, raise an army.

Under these circumstances, Herbert of Maxwell, like many others of rank and position, was led to submit to the authority of King Edward the Third. To that King he swore fealty as his liege lord in 1347. On the 20th of August that year, being about to set out for London for treating there with certain of the faithful subjects of the English monarch concerning important matters of state, he received for himself and his servants a safe-conduct from King Edward to continue to the 1st of January following.[1]

On this visit to London, having, on negotiating, come to terms with William de Bohun, Earl of Northampton, he swore allegiance to Edward, and in pledge engaged to deliver certain hostages to that Earl at the Castle of Carlaverock.

In return for this submission he received from King Edward letters of protection for himself, his men, and his Castle of Carlaverock, and the arms, victuals, cattle, etc., that were in it. The letters are in Latin, and translated, are as follows :—

The King to all his bailies and faithful subjects, as well in England as in Scotland, to whom these presents shall come, Health. Know ye that whereas Herbert of Maxwell, lately by an amicable

[1] Rotuli Scotiæ, vol. i. p. 704 a.

treaty entered into between our beloved and faithful cousin, William de Bohun, Earl of Northampton, and him, at our command, freely came into our obedience and fealty, and delivered to the foresaid Earl certain sufficient hostages to be rendered into our hands at the Castle of Carlaverock, which is in his custody : We, advisedly wishing to provide for the security of that Herbert, have taken him, and all the men that are with him in the fortification of the foresaid castle, and the said castle, with the arms and victuals, and other goods and chattels that are in the same, into our special protection and defence : And, therefore, we command you to maintain, protect, and defend that Herbert and his foresaid men, not inflicting, or allowing to be inflicted upon them injury, molestation, loss, or detriment ; and if any hurt shall be done to them, you shall cause reparation to be made to them without delay. For we are unwilling that of the arms, victuals, and goods and chattels that are in the foresaid castle, or of corn, hay, horses, carts, carriages, victuals, or other goods and chattels of that Herbert, or of his foresaid men, there may be taken any thing by our bailies, or ministers, or others whomsoever of the marches of England, or elsewhere, that are of our obedience, against the will of that Herbert, or of his foresaid men. In testimony of which thing, etc., to continue for one year, the Keeper being witness, at Gloucester, the 5th day of September [21st, Edward III., 1347.] [1]

From these letters it may be concluded that Sir Eustace of Maxwell had not completely destroyed the Castle of Carlaverock, but had only demolished the fortifications ; for we can hardly suppose that it could have been rebuilt during the short time that the Maxwell estates were possessed by his brother Sir John or by Herbert. The fortifications of the castle were, it is probable, restored either by Sir Eustace or by his brother and successor, Sir John.

In consequence of his rebellion Herbert of Maxwell was punished by King David the Second. This appears from two royal charters granting to Herbert Murray the lands and barony of Pedynane, in the county of Lanark, which Herbert Maxwell is said to have forfeited.[2]

Herbert of Maxwell obtained from King David the Second a charter, the date of which is unknown, of the discharge of the duty of Carlaverock.[3] There seems to be no evidence that the honour of knighthood was ever conferred upon him. He never receives the designation of *miles*.

Herbert died before the 1st of April 1354, at which date the Maxwell estates were in possession of Sir John Maxwell, who, we presume, was Herbert's brother.

[1] Rotuli Scotiæ, vol. i. p. 704 *b*.
[2] Robertson's Index of Charters, p. 31, No. 30, and p. 36, No. 21.
[3] Robertson's Index of Charters, p. 37, No. 12.

VIII.—2. SIR JOHN MAXWELL, KNIGHT, TENTH LORD OF MAX-WELL, AND EIGHTH OF CARLAVEROCK.

1354-1373.

CHRISTIAN HIS WIFE.

SIR JOHN MAXWELL, who succeeded to the estates of Maxwell in the year 1353 or in the beginning of the year 1354, was probably the brother of Herbert who has been now noticed.

The land and tenement of Wester-Softlaw, in the shire of Roxburgh, which had been the property of Herbert of Maxwell, ninth Lord of Maxwell, were sold either by Herbert or by Sir John to John Sadler. Robert, the son of John Sadler, having, on the death of his father, inherited them, granted these lands by charter to Roger of Auldton, with all the pertinents by which the husbandmen held them in the time of Herbert of Maxwell, lately Lord of Wester-Softlaw. Roger of Auldton and his heirs were by the charter to be free from the payment of the multure of the corn which should grow on the above-mentioned tenement, and to have right to grind "roum fre" at the mill of Maxwell after the corn of the Lord of Maxwell and after the corn which should be found in the hopper, for rendering annually a pair of gilt spurs to the lord in chief of that feu at the chief messuage, at the Feast of St. John the Baptist, and twelve pennies sterling. The lord superior was Sir John Maxwell, and his chief messuage was the Castle of Maxwell. Among the witnesses were William Abbot of Kelso, William Abbot of Melrose, John Abbot of Stirling, Bernard of Hawden and John Hessewell.[1] This charter Sir John of Maxwell, knight, and of that ilk, confirmed; and he appended his seal to the confirmation. He also granted to Roger of Auldton a remission of the annual rent of a pair of gilt spurs and of twelve pennies sterling, which were due to him from the foresaid land and tenement of Wester-Softlaw, and also full power of converting the said land and tenement to pious uses or perpetual alms.[2]

In a Council held at Inverkeithing on 1st April 1354, confirmation was made by King David the Second—though he could not have been at the

---

[1] Liber S. Marie de Calchou, vol. ii. p. 382.   [2] Liber S. Marie de Calchou, vol. ii. p. 384.

Council in person, as he was then a prisoner in the Tower of London—of the preceding confirmation and donation, which " our beloved and faithful John of Maxwell, knight, made to our beloved Roger of Auldton of the land of Wester-Softlaw," etc.[1]

On the same day Roger of Auldton, having constituted a chantry of one priest to celebrate divine service for ever at the great altar in the Church of St. James of Roxburgh, granted, for the sustentation thereof, a charter of his whole land and tenement of Wester-Softlaw, with all his rights attached thereto.[2] This charter was also confirmed at Inverkeithing on that day.[3]

In the year 1355, the Castle of Carlaverock was captured by Roger Kirkpatrick, and dismantled if not levelled with the ground.[4] The circumstances connected with its capture at this time have not been recorded.

With some of the most public and important events of the period Sir John of Maxwell was associated. He was allied with William Lord of Douglas, Roger Kirkpatrick, and Robert, Steward of Scotland, who bravely and successfully resisted Edward King of England, from whom they recovered Galloway, Nithsdale and Annandale. When, by the intervention of the Pope, peace was at last concluded between England and Scotland, he took an active part in effecting it, and in obtaining the release of King David the Second, who, as has been already stated, was taken prisoner at the battle of Durham, 17th October 1346, and imprisoned in the Tower of London, 2d January 1347. At different times treaties were proposed for King David's deliverance from his captivity in England, but it was not till the year 1357 that this was accomplished.

Sir John of Maxwell was a member of the Parliament held 26th September 1357, in which the terms proposed for the redemption of King David were agreed upon. At that Parliament the Three Estates respectively appointed special ambassadors, with full power and authority to enter into and confirm treaties made or to be made with the Council and plenipotentiaries of Edward the Third, King of England, in regard to the liberation of King David, and to engage to pay for his redemption to Edward, his heirs and successors, 100,000 merks sterling, and to make whatever agreements should

---

[1] Liber S. Marie de Calchou, vol. ii. p. 385.
[2] Ibid. vol. ii. p. 386.
[3] Ibid. vol. ii. p. 389.

[4] Extracta ex Cronicis Scocie, pp. 185, 187. Vide supra, p. 53.

be necessary for the security of the premises.   The Commissioners appointed by the clergy were William, Bishop of St. Andrews ; Thomas, Bishop of Caithness ; and Patrick, Bishop of Brechin, Chancellor of Scotland.   By the barons, who included Sir John of Maxwell, knight,[1] were appointed Patrick Earl of March ; Thomas Earl of Angus ; William Earl of Sutherland ; Sir Thomas of Murrray ; Sir William of Livingstone, and Sir Robert of Erskine, knights.   The representatives of the burghs also chose eleven of their number as Commissioners.[2]

The Commissioners met with those of Edward the Third, on the 3d of October, at Berwick-upon-Tweed, where they concluded a treaty. One hundred thousand merks were to be paid for the redemption of King David to Edward within ten years, at the rate of 10,000 merks each year, the first payment to be made at the Feast of the Nativity of St. John the Baptist (24th June) thereafter ; and a similar sum was to be paid at the same term in the succeeding years till the whole ransom was paid.   In security for the payment twenty hostages, the heirs of the greatest families of Scotland, were to be delivered to the King of England, and three of the following Lords, namely, the Steward of Scotland, the Earls of March, Mar, Ross, Angus, Sutherland, Lord Douglas, and Thomas of Murray were to remain by turns in England until the entire ransom was liquidated.   If the money stipulated was not forthcoming at the appointed terms, King David was to return to England and render himself a prisoner, there to remain till all the arrears of his ramson were discharged.[3]

For the welfare of himself and of Christian, his spouse, etc., John of Maxwell, Lord of that Ilk, granted to the Abbey of Kilwinning, in Cunninghame, Ayrshire, the patronage of the Kirk of Liberton and an acre of land adjoining, which the granter had perambulated in the presence of several persons, reserving the right of Sir Robert of Glene, rector of that kirk, until his renunciation thereof or his death.   The charter is undated, but it was probably granted soon after the succession of Sir John, as another charter to

---

[1] The barons were Robert, Steward of Scotland, who represented King David, William of Ross, Malcolm of Wigton, Donald of Lennox, Earls ; William, Lord of Douglas ; William of Keith, marshal of Scotland ; James of Lindesay, Lord of Crawford ; David of Graham, Lord of Dun-daff ; William More, Lord of Abercorn ; Roger of Kirkpatrick ; John of Maxwell ; Thomas Byset, and Patrick of Ramsay, knights.

[2] The Acts of the Parliaments of Scotland, Reign of King David the Second, vol. i. pp. 155-158.

[3] *Ibid.* vol. i. pp. 158-161.

the same monastery, by John Menteith, Lord of Arran and Knapdale, is dated 12th October 1357, and both charters were confirmed by one charter of confirmation by King David the Second, in or about the thirty-fifth year of his reign, which was the year 1363.[1]

King David the Second died in the Castle of Edinburgh, 22d February 1370-71, and was succeeded by King Robert the Second, his nephew.

Sir John of Maxwell was present at the coronation of Robert the Second, 26th March 1371, at Scone, the ceremony having been performed by William Laundelys, Bishop of St. Andrews, amidst a vast concourse of spectators, consisting of prelates, earls, barons, and many of the people who had been attracted to witness it, from all parts of the kingdom.

Sir John was one of that numerous body who, on the day after the coronation, assembled, in presence of the King, sitting on his royal seat upon the hill of Scone, as was the custom, and who made homage to him, and swore, each in succession, the oath of fidelity.[2] As Robert was the first of the Stewart line who ascended the Scottish throne, a declaration was made on the same day of the legal right by virtue of which he had succeeded David the Second, King of Scotland, his uncle and predecessor, on the ground both of propinquity of blood and of the settlement contained in certain instruments made in the time of his grandfather, King Robert the Bruce, of famous memory, which were produced and publicly read.

On this occasion Sir John also bound himself, along with others, by solemn oath, to support the claims of John, the eldest son of Robert the Second, as the true heir and successor to the throne in the event of his surviving his father. After King Robert had made a declaration to that effect, each of the prelates, earls, lords, barons, and others present declared, with a full voice, in succession, for himself, his heirs and successors, that the said Lord John, after the death of his father, should, as his lawful heir, if alive at the time, be King of Scotland, and promised, in good faith, and with hands lifted up to heaven in token of his sincerity, that he would hold him as his King, and assist and defend him against all mortals.[3]

[1] Reg. Mag. Sig., David II., p. 33, No. 86, folio, 1814.

[2] The Acts of the Parliaments of Scotland, Reign of King Robert the Second, vol. i. p. 181 ; Rymer's Fœdera, tom. vi. p. 463.

[3] The Acts of the Parliaments of Scotland, vol. i. p. 182.

To this Act, which is still extant, were attached the seals of fifty-one prelates, nobles, and barons.

The lands of Pencaitland, which had been acquired by Sir Herbert, fifth Lord of Maxwell, were sold by Sir John. He granted to Alexander Maitland his lands of Pencaitland, in the shire of Edinburgh, which had been resigned by Alice of Pencaitland, daughter and heiress of the deceased John of Pencaitland, her father, to be held for rendering to the granter and his heirs a silver penny. In the charter, which is without date, he is described "John of Maxwell, knight, Lord of Carlaverock." Among the witnesses were Sir William Waus, Sir Walter of Halyburton, Sir John of Preston, Sir William Baly, Sir David of Hanand, Sir John Herys, and Sir Robert of Levyngyston.[1]

In the Register of Dryburgh the date assigned to the charter is *circa* 1330. But this is not quite correct; for at that time, and for a considerable number of years after, Sir Eustace was Lord of Carlaverock. Though the precise date cannot be fixed, yet, from the period when the witnesses to the charter flourished, there is no room for doubt that it was made by this Sir John. One of them, Sir Walter of Halyburton, was taken prisoner at the battle of Durham in 1346, and obtained his liberty, with King David the Second, in the year 1357: he was High Sheriff of Berwick in the year 1364, and died about the year 1385. Another of the witnesses was Sir John of Preston, who was also taken prisoner at the battle of Durham, and for several years was imprisoned in the Tower of London, and who was one of the Commissioners appointed by the Parliament of Scotland for negotiating a peace with England in the year 1360. A third of them was Sir John Herys, who was a witness to and obtained charters between the years 1360 and 1369. A fourth was Sir Robert of Livingston, who was one of the Commissioners appointed in 1348 to treat with the English about the liberation of King David the Second.

Sir John and his successors retained the superiority of the lands of Pencaitland. At a later period, a dispute arose between Sir Herbert of Maxwell, knight, Lord of Carlaverock, and John the Sanceler (or Sinclair), Lord of Hyrdmanstoun, and tenant to the said Sir Herbert, of part of the lands of Pencaitland, as to Maxwell and Bekyrtoun lands in the town of Pencaitland. The dispute seems to have been as to how far the superiority of Sir Herbert in regard to these

[1] Liber S. Marie de Dryburgh, p. 270.

lands extended.   In an agreement between Sir Herbert and John Sinclair, 19th January 1427, the former engaged to give an assize to the latter, in order to determine whether these lands ought of right to be held of the lords of Max-well, as barons of Pencaitland, or were held any time of the said lords by other tenants than Dame Margaret Sinclair's predecessors, and should it be found by that assize that they were held, and ought of right to be held, of the said lords of Maxwell, that they should so remain without any claim or question of the said John Sinclair, or of any in his name, for ever in time to come.   On the 2d of June 1428, it was concluded by the assize appointed that Sir Herbert of Maxwell had more right to the two said tenandries of Maxwell land and Bekyrtoun land than the said John Sinclair, saving as much of Bekyrtoun-land as was held of the Hospitallers or Knights of St. John.[1]

On 18th September 1371, Sir John of Maxwell of Carlaverock, knight, resigned into the hands of King Robert the Second, before several nobles of the kingdom, at Kilwinning, all the lands which he held of him in chief in favour of Robert of Maxwell, his son and heir, reserving to himself the life-rent of these lands, and to Christian, his wife, the terce thereof, in case she should survive him.   In terms of this resignation a charter of these lands was given at Kilwinning, on the day after the resignation, to the said Robert of Maxwell, by Robert the Second, who designates him his beloved cousin.[2]

From King Robert the Second Sir John of Maxwell obtained a charter of the lands of Softlaw, in the barony of Maxwell, in the county of Roxburgh, which had been forfeited by William Stewart, who had yielded allegiance to Edward the Third, King of England.[3]

To provide, in the event of the death of King Robert the Second, or of that of the Earl of Carrick, his eldest son, a prince of feeble constitution, who had no lawful children of his body till the year 1378, against a disputed suc-cession, from the intrigues of the English Court or from the ambition of some of King Robert's own sons, or sons-in-law, it was judged patriotic and neces-sary to fix by an Act of Parliament the succession to the Crown in his undoubted lawful heirs, according to their respective rights and the unalterable laws of the kingdom.

[1] Original Verdict at Terregles.
[2] Reg. Mag. Sig., Robert II. p. 89, No. 312, and 122, No. 19.
[3] Robertson's Index to Charters, p. 115, No. 42.

Sir John of Maxwell was a member of the Parliament or Grand Council of King Robert the Second, held at Scone on the 4th of April 1373, by which the succession to the Crown was thus settled. By that Parliament it was declared and ordained that King Robert's sons, begotten of his first and second wives, and the heirs-male of their bodies, should successively succeed to him in the kingdom, in the following order :—1. John Earl of Carrick and Steward of Scotland, his eldest son by his first wife,[1] conformably to the declaration made in the last Parliament ; 2. Robert Earl of Fife and Menteith, his second son by his first wife ; 3. Alexander Lord of Badenoch (afterwards Earl of Buchan), his third son by the same wife ; 4. David Earl of Strathern, his son begotten of his second wife ;[2] 5. Walter, son of King Robert, brother-german to the said David ; and 6. In the event of the foresaid five brothers and the heirs-male descending from them failing, the true and lawful heirs of the blood and stock royal were to succeed to the Scottish throne.

This Statute having been ordained, Sir John of Maxwell, together with the prelates, earls, barons, etc., present, swore, touching the holy Gospels, that he would inviolably observe it for himself and for his heirs, and cause it to be observed by others, according to his ability, for ever. This was followed by the spectacle of the whole multitude of clergy and people, specially assembled in the church of Scone, before the great altar, expressing their consent and assent to the Statute, after it had been explained to them, by lifting up their hands. To this instrument the seal of Sir John of Maxwell was appended, along with the seals of the bishops and earls *ad perpetuam memoriam futurorum*.[3]

Sir John is said to have died at Carlaverock on 15th April 1373.[4] He had by his wife Christian, whose surname is unknown, one son, Robert, who succeeded him.

[1] Elizabeth Mure.   [2] Euphame Ross.
[3] The Acts of the Parliaments of Scotland, Reign of Robert the Second, vol. i. p. 185.
[4] Genealogical History of the Family.

IX. SIR ROBERT MAXWELL, KNIGHT, ELEVENTH LORD OF MAXWELL, AND NINTH OF CARLAVEROCK.

1373-1409.

OF the history of Sir Robert, who succeeded his father about the year 1373, little is known. He represented the house of Maxwell in the reigns of three monarchs, of Robert (Stuart) the Second, whose reign began 22d February 1370-71, and ended 19th April 1390 ; of Robert the Third, whose reign began 19th April 1390, and ended 4th April 1406 ; and of James the First, whose reign began 4th April 1406, and ended 21st February 1436-7. Unlike most of the representatives of the House of Maxwell, Sir Robert, though he possessed the estates about forty years, has left no mark in history. His name does not appear in connexion with any of the public affairs, civil or ecclesiastical, of the eventful period in which he lived. It rarely occurs even in family transactions, owing partly, it may be, to the paucity of the documents of that description which have been preserved.

During his father's lifetime, Robert of Maxwell, under the designation of "Lord of Mearns," granted a charter, which is dated 4th March 1371, of his lands of the Dryppys, with the pertinents, in the barony of Kilbryde and shire of Lanark, to Sir John of Maxwell, knight, Lord of Nether Pollok, his cousin, and Lady Isabella, reserving to himself and to his heirs the hill nearest the town of the Dryppys, on the summit of which a certain stone was erected. This hill the granter reserved for his courts, to be held there as often as should be required, for the administration of justice, by prosecuting the inhabitants of these lands for injuries committed by them against the granter or his heirs only.[1]

On 19th September 1371, as we have seen before, he was put in possession of the fee of the lands of the house of Maxwell on the resignation of his father, who reserved to himself the liferent, and to his spouse her terce.

He received from King Robert the Second a charter of all his lands which he held of the King in chief. In the charter he is designated "Robert of Maxwell, son and heir of John Maxwell, knight."[2]

[1] Memoirs of the Maxwells of Pollok, vol. i. p. 129.   [2] Robertson's Index of Charters, p. 131. No. 19.

About the year 1400, Sir Robert of Maxwell, knight, Lord of Carlaverock, granted a charter of donation to the Monastery of Dryburgh of that land lying in the territory of Wester Pencaitland, in the constabulary of Hadding-ton, which John Maitland, Lord of Thirlestane, held of him, and which he purely and simply resigned. The land was to be held by that monastery for rendering thence annually to the granter and his heirs one silver penny.[1] This charter he granted for the welfare of his soul, and for the welfare of the soul of Herbert of Maxwell, his son and heir, and for the welfare of all his ancestors and successors, and of the souls of all the faithful departed.

It was about this time that the lands of Balmacreuchie, in Perthshire, were acquired by the Maxwell family. It is probable that it was this Sir Robert who acquired them, and that they became his property by his marrying the heiress of that estate ; but no record of the acquisition has been discovered, or of the name of the heiress.

Sir Robert began to build the Castle of Carlaverock on the site of the present ruin—the only undertaking with which his name is associated—and it was completed by his successors.

He died before the 8th of February 1409, as we infer from a charter granted by the Earl of Douglas, 8th February 1409-10, to his son, Sir Herbert of Maxwell, who is styled "Lord of Carlaverock," a designation which would probably not have been applied to the son had the father been then alive.[2]

Sir Robert left two sons—

1. Herbert, who succeeded him.

2. Aymer.

[1] Liber S. Marie de Dryburgh, p. 273.   [2] Reg. Mag. Sig., Lib. iii. No. 153.

X. SIR HERBERT MAXWELL, TWELFTH LORD OF MAXWELL, AND TENTH OF CARLAVEROCK, FATHER OF THE FIRST LORD MAXWELL.

KATHARINE STEWART (OF DALSWINTON) HIS WIFE.

1409-1420.

SIR Herbert succeeded to his father in the year 1409, as appears from the grant in his favour of the office of Steward of Annandale, dated on the 8th of February 1409, referred to in the preceding memoir, and afterwards more particularly described. Various notices of Sir Herbert occur during the lifetime of his father.

In the year 1385 or 1386 he married, under a dispensation by the Pope, Katharine, daughter of John Stewart of Dalswinton, in the county of Dumfries. On 10th August 1386, John Stewart, Lord of Dalswinton, granted a charter of wadset, in the vernacular, for 400 merks Scots, to Sir Herbert of Maxwell, knight, the son and heir of Sir Robert of Maxwell, Lord of Carlaverock, payable from the granter's lands of Carnsalloch and Malcolme-holme and Perishede, as marriage tocher with Katharine Stewart, his daughter, spouse to Sir Herbert.[1] On 23d November 1414, a confirmation of this charter was granted by Robert Duke of Albany, Regent.

The house of Maxwell was in close friendship with the powerful house of Douglas. Sir Herbert Maxwell, knight, was one of the hostages for Archibald, fourth Earl of Douglas, a "most illustrious warrior," (as Fordun describes him,) who was a prisoner in England. That earl had been taken in the battle fought at Homildon Hill, 14th September 1402, between the Scots, under his command, and the English, headed by the Percies, but was set at liberty by Henry Percy. In a battle fought at Shrewsbury, 21st July 1403, Douglas, who now fought on the side of the Percies, was again taken prisoner. After the death of King Robert the Third, 4th April 1406, the Duke of Albany, Regent of the kingdom of Scotland, entered

---

[1] The terms of the Charter are described in the Charter of Confirmation at Terregles. In the Confirmation the grantee is designated "Herbert of Maxwell of Carlaverock."

into negotiations with the English monarch for the release of the Earl of Douglas. It was in connexion with these negotiations that Sir Herbert Maxwell went to London, in the character of a hostage, and obtained, along with others, a safe-conduct from Henry the Fourth of England, dated at Westminster, 14th March 1406-7, to come into the kingdom of England, with one servant in the company of each of them, through the castles, fortified towns, and other fortalices whatsoever, and to remain there, without harm, loss, molestation, or impediment. Among the others to whom the safe-conduct was granted were Archibald Douglas, son and heir of Archibald Earl of Douglas; James, brother of that Archibald; James, son and heir of James of Douglas, Lord of Dalkeith; John of Montgomery, Lord of Ardrossan; and John Herries, Lord of Terregles.[1] In the safe-conduct Henry promised, on the word of a king, that as soon as the Earl of Douglas, after his next passage into the parts of Scotland, should re-enter within the Castle of Durham, without fraud or guile, or should die in any way whatsoever, the foresaid Archibald Douglas, and the others before mentioned, were and should be free from all act of cautionary for the said Earl of Douglas, and that the present letters were, in that event, to have to them the force of a safe-conduct to return to the parts of Scotland with their servants,[2] for forty days from the time in which they should be fully certified of the re-entrance or death of the said Earl.

The Earl of Douglas was at length set at liberty and returned to Scotland, where he continued to signalize himself by his military valour.

Sir Herbert Maxwell obtained from Archibald, fourth Earl of Douglas, a bond, dated in the year 1407, for forty merks Scots, to be paid at Whitsunday and Martinmas, until he should be heritably put in possession of lands of twenty pounds value, in the shires of Clydesdale, Nithsdale, or Galloway. In the bond the granter describes him as his beloved cousin, Sir Herbert of Maxwell, knight, son and heir of Sir Robert Maxwell, Lord of Carlaverock. The Earl of Douglas also became bound to support and defend him in all his righteous causes, as it became him to do to any man and his cousin.[3] From this bond, as well as from other writs, in which the Earl of Douglas styles

---

[1] Rotuli Scotiæ, tom. ii. p. 182 a.
[2] *Ibid.* tom. ii. p. 182 a.   [3] Original Bond at Terregles.

Sir Herbert his cousin, it appears that they were related in that degree, although the particular link has not been ascertained.

The close identity of personal and political interests, as well as relationship in blood, which existed between the Earl of Douglas and Sir Herbert Maxwell, is further shown by the grant which was made by the Earl to Sir Herbert of the important office of Steward of Annandale. This grant was made by the Earl by a charter, dated at Linlithgow, on 8th February 1409, in favour of his beloved cousin, Herbert of Maxwell, knight, lord of Carlaverock, a designation which shows that Sir Herbert had then succeeded his father in the principal estate of the family. The grant further bears that it was made for the homage and service rendered and to be rendered to the Earl. The office is described as " officium Senescalli nostri tocius dominii nostri Vallis Annandie."

The office thus granted was hereditary in the Maxwell family, the charter by the Earl of Douglas having been confirmed by King James the Second by a charter under the Great Seal, dated 6th August 1440, in favour of Sir Herbert Maxwell, afterwards created Lord Maxwell.[1]

The office vested in the Maxwell family great power and influence over the whole district of Annandale.

The next reference to Sir Herbert after he became Lord of Carlaverock, is in the safe-conduct which was granted by King Henry the Fifth of England, at Westminster, on 3d November 1413, in favour of his son Herbert Maxwell, one of the hostages for the payment of a sum of money due by the Countess of Douglas.[2]

Sir Herbert received from Archibald, fourth Earl of Douglas, a charter, dated at Lochmaben, 18th December 1419, of the lands of Grenan, in the lordship of Galloway, constabulary of Kirkcudbright and shire of Dumfries. In this charter the grantee is named and designated Herbert of Maxwell, Lord of Carlaverock,[3] the beloved cousin of the granter. In these lands Sir Herbert was infefted on a precept by the Earl of Douglas, dated at Edinburgh, 20th March 1419,[4] in which he also styles Sir Herbert his beloved cousin.

---

[1] Reg. Mag. Sig., Lib. iii. No. 153.

[2] Rotuli Scotiæ, tom. ii. p. 208 *a* and *b*.

[3] Original Charter at Terregles.

[4] Original Instrument of Sasine, *ibid.*

Sir Herbert died before 28th October 1420, as appears from a charter of that date granted to his son Herbert, who is named and designated Herbert of Maxwell of Carlaverock, by Murdoch Duke of Albany, then Governor of the kingdom of Scotland, of the lands of Garnsalloch and of Dursqwen, in the barony of Dalswinton and shire of Dumfries, upon the resignation of Mary Stewart of Dalswinton, in her widowhood, to be held of the King, etc.[1]   That this charter was granted to the son is certain, from its being engrossed in a confirmation of it to him, 4th May 1426, by King James the First.

Sir Herbert left issue two sons :—

1. Herbert, who succeeded him, and who was served heir to his father in the lands of Mekill Dripps on 16th October 1421.[2]

2. Aymer, who is mentioned in a charter to be afterwards quoted, dated 13th January 1424-5, as the brother of Herbert, and who married Janet of Kirkconnel, from whom are descended the Maxwells of Kirkconnel, in the Stewartry of Kirkcudbright.

Aymer of Maxwell and Janet his spouse obtained from King James the Second a charter of the lands of Kirkconnel, in the lordship of Galloway and stewartry of Kirkcudbright, dated at Dumfries, 20th March 1456.   These lands, as the charter narrates, belonged to the said Aymer and Janet, and were by them resigned.   They were to be held by them, and the longest liver of them, and by the heirs lawfully begotten or to be begotten between them ; whom failing, by the lawful and nearest heirs of the said Janet whomsoever, of the King, his heirs and successors, Kings of Scotland, as the said Janet or her predecessors held them before the said resignation, by rendering annually the services due and wont.[3]

---

[1] Original Charter at Terregles ; Memoirs of the Maxwells of Pollok, vol. i. p. 155.
[2] Memorials of the Montgomeries, Earls of Eglinton, vol. ii. p. 22.
[3] Original Charter at Kirkconnel.

XI. SIR HERBERT OF MAXWELL, FIRST LORD MAXWELL.

———— HERRIES (OF TERREGLES), HIS FIRST WIFE.

KATHERINE SETON, HIS SECOND WIFE.

1420-1453.

DURING his father's lifetime, this Herbert was sent to England as one of the hostages required in security for the payment of a sum of money due by the Countess of Douglas. On 3d November 1413, a safe-conduct was granted by Henry the Fifth of England at Westminster, to " Herbert of Maxwell, son and heir of Herbert of Maxwell, knight, Lord of Carlaverock," to come into England under this character. The other hostages were Gilbert Macdowell, son and heir of Fergus Macdowell, knight, Archibald Macdowell, knight, William of Carlelle, son and heir of John of Carlelle, knight, Adam of Joneston, laird of Joneston, and Gilbert Grereson, son and heir of Gilbert Grereson, all of the kingdom of Scotland.   In terms of this safe-conduct, which was to continue to the 12th of July following, and for eight months thereafter, the persons named might come into England, together or severally, by land or by sea, with six men and their servants, horses, and goods in their company, as hostages, with King Henry's " beloved and faithful knight, John Phelip, or his attornies in this part, for 500 merks of money, English, to be paid to the same John or his attornies."[1]

Herbert succeeded his father in the year 1420.   On the 20th of October that year, "Herbert Maxwell of Carlaverock" received a precept from James Stewart, lord of Kilbride, for infefting him as heir to Sir Herbert Maxwell, his father, in the lands of Meikle Dripps.[2]

Shortly after his father's death, under the same designation, he obtained for himself and his heirs, from Murdoch Duke of Albany, then Governor of the Kingdom of Scotland, a charter, dated at Edinburgh, 28th October 1420, of the lands of Garnsalloch and of Dursquen, in the barony of Dalswinton and shire of Dumfries, upon the resignation of Mary Stewart of Dalswinton, in her widowhood, to be held of the King, etc.   The witnesses

[1] Rotuli Scotiæ, tom. ii. p. 208 α and b.

[2] Inventory of Writs of Mearns, etc., delivered up to Sir George Maxwell of Nether Pollok, 15th January 1652.

were William, Bishop of Dunblane, Alexander Stewart of Levenax, son of the said Duke, Robert Stewart of Lorn, William Lindsay of Rossy, John Forster of Corstorfyn, Keeper of the Great Seal, etc. Herbert of Maxwell was infefted in terms of the charter in the lands mentioned on 18th November 1421.[1]

That he is the person in whose favour these transactions took place, is proved from a confirmation of that charter which he received from King James the First, dated at Edinburgh, 4th May 1426. In the confirmation, Murdoch Duke of Albany, who had granted the charter, is described as deceased (*quondam*); but in it no such term is applied to Herbert Maxwell of Carlaverock, which shows that the charter and the confirmation were granted to the same person. The witnesses to the confirmation were Mr. John Cameron, provost of the collegiate church of Lyncloudane, keeper of the privy seal; John Forstar of Corstorfyn, chamberlain; Robert of Lawedre of the Bass, justiciar; and Walter of Ogilvy of Lintrethyn, treasurer of Scotland, etc.[2]

Herbert was served heir to his father in the lands of Meikle Dripps, 16th October 1421. The retour of service, translated from the original Latin, is as follows :—

An inquest was made at Kilbride before Sir John of Montegomery, bailie of the same, on Thursday, the sixteenth day of the month of October, in the year of our Lord one thousand four hundred and twenty-one, by these upright men underwritten, namely, John Lindsay, laird of Dunrod; Robert of Lekprewik, laird of the same ; Joachim of Lekprewikis, laird of Lee ; Adam More, laird of Ewirechillis ; George of Hamilton ; John of Cochrane ; Andrew Fleming ; James of Pollok ; John Brown ; John Zong ; Adam Dounyng ; William Keris ; and John Lockarde, laird of Bare : who, being sworn and carefully examined regarding the articles contained in the enclosed brief, declare that the late Herbert of Maxwell, lord of Carlaverock, father of Herbert of Maxwell, the bearer of these presents, died vested and seized, as of fee, at the peace and faith of our Lord the King, of the lands of Mekill Drippis, with the pertinents, in the barony of Kilbride, within the shire of Lanark : And they declare that the said Herbert's son is the lawful and nearest heir of the deceased Lord Herbert, his father, in the lands of Mekill Drippis, with the pertinents ; and that he is of lawful age ; and that the said lands are now worth twenty merks yearly, and were worth so much in time of peace ; And they declare that the said lands are held in chief of the lord of Kilbride by forinsic service ; and that the said lands are now in the hands of our lord the superior by recognition by a sergeant on account of the death of the said Sir Herbert of Maxwell at the time of his decease. In testimony of which retour, the seal of the bailie, together with the seals of

---

[1] Original Charter and Sasine at Terregles.   [2] Memoirs of the Maxwells of Pollok, vol. i. p. 155.

those who were present at the making of the said inquest, is affixed on the day, year, and at the place above mentioned.[1]

According to the tenor of this inquest a precept was granted, 20th October 1421, by James Stewart, lord of Kilbride, to Sir John of Montgomery, lord of Ardrossan and bailie of Kilbride, for infefting Herbert of Maxwell in the lands of Mekil Dripps.[2]

Herbert of Maxwell appears to have continued a loyal subject of King James the First during his lengthened captivity of nineteen years in England; and when that King, in 1424, obtained his liberty, Herbert took part, with others of his countrymen of all ranks, in the demonstrations of loyalty which that event called forth.

Treaties were set on foot at different times by Robert Duke of Albany, Governor of the kingdom, for the freedom of King James, but they were unsuccessful. At last a treaty for effecting that object was agreed upon by Commissioners, appointed by Murdoch Duke of Albany, who had succeeded his father, Robert, as Governor of Scotland, and the Three Estates of the Kingdom, and Commissioners from England, who met at York, on 10th September 1423. In terms of this treaty £40,000 sterling were to be paid by King James and his heirs to the King of England and his heirs, at London, in the Church of St. Paul, by equal proportions, as a reasonable sum for the expenses incurred for his subsistence and education while he was in England, though that sum was much larger than what had been expended upon him. The first payment, amounting to 10,000 merks, was to be made six months after his entrance into his own kingdom, and a like sum was to be paid in the following year, and so on during the space of six years, when the whole sum would be cleared. Before entering Scotland, King James, in security for the performance of his part of the treaty, was to give sufficient hostages, which were afterwards to be fixed upon. It was further stipulated, in order to cement and perpetuate the amity between the two kingdoms, that the Governor of Scotland should send ambassadors to London, with power to conclude a contract of marriage between King James and some English lady of the first rank. To carry into effect this

[1] Original Retour in Sir Michael Shaw Stewart's Mearns Charter-chest. Printed in Memorials of the Montgomeries, Earls of Eglinton, vol. ii. p. 22.

[2] Original Retour in Sir Michael Shaw Stewart's Mearns Charter-chest. Printed in Memorials of the Montgomeries, Earls of Eglinton, vol. ii. p. 23.

last article two new commissioners were despatched from Scotland to London to join and act with the ambassadors who had negotiated the treaty, and, on 4th December, all of them ratified the former articles, and undertook that King James should deliver his hostages to the King of England's officers, in the city of Durham, before the 31st of March following. The number of hostages, who were to be persons of rank, to be delivered up to the English, were twelve, and in case any of them should fail by death or otherwise, their places were to be supplied by others of like fortune and quality. The marriage of King James with the Lady Joanna Beaufort, daughter of John Earl of Somerset (who was a son of John of Gaunt, the first Duke of Lancaster), by Lady Margaret, daughter of Thomas Holland, Earl of Kent, brother of King Richard the Second, having been celebrated on the 1st or 2d of February 1423-4, in the church of St. Mary Overy, in Southwark, he and his Queen, accompanied with a noble retinue both of Scots and English, set out for Durham. On their arrival they found a vast number of Scottish nobility and gentlemen, with their retainers, who had come thither to attend them on their way to Scotland.

The hostages having been delivered up, as had been arranged, the English were desirous of a formal treaty of peace; but as the Scots would not agree to any terms derogatory to their engagements with France, a truce, instead of a peace, was concluded on 28th March 1424, which was to last seven years, namely, from the 1st of May following to the 1st of May 1431, that is, one year from the time fixed for the complete payment of the debt contracted by Scotland for the liberation of King James.

Herbert of Maxwell was among the number of those who had come to Durham to testify their loyalty to their sovereign. He obtained from Henry the Sixth of England letters of safe-conduct and protection to pass into the kingdom of England to the town of Durham, to the presence of the King of Scots, dated at Westminster, 13th December 1423, to continue in force until the 30th of April following. In the letters he is designated " Herbert of Maxwell of Carlaverock." Those with whom he was associated in the same letters, and in whose company he made the journey from Scotland to Durham, were Archibald of Douglas, Earl of Wigton, Herbert of Herries of Terregles, John Stewart of Dundonnald, John Stewart of Bute, John Kennedy of Carryk, who, with their horses and servants, to the number of twenty-five persons in all, obtained letters to travel to Durham and then to return to Scotland, conjunctly and severally, without disturbance or obstruction.[1] Similar letters of safe-conduct, of the same date, to continue for the same period, were granted to many other persons of distinction to proceed to the town of Durham to the presence of the King of Scots.[2]

Herbert of Maxwell was one of that large retinue who attended King James when, on the 29th or 30th of March 1424, being now at full liberty, he left Durham for Scotland.[3] On their arrival at Melrose the King, on 5th April, four days after he had passed the borders, confirmed and ratified the treaty, in terms of one of its articles. Having kept the festival of Easter at Edinburgh, they proceeded on their journey to Perth and from thence to Scone. On the 21st of the same month was solemnized the coronation of King James and his Queen, amidst the transports of joy of the numerous spectators who had assembled to witness it. The King was placed in the Chair of State by Duke Murdoch—an office which he performed as Earl of Fife—and was crowned and anointed by the Bishop of St. Andrews.

On that occasion Herbert of Maxwell was present; and he was one of those, including noblemen and young gentlemen, on whom King James, to render the ceremony of his coronation the grander, and to testify his gratitude to such as had maintained their loyalty to him during his long absence, conferred the honour of knighthood. Among the others on whom this dignity was conferred were Alexander Stewart, the youngest son of the Duke of Albany, Archibald Earl of Douglas, William Douglas, Earl of Angus, George Dunbar, Earl of March, Alexander Lindsay, Earl of Crawfurd, William Hay of Errol, Constable of Scotland, John Scrimgeour, Constable of Dundee, and Herbert Herries of Terregles.[4]

Soon after the return of King James, Murdoch Duke of Albany and his family became the objects of his signal vengeance. Sir Walter Stewart, one of the Duke's sons, was arrested 13th May 1424, and sent to the Bass, and several others were imprisoned. During the sitting of the Parliament,

[1] Rymer's Fœdera, London, 1710, vol. x. p. 308 ; Rotuli Scotiæ, tom. ii. p. 244 a.

[2] Rymer's Fœdera, vol. x. pp. 308, 309.

[3] Rymer's Fœdera, vol. x. p. 332.

[4] Extracta ex Cronicis Scocie, p. 227.

which was opened at Perth on 13th March 1424-5, Duke Murdoch himself and Sir Alexander Stewart, another of his sons, Duncan Earl of Lennox, his father-in-law, and others were arrested by the orders of the King; bold proceedings on the part of a prince who, after a protracted captivity, had been admitted so recently to the exercise of the sovereign power.

Sir Herbert of Maxwell, who, it is probable, had come to Perth to attend the Parliament, was among the number of those on whom the suspicions of the monarch fell, and who were apprehended and imprisoned. The Duke of Albany, on the same day on which he was arrested, was sent a prisoner to the Castle of Carlaverock, which of course would be seized upon by King James. The tower in that castle in which the Duke was confined is still called "Murdoch's Tower." From that tower Duke Murdoch was carried to the place of his execution at Stirling.

By the command of the King, a Parliament, or a court of justice, met at Stirling for the trial of Duke Murdoch, his two sons, Walter and Alexander, and his father-in-law, the Earl of Lennox, on a charge of high treason.[1] But the precise character of the crimes imputed to them history has not recorded. The King himself, seated on a throne, wearing his royal robes, a crown and sceptre, witnessed the trial, and the pannels were on 18th May found guilty by a jury, consisting of twelve persons of rank. On the same day on which the fatal sentence was pronounced, the sons of the Duke, Walter and Alexander, were beheaded on a hill a little way to the north-east of the Castle of Stirling. On the day after, Duke Murdoch and the Earl of Lennox were also beheaded.

By Boece and Buchanan these executions are attributed to the resentment of King James against Robert Duke of Albany, who was removed from the throne only by two princes, David Duke of Rothesay, and James, and whom they represent as having caused the first to be starved to death, and as having, during his administration, made no effort, or no earnest effort, to effect the freedom of the King. This, indeed, Murdoch accomplished; but the King, it is said, regarded what he did in this direction not as voluntary, but as extorted by the Scottish people; and he was further incensed, it is added, by discovering that the greater part of the royal revenues had been misappropriated by the governors and their dependants. The revival by Par-

[1] Extracta ex Cronicis Scocie, p. 228.

liament of the old Statutes made by King David the First and King Robert Bruce against leagues or associations, abettors of rebels, and leasing-makers, after the arrest of the Duke and his friends, has led some historians to the conclusion that he and his accomplices, upon the King's having resolved to recover the lands which the governors had alienated from the Crown, had begun to form a faction, and to plan measures, under various pretexts, for defeating that intention.

How far Sir Herbert Maxwell and the rest of the prisoners were implicated in any combination or conspiracy of a treasonable character it is impossible now to ascertain. No attempt was made to bring them to trial. They were set at liberty, the King, it would seem, being either convinced of their innocence or unwilling to shed more blood, after having got rid of the special objects of his hatred ; and they were received into the royal favour upon promise of their loyal behaviour in time to come.

Some time after, a dispute arose between Sir Herbert of Maxwell, knight, Lord of Carlaverock, and John Sinclair of Hyrdmanstoun, Sir Herbert's tenant of part of the lands of Pencaitland, in regard to Maxwell land and Bekyrtoun land in the town of Pencaitland. To determine the respective claims of the disputing parties, an assize of eight honourable and faithful men assembled in the Tolbooth of Edinburgh ; and by them judgment was given, 2d June 1428, in favour of Sir Herbert of Maxwell. To this writ, which is in the vernacular, the seals of Sir John of Carlyle, Sir Herbert of Maxwell of Collynhache, and William Gardyng, are attached in good preservation.[1]

Sir Herbert concerned himself in the affairs of State, and with those in power, he gained credit and influence by his activity and vigilance. He was frequently a member of Parliament, and in matters of the greatest importance he acted in concert with the chief men in the State. He besides distinguished himself by his skill and intrepid valour on the field of battle.

Sir Herbert is the first of the house of Maxwell on whom was conferred the dignity of the peerage. As no patent or instrument of his creation as a hereditary Lord of Parliament has been preserved, the exact date of the creation has not been ascertained. Before the return of King James the First from his captivity in England in the year 1424, there was not in the peerage of

[1] Original Verdict at Terregles.

Scotland an order known as Lords Barons of Parliament. This was a new order of Peers introduced by that Sovereign. His residence in England, where the order had been previously instituted, may have induced him to institute a similar degree of dignity in Scotland. But his unexpected assassination happened before the institution of the new dignity was completed; and the creation of Lords of Parliament appears to have been chiefly made by his son and successor, King James the Second.

As paving the way for the new order of dignity of Lords of Parliament, an Act was passed in a Parliament held by King James the First at Perth, on 1st March 1427, dispensing with the attendance of the small barons and free tenants in Parliament and general councils, and allowing the different shires to be represented by their Commissioners, but declaring that "all bischoppis, abbotis, prioris, dukis, erlis, lordis of Parliament, and banrentis, the quhilkis the King wil be reseruit and summonde to consalis and to Parliamentis by his special precep."[1]

It has been supposed that the designation applied to nine Lords in the records of Parliament in regard to a civil suit as to a right to a landed estate, affords evidence that these Lords were all created Lords of Parliament previous to 29th March 1429. Among these Lords is "Dominus de Maxwell."[2]

But as several of these nine Lords are afterwards designated in legal documents as commoners, this single designation as Lord of Maxwell seems insufficient to show that Herbert Maxwell had been created a Lord of Parliament in 1429. In the instrument of creation of the lordship of Hamilton in the year 1445, Lord Maxwell is mentioned as one of the King's cousins, and as a Lord of Parliament. He must have been created Lord Maxwell prior to that date. But the occasion on which the title was conferred upon him has not been recorded.

When the seven years' truce which had been made with England at the liberation of King James the First from his captivity was about to expire, a new truce with England was concluded, which was to continue from the setting of the sun on the 1st of May 1431 until the setting of the sun on the 1st of May 1436—a period of five years. Herbert Lord of Maxwell was one of

[1] The Acts of the Parliaments of Scotland, vol. ii. p. 15.

[2] The Acts of the Parliaments of Scotland, vol. ii. p. 28.

those who were appointed conservators of the truce, and admirals of the sea of King James, and wardens of the marches of Scotland towards England. Among those with whom he was thus associated were Walter Earl of Athole, William Earl of Angus, George Earl of March, and Alexander Earl of Mar. A special reason why King James was desirous for this prolongation of the truce was, that he might be the better able to suppress the disturbances and barbarities which in violation of all law and authority were taking place in the northern parts of the kingdom in consequence of the inveterate and ruthless feuds of clanship.

As the time approached when this truce would expire, circumstances prevented its prolongation. Hostile to the proposed match of the eldest daughter of King James with the Dauphin of France, Henry the Sixth of England and the English Court endeavoured to obstruct the voyage of the Princess to France for the completion of her marriage. Henry wrote a letter to King James, dated 8th March, desiring that the truce might be prolonged ; and Lord Scroop, the chief of the embassy which he intended to send to Scotland for that purpose, is said to have proposed a marriage between King Henry himself and the Princess, and to have made other tempting offers to Scotland. These propositions having been rejected, so incensed was Henry that, instead of renewing the truce, he threatened war. King James was barbarously murdered on the 20th or 21st of February 1437-8, by a band of conspirators, whilst at supper with his Queen and a number of courtiers in the convent of the Dominicans or Blackfriars at Perth. On the 20th of March following, King James the Second, who was not much above seven years of age, was crowned at Holyroodhouse only a month after the murder of his royal father.

Before his death, King James the First had taken measures for renewing a truce with England. On the 30th of November 1437, though then at war with England, he appointed Commissioners to join and co-operate with others, who some time previously had obtained from King Henry a safe-conduct to travel to England on that errand. The truce was renewed about six weeks after his death, and was to continue from the rising of the sun on the 1st of May 1438 to the rising of the sun on the 1st of May 1447, a period of nine years. To it the Scottish Commissioners appended their seals, at London, 31st

[1] Rymer's Fœdera, tom. x. pp. 91, 92.

March 1438.   In this truce "Herbert Lord Carlaverock" was again appointed one of the wardens of the marches of Scotland towards England.[1]

As already stated, Sir Herbert Maxwell obtained from King James the Second, on 6th August 1440, a charter of confirmation of the important office of Steward of Annandale, which was originally conferred by the Earl of Douglas on his father, Sir Herbert, in the year 1409.

Herbert Lord Maxwell built the Castle of Mearns, which stands on a rocky eminence, about a mile to the south-east of the village of Newton.   He received from King James the Second a license, in which he is designated " Herbert Lord Maxwell," dated 15th March 1449, to build a castle or fortalice on the barony of Mearns in Renfrewshire, to surround and fortify it with walls and ditches, to strengthen it by iron gates, and to erect on the top of it all warlike apparatus necessary for its defence.[2]   The site selected for its erection was the spot already described as that on which the old castle probably stood.[3]   The castle was, no doubt, built soon after the date of this license.

Mearns Castle continued to be one of the residences of the Lords Maxwell for two centuries after its erection ; but they resided more frequently at their other castles than at the Castle of Mearns, for which they appointed constables and keepers, who levied duties for the keeping of it.   A letter of bailiery, by Robert Lord Maxwell, appointing George Maxwell of Cowglen constable and keeper of the Castle of Mearns, in the shire and barony of Renfrew, with the profits thereof, for seven years, is dated at Edinburgh, 28th January 1520.[4]

In this castle Lady Elizabeth Douglas, Countess Dowager of Morton, sought a tranquil retreat in the summer of the year 1593, after the death of her husband, John, seventh Lord Maxwell, who, in December preceding, was slaughtered in a scuffle with the Johnstons.   In a letter to Sir John Maxwell of Pollok, dated 12th March 1593, she informs him that it was her purpose, God willing, to go to her lands and Castle of Mearns and to stay there during the greater part of the ensuing summer ; and she requests him to deliver the house and keys to the bearers, her servants, that the necessary repairs might be made.[5]   Soon after, it became the temporary residence of her unfortunate

[1] Rotuli Scotiæ, tom. ii. p. 310.

[2] Memoirs of the Maxwells of Pollok, vol. i. p. 167.   [3] Vide supra, p. 79.

[4] Memoirs of the Maxwells of Pollok, vol. i. p. 245.

[5] Ibid. vol. ii. p. 173.

son John, eighth Lord Maxwell, who was beheaded at the Cross of Edinburgh, on the 21st of May 1613, for having shot the laird of Johnston, on 6th April 1608, in revenge for his father's death.

The castle ceased to be the property of the Lords of Maxwell about the year 1648 or 1650, when the lands and barony of the Mearns were sold by Robert, second Earl of Nithsdale, to Sir George Maxwell of Pollok, who, however, soon after sold them to Sir Archibald Stewart of Blackhall. The castle is now the property of his descendant, Sir Michael Shaw Stewart, Baronet.

From the ruins of this castle, which are still in good preservation, a tolerably correct idea may be formed of what it originally was. It consists of a quadrangular strongly built tower, with walls about eight feet in thickness, and at irregular intervals are windows and loopholes. It was surrounded by a strong wall—of which all that now remains are some vestiges of the foundations—and a ditch, and the entrance was secured by a drawbridge, the remains of which may still be traced. It has long entirely ceased to be a place of residence ; and the doors and windows have been blocked by planks of wood. It has, however, in recent years been repeatedly the scene of festive assemblies. Several of the annual balls of the yeomanry of Mearns have been held in a spacious apartment within its walls, probably the old hall, which has undergone various repairs and alterations to render it suitable for such purposes. Descending by a narrow staircase, the visitor enters a gloomy vaulted cell below, into which the light is admitted only by a loophole in the thick wall, so narrow as only to make the darkness visible. This was apparently the dungeon of the castle, in which in olden times culprits, or such as had rendered themselves obnoxious to the lord of the manor, were imprisoned. From the battlements of the tower is obtained a magnificent prospect of the surrounding country, such as has been already described.

A view of the castle in its present state is here given.

" Herbert Lord Maxwell " was a member of the Parliament which met at Edinburgh 28th June 1445. He was witness to a charter, dated 3d July that year, by King James the Second, granting, with consent of the Parliament, to James Lord of Hamilton, knight, the lands of the baronies of Cadyhow and Mawchane, and the superiority of the lands of Hamilton farm and the lands of Corsbaskat, with the pertinents, in the shire of Lanark, and the barony of Kynneille, in the shire of Linlithgow, which lands and superiority belonged to the said James heritably, and were by him resigned into the hands of the King in the said Parliament. By this charter, these baronies, lands, and superiority were created and united into the lordship of Hamilton, and the said James was created a hereditary Lord of Parliament. Herbert, as one of the witnesses, is ranked with Duncan of Campbell, Patrick of Graham, William of Sommerveil, and Alexander of Montgomerie, as "lords of our Parliament."[1]

In the truce made between England and Scotland in 1449, Herbert Lord Maxwell was again appointed one of its conservators for the King of the Scots, and one of the admirals of the sea and wardens of the marches of Scotland towards England. The truce, to which were appended the seals of the Commissioners of the King of Scotland, in the church of Durham, 15th November that year, and the privy seal of King Henry the Sixth, 29th April 1450,[2] was to begin from the day of the date of the truce on the land, and from the Feast of the Nativity of our Lord next to come on the sea, and to continue so long as it should please Henry King of England and James King of the Scots. Each of these monarchs, in the event of his wishing to recede from the truce, was to inform the other of his purpose by his letters-patent, sealed with the Great Seal.

"Herbert Lord Maxwell" acted in the same capacity in the truce made between Scotland and England to which the seals of the Commissioners of the King of England were appended, in the church of St. Nicholas, in the town of Newcastle, in the diocese of Durham, 14th August 1451, and which was confirmed by King Henry at Westminster, 16th September following.[3] It was to begin, both on sea and land, from the rising of the sun on the 15th of August 1451, and to last to the setting of the sun on the 15th of August 1454, and thence so long as it should please the two sovereigns.

In a subsequent truce concluded between Scotland and England, Herbert Lord Maxwell sustained a similar character. By it the last-mentioned truce

[1] The Acts of the Parliaments of Scotland, vol. ii. p. 59.
[2] Rymer's Fœdera, tom. xi. p. 253; Rotuli Scotiæ, tom. ii. p. 341.
[3] Rymer's Fœdera, tom. xi. p. 300; Rotuli Scotiæ, tom. ii. p. 353.

was confirmed, and other agreements were concluded. To it the seals of the Commissioners of both kingdoms were appended at Westminster, in the diocese of London, 23d May 1453, and it was confirmed by King Henry at Westminster on the 30th of that month. This truce was to begin, both on sea and land, from the rising of the sun on the 21st of May 1453, and to continue to the setting of the sun on the 21st of the same month 1457, and thence to last as long as it should please the Kings of England and Scotland.[1]

Herbert Lord Maxwell was one of the commanders of the Scottish army at the battle of Sark, fought in the year 1448, in which the English were completely defeated. The commanders-in-chief of the respective armies were old rivals. Douglas, Earl of Ormond, led the Scots, and the English were under Percy, Earl of Northumberland. The Earl of Ormond, on approaching the English after they had passed the river of the Solway, and encamped near that of the Sark, ordered Wallace of Craigie, Sheriff of Ayrshire, to fight the left wing of the English, where was posted Magnus, one of the most celebrated of their officers, whom the Scots, in derision, called, from his long and red beard, Magnus with the red mane; and he instructed Herbert Lord Maxwell and the Laird of Johnston, ancestor of the noble family of Annandale, to attack Sir John Pennington, who headed, upon the right of the English, a numerous body of Welsh. Hollinshed says that Lord Maxwell and the Laird of Johnston commanded the left wing of the Scottish army.[2] In the genealogical history of the Maxwell family, the services rendered by Herbert Lord Maxwell on this occasion are still more favourably represented : "Having the rear, he (Lord Maxwell) wan the field, Ormond and the rest of the leaders of the army being almost discomfitt." The English sustained a loss of about three thousand men. Magnus and eleven officers were among the killed, and numerous prisoners were taken, including Sir John Pennington and Lord Percy, the latter of whom was made prisoner whilst courageously rescuing his father, the Earl of Northumberland, from the victors. The Scots did not lose above six hundred men : among whom Wallace of Craigie, who survived his wounds for three months, was the only person of distinction.

Herbert Lord Maxwell held the important office of steward of Annandale,

[1] Rymer's Fœdera, tom. xi. p. 336; Rotuli Scotiæ, tom. ii. p. 368.
[2] Hollinshed's Scottish Chronicle, vol. ii. p. 87.

as appears from his account rendered in the King's Exchequer on the 25th of November 1452.   Translated from the Latin, it is in the following terms :—

The account of Lord Herbert, Lord Maxwell, steward of Annandale, rendered at Stirling by Herbert Maxwell, namely, on the 25th day of the month of November, in the year of our Lord 1452, of all his debts and expenses by the farms and proceeds of his valley, from the 26th day of the month of June, in the year of our Lord 1449, to the present day, for three whole years to the terms of the blessed Martin, as within the account.   In the first place, the same is charged with xxxv s. of the first fruits of the manorial lands of Lochmaben of the said seven terms, within the account due to the King, because the said lands extend annually to ten pounds ; and with xxxv s. of the farms of the lands of Hetea and of Smalhame, due, *imprimis*, by the said account, because from the said lands are due to our Lord the King annually ten pounds ; and with xxxv s. of the farms of the fishing of Annand, due to our Lord the King, during the time of the account of the said seven terms, because the said fishing is annually worth ten pounds.[1]

In an agreement with Sir John Maxwell of Pollok, dated at Carlaverock, 6th February 1452-3, Herbert Lord Maxwell engaged to give him heritable possession of the lands of Nether Pollok, which were held in chief of Lord Maxwell, according to the form and tenor of the old charter given by his Lordship's predecessors to Sir John.   On the other hand, Sir John was to pay to him for these lands half a merk yearly, if asked, and to be " man to the said Lord Maxwell and to Robert of Maxwell, his son and heir," and to maintain them and their causes to the utmost of his power against all men, his allegiance to the King excepted, for the space of two years after the day on which he was put in possession of the lands of Nether Pollok.[2]

Herbert Lord Maxwell died not long after, although the exact date of his death has not been ascertained.   He was dead before 14th February 1453-4, on which date his son Robert was served heir to him.

Lord Maxwell married, first, a daughter of Sir Herbert Herries of Terregles, who attended King James the First from Durham to Scotland, was created a knight at the coronation of that King, and was one of the jury who sat on the trial of Murdoch Duke of Albany.   By her he had issue, two sons and one daughter :—1. Robert, second Lord Maxwell ; and 2. Edward, ancestor of the Maxwells of Tinwald, in the county of Dumfries, and of Monreith, in the county of Wigton ; and 3. Katherine.

[1] Captain Riddell's MS., quoted by Sir Harris Nicholas, in whose possession it was, in " Siege of Carlaverock," Preface xxi.

[2] Memoirs of the Maxwells of Pollok, vol. i. pp. 169-172.

He married, secondly, Katherine, daughter of Sir William Seton, and widow of Sir Alan Stewart of Darnley, ancestor of the Earls of Lennox and of Henry King of Scots. By her he had five sons and two daughters. The sons were—1. George, ancestor of the Maxwells of Carnsalloch, in the county of Dumfries; 2. David; 3. Adam, ancestor of the Maxwells of Southbar, in the county of Renfrew; 4. John; and 5. William. The two daughters were Janet and Marriot. All these children are enumerated in a charter of the lands of Carnsalloch, dated 20th March 1475-6.[1]

He had also a son named Gavin. In an instrument of sasine, to be afterwards more fully quoted, in favour of Robert, second Lord Maxwell, dated 28th May 1454, Gavin of Maxwell, in acting as Robert Lord Maxwell's attorney, is described as his brother.[2]

Katherine Seton, Lady Maxwell, survived her second husband, Lord Maxwell, and she was his widow for fully fifteen years. On 19th July 1468, with the consent of her eldest son George, by Herbert Lord Maxwell, she made a resignation of the lands of Hesildene and others in the Mearns, into the hands of Robert Lord Maxwell.[3] The exact date of the death of Katherine Lady Maxwell has not been ascertained; but it took place before the year 1478, in which she is referred to as deceased.[4]

Seal of Katherine Seton as Lady of Darnley, 1430, afterwards
wife of Herbert, first Lord Maxwell.

[1] Reg. Mag. Sig., Lib. vii. No. 332.

[2] Memoirs of the Maxwells of Pollok, vol. i. p. 175.

[3] Instrument of Resignation, printed in Memoirs of the Maxwells of Pollok, vol. i. p. 181.

[4] *Vide* Assignation, dated 7th February 1477-8, quoted in page 149, *postea*.

XII. ROBERT, SECOND LORD MAXWELL.

JANET FORSTAR (OF CORSTORPHINE), HIS WIFE.

1453-1485.

THE earliest notice of Robert, second Lord Maxwell, is his marriage with Janet, daughter of John Forstar of Corstorphine, Chamberlain to King James the First, by Jean, daughter of Henry Saint Clair, first Earl of Orkney. This was in the beginning of the year 1425, when he was simply Robert Maxwell, and when his father had not been elevated to the peerage. Under the designation of Robert of Maxwell, son and heir of Herbert of Maxwell, knight, lord of Carlaverock, he and Janet, daughter of John Forstar, lord of Corstorphine, obtained from Thomas of Sommerville, lord of Carnwath, cousin of Robert of Maxwell, a charter of confirmation of the lands of Libberton, in the barony of Carnwath, in the shire of Lanark, on the resignation of Herbert Maxwell of Carlaverock, for themselves and the longest liver of them, and for their heirs-male to be lawfully begotten between them; whom failing, to the foresaid Herbert and the heirs-male of his body; whom failing, to Aymer of Maxwell, brother to Herbert, and the heirs-male of his body; whom failing, to the nearest lawful heirs of Herbert whomsoever. The charter is dated 13th January 1424-5, and it was granted in presence of James, King of Scotland, Walter Earl of Athole, Alexander Earl of Mar, Henry, Earl of Orkney, James of Douglas, lord of Balveny, etc. The confirmation was given under the testimony of the Great Seal, at Edinburgh, 4th February 1424-5. Among the witnesses were William, Bishop of Glasgow, Chancellor, Henry Earl of Orkney, James of Douglas of Balveny, etc.[1]

On 20th January 1424-5 Robert of Maxwell and Janet Forstar were infefted in the lands and mill of Libberton, in the barony of Carnwath.[2]

Robert, second Lord Maxwell, succeeded his father in the year 1453-4. At Dumfries, on the 14th of February that year, he was served heir of his father, Herbert Lord Maxwell, in the lands and barony of Carlaverock, in the lands of Garnsalloch and Dursquhen, in the lands of Springkelde, and in the

---

[1] Reg. Mag. Sig., Lib. ii. No. 3, in Macfarlane's Diplomatum Regiorum Abbreviationes, vol. ii. p. 194. MS. in Advocates' Library, 35. 2.1.   [2] Original Instrument of Sasine at Terregles.

superiority of a one hundred shilling land in the territory and shire of Dumfries. Among those on the inquest were Aymer of Maxwell of Kirkconnel and Eustace of Maxwell of Collinhaith.[1] On the 21st of March following Robert Maxwell was infefted as heir of his father Herbert, in the lands of Carlaverock, at Carlaverock, the chief messuage.[2]

On 28th May 1454 he was infefted as heir of his father, Herbert Lord Maxwell, upon a precept from King James the Second, in the lands of Mearns and Netherpollok, in the barony of Renfrew, at the messuages of these lands. In the instrument of sasine, Gavin of Maxwell, who acted as his attorney, is designated his brother. In the Crown precept it is stated that these lands were held of the King in chief, as Steward of Scotland, and that in infefting Robert Maxwell in them security was to be taken for two red roses in duplication of the blench farm of the lands of the Mearns, and of £20 of relief of the lands of Netherpollok, both due to the King.[3]

During the repeated rebellions of James, ninth Earl of Douglas, against King James the Second, Robert Lord Maxwell supported the royal authority. That Earl, to avenge the death of his brother William, eighth Earl of Douglas, who was assassinated by the King in his own palace at Stirling, on 2d February 1452-3, collected forces and raised an insurrection. He was, however, afterwards reconciled to his Majesty, and was employed by him in various important transactions of State. But, in 1454, he relapsed, and rekindled the flames of civil war by his intrigues with the powerful party of the Duke of York, who then contested the English throne with Henry the Sixth, of the House of Lancaster, and whose hostile policy towards France produced hostility to Scotland, the ancient and usual ally of France. Douglas was encouraged by promises of supplies of money and troops from the York party. He and his adherents had fortified against the Government the Castles of Douglas, Thrieve, Strathaven, Abercorn, Lochindorb, and Tarnaway. But his plans were defeated by the celerity and vigour of action displayed by King James. The barons who had entered into bonds with the powerful House of Douglas were awed into submission to the Crown. The castles named were successively captured by the royal forces. At Arkinholme, in Eskdale, the Earl, at the

---

[1] Original Retour at Terregles.
[2] Original Instrument of Sasine, *ibid.*

[3] Memoirs of the Maxwells of Pollok, vol. i. p. 175.

head of a body of men who had been raised by his brothers, Archibald Earl of Moray and Hugh Earl of Ormond, was totally defeated in a conflict with the King's troops, under the command of the Earl of Angus. One of his brothers, the Earl of Ormond, was made a prisoner, and immediately put to death, and another of them, the Earl of Moray, fell on the field of battle. The Earl himself, and his only surviving brother, Sir John Douglas of Balveny, made their escape into Argyllshire.

At that engagement the royal army was powerfully assisted by the Maxwells, Scotts, and Johnstons, on the borders.

Robert Lord Maxwell was a member of the Parliament held in June 1455, by which sentences of forfeiture were pronounced on the Douglases. By this Parliament the Earl of Douglas, who had been summoned to answer before it, but who did not appear, was, on the 9th of June, declared to have forfeited his life, lands, rents, possessions, superiorities, offices, and all his goods, moveable and immoveable, for the traitorous crimes of which he was accused. In his indictment he was charged with the traitorous fortifications of the Castles of Thrieve, Douglas, Strathaven, and Abercorn; the traitorous leagues which he had made with the English; his traitorous conspiracy and insurrection with a multitude of armed people, near the burgh of Lanark, against the King; the ravages he had committed on the Grange of Henry Lord Abernethy, the King's Justiciar; and his being art and part in the burning of the burgh of Dalkeith, and in the robberies of the goods of the inhabitants of that burgh.

A similar judgment was passed on 12th June against Beatrix Countess of Douglas, mother of the Earl. Although summoned, she did not compear, to answer to her indictment for the traitorous fortification of the Castles of Abercorn, Douglas, and Strathaven; for traitorously putting the King's rebels into the Castle of Abercorn; for being art and part in the burning of the towns of Kincavill, Bonytoune, and Warnestoune, and in the rapines and depredations of the goods of the tenants of these lands; and for the traitorous counsel and assistance she had given to her sons, James, Archibald, Hugh, and John of Douglas, and their accomplices, in the crimes committed by their entering into traitorous leagues with the English. On the 12th of June, a sentence was passed against the deceased Archibald, pretended Earl of Moray, declaring that all his lands, rents, possessions, superiorities, offices, and goods, moveable and immoveable, were forfeited, for his fortification of the Castles of Lochindorb and Tarnaway, both in Moray, against the King, and for other traitorous crimes. On the same day, John of Douglas of Balveny was forfeited in his life, and in all his possessions, for the traitorous crimes he had committed by the fortification of the Castle of Abercorn, the leagues he had entered into with the English, and the support of his brother-german, the said James Earl of Douglas, and his other brothers.

To these proceedings the seal of Robert Lord Maxwell, as well as the seals of the other members of Parliament, including barons and bishops, and the seal of the burgh of Haddington, as expressing the sanction of the commissioners of all the burghs, there being no other burgh seal at hand, was appended 17th June 1455.[1]

In the new truce agreed to on 11th June 1457, between the plenipotentiaries of Henry the Sixth of England and of James the Second of Scotland, who met at Coventry, Robert Lord Maxwell was one of those appointed conservators of the truce for the King of Scotland, and admirals of the seas and wardens of the marches of Scotland towards England. All and each of the conservators had full power to repair all losses incurred and excesses perpetrated in contravention of the truce, and for the punishment of all and sundry malefactors, according to the nature of the offences committed. The truce was to continue on land from the rising of the sun on the 6th of July following, 1457, to the setting of the sun on the 6th of July 1459, and on sea from the rising of the sun on the 28th July 1457 to the setting of the sun on the 28th of July 1459, and thence to last as long as it should please the Kings of England and Scotland.[2]

At this time there were many hospitals in Scotland for the sick, the poor, and the destitute. These benevolent institutions not having been so carefully attended to as formerly, an Act was passed for their reformation in the Parliament held at Edinburgh 6th March 1457-8. The Lord Chancellor, whose office it was to visit these hospitals from time to time, was ordered to go through all parts of the kingdom in which they were established, and to see to

---

[1] The Acts of the Parliaments of Scotland, vol. ii. pp. 75-77.

[2] Rymer's Fœdera, tom. xi. p. 397 ; Rotuli Scotiæ, vol. ii. p. 383.

it that the rules of their several foundations, where they could be got, were duly observed; and where the foundation could not be had to make inquiry in the country, and to refer to the King for a remedy. For performing this work, which seemed to be too arduous for one person, there were to be joined with the Chancellor the Ordinary of each diocese and other two persons of "gude conscience." This visitation was to be made betwixt the date of the Act and Martinmas following. Among those to be joined to the Chancellor in various dioceses were Lord Maxwell and Maister John Oliver, in the diocese of Galloway.[1]

In the truce prolonged between England and Scotland, to which the seals of the Commissioners of the King of Scots were appended, in the parochial church of St. Nicholas, at Newcastle-upon-Tyne, 12th September 1459, Robert Lord Maxwell was again appointed one of the conservators of the truce and one of the admirals of the seas and wardens of the marches of Scotland towards England. At this time commenced the civil war in England between the Houses of York and Lancaster. But King James the Second and his counsellors, not taking advantage of the present unhappy conjuncture of affairs in England, readily complied with the earnest desire of King Henry the Sixth for the prolongation of the truce between the two kingdoms. The truce was to continue on land from the rising of the sun on the 6th of July next to come to the setting of the sun on the 6th of July 1468; and on sea from the rising of the sun on the 26th of July following to the setting of the sun on the 28th July 1468.[2]

On the 3d of August 1460, King James the Second lost his life by the bursting of one of his own guns, near which he was standing, at the siege of Roxburgh.[3] He had not completed the 30th year of his age. He was succeeded by his son King James the Third, who was then a child of only eight years of age.

Robert Lord Maxwell was closely allied in political affairs with the powerful house of the Boyds. He and other Scottish nobles entered into confederacies with them, each consulting his own particular advantage, and of these alliances the Boyds availed themselves for attaining that ascendancy in

[1] The Acts of the Parliaments of Scotland, vol. ii. p. 49.
[2] Rymer's Fœdera, tom. xi. p. 434.
[3] A thorn tree in the lawn in front of Floors Castle marks the spot where the King was killed.

the State which ultimately ended in their ruin.   Robert Lord Boyd, a man of
fortune and abilities, who had been elevated to the rank of a hereditary peer
by King James the Second, and who, upon the death of that King, was made
justiciary, was appointed one of the Lords of the Regency, to whom was
intrusted the administration of the affairs of State during the minority of
King James the Third.   Boyd left no arts unemployed to secure the affections of the King; and his brother, Sir Alexander Boyd, a man of chivalrous
accomplishments, who was the King's tutor in courtly and military exercises,
acquired much influence over his royal pupil.   Lord Boyd had thus little
difficulty in attaining that supremacy in the State of which he was ambitious.

Much light is thrown on the coalition formed by the Boyds and
the Scottish nobles in an indenture made at Stirling, 10th February 1465,
between Robert Lord Fleming, on the one side, and Gilbert Lord Kennedy,
elder brother of Kennedy, Bishop of St. Andrews, and Sir Alexander Boyd of
Duchol, knight, on the other.   These persons bound themselves, their kin,
friends, and men, "to stand in afald kendnes, supple, and defencs, ilk an til
odir, in all thair caussis and querrell, leifull and honest, movit and to be movit,
for all the dais of thair liffis, in contrery and aganis al maner of persones that
leiff or dee may."   Lord Fleming had, however, entered into a similar bond
with Lord Livingston and Lord Hamilton, and he excepts these noblemen in
this engagement to support Kennedy and Boyd in their quarrels lawful and
honest against all manner of persons.   Kennedy and Boyd made a similar
exception in favour of a list of persons to whom they had become bound.
In this list occur the names Lord Maxwell and others of the most powerful
of the Scottish nobility; from which it appears that they were in confederation with the Boyds.   The other nobles besides Lord Maxwell, with whom
Kennedy and Boyd were closely banded together, were the Earl of Crawford,
Lord Montgomery, Lord Livingston, Lord Hamilton, Lord Cathcart, and
Patrick Graham, Bishop of St. Andrews.

The bond into which Lord Maxwell entered with Lord Kennedy and Sir
Alexander Boyd has not been preserved.   We are therefore ignorant of the
precise character of the engagements.   If we may, however, regard the bond
between Lord Fleming and the same parties as throwing light on the subject,
it may be presumed that Lord Maxwell and the other confederate Lords

secured by their respective bonds important personal advantages. The bond between Lord Fleming and Lord Kennedy and Sir Alexander Boyd provided that Lord Fleming should be a member of the King's Council, so long as Lord Kennedy and Sir Alexander Boyd remained in that office, and that Lord Fleming should never consent to nor take any part in the removal of the King's person from the said Lord Kennedy and Sir Alexander, nor from any others to whom they may have intrusted the person of the King. Lord Fleming further engaged to counsel the King to the utmost of his power to regard with sentiments of cordiality and affection Lord Kennedy and Sir Alexander Boyd, their children, friends, and vassals. As an encouragement suitable to Lord Fleming, it was promised that should any vacant office fall into the King's hands, he should, if it was reasonable, be promoted thereto, as a recompense for his services, and should there happen to fall ward, relief or marriage, he should have it for a reasonable composition before any other.[1]

To obtain complete possession of the King's person, Lord Boyd, accompanied by Adam Hepburn, son and apparent heir of Patrick Lord Hailes, John Lord Somerville, Andrew Ker, son and heir-apparent of Andrew Ker of Cessfurd, and others, on 10th July 1466, invaded the Court at Linlithgow, where the King, who had now completed the fourteenth year of his age, was then staying, and compelled him to accompany them on horseback to Edinburgh. In this enterprise Lord Maxwell and the other Lords who had confederated with the Boyds are not mentioned as having personally been actors. But what followed affords a strong presumption that he was encouraged and supported by his party.   As there existed a Statute of Parliament lately enacted, to the effect that it would be treason to seize upon or carry away the person of the King without the express consent of the Parliament, it may be presumed that he would not have adventured on a proceeding so rash and perilous without receiving from those with whom he was in league assurances of their protection from the penalty of law. A Parliament was summoned by the King to meet at Edinburgh on 9th October 1466.   On the 13th of that month Lord Boyd appeared in the three Estates of the kingdom assembled, and falling on his knees before the King, seated on his throne, humbly prayed that it should be

---

[1] Indenture in Archives of the Earldom of Wigton, in the charter-chest of Admiral Flemyng of Cumbernauld, quoted in Tytler's History of Scotland, vol. iii. pp. 328, 507.

declared by his Highness whether he conceived any indignation or offence against him for the part he had taken in the removal of his Majesty from Linlithgow to Edinburgh. The King declared that he had conceived none, that Boyd and his friends who had taken part in that action were free from all fault, and that he regarded them as his faithful subjects. This declaration was recorded in the books of Parliament, and an instrument thereupon was granted to Lord Boyd under the Great Seal at Stirling, 25th October that year. By the Parliament he was appointed governor of the King's person and of the King's younger brothers, Alexander Duke of Albany, and John Earl of Mar, and he may be said to have had now the administration of the affairs of State wholly in his own hand. But his opponents were indefatigable in their efforts to undermine his power, and, succeeding in alienating from him the King's affections, they at last accomplished their purpose.

Lord Maxwell was a member of the Parliament which began at Edinburgh on the 12th of October 1467, in the reign of King James the Third.[1]

In the year 1468, Lord Maxwell sold to David Kilpatrik of Rokelhede, the lands of Kirkblane, in the barony of Carlaverock, and obtained from him a letter of reversion, engaging that he would quit-claim them on the payment of a certain sum. This appears from an instrument of reversion dated 23d July 1468. Among the witnesses were John Maxwell, son and apparent heir of Robert Lord Maxwell, and Robert Maxwell, also son of the said Lord, and Eustace Maxwell of Collinhaith.[2]

Lord Maxwell was a member of the Parliament which was opened at Edinburgh on the 20th of November 1469.[3] This Parliament was famous for the trial and condemnation of Robert Lord Boyd, Thomas Earl of Arran his son, and Sir Alexander Boyd his brother, with whom Lord Maxwell had been in close alliance. They had been summoned, at their principal seat at Kilmarnock, and at the market cross of the burgh of Ayr, to appear before that Parliament, to answer for traitorously seizing the person of the King at the burgh of Linlithgow, on 9th July 1466, against the will of the King, and for

---

[1] The Acts of the Parliaments of Scotland, vol. ii. p. 88.

[2] Original Instrument of Reversion at Terregles.

[3] The Acts of the Parliaments of Scotland, vol. ii. p. 93.

other treasonable actions.   Lord Boyd, discovering that, from the unrelaxing efforts of his enemies, he and his house had incurred the displeasure of the King, and forecasting the impending danger, fled into England.   His son Arran also made his escape.   Sir Alexander Boyd alone appeared before the Parliament.   In defence of Lord Boyd, and his son Arran, who in the summons is simply styled Sir Thomas Boyd, it was pleaded that the seizure of the King at Linlithgow, contrary to his declared will—the principal charge in the indictment—had been remitted by a subsequent Act of Parliament.   But that Act, it was urged in reply, having been obtained by the Boyds when they were masters of the King's person, ought not to have statutory force. All the points libelled were found proven, and Lord Boyd and Arran were, on the 22d of November 1469, sentenced to undergo, when found, the doom awarded by law for high treason.   On the same day Sir Alexander Boyd, who personally appeared before the Parliament, was declared to have been art and part in the crimes for which his brother and nephew had been criminated and condemned, and was sentenced to be beheaded upon the Castle Hill of Edinburgh ; a sentence which was duly executed.   Lord Boyd and his son Arran would doubtless have suffered a similar fate had they fallen into the hands of their enemies.   Lord Boyd died in the following year at an advanced age, at Alnwick.[1]

On the 31st of May 1474, Robert, second Lord Maxwell, obtained from William, Abbot of Sweetheart, a lease for five years of the forty-shilling worth of land called Colschangane, in the parish of Kirkpatrick and stewartry of Kirkcudbright.   The lease is dated at Carlaverock, and the witnesses were Robert of Gledstanis of that Ilk, John Maxwell of Collinhaith, Sir John Michelsone, parson of Nether Ewes, Sir John Wylde, chaplain, and others.[2]

On 1st September 1474, a precept was granted for the infeftment of Robert Lord Maxwell, in the lands of Crawfordmuir, with the castle and fortalice thereof, which had belonged to the deceased Archibald Earl of Angus.[3]

In a court of the barony of Maxwell, held 14th May 1476, Lord Maxwell, by Herbert Maxwell, bailie of the barony, assumed into his own hands all the lands of the barony, and made public intimation that whoever had any

---

[1] Buchanan's History.   [2] Original Lease at Terregles.   [3] Inventory of Maxwell Writs of 1597.

lands in lease in any part thereof, should give up possession until he took them anew from the said Lord or his bailie.[1]

At Edinburgh, on 7th February 1477-8, Robert Lord Maxwell, with the consent of John Maxwell his son and apparent heir, made an assignation to Janet Forstar, his spouse, of the terce of his lands of the Mearns, namely, the lands of Newtoune, Malisheuch, Southfelde, Schaw in the Mains, Fawside, Ryslande, the Akirdailis and Pilmur, and of the terce of the lands of Carlaverock, all which had been possessed by the deceased Katherine Setoune, Lady of Darnley and Maxwell. At the same time John Maxwell bound himself and his heirs to defend Janet his mother in the possession of her terce of the Mearns and of Carlaverock for her lifetime.[2]

Being now advanced in years, Robert Lord Maxwell executed a resignation dated at the monastery of Holyrood, 10th February 1477-8, of the barony of Maxwell in the shire of Roxburgh, the barony of Carlaverock in the shire of Dumfries, and the lands of the Mearns in the shire of Renfrew, in favour of John Maxwell, his son and heir-apparent. In the resignation he reserved to himself the liferent of the barony of Carlaverock and of the lands of the Mearns, and after his death the terce of Janet his spouse, and mother of the said John. Among the witnesses were John, Bishop of Glasgow, Archibald, Abbot of Holyrood, Andrew, Lord Avendale, Chancellor of Scotland, Colin, Earl of Argyll, Lord Lorn, William Lord Creichton, and John, Lord Carlisle.[3] At Edinburgh, on the 14th of the same month, a charter was granted by King James the Third, to the said John Maxwell, of the baronies of Maxwell and Carlaverock and the Mearns, following on the foresaid resignation.[4]

Lord Maxwell appears as a member of successive Parliaments—of the Parliament which was opened at Edinburgh 6th April 1478,[5] of that which was opened 1st June 1478,[6] and of subsequent Parliaments, respectively opened 1st March 1478-9,[7] 4th October 1479,[8] 18th March 1481-2,[9] 2d December 1482,[10] and 16th February 1483-4.[11]

[1] Original Notarial Instrument at Terregles.
[2] Ibid.
[3] Original Instrument of Resignation, ibid.
[4] Original Charter, ibid.
[5] The Acts of the Parliaments of Scotland, vol. ii. p. 115.
[6] Ibid. vol. ii. p. 116.
[7] The Acts of the Parliaments of Scotland, vol. ii. p. 121.
[8] Ibid. vol. ii. p. 124.
[9] Ibid. vol. ii. p. 137.
[10] Ibid. vol. ii. p. 142.
[11] Ibid. vol. ii. p. 153.

On 9th of May 1483, Robert Lord Maxwell, and John Maxwell, his son and apparent heir, granted, for the support of a chaplain to be at the chaplainry of the blessed Virgin Mary, in the kirk of Carlaverock, a charter of four acres of land and a particle of the lands of Kirkblane, with " sax soumes of peitt moss and turf moss," and the rents of sundry subjects in the burgh of Dumfries.[1]

On 5th June 1483, John Lord Maxwell, and Robert Lord Maxwell, his father, gave infeftment to Master David Tyndinge, chaplain of the parish church of Carlaverock, and his successors, chaplains thereof, in the lands in Kirkblane, within the barony of Carlaverock. Among the witnesses were Mr. John Maxwell, son of Robert Lord Maxwell;[2] John Maxwell, son and heir-apparent of John Lord Maxwell, and Maister Nicholas Maxwell, vicar of Carlaverock.[3]

One of those unhappy family feuds which were so common at that time existed between Robert Lord Maxwell and his friends, on the one side, and Cuthbert Murray of Cockpool and his friends, on the other. The cause in which it originated is not distinctly recorded. Like similar feuds, it had produced or threatened to lead to injuries, slaughters, and spoliation of goods, committed by the two parties on each other, and, so far as appears from extant documents, specially by the Murrays on the Maxwells.

A king's messenger was therefore sent to take assurance from the parties that they would keep the peace and allow their differences to be settled by law. For this purpose Donald M'Lyne, messenger, went to the Castle of Carlaverock, on the morning of the 22d of April 1485. On that day Robert Lord Maxwell gave assurance for himself and John Maxwell, steward of Annandale, his heir-apparent, for Thomas Kirkpatrick of Kilosberne, Edward Maxwell of Tynwald, and Robert Charteris of Amisfield, to Cuthbert Murray of Cockpool and Sir Adam Murray, his brother, their kin, friends, men, and tenants, " at the command of our Sovereign Lord's letters, that they would be skaithless of him and his, under what[soever] sums, to the feast of mid-summer next to come," if he had a like assurance from the other party for himself and his and their kin, men, friends, and tenants ; and further, that,

[1] Inventory of 1597.
[2] He was probably a natural son, as it was un-
usual to give two brothers the same Christian name.
[3] Original Instrument of Sasine at Terregles.

"with God's grace," he should attend at Edinburgh, on the 30th of May, and pursue justice.[1]

In the afternoon of the same day Cuthbert of Murray of Cockpool and Sir Adam, his brother, came to Carlaverock and gave a similar assurance.

The death of Robert Lord Maxwell took place soon after; for, on 8th May 1485, John Lord Maxwell was infefted as heir of his grandfather, Robert Lord Maxwell, in the lands of Garnsalloch, in the county of Dumfries.[2]

Robert Lord Maxwell had by his spouse, Janet Forstar, five sons, and a daughter, who was named Christian. The sons were—

1. John, Master of Maxwell, and also Lord Maxwell, who predeceased his father, having been killed in the year 1484.

2. Thomas, who is said to have married Agnes Maxwell, the heiress of Kirkconnel, in the stewartry of Kirkcudbright.[3]

3. David, who, as son of Robert Lord Maxwell, was witness to a notarial instrument of intimation made to that Lord of the assurance given by Sir Cuthbert Murray of Cockpool, and Sir Adam Murray, his brother, to the said Robert Lord Maxwell, John Maxwell, his heir, Edward of Maxwell, and others, dated at Carlaverock, 22d April 1485.[4]

4. Robert, who was witness to an instrument of reversion, formerly quoted, dated 23d July 1468.

5. Aymer, who, as son of Robert Lord Maxwell, resigned, 23d September 1473, the lands of Hesildene, into the hands of his father, in the aisle of the blessed Virgin Mary, in the parochial church of Dumfries. Among those present as witnesses was John Maxwell, son and apparent heir of the foresaid Lord Maxwell, and steward of Annandale.[5]

[1] Original Notarial Instrument at Terregles.

[2] Original Instrument of Sasine at Terregles. In the old Genealogical Account of the Maxwell family it is stated that this Lord Maxwell completed the bartizan of Carlaverock, and was slain at Bannockburn with King James the Third. The evidence referred to in the text, which proves his death took place in 1485, shows that the account—probably a tradition—that he was killed with King James the Third in 1488 is incorrect.

[3] Old Genealogical Account of the Maxwell Family.

[4] Original Notarial Instrument of Intimation at Terregles.

[5] Memoirs of the Maxwells of Pollok, vol. i. p. 185. In the old Genealogical Account of the Maxwell Family it is stated that Robert Lord Maxwell had a son *Nicol*, who was slain by the Lord of Cockpool at the football.

XIII. JOHN MAXWELL, MASTER OF MAXWELL, COMMONLY CALLED THIRD LORD MAXWELL.

JANET CRICHTON, HIS WIFE.

1454-1484.

JOHN, the eldest son of Robert, second Lord Maxwell, predeceased his father. He was commonly styled Master of Maxwell. But having been put in possession of the barony of Maxwell in the lifetime of his father, he was thereafter occasionally styled Lord Maxwell. This designation must have been applied to him as a matter of courtesy, as his father retained the title of Lord Maxwell, and the Master does not appear to have sat in Parliament as Lord Maxwell. His name first occurs in charters referring to his marriage, under the designation of "John of Maxwell, son and heir-apparent of Robert Lord Maxwell," with Janet Crichton, daughter of George Crichton, Earl of Caithness, Lord High Admiral of Scotland. In prospect of the marriage of this lady with the Master of Maxwell, her father granted to her, and her heirs to be lawfully begotten of her body, a charter, dated at Edinburgh, 29th March 1454, of the lands and barony of Tybberis, in the shire of Dumfries, in fee and heritage for ever, to be held for rendering annually to the King a red rose at the feast of the nativity of St. John the Baptist, upon the ground of the chief messuage of the said barony, in name of blench farm, if asked only. In the event of the death of Janet Crichton, that barony was wholly to return to the granter.[1]

To his daughter Janet, George Earl of Caithness also gave his lands of Barntoun, in the county of Edinburgh. She resigned these lands in favour of her son, George Maxwell, who obtained a Crown charter of them, dated 25th March 1460, to be afterwards quoted in the notice of him as one of her children.

On 14th February 1477, John Maxwell, son and apparent heir of Robert, second Lord Maxwell, obtained, upon his father's resignation, from King James the Third, a charter of the lands of the baronies of Maxwell in the shire of Roxburgh, and Carlaverock in the shire of Dumfries, and of the lands of Mearns in the shire of Renfrew, the liferent of his father in the barony of

---

[1] Original Charter at Terregles.

Carlaverock and in the lands of Mearns being reserved, and also the terce of his mother, Janet, in the event of her surviving his father.[1]

After this the Master of Maxwell received the dignity of knighthood. In the records of the Parliament opened at Edinburgh 4th October 1479, of which he was a member, he is styled "Sir John of Maxwell."[2]

After John Master of Maxwell was invested with the fee of the barony of Maxwell, on the resignation of his father, he was, as already stated, occasionally styled Lord Maxwell. In two Acts of the Lords of Council, dated 3d and 7th February 1488, John umquhile Lord Maxwell is mentioned, and also John Lord Maxwell, as son and heir to umquhile John Lord Maxwell.[3] On the 8th of February 1481, "Johannes Dominus Maxwell et de le Meyrnes," granted, as lord superior, a confirmation of a charter, dated the 6th of that month, by Sir John Maxwell of Calderwood in favour of Gavin Maxwell, his son and apparent heir, of the lands of the Dripps.[4] These writs, and others of the period which could be quoted, show that the title of Lord was occasionally used by and applied to John Master of Maxwell.

John Master of Maxwell held the office of steward of Annandale, which was hereditary in the family, after it was acquired from the Earl of Douglas in the year 1409, and confirmed by the Crown in the year 1440, as already shown. The Master is designated "Sir John of Maxwell, steward of Annandale," in a notarial certificate of agreement, dated 25th March 1482, between his procurators and the procurators of James Lord Hamilton.[5]

In an instrument of sasine, formerly described, dated 5th June 1483, in which he is called John Lord Maxwell, he and Robert Lord Maxwell, his father, gave infeftment to Master David Tyndinge, chaplain of the parish church of Carlaverock, and his successors, chaplains thereof, in four acres of land in Kyrkblane, within the barony of Carlaverock.[6]

John Master of Maxwell met with his death by the hand of violence, in the year 1484. The facts connected with his death may be briefly told. Alexander Duke of Albany and James, ninth Earl of Douglas, were then rebels against the Government. On the 22d of July 1484, which was St.

---

[1] Original Resignation and Charter at Terregles.

[2] The Acts of the Parliaments of Scotland, vol. ii. p. 124.

[3] Acta Dominorum Concilii, pp. 104, 117.

[4] Memoirs of the Maxwells of Pollok, vol. i. p. 188.

[5] Original Notarial Instrument of Agreement at Terregles.

[6] Original Instrument of Sasine, *ibid.*

Magdalene's day, they apppeared at the head of a force of five hundred horse from England, at Lochmaben, in Annandale, the annual fair there being then held, leaving in the neighbourhood a considerable body of foot as a reserve. The fair had brought together a great many people ; but the most of them, though they had been the vassals of the Duke of Albany and of the Earl of Douglas before their forfeiture, declined to join them, suspecting that their object was the plunder of the booths in the market-place and of whatever else they could carry off. A fierce conflict ensued, almost every man being then armed and able to use his weapons. The fight lasted from noon till night, both parties being repeatedly reinforced. When in danger of being worsted, the burghers

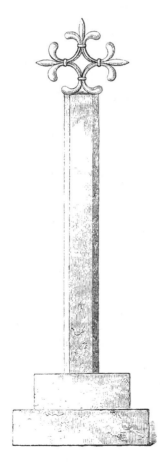

and peasantry were strengthened by a body of the King's troops, led by Charteris of Amisfield, Crichton of Sanquhar, and others ; and they ultimately gained the victory. John Master of Maxwell, the steward of Annandale, who on this occasion headed the Annandale clans, vigorously attacked the forces of the Duke of Albany and the Earl of Douglas on their retreat, near Kirtle Water, and contributed much to the defeat of the English by the Scots. The Master of Maxwell was severely wounded in the battle ; and at the close, when leaning on his sword, he was mortally stabbed, by a person of the name of Gask, a Scotsman, who, in revenge for the death of his cousin, whom the Master of Maxwell, in the administration of justice, had doomed to be hanged, came behind and inflicted the fatal stroke.[1] Lord Maxwell died on the spot. Here a column, of simple construction, having on the top a cross, formed of *fleurs de lys*, was erected. It stands on the farm of Woodhouse, in the parish of Kirkpatrick-Fleming. An engraving of the Cross is annexed. That this ancient column, which is still

[1] The Genealogical Account of the Maxwell Family states that the Master of Maxwell was struck with a whinger in the fillets under his harness.

to be seen, was a memorial intended to mark the spot where John Lord Maxwell was killed, has been the unvarying testimony of tradition. The Duke of Albany escaped by the swiftness of his horse. The Earl of Douglas, advanced in years and encumbered with his armour, was made prisoner, and carried to Edinburgh. He was condemned to imprisonment in the Abbey of Lindores: when his sentence was announced to him, the unhappy Earl muttered, " He who may no better be, must be a monk." After four years of confinement, he died in the abbey, on 15th April 1488. He was the last Earl of Douglas.

John Master of Maxwell had by his wife, Janet Crichton, eight sons and two daughters.

The sons were—

1. John, who succeeded him as fourth Lord Maxwell.

2. Robert, ancestor of the Maxwells of Cowhill, Killylung, Dinwiddie, and Broomholm, all in the county of Dumfries; and of Drumpark and Glenarm in the stewartry of Kirkcudbright. Robert was witness to the infeftment of his brother John as heir to his grandfather, Robert, second Lord Maxwell, in the lands of Carnsalloch, in the county of Dumfries, 8th May 1485.

3. James, ancestor of the Maxwells of Cavens, in the stewartry of Kirkcudbright, believed to be now extinct in the male line.

4. Homer, ancestor of the Maxwells of Portrack, in the county of Dumfries.

5. John, Abbot of Holywood, in the county of Dumfries.

6. Thomas. A precept was given by Nicholas Makgee of Balmagee, dated 11th December 1488, for infefting Thomas Maxwell, brother-german of John Lord Maxwell, in liferent in the granter's ten pound lands of Nether Camdudzale and others, of old extent, in the lordship of Balmagee and stewartry of Kirkcudbright.[1] Thomas was ancestor of the Maxwells of Glenesland, now Gleneslin, in the county of Dumfries.

7. William. In a charter by John, fourth Lord Maxwell, to his sister Christian, dated 14th October 1497, one of the witnesses was William Maxwell, the granter's brother.

[1] Original Precept of Sasine at Terregles.

8. George, who was probably named after his maternal grandfather, the Earl of Caithness, was provided by his mother to the lands of Barnton, in the county of Edinburgh. The lands were resigned by her into the hands of King James the Second, who, by a charter under the Great Seal, dated 25th March 1460, confirmed these lands to George Maxwell.[1]

The daughters were—

1. Janet, who married William Carlile, son and heir of John Lord Carlile of Torthorwald, in the county of Dumfries.

2. Christian. Christian Maxwell, sister-german to John, fourth Lord Maxwell, obtained a charter, dated at Keltoun, 14th October 1497, from Herbert Maxwell of Kirkconnel, who designates her his cousin, of his 100 shilling lands of Keltoun and Greynmarsh, in his lordship of Kirkconnel and shire of Dumfries, in liferent all the days of her life, for rendering thence annually a red rose at the feast of the nativity of John the Baptist upon the ground of the said lands, in the name of blench farm, if asked only. In the charter the granter states that, led not by force or fear, but by ardent affection, he granted it to her in her pure and honest virginity, on account of the true love which he had towards her, and for her gratuitous and meritorious counsel, assistance, and service hitherto rendered and to be rendered to him. Among the witnesses were John Lord Maxwell, Master Herbert Maxwell, vicar of Carlaverock, Thomas Maxwell, the granter's paternal uncle, William Maxwell, the granter's brother, Robert Neilson, his maternal uncle, and Robert Maxwell, his cousin.[2]

John, third Lord Maxwell, had also a son named Herbert, said to have been illegitimate, who was the ancestor of the Maxwells of Hills and Drumcoltran, in the stewartry of Kirkcudbright.

[1] Reg. Mag. Sig., Lib. v. No. 96.   [2] Original Charter at Terregles.

XIV. JOHN MAXWELL, FOURTH LORD MAXWELL.

AGNES STEWART (OF GARLIES), HIS WIFE.

1485-1513.

JOHN MAXWELL, eldest son of John Master of Maxwell, commonly called third Lord Maxwell, succeeded his father as steward of Annandale in 1484, and his grandfather, Robert, second Lord Maxwell, in the estates and honours of the house of Maxwell in 1485.

He was a man of ability. Even in the lifetime of his grandfather his name appears in connexion with the affairs of State, and he subsequently took part in some of the most important public transactions of his time.

When a truce was concluded at Nottingham between the plenipotentiaries of James the Third, King of Scots, and of Richard the Third, King of England, 21st September 1484, John Maxwell, steward of Annandale, was one of the commissioners for Scotland appointed to meet on certain days at certain places on the Borders, such as Lochmaben, Ridanburn, Dunbar, etc., for redressing offences and publishing the truce. The truce was to begin at the rising of the sun on the 29th of September that year and to last till the setting of the sun on the 29th of September 1487, a period of three years. During that term all castles, fortresses, and towns were to remain in possession of those who then held them, with the exception of the Castle of Dunbar, which the King of Scots, without violation of the truce, might attempt to recover after the lapse of six months from its date, provided he gave warning of his intention to the King of England six weeks previously.[1]

John Maxwell, as fourth Lord Maxwell, was infefted, 8th May 1485, as heir of his grandfather, Robert, second Lord Maxwell, in the lands of Carn-salloch, in the county of Dumfries, on a precept from King James the Third. Among the witnesses were Robert Maxwell, brother-german of John Lord Maxwell.[2] On the 10th of the same month he was infefted in the lands of Grenan, in the stewartry of Kirkcudbright, and, on the 11th of April 1486, upon a Crown precept, in the lands of Balmacreuchie, in the lordship of Strathardale and county of Perth.[3]

---

[1] Rymer's Fœdera, tom. xii. pp. 235-237.
[2] Original Instrument of Sasine at Terregles.   [3] *Ibid.*

At Jedburgh, 29th April 1486, he was retoured heir of his father, John Lord Maxwell, in the forty-pound lands of the barony of Maxwell, in the shire of Roxburgh ;[1] and on the 12th of May following he was infefted in these lands.

On 10th May 1486 he was infefted as the lawful and nearest heir of his grandfather, Robert, second Lord Maxwell, in the superiority of the lands of Nether Pollok, in the barony and shire of Renfrew.[3]

In the truce of three years agreed upon, 3d July 1486, by plenipotentiaries of the kingdoms of Scotland and England, beginning from that date, John Lord Maxwell was made, along with Archibald Earl of Angus, warden of the middle and western marches for Scotland. The circumstances under which this truce was concluded were these :—Richard the Third having been killed in the last battle fought between the parties, who were called respectively the Red and the White Rose, on 22d August 1485, at Bosworth, Henry the Seventh, formerly Earl of Richmond, succeeded to the throne of England. By marrying Elizabeth, the eldest daughter of Edward the Fourth, Henry reunited the pretensions of the Houses of York and Lancaster to the English throne, and put an end to a war of about thirty years' duration, in which there perished nearly a hundred thousand men. Desirous, in order the more securely to establish his throne, to live on good terms with his neighbours, he made earnest pacific overtures to the Government of Scotland. He instructed the Earl of Northumberland, warden of the marches, to open negotiations for peace with such commissioners as King James should be pleased to appoint. William Elphinston, Bishop of Aberdeen, John Ramsay of Balmain, lately created Lord Bothwell, John Lord Kennedy, and others, were despatched as ambassadors on this errand to the English Court. The result was that the truce mentioned was concluded.[4]

Amidst the tumult and violence which were so characteristic of those times, Lord Maxwell strengthened himself by cultivating relations of amity and entering into confederacies for mutual protection and assistance with other families. On 1st of August 1486 he obtained a bond of manrent from Alexander Stewart, son and apparent heir to Alexander Stewart of the Garlies, who thereby bound himself, for the space of five years from that date, to be

[1] Original Retour at Terregles.
[2] Original Instrument of Sasine, ibid.
[3] Memoirs of the Maxwells of Pollok, vol. i. p. 191.
[4] Rymer's Fœdera, tom. xii. pp. 285, 286.

leal and true to him, never to hear of his skaith or see it without warning him in all possible haste, to give him counsel when asked, to take part with him in all his honest causes and quarrels, the granter's allegiance to his sovereign lord the King and his father, Alexander Stewart, excepted.[1]

The friendly relations which subsisted between Lord Maxwell and the Stewarts of Garlies afterwards led to a matrimonial alliance of his Lordship with that house.

Reference has been already made to a feud which existed between the Maxwells and their neighbours, the Murrays of Cockpool, who were ancestors of the Murrays, Earls of Annandale. So rancorous was this feud that Cuthbert Murray of Cockpool, his brother, sons, kin and friends, who were " at the bargain of Blackschaw," waylaid Lord Maxwell as he was proceeding homeward, slew his eme, Master John of Maxwell, and others who were in his company at that time, and inflicted bodily harm on others his friends. For the reparation of these deeds of violence, an indenture was made between John Lord Maxwell, his kin and friends, on the one part, and Cuthbert Murray of Cockpool, his kin and friends, on the other, dated at Edinburgh, 4th September 1486. By this indenture it was agreed that Cuthbert Murray, his brother, bairns, kin and friends, who were concerned in the feud, should come to the market cross of Edinburgh or Dumfries, or whatever other place Lord Maxwell preferred, in their linen clothes, in the most lowly manner they could, and ask from the said Lord, his kin and friends, forgiveness of the rancour of their hearts. The said Cuthbert was also to bind himself and his heirs in special manrent and service to Lord Maxwell and his heirs, for ever, in peace and war, first and before all others, his allegiance to the King, and his service to Andrew Lord Avendale, only excepted, and should give his letters in the best form to that effect. Sir Adam of Murray, brother-german to the said Cuthbert, John of Murray, his son and apparent heir, Charles of Murray, brothers, and sons to the said Cuthbert, were also to be bound in like manner in manrent and service, first and before all others, to Lord Maxwell, all the days of their lives, their allegiance to the King alone excepted, Lord Maxwell giving, according to his own discretion, competent fee to the said Charles and Cuthbert, as such gentlemen ought to have, and

[1] Original Bond at Terregles.

letters of maintenance to all the forenamed persons, in good and secure form, if the said Cuthbert should prove that Master John Maxwell was slain against his will and without his knowledge, and that he would have saved him could he have got to him. Cuthbert Murray was, further, for the welfare of the soul of Master John Maxwell, to infeft a priest in ten pounds of annual rent in perpetuity, to sing in the kirk of Carlaverock within a year—the Lord Maxwell and his heirs to be patrons thereto,—and in the meantime was to cause a priest to sing for the soul of Master John. He was also to cause a priest to sing for a year in the said kirk for the soul of every one that was slain at the said field. Cuthbert of Murray was, besides, to cause three of the persons that were in that field to make a pilgrimage to Rome. All other persons that were in the field were to be bound to Lord Maxwell at his pleasure in manrent and service, for all the days of their lives, and Cuthbert Murray was to make amends to all that were hurt in that field by the sight and ordinance of Edward Maxwell of Tynwald, George Maxwell [of Carnsalloch] and Herbert Gledstains of [that Ilk], according to the amount of the scaith sustained.

It was also agreed that Lord Maxwell should cause a priest to sing for each of the friends of Cuthbert Murray that was slain by Lord Maxwell's friends and men, for a year in the kirk of Rivell, and should come to the , and there ask from Cuthbert and their friends forgiveness, in lowly manner, as is before said. Lord Maxwell was also to give " a sufficient letter of slains " of the deceased John Maxwell, and for all the lives of the persons that were slain with him, to the said Cuthbert and his friends, committers of the said slaughter. Cuthbert, on the other hand, was to give "sufficient letters of slains " to Lord Maxwell's folks, committers of the slaughters of the said Cuthbert's folks between the date of the indenture and Yule next to come. In regard to the spoliation of goods by any of the said parties, they were to abide by the decision of the following persons : Lord Maxwell and his friends, by that of Herbert of Maxwell, son and apparent heir to Edward Maxwell of Tenwald, Nichol M'Brair, alderman of Dumfries ; and the said Cuthbert and his friends, by that of Lyndesay of Firgarthe, and John Cairns of Orchertone : George Heries of Torauchtie was to be oversman.[1]

---

[1] Original Indenture at Terregles. This Indenture has been much injured by damp, and parts of it are now illegible.

In the conspiracy which was formed by a faction of the barons against King James the Third towards the close of his reign, there is some reason to think that John Lord Maxwell took part. The barons who at Lauder put to death the King's favourites, and who subsequently, having imprisoned their Sovereign and usurped the government, dreading that, being restored to his authority, he would proceed against them for the treason which they had committed, again rose up in arms against him ; and his son James, afterwards King James the Fourth, was forced, or permitted himself, to be seduced, by the malcontent barons unnaturally to join in the rebellion.

John Lord Maxwell was a member of the Parliament opened at Edinburgh 1st October 1487, in which the King's supporters and the conspirators tested their strength.[1] The latter proposed that a cordial understanding should be come to between them and the Sovereign, and that a full pardon should be granted to them and their associates. But to this proposition the King's adherents refused to give their consent ; whilst the King, at the same time, bestowed rewards on the chief of the barons who espoused his interest, and adopted measures for giving effect to the laws against treason.

Apprehensive of personal danger, the rebel barons assembled without delay an army ; declared that King James the Third, by his crimes and oppressions, had forfeited all claim to the throne ; and proclaimed his son, though still in his minority, by the title of King James the Fourth. An accommodation was for a short time effected ; but the hostile barons anew appeared in arms against their Sovereign ; and at Sauchie Burn, within a mile of Bannockburn, and about two miles from Stirling—hence called the Field of Stirling—the royal forces, on 11th June 1488, were routed. King James the Third, escaping from the field of battle, was put to death by an unknown hand at a hamlet called Milltown, only a short way distant. He died in the thirty-fifth year of his age, and in the twenty-eighth of his reign. His body was interred beside that of his late Queen, Margaret of Denmark, near the high altar of the Abbey of Cambuskenneth.[2]

John Lord Maxwell was a member of the first Parliament held after the

[1] The Acts of the Parliaments of Scotland, vol. ii. p. 175.

[2] To the memory of these royal ancestors, her Majesty Queen Victoria erected, in the year 1865, a monument on the spot in which their bodies are believed to have been interred.

succession of King James the Fourth, which was opened at Edinburgh 6th
October 1488, and was numerously attended.[1]　　Before this Parliament the
Earl of Buchan, Lord Forbes, Lord Bothwell, Ross of Montgrenan, the lairds
of Cockpool, Amisfield, Innermeith and Innes, Sir Thomas Fotheringhame
and Sir Alexander Dunbar, were summoned to appear to answer to the
charge of treason, for having fought on the side of the late King at the
Field of Stirling.　　Lord Bothwell, on making confession of his guilt, and
casting himself on the King's mercy, received the royal pardon.　　On
the others, who were found guilty, a sentence of forfeiture was pronounced.
In this Parliament King James the Fourth, and the nobles and barons implicated in the late rebellion, got an act of indemnity passed in their favour,
declaring that the slaughter committed in the Field of Stirling, in which the
King's father and divers barons and lieges were slain, was wholly owing to
the King himself and his wicked counsellors, and that the new Sovereign, and
the lords and barons who were with him in that field, were innocent and free
of the said slaughters.　　In the Act it is recommended, " that part of the three
estates, prelates, bishops, great barons, and burgesses, should append their
seals along with the Great Seal, to be shown and produced to our Holy Father
the Pope, the Kings of France, Spain, Denmark, and other realms."　　By
another Act of this Parliament it was declared that all justices, sheriffs,
stewards, etc., who held heritable offices, and had fought for their Sovereign, were suspended from, or deprived of, these offices for the space of
three years, and that those of the same party who held offices for life or for a
term of years, were incapable of holding them in any time coming.　　By
another Act it was declared that the heirs of all lords and proprietors of land
who had been, or might be, disinherited by their parents or predecessors for
fighting against the late King, should nevertheless succeed to and enjoy their
inheritances.

　　To put down theft, robbery, murder, and other crimes, so common at
that time, the kingdom was divided by this Parliament into districts, over
which certain earls and barons were empowered and ordained to exercise
justice, and to suppress disorders of every kind, by the discovery, trial, and
punishment of criminals, till the King should attain to the age of twenty-one

[1] The Acts of the Parliaments of Scotland, vol. ii. pp. 206-210.

years. Lord Maxwell was appointed, in conjunction with the Earl of Angus, to execute these offices in the shire of Dumfries.

To the various transactions of this Lord Maxwell, in connexion with his family estates, a few brief references will be sufficient.

On 3d November 1488 he was infefted by William Lord Sommerville in the forty-pound lands of Libbertoun, in the barony of Carnwath and shire of Lanark.[1] On 29th June 1489, as heir of Robert Lord Maxwell, his grandfather, Lord Maxwell was, on a precept of King James the Fourth, infefted in the superiority of the lands of Waranhill, in the barony of Cowantone [Colvanton] and shire of Lanark.[2] On 24th May 1490, at Renfrew, he claimed by a notarial certificate, as Lord of Mearns, the wardship and relief of the lands of Fingaltoun.[3] On 30th October 1490, he obtained a bond of manrent from Robert Hamilton of Prestoun, who "became man in manrent and service" to him for all the days of his life, his allegiance to his sovereign lord the King and to his chief Lord Hamilton excepted.[4]

A few months after that date, his marriage with Agnes, eldest daughter of Sir Alexander Stewart of Garlies, was agreed upon. In prospect and in consideration of this alliance, Sir Alexander Stewart, the father of the lady, and Alexander Stewart, her brother, gave to Lord Maxwell a bond of manrent, in which they bound themselves to assist him in all his affairs.

Lord Maxwell sold to Robert Lord Crechtoun of Sanquhar the lands of Newtoune, Brume, and Flinder, in the lordship of Mearns and shire of Renfrew; and he received, at Carlaverock, 13th July 1491, a letter of reversion from that lord for the redemption of these lands.[5] On 23d November 1491 he had an assignation from Sir William Stirling of Keir, knight, of his claim of £1000 Scots against Adam Johnstoun and Sir Adam Murray, knight.[6] As superior of the lands of Fingaltoun, he raised an action against Robert Crawfurd of Auchinamys, Sheriff of Renfrew, and obtained a decreet by the Lords of Council, reducing the service of James Lord Hamilton in these lands. A confirmation of this decreet was granted by King James the Fourth, dated at Edinburgh, 18th May 1492.[7]

[1] Original Instrument of Sasine at Terregles.
[2] Original Instrument of Sasine, ibid.
[3] Original Notarial Certificate, ibid.
[4] Original Bond of Manrent, ibid.
[5] Original Instrument of Reversion at Terregles.
[6] Original Assignation, ibid.
[7] Original Confirmation, ibid.

At Edinburgh, 30th June 1492, John Lord Maxwell obtained from Charles Pollok of Over Pollok an obligation for the payment of £10 annually out of the lands of Over Pollok.   Among the witnesses were Edward Maxwell of Tinwald, George Maxwell of Carnsalloch, William Jardane, nephew and heir-apparent of John Jardane of Apilgairth, Herbert Gledstanys of that Ilk, etc.[1]

Certain disputes in regard to property affairs arose between Lord Maxwell and John Maxwell of Pollok.   King James the Fourth gave a precept for the infeftment of the latter in the lands of Nether Pollok, in the shire of Renfrew. On 14th May 1494, Lord Maxwell, in the presence of two notaries and of witnesses, solemnly protested at these lands that whatever was done by him in the way of giving sasine in compliance with the King's precept, should not be to the prejudice of himself and his heirs.   Having made this protest he, as lord superior of these lands, infefted in them John Maxwell, in the usual way; but shortly after, he annulled the deed of infeftment by breaking a wooden platter on the said lands and at their principal mansion, on the alleged ground that the sheriff, in the direction and serving of the brieve for infeftment, and the assize, in their deliverance, had both acted irregularly.[2]

An agreement was, however, concluded in the parish church of Mearns, 20th April 1495, between John Lord Maxwell and John Maxwell of Nether Pollok, which terminated the disputes that had been litigated between them. The latter declared that he and his heirs held the said lands of John Lord Maxwell and his heirs, in ward and relief, for ever.   Lord Maxwell therefore remitted to him, and his next heir only, all rights and burdens belonging to his lordship by reason of ward and relief from the entry of the said John and his heir foresaid.   Moreover, the said John Maxwell of Nether Pollok promised, for himself and his heirs, a suit of the Sheriff-Court of Renfrew in all and sundry the Courts of the said shire, to be held there or elsewhere, for the said Lord Maxwell, by reason of ward and relief; and also engaged that he would bear all the burdens of that Court lying on the said Lord Maxwell.[3]

On 3d November 1495, John Lord Maxwell granted to John Maxwell of Nether Pollok a charter of these lands, for his meritorious services rendered in

[1] Original Obligation at Terregles.
[2] Instrument of Cassation in Memoirs of the Maxwells of Pollok, vol. i. p. 206.
[3] Memoirs of the Maxwells of Pollok, vol. i. p. 209.

many ways to his lordship's predecessors; which lands belonged to the said John Maxwell, and were by him resigned into the hands of the granter, as the lord superior, to be held in feu and heritage, for paying to him and his heirs half a merk of annual rent at Whitsunday, if asked, with the ward and relief of the said lands when they should happen, and a common suit in the Sheriff-Court of Renfrew, for the granter and his heirs, and expenses for the said lands.[1] On 4th November, John Lord Maxwell made a grant to John Maxwell of Nether Pollok, and to the next heir succeeding him, of the ward and relief of the lands of Nether Pollok.[2]

Some of the transactions of John Lord Maxwell with the neighbouring religious houses may here be noticed: On 13th May 1495, John Lord Maxwell sold the lands of Kirkblane, in the barony of Carlaverock, under reversion, to Herbert Gledstanis, and obtained from him a letter of reversion, 1st July 1498.[3] On the same day his Lordship, Robert Maxwell, his son and apparent heir, and Herbert his second son, were, by John, Abbot of Holywood, and the convent of the Abbey, constituted bailies of all the lands of the barony of the Abbey, and of all its other lands within the shire of Dumfries, for nineteen years, from the Whitsunday immediately following.[4] Again, his Lordship, Robert Maxwell, his son and heir-apparent, and Herbert Maxwell, brother to the said Robert, and the longest liver of them, obtained from John, Abbot of Holywood, 14th February 1502, a grant of the bailiery of Holywood in liferent. On 31st August 1503, a resignation was made in his favour by Robert, Abbot of Sweetheart, of the bailiery of that abbey and lands of Lochartur.[5]

He obtained from John, Abbot of Holywood, a lease of the lands of Baltersan, undated, but indorsed 1506, for nineteen years.[6] On 16th May 1507, he and Robert, his son and heir, were constituted by Robert, Abbot of Sweetheart, with the consent of the whole convent, bailies of all their lands of their barony of Lowkyndelow, in the shire of Dumfries and stewartry of Kirkcudbright, for nineteen years, immediately following the date of the grant.[7]

On 27th May 1508, John Lord Maxwell was infefted in the lands of Libbertoun, in the barony of Carnwath and shire of Lanark, by John Lord

[1] Charter in Memoirs of the Maxwells of Pollok, vol. i. p. 11.

[2] *Ibid.* vol. i. p. 215.

[3] Original Instrument of Reversion at Terregles.

[4] Original Grant at Terregles.

[5] Original Instrument of Resignation, *ibid.*

[6] Original Lease, *ibid.*

[7] Original Grant of Bailiery, *ibid.*

Somerville, lord of that barony.[1] Under reversion, he sold to Rauf Ker of Prymsideloch and Margaret Rutherfurde, his spouse, the ten-pound lands of Easter Woddane and others, in the barony of Maxwailefeild and shire of Roxburgh.   On 4th January 1508-9, he took a notarial instrument on their letter of reversion.[2]   He also sold to Raff Ker, under reversion, the twenty-pound land of the town of Maxwell, in the lordship of Maxwellfield, and took a notarial instrument, dated at Edinburgh, 1st December 1509, on the letter of reversion.[3]

A resignation was made in his favour by John Gordon of Lochinvar of the lands of Gordonstoun ; upon which he took a public instrument, dated 21st February 1509-10 :[4] and a precept was granted, dated at Edinburgh, 22d February, by King James the Fourth, for infefting him in these lands, and in others in the stewartry of Kirkcudbright.[5]

To John Lord Maxwell, King James the Fourth, for a great sum of money paid to him and his treasury by that lord, and for other considerations, gave by his letters-patent, under his Privy Seal, numerous lands within the stewartry of Annandale and shire of Dumfries, held of the Crown in chief by the service of ward and relief by the various proprietors.   These lands had been apprised to the King for payment of divers sums of money, fines, and farms due by the owners to the Crown.   They included the lands of Langreggis, Denby, and Hoddom, belonging to John Lindesay, apprised for the sum of £240, in part of the payment of £400 ; the lands of Greskin and Malinqschaw, Rontausyde, Auld Henschill, Backlaw, and Mekle Holmesyde, belonging to Andrew Lord Heris, for the sum of £266, 3s. 4d., in part of the payment of £380 ; and many other lands belonging to other persons.

Moved by paternal affection, John Lord Maxwell made an assignation to Robert Maxwell, his son and heir, of these lands, and King James granted to Robert a charter of them, dated Edinburgh, 29th November, the 23d year of the King's reign (1510).   In the charter, King James wills and ordains that the foresaid persons and their heirs, and any of them, may have full re-entrance into the foresaid apprised lands whenever they shall have paid to Robert

---

[1] Original Instrument of Sasine at Terregles.

[2] Instrument of Reversion, *ibid.*

[3] Original Instrument of Reversion, *ibid.*

[4] Original Instrument of Resignation at Terregles.

[5] Original Precept of Sasine, *ibid.*

Maxwell and his heirs the foresaid sums for which they were apprised. It was, however, necessary that they should fully make payment of the same within the space of seven years immediately following the date of the said apprisings, according to the terms of an Act of Parliament, with the expenses which had been incurred by the infeftment of the foresaid Robert Maxwell. The farms and profits of these lands were to be received in the meantime by the said Robert Maxwell and his heirs in payment of the sums and expenses before mentioned.[1]

On 3d February 1512-13, John Lord Maxwell obtained from Sir Robert Gordon of Glen, knight, a bond, by which the granter faithfully bound himself and his heirs in homage and service to his lordship and his heirs for ever, first and before all mortals, his allegiance to the King and his successors, and his service to the Earl of Bothwell for his lifetime, excepted.[2]

In little more than seven months after the date of that bond, John Lord Maxwell lost his life in the service of his Sovereign and country. The circumstances connected with his death, which form a dark and melancholy chapter in the history of Scotland, can be here only briefly stated. The accession of Henry the Eighth to the English throne, on the death of his father, Henry the Seventh, in the year 1509, was unfavourable to the tranquillity of Scotland. That monarch was proud, capricious, and tyrannical, whilst King James the Fourth was high-spirited, and little disposed to submit to the dictation of his brother-in-law. For some time the pacific relations between the two kingdoms were undisturbed. But Henry the Eighth having engaged in war with Louis the Twelfth of France, James the Fourth of Scotland, drawn by the French monarch into the quarrel, declared war against England. So popular was the King among all ranks of his subjects, that he speedily collected an army of nearly a hundred thousand men, including many of the nobility and gentry. John Lord Maxwell, with three of his brothers, joined the army, and headed a considerable body of his vassals. With this numerous force King James, who commanded in person, invaded England. On the 9th of September 1513, he encountered the English, under the command of the Earl of Surrey, at Flodden

[1] Original Charter at Terregles.
[2] Original Notarial Instrument of Bond of Manrent, *ibid.*

Field, and sustained one of the most disastrous defeats ever experienced by Scotland. The battle began between four and five o'clock in the afternoon, and was maintained with the utmost obstinacy on both sides till after night-fall—that is, for at least three hours—when it ended in the total overthrow of the Scots. From the intrepid resolution with which the Scots maintained the conflict, the loss of the English, though they gained the victory, was severe. On the side of the Scots the loss amounted to ten thousand common soldiers, the King himself, thirteen earls, fifteen lords and chiefs of clans, and a great number of gentry. That fatal day carried bereavement and mourning into almost every family, high and low, throughout the kingdom, and was remembered generations after with poignant sorrow and regret.

Among the slain were John Lord Maxwell and three of his brothers.

Lord Maxwell had possessed the family inheritance for twenty-eight years.

Agnes Stewart, Lady Maxwell, survived Lord Maxwell. She obtained from her son, Robert Lord Maxwell, a charter, dated at the Castle of Loch-maben, 29th November 1516, of the lands and barony of Mearns, in the shire of Renfrew, in liferent.[1] On the same day she was infefted in these lands, in terms of the charter.[2]

By her Lord Maxwell had five sons and four daughters. The sons were—

1. Robert, the eldest, his successor, as fifth Lord Maxwell.

2. Herbert, who is mentioned as his second son in a grant dated 13th May 1495, formerly quoted.[3] He was ancestor of the Maxwells of Clowdon, in the stewartry of Kirkcudbright.

3. John. He was Abbot of Dundrennan. King James the Fifth, from his favour for Robert, fifth Lord Maxwell, wrote a letter to the Pope for the promotion of his brother, John Maxwell, to be Abbot of the Abbey of Melrose. As, however, James Beaton, Archbishop of St. Andrews, who belonged to a different faction from Lord Maxwell in those distracted times, had written to the Pope in favour of some one else in defiance of the King's authority, the King, in a letter to Cardinal Wolsey, dated Edinburgh, 3d September 1524, begs his intercession with the King of England and the

---

[1] Original Charter at Terregles.
[2] Original Instrument of Sasine, *ibid.*   [3] *Vide* p. 165.

Pope for the advancement of John Maxwell to that dignity.[1] On 21st September 1525, the King, in the presence of a public notary and witnesses at the Palace of Holyrood, subscribed the following ratification and approval of his letter to the Pope on behalf of John Maxwell, and revocation of all letters to the contrary :—

REX.—We ratify and approvis our supplicatioun send to our haly fader the Paip for the promotioun of dene Johne Maxwell, abbot of Dundrennan, bruther germane to our cousing and counsalour Robert Lord Maxwell, to the abbacy of Melros within our realme, and revokis all lettres gif ony be send in our name incontrar our first lettres of supplicatioun send for the said dene Johne Maxwellis first promotioun, and we knaw nocht gif we haue writtin in the contrar, be this writing subscriuit with our hand at Edinburgh the xxi day of September the zeir of God 1ᵐ vᶜ xxv zeris, and for mair verificatioun of the samin I am content that this my approbatioun and reuocatioun be put in forme of instrument, as efferis.

JAMES R.

Upon all this, Robert, fifth Lord Maxwell, obtained a public notarial instrument.[2]

Margaret, Queen of Scotland, in Articles which she sent about the end of the year 1525 to her brother, Henry the Eighth of England, and his Council, and which she desired to be answered with the greatest expedition, for the furthering of a good understanding between the realms of Scotland and England, reminds him that she had written before for the expedition of the bulls of Melrose, whereby she would succeed in obtaining a pension of £1000 yearly, which would help her in some part ; and she humbly beseeches his Grace to help her in the promotion of Lord Maxwell's brother ; for until that should be sped, she would not get the pension.[3]

The Archbishop of St. Andrews, in order to defeat the appointment of John Maxwell, the brother of Robert Lord Maxwell, to the abbacy of Melrose, had written in the name of King James to Henry the Eighth of England, as he had done to the Pope, in favour of another person. To this fact particular reference is made in the

[1] Calendar of State Papers, Scotland, 1509-1589, p. 18, No. 67.
[2] Original Notarial Instrument at Terregles.
[3] State Papers, vol. iv., King Henry the Eighth, Part iv. p. 295.

instructions given in the year 1526, by King James the Fifth, to his familiar servitor Patrick Saint Klare, to be shown to Henry King of England and Cardinal Wolsey. The said Patrick was to show to Henry that the writing which was sent by King James the Fifth to him in favour of Mr. Andrew Dury did not express the mind of the King, who therein was circumvented by the Archbishop of St. Andrews, his Majesty's Chancellor;[1] and to beseech Henry to write to the Pope in favour of John Maxwell. "If they had proceded of our mynde and knowlege," to quote from the instructions, "it had been to our dishonour, considering our other letters geven by us before to Dene John Maxwel, in favour of whom we nowe, having auctorite in our hand, have wryten letters to the Pope's Holynes, conforme to our first mynde. And to this effecte the Pope's Holynes hath wryten to us, desiring us to determyne our mynde in the matier, and whom we wol be provided to the said abbay of Melrose; like as we have doon, and writen for the saide Dene John Maxwell. Praying herfor our said uncle to send his writinges to the Pope's Holynes, conforme to our letters geven in favour of the said Dene John for his promotion to our said abbey."[2]

The Archbishop of St. Andrews, however, triumphed. John Maxwell, after all, was not promoted to the office of Abbot of Melrose. That ecclesiastical dignity, to the great dissatisfaction of Lord Maxwell and of the Scottish Parliament, was bestowed upon Andrew Dury, a son of the house of Dury in Fife.

In the Parliament of Scotland, held on 14th June 1526, the matter was brought under consideration. It is recorded that the King, with the advice of the Queen-Mother and the Lords of Council, had written commendatory letters for the promotion of " his devote and weil belouit oratour, Dene Johne" Maxwell, Abbot of Dundrennan, to the vacant abbey of Melrose, but that, by surreptitious letters of the King to the Pope, Andrew Dury had been appointed Abbot; and the King declared that these letters

[1] The Great Seal was, in July 1526, taken from Archbishop Beaton.

[2] State Papers, vol. iv., King Henry the Eighth, Part iv. p. 451.

were of no effect, and ratified those he had written in favour of
Maxwell. A similar declaration was made on the 17th of November
in favour of " ane venerable fader in God, Dene Johnne Maxvell,
Abbot of Dundrinane, anent the Abbacy of Melrose, contrair Mr.
Andro Dury."[1]

Sir Christopher Dacre, in a letter to Lord Dacre, dated 2d
December [1526], thus writes on the subject :—" Druyre, a monke
of Murouse (Melrose) Abbey, has gotten the bulles of the same
Abbey at Rome, and caused them be proclamed; whiche has done
grete displeasure to my Lorde Maxwell, for it will put his broder
from the same by likelyhode, notwithstanding the King and the
Lordes at this Parliament has inacted that no Scotisman shall
prevale no benefice at the Poppe's hand, excepte that they have
licence of the King and the Lordes of the Counsaile."[2]

4. Edward. Among the witnesses to a gift by Robert Lord Maxwell,
dated at Dumfries, 16th February 1525, to John Armestrang, of the
non-entry of the lands of Mylgill and Eriswood, in the lordship of
Eskdale, was Edward Maxwell, his lordship's brother.[3] In a letter
from Lord Dacre to Cardinal Wolsey, dated Neward, 13th September [1528], mention is made of Edward Maxwell, brother of
Robert, fifth Lord Maxwell, as having, with the laird of Johnston,
lately burnt the Mote of Liddale, parcel of the King's land within
Nichol Forest, and as having, at the same burning, slain one Gilbert
Richardson.[4] In an instrument of sasine on the infeftment of Robert,
fifth Lord Maxwell, and Agnes Stewart (of Buchan), Countess of
Bothwell, his spouse, in the lands and barony of Butill, dated 1st
July 1535, " Edward Maxwell, brother of the said Lord Maxwell,"
was one of the witnesses. Among the others were John Maxwell
of Carnsalloch and Edward Maxwell of Lochruton.[5]

5. Henry. He was made a prisoner at the defeat of the Scots by the
English at Solway Moss, and was sent to the Tower of London. In

[1] The Acts of the Parliaments of Scotland, vol. ii.
pp. 301, 302, 310, 312.
[2] State Papers, vol. iv., King Henry the Eighth,
Part iv. p. 461.
[3] Original Gift at Terregles.
[4] State Papers, vol. iv., King Henry the Eighth,
Part iv. p. 507.
[5] Original Sasine at Terregles.

a contemporary paper containing the yearly value of the lands, and also the value and substance in goods of the Scottish prisoners taken at Solway Moss, the entry concerning him is "Henry Maxwell, brodyr to the Lorde Maxwell, in landes *per annum*, nothinge, and in goods nothinge."[1]   He obtained his liberty, by an agreement between ambassadors from Scotland and commissioners of Henry the Eighth of England, dated 1st July 1543, for a ransom of £100 sterling.[2]

The daughters were—

1. Mary, who married Sir John Johnstone of that Ilk, ancestor of the Marquises of Annandale.

2. Agnes, who married Robert Charteris of Amisfield, in the county of Dumfries, and had issue one son, John.

3. Elizabeth, who married Jardine of Applegirth, also in the county of Dumfries.

4. Katharine, who married John Glendonyng of that Ilk, in the county of Dumfries, and of Parton in the stewartry of Kirkcudbright, without issue.

[1] State Papers, vol. v., King Henry the Eighth, Part v. continued, p. 233.
[2] Rymer's Fœdera, tom. xiv. p. 797.

SEAL OF JOHN, FOURTH LORD MAXWELL, 1495.

XV. ROBERT, FIFTH LORD MAXWELL.

1513-1546.

JANET DOUGLAS (DRUMLANRIG), HIS FIRST WIFE.

AGNES STEWART, COUNTESS OF BOTHWELL, HIS SECOND WIFE.

THIS Lord occupied a distinguished position as a statesman, as Warden of the Marches, as a general, and as an admiral. For many years he enjoyed the favour of his Sovereign, and was one of the counsellors upon whose advice he relied ; one of the courtiers in whose society he had most pleasure. When James the Fifth deserted tried servants for a less worthy favourite, he involved himself in ruin, his country in disaster, and Lord Maxwell in trouble for the remainder of his life.

Many of the royal commissions and Crown charters which he received have been preserved. But, with the exception of a few of his letters, the whole of his correspondence has been unfortunately lost, and our only authority for many of the circumstances of his life is derived from State papers preserved in England, and we are thus in many cases left in ignorance of the motives of his actions, and of the grounds on which he might have vindicated himself from the injurious imputations which are occasionally made against him in the letters of the English ambassadors.[1]

At an early date he was employed in the public service. According to the MS. account of the Maxwell family, frequently before referred to, he " was admiral of a fleet passing to France, and upon the sea, the tyme of Flodden field, and being driven back by tempest arryved the 2d day after the battle of Kirkcudbright, where, hearing of the slaughter of the King and of his father, he seized upon the Castles Treive and Lochmaben, by the good wills of the Captains thereof."

[1] He was retoured heir to his father, John, fourth Lord Maxwell, on 4th November 1513, in the lands of Carnsalloch and Durisquen, in the shire of Dumfries, which were held of the King in chief.—(Original Retour at Terregles.) On 8th November same year, a precept of Sasine, by John Lord Sommerville, was granted to him as heir of his father in the lands of Libbertoun, in the barony of Carnwath and shire of Lanark.—(Original Precept of Sasine, ibid.) On the 10th of the same month, he was, upon a precept under the Signet of the King's Office at Perth, infefted as heir to his father in the lands of Blatoun Wester, and Balmacrewchy, in the barony of Balmacrewchy and shire of Perth. —(Original Sasine, ibid.) On 13th February 1513-14 he was infefted as heir of his father in the lands of Mearns and Nether Pollok, in the shire of Renfrew.—(Original Sasine, ibid.)

Soon after his succession to his father, in 1513, he received from Margaret, Queen Dowager of Scotland, tutor to her son, King James the Fifth, a commission, dated 26th November that year, appointing him Captain and Keeper of the Castle of Thrieve and Steward of the Stewartry of Kirkcudbright for nineteen years.[1]   Not long afterwards he was appointed Warden of the West Marches by the Duke of Albany, who informs Lord Dacre of the appointment in a letter, dated Edinburgh, 10th August 1515.   Two days after Lord Dacre expresses his approval of it in a letter to Albany.[2]

The disorders which were distracting the Borders were a great source of anxiety and annoyance to the Governments of England and Scotland, and the name of Lord Maxwell, as Warden, frequently occurs in connexion with them. In a letter, dated Naworth, 24th June 1517, Lord Dacre writes to Lord Maxwell complaining of an inroad at the West Marches, for which the latter, in his reply from Lochmaben, 26th June, promises to make redress.   Lord Dacre again wrote from Carlisle, 27th June, requesting the Scottish Warden to meet him at Lochmaben.   Lord Maxwell wished to postpone the meeting, but Lord Dacre, in another letter written from Kirkoswald, 2d July 1517, insisted on its taking place, and peremptorily demanded the fulfilment of Lord Maxwell's promises.   He appears, however, to have had little hope of this, for about the same time he appealed to the Regents for redress, and also to the Chancellor of Scotland, desiring him to stimulate Lord Maxwell, whom he blames as tardy. But they were not much more satisfactory than the Warden, for their answer consisted of a statement that the seizures complained of were lawfully made, and a promise to make inquiries.[3]

The heads of religious houses in those days commonly found it desirable, if not necessary, to intrust the government of their baronies to men of position and influence, who by their power as feudal chiefs could afford them protection, and who could prevent them from coming directly into actual collision with their vassals or other persons in the territories over which their jurisdiction extended.   Accordingly we find in Scotland, Robert Lord Maxwell acting as bailie and Justice-General over the lands, baronies, and regalities

---

[1] Original Grant at Terregles.

[2] Calendar of State Papers, 1509-1589, vol. i. p. 3, Nos. 18, 20.

[3] Index to MSS. in Cottonian Library, Caligula, B. vi. 163-171, British Museum.

which belonged to the Abbeys of Dundrennan, Tungland, Sweetheart, Holywood, the Provostry of Linclouden, and the Preceptory of Trailtrow.[1]

These offices, with that of Warden, would have made Lord Maxwell a man of great importance, but when to them were added the weight derived from his extensive landed possessions and the power which he derived from the offices of Steward of Annandale and Kirkcudbright and other districts, his influence must have been paramount in the south-west of Scotland.

Lord Maxwell was firmly attached to the interests of Margaret, Queen Dowager of Scotland, who had married Archibald, sixth Earl of Angus, grandson of the Earl popularly known as Bell the Cat. About 1518, annoyed by the neglect with which Angus treated her, Margaret began to speak of a divorce ; but her brother Henry strongly remonstrated against this step, and although Lord Maxwell, with the Earls of Argyll, Arran, Lennox, and Lords Fleming and Sempill were in favour of it, she and her husband were reconciled for a season.[2]

In the year 1523, the Queen engaged in negotiations with Dacre and Surrey for her son's assuming the sovereign power, whilst she at the head of a Council should conduct the government.[3] In 1524, when the Duke of Albany, the Regent, went to France, Lord Maxwell and the Earl of Arran, in gratification of her desire, procured that the King, though only ten years of age, should be invested with the supreme power, and the King was declared by a Council assembled in Holyrood Palace to have taken the reins of Government into his own hands.

Lord Maxwell was appointed Captain of the Guard, consisting of two hundred men, to which the care of the King's person was confided, and Henry Stewart, the Queen's favourite, was appointed his lieutenant. The constitution of this guard greatly pleased Margaret, who had great confidence in Lord Maxwell. In a letter to Norfolk, written from Edinburgh in the autumn of the year 1524, speaking of the Lords who were to remain about the person of King James the Fifth, her son, she says it was good to be well advised thereupon, and adds : " For to say that we are assured of any Lords in

[1] Original Commissions and Grants by the abbots of the religious houses mentioned, ranging from the year 1513 to the year 1544, in the Charter-room at Terregles.

[2] State Papers, vol. iv., King Henry the Eighth, Part iv., Dacre to Cardinal Wolsey, 22d October [1518].

[3] Ibid. vol. iv. p. 10.

special but my Lord of Arran and my Lord Maxwell, and their friends, we are not ;" and therefore the other Lords were not to be greatly trusted, and should not remain about the King's person as far as she could prevent it.[1] In another letter to Norfolk, she alludes expressly to the guard, saying, " for when that any disobeyed us, or did anything that might be contrary to us, we sent the said band, with their Captain, my Lord Maxwell, and put them where we pleased."

Her confidence in the guard was shared by her friends. The King's assumption of regal power was opposed by the Archbishop of St. Andrews and the Bishop of Aberdeen and others. They were therefore, by the orders of the Queen, Lord Maxwell, and the other Lords, her councillors, arrested and imprisoned, much to the joy of the English King and his Ministers of State. Cardinal Wolsey, in a letter to the Duke of Norfolk, dated 2d September [1524], after expressing his approval of all that had been done, instructed Norfolk that as the friends of these two Bishops, whilst they remained in prison in Scotland, might conspire for their release, it was the opinion of the King of England and his Council that they should, by the Queen of Scots, be sent secretly, without delay, under a suitable guard, to the town of Berwick, and that the business might be arranged by Lord Maxwell, with the guard, or part thereof.[2]

A change of parties now took place in Scotland. The Earl of Angus, who had hitherto sided with the French interest, after an absence of two years and a half returned to Scotland at the request of Henry the Eighth, and, being easily gained over to support the designs of Henry, entered into a secret treaty with that King to support them, in the hope that he and his brother, Sir George Douglas, might thus acquire supreme power in Scotland, and recover their forfeited estates. Queen Margaret, who had raised her favourite, Henry Stewart, to the office of Chancellor, opposed her husband's plans. Hitherto Arran and Maxwell had received pensions from the English Court, and in return had lent their support to the promotion of the schemes of Henry. But this did not prevent them from joining the party of the Queen, and throwing their influence on the side of France ; and strengthened by their accession for a time this party had the conduct of affairs.

---

[1] State Papers, vol. iv., King Henry the Eighth, Part iv. p. 127.

[2] State Papers, vol. iv., King Henry the Eighth, Part iv. pp. 120-123.

Magnus, in a letter to Wolsey, written from Newcastle, 10th October 1524, expresses his sorrow to hear that the Queen-mother was only advised and ordered after her own mind by the counsels of the Earl of Arran and of Lord Maxwell, and of two or three young men who were allied to the Earl of Arran, so that no justice or good order appeared about the young King.[1]

Norfolk and other English ambassadors, in a letter to Wolsey, written from Newcastle on the 23d day of the same month, assure him, from intelligence brought them, that the Queen, the Earl of Arran and Lord Maxwell had their only trust on France, and did what they could to follow that way; yet that their power was small, all the noblemen and commons desiring much the amity of England; that the commons hated the Duke of Albany, whilst the Earl of Angus was a universal favourite among them; and that the young King would gladly have had the latter as a counsellor but from fear of the Queen.[2]

As we have seen that the Queen confided in Lord Maxwell, he in turn appears to have been actuated by a sincere attachment to the young King, and the King does not appear to have been wanting in esteem for his faithful subject. Although the youthful James may not have had much to say to the earlier grants which Lord Maxwell received from the Crown, yet the later grants which he obtained show that his devotion was appreciated by the King in his riper years. Magnus, in a letter to Wolsey, from Edinburgh, 22d February [1525], says, "The Lorde Maxwell loveth the King, his Maister, as I am sure doe all the other, and therfore he repared to the Kingges presence, and also by cause he trusteth to have, for his sonne or nigh kynnesman, the Abbasy of Melroos."[3]

Lord Maxwell appears to have taken part in all important affairs of State at this time. Magnus, in a letter to Wolsey, written from Edinburgh, 24th January 1525, states that the day after his arrival, being Sunday, he went to the castle, accompanied by Lord Maxwell, the Comptroller, and other gentlemen, and found there the young King sitting at council. In this letter a description is given of the two parties which at that time existed in Scotland. In the one were the Archbishop of St. Andrews, the Earls of Angus, Lennox, and Argyll, and in the other, the Bishop of Aberdeen, the

[1] State Papers, vol. iv., King Henry the Eighth, Part iv. p. 173.   [2] State Papers, vol. iv., King Henry the Eighth, Part iv. p. 188.   [3] Ibid. p. 329.

Prior of St. Andrews, and many others, who were for a peace between England and Scotland. From her variance with her husband the Earl of Angus, though he had, without comparison, greater power than any subject in Scotland, the Queen inclined to the French party. Those whom she consulted and most confided in were the opponents of the English interest, such as the Archbishop of Glasgow, the Earl of Murray, the Bishop of Ross, as she herself confessed ; the Earl of Arran and Lord Maxwell not being inclined to that party. With the exception of these counsellors, all others, in Magnus's opinion, were disposed to join with England in a perfect amity.[1]

At this time the opinions of Luther, which were producing great commotion in Germany, had begun to attract attention in Scotland.

In the Parliament of King James the Fifth, held at Edinburgh in July 1525, at which Lord Maxwell was present, an Act was passed on the 17th of July, strongly condemning the " heretik Luther," and providing against the spread of his " filthe" from foreign parts. The Act narrates, that as the

" dampnable opunzeounis of heresy are spred in diuers cuntreis be the heretik Luther and his discipillis, and this realm and liegis has fermelie persistit in the hali-faithe sene the samin was first rassauit be thaim, and neuer as zit admittit ony opunzeounis contrar the Christin faithe, bot euer has bene clene of all sic filthe and vice : Therefor that na manner of persoun, strangears that hapnis to arrife with thair schippis within ony pairt of this realme, bring with thaim ony bukis or werkis of the said Lutheris, his discipillis, or seruandis, desputt or reherse his heresyis or opunzeounis, bot geif it be to the confusion thairof [and that be clerkis in sculis alanarlie], vnder the pane of escheting of thair schippis and gudis and putting of thair persounis in presoune : And that this Act be publist and proclamit out throw this realme, at all portis and burowis of the samin : Sa that thai may allege na ignorance thairof [And all vtheris the Kingis liegis assistaris to sic opunzeonis be pvnist in semeible wise, And the effectis of the said Act to strik apon thaim," etc.[2]]

On 21st June 1526, as King James had attained his complete majority of fourteen years, he was declared by Parliament to have assumed the government of the kingdom ; and the supreme authority, by the same Act, was placed in the hands of the Earl of Angus. Lord Maxwell was one of the Privy Council appointed to assist him as guardian of the King's person, and in the same year he obtained the office of Justiciary.[3]

[1] State Papers, vol. iv., King Henry the Eighth, Part iv. pp. 299, 305, 307.

[2] Original Acts of Parliament, MS., H.M. General Register House, Edinburgh. Printed Acts, vol. ii. p. 295.

[3] Register of Privy Seal, B. i. 6, p. 18.

His duties as Warden of the Borders caused Lord Maxwell to be frequently absent from Court.   In the MS. account of the family, it is said that he made a raid into England, 17th July 1524, and despoiled all Cumberland ; and that in 1526 he was with King James the Fifth at Melrose Bridge, at the encounter betwixt the Douglases and the Laird of Buccleuch for rescuing the King from them, and taking vengeance on the English who had burnt Dumfries.   The English Government complained of his conduct in aggravating and perpetuating these disturbances by failing to punish the Border marauders or by affording them protection.[1]

In the year 1528, he made an incursion into England and burned the town of Netherby, apparently wishing to provoke the English to a violation of a truce for three years, which Angus, and other Commissioners from Scotland, had entered into with Commissioners from England, at Berwick, 10th October 1525, to commence in the middle of January ensuing.   He was, however, forced by the Earl of Angus to compound with Lord Dacre, the English Warden, for the damages inflicted.[2]

When, to escape from the power of the Douglases, King James, in the beginning of July 1528, fled from Falkland to the Castle of Stirling, Lord Maxwell was one of the members of the Council which the King held there soon after his arrival at Stirling.

On Monday, the 6th of July, when King James went from Stirling to Edinburgh, Lord Maxwell was among the Lords who accompanied him, with their servants, to the number of three hundred spears.   On Tuesday the King remained in the lodging of the Archbishop of St. Andrews.   On Thursday following proclamation was made in the King's name, that no writing, messengers, or messages, should by any person be sent to the Earl of Angus, his two brothers, or uncle, and that none belonging to any of them should be found in the town or its precincts after four o'clock afternoon, on pain of death.   In this measure Lord Maxwell took part.   He sat in Council with the King and the other Lords on the Saturday and Monday following in the upper chamber of the Tolbooth, when it was ordained that a Parliament should meet on Wednesday, the 2d of September.   Gavin Dunbar, formerly preceptor to the

---

[1] State Papers, vol. iv., Henry the Eighth, Part iv. pp. 440, 469, 488, 492-494, 502 ; vol. v. Part iv. continued, p. 107.   [2] Pinkerton's History of Scotland, vol. ii. p. 289.

King, then Archbishop of Glasgow, was appointed Chancellor of the kingdom, and Lord Maxwell was made Provost of Edinburgh.[1] Lord Maxwell
was now associated with Queen Margaret, Henry Stewart, by this time
her husband, the Laird of Buccleuch and Sir James Hamilton, natural
son of the Earl of Arran, as the chief counsellors of the young King.[2]

While the Court made this temporary stay at Edinburgh, the Lords with
their attendants guarded the royal palace during the night from fear of the
Earl of Angus and his party. The King himself headed the guard for one
night, equipped in complete armour. On Tuesday, 14th July, he returned to
Stirling, and the Lords retired to their respective mansions, leaving Edinburgh,
as Lord Dacre says, and the country adjacent in disorder.[3]

Lord Maxwell now took active measures against Angus, from whom King
James had become wholly alienated. Roger Lascelles, steward to the Earl
of Northumberland, in a letter to his master, dated at Alnwick, 29th August
[1528], thus writes :—" Lord Maxwell, on Wednesday last, at noon, as Archibald Douglas was at dinner at Edinburgh, suddenly came in with a small
company of men ; upon which Archibald and his men hastily fled from the
town on horseback, few or none of them having been taken but horses, and
all their friends were dispersed. Had the Lord of Buccleuch come to town,
he and Lord Maxwell would have taken it."[4]

Robert Lord Maxwell was a member of the Parliament which met on
the 2d of September 1528, at which it was resolved to attaint the Earl of
Angus. A jury of eleven persons, consisting of six ecclesiastical dignitaries
and five peers, all enemies of Angus, was appointed to try the case. Lord
Maxwell was one of them. They returned a verdict of forfeiture against
the Earl of Angus and his two brothers. The two chief articles in the
indictment were that the Earl had confederated with England, and that
he had kept the King under constraint for two years, in defiance of
the laws of Scotland. The lands of Angus were divided among the chief
courtiers. Lord Maxwell received as his share the lordships of Crawfurd-
Douglas and Drumsiar.[5]

[1] State Papers, vol. iv., King Henry the Eighth,
Part iv. p. 501.
[2] Ibid. pp. 501, 502.

[3] State Papers, vol. iv., King Henry the Eighth.
Part iv. p. 502.
[4] Ibid. p. 509.   [5] Ibid. pp. 509-513.

Both the English and Scottish Borders were at this time in a state of great confusion and disturbance ; and Lord Maxwell was charged by the English with being the chief cause of this unhappy state of matters. Lord Dacre complains that though he had met with Lord Maxwell on the 2d of September, as had been appointed by him, he could obtain from him and the assizers of Scotland no redress of the bills of England, nor of the great burning and slaughter at the mote of Liddale, parcel of the King's Highness inheritance within the Nichol Forest, done by Edward Maxwell, his Lordship's brother and the Laird of Johnston.[1] The protection which Lord Maxwell afforded to the Armstrongs and other Border marauders so greatly incensed the English Government, that they threatened to terminate the peace which existed between Scotland and England, and to prevent the renewal of it.[2]

On 16th May 1529, a Parliament was held in the Tolbooth at Edinburgh, at which Lord Maxwell, along with the Earl of Bothwell, Lord Home, the Laird of Buccleuch, Mark Ker of Fernihirst, Johnston, and other principal men on the Borders, were arrested and warded in the Castle of Edinburgh,[3] to prevent them from opposing the King, who was about to undertake an expedition into Ewisdale and Teviotdale for punishing the Border thieves, whose disorders they were said to have overlooked, if not encouraged, during the time of the Earl of Angus's usurpation of the government. Two days after, most of the prisoners were sent to other prisons. But all of them were set at liberty in the course of a few months, upon giving pledges or security for their allegiance.

On the 26th of July following, the King, with an army of 8000 men, advanced into Ewisdale, and succeeded in capturing the notorious John Armstrong,[4] who had compelled the English to pay to him black mail, and

[1] State Papers, vol. iv., King Henry the Eighth, Part iv. pp. 506, 507. [2] *Ibid.* pp. 524-526.

[3] Diurnal of Occurrents in Scotland, p. 13. Calderwood gives April 1530 as the date.—History, vol. i. p. 100.

[4] Robert Lord Maxwell had various transactions with this border marauder. Under the designation of Warden of the West Marches, he granted to him a charter in the vernacular, dated 4th August 1525, of the lands of Dalbeth, the

Scheld, Dawblane, Stabilgortoune, and others.—(Original Charter at Terregles.) Lord Maxwell made a gift to him, 2d November following, of the nonentry of the lands of Dalbeth, Langholme, etc.—(Original Gift, *ibid.*) He obtained from Armstrong a bond of manrent, dated also 2d November, for the non-entries of the lands of Dalbeth, Scheild, Dalblane, Stapilgortoun, and others.—(Original Bond of Manrent, to which his seal of arms is still appended, *ibid.*) Lord Maxwell made a gift to

had greatly molested Lord Maxwell, who had befriended him on many occasions. Armstrong and a great number of his company were hanged upon the nearest trees. To render him the more odious his captors alleged that he had promised to give the English a portion of Scottish ground adjoining their borders.[1] The execution of Armstrong created some commotion, and was the theme of a popular rhyme. In the satire of the Three Estates, Sir David Lindsay alludes to

> ". . . The cordis, baith greit and lang,
> Quhilk hangit Johnie Armstrang."

The treatment which Lord Maxwell and many others experienced at the hands of the King about this time produced a coldness towards him on their part, and led the English statesmen to hold out hopes to Henry the Eighth of soon acquiring the Crown of Scotland.[2] Lord Maxwell, however, was soon reconciled to the King, and received the appointment of extraordinary Lord of Session, in which capacity he acted on 17th November 1533.

Before King James the Fifth set out on a voyage to France, in August 1536, to visit his affianced bride, Marie de Bourbon,—a journey which, however, resulted in his marrying Magdalene de Valois, eldest daughter of Francis the First, King of France,—he appointed a regency, consisting of the two arch-bishops and four noblemen, for the government of Scotland. Lord Maxwell was one of the number. The others were James Beton, Archbishop of St. Andrews, Gavin Dunbar, Archbishop of Glasgow, who was Chancellor, George Earl of Huntly, William Earl of Montrose, and Hugh Earl of Eglin-ton.[3] The King and his attendants set sail from Leith on the 1st of September following, and landed at Dieppe on the 10th. On the 26th of November he was contracted to Magdalene, and the marriage was celebrated in the city of Paris, the ceremony having been performed in the church of Notre Dame, on the 1st of January 1536-7. The King with his youthful Queen and their numerous train, having left France for Scotland, arrived at Leith on Whitsun-

---

him, 16th February 1525-6, of the non-entry of the lands of Mylgill and Eriswood, in the lordship of Eskdale.— (Original Gift, *ibid*.) A procuratory of resignation, by John Armstrong, in his favour, of the lands of Langholme, in the lordship of Eskdale, is dated 18th February 1528.—(Original Resignation, *ibid*.)

[1] Calderwood's History, vol. i. p. 101.

[2] State Papers, vol. iv., *ut supra*, Part iv. p. 598.

[3] The Commission of Regency, granted under the Great Seal, is dated at Stirling, 29th August 1536.—(Reg. Mag. Sig., Lib. xxvi. No. 1.) It was renewed 26th February 1536-7.—(*Ibid*. Lib. xxvi. No. 90.)

day Eve, 19th May 1537.[1] The Queen was in delicate health at the time of her marriage, and died in the Palace of Holyrood, on the 7th of July following.

Before Queen Magdalene had been dead a year, King James resolved on contracting a marriage with Mary of Lorraine, daughter to the Duke of Guise, and widow of the Duke of Longueville; and Lord Maxwell, then great Admiral of Scotland, was despatched in the year 1538, with David Beton, Bishop of Mirepoix, afterwards the celebrated Cardinal, and the Master of Glencairn, as ambassadors to France, to espouse her by proxy on his behalf. They arrived with her at Crail, on the coast of Fife, 10th January 1538, and King James having met her at St. Andrews, his second nuptials were celebrated in the Cathedral Church of that city, the Archbishop of Glasgow in great state and many of the nobility being present. On St. Margaret's Day following, the Queen made her entry into Edinburgh, attended by the whole nobility, coming in first at the West Port, and riding down the High-gate to the Abbey of Holyroodhouse.[2]

In regard to the disorders on the marches, Robert Lord Maxwell at this time, and for some years previously, conducted matters more to the satisfaction of the Commissioners of King Henry the Eighth than hitherto.[3] He had repeated friendly meetings with Sir Thomas Wharton, and the result of their united efforts was the restoration of the Borders to an unusual degree of peace and good order. Sir Thomas, in a letter to Cromwell, 26th December [1538], assures him that the West Marches of England, Scotland and Liddesdale were never, in the memory of any man living, in a more quiet condition than they then were.[4]

Affairs on the Borders being in this tranquil state, King James turned his attention to the isles and northern portions of his kingdom, where the chiefs acknowledged no law but their own will. To reduce them to submission, and

[1] Diurnal of Occurrents in Scotland, p. 21. State Papers, vol. v., King Henry the Eighth, Part iv. continued, pp. 59-61.

[2] Diurnal of Occurrents, p. 22.

[3] State Papers, vol. v., *ut supra*, pp. 9, 110, 111, 136-138, 140, 141, 157-159. Index to MSS. in Cottonian Library, Caligula, B. iii. 86, British Museum.

[4] State Papers, *ut supra*, vol. v. p. 145.

Lord Maxwell about this time appears as the opponent of the disciples of Wycliffe. Upon com-mandment of the Bishops, as we learn from a letter by Sir Thomas Wharton to Cromwell, dated 7th November [1538], he apprehended, at Dumfries, Frere Jerome, "a well learned man." Jerome was then lying in irons, about to suffer for the new opinions.—(State Papers, *ut supra*, vol. v. p. 141.) About this time also certain slanderous ballads which had been made by some of the Scots, in detraction of King Henry the Eighth, were in circulation. King Henry, greatly indignant, com-to insure the observance of the laws which prevailed in other parts of the kingdom, he determined personally to proceed against them with a strong force. It was intended that Lord Maxwell should act as Lord Admiral of Scotland on this occasion.[1] But he had incurred the resentment of Beton by not admitting him to attend the Queen from France, and by the management of this powerful ecclesiastic he was not called upon to take part in the expedition. The 29th of the month of May was the day finally fixed for the sailing of the fleet. The expedition was entirely successful. In a letter to Henry the Eighth of England, dated 29th July 1540, King James informs him, that as there was no complaint on the Borders he had visited the isles north and south to introduce justice and policy.

During this voyage King James had learned that his subjects in the seas of Orkney and Shetland were greatly molested by the fishing vessels of Holland, Flanders, and Bremen, who approached too near the shores for the exercise of their calling, and sometimes even compelled the Orcadians and Shetlanders to withdraw. In one instance these intruders had, by their guns, sunk a boat with a crew of twenty native sailors. It was necessary that something should be done for the protection of his Majesty's northern subjects. He accordingly commanded Lord Maxwell, as Admiral of Scotland, to conduct this mission. Finding the Dutch fishermen refractory, Lord Maxwell arrested one or two of their sailors on each vessel, and seizing one of their ships, in which they might be sent back to their own country, he brought them as prisoners

plained to his nephew, King James the Fifth. Lord Maxwell, in a letter to Sir Thomas Wharton, 30th January 1539, informs him that he had received command from the King of Scots to make diligent search for any " who had made ballettis or sangis in defamation and blasphemyng of his derrest unkle." On the following day the King himself wrote to Wharton that he had given such orders to Maxwell. Similar instructions were given by King James to his other officers on the Borders and throughout the kingdom.—(*Ibid*. pp. 148, 149.)

[1] Edward Aglionby, in a letter to Sir Thomas Wharton, Depute Warden of the West Marches of England, dated 4th May, year not stated, but evidently 1540, in giving an account of the preparations of the King of Scots for this undertaking, says, " The Lord Maxwell is not appoyntit. altho'

he be proclamyt admyrall of Scotland : the Master of Kylmawrys is appoyntyt vice-admirall vndre the Lord Maxwell, but as yet he hath no warnyng."— [From original in Cottonian MSS., Caligula, B. iii. No. 219.]

The office of Lord High Admiral was subsequently conferred on Patrick Earl of Bothwell, as a hereditary office. He died before the year 1556, when his son, James Earl of Bothwell, afterwards husband of Queen Mary, was served heir to him in that office.— (Original Retour in the Charter-chest of the Duke of Buccleuch.) In allusion to this office of Admiral, the shield of arms of James Earl of Bothwell was placed upon an anchor. A volume impressed on the side with his arms in that form, is in the library at Alnwick Castle, and another volume, similarly stamped, belongs to Mr. James Gibson-Craig, Edinburgh.

to Leith. By the Privy Council they were forbidden henceforth, under the pain of being severely punished, to invade the rights of the Orkney fishermen, and letters were despatched to the several States of Holland, intimating that it was the determination of the King of Scotland to protect his subjects in these northern parts from injustice and violence. Upon this they were dismissed and sent out of the kingdom in their own vessel.[1]

King James having been persuaded by the Bishops to refuse to meet his uncle at York in September 1541, Henry, after remaining there for several days, returned to London in great indignation, and in the following year raised an army 40,000 strong to invade Scotland, under the command of the Duke of Norfolk. This army did not enter the east borders of Scotland till the 21st of October 1542, a season of the year too far advanced for a campaign, and Norfolk, after a few days, was obliged to return to England. By this time King James had collected an army of about 30,000 men, which he assembled at the Borough Moor, on the south side of Edinburgh, and led them to Fala, fifteen miles from Edinburgh, on the road to Kelso.

Robert Lord Maxwell was in the army with a large body of his retainers; and when many of the other nobles declined to pursue the Duke of Norfolk, which the King, encouraged by the Bishops, greatly desired to do, Lord Maxwell offered to accompany him. The King, however, disbanded his army and returned to Edinburgh.

After this the King wrote to Lord Maxwell, Warden of the Western Marches, upon the subject of raising a new army to invade England upon the west coast. Chiefly by the exertions of the Warden an army of 10,000 men assembled on the Borders, led by him and others of the nobility. The King was, according to some historians, at the Castle of Lochmaben, according to others at Carlaverock, anxiously waiting the result of the invasion, when there occurred one of those unhappy divisions so frequent in Scottish history, and so natural in an army constituted as this was. Calderwood asserts that Lord Maxwell would probably have achieved some great exploit, if the King, offended at the nobility, had not given a private warrant and power of lieutenantry to his minion Oliver Sinclair, who was the third son of Sir Oliver Sinclair, to be produced at the point of joining battle, that if the war succeeded, the glory

[1] Pinkerton's History, vol. ii. p. 367.

and honour of it might not redound to the nobility.[1] The reading of the Royal Commission in presence of the army, appointing this favourite to the office of Commander-in-Chief, produced so great dissatisfaction among many of the nobility, that they declared they would not serve under him. " Thare was present," says Knox, " the Lord Maxwaill, Wardane, to whome the regiment of things in absence of the King propirlie apperteaned. He heard and saw all, butt thought more than he spak."[2] Other historians represent Lord Maxwell as having endeavoured, but without effect, to mollify the discontented nobles.[3] "The Lord Maxwell," says Knox, "perceaving what wold be the end of such begynnynges, stood upoun his foote with his freandis, who being admonissed to tack his horse and provide for himself, ansured, 'Nay, I will rather abyd hear the chance that it shall please God to send me, then to go home and thare be hanged.'"[4]

In this state of matters the whole army of the Scots fell into a state of confusion. Dacre and Musgrave, two English officers, advanced with 300 cavalry to reconnoitre the enemy, and discovering their disorganization, attacked them at once. The Scottish army, seized with panic, fled without offering resistance. Men, horses, artillery, and baggage were confusedly driven into the Solway marshes. Many of the Scots surrendered themselves to the English. A thousand of them were made prisoners, among whom was Lord Maxwell, taken by Edward Aglionby or George Foster. Others of the prisoners were the Earls of Cassillis and Glencairn, the Lords Somerville, Gray, Oliphant, and Fleming. The news of the disaster at Solway Moss, which took place on the 25th of November 1542, when brought to the King, gave a shock to his mind and frame from which he never recovered. With a spirit crushed and frenzied, he ever and anon was uttering exclamations over the flight and capture of his favourite Oliver, whose image was ever present to fancy. The tidings of the birth of his daughter, afterwards Queen Mary, shortly before his death, only intensified his agony, and he cried out bitterly—his thoughts recurring to the origin of the Royal House of Stewart, and regarding the birth of a female as a prognostication of its end—"It came with a lass, and it will go with a lass." These were the last words he uttered

[1] Calderwood's History, vol. i. p. 148.
[2] Knox's History, vol. i. p. 86.
[3] Tytler's History of Scotland, vol. iv. p. 26.
[4] Knox's History, vol. i. p. 87.

before death came to his relief, on the 14th of December, not three weeks after the fatal event which broke his spirit.

According to the orders of the English Council, on 4th December, to Sir Thomas Wharton, Lord Maxwell and twenty-four others of the chief of the Scottish prisoners were carried to London,[1] where they arrived on 19th December, wearing by King Henry's orders a red St. Andrew's cross, and were at once committed to the Tower.

On the 21st of the same month the captive nobles were conducted by Sir John Gage, Constable of the Tower, riding before them, and the lieutenant behind them, two by two, in new gowns of black damask, furred with black conies, coats of black velvet, and doublets of satin, to the Star Chamber, where Thomas Lord Audley, the Chancellor, reprimanded them, in the King's name, for the late invasion of his kingdom. He at the same time assured them that his Majesty was ready to treat them with clemency; and on receiving from them promises that they would remain true prisoners, the King ordered that they should not again be committed to the Tower, but be sent to the houses of various of the English ecclesiastics and nobility. Lord Maxwell was appointed to remain with Sir Anthony Brown.[2]

When tidings arrived of the death of the King of Scots, and of the birth of his daughter, the Princess Mary, only a few days before, Henry at once formed the design of marrying his son Edward, Prince of Wales, a child of not much more than five years of age, to the infant Princess, and of subduing Scotland to the power of England. He encouraged the Scottish prisoners in the hope of their being speedily liberated, and allowed to return to their own country upon certain conditions. He gave orders that they should attend him at Court on the 26th of the same month, when he communicated to them his intention, not limiting his demands to the proposed matrimonial alliance. He required the prisoners, by a written bond, which they were to subscribe and confirm by their oath, to acknowledge him as Lord Superior of the kingdom of Scotland, to do their utmost to put the government

[1] Haynes's State Papers, vol. i. p. 6.

[2] Calderwood's History, vol. i. p. 153. In a document giving the yearly value of the lands, and also the value and substance in goods of the Scottish prisoners lately taken at Solway Moss, is the following:—"The Lord Maxwell in landes, per annum, 4000 merks Scottisshe, which is sterling 1000 merkes, and in goodes 2000 £ Scottishe, which is sterling 500 £."—State Papers, vol. v., King Henry the Eighth, Part iv. continued, p. 233.

of the kingdom and its strongholds into his hands, and to have the infant Princess delivered to him and brought up in England. Should his demands be refused by the Scottish Parliament, they were to assist him, with all the forces at their command, in the conquest of Scotland. They were also to leave their eldest sons, or nearest relatives, as hostages for their fidelity on their obtaining their liberty. In the event of their failing to accomplish Henry's designs, they were to return to their prisons in England, on his requiring them to do so, or, if he preferred, to remain in Scotland and assist him in the war.[1]

Such is the import of the humiliating bond which Lord Maxwell and his fellow-prisoners subscribed and confirmed by their oaths in order to regain their liberty.

They commenced their journey from England to Scotland on the 1st of January 1542-3. On their way they dined at Enfield, and there saw Prince Edward. Lord Maxwell, the Earls of Cassillis and Glencairn, and Lord Fleming delivered their pledges at Carlisle to Lord Cumberland and Sir Thomas Wharton on 19th January, and the pledges were to be committed each to a certain nobleman or gentleman. Lord Maxwell's pledge, who was his eldest son, Robert Master of Maxwell, was to be committed to Sir Thomas Wharton, and his brother, Henry Maxwell, to Sir John Lamplitu.[2] In addition, Lord Maxwell was to pay 1000 merks sterling as his ransom, which was fixed at this sum on the suit of the Scottish ambassadors.[3]

Lord Maxwell and the others left Carlisle for Scotland, on the 20th of January, and arrived at Edinburgh soon after.[4] The Earl of Angus and Sir George Douglas, his brother, had left ten days before them, to introduce into the Scottish Council the projected marriage alliance between Edward Prince of England and the Princess Mary. On the arrival of the other Lords, a Council was held, on the 27th of January, by the Governor, James Earl of Arran, who being, next to the Queen, nearest heir to the Crown, was elevated to that dignity 10th January 1542-3.[5] Arran was favourable to the proposed marriage and peace, and it was agreed by the Council that a Parliament should

---

[1] Sadler's State Papers, vol. i. p. 97.
[2] State Papers, vol. v., King Henry the Eighth, Part iv. continued, pp. 234, 235, 244.
[3] Rymer's Fœdera, tom. iv. p. 797.

[4] State Papers, ut supra, vol. v. p. 244.
[5] On the 14th of the following month, February 1542-3, Robert Lord Maxwell obtained for himself, Robert Master of Maxwell, and John Maxwell, his

be called on the 12th of March, for coming to some definite conclusion on these questions.[1]

The returned prisoners, acting with great caution, were careful to conceal the ulterior designs of Henry, the knowledge of which would have caused a universal burst of indignation.[2]

During Lord Maxwell's captivity in England, many of the Scottish prisoners, who, like him, were in close communication with England, openly professed the Reformed opinions, which, however, are seldom alluded to in their secret correspondence with Henry.   Among these were the Earls of Cassillis, Glencairn, and Marishall; Lords Somerville and Crichton, the Laird of Brunston, Cockburn of Ormiston, Sandilands of Calder, and Douglas of Longniddry.[3]

In the first Parliament of Queen Mary, which met at Edinburgh on 13th March 1542-3, Lord Maxwell, who was one of the Privy Council, was present; and though there is no evidence that he embraced the new faith, he introduced the following very important bill to secure liberty to all the lieges to have and to read the Holy Scriptures in the vernacular tongue:—

" Anent the writting gevine in be Robert Lord Maxwell, in presens of my Lord Governour and Lordis of Artiklis, to be avisit be thaim gif the samen be reasonable or not, of the quhilk the tenor followis :—It is statute and ordanit that it salbe lefull to all our souirane Ladyis liegis to haif the Haly Writ, baith the New Testament and the Auld, in the vulgar toung in Inglis or Scottis, of ane gude and trew translatioun, and that thai sall incur na crimes for the hefing or reding of the samin, prouiding alvayis that na man despute or hald oppunzeonis vnder the pains contenit in the Actis of Parliament.   The Lordis of the Artiklis beand avisit with the said writting, findis the samin resonable, and thairfor thingis that the samin may be vsit amangis all the liegis of this realme, in our vulgar toung, of ane gude, trew, and just translatioun, becaus thair was na law schewin nor producit in the contrar.   And that nane of our said sourane Ladyis liegis incurr any crimes for haifing or reding of the samyn, in forme as said is, nor salbe accusit in tyme to cum; and that na personis despute, argoune, or hald oppvnionis of the samin, vnder the saidis panis contenit in the forsaidis Actis of Parliament."[4]

second son, and the longest liver of them, from Queen Mary, with the advice and consent of her tutor, James Earl of Arran, Protector and Governor of the realm, a lease of the office of captain and keeper of the Castle of Lochmaben, for the space of nineteen years from the date of these letters.   This lease was made in consideration of "the good, true, and thankful service done to her Majesty's deceased father by her cousin Robert Lord Maxwell and Robert Master of Maxwell, his son and apparent heir."   It is also stated in the preamble that the same persons had in assedation of the late King, the office of captain and keeper of the Castle of Lochmaben for nineteen years, of which divers years were yet to run.—(Original Lease at Terregles.)

[1] Keith's History, vol. i. p. 67.

[2] *Ibid.* p. 67; Tytler's History, vol. iv. pp. 268, 274, 276, 278.

[3] Tytler's History of Scotland, vol. iv. p. 355.

[4] Original Acts of Parliament, MS., H.M. General Register House, Edinburgh; Printed Acts, vol. ii. p. 415.

The measure was approved by the Earl of Arran, Governor of the Kingdom. Beton, who would have been one of the fiercest and most influential opponents of the bill, was in prison, and in his absence it was unsuccessfully opposed by Gavin Dunbar, Archbishop of Glasgow. The bill was carried, and was read and proclaimed as law at the Market Cross of Edinburgh.

The state of parties in Scotland at this time, as described by **King Henry the Eighth**, in a letter to Sadler, his ambassador in Scotland, 14th April 1543, may throw some light on the passing of this Act in regard to the Scriptures. He says that there were now two parties in Scotland, 1st, the French party, consisting of the Earls of Argyll, Murray, Huntly, and Bothwell, with all the bishops and clergy of the realm, and their partakers; and 2dly, the English party, consisting of the Earls of Angus, Glencairn, Cassillis, and Lord Maxwell, with their friends.[1] The latter party secured the passing of the Act.

"The Clargy," says John Knox, "hearto long repugned; butt in the end, convicted by reassonis and by multitud of votes in thar contrare, thei also condiscended, and so by Act of Parliament it was maid free to all man and woman to reid the Scriptures in thair awin toung, or in the Engliss toung: and so war all actes maid in the contrair abolished. . . . Then mycht have bene sein the Bybile lying almaist upoun everie gentilmanis table. The New Testament was borne about in many manis handes. We grant that some (alace!) prophaned that blessed wourd; for some that, perchance, had never it maist common in thare hand; thei wold chope thare familiares on the cheak with it, and say, 'This hes lyne hyd under my bed-feitt these ten yearis.' Otheris wold glorie, 'O! how oft have I bein in danger for this booke: How secreatlie have I stollen fra my wyff at mydnycht to reid upoun it.'"[2]

Early in the year 1543, Sadler had conferences with Lord Maxwell, the Earls of Angus, Glencairn, and Cassillis, and Lord Somerville, as to certain articles, to which the King of England was prepared to exact agreement by force. The chief of these were the marriage between Edward Prince of England and the infant Queen of Scots; her deliverance before she was ten years of age, at most, to be detained where the English King should judge most con-

---

[1] State Papers, *ut supra*, vol. v. p. 272.   [2] Knox's History, vol. i. pp. 100, 101.

venient for her safety and health ; the making of a perpetual peace between England and Scotland ; and the renunciation of the amity with France. Three earls, three bishops, and two barons, to be changed every six months, should they desire it, were to be given as pledges to England for the performance of these articles.

Sadler was instructed at the same time to require these Lords to do what they could to induce the Governor and the rest to agree to them ; to have a constant watch that the young Queen should not be removed from Linlithgow ; to order all their proceedings so that they might be masters of Edinburgh and Leith ; and to do their utmost that the Governor should not abandon their party. They were also to endeavour to get some of their trustworthy friends into the strongholds, thereby to facilitate the surrendering of them on the arrival of the English forces ; and to obtain for the English as many friends as they could, specially men of honour and good estimation.[1] They were promised a sufficient supply of English money.

Lord Maxwell also subscribed an engagement, called a " secret device," in reference to which Sadler, in a letter to the King, 17th July 1543, thus writes : " The Earl of Angus hath subscribed the articles of the device which your Majesty sent unto me with your last letters ; and the Lord Maxwell told him that as soon as he received the like articles from his Majesty, by his son, he forthwith subscribed them, and sent them to his Majesty."[2] The effect of this arrangement was similar to the articles just mentioned.

The feeling between the two parties into which the Scottish nobles were at this time divided was very acrimonious. Sadler, in a letter to Sir William Parr, thus writes from Edinburgh, 20th July [1543]: " Surelie here is greate apparence of moche myschief and rebellion, for greate preparacion is on bothe parties: the Cardinal, the Erles of Argile, Lenoux, Huntley, with their freendes of oone partie ; and the Governour, the Erles of Anguyshe, Casselles, the Lorde Maxwell, and their freendes of the other partie. What woolbe the ende I cannot yet tell ; but if I shulde saye myn owne phantasye, I thinke surelie when all is doone, they wyll not fyght for all their bragges."[3]

Lord Maxwell and Lord Somerville were the principal agents of

---

[1] State Papers, *ut supra*, vol. v. pp. 280, 284.

[2] Sadler's State Papers, vol. i. p. 237.

[3] State Papers, *ut supra*, p. 322.

Angus in conducting the intrigues for furthering Henry's projects against the independence of Scotland. On 31st October 1543 these noblemen, who were sent as ambassadors to the Earls of Cassillis and Glencairn with letters into England, were taken on their journey by the Abbot of Paisley. Lord Maxwell was imprisoned in the Castle of Edinburgh and Lord Somerville in the Castle of Blackness.[1] Upon the person of Somerville was found a band signed at Douglas Castle, the residence of the Earl of Angus, in Lanarkshire, and letters, which showed their complicity in Henry's plans. It was resolved by the Governor and Cardinal Beton that a Parliament should be summoned to meet early in December, and that its first business should be the impeachment and forfeiture of Angus and his adherents. The Parliament assembled. A summons of treason was prepared against the Earl of Angus and those of his party who had signed the band in Douglas Castle. The contract between England and Scotland concerning the marriage of Prince Edward with the infant Queen Mary was also declared to be null and void, in consequence of the conduct of the English, who had broken the peace by seizing, burning, and plundering Scottish ships.[2]

In the beginning of the year 1544,—when the state of parties in Scotland had somewhat changed, the Earl of Lennox having gone over to the English party, and Arran, the Governor, to the French,—Lord Maxwell was with the Earl of Lennox, who then held the Castle of Glasgow. On the 1st of April that year the Governor, Cardinal Beton, the Earls of Argyll, Bothwell, and many other Lords, convened by open proclamation at Glasgow, laid siege to the Castle and Steeple of Glasgow ; and after great slaughter the castle was surrendered by the Earl of Lennox. By the orders of the Governor eighteen men were hanged as traitors ; and Lord Maxwell, the Earl of Angus, James of Parkheid and James of the Water were taken, brought to Hamilton, and there imprisoned.[3] But circumstances led to their speedy liberation. Henry the Eighth, from his exasperation at the Parliament of Scotland, which had annulled the treaties then existing between Scotland and England, despatched a force of 10,000 men, embarked on board a navy of 200 ships, which made its appearance in the Firth of Forth on Saturday, 3d May 1544, and

---

[1] Diurnal of Occurrents in Scotland, p. 29.
[2] *Ibid.* p. 30 ; Tytler's History of Scotland, vol. iv. pp. 308, 309.   [3] *Ibid.* p. 31.

landed the army a little above Leith. To resist this invasion, the Governor, and others of the nobility adhering to the French party, did all in their power to collect an army; and that the differences between conflicting parties might be composed in this perilous conjuncture, Lord Maxwell and the others already named were released.[1] Lord Maxwell's commission as Warden of the West Marches had been renewed after the death of King James the Fifth, and after his release on this occasion he received another royal commission of the same office, dated 19th December 1544,[2] with a view probably to his putting the Borders under his charge in a state of defence.

This appointment, and Lord Maxwell's conduct generally, excited the suspicions of the English Government. They were not satisfied with the manner in which he had fulfilled his engagements, and doubts of his sincerity had been frequently expressed in the letters of the English ambassadors. He had offered to meet Wharton as prisoner, and Hertford had instructed Wharton to prevail upon him to do so. In a letter to King Henry, dated 8th March 1543-4, Hertford writes, "Sir John Penvan, your Majestie's chapleyn, sayeth that they [your Majesties frendes in Scotland] desyre that it may please your Majestie to call in your prysoners to theyr entrie, such as be not assured to your Highnes, as the Lordes Maxwell, whom the said Penvan can in no wyse commende, and Flemyng and the Master of Erskyn."[3] Hertford, in a letter to King Henry the Eighth, without date, but written in the year 1544, says that the servant of the Earl of Angus alleged that the Earl was abused by Lord Maxwell; and further, that the Earl of Glencairn and others told him that it was very likely that the Earl of Angus, who was a man of much simplicity, and easy to be seduced, had been deceived and brought into this captivity by Lord Maxwell, the Sheriff of Ayr and Drumlanrig, who, to colour their own falsehood, laid all the fault and untruth on that Earl.[4] By this time the Earl of Angus had deserted the English party, and gone over to the French, as appears by comparing the instructions given by the English Privy Council to Sir Thomas Wharton in April 1544, and those given to him in the month of May following. In the former he was to suggest to

[1] Keith's History, vol. i. pp. 115, 116.
[2] Original Commission at Terregles.
[3] *Vide* the King's Letter to Maxwell and Fleming. Haynes's State Papers, p. 18, and the Council's

Directions to Hertford, *ibid.* p. 15. State Papers, vol. v., King Henry the Eighth, Part iv. continued, p. 360.
[4] State Papers, *ut supra,* vol. v. pp. 381.

Angus and others the delivery of certain towns into the hands of the English, etc., and in the latter, these instructions, so far as regarded the Earl of Angus and Cardinal Beton, were cancelled.

Accordingly Lord Maxwell, not having fulfilled his engagements, as the English Government alleged, was recalled to England and once more lodged in the Tower. In March 1544-5 he complains to Secretary Paget, that he had been a long time in prison, and requests to be tried ; and denies that he has been unfaithful to the King since he has been a prisoner. If his son has not done the King's pleasure he shall get nothing which he can hold from him and shall have his malediction.[1]

Efforts were made by his son, Robert Master of Maxwell, the Earl of Cassillis, as well as by Lord Maxwell himself, to procure his liberty.

Robert Master of Maxwell, in a letter to the Earl of Lennox, dated at Dumfries, 23d February 1545, requested that the Earl would use his influence to procure the liberty of Lord Maxwell, his father ; and that the Earl would specify what services he could render to the King in order to accomplish that object. Lennox, in his answer from Carlisle, 25th February, advises the Master of Maxwell to obey his father's command by doing all he could to please the King of England, as the best means of procuring his father's liberty.[2] The Master of Maxwell, in a letter to the Earl of Cassillis, written at Dumfries, 24th March 1545, requests information relative to his father's imprisonment in the Tower. The Earl of Cassillis, in his reply, advises him, if he would effect his father's liberty, to aid in the accomplishment of the King's purpose.[3]

The Earl of Cassillis's advice appears to have had some effect on the Master of Maxwell. The Earl, in a letter from Edinburgh to Henry the Eighth, written 2d April 1545, informs him that the Master of Maxwell had come to Edinburgh, and said to him, before the Earl of Angus, that he would promote to the utmost of his power the King's purpose. Lord Angus and the Master of Maxwell both desired Cassillis to write to King Henry praying that his Highness would allow Lord Maxwell, who was still a prisoner in the Tower of London, to repair to the Borders with Sir Robert Bowis.[4]

[1] Calendar of State Papers relating to Scotland, 1509-1589, vol. i. p. 46, No. 5.

[2] Ibid. p. 48, Nos. 5, 6.

[3] Calendar of State Papers, Scotland, 1509-1589, vol. i. p. 49, Nos. 10, 10.1, 10.2.

[4] State Papers, vol. v., King Henry the Eighth, Part iv. continued, pp. 426, 427.

Lord Maxwell, in a letter to the Privy Council, without date but probably written in April, says that he counted himself a dead man without the King's pardon; begs his mercy; and promises that he would do him such service as no Scotsman should do the like on the West Borders.[1]   In another letter to the English Privy Council, from the Tower, probably in the same month, he says that he had previously written begging that they would intercede with the King for his pardon. He did not desire liberty, but that he might be held a prisoner at Carlisle, where he might, by communication with his friends, make some recompence for the great trespass which he had committed against his Majesty.[2]

The applications made to the Government of England for the liberation of Lord Maxwell were for a time unsuccessful. The English Privy Council, in a letter to the Earl of Cassillis, without date but probably written in 1545, after referring to the earnest desire of the Earl of Cassillis and the Earl of Angus for the coming home of Lord Maxwell, add that it was notoriously known in that realm how disloyally, and contrary to his former promises, Lord Maxwell had demeaned himself to the great hindrance of his Highness's affairs there, and that his Majesty thought that it would be prejudicial to his affairs to set him at liberty, as it would encourage similar disloyal attempts. Yet his case would be taken into consideration by his Majesty.[3]

At length Lord Maxwell was allowed an opportunity of vindicating his conduct; and, in April 1545, he made three confessions before the English Privy Council, in reply to charges arising out of the events which had taken place in Scotland whilst he had been there.

According to his first confession, the Queen and the Council of Scotland, both before and after the English army had arrived in Scotland, offered, if he would take their part against the King of England's army, and not return to England, to pay his ransom, which was a thousand marks sterling, and to give him a thousand marks from a benefice when it became vacant. He answered that he was the King of England's prisoner, and he trusted that they would not have him dishonoured. But if he went, what were they the weaker? They

[1] Calendar of State Papers, Scotland, 1509-1589, vol. i. p. 50, No. 20.

[2] Ibid. No. 21.

[3] State Papers, vol. v., King Henry the Eighth, Part iv. continued, p. 432.

might command his servants, who remained in Scotland, and were under their power, to do such service as they would have them to do; for using which words he cast himself upon the King's mercy. He had been desired by the Earl of Angus to sue the Queen for a safe-conduct, that he might plead before her for the life of his brother, who was a prisoner in the Castle of Edinburgh; and he obtained the safe-conduct for the Earl. When he and the Earl of Angus came to Glasgow, under this assurance, both of them were committed to prison in the Castle of Hamilton, where they remained five weeks, when the Earl was taken from thence and carried to the Castle of Blackness. All the three, himself, the Earl of Angus, and the Earl's brother, were delivered from prison on condition that they should raise their kin, friends, and retainers against the English army, which had at that time arrived in Scotland. But this condition they did not perform. He solemnly denied what had been laid to his charge, that he had commanded his son to seize his father's men and friends and to serve against the King's Majesty. It had been alleged against him that he had consented to the imprisonment of himself, the Earl of Angus, and that Earl's brother. This he solemnly denied. He had come to the Council of Scotland, trusting to their promise, and was taken deceitfully and against his will both the times that he was arrested, and for no cause but for his Majesty's sake. He further stated that his deliverance out of prison the first time was by the Queen's command, and the efforts made by her for him with the Council, and he was liberated without any condition whatever. As soon as he was released he came to the Earl of Hertford, whom he found casting down the Castle of Seaton, and burning the country thereabout, at his return from Edinburgh to England, which was eight miles on his way, and so they came through Lothian to the Borders.[1]

These confessions appear to have had a favourable effect, as shortly after they were made he was allowed by the English Government to go to Carlisle. The Earl of Hertford and Ralph Sadler, in a letter to Paget, dated from Newcastle, 8th June 1545, say that they had taken order for his conveyance thither. In this the object of the English Government was that Lord Maxwell, having there opportunity to practise and confer with the Earl of Angus, the animosity

---

[1] State Papers, vol. v., King Henry the Eighth, Part iv. continued, pp. 428-430.

which had arisen between the faction headed by the Cardinal, and that headed by the Earl of Angus and George Douglas might be intensified.[1]

The Castles of Carlaverock, Lochmaben, and Threave—places of great strength and importance—were part of the possessions of Lord Maxwell. To acquire these strongholds, and to garrison them with English soldiers, was considered essential to the execution of Henry's plan for the invasion of the west of Scotland by Lennox and the Lord of the Isles. At one time promises, and at another threats, were used to induce Lord Maxwell to surrender these castles, and aid the English against the Scots. Unwilling to act against his country, and yet extremely desirous to obtain his liberty, his conduct became inconsistent and vacillating.

The Scottish Government were quite alive to the importance of holding these castles, in order to successfully oppose an attack on their country. Accordingly, whilst Lord Maxwell remained at Carlisle a prisoner of the English, they made Robert Master of Maxwell, his son, become bound in June 1545 to keep these houses for the Queen, from their enemies of England, until Robert Lord Maxwell proved, before the Lords of Council, his innocence of conspiring with the English against his country.[2]

Various particulars regarding the imprisonment of Lord Maxwell at Carlisle at this time have been preserved, and here they may be briefly noticed. Lord Maxwell, in a letter to Lord Hertford, in June 1545, after having informed him of his son's proceedings, prayed him to beseech King Henry that he might be permitted to return to Scotland, and remain there for one month for the transaction of various matters of business with his friends. He thought that his detention at Carlisle, without more liberty, could not be so much to the advantage of the King of England's affairs as he desired. Lord Hertford, in his reply—after expressing his disapprobation of the conduct of Lord Maxwell's son, the Master, who so much forgat his natural duty towards his father as to refuse to come and speak with him upon a safe-conduct—declines to interfere in regard to Lord Maxwell's desire, that the English King should allow him to enter into Scotland, and advises him against making such a suit to the English monarch, as his doings when in

---

[1] State Papers, vol. v., King Henry the Eighth, Part iv. continued, p. 457.

[2] Regist. Secreti Concilii, Acta 1545, fol. 11, MS. in H.M. General Register House, Edinburgh.

Scotland towards his Majesty had been suspected, and until some better fruit of his service should be manifest than had hitherto appeared, this application might bring him into greater suspicion.[1]

Lord Wharton was required by the Earl of Hertford not to suffer any Scotsman to have private conference with Lord Maxwell for any purpose unless when himself or some person by his appointment was present.[2]

Yet Lord Hertford, Cuthbert, Bishop of Durham, and Ralph Sadler, thought[3] that although little was likely to be done by Lord Maxwell for the advancement of his Majesty's affairs, he might be allowed to remain for some time at Carlisle, where he was safe enough, as his presence there might serve to continue or to increase the suspicion which seemed to have arisen between the Governor, the Cardinal, and their party, and that of the Earl of Angus and others who were Lord Maxwell's friends.

The Master of Maxwell, in a letter to his father, offered to be pledge in England for his relief.[4] But he was not over hasty to perform this promise. Hertford, complaining of this, intended to send him a safe-conduct to repair to Carlisle, in order to his remaining within the realm of England as a pledge for his father, and to send Lord Maxwell back to the Tower, if the King did not countermand his orders to that effect previously given.[5] But the Master of Maxwell, though Hertford had sent him a safe-conduct, would not go to Carlisle to remain in pledge for his father. Hertford, therefore, purposed to send Lord Maxwell, who was then with him at New-castle, to the Tower of London, whither he should take his journey on the morrow under the conduct of William Brakenburye, that brought hither the King's treasure.[6]

Understanding that he was again to be sent a prisoner to the Tower, so great was the perplexity and heaviness of Lord Maxwell that he could

[1] State Papers, vol. v., King Henry the Eighth, Part iv. continued, pp. 460, 461.

[2] Letter of Hertford, dated 21st June 1545, to Paget, ibid. p. 462.

[3] Their Letter to King Henry the Eighth, dated 27th June 1545, ibid. p. 463.

[4] Communicated by the Earl of Hertford, Cuthbert, Bishop of Durham, and Ralph Sadler to Paget with a letter of their own, dated 4th July 1545, in State Papers, vol. v., King Henry the Eighth, Part iv. continued, p. 469.

[5] Letter of Hertford to Secretary Paget, written from Darlington, 19th July 1545, in State Papers, vol. v., King Henry the Eighth, Part iv. continued, p. 472.

[6] Letter of Hertford to Secretary Paget, dated at Newcastle, 27th July 1545.—(Ibid. p. 476.)

neither eat, drink, nor sleep.   He requested that he might be allowed to serve in the wars of England, wearing the red cross on his coat, as an English soldier, in which case he would prove himself to be a true Englishman ; or, if Hertford mistrusted him, that he might be imprisoned in the town of New-castle, or appointed to remain there or somewhere else in the country till Hertford should further know his Majesty's pleasure.   Hertford, finding that Lord Maxwell took this matter so much to heart, appointed him to go to York, and to remain there, in the meantime, with the Archbishop of York.   With this Lord Maxwell was satisfied ; and he departed thither the day before the date of Hertford's letter.[1]   His Majesty was pleased to stay his return to the Tower of London, and willed that he should be sent to Pomfret Castle, where he was to remain a prisoner until his Highness should otherwise determine.[2]

It did not fare well with the Master of Maxwell.   He was taken prisoner, with divers others, as Hertford informs Henry the Eighth, in a letter written from Warkeshaugh, 19th September 1545.[3]

Now that both Lord Maxwell and his eldest son were their prisoners, the English had the greater hopes that his castles would be surrendered to them. In reference to this matter, Robert, Master of Maxwell, desired that his father, Lord Maxwell, and he might be allowed to confer together with Hertford for some order to be taken for the safe custody, for his Majesty's use, of the houses of strength which they had in the West Marches of Scotland.[4]   The conference referred to took place, and the Earl of Hertford, in a letter to King Henry the Eighth, dated Newcastle, 1st October 1545, gives the particulars.   Both Lord Maxwell and his son seemed willing to deliver these strongholds into his Majesty's hands.   At the same time Lord Maxwell was urgent to be allowed to return to Scotland.   The Earl of Hertford dissuaded him from making a suit to that effect to the King until the houses should be surrendered, or until his fidelity and zeal to his Majesty should be more apparent than hitherto, as he had told him before, alleging that the houses, being in the possession of his

[1] Letter of the Earl of Hertford to Paget, dated Newcastle, 29th July 1545, in State Papers, vol. v., King Henry the Eighth, Part iv. continued, p. 479.

[2] Ibid. p. 488.

[3] Calendar of State Papers, Scotland, 1509-1589, vol. i. p. 56, No. 84.

[4] Letter of the Earl of Hertford to King Henry the Eighth, written from Newcastle, 27th September 1545, in State Papers, vol. v., King Henry the Eighth, Part iv. continued, p. 533.

son, friends and servants might be as well delivered by his command as if he went home.   This Lord Maxwell admitted, but not having much confidence in his second son, a young man, who held the Castle of Lochmaben, he would not undertake or promise that it would certainly be delivered unless he went personally to deliver it.   But he would pledge even his life that a cousin of his, then in England, named John Maxwell,[1] who was taken a prisoner with his son Robert Master of Maxwell, and was then in possession of the house of Lochmaben, would deliver it to whomsoever he would appoint for the King's behoof.[2]   John Maxwell was sent for to Carlisle, and he came the day before the date of Hertford's letter to Newcastle.   A plan was formed for his obtaining the Castle of Lochmaben out of the hands of John Maxwell, second son of Lord Maxwell, but it failed of success.   The second son here mentioned was afterwards the famous Lord Herries.

No practical result having followed, Hertford was doubtful of Lord Maxwell's sincerity in promising to deliver his castles to the English.   In a letter to Paget from Newcastle, 5th October 1545, he says that Lord Maxwell's offers to deliver his houses to the King were but practices, and came to nothing; and that his second son, John Maxwell, who had possession of them, would neither leave them nor enter himself for his father's relief.   Both Lord Maxwell and Robert, his eldest son, who were then at Newcastle, now said that they well knew that John, the second son, would not become pledge for his father, although at first they expressed no difficulty on that point; and that the only way for the King's obtaining possession of the houses was to send home Lord Maxwell, who, being in Scotland, would be able both to deliver them into his Majesty's hands and to draw the whole country to his obedience.   Hertford intended to send Lord Maxwell again to Pomfret, to remain there till the King's pleasure should be known; and to send Robert Maxwell up to the Court, as his Majesty had lately desired.[3]

Lord Maxwell's eagerness to regain his liberty appears to have increased as the chances of it diminished.   He urged on Hertford, that although the Castle of Lochmaben could not indeed be had presently, because his second

[1] John Maxwell of Cowhill.

[2] State Papers, vol. v., King Henry the Eighth, Part iv. continued, pp. 535-537.

[3] State Papers, vol. v., King Henry the Eighth, Part iv. continued, pp. 539-541.

son had it, and would neither become a pledge for his father's relief nor deliver it by his appointment, yet the house of Carlaverock, being his own by inheritance, and at that time in the keeping of a priest, who was his kinsman, might, he doubted not, be delivered into the hands of the English by that priest, at his command. This fortress, Lord Maxwell said, was stronger than Lochmaben, and a better place for a garrison.[1]

At a conference with Hertford, the Bishop of Durham, Sadler, and Lord Wharton,[2] as to how the latter castle might be surrendered, Lord Maxwell said that were he allowed to go to Carlisle with Lord Wharton, and should the priest that kept for him the Castle of Carlaverock come to Carlisle at his bidding, of which he had no doubt, he would so manage the matter as to be able to deliver the house into the hands of the King. As the priest might do more for the Master of Maxwell than for his father, as Lord Maxwell himself supposed, the Master was consulted, and, professing to be equally zealous with his father in serving the King of England, he was induced to write a letter to the priest, requiring him to come immediately to Carlisle, for the discharge of his bond, as he was a prisoner, and Robert Master of Maxwell was bound for his re-entry whenever called. He also wrote another letter, to be delivered by his father to the priest on his coming to Carlisle, to the effect that he consented to his father's device of delivering the Castle of Carlaverock to the King. As soon as the priest came to Carlisle a sufficient number were to go with him immediately to Carlaverock, in the night-time, to receive the house, wherein, if he should make any difficulty or hindrance, he should incur the penalty of death.

Hertford intended to despatch Robert Master of Maxwell from Newcastle to the Court, with Mr. Knyvet and Mr. Hobbye.

In the same month of October, Lord Maxwell was at last allowed to return to Scotland; and among his first actions after his return was his surrendering to the English, on 24th October 1545, the Castle of Carlaverock, "quhilk was a great discomfort to the countrie."[5]

[1] Letter of Lord Hertford to the English Privy Council, dated at Newcastle, 7th October 1545, in State Papers, vol. v., King Henry the Eighth, Part iv. continued, pp. 543, 544.

[2] Letter of Hertford to Paget, written from Newcastle, 11th October 1545, in State Papers, vol. v., King Henry the Eighth, Part iv. continued, pp. 545, 546.

[5] Diurnal of Occurrents in Scotland, p. 41.

But the Government of Scotland were not disposed to allow the English to remain in possession of such an important fortress. Wharton, in a letter to King Henry the Eighth, dated 28th October 1545, informs his Majesty that since his last, of the 25th, a great watch had been kept at his Highness's Castle of Carlaverock, with the Lairds Johnston, Drumlanrig, Lochinvar, and others, and the countrymen of Nithsdale, Galloway and Annandale; and he advertises his Highness that Thomas Carlton, and the others in Carlaverock, showed themselves most active in the defence of that house, and that on the day of the date of that letter he was informed that the Maxwells had begun to repent of what they had done. He was hopeful that the English would gain the Castle of Lochmaben, as they had done that of Carlaverock, if things were ordered hastily, and the Lord Maxwell was anything true.[1]

On the 21st of November, the Governor and other Lords assembled at Dumfries, and laid siege to the Castles of Lochmaben and Threave, which were in Lord Maxwell's possession, and were held by his sons. Two or three days after, these castles were surrendered. Lord Maxwell was taken prisoner and carried to Dumfries, as a traitor, with certain of his English confederates. The Laird of Lochinvar[2] was made captain of Lochmaben, and the Laird of Garlies captain of the Threave. The Earl of Angus came not to the raid, because Lord Maxwell was his father-in-law.

Lord Maxwell had now to conciliate the Government of Scotland, to which, by the treasonable bond he had entered into with the English, he had made himself obnoxious; and for this purpose he made a solemn protestation in his new house of Dumfries for his exculpation, dated 28th November 1545. In the presence of a public notary and witnesses he declared that, when a prisoner in England, under the power of King Henry, he had, from fear and danger of his life, and from no other motive, consented that the Castle of Carlaverock should be delivered into the hands of officers commissioned by that monarch, and had bound himself to him by other obligations, by word and writing, against the authority of law and the will of his most gracious Princess the Queen of Scotland, for which he had obtained writings and

---

[1] State Papers, vol. v., King Henry the Eighth, Part iv. continued, p. 552.

[2] Lochinvar and Johnston were the greatest enemies of Lord Maxwell in the west of Scotland, as Wharton states in a letter to the King, 30th October 1545. Their enmity arose from their wish to supplant Maxwell in the offices he held in Galloway and Annandale.

letters of the King of England, to his advantage ; and solemnly protested that whatever was thus done by him should not tend to his loss or prejudice in the future, since immediately on his arrival in his native kingdom of Scotland, after being delivered from captivity, he had revoked and renounced all such obligations, wishing that henceforth they should have no effect; promising that he would live and die a faithful and an obedient subject to her Highness and to the Protector and Governor of her kingdom.[1]

Having made this protest, he received from Queen Mary, with consent of her tutor, James Earl of Arran, and the Lords of her Privy Council, a remission, dated at Linlithgow, 12th January 1545-6, for his intercommuning with the English at the time of their burning Leith, and for delivering to them the Castles of Carlaverock and Lochmaben while he was their prisoner in England.[2]

Lord Maxwell was too powerful, and his influence in Scotland, particularly on the Borders, was too great to allow of his being unemployed by the Government. He obtained from Queen Mary a commission as Chief-Justice of Annandale, Kirkcudbright, Wigtoun, and Dumfries, dated at Linlithgow, 12th January 1545-6.[3]

He was also reappointed to his old office of Warden of the West Marches by a commission from Queen Mary, dated at Perth, 3d June 1546 ; and on the 11th of the same month, at Stirling, in presence of the Queen, the Lord Governor, and the Lords of Council, he declared that, having now been reinvested with the office of Warden of the West Marches of Scotland, he could not well execute that office unless he was again put in possession of the Queen's house of Lochmaben. It was accordingly delivered to him, and he engaged to keep it from the English, and from all others, to be forthcoming to the Queen, the Lord Governor, and the Government, upon his life and heritage. Should he be charged to enter again into England, he was to give the Lord Governor a warning of fifteen days to receive that house, and was to deliver it to him or to whomsoever he should appoint ; and should a great English army come upon him, which he could not effectively resist, he was to give to the Lord Governor premonition to receive Lochmaben, and deliver

[1] Original Instrument at Terregles.
[2] Original Remission, *ibid.*
[3] Original Commission at Terregles.

it to him. Should he be pleased to cease from keeping that house, he was to advertise the Lord Governor of his intention fifteen days previously, and to deliver it to him. Lord Maxwell's cautioners for his fulfilling this agreement were Archibald Earl of Angus, Gilbert Earl of Cassillis, Malcolm Lord Fleming, and James Douglas of Drumlanrig, who bound themselves, conjunctly and severally, under the pain of £22.[1]

On the same day Lord Maxwell, along with other Lords, Archibald Earl of Angus, Gilbert Earl of Cassillis, and Sir George Douglas, in presence of the Queen, the Lord Governor, and Lords of Privy Council, ratified and approved the Act of Parliament made in December 1543, for the dissolution of the peace that had been made between England and Scotland, and of the contract of marriage between Prince Edward of England and Mary Queen of Scots; and annulled all the bonds by which they had bound themselves to the King of England.[2]

The troubles through which Robert Lord Maxwell had passed had worn him out. He did not long survive his renewed prosperity, having died within a month of his recovering the Castle of Lochmaben.

Lord Maxwell received many tokens of royal favour. By a commission granted by King James the Fifth, with consent of the Regent Albany, dated 7th October 1522, Lord Maxwell was appointed Keeper of the Castle of Lochmaben for nineteen years. The grant bears that Lord Maxwell was then in possession of the castle of Lochmaben by a previous grant under the Great Seal.[3] By another commission, dated 18th August 1524, he was made provost of Edinburgh in the room of Mr. Francis Bothwell, who was deprived of that office.[4] As provost of Edinburgh, Lord Maxwell was elected one of the Lords of the Articles for the Commissioners of Burghs, a rare, if not the only, instance of a nobleman having been so elected. Lord Maxwell was constituted warden of the West Marches[5] by King James the Fifth, by a commission dated 28th January 1525. On the same day a lease was granted to him by the King, with consent of the Lords of Secret

---

[1] Regist. Secreti Concilii, Acta 1546, fol. 31, MS., in H.M. General Register House, Edinburgh.

[2] *Ibid.* fol. 32.

[3] Original Grant at Terregles.

[4] Diurnal of Occurrents in Scotland, p. 9.

[5] Original Commission at Terregles.

Council, chosen by Parliament, for nine years, of the lands of Wauchopdale, in the lordship of Eskdale and shire of Dumfries, forfeited by John Lindsay of Wauchop.[1]   After King James the Fifth attained his lawful age he granted, on 22d June 1526, a confirmation, under the Great Seal, to Robert Lord Maxwell, of his rights of the stewardships of Annandale and Kirkcudbright, and the keeping of the castles of Lochmaben and Trief.[2]   By a commission under the Great Seal, 21st August same year, King James the Fifth appointed Lord Maxwell Master of the Royal Household for life.[3]   Lord Maxwell received from the King a charter, under the Great Seal, on 16th November 1526, of the offices of steward of Kirkcudbright and Keeper of the castle of Treif, and also of the lands of Duncow, Treif-Grange, etc., and he was infefted therein on 31st of January thereafter.[4]   He obtained a commission from the King, under the Great Seal, 4th July 1528, as chief carver to the King, or in the words of the grant, "nostrum principalem incisorem vulgo carvour nuncupatum."[5]   A royal charter was granted to him, 5th September same year, of the lands of Crawfurdmure and half of the lands and barony of Dunsyre, in the shire of Lanark, being a part of the forfeited estates of Archibald Earl of Angus.[6]

A precept of sasine, dated 1st January 1530, was granted by King James the Fifth to Robert Lord Maxwell, of the lands and barony of Crawfurdmure, the lands of Bonyntoun and Hyndfurd, in the shire of Lanark, and the lands of Halkschawis, in the shire of Peebles, forfeited by Archibald Earl of Angus.[7]

On 28th July 1534, he obtained from King James the Fifth a charter renewing and confirming the grants of the £40 lands of the barony of Maxwell, in the shire of Roxburgh; the lands and barony of Carlaverock, in the shire of Dumfries; the lands of Springkell, in the lordship of Annandale; the offices of steward of Annandale and Kirkcudbright; the lands of Carnsalloch and Dunsquhen and the superiority of the £5 lands in the burgh of Dumfries in the shire of that name; the lands and barony of Balmacreuchie, in the shire of Perth; the lands of Gordonston and Grennan, in the stewartry of Kirkcudbright; the lands and barony of Mearns, and the lands of Nether Pollok, in the shire of Renfrew; which lands were held of the King, except

[1] Original Lease at Terregles.
[2] Original Confirmation, *ibid.*
[3] Original Commission, *ibid.*
[4] Original Sasine, *ibid.*

[5] Original Commission at Terregles.
[6] Original Charter, *ibid.*
[7] Original Precept of Sasine, *ibid.*

the barony of Mearns and Nether Pollok, which were held of him as steward of Scotland. These lands, baronies, and offices belonged to Robert Lord Maxwell, and his predecessors, except the half of the lands and barony of Mearns, and the lands of Nether Pollok (which belonged to Robert, his son and apparent heir), having been formally resigned by him; and the half of the barony of Mearns, having been similarly resigned by his son Robert into the hands of the King at Falkland, were of new created, united, and erected into one free lordship and barony, to be called the LORDSHIP AND BARONY OF MAXWELL, and the CASTLE OF CARLAVEROCK was declared to be the principal messuage. This charter was granted in consideration of the long and faithful services rendered by Lord Maxwell, in the tender age of the King, who styles him "carvour."[1] A confirmation of this charter, and other royal charters, in his favour was made by the King, 19th July 1537.[2]

Lord Maxwell also obtained from King James the Fifth another charter, dated at Edinburgh, 6th June 1540, granting of new, and confirming to him, upon his resignation, the lands, lordships, baronies, and offices mentioned in the charter dated 28th July 1534, with various additions, Louthirwod being added to the barony of Carlaverock, and Natone and Logane to the lands of Spring-kell, there being also added the fourteen merk lands of Dunsire, Westoun, Todholis, and the half of the dominical lands thereof, in the shire of Lanark, the lands of Spottis, in the stewartry of Kirkcudbright, and Drippis, in the shire of Renfrew; and of new erecting the foresaid lands, lordships, offices and baronies, except the lands and barony of Mearns, Drippis, and Nether Pollok, into one entire lordship and free barony, to be called the BARONY OF MAXWELL, of which the CASTLE OF CARLAVEROCK was to be the principal messuage. This charter was granted to "our cousin" Robert Lord Maxwell, and after his decease to Robert Master of Maxwell, his son and heir-apparent, and to the heirs-male of his body; whom failing, successively to John Maxwell, his second son, and the heirs-male of his body; whom failing, to Edward Maxwell of Tynwald, Edward Maxwell of Lochrutoun, John Maxwell of Cowhill, and the heirs-male of their bodies; whom failing, to Herbert Maxwell, brother-german " of our foresaid cousin;" whom failing, to Edward Maxwell in like manner, his brother-german; whom all failing, to the lawful and nearest

---

[1] Original Charter at Terregles.   [2] Original Confirmation, ibid.

heir-male of the blood, house and surname of Maxwell bearing the arms thereof; whom failing, to the lawful and nearest heirs " of our said cousin " whomsoever.[1]

Cultivating friendly relations with other families, he received from many proprietors of the soil bonds of manrent, which served the more effectually to protect both parties in those turbulent times, when justice was but feebly administered. During the seventeen years between 1514 and 1531, Lord Maxwell received twelve bonds of this description from the families of Murray of Cockpool, ancestor of the Earl of Mansfield ; Douglas of Drumlanrig, ancestor of the Dukes and Marquises of Queensberry ; Stewart of Garlies, ancestor of the Earls Galloway ; Johnston of Johnston, ancestor of the Marquises of Annandale ; Gordon of Lochinvar, ancestor of the Lords Kenmure, and from other Nithsdale and Galloway families.[2]

This Lord Maxwell built the Castle of Langholm, which was one of the houses of the family for many generations. He also built a castle in Dumfries, with a bartisan about the same.[3]

Although it is not recorded in any of the family muniments, it is very probable that the large and finely executed armorial stone which is still above the principal entrance to Carlaverock Castle, was placed there by this Lord Maxwell. The carving and lettering of the stone indicate that they were executed in his time, and the initials 'R. M.' probably refer to him. The arms of Stewart of Garlies are in one of the shields on the stone, owing to the mother of this Lord having been a daughter of that house. If this conjecture as to the armorial stone is correct, the fifth Lord is the first who is known to have adopted the stag for his crest, and the holly as the Maxwell badge.

Robert, fifth Lord Maxwell, was twice married.

During his father's lifetime he married Janet Douglas, daughter of Sir William Douglas of Drumlanrig, knight. In the year 1509, his father, John Lord Maxwell, by an indenture made between him and Sir William Douglas, bound himself that Sir Robert Maxwell, knight, his son and apparent heir, should, God willing, marry Janet Douglas, daughter of Sir William, between

---

[1] Original Charter of Confirmation at Terregles.
[2] Original Bonds of Manrent, *ibid.*
[3] MS. History of the Family. This is probably the " new house" in which, on 28th November 1545,

Lord Maxwell made a notarial protest against the exactions of King Henry the Eighth during his Lordship's captivity

the date thereof and Candlemas (2d February) next. He also bound himself that, within forty days after the completing of the marriage, he should
give conjunct infeftment to Sir Robert and Janet, and to the longer liver
of them, and to the heirs of their marriage, the lands of Hessilden, and
others, in the barony of Mearns and shire of Renfrew, with the lands of
Glencapil, Glenhowane, and Langside, in the barony of Carlaverock, in the
shire of Dumfries. In consideration of all this, Sir William Douglas became
bound to pay to John Lord Maxwell one thousand pounds Scots, as tocher
with his daughter. The obligation is dated at Gleneslan, 4th June 1509.[1]

Robert, fifth Lord Maxwell, married, secondly, Lady Agnes Stewart,
daughter of James Earl of Buchan, and widow of Adam, second Earl of
Bothwell, without issue.[2]

Robert, fifth Lord Maxwell, died at Logan, on the 9th of July 1546,[3]
leaving by his first wife two sons and one daughter.

1. Robert, who succeeded him as sixth Lord Maxwell.
2. John, who, after his marriage with Agnes, the eldest daughter and
   coheiress of William, third Lord Herries, became Sir John Maxwell
   of Terregles, and afterwards the first LORD HERRIES of the house
   of Maxwell. On the failure of the male descendants of his elder
   brother Robert, sixth Lord Maxwell, in the person of Robert, second
   Earl of Nithsdale, in 1667, the male descendants of Lord Herries
   became the representatives of the noble family of Maxwell as well
   as heirs-general of the noble house of Herries.[4]

Margaret, who married, before 9th August 1543, first, Archibald Douglas,
   sixth Earl of Angus, by whom she had one son, James Douglas,
   Master of Angus, who predeceased his father. Wharton, in a letter
   to Suffolk and others, dated at the King's Castle at Carlisle, 2d
   February 1542-3, informs them that his servant, Edward Storye,

[1] Original Obligation at Terregles.
[2] Robert Lord Maxwell and Agnes Stewart, Countess of Bothwell, his spouse, received several charters, and were associated in many property transactions, ranging from the year 1529 to the year
1541.—(Original Charters at Terregles.)
[3] MS. History of the Maxwell Family. In the
retour of Robert, sixth Lord Maxwell, to his father,

expede on 5th August 1550, it is stated that the
lands have remained in the hands of the superior
for four years.—[Record of Retours in H.M. Chancery, Edinburgh, vol. i. 167.]
[4] Robert, fifth Lord Maxwell, also had a natural
son, of whom the Maxwells of Logan are descended.
—[MS. History of the Maxwell Family.]

from Edinburgh, said that upon Sunday, the 4th of this instant [February], the Earl of Angus will marry the daughter of Lord Maxwell [State Papers, *ut supra*, p. 252]. Margaret Maxwell, Countess of Angus, married, secondly, Sir William Baillie of Lamington, in the county of Lanark.

TWO SEALS OF ROBERT, FIFTH LORD MAXWELL, appended to Charters dated 3d May 1538 and March 1543, Nos. 176 and 216 of Maxwell Muniments.

SIGNATURE OF ROBERT, FIFTH LORD MAXWELL, 1521.

SIGNATURE OF ROBERT, FIFTH LORD MAXWELL, 1536.

XVI. ROBERT, SIXTH LORD MAXWELL.

Lady Beatrix Douglas (of Morton), Lady Maxwell.

1546-1552.

THIS Lord appears to have been a man of a courageous, impetuous, and energetic character; but his early death prevented his attaining the conspicuous and influential position which his father held.

During his father's life, various notices of this Lord, when Master of Maxwell, occur in the family papers, and in records of the period.[1]

He married Lady Beatrix Douglas, second daughter of James, third Earl of Morton, and coheiress of the Earldom. The mother of Lady Beatrix was Lady Katherine Stewart, daughter of King James the Fourth. Lady Beatrix was the immediate elder sister of Lady Elizabeth Douglas, who married, in 1542, James Douglas, nephew of Archibald Earl of Angus, who became through her the fourth Earl of Morton, and was the famous Regent. Negotiations as to the marriage of the Master of Maxwell took place in the year 1528. Licence for a contract of marriage between the Master and a daughter of the third Earl of Morton was asked by that Earl from King James the Fifth. The King, in a letter to the Earl, 17th June (1528), expresses himself as heartily content with the proposed marriage of his niece, made known to him by a previous letter; and in another letter to the Earl and his Countess, dated 21st July (1528), his Majesty, who calls the affianced lady their "youngest doughter," similarly expresses his approval of the contemplated matrimonial alliance, and would rather that she should be married to "Robert Maxwell, sone to our cousing Lord Robert Maxwell," than to any other, "for," he adds, "we purpose to tak him fra his fadir and bring him vp in our awne house."[2] At the date of that letter, Lord Maxwell was Master of the Royal

---

[1] On 5th August 1550, Robert, sixth Lord Maxwell, was served heir to his father, Robert, fifth Lord, by six separate retours in the baronies of Maxwell and Carlaverock, and in the other Maxwell lands and estates in the counties of Dumfries, Roxburgh, Kirkcudbright, Perth, and Renfrew. — [Printed Retours.] The sixth Lord was infefted in these baronies, etc., chiefly in November 1551.—[Sasines at Terregles.]

[2] Vide vol. ii. pp. 1, 2.

Household ; and the intention of the King to take the Master into the palace shows his Majesty's affection for his father.   The marriage of the Master of Maxwell and Lady Beatrix Douglas probably took place in the year 1530, as on the 25th of July that year the Master infefted her in the barony of Mearns.[1] At the time of his marriage, the Master of Maxwell was probably about twenty years of age, his parents having been married in the year 1509.

Any notice of the connexion of the House of Maxwell with the John-stons of Annandale acquires interest from the mortal feud which at a subse-quent period broke out between them, and issued in tragic events that are remarkable even in Border history.   Robert Master of Maxwell granted a bond of manrent to John Johnston of that Ilk, dated at Edinburgh, 3d January 1542-3.   The bond narrates that Johnston was bound in manrent, during all the days of his life, to Robert, fifth Lord Maxwell, before the imprisonment of his Lordship.   That bond being still binding, although Robert Lord Maxwell, with other noblemen of the realm of Scotland, was a prisoner in England, Johnston became bound to keep it in all points to Robert Master of Maxwell during the time of his father's imprisonment in England, by taking his plain part in all his just and honest actions, giving him his best counsel, assisting him in the punishment of offenders, and promoting the common weal of the realm, even as he was obliged to his father.   For these causes Robert Master of Maxwell promised faithfully to assist Johnston in all his just and honest actions conformably to his father's bond, given to him before; and, until his father's home-coming, to cause Johnston to obtain the maills, grassums, profits, and duties of the ten merk lands of Dryfsdale, claimed by him, and to be paid his £40 yearly of feu, contained in his father's bond.[2]

When Lord Maxwell was liberated from the Tower of London, Robert Master of Maxwell was, on the 19th of January 1543, delivered by him as his hostage, at Carlisle, to Lord Cumberland and Sir Thomas Wharton, English Warden of the West Marches, and he lay in pledge with Sir Thomas Wharton.[3]

The Master was afterwards permitted to return to his native country on

[1] Reg. Mag. Sig., Lib. xxiii. No. 203.
[2] Original Bond of Manrent at Terregles.

[3] State Papers, vol. v., King Henry the Eighth, Part iv. continued, p. 234.

his promising that when there he would promote the designs of Henry against Scotland.   Hertford, in a letter to King Henry in April 1544, would have his Majesty to grant "assurance to Robert Master of Maxwell for eight days, and so from eight days to eight," that is, liberty to remain in Scotland by successive grants, each grant being limited to these short periods, so long as he showed himself for his Majesty.   In another letter to King Henry, indorsed "depeched xiiii April, at ii after noone," he states, that Robert Maxwell desired not only assurance for himself and his friends, upon four days' warning, but also some entertainment, that is, pecuniary assistance, from his Majesty, to enable him the better to fortify, defend, and keep himself and his houses out of the hands of the Governor and Cardinal, with their adherents.   He and his fellow-ambassadors were of opinion that Robert Maxwell, and Drumlanrig, who had made a similar request, considering the benefit which they had already received from his Majesty, for which they had done no manner of service,— giving reason to conclude that they sought only their own interest,—should not obtain what they prayed for, unless they openly declared themselves to be for his Majesty by some honest service.   Should the Master of Maxwell now deliver Lochmaben to his Highness's use, that would be a good declaration on his part, for which he would be worthy of the liberality of his Highness.   Instructions had been given to Mr. Bowes that he and Lord Wharton should have a meeting and conference with the Master of Maxwell, when they should remind him of the great benefits which his father and he had received from the King of England, whilst they had hitherto done little or no service whatever in return, and should sound his inclination regarding the delivery of the Castle of Lochmaben, telling him that thereby he should obtain such favour from the King of England as should turn out to his great advantage.[1]

On 19th December 1544, Robert Master of Maxwell obtained from Queen Mary, with the consent of the Regent Arran, a commission as Guardian of the West Marches of Scotland against England, within the bounds of Annandale, Eskdale, Ewisdale, Nithisdale, and Galloway, as well above as below the Water of Cree; and also to be Justiciar within the same bounds,[2] instead of his

[1] State Papers, vol. v., King Henry the Eighth, Part iv. continued, pp. 370, 374.
[2] Original Commission at Terregles.

father, who was then a prisoner in England. The Regent Arran, from whom this appointment really flowed, was the brother-in-law of Robert Master of Maxwell, their respective wives being the daughters of the third Earl of Morton.

The bloody feud between the Johnstons and the Maxwells we shall afterwards have occasion to relate in detail. At this time Sir Thomas Wharton, in order to weaken the power of the Scots on the Borders, was very active in exciting animosity between the Laird of Johnston and Robert Master of Maxwell, who, had they been united in defence of their country, might have made his expedition against the Scottish borders much more difficult and costly. Speaking of this, Wharton, in a letter to the Earl of Shrewsbury, dated 10th February 1545, informs him that he had long used a follower as an emissary to create discord between the chief of the Johnstons and Lord Maxwell's son,—Lord Maxwell himself being at this time a prisoner in England. A feud had in consequence broken out between them, which the Scottish Privy Council found it impossible to allay. Wharton had offered Johnston 300 crowns ; his brother, the Abbot of Soul Seat, 100 ; and his followers 100 ; on condition that the Master of Maxwell should be put into his power. Johnston, he says, had entered into the plot, but he and his friends " were all so false that he knew not what to say." He placed very little confidence in them. But he would be " glad to annoy and entrap the Master of Maxwell, or the Laird of Johnston, to the King's Majestie's honour and his own poor honesty."

On this occasion the Laird of Johnston acted in violation of the bonds of manrent before mentioned, by which he bound himself to assist Robert Lord Maxwell and Robert Master of Maxwell in all their just and honest actions. But at that period it was common among the chief men of the kingdom of Scotland, from the overwhelming power of England, to bring themselves under dishonourable engagements to the English sovereign.

When his father, in the beginning of the year 1545, was recalled to England as a prisoner, and re-committed to the Tower, Robert Master of Maxwell made efforts to obtain his father's liberation ; and to accomplish that object he promised to the English ambassador to do his utmost to advance the interests of Henry in Scotland.

Though anxious to procure his father's liberty, and though he even engaged to become a hostage for him, he hesitated to deliver himself up. He was indeed rather in a difficulty, for while the Government of England desired to secure him as a hostage for his father, that through his influence they might secure the important Border fortresses belonging to his family, the Government of Scotland, equally alive to the value of these fortresses, were not less anxious to keep him in his native country.

Whilst his father was still a prisoner in England, the Master of Maxwell became bound in June 1545, in presence of the Queen, the Lord Governor and the Lords of Council,[1] loyally to keep the houses of Carlaverock, Lochmaben, and the Threave for the Queen, the Governor, and the government, from their enemies of England, until Lord Maxwell himself should personally appear before the Lord Governor and Lords of Council, and declare his innocence in regard to his conspiring with the English against his country, and purge himself of the suspicions which they had against him in that respect ; and until he was attacked by an English army so great that it was impossible for him to resist it, but in that case the Lord Governor and Council were to be advertised thereof.

His pledges for the fulfilment of this bond were James Douglas of Drumlanrig, James Gordon of Lochinvar, Alexander Stewart of Garlies, John Johnston of that Ilk, John Grierson of Lag, Thomas Kirkpatrick of Closburn, and Kirkpatrick of Ross. They became bound respectively upon their lives and heritages to have no intelligence with England. The Lord Governor and Lords of Council, at the same time, promised to supply the Master of Maxwell with men and arms to assist in the defence of these houses.[2]

The inclinations of the Master of Maxwell and his father were undoubtedly patriotic, although their conduct was not always at first sight consistent with a love of their country, but the submissions they made to the English were extorted by the pressure of a power against which they felt themselves unable to contend. It is clear that Henry and his ambassadors never trusted them,

---

[1] At this meeting of Council were present, besides the Queen and Governor, the Cardinal, who was Chancellor, the Bishops of Dunblane and Orkney, the Earls of Huntley, Bothwell, Glencairn, Cassillis, Montrose ; the Abbots of Dunfermline and Couper ; Lords Fleming, Ruthven, Elphinstoun, Lord Stewart of Ochiltree and Methven.

[2] Regist. Secreti Concilii, Acta, 1548, MS., fol. 11, in the General Register House, Edinburgh.

and they frequently expressed their belief that both father and son were acting insincerely; nor ought it to be forgotten that, with the lax morality of the age on such subjects, their own countrymen readily overlooked and forgave their compliances with the demands of a superior power.

Henry, to punish the Scotch for their violation of the treaty of peace and their rejection of his proposals for the marriage of their Queen to his son, sent an army to invade Scotland in September 1545. One section of his army entered by the Eastern Borders, and by it the Abbey of Kelso was taken, and the Abbeys of Dryburgh, Melrose, and Jedburgh burned, as were also the towns of Melrose and Jedburgh and many villages.[1]

In the meantime the Earl of Bothwell, Lord Home, the Master of Home, the Abbots of Jedburgh and Dryburgh, with two or three thousand men, entered Northumberland and burned a town called Horneclyff. Upon this the garrisons of Berwick, Norham, Warke, Cornehill, Etill, and Forde, to the number of 600 or 700 horsemen, which Hertford had left for the better protection of the frontiers in his absence, along with the countrymen, who immediately arose and repaired to the fray, attacked the Scots, chased them over the Tweed, and in the pursuit slew about fifty, and took 149 prisoners.[2]

Whilst these events were taking place at the Eastern Marches, Wharton, at the head of an English force, was committing similar depredations in the Western Borders,[3] assisted by some of the strongest of the predatory tribes, on the Scottish side, such as the Armstrongs, the Beattisons or Beatties, the Thomsons, the Littles, and others whom he had gained over.

To resist Wharton, Robert Master of Maxwell had collected a considerable

[1] State Papers, vol. v., King Henry the Eighth, Part iv. continued, pp. 513, 518.

[2] Ibid. pp. 521-524.

There is some confusion in the narrative of this raid on the East Borders, as given by Hollinshed in his History, vol. ii. p. 228. He says that Maxwell (meaning probably Lord Maxwell, but by mistake, as that Lord was then a prisoner in England), Lochinvar and Johnston were leaders in this expedition. But the English ambassadors, who are minute in their details, and who specially mention the leaders, do not name these chieftains of the west. Hollinshed states only 300 or 400 as the number of the Scotch who attempted to enter into England, whilst the English ambassadors make them 2000 or 3000. Hollinshed gives 16th September 1545 as the date of the raid, which is probably the true one. He is also correct in saying that the Scotch were assisted by some Frenchmen, and that "among others that were taken one of the sons of Lord Hume, with a French capteine, and George Elphinston, archer of the corps to the French King, were accounted the chiefe."

[3] Haynes's State Papers, pp. 43-51.

although insufficient force. In the MS. History of the House of Maxwell this adventure is told with various particulars not elsewhere to be found. It is there said that, in the discharge of his duty as Warden of the Marches, the Master of Maxwell had undertaken this expedition for the apprehension and punishment of the inhabitants of Staikheuik, a place in Langholm, who, at that time, were treasonable fugitives from Scotland ; and that in this expedition he was unsuccessful, having been met and resisted in his progress by the Grahams and other borderers of England, assisted by the Littles and Johnstouns, Christopher Armstrong, and other border marauders in Scotland. At the Yellow Sykehead in Wauchopdale he fell into the hands of the enemy, with sundry of his men, and was carried to London, where his father had already been a prisoner for some time. He remained in England till the year 1549, when he was exchanged for an Englishman called Sir Thomas Palmer, who had been taken the year before at the siege of Haddington, by one Hamilton, from whom John Maxwell, the younger brother of the Master, had bought him for £1000. Whilst his father and brother were in captivity, John Maxwell governed the estates of Maxwell ; and during that time he obtained in marriage Agnes Herries, the heiress of Herries, from the Earl of Arran, Governor, for expelling the Earl of Lennox and the English army out of Scotland, making the rivers of Solway and Esk the marches thereof as before.[1]

Hertford, in a letter to King Henry the Eighth, dated from the camp at Warkeshaughe, 19th September 1545, informs him of the unsuccessful character of an adventure made by Robert Maxwell, who was taken, and was then in his Majesty's hands, with divers others.[2] The Scots at this time had been unfortunate in their enterprises, both at the East and West Marches, and had also been " sufficiently well scourged at home, whereof we thanke God," says Hertforde, " and take the same to be his just judgement and castigation for theyr great untrouthe." He desires to know his Majesty's pleasure as to what should be further done with Robert Maxwell and such of the best reputation as had been taken prisoners. His Majesty ordered that the Master of Maxwell should be sent up to the Court. Hertford, therefore,

[1] MS. History of the Family of Maxwell.
[2] State Papers, vol. v., *ut supra*, pp. 525, 526.

in a letter to Paget, dated Newcastle, 11th October 1545, says, "For Robert Maxwell I intend to despatch him from hence to the Court, with Mr. Knyvet and Mr. Hobbye."[1] After the battle of Pinkie, Dumfriesshire was at the mercy of the English Sovereign, and the landholders generally submitted to him. In a list of those who did so in that county and in East Galloway, Lord Maxwell's followers are stated at more than one thousand, a much larger number than those of any other chief.[2]

As was the custom in his time, Lord Maxwell endeavoured to strengthen himself for defence or attack by entering into bonds of manrent with neighbouring proprietors, who placed at his service their kin, friends, servants, and retainers. In the years 1549 and 1550 he received a bond of this description from Thomas Makclellan of Auchlane, tutor of Bombie, and other Makclellans, to continue during the minority of Thomas Makclellan of Bombie, their chief; and others from William Kirkpatrick of Kirkmichell, John Grierson of Lag, Alexander Stewart of Garlies, John Crichton, brother to the late William Lord Crichton of Sanquhar, and nine more of his family and name, and Thomas Kirkpatrick of Closeburn.[3]

After his return to Scotland, from his captivity in England, Lord Maxwell went to France with the Queen Regent, in the year 1550, and was there most courteously welcomed and entertained by King Henry the Second, as a constant adherent to the ancient league between Scotland and France. By that monarch he was made a gentleman of the royal chamber, with a pension of 300 merks yearly from the French Exchequer. The King also presented him with an elegant and sumptuous gold chain, which, with his own hand, he put about his neck, in token of greater distinction.[4]

From Queen Mary and his brother-in-law, the Regent Arran, Lord Maxwell obtained a renewed commission, dated 29th March 1550, as Warden of the West Marches, within the bounds of Annandale, Ewisdale, Nithsdale, Eskdale, and Galloway, and as Justiciar within these bounds.[5]

On 20th April 1550, Arran, Lord Governor of the kingdom, and the Lords of Secret Council ordained that the house and place of Mousewald, which was

---

[1] State Papers, *ut supra*, vol. v. p. 546.
[2] Nicolson's Cumberland, lv.
[3] Original Bonds of Manrent at Terregles.

[4] MS. History of the Family of Maxwell.
[5] Original Commission at Terregles.

then in the hands of Lord Maxwell, should be delivered to Sir James Douglas of Drumlanrig, knight, who had received a gift of the ward and marriage of Mousewald.[1]

The Debateable Land upon the West Borders between Scotland and England had long been the refuge of a great number of thieves and traitors, both English and Scotch, who, banding together, issued from their strongholds and inflicted serious injuries on those dwelling on either side of the Border. To remedy this evil, Commissioners from the two countries were appointed for dividing equally the debateable ground, in the hope of securing the tranquillity of the whole district. Lord Maxwell was one of the Commissioners thus appointed by the Queen, the Lord Governor, and the Lords of the Privy Council at Stirling, 20th March 1550-1. The other Commissioners who were to act with him were Gilbert Earl of Cassillis, Sir James Douglas of Drumlanrig, and Mr. John Bellenden of Auchnowll, Justice-Clerk.[2]

The instructions given to the Commissioners were in the following terms :—

In the first ze sall convene with the commissionaris of Ingland at sik day and place as ze appoynt amangis zourselffis in writing : and first it is thought expedient, becaus ther is na perfyt euidentis to clere the boundis of the said debatabill ground and merchis of the samyn, that ther be ane certane nowmer of the maist honest men of the bordouris for the part of Scotland, and siclik for the part of Ingland, to equale nowmer, chosin and sworne to declair the saidis merchis, and that ther be ane scribe for zour part, as the commissionaris of Ingland will put ane of theris to writt the saidis merchis ; and giff ther men aggreis nocht, ze sall tak sik vther tryall as ze and the saidis commissionaris can aggre for decyding of that land that is indifferent, sua that for ane litill valour nocht leif the landis vndevidit, or giff ze think vtherwais, that land that is in contrauersy, to devyd the samyn, providing alwayis that ze enter nocht to na diuisioun of the landis of the priorye of Caunoby as debatabill.

Item, quhen ze haif aggreit vpoun the merchis of the said debatabile ground, than ze sall proceid to the diuisioun of the samyn, in ane equale maner, or therby, as ze can aggre, be zour awin discretioun : That ane half to pertene seueralie to Scotland and that vther to Ingland, in tymes cuming, and to mak ane perfyt euident betuix zow and the saidis commissionaris of Ingland, quhilk sall nocht allanerlie contene the hail merchis and methis of the debatabill, bot alswa of twa halffis, as beis diuidit vnder zour selis and subscriptionis as the maner is.

---

[1] Regist. Secreti Concilii, Acta, 1550-1553, fol. 12.

From the Drumlanrig Muniments it appears that the heiress of Mousewald, of the surname of Carruthers, who was in ward of Sir James Douglas, declined the husband who was offered to her by Sir James, and rather than accept of him threatened to commit, if she did not actually commit, suicide by leaping over a precipice.

[2] Regist. Secreti Concilii, Acta, 1550-1553, fol. 45.

Item, to desir that the Indent proport that it sall nocht be lesum to ather of the princes nowther of Scotland nor Ingland, nor successouris, to big ony strenth vpoun ony part of the said debatabill land in ony tymes to cum, bot the samyn to be occupyt and manurit in maner of husbandrie, and gif this can be obtenit consent to the downputting of baith the stane houss that is biggit vpoun the debatabill, and howbeit it be nocht obtenit, leif nocht the said debatabill vndeuidit.

Item, giff it be desyrit at zow that the inhabitantis now for the part that happynnis to Scotland to remane vpoun the samyn ze sall appoynt and concord that samony as will cum Scottismen and giff ther aithis be plege for dew obedience and gud reule salbe ressauit as Scottismen to the Quenis pardoun, as samony as the lordis commissionaris permittis pardoun, and remitt vnto thais personis sall haif the quenis Grace and my Lord gouernouris pardoun and remitt.

Item, in deviding of the said debatabill, giff ze can aggre with the saidis commissionaris of Ingland that the samyn be done be the sicht and estimatioun of Eee. It is best sa and maist equale vtherwyis to cast cavillis quha sall devyd the samyn and the vther to tak ther chois quhen it is sa diuidit.

Item, to vnderstand at zour conventioun that the saidis commissionaris of Ingland haif power of the King their maister to giff zow saulff conduct to pas with tham to Carlile, and gif thai haif it nocht, that thai send for the samyn, for ze haif power to gif tham conduct and selfgard to cum to Drumfreis for the treating of the said besynes.[1]

The Debateable Land was situated along the Scottish side of the rivers Esk and Liddell. It extended in length to eight miles, and in breadth to four miles, and was bounded on the west by the river Sark. This tract originally belonged to Scotland, as appears from charters, from the twelfth to the fourteenth centuries. But in the course of the long-continued Border warfare, it was frequently possessed by England, and in the end came to be claimed by both countries. During the infancy of Queen Mary, the overbearing monarch of England compelled the inhabitants of this district to submit to his power.

Following the explicit instructions which they had received, the Commissioners had no difficulty in coming to a settlement. Their arrangement for the division of the Debateable Land was very simple. They drew a line of intersection from the Sark on the west to the Esk on the east. The northern half or parish of Canonby was assigned to Scotland, and the southern half or parish of Kirkandrews to England. The division was made according to a *plot* or plan, and the partition line was marked by stone pillars, bearing the armorial ensigns of England and Scotland, placed on the south and north sides respectively.

[1] Regist. Secreti Concilii, Acta, 1550-1553, fol. 46.

Lord Maxwell was also one of the Commissioners appointed by Queen Mary, under the Great Seal, 8th May 1551, with the consent of James Duke of Chatelherault, her tutor, and Governor of the kingdom, to conclude a treaty with the Commissioners of Edward the Sixth, King of England, for the settling of questions, and controversies between her Majesty and the sovereign of England, in regard to the limits of the two kingdoms, and all other causes tending in any way to the rupture of the treaty of friendship and peace entered into and confirmed between her Majesty and King Edward. The other Commissioners from Scotland were Robert Bishop of Orkney, Thomas Master of Erskine, Louis de St. Gelays, and Robert Carnegie of Kinnaird. The treaty was concluded at the church of Norham, 10th June 1551, and confirmed in the same month by Edward the Sixth.[1] It comprehended within its provisions the final settlement for the division of the Debateable Land between Scotland and England.

Robert Lord Maxwell being involved in a serious feud with the Grahams on the English side of the Border, as a means of defence against them built a tower at Annan, which town his brother afterwards strengthened by causing dykes to be cast.[2]

On 12th July 1552, only two months before his death, Lord Maxwell entered into a bond, made at Dumfries, with Alexander Stewart of Garlies, James Douglas of Drumlanrig, John Gordon of Lochinvar, John Crichton, tutor of Sanquhar, John Maxwell of Terregles, John Grierson of Lag, John Charteris of Amisfield and others, for mutual defence against the Grahams.[3]

Robert, sixth Lord Maxwell, died at Dumfries, on 13th September 1552,[4] leaving his widow, Lady Beatrix Douglas, who survived him many years, and was alive on the 21st of October 1583, when King James the Sixth required John Earl of Morton, Lord Maxwell, to admit her as tenant to him in the lands of Kilbocke, and others, in the shire of Peebles, which had been disponed to her by her late father, James, third Earl of Morton. In these lands she was infefted on the 31st of the same month.[5]

---

[1] Rymer's Fœdera, tom. v. p. 263.
[2] MS. History of the Family of Maxwell.
[3] Original Bond at Terregles.

[4] MS. History of the Family of Maxwell.
[5] Original Letters and Instrument of Sasine at Terregles.

Robert sixth Lord Maxwell and Lady Beatrix Douglas had a family of two sons,—

1. Robert, their elder son, who succeeded his father as seventh Lord Maxwell, but who died, when only four years of age, in the mansion-house of the Hills.

2. John, a posthumous child. After the death of his brother Robert, he became eighth Lord Maxwell, and was afterwards created EARL OF MORTON.[1]

[1] Robert, sixth Lord Maxwell, had also a natural son, named Robert Maxwell of Castlemilk, in the county of Dumfries. He was frequently involved in feuds with the Johnstons and others, as appears from several entries in the Records of the Privy Council in the years 1579 and 1580.—Regist. Secreti Concilii, Acta, 1577-79, fol. 106, 236; 1579-81, fol. 411, 421.

SEAL OF ROBERT, SIXTH LORD MAXWELL, appended to Obligation, 24th June 1551.

SIGNATURE OF ROBERT, SIXTH LORD MAXWELL, to Obligation, 24th June 1551.

XVII. 1. ROBERT, SEVENTH LORD MAXWELL.
1552-1554.

ROBERT, SEVENTH LORD MAXWELL, was a child of only about two years of age when on his father's death he succeeded to the extensive possessions of the House of Maxwell. He was under the guardianship of his paternal uncle, Sir John Maxwell of Terregles, afterwards well known as Lord Herries.

On 16th June 1553, he was infeft, on a precept of sasine by John, Abbot of Sweetheart, and the chapter thereof, as heir to his father in the lands of Kirkpatrick-Durham; and, on the 21st of June, a confirmation of the Abbot's charter of these lands was granted by John, Archbishop of St. Andrews, the Pope's legate *a latere*, to him, and the heirs-male of his body, whom failing, to his brother, John Maxwell, and the heirs-male of his body.[1]

This Lord obtained a precept of sasine, dated at Edinburgh, 4th December 1553, from Patrick Earl of Bothwell, Lord Hales and Crichton, for his infeftment in the lands of Turmour and others; and he was infeft in these lands on 22d December same year.[2]

A bond of manrent was granted, on the 25th of the same month, by Thomas Makclellan, tutor of Bombie, and other Makclellans, for themselves and their kin, to Sir John Maxwell of Terregles, that they should serve Robert Lord Maxwell, a pupil, until he should attain the age of eighteen years, and that during the minority of Thomas Makclellan of Bombie, their chief.

About two years after his succession to his father, Robert, seventh Lord Maxwell, died, when a child of four years, in the mansion-house of the Hills, where he resided. He died before 16th January 1554-5, and was succeeded in the title and estates by his brother John.[3]

[1] Original Precept of Sasine and Confirmation at Terregles.

[2] Original Precept of Sasine, *ibid.*

[3] An Original Precept of Clare Constat, by John, Abbot of Sweetheart, for infefting John Lord Maxwell, as heir to his grandfather, Robert, fifth Lord Maxwell, in the bailiery of Sweetheart, etc., is dated 16th January 1554-5. At Terregles.

XVII. 2. JOHN, EIGHTH LORD MAXWELL,
CREATED EARL OF MORTON.

LADY ELIZABETH DOUGLAS (OF ANGUS) HIS WIFE.

1554-1593.

JOHN, EIGHTH LORD MAXWELL, younger son of Robert, sixth Lord Maxwell, who, on the death of his elder brother Robert, seventh Lord Maxwell, in infancy, inherited the estates and title of the house of Maxwell, was a posthumous child. He was born on 24th April 1553, little more than six months after his father's death; and he was less than two years of age on his succession. His position was a critical one, considering the unsettled times in which he was born; and the results of a long minority might have been very disastrous to the interests of his family, had he not fortunately been placed under the care of guardians who conducted his affairs with eminent prudence and honour, and under whose administration the possessions and power of the house of Maxwell suffered no diminution.

During his minority the infant lord had for his guardian his uncle, a younger brother of his father, Sir John Maxwell of Terregles, afterwards Lord Herries, who, being the nearest heir of his nephew, was styled Master of Maxwell. On reaching the age of puberty, Edward Maxwell of Tinwald, Robert Maxwell of Cowhill,[1] and William Douglas of Whittingham, were appointed his curators.[2] Through his mother, Beatrix Douglas, he was connected with the Hamilton and the Douglas families, his mother's eldest sister, Lady Margaret, having married James Earl of Arran and Duke of Chatelherault, and her youngest sister, Lady Elizabeth, having married James Douglas (brother of David, seventh Earl of Angus), afterwards Earl of Morton and Regent of Scotland.

---

[1] To these two, under the designation of the curators of John Lord Maxwell, was delivered an extract from the Steward Court Books of Kirkcudbright of an inventory of the evidents, writings, etc., 24th May 1569, by Sir William Maxwell of Aven, knight, Master of Herries, and Sir John Bryce, vicar of Dumfries, on the part of John Lord Herries.—Extract at Terregles.

[2] William Douglas of Whittingham is so called in a charter, dated 6th February 1571, to be afterwards quoted.

Whilst a minor, he was infefted between the years 1555 and 1576 as heir to his grandfather, father, or brother in the lands and baronies of Maxwell, Carlaverock, and others, and in the bailieries of Sweetheart, Dundrennan, Holywood, and Lincluden.[1]

John Lord Maxwell early joined the ranks of the supporters of Queen Mary in opposition to the government which acted in the name of her son, King James the Sixth. Those on the side of Mary included the Duke of Chatel-herault, the Earls of Argyll, Athole, Huntly, Crawford, Rothes, and Cassillis, Lords Seton, Boyd, Gray, Livingston, and Fleming, and the Lairds of Buccleuch, Ferniehirst, with Secretary Maitland and Kirkcaldy of Grange, one of the most distinguished soldiers of his age. The King's party included the Earls of Lennox, Morton, Mar, and Glencairn ; Lords Lindsay, Glammis, Semple, Methven, Ochiltree, Cathcart and Ruthven. The nobles attached to this party were fewer in number and less powerful than the nobles who adhered to Queen Mary ; but they were assisted by Queen Elizabeth, and supported by the Kirk and the people.

After the assassination of Regent Murray, at Linlithgow, in January 1569-70, Queen Elizabeth, to whom his death was a heavy blow, sent Lord Scrope, a warden of the English marches, into Dumfriesshire to lay waste the lands of all who were attached to Queen Mary. Lord Maxwell, who was then only seventeen years of age, mustered a considerable body of men, and, accompanied by the magistrates and many of the people of Dumfries, advanced to oppose Lord Scrope. They met and repeatedly attacked his cavalry, who in the end drove them off, and took a number of prisoners, including the Provost and some of the burgesses of Dumfries.[2] Lord Scrope, in a letter to the Earl of Sussex, Queen Elizabeth's lieutenant on the Borders, dated Carlisle, 21st April 1570, in reporting the movements of the English troops in this foray into Scotland, mentions three conflicts with Lord Maxwell, the flight of Maxwell, and the number of the prisoners taken.[3]

Lord Maxwell and his friends suffered severely for the part which they took on this occasion. To maintain the government established in the name of King James the Sixth in opposition to his mother, Queen Mary, Scotland was invaded

[1] Maxwell Muniments at Terregles.
[2] The Cabala, pp. 164, 165.
[3] Calendar of State Papers, Scotland, 1509-1589, vol. i. p. 282, No. 60.

by an English army of 15,000 men, under the command of the Earl of Sussex, who, with a part of his forces, 4000, advanced from Carlisle into Scotland, committing ravages in his progress ; and, between the 22d of August 1570, when he entered Scotland, and the 28th, when he returned to Carlisle, to quote from his own report in a letter to Queen Elizabeth, he threw down the castles of Annand and Hoddom, belonging to Lord Herries, the castles of Dumfries and Carlaverock, belonging to Lord Maxwell, the castles of Tynwald and Cowhill, belonging to the lairds of Tynwald and Cowhill, etc.   In a letter to Cecil, he takes credit for having avoided, as much as possible, the burning of houses and corn and the spoiling of cattle and goods ; yet, in his letter to Queen Elizabeth, he says that he had not left a stone house to an ill neighbour within twenty miles of this town (Carlisle).[1]

Lord Maxwell was suspected of favouring the insurrection raised by Leonard Dacre, titular sixth Lord Dacre of Graystock,[2] in the years 1570 and 1571, and of intending to bring a body of men to his assistance.   Dacre was suspected by the Government of Queen Elizabeth of having been a confederate of the Earls of Northumberland and Westmoreland in the rebellion raised by them in the north of England in the year 1569, to restore that kingdom to the obedience of the Holy Roman See ; and, although he did not appear in the field with them in Durham,[3] orders were given for his apprehension.[4]   Having strongly fortified his house of Naworth, and furnished it with men and provisions, he assembled, 18th February 1570-71, upwards of 3000 men, English and Scots, against the Queen, under colour of defending his tenants of Gillesland, and of simply maintaining his title and keeping his possessions, which otherwise would have been forcibly taken from him.[5]   There is reason to believe that Dacre expected to be assisted in this rash enterprise by Lord Maxwell and other Lords in Scotland.   Lord Scrope, in a letter to Sir William Cecil, dated midnight, Carlisle, 18th February that year, says that Dacre looked for the friends and forces of the Lords Herries and Maxwell ; and that Lords Home,

[1] Tytler's History, vol. vi. p. 144.

[2] Leonard Dacre was the second son of William, third Lord Dacre.   The eldest son was Thomas, fourth Lord Dacre, who had a son, George, and three daughters.   He was succeeded by his son George, fifth Lord Dacre.   Upon the death of George, who died in his minority, leaving his sisters as his co-heirs, Leonard claimed the title as heir-male.

[3] Calendar of State Papers, Domestic Series, Queen Elizabeth, Addenda, 1566-1579, pp. 90, 106, 119.

[4] Ibid. pp. 185, 193.

[5] Ibid. pp. 219, 220, 237, 243, 244.

Cessford, Buccleuch, and other Lords of Teviotdale willed him to keep his house, and promised to come in person, with their men, to his relief.[1] Sir Thomas Gargrave also, in a letter to Sir William Cecil, dated York, 2d March, thus writes :—" I enclose letters from Sir John Forster, Lord Warden of the Middle Marches, and Simon Musgrave, Captain of Bewcastle. It seems that the frontiers are in peril of spoil, and unless foreseen, all the frontiers of Scotland will join our rebels against the state lately established in that realm. Lord Hume has forsaken religion, and hears two or three masses daily with Lady Northumberland ; so being revolted and joined with Buccleuch and the Carrs, Lord Maxwell and Herries may join them, and, with the assistance of the rebels, they will hurt the frontiers unless prevented. They are well horsed with the rebel's horses, and ours are spoiled, so that if any thing is done horsemen must be provided elsewhere."[2]

There is, however, no evidence that Lord Maxwell gave any assistance to Dacre, although it is certain that they had communications with each other.

Leonard Dacre, when in need of money, thus writes in a letter to his brother Edward, dated Mechlin, 22d January 1571-2 :—" I received your letter by my man William. . . . Whatever fair promises William had, I have never heard nor received anything from that side the seas, and so remain without hope of good. . . . If any will help me, they must deliver it to you, and you send it hither by Lord Maxwell's means, with some merchant of Dumfries. . . . Tell Lord Maxwell that I will send copies of the writings between him and Laird Johnston with the first Dumfries merchant that I can learn of."[3]

At this period Lord Maxwell, though only eighteen years of age, took an active part in the cause of Queen Mary. When her friends assembled at Edinburgh in 1571, Lord Maxwell, his uncle, Lord Herries, and the Laird of Lochinvar, came to the capital on the 14th of April, about ten o'clock at night, and alighted at the Castle gate. Upon Tuesday the 17th of that month, Lord Herries and Lochinvar went home, and Lord Maxwell on the following day.[4]

Conflicting Parliaments were held by the two parties. Matthew Earl of Lennox, the Regent,[5] not being in possession of the town of Edinburgh,

[1] Calendar of State Papers, Domestic Series, Queen Elizabeth, Addenda, 1566-1579, pp. 237, 239, 240.

[2] Ibid. p. 249.   [3] Ibid. p. 381.

[4] Calderwood's History, vol. iii. p. 60.

[5] He was elected Regent by a convocation of the Estates, held at Edinburgh on the 12th of July 1570.

held a Parliament at the head of the Canongate, above St. John's Cross, on the 14th of May same year.

The friends of the Queen held their Parliament in her name in the Tolbooth of Edinburgh, with the crown, sceptre, and sword, and prorogued it to the 12th of June. To attend the Parliament, Lord Maxwell, along with his uncle, Lord Herries, and Lochinvar returned to Edinburgh, accompanied by more than two hundred horse. After the prorogation of the Parliament, they left the capital, and returned again to hold it on the 12th of June. On that day the Earls of Lennox and Huntly, Lords Home and Maxwell, Lord Claud Hamilton, the Prior of Coldingham, the Abbot of Kilwinning, the Bishop of Galloway, the Laird of Ferniehirst, and some other barons, walked from the Castle to the Tolbooth. A letter was presented to them, said to be from the Queen, but forged in the Castle of Edinburgh, requesting that all former proceedings touching her extorted demission of the kingdom of Scotland in prison, and the consequent coronation of her son, and the authority usurped by some under his name, should be declared null and void, and all the subjects of the realm of Scotland bound to acknowledge their allegiance to her Majesty as their only and undoubted Sovereign. An Act to this effect was made in this Parliament. After a sitting of about two hours and a half, the members left the Tolbooth, riding in order, some of the chief of them bearing the sword, the sceptre, and the crown, which the captain of the castle delivered to them. He had refused to deliver these insignia of royalty out of the castle to the Earl of Lennox, Regent, when he previously held his Parliament.[1]

The Regent Lennox was assassinated at Stirling, 4th September 1571, and was succeeded in the Regency by John Earl of Mar, who was chosen on the following day. The efforts of Mar, who was a nobleman of great moderation and integrity of character, were directed to the reconciliation of the two factions—those who adhered to Queen Mary, and those who supported the Government of her son, King James the Sixth. But these efforts were defeated by his early death on 28th October 1572, and by the ambition of Morton and many of the nobles.

The clan Maxwell beheld with pride the indications which their chief

---

[1] Calderwood's History, vol. iii. pp. 91-96.

gave of possessing the valour and intrepidity which had distinguished his grandfather. Their future safety might greatly depend on their union, and as a means of the maintenance of concord with one another, a number of them entered into a somewhat peculiar bond of manrent with him, as head of the family, in testimony of the confidence which they placed in his abilities. At Dumfries, 20th November 1571, Robert Maxwell of Cowhill, and many other persons of the name of Maxwell, in conformity with the lawful custom of their forefathers, the observance of which they believed would be to their advantage, promised truly to stand by the judgment of their chief, John Lord Maxwell, in all differences that should arise between them or any two of them, so that thereafter no other judgment of the law should be sought, provided two Maxwells were chosen by either party to assist and concur in counsel with Lord Maxwell. They bound themselves truly to serve and obey him as their chief in all his honest causes against whomsoever, and to give him their upright counsel in all causes, when he should require it. Lord Maxwell also bound himself to do equal justice, without respecting one party above another, and to defend them to the utmost of his power in all their honest and lawful causes.[1]

Lord Maxwell also obtained, on 11th January 1572, a bond of manrent from John Maxwell, tutor of Kirkconnell, acknowledging him as his only chief and master; and another, on 11th June 1574, from Robert Charteris of Kelwood.[2]

Although the ward and marriage of Lord Maxwell had been granted to Jane Fleming, daughter of James Lord Fleming,[3] probably with a view to their marriage, Lord Maxwell married Lady Elizabeth Douglas, youngest daughter of David, seventh Earl of Angus. Their marriage-contract is dated at Leith, 13th January 1571-2.

With consent of Edward Maxwell of Tinwald, Robert Maxwell of Cowhill, and William Douglas of Whittingham, his curators, Lord Maxwell granted a charter in favour of Lady Elizabeth Douglas, sister to Archibald Earl of Angus, his intended spouse, in implement of the contract of marriage, of a liferent in the barony of Mearns, Drippis, and Nether Pollok, in the shire

---

[1] Original Bond of Manrent at Terregles.
[2] Original Bonds of Manrent, *ibid.*
[3] Discharge by Jane Fleming at Terregles. She married Lord Chancellor Thirlstane.

of Renfrew.   This charter was confirmed by King James the Sixth at Leith on the 6th of February following.[1]

On this occasion James Earl of Morton, who was married to Lord Maxwell's maternal aunt, and who was paternal uncle of his Lordship's bride, prepared for his niece and her husband a sumptuous feast at his castle of Dalkeith ; but Queen Mary's party, who held the Castle of Edinburgh, mischievously marred the festivities by seizing upon the wine and provisions when on their way to Dalkeith.[2]

By his marriage, Lord Maxwell became still more closely connected than before with the houses of Hamilton and Douglas, and also with the Scotts of Buccleuch and the Earl of Bothwell.   Lady Margaret Douglas, the sister of Lady Maxwell, married, first, Sir Walter Scott of Buccleuch, and secondly, Francis Stewart, Earl of Bothwell.

Not long after his marriage, Lord Maxwell submitted to the Government conducted in the name of King James the Sixth.   Sir William Drury and Mr. Randolph, in a letter to Lord Hunsdon, dated Leith, 10th April 1572, say that Herries and Lord Maxwell were about to submit, and that Maxwell denied that he had supported Edward Dacre.[3]   Maxwell's actual submission is reported in a letter by James Earl of Morton to the Earl of Sussex, written from Leith, on the 28th of the same month, requesting his intercession with the Queen of England for the redress of certain losses sustained by his servants at Preston in Galloway, and for restraining English subjects from invading Lord Maxwell, who had submitted to the King's authority.[4]   On the death of the Regent Mar, James Douglas, fourth Earl of Morton, was chosen Regent on the 24th of November same year.

Soon after, Lord Maxwell obtained from the new Regent the office of Warden of the West Marches.   His commission under the Great Seal is dated at Holyroodhouse, 26th August 1573.[5]   This office had been held from the death of his father, in September 1552, by his uncle, Sir John Maxwell of Terregles, till after the battle of Langside in 1568, when, having fought on the side of Queen Mary, he was deprived by the Regent Murray, who

---

[1] Original Charter of Confirmation at Terregles.

[2] History of King James VI., p. 160.

[3] Calendar of State Papers, Scottish Series, 1509-1589, vol. i. p. 345, No. 70.

[4] Calendar of State Papers, Scottish Series, 1509-1589, vol. i. p. 349.

[5] Original Commission at Terregles.

bestowed the office on Douglas of Drumlanrig, by whom it was held for five years.

As the possession of the Castle of Lochmaben by the Warden of the West Marches was necessary, in order to the successful discharge of the duties of the office, Lord Maxwell obtained from King James the Sixth, with the advice and consent of the Regent Morton, a commission, dated 26th October 1573, as captain and keeper of that castle.[1]

The bad feeling which existed between the Maxwells and Johnstons began to show itself about this time, although not to the extent which it did some years later. Some altercations, accompanied with violence, having taken place between Lord Maxwell's brother, friends and servants, and the friends and servants of Johnston of that ilk, Lord Maxwell, Warden of the West Marches, made a complaint to the Privy Council held at Dalkeith, 28th November 1574, against Johnston, for the non-compearance of his friends and servants at the Steward Court of Annandale. The Regent Morton and the Lords of Secret Council found and declared that Johnston's friends and servants should compear at that Court, as others of his Majesty's lieges, within the bounds of the stewartry of Annandale, and ordained Lord Maxwell to find surety that none of them should be molested in coming to and passing from that Court. Johnston promised to cause all his friends or servants within Annandale, who had not previously found security, to find it. He and Lord Maxwell, in order to the hearing, trying, and composing of all debates and unkindness which either of them had, or might pretend to have, against the other, nominated respectively certain noblemen and friends, of whom any four, three, or two on each side should convene for that purpose in the burgh of Edinburgh, on the 15th of February next; and both parties in the meantime promised to keep good rule in the country, as they would be answerable.[2]

[1] Original Commission at Terregles.

[2] Regist. Secreti Concilii, Acta, 1572-1575, fol. 274. The friends nominated by Lord Maxwell were John Lord Glammis, Chancellor of Scotland, Robert Lord Boyd, John Lord Herries, James Douglas of Drumlanrig, Alexander Stewart of Garlies, William Douglas of Whittingham, John Mure of Rowallan, Robert Maxwell of Cowhill, and Edward Maxwell of Drumcoltrane.

Those nominated by Johnston were Andrew Earl of Rothes, Commendator of Dunfermline, Sir James Balfour of Pittendreich, Sir James Hamilton of Craufurd-John, William Livingstoun of Jerviswood, John Johnston of Newby, Thomas Johnston of Craighopburne, Robert Douglas of Cassehogill, Walter Scott of Goldelandis, and Walter Scott of Tuschelaw.

Lord Maxwell having attained his majority, his uncle, John Lord Herries, who had been his tutor, made, 14th April 1575, an assignation to him of lands held during his minority, for the terce and courtesy of his mother, Lady Beatrix Douglas.[1]

The commission of Lord Maxwell, as Warden of the West Marches, was renewed by King James the Sixth on 4th June 1575.[2] Lord Scrope, the Warden on the English side directly opposite, testifies to the efficient manner in which he discharged the duties of this office in a letter to Lord Burghley, dated Carlisle, 29th November 1576 :—" On the 22d instant," he says, " Lord Maxwell and I met at a day march, where we made delivery of forty-two bills; the like example of justice done in one day has not been seen or heard of in these borders." [3]

In the discharge of his duties as Warden, Lord Maxwell was not, however, encouraged and assisted as he had a right to expect. Not only the yeomen within his Wardenry, but the barons and landed proprietors absented themselves from attending him on the days of truce, in consequence of which the King's authority and service were impaired, and acts of theft and other enormities were multiplied. The Regent and Privy Council, therefore, at Jedburgh, 5th December 1576, to enable Lord Maxwell the more effectively to discharge the duties of his office as Warden, ordained that an Act made by Queen Mary, with advice of the Lords of Secret Council, 12th December 1564, relating to the office of Warden, should be proclaimed at the market-cross of the burgh of Dumfries and other places needful, commanding all earls, lords, barons, freeholders, gentlemen, and substantial yeomen, without exception, dwelling within the bounds of the Wardenry of the West Marches, under the penalties contained in that Act, to meet and accompany Lord Maxwell, Warden, on all days of truce or other conventions which he should appoint by open proclamation, or by the Warden officer, or by missive letters for arresting disorders and preserving the country in peace.[4]

Though Lord Maxwell and the Regent Morton were closely connected, the claim which the former put forward to the Earldom and title of Morton

[1] Original Assignation at Terregles.
[2] Original Commission, ibid.
[3] Calendar of State Papers, Domestic Series, Queen Elizabeth, Addenda, 1566-1579, p. 506.
[4] Regist. Secreti Concilii, Acta, 1575-1577, fol. 29.

caused a jealousy on the part of the latter. The title was created by King James the Second in the year 1458, in favour of James Douglas, Lord of Dalkeith, on whose behalf the Lord Chancellor declared in Parliament that the Lord of Dalkeith was not to receive his title in the Earldom for the lands of Morton in the lordship of Niddisdale, but for the lands of Morton in the territory of Caldercleir.[1] This declaration was made in consequence of a demand by Janet Borthwick, Lady Dalkeith, on behalf of her son, William de Douglas of Morton.

The title of Earl of Morton was afterwards held by the son and grandson of the first Earl. James, the third Earl, left three daughters, Ladies Margaret, Beatrix, and Elizabeth, but no son. The eldest daughter became Duchess of Chatelherault, as the wife of the Duke ; the second daughter became Lady Maxwell, as the wife of Robert, the sixth Lord ; and the third daughter married James Douglas (brother of David Earl of Angus), afterwards the famous Regent. Owing probably to his eldest and second daughters being married to peers, whose sons would inherit their dignities, and the husband of his youngest daughter being a commoner and a Douglas, James settled his earldom and estates upon James Douglas and Lady Elizabeth, his wife, and their male children ; whom failing, upon David Douglas, brother of James, George Douglas, father of James, Archibald Earl of Angus, and other persons of the name of Douglas in succession. This settlement was confirmed by the Crown in the year 1543. Lord Maxwell, as representing the second daughter of the Earl, considered this settlement unjust ; and instead of acquiescing in it, asserted his right to the earldom, resting his claim on the ground that, as heir to his mother, he was entitled to one-third of the earldom ; that he had a right to another third by the demission executed in his favour by Margaret Duchess of Chatelherault, with consent of her husband, and the Earl of Arran, his son, but of which demission there is no proper evidence ; and that he was heir-apparent to Lady Elizabeth, who had no issue.

The Regent, doubtful of the legality of his own title as Earl of Morton,

[1] Notwithstanding this statement it is probable that the Morton title was suggested by the ancient stronghold and lands of Morton, in the parish of Morton, which were then the property of the Douglas family. Morton Castle is now in ruins, and forms part of the Drumlanrig estates of His Grace the Duke of Buccleuch and Queensberry.

and apprehensive that Lord Maxwell would press his claims, used every means to induce him to renounce them, but without success.[1] In his indignation, the Regent had recourse to severe proceedings against him. He first deprived him of the office of Warden of the West Marches. By an Act of the Privy Council, dated 11th June 1577, Archibald Earl of Angus is said to have been made lieutenant-general over all the Marches and Warden of the West Marches by the Lord Regent Morton. In the King's letters in regard to the appointment of Angus, Lord Maxwell is represented as having voluntarily demitted his office of Warden.[2] This, of course, was Morton's version of the matter, but there seems little reason to doubt that Lord Maxwell was forced to resign the Wardenship. At this meeting of Council he and Herbert Anderson, his clerk, as they had been charged, appeared personally, and produced certain books, scrolls, evidents, and other writs, concerning the Wardenry, in order to their being delivered to Archibald Earl of Angus, upon the production of which they asked instruments.

A few weeks after, on the 22d of July, Lord Maxwell was warded in the Castle of Edinburgh. He was next sent a prisoner to the Castle of Blackness.

In the beginning of August of the same year, we find him warded in that castle, with the liberty of two miles around it. His letter to his kinsman, Sir John Maxwell of Pollok, with whom he lived on terms of friendship and maintained frequent correspondence, requesting him to become one of his cautioners, is dated 1st August.[3] On the 1st and 3d of the month, Sir John Maxwell of Pollok, Patrick Houston of that Ilk, and George Maxwell of Newark, bound themselves that Lord Maxwell, then committed to ward within the Castle of Blackness, should not escape from it, and two miles thereabout, until he was liberated by the King and the Regent, under the pain of £10,000 Scots.[4]

In the beginning of September he was released from the Castle of Blackness, but was required within four days after his release to re-enter his person within the city of St. Andrews, and to remain in it, and three miles thereabout,

---

[1] MS. History of the Family of Maxwell.

[2] Regist. Secreti Concilii, Acta, 1575-1577, fol. 48.

[3] Memoirs of the Maxwells of Pollok, vol. ii. p. 142.

[4] Regist. Secreti Concilii, Acta, 1575-1577, fol. 50.

until he was freed by the King and the Regent. On the 2d of that month, John Blair of that Ilk, James Maxwell of Calderwood, and Roger Grierson of Lag, bound themselves, under the pain of 20,000 merks Scots, that Lord Maxwell should comply with these requirements.[1]

Lord Maxwell appears to have been implicated in a conspiracy which was formed by a number of the nobility to deprive Morton of his power. The other nobles involved were Argyll, Athole, Glammis, the Chancellor, the Abbot of Dumfermline, Secretary; Tullibardine, the Comptroller; with Lords Lindsay, Ruthven, and Ogilvy. That Lord Maxwell was at least believed by the party to be favourable to their design, may be inferred from his having been invited to the Convention which was to be held on the 10th of March 1577-8, by the nobles who had plotted to remove Morton from the Regency, at Stirling, where King James then was, under the care of Alexander Erskine, his governor, and commander of Stirling Castle, one of the conspirators. Morton resigned his office on the 12th of that month. On the same day it was publicly proclaimed that King James the Sixth, at that time only in the twelfth year of his age, had assumed the government of the kingdom, at the earnest desire of the nobility, Morton being present at the proclamation; and a new Council of twelve was appointed, consisting of the Earls of Argyll, Athole, Montrose, and Glencairn; the Lords Ruthven, Lindsay, and Herries; the Abbots of Newbattle and Dunfermline; the Prior of St. Andrews, with George Buchanan, the King's tutor, and James Makgill, the Clerk-Register.

Morton being now deprived of the Regency, Lord Maxwell found himself at liberty. In a petition which he presented to the King, nobility, and Estates, and which was read and considered by them at the Castle of Stirling, 13th March 1577-8, he complains that he had been detained by James Earl of Morton, late Regent, in ward within the Castles of Edinburgh and Blackness, and last of all in the city of St. Andrews, since the 22d of July last, for what cause he knew not; and that, before his coming out of the Castle of Blackness and entering into St. Andrews, he was compelled to find cautioners that he would not depart from the city of St. Andrews until he was freed by the King or the late Regent, under the pain of 20,000 merks; and since now he had repaired to Stirling, in obedience to his Majesty's letter, ready to do his

[1] Regist. Secreti Concilii, Acta, 1575-1577, fol. 53.

Majesty's service, he humbly desired that he and his cautioners might be discharged of that obligation.

The King, with advice of his nobility and Estates, declared that Lord Maxwell had done good and thankful pleasure to his Majesty in repairing to him conformably to his letter to that effect, and granted the prayer of the petition.[1]

Morton soon after—early in the month of May—recovered his power, though he did not again acquire the Regency.

A Parliament was summoned to be held at Edinburgh, on 10th July 1578. Lord Maxwell was commanded by the King to be present ; and his Lordship, deeming it expedient that he should be accompanied there with his friends, wrote from Carlaverock, on the 30th of April, to Sir John Maxwell of Pollok, desiring that, as one of his friends, he should make ready to go with him.[2]

Morton, although he obtained, from a convocation of the nobility at Stirling, a new Council, was unwilling to leave the King, who was at Stirling, and to come to the Parliament in Edinburgh, where he knew he was unpopular ; and by his persuasion a royal proclamation was issued, commanding that the Parliament should be held in the Castle of Stirling.

To oppose the meeting of this Parliament, Lord Maxwell, along with Argyll, Montrose, Herries, and others of their friends, assembled in Edinburgh in the beginning of July, declaring that they could not attend a Parliament held in a garrisoned fortress, where it was not to be expected that freedom of discussion would be allowed. The Parliament, however, having been opened on the 10th of July, in the Tolbooth of Edinburgh, was continued till the 25th of July, when, in terms of the King's proclamation, it was transferred to the Castle of Stirling. Lord Maxwell, Argyll, Athole, and their adherents did not go to the Parliament, but sent the Earl of Montrose and Lord Lindsay as their commissioners to protest against its proceedings, as it could in no sense be called a free Parliament.[3]

The differences between these factions threatened to produce a civil war.

In August 1578, John Lord Maxwell, once more Warden of the West Marches, combined with the Earl of Athole, Chancellor, Earl of Argyll,

[1] Regist. Secreti Concilii, Acta, 1577-1579, fol. 4.
[2] Memoirs of the Maxwells of Pollok, vol. ii. p. 143.
[3] Calderwood's History, vol. iii. pp. 409, 410 ; Tytler's History, vol. vi. pp. 247, 248.

Chief-Justice, and the Lairds of Coldingknowes and Cessford, for relief of the King, whom they regarded as held captive by the Earl of Morton, and the Abbots of Dryburgh and Cambuskenneth ; the Master of Mar, who was captain, being shut out of the castle.   At Falkirk they mustered, on the 13th of that month, 7000 strong.   They carried a banner of blue sarcenet, on which was painted the device of a boy within a grated window, with the motto,

> " Liberty I crave,
> And cannot it have,"

in allusion to the alleged thraldom of the King.   To meet them the Earl of Angus, recently proclaimed Lieutenant-General to the King, appeared at the head of 5000 men.[1]   When the skirmishing between the two armies had commenced, Sir Robert Bowes, Queen Elizabeth's ambassador, offered himself as a peacemaker, in her name, and succeeded in reconciling the two factions.

Shortly after, a summons was raised by John Bek, taskar, against Lord Maxwell for personal maltreatment.   The summons makes mention that in the month of August 1578 Lord Maxwell, by the persuasion of Robert Maxwell of Cowhill, took and put the complainer in prison, in the place of Carlaverock, in which he was detained for ten days, and at last taken out and conveyed to a wood-side adjoining, where he was bound hand and foot to a tree, and then a small cord, being tied about his head, was twisted round with a pin until his " ene lapend vpoun his cheikis ;" all which was done to him simply because he would not bear false testimony against John Schortrig of Mareholme as to alleged wrongs done by him to Lord Maxwell, in reference to certain corns.   After this cruel handling, Bek was again, by the persuasion of Robert Maxwell of Cowhill, committed to prison, where he still lay on 16th October.   The summons charged Lord Maxwell to bring and exhibit the complainer before the King and the Lords of Secret Council, and to hear and see him decerned to be set at liberty, as one of his Majesty's free lieges, or else to show a reasonable cause to the contrary, under the pain of rebellion and putting him to the horn.   The case came before the Privy Council at their meeting at the castle of Stirling, on the 16th of October ; and Lord Maxwell not compearing, the Council ordained letters to be directed to him, charging

---

[1] MS. History of the Maxwell Family ; Tytler's History of Scotland, vol. vi. p. 250.

him to set at liberty John Bek, taskar, within three days after the charge, under the pain of rebellion.[1]

In January 1578-9, Lord Maxwell was summoned to appear before the King and the Privy Council for neglecting the duties of his office as Warden of the West Marches,—a charge which was often brought against his grandfather, Robert, fifth Lord Maxwell, and of which an extenuation might almost at all times have been found in the arduous nature of the duties of that office. He pleaded in defence the limitations of his commission.

The opinion and advice of Lord Herries, a man of eminent reputation, who had long enjoyed the office, were asked. He gave in to the King a statement, which contains much information concerning the past and present condition of the West Marches, and his judgment as to the best means of maintaining good order within them, and as to the duties of the office of warden and justiciary of these parts.

In this document Lord Herries attributes the origin of the disturbances, for which the Borders were so notable, to some disaffected Scotsmen, who, in the time of King James the Fifth, had settled on the English frontiers, and who, enjoying the protection of the English, made incursions into Scotland, and gradually became formidable from their number, wealth, and fortified places.

The attention of King James the Fifth, he informs us, was turned, a little before his death, to a few of his disloyal subjects, who, having planted themselves on the frontiers of England, in the opposite wardenry, had made sundry inroads into Scotland, and, supported by the English, were growing in number and in power ; and that monarch sent a great company of nobles and others to punish them by fire and sword. From lack of government and of military knowledge, and having no provisions, this company fled. By their defeat, the Grahams and their marauding associates, the inhabitants of Esk, Levin, and Sark, whom they were sent to destroy, got from the ransoms of the chiefs of that company, and by plunder, 100,000 merks, with which, aided further by more than £100,000 Scots, which they subsequently obtained in Scotland, they built upon the Scottish frontiers eight or nine great stone houses, impregnable to the Warden of Scotland. They further strengthened themselves by matrimonial alliances with most of the Scottish Borderers adjacent to them,

[1] Regist. Secreti Concilii, Acta, 1577-1579, fol. 77.

who, to secure themselves from plunder, were glad to take the daughters of these marauders in marriage without tocher.

In the year 1542, when King James the Fifth died, they did not exceed in number twenty or thirty, but, at the time when Lord Herries wrote, they had, with their plundering accomplices, increased to sixteen or eighteen score, ready, at an hour or a half-hour's warning, all well-horsed men, to commit their depredations in Scotland. In addition to their deeds of spoliation they had perpetrated outrageous slaughters on more than a hundred Scotsmen and burned much of the country. Besides, England had destroyed the House of Annand, burned Dumfries, the principal town within the West Marches, and the houses of loyal subjects, built on the Scottish frontiers, for their protection, so that within twenty miles of the marches of England, on the Scottish side, there was no strong place in which a loyal subject could remain secure.

The thieves already mentioned, with the assistance of English accomplices, had slain the principal Scottish barons that were nearest to the marches, such as Lord Carlisle, the lairds of Mousewald, Kirkmichaell, Kirkconnell, and Logan, in Annandale, with many other sober landed men, and had planted and occupied the most part of their lands. The Warden, therefore, lacking the substantial households of the honest men that were ever helpful to him and true as his own household, dared not approach the frontiers of Scotland to do his Majesty's service, in the exercise of his office, unless he was accompanied with others besides the inhabitants of that country. The West Marches of England were planted to the very frontiers with strongholds. The city of Carlisle, with a strong castle, well munitioned, the constant residence of the English warden, was within four miles of the marches of Scotland. The Castle of Rockleiff, which could sufficiently lodge a hundred horse and men, was only about three-quarters of a mile from the Scottish Borders, and there were many strong stone houses along the English marches, fronting the realm of Scotland. Further, the English frontier had a fruitful soil, abounded in good corns, was governed by good laws, and had obedient subjects. The frontiers of Scotland, on the contrary, were pasture ground, which was very bare, and until it came far within the realm, was in a great measure fit only for cattle, one man requiring ten times more such land in order to be equally sustained with a man that lived on corn ground. For this reason the West Marches of England were much more populous than those of Scotland.

In his advice for maintaining good order in the West Marches, Lord Herries recommended much that was most important, though his nephew, as we shall afterwards see, took exception to several of his recommendations.

At a meeting of the Privy Council at the Castle of Stirling, 20th January 1578-9,[1] Lord Herries presented to the King the paper now referred to, which was read in presence of the King and Council. This document Lord Maxwell termed "a pernicious council, rather inventit vpoun malice than ony favour to the commoun weill." It contained, he said, recommendations injurious to him, and he required to consider it. It was therefore delivered to him, in compliance with his request. Having declared to Lord Ruthven, lieutenant at Dumfries, that he had not actually accepted the charge of the Wardenry of the West Marches, but was only induced to continue to retain it until his coming to the King, when he would either assume or resign it, he was required by the Council presently to say whether he would retain that office or not. He promised to give a written answer on the morrow ; and, to enable him the better to understand the state of the country, and those who were obedient or disobedient, the book of pledges was delivered to him.[2]

At a meeting of the Council at the Castle of Stirling, the day after (21st January), he presented a roll of the names of the disobedient within the bounds of the West Marches, amounting to upwards of 500, and also delivered a written answer in regard to his retaining the office of Warden. He expressed his willingness to retain it on certain conditions. He required from his Majesty and the Council security that he should be obeyed by all his Majesty's subjects, without exception, within that jurisdiction ; and that any nobleman, baron, or others his Majesty's immediate tenants within it who failed to fulfil his general bond, should, on complaint being made to his Majesty, and after due trial, be punished. Since there remained a great number of fugitives disobedient, with whom no baron nor other of his Majesty's loyal tenants might

---

[1] The sederunt at this meeting of Council were John Earl of Montrose, Andrew Earl of Rothes, William Earl of Glencairn, William Lord Ruthven, the Commendator of Dumfermline, and the Commendator of Cambuskenneth.—Regist. Secreti Concilii, Acta, 1577-1579, fol. 108.

[2] Regist. Secreti Concilii, Acta, 1577-1579, fol. 108, 109.

justly be burdened upon the general band, he thought it requisite that a company of horsemen should be levied and maintained, according to the number of these fugitives, for reducing them to obedience. He also desired that he might obtain from his Majesty as ample a commission as any of his predecessors in the said office had possessed, and that no fugitive, being once denounced, should be received again to peace but by him, or at least without his advice. Lastly, he would accept the office of Warden only on condition that he should receive payment of his fees and duties bygone and to come during his service in that office.[1] He added, that if it should please his Majesty to cause his Majesty's house in Annand to be built, it would much further obedience in time of peace, and strengthen the Borders in time of war.

At the meeting of the Council at the Castle of Stirling, 22d January 1578-9, Lord Maxwell presented an answer to the discourse and advice of his uncle, Lord Herries, in reference to the Borders, so far as it touched himself, and it was read in audience of the Council.

In his advice for maintaining good order in the West Marches, Lord Herries recommended that the Warden, who was Justiciary-General, should reside with his household at Lochmaben, and that, should he remove from it in winter to Dumfries, he should always have a deputy in Lochmaben. He further recommended that the Justice Court, or Steward Court, as it was called, should be held weekly in the town of Lochmaben ; that every landed man should present his tenants when he was required ; and that, to assist the Steward, there should be five or six of the wisest men of the country as deputies, of which number there should be two Johnstons. He again suggested that the Laird of Johnston, to give him no occasion to think that the correction of his thieves was done either from greed or from any improper cause, should have the one-half of the escheats of such of his men for whom he was bound as were convicted and executed, and that the other half should be divided equally between the wife and children of the culprits, if any, and the officers who made the search. He was also of opinion that his Majesty should grant a worthy gentleman as captain, and wages to twenty-four well horsed men, to lie at his Majesty's destroyed town of Annand, for the punishment of those disloyal subjects ; and that the captain should have for

---

[1] Regist. Secreti Concilii, Acta, 1577-1579, fol. 109.

his yearly salary £200, with eight great bolls of oats, and each of his soldiers £100, with several bolls of oats ; the oats to be taken up from the Grange of Lochmaben.   He further judged it expedient that Lord Maxwell, whose grandfather obtained the most part of the lands of Eskdale, Ewisdale, and Wauchopdale from King James the Fifth, should, if he was Warden, and remained at Lochmaben, have a suitable person to be deputy and captain in the Langholm.   To this deputy and to his household Lord Maxwell should allow the whole of his mails, multures, and other duties of his lands there, and all the profits of the kirks of Watsticker, Stabilgortoun, Wauchope, and Nether kirk of Ewis, it being always understood that the ministers of the Church were to be first sustained.   In this way twelve horsemen with their captain might be maintained.

Lord Maxwell regarded these recommendations of his uncle as extremely detrimental to his interests, and in an answer to them, which he addressed to the King, he complains of their injustice.

In objecting to the advice of Lord Herries, that the Warden should reside in the Castle of Lochmaben, Lord Maxwell urged that the custody of that castle was by itself an office having fees and duties appropriate thereto, and of long time had belonged to him as to his predecessors.   He affirmed that, for due obedience to the Steward Court of Annandale, held weekly in the town of Lochmaben, it was most needful that the castle should be committed to him, as most convenient for his residence as Steward.   He maintained that the most proper place for the residence of the Warden in that country was Annan, where he would have the same advantage on the Scottish side, which the English Warden had on the other side, directly opposite, by residing at Carlisle, Annan being of the like distance with Carlisle from the frontiers.

Lord Maxwell further objected to his uncle's proposed division of the escheats of the Laird of Johnston's men who were executed by justice.   Should the Laird of Johnston, he argued, have this reward for his disobedience, other barons might thereby be encouraged to disobedience in order to their obtaining the same advantage, and there was no good reason why the casualties of the country should be taken from his Majesty's officers.

In regard to the advice that the farm-corn of Lochmaben should be supplied to the garrison for their horse-corn, he answered that the corn which his uncle would appropriate in this way was the chief fee annexed for the custody of the Castle of Lochmaben; and should his Majesty, like his predecessors, be pleased to repair to that country, where should his horses' corn be had?

To the advice that he should provide a captain in the Langholm, who was to have the revenues specified, he replied that, since he had bound himself as strictly for his lands and servants to the King as the other freeholders within the Wardenry had done, it was unjust to impose such burdens specially upon him.[1]

On the same day on which Lord Maxwell gave in to the Council this answer, the Council agreed upon certain conditions, which were to be accepted by the Warden of the West Marches. These conditions, with some qualifications, amounted to a concession of what Lord Maxwell desired as the terms of his accepting that office. They are as follows:—

The Kingis maiestie will se his Wardane to haue vniuersale obeydience of all his Maiesteis subiectis within the jurisdictioun of the west Wardanerie, without exceptioun; the Wardane doand equale and indifferent iustice to all personis be the gude aduise of sic baronis of the cuntrie as his Maiestie and the counsale sall appoint.

Sic nobilmen or baronis as failzeis in fulfilling of thair generall band vpoun complaint of the Wardane salbe callit befoir his Maiestie and his counsale, and eftir dew tryell the failzear salbe puneist as appertenis.

Sic securitie as is for all the Kingis subiectis within the west Wardanry be the bandis of thair landislordis plegis or vtherwayis the Wardane salbe informit of, and for the suppressing of ony sic as ar [or] salbe dissobeydient his Maiestie will grant a cumpany of xxiiii horsmen and a capitane, with sic pay and for sic space as his Hienes sall think expedient, and that they and thair capitane salbe at commandiment as his Hienes may haue occasioun vtherwayis to employ thame.

The Wardane sal haue als ampill commissioun as ony that hes seruit in that office of befoir, and na fugitives anis lauchfullie denuncit salbe takin in or ressett to peax quhill warning be gevin to the warden and his aduise socht, prouiding he denunce and mak na fugitiuis without gude and deliberat aduise of the baronis, and signifie his denunceatioune to the King and counsale.

The Wardane sall tak or apprehend na landit mannis man or seruand for quhome thair maisteris standis bound, except they be taikin reid hand, quhill his maister be first dewlie chargit for his entrie or be fund to haue faillit in his band or promeis, or that he haue na maister or landislord that will tak on hand to enter him, or that the Warden and iustice haue a speciall

---

[1] Lord Herries's Discourse and Lord Maxwell's Answer are registered at length in the Minutes of the Privy Council, as ordained by them, at the meeting at the Castle of Stirling, 23d January 1578-9. —Regist. Secreti Concilii, Acta, 1577-1579, fol. 113.

or particular warrand and directioun frome the Kingis Hienes, with auise of his Counsale, for the said apprehensioun.

The Wardane salbe thankfullie answerit of his feis and dewis according to the tyme of his seruice.   His Maiestie wilbe cairfull for the reparatioun and bigging of his houss of Lochmaben and Annand how sone the commoditie may convenientlie serue.

These conditions having been read to Lord Maxwell, and the question having been put to him, whether he would retain the office of the West War-denry upon such conditions, he answered in the affirmative, on the under-standing that he should have such liberties and privileges as were enjoyed by his ancestors who had served in the office.[1]

Yet on the same day, at the request of the King and the Privy Council, Lord Herries accepted the office of Warden of the West Marches ; upon which John Lord Maxwell protested that he had offered himself as ready to retain and to serve the King in that office.[2]

It was most important for the good rule of the Borders that frequent meetings should be held and friendly co-operation maintained between the Wardens of Scotland and England at the West Marches.   These meetings were usually held on the field, and there was, of course, great difficulty in holding them in the short winter days, when there was barely sufficient light for the Wardens to reach their usual place of meeting and return to their homes on the same day, without allowing for time to be spent in the admini-stration of justice ; and there not being any good lodging by the way, it was very inconvenient for them to remain out for the night.   To meet this diffi-culty, the King with the Privy Council, on 23d January 1578-9, declared it expedient that, whenever his Warden of the West Marches found it needful, he should repair to Carlisle, or any other place within the West Marches of England, on a safe-conduct from the English Warden opposite, to whom he might grant the like safe-conduct, to come with his company to Dumfries, or to any other part within the West Marches of Scotland.[3]

At the same meeting of Council Lord Maxwell bound himself to enter Edward Armstrong before the King and Council, on the 20th of February next, under the pain of £2000.   On the same day six persons, three of them of the name of Beattie, who had been detained as pledges, were allowed to

[1] Regist. Secreti Concilii, Acta, 1577-1579, fol. 111.   [2] Ibid. fol. 112.   [3] Ibid. fol. 113.

go home to him, at his suit, on his becoming bound that, if any of those for whom they had lain as pledges should hereafter not answer the laws, he should again enter them as pledges, under the pain, for each, of £2000.

On the 24th of January 1578-9, King James the Sixth revoked the lease made in his minority to John Lord Maxwell, Warden of the West Marches, of the Castle of Lochmaben, lands, rents, fishings and possessions belonging thereto ; and the keeping of that castle was thereafter committed to John Lord Herries, then Warden of the West Marches.[1]   On the 27th of the same month, Lord Maxwell became bound, before the Privy Council, at Stirling Castle, to cause that Castle, with all scrolls, rolls and bands made to him as Warden, for the entry of any person whomsoever, and of all prisoners then remaining in the Pledge Chamber, to be delivered to John Lord Herries on the 2d of February next, under the pain of 2000 merks, and to remain within the burgh of Stirling until he found surety to that effect.[2]   Having, at the time fixed, in terms of this obligation, delivered the Castle of Lochmaben, etc., to Lord Herries, he obtained from the Privy Council, 11th April 1579, on showing his discharge, a decreet declaring that he had fulfilled the command of the Act of Council, and exonering him of that Act and of all pains contained therein.[3]

On the same day Lord Maxwell promised to present John Armstrong of Caffield before the King and the Privy Council on the 1st of May next, under the pain of £2000.[4]   He also submitted himself to such advice and order as the King and Lords of Council should give to him in regard to the Armstrongs of the Gyngillis and their accomplices.   In the meantime, as a means of more effectually maintaining quiet government on the Borders, it was ordained that Lord Herries should take assurance between the Armstrongs of the Gyngillis and the Elliots of Ewisdale until the 31st of that month, or until midsummer, and bring four or half-a-dozen of the principal of each party with him, that the King and his Council might cause their offences to be considered, and obtain requisite security for the performance of what they had promised.

[1] These facts are narrated in an Act of Privy Council, 16th February 1578-9, ordaining letters to be directed charging the tenants and intromitters with the mails, etc., of the said Castle of Lochmaben, lands, etc., to make payment to Lord Herries, his factors or servants, of the same, within ten days thereafter, so far as resting or intromitted with by Lord Maxwell at the time of the revocation mentioned in the text.—Regist. Secreti Concilii, Acta, 1577-1579, fol. 132.

[2] Regist. Secreti Concilii, Acta, 1577-1579, fol. 129.

[3] Ibid. fol. 195.

[4] Ibid. fol. 195.

Lord Maxwell, on the King's command, promised not to disturb the Armstrongs in occupying their rooms.[1]   He was also ordered to bring and present Robert Maxwell, his brother-natural, before the King and the Council, on the 20th of May, to answer to such things as should be laid to his charge.[2]

The Council having charged the tenants and intromitters with the mails, etc., of the Castle of Lochmaben, lands, etc., to make payment thereof to Lord Herries, Lord Maxwell resisted this order of the Council.   At their meeting, 11th April 1579, he produced certain leases made to his grandfather and himself of the castle, its lands, profits and fishings, alleging that these leases were a sufficient right for his intromitting therewith, notwithstanding his Majesty's revocation, and command to him to answer Lord Herries, then Warden of the West Marches.   The King and Council ordained the dates of these leases to be noted, and deferred the determination of the question whether Lord Maxwell's pretended title was valid in law against his Majesty's revocation to the 20th of May next.   In the meantime they commanded that Lord Maxwell should in nowise intromit with the Castle of Lochmaben, its fruits, rents and profits until the decision of the King and Council.   Lord Maxwell protested that his Majesty's command and ordinance foresaid should in nowise prejudge his title and possession of the castle, its fruits, rents and profits.

On the 25th of May 1579, Lord Maxwell and Lord Herries having appeared personally before the Council, Lord Maxwell protested that before being prejudged of his lease of the Castle of Lochmaben, lands, profits and fishings belonging thereto, he might be treated in conformity with law, that is, lawfully summoned before a judge competent; and, if he should be presently proceeded against contrary to this right, he protested.   The King and Lords of Council found that they were judges competent in this matter, and that the keepers of his Majesty's castles might, according to the laws of the realm and Acts of Parliament, be removed according to his Majesty's good pleasure.   They decerned that the letter of lease or commission made by the King in his minority, with advice of James Earl of Morton, Regent, of the Castle of Lochmaben, lands, profits and fishings belonging thereto, fell under the King's revocation upon the 24th day of January bypast, and that the letter of lease had no further strength after the date of that Act.   They

[1] Regist. Secreti Concilii, Acta, 1577-1579, fol. 106.			[2] *Ibid.* fol. 106.

therefore ordained that the tenants and intromitters with the mails, etc., of the lands, rents, fishings and possessions belonging to the Castle of Lochmaben should make payment thereof, in terms of the Act passed against them on 16th February last.[1]

In the beginning of August 1579 Lord Maxwell was again committed to prison by the Earl of Morton. In November he was transferred as a prisoner from the Castle of Blackness to the burgh of Edinburgh. On the 25th of that month Thomas MacClellan of Bomby and James Maxwell of Calderwood became bound, as cautioners for him, that, being freed from his ward within the Castle of Blackness, he should immediately repair to the burgh of Edinburgh, within which, and one mile thereabout, he should remain, until he was released by the King, under the pain of 20,000 merks.[2]

Lord Maxwell was, however, shortly after allowed by the King to go home for the better performing of such directions as his Majesty, with the advice of his Council, had given him for the furtherance of his Majesty's service. In consideration of this, Thomas MacClellan of Bomby and John Maxwell of Pollok, as Lord Maxwell's cautioners, became bound before the Council, held at Holyroodhouse on the 11th of December, that his Lordship, his men, tenants and servants for whom he was bound by the general band, should behave themselves as dutiful subjects to the King; that he should obey and assist the King's Warden in the exercise of his office; and that he should enter his person again in ward in the Castle of Blackness between the date of that Act and the 8th of February following, until the obligation to enter should be removed from him, and thereafter until he should be lawfully liberated, under the pain of 20,000 merks.[3]

On the same day Lord Maxwell became bound, as cautioner for Robert Maxwell of Cowhill, then in ward within the Castle of Inverness, that being set at liberty he should keep ward within the burgh of Edinburgh, and three miles thereabout, until freed by the King, under the pain of £2000.

Lord Maxwell's illegitimate brother, Robert Maxwell, and Archibald Maxwell of Cowhill, had, about this time, inflicted personal injury on Robert Johnston of Carnsalloch, whom they pursued and hurt within the burgh of Dumfries, to the effusion of his blood in great quantity; and at the same

---

[1] Regist. Secreti Concilii, Acta, 1577-1579, fol. 245.   [2] Ibid. 1579-1581, fol. 370.   [3] Ibid. fol. 381.

time Archibald Maxwell suffered bodily harm. The King and the Lords of Council, in order to try the case impartially, considered it necessary that assurance should be taken between both the parties and their principal friends that nothing should in the meantime be attempted to hinder the trial. They therefore, at Holyroodhouse, on 9th February 1579-80, ordained letters to be directed to John Lord Maxwell and Robert Maxwell, his brother, on the one part, and John Johnston of that Ilk and Robert Johnston of Carnsalloch on the other part, charging them within twenty-four hours to confirm, under the pain of rebellion, such form of assurance as should be presented to them, noted by the Clerk of Council, to continue to the 1st of August next.[1]

On 14th February 1579-80, Lord Maxwell became bound as cautioner that Robert Maxwell of Cowhill should repair from the burgh of Aberdeen to that of Edinburgh, and keep ward within it, and a mile thereabout, until he was freed by the King, under the pain of £2000.[2]

On the same day the Lords of Secret Council dispensed with the entry of John Lord Maxwell within the Castle of Blackness to the 1st of May, that he might pass home to his own dwelling-house, provided the sureties found by him on the 11th of December last should stand bound for his entry within the Castle of Blackness on the day appointed.[3]

On 4th March following he became bound as cautioner, under the pain of £1000, that Robert Maxwell, his brother-natural, then in ward within the Castle of Dumbarton, should, on being set at liberty, immediately repair to the burgh of Edinburgh, and keep ward within it and a mile thereabout, until he was freed by the King and Lords of Council.[4]

John Lord Herries having ceased to be Warden of the West Marches, the office was conferred upon John Johnston of that Ilk. Johnston appears as holding that office on 4th May 1580. The conferring upon a rival an office which Lord Maxwell's ancestors had held for ages was regarded by him as a studied affront, and the angry feeling which already existed between their families was much aggravated, and was the origin of many disastrous conflicts, calamitous not only to the families themselves, but to the whole shire of Dumfries.

[1] Regist. Secreti Concilii, Acta, 1579-1581, fol. 411.   [3] Regist. Secreti Concilii, Acta, 1579-1581, fol. 414.
[2] *Ibid.* fol. 413.   [4] *Ibid.* 1579-1581, fol. 421.

Letters were raised at the instance of John Johnston, Warden of the West Marches, against John Lord Maxwell, formerly Warden of these Marches, and Robert Maxwell of Cowhill, his deputy, charging them to deliver to the present Warden certain English bills filed by them on the 6th of May 1578, and also a note of the Scottish bills filed at the same time by Lord Scrope, Warden of the English Marches opposite, that the present Warden might give redress to the English, and obtain redress to his Majesty's subjects of Scotland.

The case came before the Lords of Privy Council, of which James Earl of Morton, Lord Maxwell's enemy, was still a conspicuous member, his name appearing first on the roll, at their meeting in the Castle of Stirling, 4th May 1580. John Johnston, the Warden, Lord Maxwell personally, and Robert Maxwell by his procurator, compeared before the Council; and the parties having been heard, the Council determined in favour of Johnston in terms of the summons against Lord Maxwell and his deputy, charging them to deliver to Johnston the documents within ten days after their being charged to do so, under the pain of rebellion and being put to the horn.[1]

At the same meeting of Council a complaint was made to the King and Council by Johnston against Lord Maxwell, to the effect that he had convened his Majesty's lieges in warlike manner, and committed, with his accomplices, sundry crimes upon the complainant, his friends, servants and assisters, in violation of the assurance by which they had pledged themselves to each other. The Council admitted the complaint in so far as it related to the breach of the assurance on the part of Lord Maxwell, and assigned to Johnston the 21st of May for proof thereof. They further ordained that the assurance by which the said parties had been bound to each other for themselves, their kin, friends, servants, tenants and assisters, should have full force, to the 1st of August following, notwithstanding the complaint.[2]

On the 7th of May, Lord Maxwell became bound that he should compear personally before the King and Lords of Council on the 15th of June next, and remain thereafter with his Majesty, until he was set at liberty. His cautioners were James Campbell of Ardkinglas, and John Campbell of Calder, knight. The penalty was 20,000 merks in case of failure. The

[1] Regist. Secreti Concilii, Acta, 1579-1581, fol. 437.   [2] Ibid. fol. 437.

sureties formerly found for his entering himself in ward within the Castle of Blackness were *simpliciter* discharged.[1]

By the procurement of John Johnston of that Ilk, Lord Maxwell and Robert Maxwell of Cowhill were denounced rebels and put to the horn for not having obeyed the summons formerly mentioned by delivering to Johnston, as Warden of the West Marches, the scrolls and bills filed by Lord Maxwell during the time that he was Warden, together with notes of English bills said to be in his hands.

Lord Maxwell and Robert Maxwell of Cowhill raised counter letters against Johnston, wherein they pleaded that they had left nothing undone in regard to the delivering of these scrolls and bills to Johnston, and charged Johnston to compear before the King and Council, and produce the letters of horning against them, with the execution thereof, and to hear and see them suspended *simpliciter*. The case came before the King and Lords of Council on 29th July 1580. Lord Maxwell and John Johnston appeared personally. Lord Maxwell produced the English bills, which, he alleged, had presently come into his hands, and also a note of the Scotch bills filed by Lord Scrope, with the names of the persons upon whom the English bills were filed. The Council found that, as the English and Scotch bills had not been delivered to Johnston within the time prescribed by the letters executed upon Lord Maxwell, the letters had been orderly executed upon him, and ordained that the bills, notes, and other writs produced by Lord Maxwell should be delivered to Johnston, for the better discharge of his office, to be however again returned to Lord Maxwell for his relief.[2]

These bills having been produced, the Council, on 30th July, suspended *simpliciter* the letters of horning procured by Johnston against Lord Maxwell and Robert Maxwell of Cowhill.[3]

The dispute between Lord Maxwell and Johnston of that Ilk had now become so serious, and the Government was so desirous to have it settled, that the Privy Council interposed, and brought them to subscribe, in their presence at Holyroodhouse, 2d September 1580, a mutual assurance, whereby they became bound that the kin, friends, men, tenants, servants, assisters

---

[1] Regist. Secreti Concilii, Acta, 1579-1581, fol. 440.		[2] Regist. Secreti Concilii, Acta, 1579-1581, fol. fol. 453.		[3] *Ibid.* fol. 454.

and partakers of the one should not hurt or molest those of the other in time coming, for whatsoever cause or quarrel preceding that date, otherwise than by order of law and justice, to the 1st of April next, under the pain of perjury, and loss of honour, in time coming.[1]

On the same day Lord Maxwell, at command of the King and Lords of Council, subscribed a similar assurance to Edward Maxwell of Tinwald, James Maxwell of Portrak, and Archibald Newall in Dumfries, to continue until the 1st of April. At the same time, John Johnston of that Ilk declared that the three persons to whom this assurance was given then were and had been his assisters in the quarrels standing between him and Lord Maxwell, his kin and friends,[2] and therefore protested that they should be held as his assisters, as if they had been specially mentioned in the assurance subscribed by him and Lord Maxwell. But Lord Maxwell protested that, as he had given and subscribed a special assurance to Edward Maxwell, James Maxwell, and Archibald Newall and others, their kin and friends, he should not be bound to them by any other assurance.[3]

After the arrival in Scotland of Esme Stewart, Lord d'Aubigny, from France, on 8th September 1579, Lord Maxwell became closely associated with that nobleman.

Esme Stewart was young, graceful, and accomplished, and immediately rose into high favour with his kinsman, King James, by whom he was first made Earl, and, on 25th August 1581, Duke of Lennox. Captain James Stewart, afterwards Earl of Arran (second son of Lord Ochiltree), a man of courtly address, but profligate, rapacious, intolerant and unprincipled, was also a favourite of the King. The ascendancy acquired by these men over the royal mind produced a great change in the administration of public affairs, which proved favourable to Lord Maxwell, and fatal to his enemy, the Earl of Morton.

One of the first proofs of this change produced was the depriving Johnston of the Wardenship of the West Marches, and the restoration of Lord Maxwell to that office.

---

[1] Regist. Secreti Concilii, Acta, 1579-1581, fol. 460.

[2] A mutual bond to that effect between Johnston and Edward Maxwell of Tinwald, and James Maxwell of Portrak, is dated 8th April 1580.—Original Bond at Raehills.

[3] Regist. Secreti Concilii, Acta, 1579-1581, fol. 460.

Sundry reports were made to the King that Johnston had of late conducted himself less dutifully than hitherto towards his Majesty; and that he had especially shown favour to certain disloyal persons. As, however, Johnston was his Majesty's officer, and had in time past acted faithfully in his office as Warden of the West Marches, to the quietness of the country, his Majesty and the Lords of Secret Council were not inclined hastily to give credit to these reports, and charged him to compear before them at Holyroodhouse, on the 22d of April 1581, to certify whether or not they were true.

Johnston, who probably believed that his deprivation and the substitution of Lord Maxwell in his place was determined upon, failed to appear before the Lords of Council; and they thereupon ordained letters to be directed to the Sheriff's officer for denouncing him his Majesty's rebel, and putting him to the horn.[1]

Lord Maxwell was restored to his office of Warden of the West Marches by two separate commissions, the one dated at Edinburgh on the 27th, and the other at Dalkeith on the 30th, of April 1581.[2] On the 29th of the same month the King ordained that his Sheriffs in that part should pass to the Market Cross of Dumfries, and other places needful, and there by open proclamation, in his Majesty's name, command all the inhabitants within the Wardenry to obey Lord Maxwell in all things tending to the furtherance of his Majesty's service in the punishment of offenders, the redress of grievances both to the subjects of England and Scotland, and the preservation of good order.[3]

Lennox and Arran set their minds upon the destruction of Morton, and by their contrivance he was brought to trial on the 1st of June 1581. The chief article in his indictment was that he had been accessory to the murder of the King's father, Lord Darnley. He confessed that, though he had neither contrived nor given his consent to that murder, he yet knew, but had concealed it, and on this confession he was convicted by a jury. He was beheaded on Friday the 2d of June, by the machine called the "Maiden," which he had

---

[1] Regist. Secreti Concilii, Acta, 1579-1581, fol. 558.

[2] Original Commissions at Terregles.

[3] Regist. Secreti Concilii, Acta, 1579-1581, fol. 560.

introduced into Scotland. His body was interred in the Greyfriars' Church-yard at Edinburgh. No monument marks his grave.

In anticipation of this event, when Morton was in prison awaiting his trial for treason, a remarkable agreement was entered into, on 29th April 1581, between Esme Earl of Lennox, then the Great Chamberlain of Scotland, and Lord Maxwell, son and apparent heir to Dame Beatrix Douglas, daughter, and one of the three heirs of the deceased James Earl of Morton, and thereby " maist abill" to succeed to him. The agreement provided that Lennox should endeavour to get Maxwell appointed Chamberlain on the Earldom of Morton ; that brieves of idiotry should be raised against the three daughters of the late Earl of Morton ; and that Maxwell should be made tutor to them. If the late Regent was convicted, Lennox promised to use his influence to obtain for Maxwell a grant of the earldom of Morton, etc. There were to be excepted the baronies of Dalkeith and Aberdour, and the lands of Caldercleir, which were to be the property of Lennox.[1]

The forfeiture and execution of Morton having followed, Lord Maxwell obtained from King James the Sixth a grant of the Earldom of Morton by two charters. The first is dated at Holyroodhouse, 5th June 1581, and grants to him the lands, baronies, earldom, regality, and annual rents of Morton, as particularly described, which had fallen into the hands of the King, and were at his disposal, through the forfeiture of the deceased James, formerly Earl of Morton, for the crimes of lese-Majesty committed by him, of which he had been convicted.[2] It does not, however, contain any grant of the title of honour of Earl of Morton.[3] In terms of this charter, John Lord Maxwell, on 17th June 1581, was, on a precept of sasine by King James the Sixth, infeft in the barony of Morton.[4]

John Lord Maxwell was created Earl of Morton, Lord Carleill and Esk-

---

[1] Original Agreement at Terregles. The signatures have been torn away, along with part of the Agreement adjoining them.

[2] Original Charter at Terregles.

[3] At this time Lord Maxwell was in need of money, and he borrowed from George Heriot, goldsmith in Edinburgh, 1000 merks. For this money Heriot was to receive an annual rent of 120 merks Scots, out of the lands of Mollattisheuch and Newtoun, in the barony of the Mearns and shire of Renfrew. In terms of a letter of reversion from Heriot and Katherine Asloane, his spouse, to Lord Maxwell, dated at Edinburgh, 14th June 1581, the principal sum of 1000 merks was to be repaid in currency of the time, "that cunze callit stampit plakkis and stampit penneis alwys exceptit."— Original Instrument of Reversion at Terregles. The seals of Heriot and his wife are appended, and both are entire.

[4] Original Instrument of Sasine at Terregles.

daill, etc., in the month of October 1581. An original extract from the records of the Lyon Office bears that the creation took place at Holyroodhouse, on 29th April 1581.[1] It is, however, certain that 29th April is a mistake for 29th October. In a decreet of the Privy Council, dated 11th January 1621, decerning that Robert, first Earl of Nithsdale, should enjoy the precedency of an Earl from the date of the creation of his father, John Lord Maxwell, as Earl of Morton, it is particularly and repeatedly stated that his said father was created by the King Earl of Morton in the month of October 1581.[2] The purport of the patent of his creation, which is there given, bears the same date.

In the memoirs of Moysie it is said that John Earl of Morton was one of the five Peers who were belted at Holyroodhouse upon Sunday the 29th of October 1581. The belting of Lord Maxwell as Earl of Morton, and other five earls at the same time, after formal charters of creation had been expede in favour of some of these earls, shows the importance then attached to the solemn form of belting, as it is called in an old Act of Parliament.

In the decreet above quoted, it is further stated that Robert Earl of Nithsdale, for verification of his claim of precedency, produced before the Lords of Council a note under the hand of Sir George Hay of Netherliff, knight, Clerk of Register, extracted out of the Books of Parliament, bearing that in the Parliament held at Edinburgh in the month of October 1581, the Earl of Morton, his father, was present, and sat and was ranked among the Earls, and was upon the Articles.

In the second charter referred to, by which the earldom of Morton was granted to John Lord Maxwell, dated 9th November 1581, the grantee is designated John Earl of Morton, Lord Maxwell. This second charter confirms the first, but it does not contain any creation of the title of honour, which had taken place previous to the date of the charter.

Soon after the second charter was granted, an Act of Parliament was made, on 29th November 1581, in favour of John Earl of Morton, Lord Maxwell, ratifying his charter and infeftment of the earldom of Morton.

---

[1] The extract was made at Edinburgh on 11th January 1621, by Thomas Dryisdaill, Ilay Herald, Keeper of the Records of the Lyon King-at-Arms. —Original Extract at Terregles.

[2] Extract Decreet at Terregles.

The first and second charters are engrossed in the Act, which also contains the following clause of creation of the title of honour :—

" And further, our said Souerane Lord, being of guid will and mynd that the honour of his rycht traist cousigne and counsalour, be his Majesteis benefite, sall incresce and be augmentit, in sa far as the erledome, landis, baroneis and regalitie foirsaid, contenit in the said infeftment, ar already disponit to his richt traist cousigne and counsalour be his said chartour and infeftment ; as alsua, in consideratioun that his Hienes cousigne and counsalour foirsaid is oy and apperand air to vmquhill James Erll of Mortoun, his guidschir, and thairby maist able to succede to him, his landis, honouris, and dignities, his Maiestie thairfoir is maist willing that he bruik the samyn with all honouris, dignitie and preeminenceis quhilk his said vmquhill guidschir, James Erll of Mortoun, and his predecessouris of the said erledome, landis and baroneis, brukit the samin befoir : And thairfoir our souerane Lord, with auise and consent foirsaid, of new hes ratefeit the erectioun and creatioun of the erlldome of Mortoun, with all landis, baroneis and vtheris apertening thairto : Likeas his Maiestie, be the tennour heirof, of new erectis and creatis the saidis landis and baroneis, with thair annexis and pertinentis specefeit in the said infeftment, in ane frie erldome and regalitie, in all tymes cumming, to be callit the erledome and regalitie of Mortoun, and hes creat and constitute, likas his Hienes creatis and constitutis his said rycht traist cousigne and counsalour and his airis maill Erllis of Mortoun : And ordinis his richt traist cousigne and counsalour, and his airis abone mentionatt, in all tymis cumming to be intitulatt, callit and styllit Erllis of Mortoun, and to haue vote in Parliament, generall counsellis, conventionis and generall assembleis, as ony vther Erll or Lord of Parliament had, hes, or may haue within this realme : And namelie the samyn place, rank, ordour and degrie quhilk his said vmquhill guidschir, James Erll of Mortoun, and his predicessouris of the said realme, haue had in ony tyme heirtofoir : And that his said rycht traist cousigne and counsallour, and his airis abone rehersit, in all tymes cumming, sall haue, bruik and inioy all dignities, honouris and preeminenceis pertening to ane Erll and Lord of Parliament, and speciallie in the place and degrie quhilk his said vmquhill guidschir, James Erll of Mortoun, occupyit of befoir." [1]

Thus was Lord Maxwell formally created Earl of Morton, the first title of Earl conferred on the Maxwell family.

This creation greatly excited the resentment of Archibald Earl of Angus,[2] in favour of whom the late Regent had made an entail of the estate and honours of Morton, which became inoperative in consequence of the forfeiture of Morton. Angus had been forced to flee to England after his attempt to release Morton from prison, but his rage against the new Earl led him to make an incursion from that country upon the lands of Maxwell, which he laid waste, and to make an attack upon the Castle of Langholm, which, however, was unsuccessful.[3]

On Monday, the 6th of August 1582, a Chamberlain Air was proclaimed

[1] The Acts of the Parliaments of Scotland, vol. iii. p. 262.

[2] Moysie's Mem. pp. 55-57.

[3] History of King James VI., p. 287.

to be held at Edinburgh, on the 27th of that month, by the Duke of Lennox. To prepare for this Court, the Duke provided a great number of armed men. Lord Maxwell was advertised, 21st August, of the meeting of the Court, and was required by the Duke to bring with him all his friends and kin to attend his Grace at the opening of the Court. He accordingly, in a letter to Sir John Maxwell of Pollok, written on the 21st of August, earnestly desired him to meet him, accompanied with his friends and servants, in such reasonable number as opportunity and the shortness of the time allowed, at Biggar, on the 26th of that month.[1]

The purpose of the Duke of Lennox, as afterwards discovered, was to bring in to Edinburgh, on the day of the meeting of the Chamberlain Air, Maxwell, Livingston, Seton, Herries, Captain Crawfurd, Hume, Scott, Newbottle, Ferniehirst, etc., with their forces, and, after occupying the gates of the town and the streets, to forbid any to appear in the streets but such as were either sent for by the Chamberlain's officer, or were summoned upon the assizes.[2] His object was defeated by the "Raid of Ruthven;" a conspiracy formed by many of the nobles, and headed by the Earl of Gowrie, against Lennox and Arran, and especially the latter, who, from his unprincipled character, was universally detested. When the King was in Perthshire hunting, separated from Lennox, who was then at Dalkeith, and from Arran, who was then at Kinneil, in the shire of Linlithgow, some of the conspirators, Gowrie, Mar, Lindsay, and the Master of Glammis, having assembled a thousand men, made themselves masters of his person in the Castle of Ruthven, 22d August 1582, and thus deprived Lennox and Arran of all power in the State, and acquired the direction of the Government, which they exercised in the name of the King.

On Sabbath, 21st August, the day before the "Raid of Ruthven," Lord Maxwell, now Earl of Morton, who was in close confederation with the Duke of Lennox, came to Edinburgh with sixty armed men to wait upon him. There resorted also to the Duke at this time Lords Herries, Hume, Seton, Newbottle, the Master of Livingston, and the Laird of Ferniehirst.[3]

Whilst, in September of the same year, Lord Maxwell was with the Duke

[1] Memoirs of the Maxwells of Pollok, vol. ii. p. 149.
[2] Calderwood's History, vol. iii. p. 635.   [3] *Ibid.* vol. iii. p. 643.

of Lennox, and his party in Edinburgh, endeavours were made by them, but without success, to effect a reconciliation between the Duke and his adversaries. The Duke was commanded to depart out of Scotland within fourteen days, to remain at Dalkeith or Aberdour, accompanied with only forty persons, till his departure, and immediately to surrender the Castle of Dumbarton.

When the Duke of Lennox found himself unpopular in Edinburgh, he left the town, on the 6th of September, accompanied by the Provost, bailies, and 500 men, and went in the direction of the Sciennes, ostensibly going to Dalkeith, but really with the design of going to Glasgow, which he did after staying for some time on the south side of Boroughmoor, having been joined by Lord Maxwell and other friends, including the Master of Livingston, the Master of Eglinton and Ferniehirst.[1]   In the beginning of December he went to Callander, and thence to Blackness on the 4th of that month, with the intention, it was reported, of seizing upon the Palace of Holyrood and the town of Edinburgh by a surprise, in which Lord Maxwell and others of his confederates were to assist him with their armed men.   But whatever his designs were, they came to nothing.   Strict watch was kept both in the town and in the Abbey.   Colonel Stewart, with the soldiers recently levied, watched in the Abbey, and within the iron gate.   The Lords suspecting some treachery among themselves, resolved that Maxwell with some others should, in the meantime, be apprehended.   Maxwell escaped from the town upon Tuesday at night, although it was believed that he returned secretly on the following day.[2]   The Ruthven Lords having the King in their power now had everything their own way, and Lennox was commanded by a herald, in name of the Council, to leave the kingdom, under pain of treason.   At the close of the year 1582 the Duke found it necessary to leave Scotland.[3]

Frequent complaints of the disturbed state of the Borders were at this time made to the Government.   To enable them to judge what was the fittest course to be followed for the staunching of the slaughters and open robberies of the thieves and broken men, inhabitants of the Borders, and for reducing them to his Majesty's obedience, the Council summoned John Earl of Morton, John Lord Herries, James Douglas of Drumlanrig, Master Robert Douglas,

[1] Calderwood's History, vol. iii. p. 648.
[2] Ibid. vol. iii. p. 691.

[3] He went to France, where he died in the summer of the year 1583.

Provost of Lincluden, John Johnston of that Ilk, and Alexander Jarden of Applegarth, to compear personally before them, to give their advice, under the pain of rebellion and putting them to the horn. At the meeting of the Council, held at Holyroodhouse on 12th November, all these persons, with the exception of John Earl of Morton, gave in their advice touching the quieting of the Borders ; John Lord Herries by his son William Master of Herries, and the others personally. John Earl of Morton not having compeared, the Lords of Council ordained that the Sheriff's officers of those parts should be charged to denounce him rebel.[1]

Shortly before, there had occurred one of those scenes of plunder and violence so frequent in the history of the Borders, perpetrated by the household men, servants, or tenants of John Earl of Morton, Lord Maxwell, Warden and Justice of the West Marches, dwelling upon his lands or within the jurisdiction of his Wardenry, many of them being of the name of Armstrong, accompanied by some of the Grahams, Englishmen, and others, their accomplices, common thieves, to the number of nine score persons. On 30th October 1582, they went, under silence of night, first to the lands of Easter Montberengier, and carried off eighteen score of sheep, with plenishing, estimated at the value of 200 merks, belonging to Marjory Lowis, relict of John Scott in Easter Montberengier, William Scott there, and Adam Scott, his sons, tenants of his Majesty's lands of Ettrick Forest. Immediately after, on the same night, they proceeded to the lands of Dewchar, from which they stole twenty-two score of sheep, twenty-four kye and oxen, and plenishing worth 100 merks, belonging to Thomas and John Dalgleish ; and the lands of Whitehope they despoiled of two hundred sheep, and oxen and three horses, with plenishing worth 100 merks, belonging to John Dalgleish in Whitehope. The same persons, at the same time, seized upon Thomas Dalgleish and Adam Scott, and forcibly carried them into Annandale, in which, and sometimes in England, and in other parts, they kept them in strait prison in irons, and shamefully bound the said Thomas to a tree, with fetters, intending to compel them to pay exorbitant ransoms.

These violent deeds, as might have been expected, brought into disrepute Lord Morton's administration as Warden of the West Marches. He was

[1] Regist. Secreti Concilii, Acta, 1581-1585, fol. 34.

summoned by the sufferers to compear before the Privy Council, and to enter and present the persons who had committed the said crimes. He failed to compear. The Council therefore, on 16th November same year, ordained letters to be directed to denounce him rebel, and to put him to the horn.[1] On the same day, not having, as bound when required, upon six days' warning, presented Cristie Armstrong of Auchingavill, and Robert Armstrong, his brother's son, before the King and Council, or before the King's lieutenant, warden or justice, or his deputies, under the pain of £2000 for each of them, according to an Act of Council, 15th October 1580, he was decerned by the Council to have incurred that penalty, and letters of horning were ordained to be issued for uptaking it.[2] He was also found to have incurred the pain of £1000 for each of three persons, two of the name of Armstrong, and one named Beattie, whom, though similarly bound, he had failed to present before the King and Lords of Council, or before the justice or his deputies, to underlie the law for all the crimes that could be laid to their charge.[3]

By his friendship for the Duke of Lennox, Lord Morton having rendered himself obnoxious to the conspirators of Ruthven, they caused the King to deprive him of the office of Warden of the West Marches, and to grant a commission in favour of the Laird of Johnston.[4]

The King, with advice of the Lords of Council, 16th November 1582, ordained letters to be directed to John Earl of Morton, late Warden and Justice of the West Marches, charging him, under the pain of rebellion, to deliver to John Johnston of that Ilk, "present" Warden, or his successors, in his name, all books, scrolls, rolls, indents, and other writs concerning the Wardenry, that he might use them for his better information, both as to what he had to answer for and what to crave, and for the more effectual discharge of his office.[5]

King James having effected his escape from the Ruthven Lords in June 1583, Stewart, Earl of Arran, returned to Court, and became as powerful as ever.[6]

The character of Stewart, Earl of Arran, who was thus a persecutor of Lord Maxwell, has been painted in very different colours by two writers of the

[1] Regist. Secreti Concilii, Acta, 1581-1585, fol. 35.
[2] Ibid.   [3] Ibid.
[4] Spottiswoode's History, vol. ii. p. 299.

[5] Regist. Secreti Concilii, Acta, 1581-1585, fol. 39.
[6] Tytler's History of Scotland, vol. vi. pp. 359, 360.

same name. Principal William Robertson says that he was remarkable for all the vices which render a man formidable to his country, and a pernicious counsellor to his Prince; nor did he possess one virtue to counterbalance these vices, unless dexterity in conducting his own designs, and an enterprising courage, superior to the sense of danger, may pass by that name. Unrestrained by religion, regardless of decency, and undismayed by opposition, he aimed at objects seemingly unattainable; but under a prince void of experience, and blind to the defects of those who had gained his favour, his audacity was successful; and honour, wealth, and power were the reward of his crimes.[1] In subsequent passages the same distinguished author refers to the elevation of Stewart to the office of Lord Chancellor, and to his scandalous venality as a judge and his insatiable rapacity as a minister. He required Lord Maxwell to exchange part of his estate for the forfeited lands of Kinneil, and because he was unwilling to quit an ancient inheritance for a possession so precarious, he stirred up against him his hereditary rival, the Laird of Johnston, and involved that part of the kingdom in a civil war.[2] There is not, perhaps, in history an example of a minister so universally detestable to a nation, or who more justly deserved its detestation.

The other writer referred to describes Stewart as " the ablest statesman and one of the best patriots in Scotland since the death of Cardinal Beaton."[3]

A conspiracy having been formed against King James the Sixth, early in the year 1584, by the Earls of Mar and Angus, the Master of Glammis, and others, who entered Stirling with five hundred men, and took possession of the castle, King James, without delay, mustered a strong army to oppose them. In levying men he wrote a letter to Lord Morton, requiring him to attend upon him with all possible diligence, accompanied with his whole friends and forces, horse and foot, in their best array. To support the King, Lord Morton in a letter to Sir John Maxwell of Pollok, dated 22d April 1584, desired him, as his kinsman, whom he specially esteemed, to be ready with such friends and servants as he could procure to meet him at Linton, upon Friday, 1st May next, with fifteen days' furnishing; and also to take order that his Lordship's

---

[1] Principal Robertson's History of Scotland, vol. ii. p. 241.

[2] *Ibid.* vol. ii. p. 290.

[3] Miscellany of the Maitland Club, edited by Mr. Joseph Robertson, vol. iv. Part i., 1847, p. 126, note.

whole folk of the Mearns should be with him.[1]   The King having advanced to Stirling at the head of an army of twelve thousand men, the insurgent lords fled into England, and solicited the protection of Queen Elizabeth.[2]

In the same year, Lord Morton incurred the deep resentment of Stewart, Earl of Arran, by his refusal to exchange the barony of Mearns and the lands of Maxwellheugh for the barony of Kinneil, which Arran had acquired by the forfeiture of the Hamiltons.   Under any circumstances Lord Morton might not have been disposed to part with the old inheritance of his family ; but to exchange it for lands which by a revolution of political parties might be restored to the rightful owners, he did not consider it to be just on the part of Arran to ask, nor prudent for himself to concede.   He therefore declined the proposed bargain.

Not to be defeated in his object, the unscrupulous upstart, Stewart, Earl of Arran, purposed to adopt some indirect means by which he might force the Earl of Morton to make the exchange.   With this view he prevailed upon the wife of Lord Morton's rival, the Laird of Johnston, who was at Court, to induce her husband to accept of the post of Provost of Dumfries ; and at Michaelmas election (September) Arran sent a letter in the King's name to the electors, requesting them to elect, in the room of John Maxwell of Newlaw, a natural son of John Lord Herries, and a staunch supporter of Lord Morton,[3] the Laird of Johnston, who, being Warden of the West Marches, would, he said, if Provost of Dumfries, occupy a position which would enable him the more effectively to maintain order on the Borders.   But Morton, who readily perceived that this extrusion of his family from the Provostship was intended to disgrace him, assembled his forces at the time of the election, prevented Johnston from entering the town, and secured the re-election of Maxwell of Newlaw to that office.

Johnston immediately complained to Arran of the wrong done to him, and said that tranquillity was not to be expected in those parts unless the power of Morton was restrained.[4]

Arran still persevered in his efforts to curb the power of the Earl of

---

[1] Memoirs of the Maxwells of Pollok, vol. ii. p. 155.

[2] Tytler's History, vol. vi. p. 379.

[3] John Maxwell of Newlaw commanded a troop of horse for the Earl of Morton at the raid to Stirling, and special mention is made of him as one of the Earl's chief friends in the Act of Oblivion.

[4] Spottiswoode's History, vol. ii. pp. 325, 326.

Morton. This will be seen from the strong measures adopted against him by the Secret Council. On 26th February 1584-5 it was ordained by the Council that Lord Morton should be denounced his Majesty's rebel for not having, when summoned, presented before the Council two persons of the name of Armstrong, who were in the Pledge Chamber of Dumfries, and whom he was accused of having protected in their depredations. It was also ordained that he should be charged to enter his person in ward in the Castle of Blackness, within six days after he was charged, under the pain of treason, to remain therein, at his own expenses, until he was set at liberty by the King. It was further ordained that he and all other keepers of the Castle of Carlaverock, the Threave, the houses in Dumfries, Mearns, and Goatgellis, should be commanded to deliver them up, and to remove themselves and their servants forth thereof, within twenty-four hours after their being so commanded, under the pain of treason. It was besides ordained that letters should be directed charging the Earl's friends of the West Borders, whose names should be given in, to compear personally before John Johnston of that Ilk, Warden of the West Marches, upon a certain day, to give security for their due obedience and relief of the King and Warden, under the pain of rebellion.[1]

Arran, besides the severe measures now narrated, procured a commission for the Laird of Johnston to pursue Lord Morton, and despatched against him two companies of hired soldiers, under the command of two captains, Lamby and Cranston.

Informed of these hostile measures, Lord Morton brought together his forces ; and sent his natural brother, Robert Maxwell of Castlemilk, a man of a daring and intrepid spirit, with a detachment to intercept the two captains before they should join with Johnston. The hostile parties encountered each other in Crawford Moor ; and after a sharp conflict Johnston's captains were defeated. Lamby and most of his company were killed, and Cranston and several others were taken prisoners.

It was the interest of Arran to weaken Lord Morton in every possible way ; he accordingly incited the Johnstons to continue their attacks upon him.

[1] Regist. Secreti Concilii, Acta, 1581-1585, fol. 122.

Johnston made a raid on the lands of Maxwell, on which he committed great depredation, burning Cummertrees, Duncow, and Cowhill.

Lord Morton retaliated. On 6th April 1585, his brother, Robert, with David Maxwell, at the head of one hundred and twenty English and Scotch rebels, invaded, during the night-time, the house of Lochwood, the principal residence of Johnston, and burned it, boasting that he would give Lady Johnston light enough by which to " set her hood."[1] This calamity unhappily involved in destruction not only the household furniture but also the charter-chest of the Laird of Johnston, the depository of the whole muniments of the family, containing many valuable papers, relating not only to the house of Johnston but to the history of the Borders. At the same time Robert Maxwell killed several of the Johnstons of Annandale, and took many of them prisoners.[2] Johnston had to surrender at Bonshaw Tower, the property of Irving of Bonshaw, one of his partakers, whither he had fled. Cannon were brought by the Earl of Morton against it. When it could hold out no longer, an agreement, through the mediation of Lord Scrope, was come to between Johnston and the Earl. Of this raid, which intensified the indignation of Arran, and greatly incensed the King, an account is given in an Act of Secret Council, 9th April 1585. It is there stated that John Earl of Morton had not only failed to compear personally before the Council as charged, and to enter certain persons of the surname of Armstrong, and others, for whom he was bound, before the Council, but, in further contempt of his Majesty and his authority, had since caused some pledges and malefactors, who were in the Pledge Chamber of Dumfries, to be set at liberty, and had persuaded them, with other broken men of both realms, to take arms, and, accompanied with some of his own principal friends, hounded them on to pursue his Majesty's good subjects with all kind of force and warlike ingyne. It is added that they had treasonably burned the house of Lochwood, after they had despoiled it, and other rooms belonging to Sir John Johnston of that Ilk, knight, Warden and Justice of the West Marches, slain some of his friends, taken others of them prisoners, whom they transported into England, and, finally, had done, and still continued to do, all that they could to stir up rebellion, and to bring on

[1] Minstrelsy of the Scottish Border, vol. i. p. 291.   [2] Moysie's Mem., p. 95.

open war.[1] To prevent their treasonable intention from taking effect, his Majesty, with advice of the Lords of Council, and of some of the principal barons of the West Marches, ordained, at Holyroodhouse, 9th April 1585, that the Provosts and bailies of the burghs of Dumfries, Kirkcudbright, Wigton, Peebles, Lanark, Selkirk, Hawick, and Jedburgh, and all others his Majesty's lieges, should, by open proclamation at the Market crosses of these burghs, and other places needful, be forbidden to assist or intercommune with John Earl of Morton, Robert Maxwell, his brother-natural, or others their accomplices, in their rebellion, or to reset them, their wives, children, servants, goods or gear.[2]

On the same day the King, taking advantage of the privileges granted to him and his predecessors by the common law and acts of the realm of revoking whatever was done in his minority, revoked and annulled, with advice of his Council, the gift granted by him to John Lord Maxwell and his heirs-male of the lands, earldom, barony, and regality of Morton.[3]

The following is the Act of Revocation :—

" We vndirstanding the priuilege of the commoun law, actis and statutis of oure realme, grantit alsweil to ws and oure predicessouris in oure minoriteis, as vtheris minoris in thair leseage within the samin, to revoik, cas and annull quhatsumeuir thingis done be ws in oure minoritie and leseage, for diuers ressonable causs and considerationes moving ws, with auise of the lordis of oure secrete counsall, revoikis, cass and annullis the gift and infeftment grantit be ws, with auise foirsaid, to Johnne Lord Maxwell, his airis maill, and assignayis quhatsumeuir, off all and sindrie the landis, baroneyis, erldom, regalite, annualrentis, and vthiris respectiue eftir specifeit, that is to say, all and haill the landis, erldome, barony and regalitie of Mortoun, with the castell, tour, fortalice, maner place, orcheardis, zairdis, woddis, mylnis, fischeingis, tennentis, tenandreis, seruice of free tennentis of the same, outsettis, partis, pendiclis, annexis, connexis, aduocatioun, and donatioun of kirkis and chaiplanreis of the samin, and all thair pertinentis lyand within the Schirrefdome of Drumfreis ; the landis and barony of Prestoun, the landis of Brog, with castell tour, fortalice, maner place, woddis, mylnis, fischeingis, . . . within the stewartrie of Kirkcudbright ; the landis and barony of Hutoun vnder the mure ; the landis of Moffet-daill, with the maner place, orcheardis, . . . within the stewartrie of Annanderdaill and shirrefdome of Drumfreis foirsaid ; the landis and baronyis of Newlandis, Lyntoun, and Killotho, with castellis,

[1] In one of the conflicts between the two parties Johnston was made a prisoner. Johnston, having soon fallen away from the agreement made in 1580 (p. 250), was taken by Carruthers of Holmends, as he was lying in ambush a short way from Dumfries, to attack Robert Maxwell, brother of the Earl of Morton, who was expected to pass that way going to Langholm. This defeat so affected Johnston that shortly after his liberation he died, in the beginning of the year 1586.

[2] Regist. Secreti Concilii, Acta, 1581-1585, fol. 126. [3] Ibid. fol. 127.

touris, fortalices, maner places, orcheardis, . . . aduocatioun and donatioun of the kirkis of New-landis and Killotho, and all vtheris kirkis and chaiplanreis of the saidis landis and baroneyis . . . lyand within the shirrefdome of Peblis ; pairt of the landis of Kirkwod and Lochwod ; . . . the landis of Escheill, the landis of Quilt and the landis of Sethame, with touris, fortalices, maner places, woddis ; . . . sax pundis threttene schillingis four penneyis [Scots] money of annuelrent to be zeirlie tane and vpliftit, of all and haill the landis of Horsburgh ; . . . sex pundis xiii s. iiii d. money foirsaid of annuelrent, to be zeirlie tane and vpliftit, of the landis of Hopcalzie ; . . . foure pundis money abonespecifeit of annuelrent, to be zeirlie tane and vpliftit of the landis of Newbie, . . . lyand within the said sherefdome of Peblis ; the landis and barony of Robertoun, with the fortalice, maner place, orcheardis, . . . within the Shirefdome of Lanerk ; and the landis of Edmestoun, with the maner place, . . . within the barony of Beggar and Shirrefdome of Lanerk foirsaid, as at mair lenth is contenit in the said gift and infeftment grantit be ws to the said Lord Maxwell thair-vpoun : And decernis and declairis the same gift and infeftment, with all that hes followit, or may follow thairvpoun, to haue bene frome the begyning, and to be in all tyme cuming, null and of nane availl, force, nor effect : And siclik we, with aduise foirsaid, willis and declairis that this our reuoca-tioun salhaue als grite effect, and be als largelie extendit in generall, and in speciall, as ony vther oure reuocationes hes, or mycht haif bene in ony tyme heirtofoir, and consentis and ordainis that the samin be insert and registrat in our buikis of Secrete Counsale and Sessioun, and haue the strenth of ane act and decrete of oure Lordis thairof, and thair authoriteis respectiue, to be inter-ponit thairto, and lettres of publicatioun to be direct thairvpoun, in forme as efferis : Subscryuit be ws, and lordis of oure Secrete Counsale, at Haliruidhous, the nynt of April." [1]

Upon the Earl of Morton's becoming obnoxious to the Government, numbers of his family came forward to disown all connexion with his proceed-ings.   William Lord Herries, and sundry gentlemen of the name of Maxwell, upon the knowledge of the first disobedience of Lord Morton, offered to his Majesty their service in all things tending to the quieting of the country. As his Majesty could not impute any part of the undutiful doings of Lord Maxwell to them, who would rather have withstood the burning and harrying of their lands and bounds, he took, with the advice of his Council, 30th April 1585, William Lord Herries, etc., their tenants and servants, and all others their friends and proper dependers, under his special protection.[2]

To put down the Earl, £20,000 was granted by a Convention of the Estates for levying soldiers.   All that could bear arms on the south of the Forth were commanded, by proclamation, to be prepared to attend the King in an expedition into Dumfriesshire against him.   The expedition was, how-ever, deferred for some months, and came to nothing, in consequence of the

[1] Regist. Secreti Concilii, Acta, Dec. 1581,—Ap. 1585, fol. 127.   [2] *Ibid.* 1581-1585, fol. 132.

breaking out of the plague in Edinburgh, where it raged during the whole summer of the year 1585.[1]

So formidable was Lord Morton, that the Johnstons thought it necessary to make preparations in the expectation of his attacking them. The Laird of Johnston, in a letter dated Lochmaben Castle, 15th May 1585, wrote that Lord Maxwell thought to be within the country of the Johnstons shortly ; and desired his correspondent to meet him at the kirk of Applegarth on Monday next, with as many horse and foot as he could, that they might be able to defend themselves from his invasion.[2]

The invasion actually took place, and renewed depredations were committed upon the barony of Johnston on or about the 15th and 16th days of May. This raid, and the burning of the house of Lochwood on 6th April preceding, are particularly narrated in a paper setting forth the claims of Sir James Johnston of that Ilk upon Lord Maxwell, which were submitted to arbitration. This document is as follows :—

" Thir ar the aclaimes that I, James Johnstoun of that Ilk, askis and clames off Jhone Lord Maxwell for an part to be decernit and discussit be zow gude men arbitouris :—

" Item, In the first, that quhair it is of verrittie that Robert Maxwell, brother naturall to Jhonne Lord Maxwell, and wmquhill Mr. David Maxwell, with thair compleces, Engless and Scottis rebellis, to the number of sax scoir personis, came to the place of the Lochwoid, vpone the saxt day of Appryle or thairby, in the zeir of God four scoir four zeiris, and ther in thair pretendit maner tressonablie brint the place, mantioun and haill houss thairof, with the haill insycht thairin, bedding, plenesching, and brint and distroyit my chartour kist, with my haill evedentis and wreittis, besyd my jewellis, committit wnder silence of nycht be the command and spetiall directioun of the said Jhonne Lord Maxwell and be his hunding, sending and command.

" Secundle, It is of verretie and to rateffe this formar interpryss, the said Lord Maxwell him sellff in proper persone, wpone xv and xvi dayis of May, in the zeir of God foirsaid, with his haill forces come to my barony of Johnstoun, and wtheris, rowmes of my freindis, seruandis and dependaris, and thair brint, slew, herreit, sackit my haill barony, landis, rowmes, and possessiounis within Anerdaill and Neidisdaill, and his said forceis, reft and away tuik, beand baith Engless men and Scottis, thair haill quick guiddis, thair insycht and planesching, in greit quantite, besyd the waisting of my haill heland rowmes, this fyve zeir bigane, my haill skaith extending abone a hunder thousand merkis, thir tymes abone speceffeit, quhilk I craiff to be repairit for the present.

" JOHNSTOUNE."[3]

A plot was formed in the beginning of the year 1585 by the Master of

[1] Spottiswoode's History, vol. ii. pp. 325, 326.
[2] Calendar of State Papers, Scottish Series, 1509-1589, vol. i. p. 495, No. 42.
[3] Johnston Papers, at Raehills.

Gray, then in England at the Court of Queen Elizabeth, with the assistance of Walsingham, for the destruction of Arran; and in this plot Lord Morton, who, as we have seen, was at deadly feud with Arran, and had incurred the resentment of King James the Sixth, was easily induced to embark. To carry it into execution, Edward Wotton was despatched by Queen Elizabeth to the Court of Scotland. On his arrival in Edinburgh, he found that the question engaging the attention of the Master of Gray and his fellow-conspirators was whether they should arrest their enemy and expel him from the Court, or whether they should terminate his career by assassination. The more desperate course might have been followed, had the Master of Gray received from Wotton assurances of the protection of Queen Elizabeth. But Wotton had been instructed not to implicate Queen Elizabeth by any promises of that description. Receiving a visit from Arran's intended murderer, said to have been Douglas of Lincluden, Wotton, to whom he had revealed his purpose, and whom he conceals under the figure 38, writes, in a letter to Walsingham, dated 1st June 1585, that he asked him whether Arran might not rather be discourted? "Yea," quoth he, "worthily for twenty offences; but the King will not admit such proceedings." "Then," says Wotton, "I asked if 20 [Morton] might not attempt it, seeing he was already engaged; but that, for want of secrecy," he said, "and distance, was full of danger." From this conspiracy Arran was so fortunate as to escape by his own vigilance, and by the refusal of the English ambassador to promise the conspirators the protection of Queen Elizabeth.[1]

Some persons at this time wrote a forged letter, in name of Queen Elizabeth, to Lord Morton, with the view of bringing him over to the English interest. Wotton, in a letter to that Queen, dated Edinburgh, 13th June 1585, says that the King promised to find out the author of the letter written in her Majesty's name to Lord Morton.[2]

From Lord Morton's indomitable energy and power of resistance, Arran seemed desirous to be reconciled to him, though in this he was unsuccessful, probably from not being sufficiently in earnest. Wotton, in a letter to Sir Francis Walsingham, dated Dunfermline, 27th of the same month, refers to

[1] Tytler's History of Scotland, vol. vi. pp. 428-437.

[2] Calendar of State Papers, Scottish Series, 1509-1589, vol. i. p. 497, No. 63.

the King's dislike of the exiled Lords, and to Arran's tampering with Lord Maxwell.[1] Reports were current, as Wotton mentions in another letter to Walsingham, from Falkland, 22d July, that Maxwell had made, or was about to make, overtures to the King for a pardon, and that he had the prospect of obtaining it.[2]

When, in August, same year, a new plot was formed against Arran, the Earl of Morton, against whom the King, for the reasons before stated, had resolved to lead an army, readily joined in this conspiracy also, when overtures were made to him by the Master of Gray. Their scheme included an invasion of Scotland, to be made by the banished Lords—the Earls of Angus and Mar, and the Master of Glammis and their friends, who were then in England. They were to be joined by Lords Claud and John Hamilton, the mortal enemies of Arran, who had been in exile since the year 1579, when they were forfeited for the murder of the Regents Murray and Lennox, but who now, though they had been at feud with the Earl of Angus and his party, united against Arran, their common foe.

To this plot reference is made in a letter, by an unknown correspondent, to Archibald Douglas, in [August] 1585, in which the writer promises the banished Lords the assistance of Lord Maxwell and others, if they can levy some men, and come to the Borders, as the King must then either yield or leave the country. He adds that the King would by no means deliver Arran into England.[3]

The accession of the Earl of Morton, " whom few noblemen in Scotland could surpass in military power and experience,"[4] was regarded as a great acquisition, and the fact was communicated in a letter, 30th September that year, by Wotton to Walsingham. He had already raised a powerful force, which he intended to employ against the Johnstons, and this could be made immediately available for the purposes of the conspirators.

Morton was meanwhile denounced a rebel, and put to the horn. To suppress his power all the lieges were commanded, by proclamation, to meet the King upon Crawford Moor on the 24th of October. Wotton, in a letter to

---

[1] Calendar of State Papers, Scottish Series, 1509-1589, vol. i. p. 499, No. 79.

[2] *Ibid.* vol. i. p. 501, No. 97.

[3] Calendar of State Papers, Scottish Series, 1509-1589, vol. i. p. 503, No. 1.

[4] Tytler's History of Scotland, vol. vi. p. 444.

Walsingham from Stirling, 30th September, speaks of the King's preparations to go against Maxwell;[1] and in another to Lord Scrope, Warden of the West Marches, from Stirling, 4th October, he says that it was reported that the King intended to go in person with an army against Lord Maxwell, and sent this information that the Borderers might be ready.[2]

Early in October the banished Lords, who were then in London, the Earls of Angus and Mar, and the Master of Glammis, having received permission from Queen Elizabeth to return to Scotland, made their journey homeward. Having come to Kelso, they remained a few days with the Earl of Bothwell, during which time they met with Lord Hume, Wedderburn, Cessford, Coldingknowes, and other barons and gentlemen who were favourable to their enterprise. On the 25th of October they went to Jedburgh, thence to Peebles, and then to Lanark, where they were to join Hamilton and Maxwell's forces, and with them to proceed to Stirling. For their vindication, they issued a proclamation at the burgh towns in their progress, declaring that their object was simply the defence of the truth, the deliverance of the King from evil counsellors, and the preservation of amity with England.

Maxwell's soldiers numbered 1300 foot and 700 horse, whilst, according to Spottiswoode, the forces of all the others, Bothwell, Home, Yester, Cessford, Drumlanrig, etc., who had joined them, scarcely equalled that number.

In the prosecution of their enterprise, these parties may have been impelled by different motives, but upon one thing they were all agreed, namely, the banishment of Arran from the presence of the King. On 31st October their whole forces assembled at Falkirk.[3] Being within five miles of the enemy, they kept a strong watch. Lord Maxwell had the charge of the hired soldiers on the watch, and he made choice of "Saint Andrew" as the watchword, which, says Hume of Godscroft, was suspected as "smelling of his superstitious disposition."[4] On 1st November the army pitched their tents at the chapel of St. Ninians, within a mile of Stirling.[5] Next morning, at break of day, they advanced to that town, and without difficulty took it and the

---

[1] Calendar of State Papers, Scottish Series, 1509-1589, vol. i. p. 510, Nos. 70, 71.

[2] Ibid. vol. i. p. 510, No. 75.

[3] Spottiswoode's History, vol. ii. p. 330; Tytler's History, vol. vi. pp. 450, 451.

[4] The History of Douglas and Angus, by Mr. David Hume of Godscroft, 1644, fol. p. 404.

[5] Calderwood says that their number there amounted to 9,000 or 10,000.

castle. Having appointed some to make a show of entering the town by an orchard on the west, and others to advance by the ports, as if to assault it upon the castle side, the Lords themselves, with the body of their army, at the same time marched upon the other side to enter the town. The hired soldiers of Lord Maxwell, who were under the command of his natural brother, Robert Maxwell, were ordered to go before, shooting any one that should offer resistance. Having entered the town, the Border men of Annandale, who attended upon Maxwell, true to their predatory character as Borderers, took by violence the gentlemen's horses, respecting neither friend nor foe, for the gentlemen had alighted and committed their horses to their valets, and what was worse, robbed the sick in the pest-lodges that were in the field about Stirling, and carried away the clothes of the infected.[1] The banished Lords, to whom the gates of the Castle of Stirling were opened, entered on the 4th of November about the evening; and being admitted into the presence of the King, who was attended with many lords, barons, and gentlemen, they sought his Majesty's pardon, vindicated themselves from all imputations, and disclaimed any intention of disloyalty towards his Majesty.

Meanwhile Arran had secretly fled, accompanied only by a single horseman. The Lords were pardoned by the King, and their pardon was proclaimed by sound of trumpet.[2]

Proclamation was made by Lord Maxwell, in the West Marches of Scotland, for keeping the peace with England, dated at Dumfries, 15th November 1585.[3]

He sat as Earl of Morton in the Parliament held at Linlithgow on 1st December 1585.[4] In that Parliament was passed a general Act, by which all persons who had been forfeited in the King's minority since his coronation, for whatsoever offence, were restored to all their lands, honours and possessions, excepting those on whom sentence of forfeiture had been pronounced for their being art and part in the most cruel murder of the King's dearest father.[5]

[1] Hume's History of Douglas and Angus, p. 408.

[2] Calderwood's History, vol. iv. pp. 381-392; Spottiswoode's History, vol. ii. pp. 333, 334.

[3] Calendar of State Papers, ut supra, vol. i. p. 512, No. 98.

[4] The Acts of the Parliaments of Scotland, vol. iii. p. 373.

[5] Noted in royal letter restoring Archibald Earl of Angus to the earldom and title of Earl of Morton, 29th Jan. 1585.—Reg. Mag. Sig., Lib. xxxvi. No. 549.

On 10th December, same year, John Earl of Morton sat in the same Parliament at Linlithgow. An Act was then passed by the Parliament in favour of him, his kin, friends, servants and dependers, granting them indemnity for all their unlawful doings within the kingdom, from April 1569 to the date of the Act. In this Act, besides many others, there were named 600 men from Lord Morton's estates in Nithsdale and Galloway, and 600 from his estate in Eskdale, Ewesdale, Wauchopdale, mostly Beatties, Littles, and Armstrongs.[1]

At the same time an Act was passed in favour of the town of Dumfries. The Act narrates that the King and the three Estates of Parliament understood that his trusty cousin and counsellor, John Earl of Morton, Lord Maxwell, with his haill kin, friends and servants, during the time of the feud and late troubles betwixt him and Sir John Johnston of Dunskellie, knight, specially repaired to the town of Dumfries, which they stuffed and garnished with men of arms, victual and all other furniture needful for their defence, and that the inhabitants were prevented from offering opposition from the multitude of the said Lord's friends dwelling around and within that burgh. The King, there-fore, of his special favour and clemency, granted to the Provost, bailies, council and community of the burgh of Dumfries, the benefit of the general pacification granted in that Parliament in favour of John Earl of Morton, and others. The Act further declared that the election of John Maxwell of Newlaw as Provost of the burgh of Dumfries was good and sufficient in itself, and was to stand for him and his successors, so long as he should be authorized by the common election or consent of the inhabitants.[2]

At Christmas (24th, 25th, and 26th December) 1585, John Lord Maxwell, having assembled a number of people, marched in procession from Dumfries to the kirk of Lincluden, in which he caused mass to be openly celebrated. Stringent laws had been enacted against the celebration of mass ; and for violating these he and the rest of the hearers were charged to compear before the Privy Council. He compeared and offered himself for trial.[3]

By a royal letter under the Great Seal, dated at Holyroodhouse on 29th January 1585-6, King James the Sixth, with the advice of the Lords of

[1] The Acts of the Parliaments of Scotland, vol. iii. pp. 387-395.
[2] Ibid. pp. 398, 399.   [3] Calderwood's History, vol. iv. p. 489.

Secret Council, rescinded the forfeiture of James Earl of Morton, the late Regent, and thereby restored his heirs and posterity to his honours, lands, offices, and possessions. The letter of restoration decerned and declared that Archibald Earl of Angus, as the nearest heir of line and tailzie of the Regent, should succeed to the earldom of Morton, the lands, lordships and possessions thereof that belonged to the said Earl and earldom, and enter into the same by brieves and by any other similar way, as freely as if the said sentence of forfeiture had not been pronounced against the said deceased Earl of Morton, notwithstanding whatever infeftments, charters and dispositions may have been made by his Majesty to any person or persons.[1] The King reserved to himself the castle and place of Dalkeith, with the gardens, etc. This grant the King promised to confirm in his next Parliament.

In the preamble to the royal letter it is stated that, although in the general indemnity granted by the King and Parliament at Linlithgow, 1st December 1585, those who had been forfeited as being art and part in the most cruel murder of the King's dearest father were excepted, yet Douglas Earl of Morton, who had been condemned for that crime, and his heirs, were admitted to the benefit of the indemnity on account of the good, faithful and gratuitous services which he had rendered to the King during his minority in the government of the kingdom, and because he was not guilty art and part in the said crime, to the perpetration of which he had not given his consent, but only knew and concealed it.

Neither by this Act nor by any other was John Lord Maxwell deprived of the title of Earl of Morton. On the contrary, he not only continued to use this title till his death, but it was, subsequently to the above Act, given to him in royal charters and commissions. That he was never deprived of the title of Earl of Morton is evident from the terms of the patent granted to his son Robert in 1620, creating him Earl of Nithsdale. That patent expressly declares that the restitution of Douglas Earl of Morton to his former honours and dignities could no ways prejudge the deceased Lord Maxwell, who was created Earl of Morton in October 1581, nor his heirs, of the honour of Earl, then given to him by his Majesty, and that by the patent there was simply a change of the title of Earl of Morton into that of Earl of

---

[1] Reg. Mag. Sig., Lib. xxxvi. No. 549.

Nithsdale, this change being necessary, as it could not stand with the order and custom of the country to honour two Earls with one title. In conformity with this view of the case, the precedency of Robert Earl of Nithsdale took date from his father's creation as Earl of Morton, in the year 1581.[1]

Shortly after, we find John Earl of Morton, Lord Maxwell, a prisoner in the Castle of Edinburgh. But the Privy Council, about the middle of March, agreed to release him on his giving bond that, being released from the Castle of Edinburgh, where he then remained, he should immediately repair to the burgh of Edinburgh, and keep ward therein, and one mile thereabout, until he was liberated by his Majesty. He bound himself to that effect, and Robert Lord Seytoun, Sir Patrick Vaus of Barnbarauch, knight, James Douglas of Drumlanrig, and Edward Maxwell, fiar of Lamyngtoun, became bound as cautioners for him, under the pain of 100,000 merks. The bond was subscribed at Edinburgh, Castle of Drumlanrig, and Lamingtoun, on 13th, 14th, 19th and 20th, and acted and registered in the books of Council on 22d March 1585-6.[2]

By the Lords of Council he was required to compear before the General Assembly upon the 13th of May next, to satisfy the Kirk for whatever could be laid to his charge in regard to the hearing of mass, or for any other thing done by him slanderous to the Kirk. He was also required to find a cautioner that he would do so, and would behave himself in time coming as a dutiful subject to his Majesty, and should attempt nothing prejudicial to the royal authority, or to the true preaching of the Evangel then professed within the realm, under the pain of £1000; and that he should accept of a minister, with whom he might confer, for his better resolution, on the head of religion. His cautioner, Sir James Maxwell of Calderwood, knight, became bound to that effect before the Privy Council, 13th April 1586.[3]

The Earl and his cautioners having by the King been relieved of their bond for his keeping ward within the burgh of Edinburgh, and one mile thereabout, under the pain of 100,000 merks, he was required by the Council to find cautioners to give bond, under the penalty of 20,000 merks, that he

---

[1] The purport of the patent is contained in a decreet of the Privy Council, dated 11th January 1621, relating to the precedency of Robert, first Earl of Nithsdale, at Terregles.

[2] Regist. Secreti Concilii, Acta, 1585-1587, fol. 172.

[3] *Ibid.* fol. 172.

should keep ward within the burgh of Edinburgh, and four miles thereabout; and further, that he should make redress for all attempts committed by those for whom he was answerable since last Parliament at Linlithgow, 10th December 1585, and should enter them before the Warden, Justice, or his deputies, or do his diligence against them. This he did. His cautioners were Edward Maxwell, fiar of Lamington, and Sir Robert Maxwell of Dinwooddie, knight. The bond is dated at Edinburgh, Lamington, and Tinwald, 12th, 13th, and 14th May 1586, and it was registered in the Books of Secret Council on the 27th of that month.[1]

Lord Maxwell was soon after set at liberty.

At a convention of Estates, 18th September 1586, a taxation of £15,000 having been granted to provide horse and foot to assist the lieutenant, the Earl of Angus, in repressing thieves on the Borders, Lord Maxwell was charged to compear before the King and Council on the 10th of November, to be examined as to what obedience he would promise in name of his tenants. He excused himself for his non-compearance by pleading an appointment which he had with an English nobleman, and at the request of Lord Hamilton, his compearance was continued till the 27th of that month.[2]

Soon after, John Earl of Morton, Lord Maxwell, was appointed by the King, with advice of his Council, Warden and Justice of the West Marches, to hold Justice Courts within the bounds thereof, and to receive pledges of sundry broken men for the better observance of the peace of the country.

By an Act of Council at Falkland, 4th October 1586, in which his appointment is mentioned, it was ordained, in order to the removal of all impediments to his performing the duties of the office of Warden, that he should be relaxed by open proclamation at the Market Cross of Dumfries, and other places needful, from whatever process of horning had been led against him for any cause bygone.[3]

At the same meeting of Council, and at their meetings on 21st October and 2d of November, it was ordained that John Earl of Morton, Lord Maxwell, James Douglas of Drumlanrig, Alexander Jardine of Applegarth, and Sir

[1] Regist. Secreti Concilii, Acta, 1585-1587, fol. 179.
[2] Calderwood's History, vol. iv. pp. 602, 603.
[3] Regist. Secreti Concilii, Acta, 1585-1587, fol. 200.

John Johnston of Dunskellie, knight, should be charged to compear before his Majesty and the Council, at Holyroodhouse, on the 15th of November, to give in and pursue their actions in relation to the breaking of the assurances which had passed between them, and others their friends and assisters, that the same might be tried, and order taken concerning them. As some of the said persons might excuse themselves for their non-compearance in consequence of the process of horning which had been led against them for certain causes, civil and criminal, the Privy Council, on 4th November, ordained letters to be directed to relax them from the process of horning, for whatsoever cause, till the 1st of December next.[1]

On receiving intelligence of the death of his mother, King James was greatly excited, and immediately sent for Lord Maxwell, Ker of Ancrum and Ferniehirst, the most powerful and resolute of the Border chieftains, and well-known adherents of Queen Mary, and with them held confidential consultation.[2] But if this was with a view to avenging the death of his mother, which seems likely, nothing was done. Probably as James's anger cooled, the fear of being excluded from the succession to the Crown of England, in the event of the death of Queen Elizabeth, gained force. At all events he still maintained amicable relations with her.

On the other hand, Lord Maxwell and the Catholic Lords, Huntly, Errol, and Angus, made no secret of their joy at the vast preparations which it was known Philip the Second of Spain was making against England, and the English Queen, whom they regarded as the murderess of their Sovereign, and the irreconcilable foe of their faith.

In April 1587, John Earl of Morton received license from the King to depart from the realm to whatever parts beyond sea he chose. He was, however, required to give bond, with cautioners, that he should use his license within the space of a month at the furthest, after its date ; that in the meantime he should not attempt, by himself, nor by any other party, to trouble his Majesty or his realm ; that whilst he remained in foreign parts he should, neither privately nor publicly, directly nor indirectly, practise anything prejudicial to the true religion, presently professed within this realm ; and that

[1] Regist. Secreti Concilii, Acta, 1585-1587, fol. 200, 201.

[2] Lord Scrope to Walsingham, 21st February 1586-7, in Wright's Elizabeth, vol. ii. p. 333.

he should not return to Scotland without obtaining his Majesty's special permission. He and his cautioners gave a bond to this effect, under a penalty of 10,000 merks, dated 12th April 1587.[1] His cautioners were John Lord Hamilton, William Lord Herries, and Sir John Gordon of Lochinvar, knight.[2]

In the month of May that year the Earl of Morton left Scotland and went to Spain. Whilst he was abroad, ratification was made on 29th July 1587, by the King and the Three Estates of Parliament, of the letters granted under the Great Seal to Archibald Earl of Angus, rendering him capable of succeeding the late James Earl of Morton in his lands, heritages, rooms, and possessions.[3]

On the same day Claud, Commendator of Paisley, and William Baillie of Lamington, protested, in name and behalf of John Earl of Morton, Lord Maxwell, before the King and the Estates of Parliament, that that Earl, by the rehabilitation granted to Archibald Earl of Angus, as nearest heir to succeed to the deceased James Earl of Morton to the earldom of Morton, etc., should not be prejudiced of that part of the lands, earldom and regality of Morton belonging to him lawfully by birthright, either as heir to the deceased James Earl of Morton, Lord of Dalkeith, his grandfather, or as heir to Beatrix Douglas, Lady Maxwell, his mother. They also protested that the premises should not alter or infringe on the license granted to Lord Maxwell before his departure out of the realm in May last, and that nothing done in that Parliament might be prejudicial to him.[4]

During the Earl of Morton's stay in the kingdom of Spain he was in active communication with the Spanish Court, which was then contemplating the invasion of England, and not only saw the preparations that were making for that enterprise, but promised his assistance.[5]

He had been deprived of the Wardenship of the West Marches, but the precise date when he ceased to hold that office is uncertain. William Lord Herries, however, held it 2d February 1587-8. On that day the Lords of

[1] Calderwood, in his History (vol. iv. p. 489), incorrectly places the departure of Lord Maxwell from Scotland for the Continent under the year 1586.

[2] Regist. Secreti Concilii, Acta, 1585-1587, fol. 125.

[3] The Acts of the Parliaments of Scotland, vol. iii. p. 472 ; Calderwood's History, vol. iv. p. 640.

Archibald Earl of Angus was retoured heir-male and of tailzie to James Earl of Morton, his paternal uncle, 12th September 1587, in the lands of Dalkeith, Morton, and many others.—Original Retour at Terregles.

[4] The Acts of the Parliament of Scotland, vol. iii. p. 470.

[5] Tytler's History of Scotland, vol. viii. p. 137.

Council, before whom, under that designation, he had been summoned to compear to give his advice in such things as concerned the West Marches, and the quieting thereof, ordered him, in consequence of his non-compearance, to be declared rebel, and put to the horn.[1] He was, however, released by the Council, 3d March 1587-8, from the process of horning led against him.[2]

Lord Maxwell landed at Kirkcudbright from Spain about the end of April 1588.[3] Calderwood says that he was accompanied by Captain Sempill. Contrary to the assurance he had given, he returned without the King's license. His Majesty having been informed of this, and his Lordship not having appeared personally before his Majesty, nor by his letters or message assigned any lawful excuse or cause for his return, his Majesty suspected that his intention was to put in execution such treasonable purposes as he had been occupied with during his absence from the realm, tending to the overthrow of the true Christian religion professed. The King, therefore, and the Council, at a meeting at Jedburgh, 25th April 1588, ordained that all his Majesty's subjects should by open proclamation be forbidden to reset or intercommune with him, under the pain of being held as art and part with him in his treasonable practices.[4]

The advice of the Catholic Lords of Scotland to the Spanish monarch and to the Duke of Parma was that England should be invaded through Scotland ; and they offered immediately on the landing of the Spanish army to strengthen it by the accession of a numerous body of soldiers. It was expected that the Spanish navy would first sail to the west coast of Scotland, and then enter into England. In this hope Lord Maxwell, from his zeal on behalf of the contemplated enterprise, hired soldiers to be in readiness to join the Spanish army whenever they should land. But other counsels were followed.

Upon his return to Scotland, Lord Maxwell was joined by numbers of broken men and country people. Lord Herries, afraid lest, should there be any disorder, it should be imputed to him, warned the King of the trouble likely to arise. Lord Maxwell was immediately summoned to appear before the Privy Council. He paid no attention to the summons, and the Council,

[1] Regist. Secreti Concilii, Acta, 1585-1587, fol. 270.
[2] Ibid. 1587-1589, fol. 5.
[3] Calderwood's History, vol. iv. p. 547. This historian incorrectly gives the date of Lord Maxwell's return to Scotland as about the month of April 1586.
[4] Regist. Secreti Concilii, Acta, 1587-1589, fol. 30.

therefore, 8th May 1588, ordained letters to be directed to Sheriff-officers in that part charging them to denounce him, and put him to the horn.[1] In defiance of the Council, he fortified his castles, and levied some companies of foot and horse. Receiving intelligence of this, King James, to punish his rebellious subject, and to show his hostility to the Spanish invasion of England, the success of which would destroy all hopes of his succession to the English throne, as well as endanger that of Scotland, and to convince Queen Elizabeth of the sincerity of his hostility to her enemies, adopted severer measures against Lord Maxwell. He was charged with having, notwithstanding the many great favours bestowed by the King upon him since his return to Scotland, given manifest demonstration of his ingratitude, inasmuch as he had conspired to alter the quiet estate of the realm and of the true Christian religion professed by his Majesty and all his faithful subjects, by drawing in strangers, and in order to provide for their arrival, had caused his kinsmen and household servants to surprise and to occupy the King's own houses, and to stuff them with victuals and men of war, treasonably raised and paid by him. The King and Council, therefore, 30th May 1588, ordained letters to be directed to make proclamation of the Earl's treasonable course, and to forbid all and sundry his Majesty's lieges, as before, to reset or intercommune with him or with Robert Maxwell, his bastard brother, or with Mr. David Maxwell, brother-natural to the deceased Sir Robert Maxwell of Dinwooddie, knight,[2] or any who had assisted them, either on horse or foot, since their late public rebellion, under the pain of being held as art and part with them in the treasonable crimes which they had committed.[3]

The King further summoned his forces in order to take the Castle of Lochmaben, which was held by Lord Maxwell. In the month of May 1588 the lieges within the shires on the south of the Forth, the shires of Perth and Forfar, and the stewartries of Strathern and Menteith, were commanded by open proclamation to repair to Biggar on the 25th of May with ten days' victual.

The King, accompanied with such forces as he could suddenly bring together, hastened to Dumfries. Lord Maxwell, who was in his house in that town, received warning of the King's advance only an hour before, and was

[1] Regist. Secreti Concilii, Acta, 1587-1589, fol. 30.

[2] The same as David Maxwell, brother to the Laird of Cowhill, mentioned in next page.

[3] Regist. Secreti Concilii, Acta, 1587-1589, fol. 30.

almost surprised by the royal troops. A large party of the burgesses of the town having resisted them, ignorant of the King's presence, Lord Maxwell effected his escape. He hurried on horseback to Kirkcudbright, and there procured a ship, in which he put to sea.

When the King was in Dumfries, the houses of Lochmaben, Langholm, Threave, and Carlaverock were summoned by the royal heralds to surrender. They all obeyed except the Castle of Lochmaben. In the meantime, Sir William Stewart, brother to Captain James Stewart, sometime Earl of Arran, was despatched by the King to pursue Maxwell. And having learned that he had taken to sea in a small bark, he followed in a ship rigged forth by the town of Ayr. To escape from the close pursuit of Stewart, Maxwell left the ship to which he had betaken himself, for the ship's boat, and fled for land. Having seized on the ship, Stewart followed Maxwell to land, and apprehending him in a cothouse brought him to Dumfries. Maxwell was in the meantime committed to the keeping of Douglas of Drumlanrig. According to another account, Maxwell left the ship with only one attendant in a cock-boat for Ailsa Craig, and on the back of that isle finding a fishing-boat he came to land opposite to the Abbey of Crossraguel, in Carrick. Not obtaining admission into the Abbey, he went to an inn in the town, in which, whilst he was dining, six or seven persons, beginning to break open the doors of the house, he fled to the wood, where he was taken in a cave, on 5th June 1588, by Sir William Stewart.[1]

The King himself accompanied his troops to the Castle of Lochmaben, and commanded its captain, David Maxwell, brother to the Laird of Cowhill, to surrender. Maxwell refused. The castle was immediately invested, and as the Royal forces had no ordnance sufficiently heavy to make an impression on its walls, a post was sent to borrow heavier guns from the English Warden. This, being speedily obtained, was so effective that the garrison were constrained to capitulate. Sir William Stewart, in a written document, which he said was in the handwriting of the King, offered to the Captain, David Maxwell, and his company, their lives, on condition of their capitulating. The Captain surrendered on Sabbath the 9th of June. But the promise made by Stewart was shamefully violated, the King alleging that it was a forgery.

---

[1] Calderwood's History, vol. iv. p. 678 ; Spottiswoode's History, vol. ii. pp. 383, 386.

The Captain, because he had refused to surrender to the King at first, and five of the chief of the garrison, were hanged before the castle gate. The rest, whose lives were spared, were sent to Dumfries ; seventeen that were in the ship with Lord Maxwell were also doomed to the gallows.[1]

Meanwhile Robert Maxwell, brother to Lord Maxwell, devastated the surrounding country. The Government being unable to put a stop to his proceedings, thought to get hold of him through the treachery of some of his followers, and the King, at Dumfries, 23d June 1588, ordained that proclamation should be made at the market cross of Dumfries, Lochmaben, Annan, and other places needful, forbidding that any should reset or intercommune with him under the pain of being held as partakers with him in all his treasonable deeds, and punished with all rigour. He further faithfully promised, on the word of a prince, that any person or persons who were rebels and fugitives that would bring the said Robert Maxwell quick to his Majesty, or, he being slain, would bring his head, should receive his master's pardon, with a thousand pounds of reward, and that whosoever of his Majesty's obedient subjects should perform the said service should have two thousand pounds of reward thankfully paid to them without delay. In the preamble to this decree it is said that in the late rebellion raised against his Majesty within the West Marches, in fortifying and withholding his Majesty's own houses against him, fire-raising, depredations, and sundry other treasonable enterprises, Robert Maxwell of Castlemilk had shown himself a principal inventer, hounder, and stirrer up of broken men, and others to cast off their due obedience and to continue rebellious, for which he deserved the due punishment of his demerits.[2]

Fearing that the temptations held out by this proclamation might tempt some of his own party to betray him, Robert Maxwell secretly left them. The King, who was in the south till the 27th of June, then intrusted the government of the country to the Earl of Angus ; and returning to Edinburgh he brought with him Lord Maxwell, who was warded in Robert Gourlay's house in Edinburgh, and committed to the custody of Sir William Stewart.[3]

With the success and severity of these proceedings against Lord Maxwell and his friends Queen Elizabeth was delighted, and she despatched William

[1] Spottiswoode's History, vol. ii. pp. 383, 386.
[2] Regist. Secreti Concilii, Acta, 1587-1589, fol. 58.
[3] Spottiswoode's History, vol. iv. pp. 678, 679 ; Historie of James the Sext, p. 236.

Ashby to the Court of Scotland to convey to the King her thanks and congratulations.[1]

Even after the terrible disasters which had befallen the celebrated Spanish Armada, which in 1588 attempted the invasion and conquest of England, Lord Maxwell, who when in Spain was privy to the plans of Philip the Second, and other Catholic Scottish nobles, encouraged the Spanish monarch to renew the enterprise. A letter to that effect, addressed to the King of Spain, dated Edinburgh, 24th January 1589, and written in French in cipher, is subscribed by Lord Maxwell, Lord Claud Hamilton and George Earl of Huntly, " in name of the Lords Catholics in Scotland."[2]

They begin with lamenting the terrible calamity which had befallen the Armada, and with expressing their regret that it had not visited Scotland on its way to England, in which case it would have received assistance from a more numerous body of Catholic friends than the Catholics who assisted in England. " We cannot sufficiently express by speech the great regret we have conceived, being frustrated of the hope we have so long had, to see (this year past) the desired effects fall out, which we expected of your Majesty's preparations ; and our displeasure hath been so much the greater, that your army naval should have passed by so near us, unvisiting us, who expected the same, with sufficient forces for the peaceable receipt and assisting thereof, against all enemies, in such sort, as it should have had no resistance in this country, and with our support, should have given enough ado to England. At least, if it had come here for refreshment, it had preserved a number of vessels and men, which we know have perished near our isles and upon the coast of Ireland ; and had discovered an incredible number of friends in full readiness to have run the same fortune with it, in such sort as, we dare well affirm, it should not have found half so many in England, for all that is spoken by the English Catholics refuged there, who by emulation, or rather by unchristian envy, undervalue our means to aid you, to magnify their own only, and to make themselves to be esteemed able to do all, to advance themselves thereby in credit with your Majesty and such as are about you. But the experience

[1] William Ashby to Lord Burleigh, 6th August 1588, State Paper Office, quoted in Tytler's History, vol. vii. p. 140.

[2] The letter was intercepted in the same month, deciphered and translated.

of this year past hath sufficiently testified that they have not shown themselves in such number to assist your forces as we have done . . . We remit
to the declaration of some of your own subjects that have been here, the
advantages of landing in Scotland, where the expenses bestowed upon the
equipage of one galliasse shall bring more fruit to your service than you may
have of ten upon the sea."

They next assure Philip that he would be successful in raising troops
in Scotland. "And we may assure your Majesty, that having once six
thousand men here of your own, with money, ye may list here forces in this
country as freely as in Spain, who will serve you no less faithfully than your
own natural subjects."

They further point out how the errors committed in the first invasion
might be avoided in a second : "The over-late arrival of your army in our
waters took from it the advantage of retiring in such safety as it might
have done had it come sooner, by reason of the great winds that are ordinary
here in harvest: as also lack of experienced pilots upon the coasts of England,
Scotland and Ireland, appears to have bred great harm to the said army ; for
which we could have provided a remedy in regard to Scotland, by sending
pilots from this, had your Majesty been pleased to have served yourself with
them."

They next suggest how the second enterprise should be conducted in
order to insure its success. They would have a part of Philip's forces sent to
Scotland, and the other sent direct to England, and that secretly by the back
of Ireland. Philip would thus compel the enemy to divide their forces, and in
order to resist Philip's landing and invasion on the Scottish coast, might cause
them send the greater part of them to Scotland, whither he might make
them believe the most of his forces had arrived. "And we may well promise,"
they say, "that having here six thousand of your men, and money to list
others, we should, within six weeks after their arrival, be well far within
England, to approach and assist the forces which your Majesty should cause
enter there."

They add that Sir William Semple, Colonel, could show his Majesty the
whole. They had also caused letters to be written both before and since his
departure, intrusted to Mr. Robert Bruce, and addressed to the Duke of

Parma, to whom Philip had remitted them from the beginning of these affairs.[1]

But so severely had Philip's ambition been mortified by the terrible fate of his fleet, and so great were the difficulties and dangers of renewing the enterprise, that the idea of attempting it was abandoned.

Mr. Robert Bruce, a Jesuit, who was secretly engaged in Scotland in intrigues on behalf of Spain, and for the re-establishment of the Roman Catholic faith in Scotland, in a letter to the Duke of Parma, ciphered in French, dated Edinburgh, 24th January 1589,[2] thus writes concerning John Earl of Morton, Lord Maxwell :—" The Earl of Morton,[3] to whom I have given consolation by writ in prison, hath instantly prayed me, also by writ, to remember his most affectioned service to your Highness, finding himself greatly honoured by the care it hath pleased you to have of him.   By the grace of God, he is no more in danger of his life by way of justice, it not being possible to his enemies to prove against him anything which they had supposed in his accusation ; as also the King's affection [is] not so far alienated from him as it hath been heretofore.   And in case they would annoy him, or that it were presently requisite for the weal of our cause to deliver him, we have ever means to get him out of prison, and in the meantime abide only the King's will towards his liberty, in order to avoid all pursuit that they would make if we delivered him extraordinarily.   When they offered him, in the King's name, his liberty if he would subscribe the Confession of the heretic's faith, he answered, that he would not do it for the King's crown, nor for an hundred thousand lives, if he had them to lose ; and hath offered to confound the ministers by public disputation. I shall solicit the Lords, his friends, to procure of the King his liberty very soon, for he importeth the weal of our cause more than any of the rest, by reason of his forces, which are near England, and the principal town of Scotland, and the ordinary residence of our King ; as also he is the Lord the most resolute, constant, and of greatest execution of any of the Catholics."[4]

On the 12th of September 1589, Lord Maxwell was liberated from the Castle of Edinburgh to attend the Queen upon her arrival.   On his being

[1] Calderwood's History, vol. v. pp. 14-16.

[2] This letter was intercepted in January 1589, before the road of the Bridge of Dee, and was deciphered.

[3] *Alias* Lord Maxwell, note in Calderwood's MS.

[4] Calderwood's History, vol. v. p. 24.

liberated, he subscribed the following bond, by which he promised to conduct himself as a loyal subject :—

" Be it kend till all men be thir present lettres, me, Johnne Lord Maxwaill, that forsamekle as it hes plesit the Kingis Maiestie, oure Souerane Lord, of his fauour and clemency, to putt me to libertie and fredome oute of my present warde, thairfoir to be bundin and oblissit, and be the tennour heirof vpoun my faith, honnour, and allegeance, bindis and oblissis me and my airis that I sall frome this furth continew loyall and obedient subiect to oure said Souerane Lord and his auctoritie, and sall nawayes practize, do, nor procure, directlie nor indirectlie, be my selff or ony that I may latt, ony thing tending to the trouble or alteratioun of the state of religioun presently professit and be law establisset within this realm, nor to the hurte and preiudice of his Maiestie, his auctorite, and the present Estate, vndir the pane of ane hundreth thousand pundis money of this realme, to be payit to his Hienes, his airis and successouris, in cais of my failzie in the premiss, to the payment quhairof I oblis me, my airis and assignayis, oure personis, landis, and guidis, movable and vnmouable, present and to cum, and is content and consentis that this oure band and obligatioun be actit and registrat in the Buikis of Secret Counsaill, to haue the strenth of ane act and decrete of the Lordis thairof, and that lettres and executoriallis be direct thairupoun, gif neid beis, in forme as effeiris. In witnes heirof I haue subscryuit this my band and obligatioun with my hand, at the Castell of Edinburgh, the   day of September, the zeir of God Iᵐ vᶜ lxxx nyne zeiris, befoir thir witness, Johnne Lord Hammiltoun, Schir James Hwme of Coldenknowis, knycht, capitane of the said castell, Schir James Maxwell of Calderwode, knycht. Sic subscribitur, Johnne Maxwell, J. Hammiltoun, witnes ; J. Calderwode, knycht, witnes ; Thomas Hammiltoun, witnes." [1]

For the reason assigned for the release of Lord Maxwell, the rest of the Earls were set at liberty about the same time.[2]

King James, when about to set sail for Norway to be united to his affianced bride, Princess Anne of Denmark, made provision for the government of the kingdom during his absence. Lord Hamilton was invested with the military power as Lord Lieutenant, in which office he was to be assisted by Lords Boyd, Herries, Maxwell, Home, Cessford, and other principal barons on the Borders. The following is the letter of the King on this subject :—

" Trustie and well beloved cosin we greet you hartelye well,
Upon occasion of the impediments objected toward the transportinge hether of the Quene our spous in this season, we have taken present purpose to passe to Norroway our selfe, where she presentlie remaines, and wher, God willinge, our tarrye shall be very short, winde and weather servinge. In the meantime we have declared our will how things shall be governed in our absence ; and specially conserning the keepinge of good reule on the borders : havinge committed the chefe

[1] This bond was ordained by the Privy Council, in the same month, to be acted and registered in the Books of Secret Council, to have the strength of an act and decreet of the Lords thereof.—Regist. Secreti Concilii, Acta, 1587-1589, fol. 241.
[2] Calderwood's History, vol. v. p. 59.

care and oversight of them to our cousinge the Lord Hammelton, a nobleman verye well affected to justice, and interteyninge of the amitie betuixt the realmes : and therewithall hath derected and admonished the Lord Maxwell, with the others noblemen, barons and gentlemen inhabitinge the whole merches, but specialye that our west merches foranent you, to take speciall diligence that the committing of disorders by their men and dependers be left off and forborn, and quietnes and good neighberhode to be kepte, principallye till our returninge, that we may resolutely establish the Justiciarie and Wardanrie theire, being constrained upon necessary respects to take Carmichaell present off in our awne companye : Wherfore our lippininge ys, according to your accustomed good will, for keeping of the peace and amitie ever declared, That you will do your uttermost endevoure to interteyne the quietnes, and restraine the troublesome men under your charge by your auctority and wisedome att this time, as also to cause the good people under your reull to stand the better on their awne garde, in caise our disorderte subjects wolde take occasion uppon our absence to make further breake, wherin we doubte not yt shall be verye acceptable ; since to the Queen your Soveraigne, our dearest sister and to us, it will be right thankfull pleasure ; so we committ yow to the protection of Almightie God.

Your loving freind,   JAMES R.[1]

" Att Leith, the xxii. day of October, 1589."

On the day on which this letter was dated, King James embarked at Leith for Norway, attended by Chancellor Maitland, Mr. David Lindsay his chaplain, and a retinue of his nobility ; and on the fifth day he arrived at Upsal.   His marriage with Princess Anne of Denmark was celebrated at Upsal on the 23d of November 1589, the ceremony having been performed by Mr. David Lindsay.   The King accompanied by his own retinue, and his Queen attended by a train of Danish nobles and ladies, landed at Leith on the 1st of May 1590.

The ill feeling which continued to exist between Lord Maxwell and the Johnstons showed itself during the King's absence.   Lord Maxwell obtained a letter, subscribed by the King and his Chancellor, at Craigmillar, 29th September 1589, forbidding any to intrude into his Lordship's lands, livings, and offices.   By virtue of this letter Lord Maxwell charged James Johnston of that Ilk and Andrew Johnston of Mungebank, on 1st November 1589, by a messenger, to desist from any exercise of his Lordship's offices whatsoever, and for their alleged disobedience he was about to denounce them rebels and put them to the horn.   The letter was directed against certain persons specially named, who were charged with intruding into Lord Maxwell's lands, livings, and offices.   James Johnston of that Ilk and Andrew Johnston were not

[1] Rymer's Fœdera, tom. xvi. p. 27.

specially named in them ; but their names were interlined on the margin in the handwriting of Lord Maxwell.   They, therefore, complained to the Privy Council, and urged that by the laws of the realm the pretended horning by virtue of such a letter should not be effectual against them, but should be suspended *simpliciter*.   They further pleaded that James Johnston of that Ilk had not kept a Steward Court, nor had otherwise intruded himself into any of Lord Maxwell's offices or possessions whatsoever, but that he had held only such Courts as he was authorized to hold by his Majesty's Commission, dated at Holyroodhouse, 8th April 1588, on his own lands and bailieries, and upon his own friends, servants and dependers, for preserving good order, and as the King before his departure from the realm had personally commanded him to do.   This complaint was brought before the Privy Council at their meeting at Edinburgh, 4th December 1589, at which James Johnston of that Ilk and Lord Maxwell appeared personally, and the Council suspended the foresaid letters and the process of horning contained therein upon James and Andrew Johnston, *simpliciter*, and ordained letters to be directed to relax them from the process of horning.[1]

By a deed subscribed at Dumfries and Lochwood, 12th and 13th of March 1589-90, John Earl of Morton, and James Johnston of that Ilk, each for his kin, friends, men, tenants, servants, assisters, partakers and dependers, made a submission of all questions, quarrels and debates between them to certain arbiters whom they had respectively chosen, and who were to meet on the 17th of that month, and to give their final decreet between that date and the 21st of the same month.[2]

Early in the year 1592, it seemed as if the feud between Lord Maxwell and the Johnstons would at last give place to a permanent reconciliation and friendship.   On the 1st of April that year, John Earl of Morton and Sir James Johnston of Dunskellie, knight, who is described as "the said noble Lord's dear cousin," entered into an agreement to that effect, so full in its provisions, that apparently every difficulty was met, and all future misunderstanding provided against.   By this agreement, moved by the fear of God, in obedience to the King, for the common weal of their native country, and from

---

[1] Regist. Secreti Concilii, Acta, 1587-1589, fol. 276.

[2] Original Submission amongst the Johnston Papers at Raehills.

a special respect to propinquity of blood, affinity, habitation and the ancient amity between them and their ancestors, each taking the burden on himself, for his kin, friends, men, tenants, servants, dependers and partakers, freely remitted and forgave all rancour of mind, grudge, malice and feuds that had passed or fallen forth betwixt them or any of their forbears in any time bygone, with all slaughters, herschipps and reiffs that had followed thereupon. They also became bound that they themselves, their kin, friends, etc., should in all time coming live together in sure peace and amity, and that they should not hurt, invade, quarrel or pursue one the other in body, lands or goods hereafter, otherwise than by order of law. For avoiding all suspicion of partiality, the Earl of Morton was to constitute two discreet friends, whom Sir James Johnston should nominate, to be stewart-deputies of the stewartry of Annandale in all causes concerning Sir James or any of his kin, friends, men, tenants, etc., for whom he stood bound by the Acts of Parliament and general band to make answerable, and that no decreet pronounced by any other stewart-deputy of the stewartry should be valid against them without the consent of these two deputies, who should be responsible to Lord Morton for the due administration of their offices. It was also agreed between the parties that they should account any of their kin, friends, etc., who would not consent to this agreement, common enemies to them both, and should prosecute them with all extremity until they were reduced to submission. They also agreed that should any controversy or questions arise between them hereafter on this contract, or any point thereof, it should be decided by eight friends, of whom four were to be Maxwells chosen by the said noble Lord, and four Johnstons chosen by Sir James; and that in case of variance among these eight friends, the King should be oversman, to whose decision they bound themselves to submit *simpliciter*.[1]

Having regained his place in the royal favour, Lord Maxwell, on 28th July 1592, received a commission from King James the Sixth to be Warden of the West Marches upon the demission of Sir John Carmichael of that Ilk, knight. In the commission he is styled John Earl of Morton.[2] Under the same designation he obtained a gift, having the same date, from the King, of

---

[1] Original Agreement at Raehills.
[2] Original Commission at Terregles ; Pitcairn's Criminal Trials, part ii. p. 275.

the hereditary keepership of the Castle of Lochmaben, and was infefted therein on 12th August following.[1]

In the commission granted to Lord Maxwell over the whole lands of Annandale, Eskdale, Ewesdale, Nithsdale and Galloway, as well above as beneath Cree, unusually ample justiciary powers were inserted. The barons, freeholders and heritors within the bounds of Nithsdale and Galloway, afraid that these powers would be abused, complained to the King, who, on 19th September, ordered that the powers of justiciary should be withdrawn, leaving to Lord Maxwell only the usual powers of Warden.[2]

Lord Maxwell was a member of the Parliament which met in October 1591. In a letter to Sir John Maxwell of Pollok, dated 9th October of that year, from Dumfries, he writes that, as it was requisite he should be accompanied by his kin, friends, vassals, servants and dependants during the time of Parliament then approaching, at which he was requested by the King to be present, he desired Sir John to be with him in Edinburgh on the 21st instant.[3]

On Friday, 26th January 1592-3, Lord Maxwell, whether from policy or conviction may be questioned, subscribed the Confession of Faith with his title of Earl of Morton, before the Presbytery of Edinburgh. He frankly promised to be ready whenever the Kirk should employ him. At this time so much was he in disfavour with the barons and gentlemen of Galloway, that on the previous day they boldly said to King James that they would not have one of their own companions, meaning Maxwell, to be their King; and that if his Majesty denied them his protection, they would submit themselves to a foreign sovereign.[4]

On Friday, the 2d of February following, a tumult was raised by Maxwell and William Douglas of Lochleven, who, on the death of Archibald Earl of Angus and Morton in 1588, had succeeded him as Earl of Morton, each striving for precedency in the kirk of Edinburgh. Before they had time to draw their swords they were parted by the Provost, and conveyed under a guard to their lodgings, as was also Lord John Hamilton for having assisted Maxwell. Maxwell came into the kirk first, as if to dispute precedency with Morton.[5]

---

[1] Original Gift and Sasine at Terregles.

[2] Original Order, *ibid.*

[3] Memoirs of the Maxwells of Pollok, vol. ii. p. 167.

[4] Calderwood's History, vol. v. p. 222.

[5] *Ibid.* vol. v. pp. 221, 222. In an advertisement to the ministry of Edinburgh, affixed to the kirk door, Cross, or Tolbooth, on the 17th of

When George Earl of Huntly, who was warded, 10th of March 1592-3, in the Castle of Blackness for his implication in the burning of the house of Donnybrissell, and the murder of the Earl of Murray on 8th February preceding, was released, in answer to his supplication to the King and Council, on finding security that he would re-enter, Lord Maxwell was one of his sureties. The other two were Lord John Hamilton and the Earl of Montrose. They were bound under the pain of £20,000.[1]

In March 1592-3, Lord Maxwell and Sir James Johnston of Dunskellie continued to cultivate friendly relations with each other. On the 13th of that month they entered into a contract, each binding himself, his kin, friends, tenants and servants, dependers and partakers, not to traffic or agree with Sir James Douglas of Drumlanrig, knight, his kin, friends, etc., without the special advice and consent of the other; and should any of them have an action of law against Sir James Douglas, his kin, friends, etc., the one was to assist the other to the utmost of his power against him, his kin, friends, etc., until the parties at feud were reconciled.[2]

But circumstances soon after brought them again into hostile collision. In those times the impatience of clans at feud could not wait for the slow determinations of law. They often took a more summary method of obtaining the redress of real or supposed wrongs. In the year 1593 a party of the clan of the Johnstons and their friends, headed by William Johnston of Wamphray, made a predatory incursion into the lands of Lord Crichton of Sanquhar, with whom they were at variance; and, their leader having been captured and hanged by the Crichtons, they invaded, under a new commander, with increased force, the tenantry of the Crichtons, committing ruthlessly their devastations, and killing a number of those obnoxious to their vengeance; and on their way to their homes they left, like locusts, the devastating marks of their presence. This Border foray attracted the notice of Sir Walter Scott, and it forms the theme of one of his metrical legends of the Borders, entitled "The Lads of Wamphray."[3]

The proprietors and tenants whose lands had been laid waste, and whose

February 1592-3, it is complained that Maxwell and Home, who were considered to be of the Spanish faction, were in great credit at Court.—*Ibid.* vol. v. p. 232.

[1] Calderwood's History. vol. v. pp. 144, 149.
[2] Original Agreement at Raehills.
[3] Minstrelsy of the Scottish Border, vol. i. p. 308.

property had been seized and carried off, and those whose relatives had been slaughtered, appealed to Lord Maxwell, Warden of the West Marches. They also complained to the King and the Privy Council. A deputation, consisting of poor women, undertook a long journey from Nithsdale to Edinburgh, carrying with them fifteen bloody shirts which had belonged to their husbands, sons, brothers or other friends, who had been cruelly slain, and implored the King and the Privy Council to cause justice to be done upon the Johnstons, by whom their friends had been killed. The petition was coldly received by the King and Council, and there seemed little prospect of their obtaining redress. On the 23d July 1593, by the advice of their friends, they went in procession through the streets of Edinburgh, with the bloody shirts carried in front of them. The crowd who witnessed this strange spectacle were moved to indignation against the King and Council for their apathy, and cried out for vengeance upon them. So strong was the feeling thus raised, that the Government was constrained to take proceedings against the Johnstons. The Government was thus compelled to listen to the prayer of the women's petition, and to do something.[1]

The King issued a special commission, and commanded Lord Maxwell to execute justice on the clan of the Johnstons for the depredations and slaughters which they had committed. At the same time the proprietors and others who had suffered bound themselves to assist Lord Maxwell in all his quarrels, provided he would, in the exercise of his office, inflict merited punishment on the Johnstons who were concerned in these predatory and bloody transactions. On the 23d of October 1593, at Blackwoodhead, a bond was entered into by Sir James Douglas of Drumlanrig, Robert Maxwell of Castlemilk, brother of Lord Maxwell, and Thomas Kirkpatrick of Closeburn, binding themselves to stand firmly by each other in the execution of the Royal Commission for the apprehension of Sir James Johnston of Dunskellie, and to defend each other against him and the rest of the name of Johnston and their partakers, except so many as assisted them in his apprehension. The bond particularly narrates that the King had given special authority to John Earl of Morton, Warden of the West Marches of Scotland directly opposite to England, and Justice within the whole bounds thereof, and Steward of Annandale, to apprehend Sir

---

[1] Calderwood's History, vol. v. p. 256; Chambers's Domestic Annals, vol. i. p. 250.

James Johnston of Dunskellie, knight, his Majesty's rebel, for divers odious crimes, and for reset of the murderers of the men of Sanquhar and sundry other fugitives in his house of Lochwood; that Lord Maxwell had employed Robert Maxwell of Castlemilk, with the concurrence of Thomas Kirkpatrick of Closeburn, and such others of the barons within the wardenry as might be moved to advance the King's service; and that Sir James Douglas of Drumlanrig had promised to embark in the expedition.[1]

The Laird of Johnston having got possession of the bond of agreement entered into between Lord Maxwell and the gentlemen of Nithsdale, which had been carelessly kept,[2] discovered the danger impending over him and his clan, and immediately made vigorous preparations for defence. From his maternal relatives, the Scotts of Eskdale and Teviotdale, he received 500 men, headed by Sir Gideon Murray of Elibank, in place of the Laird of Buccleuch, who was then abroad. He was also assisted by the Elliots of Liddesdale, the Grahams of the Debateable Land, and other Border tribes.

Commissioned by the King, and supported by the sufferers of Nithsdale, Lord Maxwell proceeded to action. He first summoned Sir James Johnston of Dunskellie to surrender in the King's name, and submit himself to trial. As might have been expected, the summons was treated with contempt. Maxwell now had no alternative but to endeavour to secure obedience to his authority by force of arms. As Warden of the Marches, according to a contemporary authority, he had, in foot and horse, 1500, whilst the Laird of Johnston, with the Scots, numbered 800 men or thereby.[3]

Early in the month of December 1593, Lord Maxwell marched with his forces from Dumfries into Annandale. To observe the motions of the enemy, he sent out a reconnoitering party under the command of Captain Oliphant. This party was suddenly overpowered by a strong body of the Johnstons near Lochmaben, and many of them were slain, including their leader. Others sought shelter in the parish church, but the Johnstons having set fire to it, they were soon compelled to surrender.

Nothing discouraged, Lord Maxwell crossed the Lochmaben hills, on the

[1] Original Bond at Raehills.
[2] Spottiswoode's History, vol. ii. p. 446.
[3] Contemporary account, MS. in Advocates' Library, supposed to have been written by Robert Johnston, a learned historian, who died about the year 1630; and Chambers's Domestic Annals, vol. i. p. 252.

6th of December 1593, and encamped during the night on the heights of Skipmyre. On the forenoon of the following day, advancing to the river Annan, which was at some distance, they crossed that river, and found themselves face to face with the Johnstons, who had taken up their position on elevated ground, now a portion of the parish glebe, which sloped gradually away southward. It was a proof of the military skill of Sir James, thus to force Lord Maxwell into an engagement on ground so disadvantageous that he could never bring into action more than the half of his men. Lord Maxwell, from rash confidence in his superior forces, had not kept himself sufficiently informed as to the movements of his enemy, and his forces having been thrown somewhat into disorder through crossing the river, he and the advanced part of his army found themselves in a position in which he had no alternative but to fight or to make a disastrous retreat. To force him to fight, Johnston "sent forth some prickers to ride and make provocation," challenging to the conflict, and shouting the Johnstons' war-cry, "Ready, aye ready!" Maxwell, exasperated, sent forth a strong detachment of his men, crying "Wardlaw! Wardlaw! Wardlaw! I bid you bide, Wardlaw!" the slogan of the Maxwells. This detachment was suddenly surrounded and attacked on all sides by a larger body of Johnstons, which in addition to its greater number had the advantage of a more favourable position. The Maxwells broke up and fell back on the main body, which was thus thrown into confusion. The Johnstons, seeing this, rushed down from their elevated position with their whole force upon their enemies, who never rallied from the disorder into which they had fallen. Lord Maxwell and his army were thrown into a panic, and fled in confusion, the most of them falling back upon and recrossing the water of Annan.

The fate of Lord Maxwell was tragical. It is said that some days before the battle he had promised a reward of a ten pound land, that is, land valued to the King at that yearly rental for taxation purposes, to any person who should bring to him the head or hand of the chief of the Johnstons. In retaliation the chief of the Johnstons said that he had not a ten pound land to give, but he offered a farm of the half of that value to the man who should bring to him the head or the hand of Maxwell. "The Lord Maxwell," says Spottiswoode, the only writer of the time who gives some details of Lord Maxwell's death, "a tall man and heavy in armour, was in the chase overtaken and stricken from his horse."[1]   Other particulars are told by tradition.   Lord Maxwell, it is said, was overtaken about half a mile below the old churchyard by William Johnston of Kirkhill, who, on coming up to him, struck him from his horse, and disregarding his prayer for mercy, on the ground that in similar circumstances he had treated the chief of the Johnstons with clemency, cut off his hand, and put him to death.   This account is said by Sir Walter Scott to be that of the daughters of William Johnston of Kirkhill, derived from their father.   There is another tradition which represents Johnston as having indeed cut off the hand of Maxwell, and left him mutilated but alive.   Shortly afterwards the wife of James Johnston of Kirkton, who had gone out of Kirkton Tower with a few female attendants to search for her husband, and to afford relief to the wounded on the field, having discovered Maxwell, despatched him by repeatedly striking him on the head with the keys of the tower, which she had suspended to her girdle on locking the tower.   The probability is that Johnston of Kirkhill did not leave Maxwell till certain of his death, and that he carried the arm and head of Maxwell to his chief.[2]

In a contemporary account, formerly quoted, after stating that Lord Maxwell was slain with the Laird of Johnston's own hand,[3] it is added, " Never ane of his awn folks remained with him (only twenty of his own houshold), but all fled through the water; five of the said Lord's company were slain, and his head and right arm were taken with them to the Lochwood, and affixed on the wall thereof.   The bruit ran, 'that the said Lord Maxwell was treacherously deserted by his awn company.'"[4]   This account gives evidence at least as to reports of treachery, but no particular parties are named, although in Lord Maxwell's " Gude Night," to be afterwards quoted, the Lairds

[1] Spottiswoode's History, vol. ii. p. 446.

[2] Two large thorn trees, called " Maxwell's thorns," long marked the place where Lord Maxwell was slain ; but about half a century ago they were swept away when the waters of the Dryfe were greatly swollen.

[3] At this part of the manuscript history there is an interlineation by another hand,—"or, as is alleged, by Mr. Gideon Murray, being servitor to Scott of Buccleuch."

[4] Printed from Johnston's MS. History, Advocates' Library, in Chambers's Domestic Annals, vol. i. p. 252.   Robert Johnston and Spottiswoode are the only contemporary writers who give an account of this battle.   In those points as to which they differ, the former is probably the more trustworthy, as his narrative was written earlier than that of the other, and he had better opportunities of obtaining correct information, as his friends were likely engaged in the battle.

of Drumlanrig, Closeburn, and Lag are directly charged with the desertion of Lord Morton.

The battle, which was fought on the 6th of December 1593, is usually called the battle of Dryfe Sands, from its having taken place upon the sands bearing that name, formed by the floods of the river Dryfe as it falls into the Annan. In the battle itself only a few on either side fell. It has been asserted by some writers that some hundreds of Lord Maxwell's men were slain in their flight, that many of them were made prisoners, that others of them were drowned in the Annan, whose waters were then swollen, and that seven hundred of them are believed to have perished on this occasion.[1] This we take to be a great exaggeration. Johnston, in his narrative, records that only five of Lord Maxwell's company were slain in the battle. But the official records of the time, a more trustworthy authority than even Johnston, though a contemporary, lead to the conclusion that the battle, though not involving so great a loss as some modern writers represent, was yet of a more serious character than Johnston's narrative would seem to imply.

In a commission[2] appointed 22d December 1593 by the King, for establishing good order upon the Western Marches, in consideration of their troubled state, and of the treasonable rebellion of Sir James Johnston of Dunskellie, he and his accomplices are charged with "murdering the trew men induellaris in the Sanquhar, in the defens and saulftie of thair awne guidis ;" burning the parish kirk of Lochmaben, and the slaughter of some of his Majesty's subjects, sent thither by John Lord Maxwell, the King's Warden and justice, and for having appeared in arms against the Warden "umbesett, invadit, persewit, and maist cruellie and outragiouslie slew him, and sindrie gentilmen of his name, and vtheris his Majestie's obedient subjectis ; drownit, hurte, lamyt, dememberit, and tuke a grite nowmer of prisonaris, reft and spuilzeit thair horsis, armour, pursis, money, and vtheris

---

[1] M'Dowall's History of the Burgh of Dumfries, p. 322. Sir Walter Scott, in his Tales of a Grandfather, is incorrect in this and other particulars in reference to this battle, adopting too implicitly the loosest of traditions, and drawing too much on imagination. Other writers, trusting to him as an authority, have repeated his mistakes.

[2] The commission consisted of William Lord Herries, Sir John Gordon of Lochinvar, Alexander Stewart of Garlies, James Douglas of Drumlanrig, Thomas M'Lellan of Bombie, Thomas Kilpatrick of Closeburn, William Grierson of Lag, Alexander Jardine of Applegarth, John Charteris of Amisfield, and Charles Murray of Cockpool.

guidis."[1] It has been said by some historians that many of them fled in the direction of Lockerbie, and were so severely wounded as to give rise to the proverbial expression of " Lockerbie licks."

In an Act of Parliament, passed on 29th June 1598, Johnston is charged with the slaughter of the King's lieutenant and officer for the time, and the Laird of Nether Pollok, with sundry others, barons and gentlemen, to the number of thirty or forty. These numbers include those who were slain with Lord Maxwell in 1593, and in the raid by William Lord Herries in 1595.[2]

The fate of Lord Maxwell was lamented by all who knew him ; for though possessing a certain turbulence of character which was constantly involving him in difficulties, he was regarded, as Spottiswoode observes, as a nobleman of great spirit, humane, courteous, and more learned than noblemen commonly are. Having had a long minority under the care of his uncle, Lord Herries, Lord Maxwell was probably educated under Catholic clergymen. His correspondence, still preserved, shows his learning ; and his heraldic seals, which are the finest examples of the " noble science " in the family muniment room, show that his refined tastes were not destroyed by his rough Border life. " His fall was pitied of many, for that he was not known to have done much wrong in his time, and was rather hurtful to himself than others."[3] He fell in the prime of life, being only forty years of age.[4] His remains were interred in the College of Lincluden, on the 30th of December 1593.

The following is a letter of invitation to his funeral, written by William Lord Herries, to Sir John Maxwell of Pollok :—

" Rycht honorable and my verie guid freind, efter my hartlie commendationis,—Ze have hard of the infortunat slauchter of zour cheiff, my Loird Erle of Mortoun.[5] I, with advyis of his freindis heir, hes thocht meit that the buriall of his body salbe vpon Soneday, the penult of December instant; and becaus ze ar ane of his speciall friendis, quhais presence is maist requisite, bayth for

[1] Regist. Secreti Concilii, Acta, 1591-1594, fol. 270 ; Pitcairn's Criminal Trials, vol. i. part ii. p. 304.

[2] The Acts of the Parliaments of Scotland, vol. i. p. 166.

[3] Spottiswoode's History, vol. ii. p. 447.

[4] Sir Walter Scott incorrectly represents him as being an elderly grey-haired man.—Tales of a Grandfather, p. 153.

[5] This designation shows that the Morton title was generally accorded to Lord Maxwell many years after he was deprived of the earldom. Had he survived, it is probable that he might have obtained, as his son did, the title of Earl of Nithsdale, in substitution for that of Morton. His battles with the Crown in his lifetime, and his early death, prevented any such arrangement.—Memoirs of the Maxwells of Pollok, vol. ii. p. 170.

the furthset of the buriall, and for zour counsell to be had anent the taking ordour with his Loird-shippis bayrnis, leving and freindis.   Thairfoir I desyir zow effectuouslie to keip the said day, as ze respect the honour of that hous and standing of his bayrnis and leving.   Sa I commit zow to the protectioun of God.   From Drumfreis, the xi day of December 1593.

Zour loving and assurit freind,

HERYS.

" To the honorable and my assurit guid freind, the Layrd of Pollok."

Intelligence of the disastrous defeat of his lieutenant of the Western Marches having reached King James the Sixth, he was much exasperated, and Sir James Johnston and his accomplices were immediately put to the horn, declared to be rebels, and all were forbidden to intercommune with or harbour them under the pain of being treated as traitors to the King.

Among the prisoners taken by the Johnstons at Dryfe Sands, were Amer Maxwell of Carnsalloch, George Maxwell of Drumcoltran, William Maxwell of Tinwald, younger, John Maxwell of Portrack, and Mungo Maxwell, there.   In a bond which they gave to Sir James Johnston of Dunskellie, dated at Loch-wood, 10th December 1593, in which it is narrated that they were taken prisoners by him, they bound themselves, under the pain of treason, that they should enter into the house of Lochwood on the 8th day of January, and there remain until lawful entry should be taken of them by Sir James.[1]

The resentment of the King on account of the slaughter of his Warden appears to have been soon appeased.   A warrant was obtained by Sir James Johnston, under the King's sign-manual, ordaining a respite to be made under the Privy Seal, in favour of Sir James, for the "tresonable slauchter of Lord Maxwell."   The date of the slaughter is there stated to have occurred on the 6th of December.   The date of the royal warrant itself is left incomplete, but it appears to have been granted in the year 1594, as a respite passed the Privy Seal at Holyroodhouse, 24th December that year, in favour of Sir James Johnston of Dunskellie, John Carmichael of Medowflatt, Robert Johnston of Raycleuch, Symoun Johnestoun, brother to the Laird of Johnestoun, and other Johnstouns, and others therein named, to the number of one hundred and sixty, for the pursuit and slaughter of John Lord Maxwell, his Majesty's lieutenant and Warden for the time, and of sundry others his Majesty's subjects, who were in company with him ; the mutilation and hurting of others committed

---

[1] Original Bond amongst the Johnston Papers at Raehills.

in the month of December 1593 ; the raising and burning of the kirk of Loch-maben, and the slaughter of Captain Oliphant and others. The respite was for the space of five years after the date.[1]

By his spouse, Lady Elizabeth Douglas, Lord Maxwell had three sons and four daughters. The sons were—

1. John, who succeeded his father as ninth Lord Maxwell.

2. Robert, who succeeded his elder brother John as tenth Lord Max-well, and who was created Earl of Nithsdale.

3. James of Springkell, styled Master of Maxwell. Captain James Maxwell, brother of Robert Earl of Nithsdale, as principal, and John Lord Herries as cautioner, became bound to Sir John Hep-burn, knight, colonel of a regiment of Scotsmen serving the King of France, to raise, and have in readiness 150 good and able Scotsmen, sufficiently clothed and armed with swords and hats, and that at least sixty should have blue or red cloth "cassiks," to serve in the wars under that colonel, and to transport them to Dieppe, before the 1st of March 1635. On 21st December 1634, a bond was granted by the said Captain James Maxwell to John Lord Herries, relieving him from all loss by his cautionery.[2] He died without male issue, before 5th October 1667, when his nephew's titles and estates passed to John, fourth Lord Herries. The Master left a daughter, Jean Maxwell.[3]

The daughters of Lord Maxwell were—

1. Elizabeth, who married John Maxwell, Lord Herries, grandson of the celebrated John Lord Herries. Allusion is made to some love affair of this lady in a letter from her father to Sir John Maxwell of Pollok, dated 6th June 1593. " My las Elizabeth," he says, " hes lattine me sie zour lettre, quhairbe I do vnderstand zour cairfull mynd toward the weilfair of my bairnes. . . . As ze find oportunytie, lat word cum, that I may mak hir to do that quhilk womanlie modestie wil permit on hir parte. Marye, ze knaw that it is a grit disgrace for ane gentill woman to wowe and than be disapoyntit."[4]

[1] Regist. Secreti Sigilli, vol. lxvii. fol. 43.   [3] Memoirs of Maxwells of Pollok, vol. i. p. 446.
[2] Original Bond at Terregles.   [4] Ibid. vol. ii. p. 168.

Sir John Maxwell, in a letter to her, 13th March 1593-4, after referring to his losses through her father's death, says that he had been as steadable and ready to serve her late father and her mother as any Maxwell in Scotland, and should be as ready for his sake to do her, her brothers and sisters, honour and service, as any of that name, according to his simple power. He would have her mother to do her duty to him, otherwise kindness would not stand that was altogether on the one side. If his counsel was followed, he would wish that Lord Herries and her mother should assign a reasonable part of her late father's living, for a certain number of years, to be tocher to her, and her sisters, and that a trusty friend should be appointed collector thereof.[1]

2. Margaret, who married John Wallace, younger of Craigie. Their marriage-contract is dated 15th December 1597, and was registered in the books of Council on the 10th of July 1598. In this contract John Lord Maxwell as principal, and his cautioners, John Maxwell of Kirkconnell, George Maxwell of Drumcoltrane, and others, became bound to pay to John Wallace, younger of Craigie, 7000 merks Scots, within the parish kirk of Ayr, upon the 10th of November 1599, as tocher, with Margaret Maxwell, his sister. The right to this sum was afterwards transferred to Katherine Wallace, daughter of John Wallace of Craigie, who was made cessioner thereto by John Wallace, younger of Craigie. This lady, by a legal action, compelled George Maxwell of Drumcoltrane, one of the cautioners, to pay the said 7000 merks to her and William Wallace, younger of Ellerslie, her husband. This sum was afterwards paid to Edward Maxwell of Drumcoltrane, son of the said George, by Robert, first Earl of Nithsdale, who obtained from him a discharge, dated 17th January 1631.[2]

3. Jean, who died unmarried.

4. Agnes, who married William Douglas of Penzerie.[3] Mrs. Agnes Maxwell, lawful daughter of the deceased John Lord Maxwell, in

---

[1] Memoirs of the Maxwells of Pollok, vol. ii. p. 174.

[2] Original Discharge at Terregles.

[3] MS. Account of the Herries Family.

an instrument of requisition, dated 9th April 1612, to George Cran-stoun, in Edinburgh, desired him to receive payment of 500 merks Scots, and to deliver certain " cannabies" and " courteins" therein described, and " a woman's goun of purpour satyne, conteining nyne breidis thairin," all in a coffer, and laid in wad, for the said sum.[1]

The father of these ladies, at Dumfries, on 6th August 1592, made an assignation of the 35,000 merks, due to him for exercising the office of Warden of the West Marches, in favour of his three daughters, Elspeth, Margaret and Agnes, the first to receive £10,000, and the other two 10,000 merks each.[2]

John Lord Maxwell had also an illegitimate son, of whom was descended Maxwell of Middlebie. John Maxwell, brother-natural to the Earl of Niths-dale, was witness to an assignation by David Makghie, with consent of Adam Cunningham, advocate, Prebendar of Lincluden, of a lease of the prebend thereof, by him, dated 10th July 1623.

Lady Elizabeth Douglas, after the death of her husband, John Lord Maxwell, married, secondly, Alexander Stewart of Garlies (father of the first Earl of Galloway), who died on 9th October 1596, without issue by her, and, thirdly, about 1598, John Wallace, elder of Craigie, in the county of Ayr.

On 21st December 1605, a discharge was granted by John Lord Maxwell to Dame Elizabeth Douglas, Lady Maxwell, his mother, and John Wallace of Craigie, her spouse, for the delivery of the inventories of deeds belonging to his deceased father.[3] In a contract, 22d September 1607, between John Lord Maxwell and Patrick Maxwell of Newark, his cousin, the former, in binding him-self to dispone to the latter certain lands in the barony of Mearns, reserved the rights of Dame Elizabeth Douglas, Lady Maxwell, his mother.[4] On 13th December 1609, King James the Sixth made a gift to Sir James Richardson of Smeatoun, knight, of the liferent escheat of John Wallace of Craigie, *jure mariti*, as spouse to Dame Elizabeth Douglas, which belonged to her by the disposition and decease of John Lord Maxwell, her first husband, the same having fallen to the King through John Wallace's being denounced rebel and put to the horn for non-payment of debt.[5] At the instance of Dame Elizabeth

[1] Original Instrument of Requisition at Terregles.
[2] Original Assignation, *ibid.* [3] Original Discharge, *ibid.*
[4] Original Contract at Terregles.
[5] Original Gift, *ibid.*

Douglas, a summons of removing was raised against certain tenants in Maxwellheuch, dated 3d and 4th July 1629.[1] This lady died at Edinburgh, in the year 1637. Robert, first Earl of Nithsdale, her son, gave her a sumptuous funeral, and afterwards transported her remains to the College Kirk of Lincluden, to be interred in a vault beside those of her first husband, John Earl of Morton.[2]

[1] Original Summons at Terregles.　　　　　[2] MS. Account of the Herries Family.

SEALS AND SIGNATURE OF JOHN EARL OF MORTON, LORD MAXWELL.

XVIII. 1. JOHN, NINTH LORD MAXWELL,

SECOND EARL OF MORTON.

LADY MARGARET HAMILTON, DAUGHTER OF JOHN MARQUIS OF HAMILTON.

1593-1613.

JOHN, NINTH LORD MAXWELL, was born about the year 1586. In " a Note of the especiall particularities concerning the present estate of the nobility here in Scotland, 10th April 1589," he is said to have been then three years of age. He was therefore about eight years of age at the time of his succession to his father's estates and title in the year 1593.[1] His tutor was William Maxwell, Lord Herries, to whom, in that capacity, Dame Elizabeth Douglas, Dowager Countess of Morton, the mother of Lord Maxwell, delivered an inventory of writs of the Maxwell estates at Dumfries on 3d August 1594.[2] His curators, in the year 1601, were John Earl of Cassillis, Sir James Maxwell of Calderwood, Patrick Maxwell of Newark, John Maxwel of Kirkconnel, and Sir Robert Hamilton of Goslington.

On 10th March 1596-7, Lord Maxwell was served heir to his father in the lordship of Maxwell and other lands. Between April 1601 and September 1604 he was served heir to his father in the office of bailie of the Provostry of Lincluden and in the lands of Numbellie and others ; in the office of heritable keeper of the castle of Lochmaben, with lands, fishings, and other privileges ; in sundry lands and fishings in Annandale ; in the lands of Duncow, Keir, Bardannoche and others in the barony of Holywood, the lands of Tinwald, Broomholm and Arkinholm, Wauchopdale and others ; in the barony of Buittle, lands in Kirkpatrick-Durham, Trevegrange, the offices of steward of Kirkcudbright and keeper of Threave Castle, bailiery of Sweetheart and lands of Locharthur, bailiery of Dundrennan, and the lands of Mullock and isle of Hestan.[3]

As heir to his father, he was, in April 1605, infeft in the lands of the lordship and barony of Buittle, including Munches, Barscheane, Castlegour,

---

[1] Letters of John Colville, Bannatyne Club, 1858, Appendix, p. 327. Lord Maxwell was still under curators in the year 1601, but he was of age in the year 1608, when he granted charters without the consent of his curators.

[2] Original Inventory at Terregles.

[3] Original Retours, *ibid.*

Balgredden, etc., in the lordship of Galloway and Stewartry of Kirkcudbright ; and in other lands.[1]

While still in his minority, and probably when he was only about twelve years of age, a marriage was arranged between him and Lady Margaret Hamilton, only daughter of Lord John Hamilton, afterwards created Marquis of Hamilton. The contract for this is dated at Hamilton, the 9th of August 1597, and was recorded in the books of Council 1st April 1598. In it the lady is styled " Mastres Margaret Hamilton, dochtir liberall " to the Marquis and Dame Margaret Lyoun his spouse. A discharge, granted by Lord Maxwell and his curators, on 29th October 1601, for 9000 merks Scots, in full payment of the 20,000 merks promised as tocher, states that the marriage had been solemnized after the date of the contract, and that the lady was then the spouse of Lord Maxwell.[2]

The feud between the Johnstons and Maxwells was only aggravated by the death of Lord Maxwell's father, and, guided by the headstrong Laird of Johnston, the former lost no opportunity of molesting their ancient enemies. When William Maxwell, Lord Herries, in the performance of his duty as Warden of the West Marches, went, in the end of October 1595, to Lockerbie, accompanied by 300 men, and seized upon some malefactors, he was attacked by a party of the Johnstons, who rescued the prisoners, and forced him to retire, leaving on the field about a score of his men dead or mortally wounded, amongst whom was Sir John Maxwell of Pollok.[3]

The Government endeavoured to allay these mortal feuds, which so greatly disturbed the peace of the kingdom.

Mr. John Colville, in a letter to Robert Bowes, 25th October 1595, informs him that the Convention appointed to meet on the 24th of that month was delayed to the 1st of the following month, when it was expected that some order should be set down for quieting the deadly feud between Maxwell and Johnston, who, on the 17th of October, had met in Annandale, Johnston's bounds ; that Lord Hay with Drumlanrig, accompanied by nearly 2000 men, ran a foray in Annandale, and took away a great booty of goods, which were restored.[4] In a letter to Bowes, 29th December same year, Colville writes

[1] Original Retours at Terregles.
[2] Original Discharge at Kirkconnel.
[3] Memoirs of the Maxwells of Pollok, vol. i. p. 42.
[4] Colville's Letters, p. 184.

that his Majesty intended to compose generally with all, except Papists and actual murderers, the deadly feuds which so abounded that no man could safely go a mile from his own house ; and that the three mortal feuds which were the principal, namely, those betwixt Maxwell and Johnston, Maguire (Montgomerie) and Cunynghame, the Earl of Mar and Leviston were to be pacified about the 16th of the next month, and whichever of the parties refused should be the worse liked of his Grace.[1]   In another letter to Bowes, 7th December 1595, a mistake for January 1595-6, Colville writes that in that week pledges were to be taken of Maxwell, Drumlanrig, and Johnston for keeping good order, and a Warden was to be nominated, who he thought should be Carmichaell.[2]

But the efforts of the Government to reconcile the conflicting clans had little effect.   The feud was still further embittered by the appointment of Sir James Johnston of Dunskellie, knight, in April 1596, to be the Warden of the Western Marches, in the room of William Lord Herries, who had been deprived of the office.   It was soon discovered that this appointment only increased the disturbances which it was so difficult to quell, and in November in the following year the office was conferred upon Andrew Lord Stewart of Ochiltree, in the hope that this would conduce to restore and maintain tranquillity on the Borders.

Such was the annoyance which Johnston, by his acts of outrage and blood, gave to the Government, that on 27th May 1598 he was declared rebel, and his portrait hung at the cross of Edinburgh, with his head downwards.[3] So heavy were the complaints made against him by the inhabitants of the West Marches, that, in compliance with their supplication, the Parliament, on 29th June, passed an Act forbidding all persons to receive, assist, or intercommune with him.   In the Act he and his friends are charged generally with great, odious, and detestable slaughters, murders, bloodsheds, and enormities ; and specially with having first most cruelly and unmercifully slain and murdered the late John Lord Maxwell, his Majesty's lieutenant, with the Laird of Pollok, and sundry other barons and gentlemen, to the number of thirty or forty ; and next a great number of honest men of Sanquhar, and sundry gentle-

[1] Colville's Letters, p. 188.
[2] Ibid. p. 190.
[3] Birrell's Diary, quoted in Pitcairn's Criminal Trials, vol. iii. p. 29.

men and others since that time, to the great contempt of God, his Majesty, all form of law and justice, and disquiet of the country. Johnston is said to be still prosecuting a most wild and bloody course, without regard to assurance, oath, or promise, or duty towards God and his Majesty, or charity towards his neighbour. The Act bears the subscription of King James the Sixth.[1]

Lord Maxwell was a member of the Convention of the Nobility and Estates, held at Holyroodhouse, at which this Act was passed.[2] For the purpose of keeping peace on the West Borders, it was ordained by Parliament, on 31st July 1599, that William Lord Herries, Sir James Douglas of Drumlanrig, and Sir James Johnston of Dunskellie, should be warded. Their imprisonment was to continue till the Warden and Barons of the West Marches should advise with the King and Council regarding their liberation.[3]

Sir James Johnston was liberated before 2d July 1600, when he was restored to his honours at the cross of Edinburgh, by the proclamation of a herald and four trumpets.[4] On 13th July, same year, he was again appointed Warden of the West Marches and Justiciar; an appointment which aggravated still more the ill feeling between the Maxwells and the Johnstons.

These brief notices of Sir James Johnston show that he was not a man whose temper and actions were likely to conciliate Lord Maxwell; and that the feud between them was more likely to burst forth, under certain circumstances, with renewed and fatal violence, than to be allayed or removed.

It is notable that when William Lord Herries subscribed, at the King's special command, a submission between him and the Laird of Johnston for his own feud, he protested before the Privy Council, 7th March 1600, that he reserved his duty of blood and friendship to Lord Maxwell; a protestation which was admitted by the King. Lord Herries had been warded by an Act of Parliament, 31st July 1599, till he became bound for the peaceable behaviour of his men, tenants, and servants, and was allowed to go forth from his ward within the Castle of Tantallan on 15th September.

Lord Maxwell was a steadfast adherent of the Roman Catholic religion, and in the part of the country where he resided, particularly at Dumfries, mass

[1] The Acts of the Parliaments of Scotland, vol. v. p. 166.

[2] Ibid. vol. iv. p. 158.

[3] The Acts of the Parliaments of Scotland, vol. iv. p. 182.

[4] Birrell's Diary, quoted in Pitcairn's Criminal Trials, vol. iii. p. 29.

was celebrated by seminary priests, and attended by sundry persons of quality, contrary to the laws then in force. For the violation of these laws he was declared rebel, and put to the horn, before the year 1600.

The following petition, without date, from Lord Maxwell to the King, preserved among the papers of James Lord Balmerino, Secretary of State to King James the Sixth, an office to which he was appointed in 1598, praying for his Majesty's forgiveness, probably belongs to this period :—

" PLEASE YOUR MAJESTIE,—I, your Majestie's most humble and obedient subiect, as I desyred my louing cousen, the Maister of Paisley, to enforme your Majestie of my comming towardes your Highnes, in all humility and repentaunce for my greate ouersight of dewty towardes your Highnes, my most gratious Prince, not being able to make satisfactioun for the same, I am to flie to your Highnes clemency and mercy (only for my refuge) to be vsed towardis me, casting my self fullie at your Highnes feete of purpose, be Gode's grace, to obey in all thinges sa far as in me lyes your Highnes wille and commandements ; and to assure your Highnes the farther I haue tane the boldnes to testifie this by this my hand writte, and for your Majestie's obedience in the particulare betwixte me and my party, wherein with my losse your Majestie's honour is conioyned, I am content to refere my selfe simpliciter in your Majestie's wille, not doubting but your Majestie will haue consideration of the great wrong I and my freindes haue susteyned ; and in the meanetyme I shall keepe your Majestie's peace and await your Majestie's sacred wille.

" Your Highnes maist humble and obedient subiect,

" J. MAXUELL."

(Indorsed)—Coppie of the Lord Maxwell his Letter to his Majestie.[1]

In March 1601 Lord Maxwell was imprisoned in the Castle of Edinburgh for favouring Popery. " Mr. Johne Hammiltoun," says Calderwood, " the Apostat taught in Maxwell's galrie publictlie a little before, upon Luke ix. 58, ' The foxes have holes,' " etc.[2]

By the General Assembly, which met in the Royal Chapel at Holyrood-House, 10th November 1602, ministers were appointed to wait upon the noblemen who professed the Roman Catholic religion, and to remain for a quarter of a year continually with them, to confirm them and their families in the truth. Mr. Henry Blyth was to attend upon Lord Maxwell so long as he remained in the Castle of Edinburgh.[3]

On 12th January 1602 Lord Maxwell made his escape from the Castle of Edinburgh. On the 17th of the same month a proclamation was issued for-

[1] Contemporary Copy in Lord Elphinstone's Charter-chest.

[2] Calderwood's History, vol. vi. p. 146.
[3] Ibid. vol. vi. p. 166.

bidding all his Majesty's subjects to reset, harbour, or give any entertainment to him under the pain of treason.[1]

Soon after Lord Maxwell proceeded to active hostilities against the Johnstons : In February 1602 he set out, accompanied by Charles Maxwell of Kirkhouse, Robert Maxwell of Dinwooddie, and a party of his friends, amounting in all to twenty, with helmets, lances, coats of mail, muskets, harquebuses, and other prohibited arms, against William Johnston, brother of William Johnston of Elcheschellis, and John Johnston, brother of James Johnston of Hisliebray, on account of the deadly enmities between the Johnstons and the Maxwells. They went to the town of Dalfibble, in the parish of Kirkmichael and shire of Dumfries, where they cruelly attacked William Johnston, who was living quietly and peaceably in the town of Dalfibble, suspecting no injury, treachery, or invasion, drove him within his house in that town, purposely set fire to the house, and, when the violence of the fire compelled him to come out, cruelly slew him. Then coming immediately to the house of Cuthbert Bratten, in the same town, they, with equal cruelty, set fire to it, burned James Johnston, called of Briggis, alive within it, and wholly consumed in the flames the house of the said Cuthbert.

A little more than two years after, a professed reconciliation took place between Lord Maxwell and the Johnstons, by the friendly offices of the Privy Council, who prevailed upon Lord Maxwell to execute, upon 11th June 1605, " letters of Slannis" in favour of Sir James Johnston of Dunskellie, knight. By these letters Lord Maxwell, for himself, and taking burden for all others concerned, forgave Sir James Johnston of Dunskellie, knight, his kin, friends, servants, and dependants, all hatred, rancour, grudge and quarrel which he had against them for the slaughter of John Lord Maxwell, his father, and all other slaughters, mutilations, and insolencies which followed thereupon.[2] It may, however, be doubted whether Lord Maxwell really felt the placable spirit which these letters seem to breathe.

Soon after, by the orders of the Lords of the Privy Council, the " letters of Slannis," signed by Lord Maxwell, were ordained to be delivered by the Chancellor to Sir James Johnston of Dunskellie, in consideration of his having

---

[1] Balfour's Annals, vol. i. p. 411.

[2] Inventory of Annandale Family Papers, p. 470 ;

The Acts of the Parliaments of Scotland, vol. iv. p. 415.

obeyed a former Act of Secret Council by the exhibition before them of Christie Armstrong of Barnscallow.[1] On 28th September 1605, a remission was granted under the Great Seal to Sir James and others his friends for being art and part in the burning of the kirk of Lochmaben, and for the slaughter of John Lord Maxwell.[2]

Lord Maxwell was a member of the Parliaments which sat at Edinburgh 20th March and 13th May 1606.[3]

In a Convention held at Linlithgow, 10th December 1606, in which it was ordained that the noblemen suspected of Popery should be confined in certain towns, Lord Maxwell was to be confined in Leith ; the Earl of Sutherland, his wife and mother, were to be confined in Inverness ; the Earl of Caithness and his Countess in Elgin ; the Marquis of Huntly, his Marchioness and children, in Aberdeen ; the Earl of Angus, his Countess and children, in Glasgow ; the Earl of Hume and Lord Herries in Edinburgh; and Lord Sempill in Irvine.[4]

By asserting his claim to the title of Earl of Morton, as inherited from his father, and by holding courts in Eskdale muir, which was part of the earldom of Morton, Lord Maxwell was involved in disputes with William Douglas of Lochleven, who became Earl of Morton in 1588, on the death of Archibald Earl of Angus, who was rehabilitated in the earldom and title of Earl of Morton on 29th January 1585-6. To maintain their claims and their respective jurisdictions in Eskdale, Maxwell and Morton mustered their forces in the field. They were commanded by the Privy Council to dismiss their forces. Lord Maxwell disregarded the order, and challenged the Earl of Morton to determine the controversy by single combat. For this violence and contempt of the authority of the State, Lord Maxwell was again imprisoned in the Castle of Edinburgh, by order of the Parliament held at Edinburgh, 11th August 1607, by Ludovick Duke of Lennox, the King's commissioner.

About eight weeks after his imprisonment, Lord Maxwell, having planned his escape from the Castle of Edinburgh, accomplished it with characteristic daring and determination, along with Sir James M'Connell, knight,

---

[1] Inventory of Annandale Family Papers, p. 471.
[2] Ibid. p. 471.
[3] The Acts of the Parliament of Scotland, vol. iv. pp. 277, 278.
[4] Calderwood's History, vol. vi. p. 608.

and Robert Maxwell of Dinwooddie, his fellow-prisoners. About four or five o'clock on the afternoon of Friday, 4th of October, coming into Sir James M'Connell's chamber, as if to pass the time, according to his custom, he sat down beside him, and, after smoking two pipes of tobacco, told him that it was his purpose to make his escape on that very night, and desired him to be prepared to share in the adventure, for he had men at the gates ready to hold them open, and horses waiting upon the fields to carry them away. Sir James, hesitating, urged the need of good advice and deliberation. "Tushe man!" replied Lord Maxwell, "sic interpryses ar nocht effectuat with deliberationis and advisments, but with suddane resolutionis!" There were present, besides Sir James M'Connell, young Closeburn, Robert Maxwell of the Tour, William Armstrong of the Gingillis, William Maxwell of Kirkhouse, Lord Maxwell's servant, and two soldiers, the one the keeper of Lord Maxwell, and the other of Sir James M'Connell. His Lordship caused two quarts of wine to be brought in, and all were excited by drinking freely.

Rising up and walking about the room, Lord Maxwell suddenly turned upon the soldier who was Sir James M'Connell's keeper, and attempted to wrest from him his sword. Being resisted, he took from William Maxwell his "quhinger," with which, holding it to the soldier's breast, he swore that if he yielded not he would stab him. From fear of his life the soldier delivered up to him his sword. Lord Maxwell, in like manner, forced his own keeper and William Armstrong to surrender to him their swords. He gave one of the swords to Sir James M'Connell, another to Robert Maxwell, and kept the third for himself, calling out, "All gud fellowis that luiffis me, follow me! for I sall ather be furthe of the Castell this nycht, or ellis I sall loise my lyiff!" He then with his companions went out of the room; and closing the door upon young Closeburn, who had refused to accompany him, and William Armstrong, he fastened it on the outside "with the catbande," vowing to God that should any of them cry out, he would come back and despatch them. The soldier whose sword Lord Maxwell had first taken, having made the door fast within, gave alarm by crying out at the south window towards the West Port, "Treason! treason!" Coming to the guard-house at the inner gate, where the master porter of the Castle was sitting, William Maxwell of Kirkhouse desired him to open the gate. Lord Maxwell immediately made a similar demand, and on the refusal of the porter, he smote him with a drawn sword on the arm. He would have repeated the blow but for William Maxwell of Kirkhouse, who threw to him the keys, with which he opened the gate. Lord Maxwell and his companions had next an encounter at the second gate with the under porter. William Maxwell of Kirkhouse, to whom the porter opened the inner wicket, put his back to it on passing, to prevent its being closed. As the porter was pressing to close it, Lord Maxwell, Sir James M'Connell, and Robert Maxwell of Tour, came to him with drawn swords in their hands. They wounded him; and the two former, whilst he was in conflict with Robert Maxwell of Tour, escaped by the inner gate. Upon this the porter locked the gate, and held in Robert Maxwell, who, however, immediately escaped by leaping over the west castle wall that goes to the West Port of Edinburgh. Having climbed the wall, Lord Maxwell hastily made his escape upon a horse, which had been kept in readiness for him. There was an immediate pursuit. The Constable of the Castle, with other keepers, apprehended Sir James M'Connell, who, having irons upon him, wrested his ankle in leaping, which prevented his escape, and he was found lying on a dunghill, to which he had crept. Sir James was brought back to the Castle of Edinburgh, and put in irons. William Maxwell, who had left Lord Maxwell at the outer gate, was there taken. This was in the gloaming.[1]

On receiving intelligence of the escape of Lord Maxwell from the Castle of Edinburgh, the King was greatly incensed. In a letter to the Privy Council, dated 14th December 1607, he required them to order the publication of a proclamation, which he had sent them, at all places needful, and thereafter to take order for the prosecution of all resetters of Lord Maxwell. He further charged them to send summonses of treason for the rendering of his castles and houses; to put garrisons and keepers in each of them, to be entertained upon the rents belonging to the houses, until such time as his Majesty took further order therewith; and to give orders to such as should receive the Castle of Lochmaben, to deliver it to the Earl of Dunbar, or to any whom he should appoint for that purpose. He commanded them also to charge the principal of Lord Maxwell's name and followers to find surety, under pecuniary penalties, that they should not reset, supply, nor inter-

---

[1] Calderwood's History, vol. vi. p. 686.

commune with him ; and that they should give order to the garrisons under the command of the Lord of Scone and Sir William Cranstoune, to make special search in order to the apprehension of Lord Maxwell, and to omit nothing that might hasten the infliction of exemplary punishment upon him.[1]

Sir Thomas Hamilton was then Lord Advocate. He had heard that it was the opinion of some that unless the crimes for which Lord Maxwell was imprisoned were treasonable, his breaking of ward could not involve treason. He was therefore solicitous to ascertain what were his lordship's other offences which might be found treasonable in law, in order to the discharge of his duty in pursuing Lord Maxwell for treasonably making his escape from the Castle of Edinburgh. He accordingly, in a letter to the King, dated Edinburgh, 28th January 1608, requested instructions on this point. " As to the Lord Maxwell," he says, " I haue hard of his raising of fyre at Dalfibbill, whan he slew Willie Johnestoun, callit of Eschiescheillis, and ane vther Johne-stoun ; bot becaus he hes sensyne had the honour to be admitted to your royall presence, I wald not presume to summond him for that fact, whill first I sould knaw your Maiestie's mynde thairanent, the knawledge whairof sall lead me to proceid or desist."[2] The King's answer has not been preserved, but that it was unfavourable to Lord Maxwell there is no reason to doubt.

After his escape Lord Maxwell, notwithstanding the proclamations issued for his apprehension, openly travelled through the country, accompanied by not fewer than twenty horse, in defiance of his Majesty's authority, and repaired at sundry times to Dumfries. The King therefore, in a letter to the Privy Council, dated Whitehall, 2d February 1608, after stating these facts, informed them what they were to do. He commanded them to direct the King's Guard, under Lord Scoone, to repair to Dumfries, and with the guard under Sir William Cranstoune, to make diligent search for Lord Maxwell, and either apprehend him, or put him out of those bounds. He also ordered that the bailies of Dumfries should be charged to compear before the Council. If the Council found that they had knowledge of Lord Maxwell's being in town, they were to inflict exemplary punishment upon them, both by fines and imprisonment, and were rigorously to proceed against all who

[1] The Earl of Haddington's Collection of State Papers, in the General Register House, quoted in   Pitcairn's Criminal Trials, vol. iii. p. 38.
[2] Melrose Papers, vol. i. p. 38.

should reset his Lordship.[1]   One of his retreats was a certain cave in Clawbelly Hill, in the parish of Kirkgunzeon, which is still called "Lord Maxwell's cave." The Privy Council informed the King of this hiding-place of the rebel Lord.

Lord Maxwell's situation as a declared traitor was felt by him to be a very unhappy one. To escape being arrested, he had either to seek shelter as a fugitive, or to defy the Government by going about attended with an armed force. This caused him constant disquietude. A reconciliation between him and the Laird of Johnston was extremely desirable. Both of them seem to have been convinced of this; and to accomplish so good an object, the mediation of Sir Robert Maxwell of Spottis, or Orchardtoun, Lord Maxwell's cousin, and Johnston's brother-in-law, was specially employed. The proposition for peace seems to have come first from Johnston.

Sir Robert, when on one occasion at Lochwood House, was desired by the Laird of Johnston to embrace the first favourable opportunity to speak with Lord Maxwell about the effecting of some good understanding between them. He excused himself by pleading that he was a sickly man, and had no credit with Lord Maxwell, who had always disliked him, because he had married Johnston's sister; nor did he wish to meddle in their quarrel, as it was dangerous to have anything to do with such a man. About the end of March 1608, Sir Robert Maxwell visited Lord Maxwell at his request. On their meeting Lord Maxwell explained why he wanted to see him. "Cosine," he said, "it wes for this caus I send for zow. Ze see my estait and dangour I stand in; and I wald crave zour counsell and avise as ane man that tenderis my weill." Sir Robert advised him to keep himself quiet, and to do nothing which might still more offend the King. He also promised that he would endeavour to move the noblemen who were his friends at Court and Council to report the best concerning him to the King and Council. He expressed his willingness, if his Lordship was disposed to forgive the Laird of Johnston, to do what he could to compose their differences. Lord Maxwell, if he saw any disposition on the part of the Laird of Johnston to do his duty to him, was willing to overlook the past, and would, if he received a reasonable answer from him, be ready to meet him at any convenient place, with a view to their

---

[1] Haddington MSS., General Register House, quoted in Pitcairn's Criminal Trials, vol. iii. p. 49.

being reconciled. Sir Robert received a letter on the subject from the Laird of Johnston, with which Lord Maxwell was entirely satisfied.

In prospect of the meeting together of the parties for this amicable purpose, Sir Robert exacted from Lord Maxwell a promise and oath with his Lordship's hand " strekit " in his hands, that neither he himself, nor his attendant, should do any wrong, whether they came to an accommodation or not.   They fixed the tryst to be on Wednesday, 6th April, beyond the house of Beal, between three and four o'clock in the afternoon.   Each party was to be accompanied by only one attendant, and no other person except Sir Robert, who was to mediate between them, was to be present.   Lord Maxwell promised to bring with him Robert Maxwell of the Tour, or some other person who would be equally acceptable to Sir Robert, and for whose fidelity he should be answerable.

On the 6th of April, the Laird of Johnston, leaving his best horse behind him, set out for the tryst on "ane amling naig," for the sake of secrecy, with Sir Robert, and William Johnston of Lockerbie, who, happening to come to Lochwood about one o'clock in the afternoon of that day, had been chosen as the Laird's attendant.   When they were about a mile from the place appointed, Sir Robert observed that Lord Maxwell and his attendant, both riding on horseback, were advancing.   He desired the Laird of Johnston and his friend to stop where they were until he returned to them or else gave them a sign to come forward by holding up his napkin upon the point of his riding-switch.   Riding forward to Lord Maxwell, he told him that the Laird of Johnston was coming, accompanied by William Johnston of Lockerbie.   Sir Robert felt regret on discovering that Lord Maxwell's attendant was Charles Maxwell, from whose character he was somewhat apprehensive that the meeting might not be so successful in composing differences as he would otherwise have anticipated.   He, however, did not express his apprehensions, but again required, as he had previously done, that Lord Maxwell should renew his oath and promise of strict fidelity.   With this request his Lordship at once complied.   He also promised to be answerable for Charles Maxwell.   Sir Robert, then leaving Lord Maxwell, when about midway between the two parties, held up his napkin on the point of his switch, upon which the Laird of Johnston and William Johnston rode forward to Sir Robert, who told the Laird that Lord

Maxwell, accompanied with Charles Maxwell alone, was at the place appointed waiting for them.   The Laird of Johnston declared himself satisfied with Charles Maxwell in preference to any other person, because he was John Murray of Cockpool's sister's son.   Sir Robert took the Laird of Johnston's oath and promise of fidelity, as he had done Lord Maxwell's, for himself and his man, by his hand laid in his, whether an agreement was come to or not.   The attendants of both parties were commanded by their respective chieftains to ride off from them and also from each other.   On meeting, Lord Maxwell and the Laird of Johnston, after mutual salutations, rode together, Sir Robert being in the middle, suitably to his character as mediator between them, and doubtless urging upon both the wisdom of forgetting the past and the advantages of cultivating a true friendship in the future.   Whilst their backs were turned to the two attendants, Sir Robert, looking behind, saw Charles Maxwell go, evidently from a hostile purpose, from the place where he was ordered to stay, towards William Johnston.   Immediately an altercation took place between the two attendants.   " Gif I had knawin of this tryist," said the former to the latter, " the Lord Maxwell nather culd nor suld haif brocht me heir."   " I hoip in God, Charlis," returned the other, in a conciliatory tone, " ze sall nocht rew of zour cumming heir!   For thir twa noble men hes bene lang in variance, and I hoip now thai sall aggrie."   " The Lard of Johnstoune," said Charles Maxwell, evidently in irritation, " is nocht able to mak ane amendis, for the great skayth and injurie he has done to tham!"   The other answered coolly and hopefully, " The Lard will do to his powar to satisfie the Lord and his freyndis."   But Charles Maxwell, who seemed intent on fastening a quarrel on his fellow-attendant, was not to be soothed down, and so bitter were his words and so irritated his temper that at last he fired a pistol on William Johnston and shot him through his cloak.   In retaliation William Johnston attempted to fire with his pistol, but it did not go off, and he cried out " Treason."   Thereafter Sir Robert, afraid of the consequences, endeavoured to seize the bridle of Lord Maxwell's horse, but missing it, caught his Lordship's cloak, which he held, with the design of restraining him from any act of violence, and deprecatingly said to him, " Fy! my Lord.   Mak not zour selff a tratour and me baith."   " I am witles," answered Lord Maxwell. Johnston in the meantime stole away, and was riding for the relief of his own man, when Lord Maxwell, bursting from the grasp of Sir Robert, impetuously hastened towards the Laird of Johnston and fired a pistol after him, with fatal effect, after which he rode away.   Johnston was mortally wounded.   He kept his seat on his palfrey for a short time, but the animal growing restive, the girths broke, and the Laird fell to the ground.   He again got up on his feet, and while William Johnston, who had come to his help, was standing with him, Charles Maxwell again fired at them.   William endeavoured to put his wounded chief on horseback, but unable to do this he set him on the ground, and holding him up, inquired what he had to say.   Looking up to heaven, the Laird of Johnston said, "Lord have mercy on me!   Christ have mercy on me!   I am deceived," and soon after expired.   "Come away!" cried Lord Maxwell to Charles.   "My Lord," answered Charles, remorselessly, "will ye ride away and leave this bloody thief behind you?"   "What rak of him," said Lord Maxwell, as if his thirst for blood had been slaked by the death of the slayer of his father, "for the other has enough."   Then they rode away together.

On the 6th of April 1608, the very day on which this tragic scene occurred, Lord Maxwell granted at Lincluden to Charles Maxwell (brother of William Maxwell of Kirkhouse), and his heirs, without reversion, a charter of the five pound lands of Numbellie, in the provostry of Lincluden, parish of Kirkbean and stewartry of Kirkcudbright, for a certain sum of money paid to him by the said Charles Maxwell, and also for good, faithful and gratuitous services rendered and to be rendered to him by the grantee.   The witnesses to this transaction were William Douglas, heir-apparent of Lincluden, David Maxwell of Kilmacolme, Herbert Cunningham, by whom the deed was written, and George Maxwell, writer.   To the charter is appended in a broken condition an impression on wax of the beautiful seal which was engraved for his father, the Earl of Morton.   The granting of such a charter for services rendered, or to be rendered, on the very day when the granter made such dire use of the services of the grantee, is somewhat suspicious, although it is just possible that it was only a singular coincidence.[1]

From his violence Lord Maxwell had created many enemies, who now united with the relatives and friends of the deceased Laird of Johnston in

[1] Original Charter at Carruchan.

loudly demanding the infliction of the last penalty of the law on the murderer of their chief.

Foremost among his enemies was James, second Marquis of Hamilton, whose only sister, Lady Margaret Hamilton, was the wife of Lord Maxwell. Lord Maxwell had raised a process of divorce against her, during the dependence of which she died. This proceeding, the history of which is involved in much obscurity, gave great offence to the Hamiltons, who were afterwards the enemies of Lord Maxwell.[1]

Soon after the death of the Laird of Johnston " proclamation was made, by sound of trumpet at the cross of Edinburgh, that none, under pain of death, should transport or carry away the Lord Maxwell out of the country, in ship or craer, seeing the King and Council were to take order with him for the traitorous murdering of the Laird of Johnston and his other offences." [2]

Great efforts were made to capture Lord Maxwell and to bring him to justice, but he eluded his pursuers, and made his escape to France, where he remained for several years. His flight, after the perpetration of this deed of blood, is commemorated in a poem, entitled " Lord Maxwell's Goodnight," in which he takes farewell of his mother, his sisters, and his Lady, Drumlanrig, Closeburn, and Grierson of Lag, the town of Dumfries, the fortresses of Carlaverock, Threave, Lochmaben, and Langholm, in which he and his ancestors had often found protection, and the Eskdale, in which his lands were situated.

The poem is as follows :—

LORD MAXWELL'S GOODNIGHT.

Adieu ! madame, my mother dear,
　But and my sisters three ;
Adieu ! fair Robert of Orchardstane,
　My heart is wae for thee.
Adieu ! the lilye and the rose,
　The primrose fair to see ;
Adieu ! my ladye, and only joy,
　For I may not stay with thee.

---

[1] MS. History of the Maxwell Family.　　　　[2] Calderwood's History, vol. vi. p. 704.

Though I hae slain the Lord Johnstone,
    What care I for their feid ?
My noble mind their wrath disdains :—
    He was my father's deid.
Both night and day I laboured oft
    Of him avenged to be ;
But now I 've got what lang I sought,
    And I may not stay with thee.

Adieu ! Drumlanrig, false wert aye,
    And Closeburn in a band ;
The Laird of Lag, frae my father that fled,
    When the Johnstone struck aff his hand.
They were three brethren in a band—
    Joy may they never see !
Their treacherous art, and cowardly heart,
    Has twin'd my love and me.

Adieu ! Dumfries, my proper place,
    But and Carlaverock fair !
Adieu ! my castle of the Thrieve,
    Wi' a' my buildings there :
Adieu ! Lochmaben's gates sae fair,
    The Langholm-holm where birks there be ;
Adieu ! my ladye, and only joy,
    For, trust me, I may not stay wi' thee.

Adieu ! fair Eskdale up and down,
    Where my puir friends do dwell ;
The bangisters[1] will ding them down,
    And will them sair compell.
But I 'll avenge their feid mysell,
    When I come o'er the sea ;
Adieu ! my ladye, and only joy,
    For I may not stay wi' thee.—

" Lord of the land !"—that ladye said,
    " O wad ye go wi' me,
Unto my brother's stately tower
    Where safest ye may be !

---

[1] Bangisters—the prevailing party.

There Hamiltons and Douglas baith,
    Shall rise to succour thee."—
—" Thanks for thy kindness, fair my dame,
    But I may not stay wi' thee."—

Then he tuik aff a gay gold ring,
    Thereat hang signets three ;
—" Hae take thee that, mine ain dear thing,
    And still hae mind o' me ;
But, if thou take another lord,
    Ere I come ower the sea—
His life is but a three days' lease,
    Tho' I may not stay wi' thee."—

The wind was fair, the ship was clear,
    That good Lord went away ;
And most part of his friends were there,
    To give him a fair convey.
They drank the wine, they did na spair,
    Even in that gude lord's sight—
Sae now he 's o'er the floods sae gray,
    And Lord Maxwell has ta'en his Goodnight.[1]

By a summons of treason and forfeiture against him, dated 26th January 1609, Lord Maxwell was ordered to be summoned personally, if access could be had to him, and if not by public proclamation at the market crosses of Edinburgh and Dumfries, and at the castles of Carlaverock and Dumfries, and his residence, before his rebellion and flight, and at the shore and pier of Leith, and other necessary places, upon a premonition of sixty days, because he was believed to be without the kingdom of Scotland, to appear before the King, the King's Commissioner and Justiciary, and nobles of the kingdom of Scotland, and the Parliament at Edinburgh, to be held on 12th April following, to answer for the crimes of lese-Majesty committed by him.

In the summons he is charged with having from his youth been given to contumacy, rebellion, contempt of his Majesty's laws and authority, both by nature and depraved custom. Though he had been commanded by several

---

[1] Minstrelsy of the Scottish Border. Edinburgh, 1810, vol. i. p. 290. The above ballad is published from a copy in Glenriddel's MSS., with some slight variations from tradition. Its historical accuracy in some particulars may be disputed. As it contains no allusion to Lord Maxwell's death in 1613, it was probably composed before that event.

Royal letters, in the years 1598-1602, to appear before the Lords of Council, to answer for his contempt, rebellion, and breaking of his Majesty's prisons, yet, pertinaciously despising the King's authority, he committed flagitious crimes, which deserved the extreme punishment of the laws. He is accused of having, with his accomplices, committed the crimes of fire-raising and the slaughters already mentioned at the town of Dalfibble ; of the murder, under trust, credit and assurance, of Sir James Johnston, by means of two poisoned bullets,[1] contrary to the faith given and the friendship entered into before the Lords of Council and Sir Robert Maxwell, by the repeated intervention of Lord Maxwell's oath ; and of breaking ward by escaping from the Castle of Edinburgh, with Sir James M'Connell of Dwnyveg, knight, and Robert Maxwell of Dinwooddie, in December 1607.[2]

The summons of treason was executed on 27th January 1609 at the market cross of Edinburgh, on the 28th of that month, at the pier and shore of Leith, and on the 4th and 5th of February thereafter at the Castles of Carlaverock, Langholm, and Dumfries, and the market cross of Dumfries.

On 12th April the Parliament met, but only to adjourn. On 17th June following the case was taken up by the Parliament. The summons of treason against Lord Maxwell having been read in presence of the Estates of Parliament, he was thrice called at the Tolbooth window by Sir David Lindsay of the Mount, knight, Lyon Herald, and his brother colleagues, to answer to the summons. He did not compear. But the only thing done in the prosecution by the Parliament on that day was the verification of the execution of the summons of treason.[3]

The trial was continued on 24th June 1609, when the summons of treason was read by Sir Thomas Hamilton of Bynnie, knight, King's advocate, in presence of George Earl Marischal, the King's Commissioner, and the Estates of Parliament. Lord Maxwell was thrice called, as before, at the Tolbooth window of the burgh of Edinburgh, to compear, to defend himself, and not compearing the summons was found relevant, and the King's advocate, to prove the points contained in the summons, repeated all the depositions

---

[1] No evidence was ever adduced to prove that the bullets with which Lord Maxwell shot the Laird of Johnston were poisoned.

[2] The Acts of the Parliaments of Scotland, vol. iv. p. 414.

[3] Ibid. vol. iv. pp. 411, 412.

of the witnesses examined before the Lords of Articles and the Secret Council, together with divers Acts of Parliament, laws and constitutions of the realm, relating to the case. The Lord Commissioner and Estates of Parliament found, decerned and declared, that John Lord Maxwell had committed open treason in all the articles set forth in the summons. Upon which sentence was pronounced by David Lindsay, dempster of Parliament, to the effect that John Lord Maxwell should suffer the pains of law for the crimes of treason and lese-Majesty, to wit, the tynsall and confiscation of his life and all his goods, moveable and unmoveable, lands, tenements, dignities, offices, rights, and all other things belonging to him.[1]

In June 1609 an Act of Parliament was passed in favour of Lord Maxwell's vassals, freeholders and tenants, who held any lands and possessions of him by heritable infeftment, wadset or tack, as their lord superior, declaring and ordaining that his forfeiture should in no way derogate from any securities, rights, infeftments, or tacks made in their favour. In this Act the Parliament draws the following by no means flattering picture of Lord Maxwell :—

"Thair is nane ignorant what just cause his Majestie hes to be incensed aganis that Lord Maxwell, wha nocht contenting him self to haue done these villanous deidis (the just ressones moveing his Majestie to proceid thus hardlie aganis him), did alsua maist contempteouslie, and in a bragging maner, as gif thair had bene na king in Isriell, nor na pvnishment for offence, remane still in this kingdome, rather glorying in his villany then schawing ony tokin of penitencie, nocht allone, bot often verie weill accompanyit, sa as how soeuir the first crymes quhairvpoun his sentence of foirfaltour is deducit mycht haue bene personall (albeit na doubt they had thair awin assisteris), zit this subsequent could nocht fall out without help and supplie of sum wha by all presumptioun must haue bene sum of these his vassellis and tennentis, wha na doubt ar now na les curious to be reseruit and comprehendit in the generall clause, then these wha ar maist innocent, as lykwayes it is notorious to the haill Estaittis of Parliament, what the conditioun had bene of the said Lord Maxwell sum yearis befoir his maioritie, and euir sensyne, alsua nevir being sex monethis togidder answerable to oure souerane lordis lawes, still rynning heidlong in a disperat course for his awin vndoing, whilk had maid him, bot specialie sen the tyme of the committing of his tressonable crymes, verie prodigall of his estait, without all respect, nocht regairding wha wer benefitit theirby, sa as he micht mak it vnproffitable to oure souerane lord."[2]

After the forfeiture of Lord Maxwell, his lands were bestowed upon various favourites of the Court. William Lord Cranstoun obtained the lands

<hr>

[1] The Acts of the Parliaments of Scotland, vol. iv. p. 419.

[2] The Acts of the Parliaments of Scotland, vol. iv. p. 451.

of Langholm and others ; Sir Gideon Murray of Elibank, knight, the lands of Murtholme and others in Wauchopedale ; Sir Patrick Murray, heir-apparent of Elibank, the keepership of the castle of Carlaverock and lands thereof ; James Maxwell of Kirkhouse, one of the gentlemen of his Majesty's bed-chamber, the lands of Curclewthe and others, in the shire of Dumfries ; and Edward Maxwell of Hills,[1] the lands of Keltoun and Halmyre, in the parish of Keltoun and stewartry of Kirkcudbright. They obtained these lands between the 6th of February 1610 and 16th April 1614.[2]

Lord Maxwell ventured to return to Scotland in March 1612, with two or three persons, outlawed like himself, without the King's licence.[3]   But time had not mollified the resentment of his enemies, who were powerful, and he had to lead the life of a hunted fugitive. Great search was made for him, and so hard was the pursuit after him on the Borders, and so unable was he, from poor health, caused by hardships, to sustain the harassments to which he was now subjected, that he purposed to embark for Sweden. His relative, George Sinclair, fifth Earl of Caithness, under professions of warm concern for his safety, dissuaded him from executing his design, and promised to afford him secrecy and shelter in the Castle of Sinclair until he could with less danger effect his escape from the kingdom. Maxwell accepted this apparently generous offer, deeply penetrated with sentiments of gratitude, but was doomed to fall a victim to the treachery of the Earl, who intended to deliver up his guest to the Government, in order thereby to obtain the favour of the Court. To escape the odium of having violated the laws of hospitality, the Earl contrived that Maxwell should leave Caithness and pass through Sutherland, in order to his being taken there. But so intent were the Earl's servants upon the execution of their commission that they arrested him within the county of Caithness, took him to Thurso, where, upon his arrival, he was carried by Captain George Sinclair a prisoner to Castle Sinclair. By the orders of the Privy Council he was brought by sea to Leith, and warded in the jail of Edinburgh, on the 19th of September 1612.[4]

1 As Edward Maxwell of Lochrutton, the grandfather of this Edward, possessed the contiguous lands of Bordland of Gelston, holding of the Crown, this royal charter, granted in his favour, may be merely the consequence of the Act of June 1609 in favour of Lord Maxwell's vassals.   The same may have been the case with Kirkhouse.

2 Original Charters and Sasines at Terregles.

3 Calderwood's History, vol. vii. p. 165.

4 *Ibid.* vol. viii. p. 165.

The treacherous conduct of Sinclair was worthy of such a base character. He had himself been guilty of the foul murder of David Hume of Crewshaws and others, for which he obtained a remission, under the Great Seal, on the 19th of May 1585. In this respect he was more fortunate than the victim who had confided in him. But it is a satisfaction to know that Sinclair was unsuccessful in obtaining from the Government any reward for this base treachery, which entailed indelible infamy on himself, and brought reproach upon his family.[1]

When Lord Maxwell was now in the hands of the Government, Sir James Johnston, afterwards first Lord Johnston, his mother and grandmother, presented a petition to the King, praying that justice might be executed upon him for the slaughter of the late Laird of Johnston. They all came to Edinburgh to insist with the Government on the prosecution of Lord Maxwell, according to the tenor of their petition. Sir James, with his mother and tutor, having appeared before the Privy Council, declared that such was their object in coming to Edinburgh. The grandmother, who with great difficulty had made the journey on the same errand, being unable, in consequence of sickness, to compear before the Council, the Lords of Council sent the Bishop of Caithness, Lord Kildrymmie, and the Lord Privy Seal, to learn from herself what was her pleasure. She declared that she had no other purpose in coming to the capital. Under these circumstances the Privy Council, in a letter to the King, dated 28th April 1613, prayed for instructions before they proceeded further.[2]

Lord Maxwell's friends, to effect a reconciliation between him and the relatives of the deceased Laird of Johnston, committed to writing certain offers in his name to be presented to them. That these offers might have the greater effect, they besought certain of the ministers of Edinburgh, and some of the bishops, to present them to the persons for whom they were intended. This, however, the ministers and bishops, and all other persons of quality, refused

[1] Sir Robert Gordon's Genealogy of the Earls of Sutherland to the year 1630, pp. 287, 289. Sir Robert explains that the chief instrument of the Earl of Caithness in his treacherous conduct to Lord Maxwell was his bastard nephew, Captain George Sinclair, who, according to Sir Robert, came to his deserved end by being " miserablie cut to pieces by the boors of Norway."

[2] Original Denmylne MSS., Advocates' Library, quoted in Pitcairn's Criminal Trials, vol. iii. p. 50 ; Melrose Papers, vol. i. p. 108.

to do unless they had the warrant of the Privy Council. Accordingly, on the same day, a petition was given in to the Council by Robert Maxwell, brother to the late Lord Maxwell, in which he prays that they would give directions to some of the ministers of Edinburgh to present these offers to the parties, or that they would call the parties into their presence to that effect, and further, that they would inform his Majesty that his brother was willing to satisfy the parties offended,—the Marquis of Hamilton and his friends, and the Laird of Johnston and his friends, and most humbly to submit himself to his Majesty.[1]

In the first of these offers Lord Maxwell humbly confessed and craved mercy for his offence against God, the King, and the surviving relatives of Sir James Johnston, for the unhappy slaughter of Sir James. He testified by his solemn oath, upon his salvation and condemnation, that that unhappy slaughter was in no respect committed by him upon forethought, felony, or set purpose, but upon mere accident. For the clearing of this he was content to purge himself by his great oath in public, where it should please the parties to appoint, and to do what further homage should be thought expedient.

Secondly, he was contented, not only for himself, but for his whole kin and friends, to forgive the slaughter of the late John Lord Maxwell, his father, committed by the deceased Laird of Johnston and his accomplices,[2] and to give security for the safety of all persons who were either personally guilty of, or were art and part in the said slaughter, so that none of them should ever be troubled for it by him or his kin and friends, directly or indirectly.

Thirdly, as   [3] Johnston, daughter to the deceased Sir James, was, by the sudden and unhappy slaughter of her father, left unprovided with a sufficient tocher, he was willing, the better to avoid all enmity that might arise between the houses of Maxwell and Johnston, and to establish friendship between them in time coming, to marry and take for his wife the said daughter without any tocher.[4]

[1] Denmylne MSS., Advocates' Library, quoted in Pitcairn's Criminal Trials, vol. iii. p. 52.

[2] This fixes the slaughter of John Lord Maxwell on the Laird of Johnston alone, and confirms the belief that the tradition that Lady Johnston of Kirkton killed him by repeated blows on the head with the key of her castle is an unveritable legend.

[3] The Christian name of the lady is omitted in the original.

[4] It appears from this offer that Lady Maxwell was by this time dead. According to the MS. family history, which at this period seems so generally correct, her death took place before Lord Maxwell had to fly the country. The offence he had committed against the Marquis of Hamilton and his friends, referred to in his brother Robert's petition to the Privy Council, probably related to his bad treatment of this lady.

Fourthly, he desired that the Laird of Johnston should be married to Dame Maxwell, daughter to John Lord Herries, and sister-daughter to Lord Maxwell, who was a person of like age with the Laird of Johnston. He also became bound to pay to the Laird of Johnston, in name of tocher, with his said sister-daughter, 20,000 merks Scots, and whatever additional sum should be thought expedient by the advice of friends.

Lastly, he was content, for the further satisfaction of the house of Johnston, to be banished from his Majesty's dominions for the space of seven years, or longer, at the will and pleasure of the Laird of Johnston.

These offers were to be augmented at the discretion of common friends, to be chosen for that purpose.[1]

It does not appear that any attempt was made by the Privy Council to bring these offers before the relatives of the deceased Laird of Johnston, who would probably have rejected them. It was the purpose of the Government that the sentence formerly pronounced upon Lord Maxwell in his absence should be carried into effect.

On 18th May 1613 a warrant was issued by the Privy Council to the Provost and Bailies of Edinburgh to take Maxwell to the market cross, upon the 21st of that month, and there to cause his head to be stricken from his body. To afford him leisure to be resolved, and to give the ministers time to confer with him for his better resolution, a delay of two days was granted.

On the same day Maxwell was informed by the bailies of Edinburgh that Friday, the 21st of that month, was the day fixed for his execution, and he was exhorted to prepare for the sad fate awaiting him. He received the announcement with calmness, and expressed himself as resigned to the good pleasure of God and his Prince.

Such of his friends as he desired and named were, by a license granted to him by the Council, to be admitted to converse with him. He had divers conferences with sundry of his friends, in presence of one of the bailies, but he refused to receive any religious instruction or consolation from the ministers, declaring that he was a Catholic man and not of their religion.

The bailies and others, apprehensive lest, if he should speak on the subject of religion before the people on the scaffold, some disturbance might be

[1] Sir James Balfour's MS. Collections, Advocates' Library ; Melrose Papers, vol. i. p. 110.

created, expressed to him their desire that he should forbear all mention of his peculiar religious opinions, simply professing his belief in the Christian faith. He made a promise to them to that effect, of which he is said to have afterwards repented.

On the 21st of May he was brought from the Tolbooth of Edinburgh to the market cross, the place of execution.[1] None of the ministers of Edinburgh were present with him, as he did not desire their presence. On the scaffold he acknowledged that he justly deserved the punishment which he was about to undergo, and was prepared patiently to suffer it, asking mercy from God for his sins, and heartily wishing that his Majesty would be graciously pleased to accept his life and blood as a sufficient punishment for his offences, and to restore his brother and house to the rank and place of his predecessors, hoping that his brother would do his Majesty good and faithful service, as his ancestors had done to his Majesty's royal predecessors. He next asked forgiveness of the Laird of Johnston, his mother, grandmother, and friends, acknowledging the wrong he had done to them, and protested that it was without dishonour or infamy " for the worldlie pairt of it," which were the words he used. He likewise craved pardon of Pollok, Calderwood, and his other friends who were present, acknowledging that while he ought, from his position, to have contributed to their honour and safety, he had procured them harm and discredit. He then retired near the block, and, after passing some short time in devotion, he took leave of his friends and of the bailies of the town, and, suffering his eyes to be covered with a handkerchief, he offered his head to the fatal axe. The execution took place at four o'clock in the afternoon.[2]

The body of Lord Maxwell, as stated in the MS. History of the Family of Maxwell, was interred in the Abbey of Newbottle, belonging to Mark Ker, who was created successively Lord Newbottle and Earl of Lothian, and whose Countess, Margaret Maxwell, was the daughter of Lord Herries, the granduncle of the beheaded Lord Maxwell.

" The execution of Lord Maxwell," says Sir Walter Scott, " put a final end to the foul debate betwixt the Maxwells and the Johnstons, in the course

---

[1] " This execution," says Calderwood, " was procured by the Laird of Johnston's friends, specially by Sir Robert Ker, Earl of Rochester, the chief Guider of the Court at that time."—History, vol. vii. p. 177.

[2] Denmylne MSS., Advocates' Library, in Pitcairn's Criminal Trials, vol. iii. p. 52.

of which each family lost two chieftains : one dying of a broken heart, one in the field of battle, one by assassination, and one by the sword of the executioner."

In the following chapter an account will be given of the restoration of the estates and honours of the house of Maxwell.

SEAL AND SIGNATURE OF JOHN, NINTH LORD MAXWELL, SECOND EARL OF MORTON.

THE FIVE EARLS OF NITHSDALE.

XIX. 2. ROBERT, TENTH LORD MAXWELL,
AND FIRST EARL OF NITHSDALE.

ELIZABETH BEAUMONT, HIS COUNTESS.

1613-1646.

ON the death of John, ninth Lord Maxwell, under the unhappy circumstances which have been narrated, the representation of the House of Maxwell devolved on his younger brother, Robert. But as the estates and titles of John, ninth Lord Maxwell, were forfeited to the Crown, and portions of the estates gifted to various parties, it was some time before Robert succeeded in obtaining a restoration of the titles and possessions of his ancestors.

In the year 1607, Robert Maxwell, under the designation of Master of Maxwell, appears as Provost of the burgh of Annan. In that capacity he granted a charter, dated in that year, to John Cousin, burgess of Dumfries, of a ten pound land of the common burgage and town-land therein described.[1]

During the lifetime of his brother, John Lord Maxwell, Robert obtained from him a charter, without date, of the six merk land of Capenoch, in the barony of Keir, parish of Holywood and shire of Dumfries, and of the mill of Keir.[2]

He also obtained from his brother John, with consent of his curators, to himself and the heirs-male of his body, a charter of the ten merk lands of Castlegour, in the barony and parish of Butill and stewartry of Kirkcudbright, dated at Kirkcudbright, the year left blank; and he was infefted therein on 16th July 1612, in terms of a precept in the charter.[3]

On a precept of sasine from King James the Sixth, Robert Maxwell was also infefted, on 28th, 29th, 30th, and 31st August 1615, in the barony of

[1] Original Charter at Terregles.
[2] Original Charter, *ibid.*
[3] Original Charter and Instrument of Sasine at Terregles. The Sasine has "the six merk land of Castlegour."

Carlaverock and other lands therein described, as heir to John Lord Maxwell, his father.[1]

By an Act of Parliament passed on 28th June 1617, he was declared to be capable of possessing all lands, heritages, teinds, houses, woods, fishings, patronages, etc., belonging to his brother John, sometime Lord Maxwell, that were disponed by his Majesty to him (Robert Maxwell), or that were already, or should hereafter be, acquired by him from any other person, or that were as yet in his Majesty's hands, by virtue of John Lord Maxwell's forfeiture, undisponed before the date hereof.   From this Act were excepted all titles and honours that formerly belonged to the house of Maxwell, and the offices of the stewartries of Annandale and Galloway, that were held immediately of the King or his predecessors.   There were also excepted the lands disponed by his Majesty to the lairds of Lochinvar and Lag through the forfeiture, and the lands of the living of Maxwell, disponed by the King to Lord Cranstoun, until Robert Maxwell and Lord Cranstoun should come to an agreement. There were further reserved all other men's rights acquired to any part of the lands and living of the lordship of Maxwell from the King, through the forfeiture, at any time preceding the date of the Act, not yet re-acquired by Robert Maxwell, until they should be acquired by him, his heirs and successors.[2]

To acquire the forfeited Maxwell estates was an object upon which Robert Maxwell was naturally very intent, and he had various friends who were ready to assist him in making this acquisition.   The difficulties were numerous, for many of the lands were granted by the Crown to persons of influence, and he was deficient in pecuniary resources.   He, however, gradually surmounted obstacles, and recovered the possessions of his ancestors.

Under the designation of the Honourable Robert Maxwell of Carlaverock, he obtained a discharge and procuratory of resignation from William Lord Cranstoun, and Sir John Cranstoun, his son, of the lands and barony of Langholm, and others, dated 14th December 1617.[3]

Pecuniary assistance was in the meantime afforded him.   King James the Sixth, commiserating his pecuniary embarrassments, ordered, by a precept,

[1] Original Instrument of Sasine at Terregles.

[2] The Acts of the Parliaments of Scotland, vol. iv. p. 561.

[3] Original Procuratory of Resignation at Terre-

gles. The barony of Langholm was erected by a charter by King James the Sixth, dated 7th July 1615, in favour of Sir John Cranstoun, knight, son and heir-apparent of William Lord Cranstoun.

addressed, about October 1616, to the Commissioners of the Royal Rents, £2000 sterling to be delivered to him out of the Royal Exchequer of Scotland. The Earl of Mar, then High Treasurer of Scotland, not judging this to be a sufficient warrant for paying the money, the King, in a letter to that Earl, dated 23d October 1617, renewed the precept, requiring the Earl to cause payment to be made with all expedition to Robert Maxwell of Carlaverock of the sum contained therein.[1]

Robert Maxwell was also relieved by a loan of £11,000 from Sir William Graham of Braco and Mary Edinestoun, his spouse, for which he gave them a bond, with cautioners, dated at Edinburgh, 9th, 12th, 16th, and 18th June 1618. He also obtained the loan of 3000 merks Scots from Marion Adinstoun, relict of John Cleaves, and Patrick Levingston of Saltcoats, her husband, for which he gave them a bond, with cautioners, dated at Edinburgh, 2d July same year.[2]

The King, by three letters-patent under the Great Seal, restored to Robert Maxwell the lands, rents, living, teinds, offices and dignities that belonged to his predecessors. One of them is dated at Roystoun, 5th October 1618 ; another at Newmarket, 13th March 1619 ; and the third at Fernehame, 29th August 1620.[3]

The last-mentioned patent bears that as the late John Lord Maxwell, father to Robert, now Lord Maxwell, had been created by his Majesty, on 29th October 1581, Earl of Morton, and as the restitution of the Earl of Morton, Douglas, to his former dignities was to be in no respect to the prejudice of the said Lord Maxwell as to the honour of Earl bestowed on his father, his Majesty was graciously pleased to continue the dignity conferred on him to his son, Robert Lord Maxwell, and his heirs-male, from the date of the creation of his father as Earl.

It had been always his Majesty's care, the patent narrates, to remove differences between his subjects; and, calling to remembrance the constant hatred between the families of Morton and Maxwell, and also its being un-usual in his Majesty's kingdoms for two earls to wear the same title, his Majesty, by his sole authority, changed the title of Earl of Morton, which he

---

[1] Original Royal Letter in the Mar Charter-chest.
[2] Original Bond at Terregles.
[3] The Acts of the Parliaments of Scotland, vol. iv. p. 635.

had conferred on the said deceased Lord Maxwell, into that of Earl of Nithsdale, which he now conferred on Lord Maxwell, his son, whose designation would be Lord Maxwell, Lord Eskdale and Carlisle, and Earl of Nithsdale.   This was done without prejudice to the antiquity of the dignity granted to his father, and now continued and confirmed to him and his heirs-male ; nor should it be reckoned or supposed that the change of the said title constituted any new creation.   It only amounted to a regrant and confirmation of a former dignity ; and consequently the date of the creation of Robert Lord Maxwell as Earl of Nithsdale should be computed from the 29th of October 1581.[1]

An Act was passed by the Privy Council, appointing that two hundred merks should be paid as a duty to the Lyon-King-at-Arms by all who were pre-ferred to the dignity of a Lord of Parliament after his Majesty's accession to the Crown of England.

Letters were raised, at the instance of the Lyon-King-at-Arms and his brethren, heralds and pursuivants, against Lord Maxwell, charging him to make payment to them of that sum as the fee due for his being, as they alleged, newly created and preferred to the dignity of a Lord of Parliament.   This sum Lord Maxwell refused to pay.   He raised letters against Robert Winrahame, herald, and Walter Ritchie, collector of the Lyon-King-at-Arms, in which he maintained that the foresaid Act ought not to take effect against him, on the ground that the dignity of a Lord of Parliament conferred on him was not a title and dignity newly bestowed by his Majesty since his accession to the Crown of England, but was merely the restoration of the ancient dignities of the house of Maxwell.   He therefore argued that the Act was not to be extended against him.   If it were so, the Lyon-King-at-Arms and his brethren, he said, might exact the same duty of every lord that should be served heir to his father in his lands and dignities.   Such was not the meaning of the King or his Council, who intended the Act to apply only to such as received their honours since his Majesty succeeded to the throne of England.

At a meeting of the Privy Council, on 29th July 1619, Lord Maxwell having appeared by his procurator, and the defenders, though often called, not compearing, the Council suspended *simpliciter* the process of horning against

---

[1] Original Patent at Terregles.   The substance of the Patent is engrossed in Act of the Privy Council, dated 11th January 1621, in extract at Terregles.

him, and declared that the effect and execution thereof were to cease in all time coming, for the reasons mentioned in Lord Maxwell's summons, which were found to be relevant.[1]

King James the Sixth in a letter to the Earl of Mar, dated 11th July 1621, after informing him that he had signed a signature to the Earl of Nithsdale for a general infeftment in all his lands, required him to allow upon reasonable composition that it might be expede in the usual way.[2]

In August following, the letters-patent now mentioned were confirmed by the King, with advice of the Estates of Parliament. At the same time the sentence of forfeiture against the late John Lord Maxwell was rescinded, and Robert Earl of Nithsdale, his heirs and successors, were restored to all lands, rents, teinds, offices, and dignities that had belonged to his predecessors before the forfeiture.

This was done on the ground that the sentence of forfeiture had not been pronounced against John Lord Maxwell for crimes committed against his Majesty's sacred person or the estate of the country (which might justly have excluded Lord Maxwell's posterity from his Majesty's favour), and that the said Robert Maxwell had given good proof of his loyalty and affection towards his Majesty and the kingdom. Letters of horning were ordained to be directed hereon on a simple charge of ten days against all the possessors of the lands, rents, teinds, offices, and dignities, in order to the Earl of Nithsdale's being put in possession of them. From this order were excepted the lands which his Majesty disponed by virtue of said forfeiture to William Lord Cranstoun, Sir John Cranstoun, his son, Sir Gideon Murray, Sir Patrick Murray his son, and the lands disponed to Sir Thomas Penrodoke and to James Maxwell, by a charter dated 28th June 1621, only for their good service.[3]

The title of Nithsdale was even more appropriate as a family title of honour than that of Morton, for which it was exchanged. Morton had not been previously in the family as a territorial possession, and they acquired only a *quasi* right through the marriage of a co-heiress.[4]

---

[1] Regist. Secreti Concilii, Decreta, Nov. 1618-Feb. 1620, fol. 177.

[2] Original Royal Letter in the Mar Charter-chest.

[3] The Acts of the Parliaments of Scotland, vol. iv. p. 635.

[4] Several places in Nithsdale have afforded names of titles to the Scottish nobility, including those of Duke, Marquis, and Earl of Queensberry, Earl of Dumfries, etc.

On the other hand, the rich and beautiful vale of the Nith in Dumfries-shire, through which the river Nith flows, was historically associated with the Maxwells.   From a very early period they owned, as we have seen, the Castle of Carlaverock, which was the key to the whole of that district.   The family also, through its heads and branches, had long possessed large territories on both banks of the Nith, from its mouth, where it falls into the Solway Firth, about six miles below the town of Dumfries, to nearly the source of that river in the parish of Dalmellington, in Ayrshire, a course of about fifty miles, measured by a direct line, but of nearly a hundred if the windings of the river are included.   The first territorial chieftain of Nithsdale who appears in the ancient chronicles is Dunegal of Stranith, who flourished in the reign of King David the First; probably the most powerful man in Nithsdale.   He was witness to a grant made by that King to Robert Bruce of Strathannand, or Annandale, about the year 1124.   He left four sons, among whom, upon his death, his extensive territories were divided.   Randolph, the eldest, inherited the largest portion of Stranith.   As superior of Dumfries he granted a portion of land near the town to the Abbey of Jedburgh, in the year 1147.   Randolph had three sons, Duncan, Gillespie, and Dovenald.   Dovenald received from his father Sanquhar and other lands.   One of Dovenald's sons was Edgar, who flourished in the reigns of King William the Lion and Alexander the Second. His children adopted the name of Edgar.

A grandson of Edgar's, Donald Edgar, obtained from King David the Second the captainship of the Macgowans, a clan of the district.[1]

The great-grandson of Dunegal of Stranith married the sister of King Robert the Bruce ; and from that monarch he obtained the earldom of Murray, on his resigning to him the castle and estate of Morton.[2]   Randolph Earl of Murray was one of the foremost of the heroes who were illustrious in the days of Bruce.

In the Register of the Armorial Bearings of the Nobility and the lesser Barons of Scotland, by Sir David Lindsay, Lyon King of Arms, in 1542, the bearings are given, page 64, of the " Lord of Nyddisdaill of Auld."   Sable, a lion rampant argent.

During the last half of the fourteenth century Sir William Douglas,

---

[1] Robertson's Index to the Missing Charters, p. 39, No. 54.   [2] Grose's Antiquities, p. 148.

natural son of Archibald, third Earl of Douglas and Lord of Galloway, having married Egidia, daughter of King Robert the Second, acquired with her the lordship of Nithsdale and the office of Sheriff of Dumfries.[1]   He was killed at Dantzic in 1390.   His only daughter, Giles, celebrated as the Fair Maid of Nithsdale, married Henry Sinclair, Earl of Orkney, and by him had a son, William Earl of Orkney, who inherited Nithsdale and the office of Sheriff of Dumfries, but who resigned them in August 1455, into the hands of King James the Second, for the earldom of Caithness.   In the Ancient Register of the Armorial Bearings before referred to are entered the bearings of " Dowglas, Lord of Niddisdaill."   Quarterly, 1st and 4th argent a human heart ducally crowned, gules, on a chief azure, 3 mullets of the first, and over all a ribbon, or : 2d and 3d sable, a lion rampant argent.   This is one of the earliest instances of the Douglas heart being crowned.

Whether from extensive territories in the district, and the command of castles which dominated it, or from the high office of Warden of the West Marches, which included Nithsdale, the title Earl of Nithsdale was appropriately granted to Lord Maxwell in exchange for his earlier title of Earl of Morton, after that title was restored to the family of Douglas.

On the creation of Robert Maxwell as Earl of Nithsdale, a claim of precedency before him was set up by some earls who had been created since his father was advanced to the dignity of Earl of Morton in October 1581. These were the Earls of Wintoun, Linlithgow, Perth, Wigton, Kinghorn, Abercorn, Lothian, Tullibardin, Roxburgh and Buccleuch.   To terminate this contention the Privy Council called these Earls before them, and informed them of the King's letter to the Lord Chancellor, and of the Earl of Nithsdale's patent, which contained the just reasons of his Majesty's determination as to precedency.   The opposing earls alleged that all this had been done without their having been heard for their own interest, but they expressed their assurance that his Majesty did not intend thereby to do them any prejudice in regard to the precedency with which he had honoured them or their predecessors.   They argued that, after the restoration of the Earl of Angus to the dignity of Earl of Morton, the Earl of Nithsdale's father had not possessed that dignity, and that his brother had sat

[1] Godscroft, 109.

and voted in Parliament among the Lords. The Earl of Nithsdale in self-defence maintained that his father to the close of life had held the place and dignity of an earl, and that the neglect of his brother to assert his right could not prejudice him in a right which he claimed as heir to his father, and which was strengthened by his Majesty's just declaration. His opponents requested that the place which they had long possessed should not be taken from them until their right should be decided by the Judge Ordinary. The Council appointed some to deal with them, with the view of inducing them to yield in the meantime to the Council's advice, with an assurance that this should not prejudice their rights when they came to be tried by the Judge. But these endeavours were without effect. The Earl of Nithsdale with greater facility of disposition offered to accept of such a place as the Council should assign him, provided they would testify to his Majesty by their letter that he had done this in obedience to them and for the furtherance of his Majesty's service. "So by his discretion," says the Earl of Melrose, in a letter to King James the Sixth, 23d November [1620], "the present contention is declined until your Majesty's known will shall prescribe a clear expedient in their controversy."[1]

Finally to settle this question, the King, by a missive letter, commanded Thomas Earl of Melrose, President of the Council, and Secretary of the Kingdom of Scotland, to write to all the noblemen who pretended to have an interest in opposing the Earl of Nithsdale's precedency as dating from his father's creation as Earl of Morton in October 1581, requesting them to appear before the Council, 11th January 1621, to hear his Majesty's pleasure declared touching the point of his precedency.

In obedience to his Majesty's command, the Earl of Melrose, as he informs his Majesty in a letter to him, dated 22d December [1620], wrote to these noblemen to that effect.[2]

At the meeting of the Council, 11th January 1621, the Earl of Melrose having read the King's missive in their audience, and the noblemen above mentioned having been called, the Earls of Nithsdale, Wintoun, and Roxburgh compeared personally, whilst some of the others sent excuses for their absence, promising to conform themselves to whatever course and order the Lords of

[1] The Melrose Papers, vol. ii. pp. 374-376.   [2] Ibid. vol. ii. p. 388.

Council should be pleased to take in that matter.   The Earl of Nithsdale, for the verification of his right and claim of precedency before the noblemen already named, and others who had been advanced to the dignity of an Earl since October 1581, produced before the Lords of Council two notes extracted out of the book of Parliament, bearing that in the Parliaments held at Edinburgh in that year and month, and in May 1584, the Earl of Morton, his father, was present, was ranked among the Earls, and was upon the Articles.   He also produced a patent given to him by the King under the Great Seal, dated at Ferneyhame, 29th August 1620, granting him precedency as Earl of Nithsdale from his father's creation as Earl of Morton in 1581.   This patent and the notes foresaid were read and considered by the Council, and the reasons of the parties present were heard.   The Lords of Council found and declared that the dignity of an Earl, to which his Majesty was pleased to advance John Lord Maxwell, should remain with Robert Earl of Nithsdale, his son, and his heirs-male, according to the tenor of his patent, and that no opposition should be made to his Majesty's pleasure on that point.   They ordained that that Earl should enjoy his dignity and precedency in sitting, ranking, and voting among the nobility in all Parliaments, Conventions, and General Councils of this kingdom, from the date of his father's creation as an earl, as before stated, until the person or persons interested, or aggrieved, should, by the ordinary course of law and justice, before the judge competent, find redress, either by reduction or by such other form as the laws and practice of the kingdom of Scotland admitted.[1]

The Earl of Nithsdale was a member of the Parliament which met on 25th January 1621.   By this Parliament it was concluded that some twelve or fourteen of the ripest judgment and experience should convene upon the following day to advise upon the best means of giving to the King a voluntary contribution for the defence of the kingdom and as a dowry to his daughter and grandchildren.   The Earl of Nithsdale was included in this committee. The others nominated were the Lords Chancellor and Treasurer, the Archbishops of St. Andrews and Glasgow, the Earls of Angus, Morton, Roxburgh, the Lords Ogilvy, Scoone, Cranstoun, and Carnegie, and the Bishops of Aberdeen and Ross, without excluding such others of the nobility as pleased

---

[1] Extract from Decreet of Privy Council at Terregles.

to attend; and the committee was ordained to report to the meeting of Parliament to be held on the following day.

On 26th January the committee, after deliberation, concluded that choice should be made of some fit persons to wait upon his Majesty, to assure him of the hearty affection of the nobility, and of their willingness to give him such a large and seasonable supply as would be creditable to the country, which could only be obtained by a taxation imposed impartially upon the whole body of the estate.[1]

The Earl of Nithsdale was present at the Parliament which met at Edinburgh 25th July same year, and he was appointed one of the Lords of Articles.[2]   At the meeting of the Parliament, 4th August following, he voted for the ratification of the five Articles of the General Assembly of the Kirk, held at Perth in August 1618.   These Articles were, kneeling at the Eucharist; private Communion; private Baptism; Confirmation; the observance of our Lord's Nativity, Passion, Resurrection, Ascension, and the day of Pentecost, as holidays.[3]

On 12th August 1621, the Earl obtained from William Lord Cranstoun a resignation in his favour of numerous lands in the shire of Dumfries, which formed the barony of Langholm.[4]

We have seen before that a feud existed between the Maxwells and the Murrays of Cockpool.   But the first Earl of Nithsdale, who, unlike his brother, was peaceably disposed, came to an amicable understanding with the representative of the Murrays of Cockpool.   He was on terms of sincere friendship with John Murray of Lochmaben (brother of Sir Robert Murray of Cockpool, to whom he was served heir in 1637), one of the gentlemen of the Bed-Chamber of King James VI. and Master of the Horse, who was eminent for his worth and accomplishments, and who, by letters-patent, dated 13th March 1624, was raised to the peerage, under the titles of Viscount Annan and Earl of Annandale.   The Earl of Melrose, in a letter to John Murray of Lochmaben, dated Edinburgh, 28th May [1621 ?], says, " I am glade ye haue setled with the Earle of Niddisdaill ;"[5] and in a letter to him, dated Edinburgh, 19th June

---

[1] The Acts of the Parliaments of Scotland, vol. iv. pp. 589, 590.   [2] *Ibid.* vol. iv. pp. 593, 594.
[3] *Ibid.* vol. iv. pp. 595, 596.

[4] Original Resignation at Terregles.
[5] The Melrose Papers, vol. ii. p. 399.

[1622], he writes, " All that loue yow will allow the good course taken by yow for setling freindship with the Earle of Niddisdaill." [1]

With the view of promoting the peace of the country by removing the causes of new disturbances, the Privy Council granted to the Laird of Johnston exemption from the Earl of Nithsdale's jurisdiction over the middle shires, notwithstanding the Earl's opposition. The King, however, apprehending that this exemption would have a contrary effect, required the Privy Council of Scotland, in a letter dated 7th August 1622, to delete the exemption from their books. On receiving his letter, the Council considered that, from the importance of the matter, the Laird of Johnston should be heard before them, and they appointed that day eight days for the purpose. On his appearance the Council showed him the equity of his Majesty's command, grounded upon the reconciliation made between the Earl and him, and upon his Majesty's belief that the Earl would strive to merit still further the favour of his sovereign by his honourable and upright behaviour in that business. The Laird of Johnston gave his answer in writing. He did not distrust the honour of the Earl of Nithsdale, and would take no exception against him ; but he urged that the malice of certain of the Earl's friends and followers against some of the name of Johnston was as fresh and violent as ever. In proof of this he adduced two instances of wrongs committed against some of his friends by John Maxwell of Castlemilk, whom the Earl had specially intrusted with the execution of some parts of his commission. In arguing against the recalling of the exemption, he expressed a strong apprehension that the public tranquillity might be endangered should any of the Earl of Nithsdale's friends and followers be armed with the King's authority over him and his friends whom he had become bound to exhibit at their trial before the rest of the Commissioners.

The Privy Council, on 31st March 1623, laid these facts before his Majesty, and promised to obey him in whatever he should therein be pleased to command. [2] The King, in his reply, 29th May, willed the Privy Council to call before them the Earl of Nithsdale and the Laird of Johnston, and, if they found any cause of quarrel remaining between them or any of their friends, to interpose their authority in order to remove it and

[1] The Melrose Papers, vol. ii. p. 463.   [2] Ibid. vol. ii. pp. 509-511.

to restore them to friendship, and to abrogate the exemption of the Laird of Johnston from the jurisdiction of the Earl of Nithsdale, as being a special means of fostering deadly feud.[1]

The Earl of Nithsdale obtained from the King a grant of the non-entry of all his own lands for all the years during which they were in non-entry ; and the Earl of Mar, as Treasurer, was required, in a letter from the King, dated 24th April 1623, to allow that grant to be expede through his Majesty's seals, according to the accustomed form, with all convenient despatch. In the same letter the Earl of Mar was required to dispone the escheat and liferent of Lord Borthwick, which "were sought by divers to his utter overthrow," to none but such as the Earl of Nithsdale and Viscount Annan should nominate for his behoof.[2]

On 17th June same year the Earl of Nithsdale and James Johnston of Westraw, having appeared before the Privy Council, agreed to be reconciled, and in testimony thereof " choppit hands." The Laird of Westraw, as well as the Laird of Johnston, consented to the withdrawment of the exemption formerly granted to them from the jurisdiction of the Earl, under his commission for the middle shires. He, however, represented that he stood in a different position from the Laird of Johnston, since he had been sundry times upon the ground, when hurt was both given and received in the feud between the two families, and that though he had perfect confidence in the honour of the Earl of Nithsdale, he was suspicious of his followers, were they armed with power to search his house on pretence of seeking for fugitives. The Earl of Nithsdale therefore promised, on his honour, that no one against whom Westraw could take exception should search his houses ; that, under his commission, he would never sit in judgment in any case affecting Westraw's life ; and that his (the Earl's) brother, the Sheriff of Dumfries, should never judge in any civil action in which Westraw was concerned.[3]

The Earl of Melrose was disposed to promote the interests of the Earl of Nithsdale. He respected him personally, and he had received favours from the Duke of Buckingham, to whom Lord Nithsdale was nearly related by marriage. Nor did he think that his friendship with the house of Johnston, to whom he was bound, would be considered by the Earl of Nithsdale, from the

[1] The Melrose Papers, vol. ii. p. 4.
[2] Original Royal Letter in the Mar Charter-chest.
[3] Extract Minute of Privy Council at Terregles.

discretion of his character, incompatible with maintaining relations of amity with him. In a letter to their common friend, the Viscount of Annan, dated Edinburgh, 1st July 1623, the Earl of Melrose thus writes :—" I thank your Lordship for showing to the Earle of Niddisdaill the truth of my dealing. Many times I told him, that beside the respect I did beare to his owne place and worth, that I wes infinitlie bound to the Marquis of Buckingham's many great and vndesserued fauours ; and finding my self vnable to requit them by any seruice to him self, God having so blessed him, as he neither needed the prouffes of my seruice, nor did I see anyway to testifie my thankfull minde to him self, I would striue to embrace all occasions to make it knowne by my dutie to his lordship's freinds in this countrie, and chieflie to the Earle of Niddisdaill, who had the honour to be nearer to him by alliance. . . . My remembrance of the freindship which wes betwix the Laird of Johnston and me, binding me to keep dutie to his sone, will moue some of my lord's freinds to think and prease to persuade him that I can not be dutifull to him, but knowing that his lordship is honorable and wise, I assure myself that he will think that I may discharge honest dutie to both."[1]

In a Justice Court held at Dumfries, 5th August 1623, a hot altercation took place between the Earl of Nithsdale and Sir William Seton, a commissioner for the middle shires.[2] Of this dispute the Earl of Melrose, in a letter to the Viscount of Annan, dated Edinburgh, 12th August, gives the following account :—" I am sorie to heare that maters went crosse betuix the Earle of Niddisdaill and Sir William and the maister of Jedburgh, by occasion of there contrare opinions, in a repledgration soght by vertue of Drumlanrik's regalitie, which my lord tooke in ill pairt, and promised to aduertise his Maiestie. It is reported that the laird of Lag agried in opinion with the other two, but because I know not the certantie, I remit it to the parties owne informations."[3]

The Earl of Nithsdale, in a letter to the Viscount of Annan, dated Dumfries, 29th September, gives additional particulars regarding the dispute :— " I have sent the letter anent that disput betwixt the Commissioners and me. Drumlenrik, in that matter, can pretend no ignorance, for, a fourtnight befoir

[1] The Melrose Papers, vol. ii. pp. 525, 526.   [2] Ibid. vol. ii. p. 539.   [3] Ibid. vol. ii. p. 538.

the court, in ane discours betuixt him and me, he said that he wald account him selfe no moir oblissed to anie man wald bring his regalatie in question, then he intendit to cut his throt ; wherto I ansuered, that I sheuld be lothe to be wpon knoledge of cutting his throt, bot my maister's direction wald make me wse noe serimonie to refuse repledging; 'for,' said I, 'what reason can yow have now to tak exseptions moir then yowr father did, in the tyme of the Earle of Dumbar ? ' His ansuer was, thoght it was his father's pleasor to doe so to the Earle of Dumbar, it was nocht his pleasor to doe so with me."[1]

Sir George Elphinston proposed that the Earl of Nithsdale and his wife should come up to London. But the Earl's past experience of the expense of such journeys was not encouraging. He had found, as he states in a letter to the Viscount of Annan, dated Dumfries, 29th September 1623, " the smart of wasturrie in that pert suffisientlie allredie ;" nor did he intend that his wife should go up to the Court, unless he was assured from the Duke of Buckingham of being bettered by the voyage. " For my oune wpcuming, if yowr lordship sall think it fit, efter yow haue spokin my Lord Bukinghame, short advertisment sall serve."[2]

Under his pecuniary difficulties the Earl of Nithsdale applied for pecuniary assistance to George Heriot; but the wealthy jeweller was cautious and doubtful. " I am sorie," says the Earl in the same letter, " that George Hariot is put in such fear and distast with me, as I heer be Sir George he is, for his securitie may be good enough, if he wald be pleasit to furnis sum munie."

He adds in a postscript that he had caused to be proclaimed a Justice Court, to be held on the 16th day of the next month. The outcry of poor prisoners and of the town of Dumfries in maintaining them had made him hasten the same.

The Earl of Nithsdale and John Murray, Viscount Annan, obtained from the King a gift of the escheat and liferent of James Johnstoun of Thornick, called Captain Johnstoun, a fugitive from law, and of such lands as he had held immediately of the Crown before his rebellion. Against Johnstoun criminal letters had been raised, dated Edinburgh, 12th July 1623. The King in a letter to the Earl of Mar, the Treasurer, 20th March 1624, required him to sign the royal signatures for these gifts without taking

---

[1] The Melrose Papers, vol. ii. p. 542.   [2] Ibid. vol. ii. p. 544.

any composition.[1] In terms of the gift, a charter was to be passed under the Great Seal in favour of the Earl of Nithsdale and Viscount Annan, disponing to them the said lands equally between them.[2] But this arrangement was departed from, and the lands were wholly given to the Earl of Annandale, as we are instructed in a letter from the King to the Privy Council, dated 23d September 1624.[3]

In the summer of that year the Earl of Nithsdale intended to go abroad. The letter from King James the Sixth, granting him license to travel and be absent from his Majesty's dominions for some time, is dated 21st May 1624. It is addressed to Sir George Hay, Knight, Chancellor, and the Earl of Melrose, Principal Secretary of Scotland. It requires them to have a special care that, during his absence, he should receive no wrong either in the matter of judicatory or otherwise ; and especially that should any of his creditors crave their principal sums, they would deal with them to accept of their just annual interest for a reasonable time, at least for one year.[4]

On his arrival in London the Earl wrote a letter to the Earl of Annandale, dated Denmark House, 28th May. In the letter he says, —"Yow must leykweyse procur my lord Duck's letter to send home to comfort my wyfe, with letters to the Chansaller and Presedent of Scotland, shewand that, durand my absence, his grace will be protector of what conserns me, and, in that kynd, intreats their favor. What other thing sall occour quherinto yow think fitt to be trubilsome to his grace at his Majestie's hand, I know yow will find noe lothing at his hands if it conserns me. Thoght yow apprehend that discontented humors possessis me, I craue no moir at God's hands, for the weall of my hous and cheyld, bot that his grace may have long and good healthe. My Sacred Maister, and our prinse, whom God long preserve ! being alyve, in yowr brotherlie cair, I haue full confidence, and remits to yowr selfe all my privat affairs, to be disposed as yowr lordship thinks fitt."[5]

To afford the Earl of Nithsdale relief in his embarrassed circumstances, when now absent from Scotland, King James was desirous that all legal

[1] Original Royal Letter in the Mar Charter-chest.
[2] Original Gift at Terregles.
[3] Original Letter in Mar Charter-chest.
[4] The Melrose Papers, vol. ii. p. 560.
[5] Ibid. vol. ii. p. 561.

proceedings against him should be prevented or rendered ineffectual. With this view he sent a letter to the Privy Council of Scotland, dated 7th July 1624. "Whereas we haue bene crediblie informed," he says, "that the creditors of the Earle of Nethesdale, more oute of rigor then of anie necessitie, haue putte himselfe and diuers his cautioners to our horne, and because there may be, as well in his owne person as in those of his cautioners, diuers tackes, whereof the rigor may be exacted if they come in other men's handes, wee haue therefor thoughte good, by these presentes, to wille and require yow not to dispose of the eschetes eyther of the said Earle of Nethesdale or of anie of his cautioners, but to reteyne the same in your owne handes til by our selfe yee shall vnderstande our furder pleasor concerning them."[1]

Before receiving this letter the Council, his Majesty's Chancellor and Secretary, had dealt at divers meetings with the Earl's creditors for a delay of personal execution against his cautioners till Martinmas. After the receipt of the King's letter, they brought the Earl's creditors before them, pressed upon them forbearance, and from the near approach of the term would have them to delay the matter till Whitsunday, promise being made to them of the payment of their annuals. Some of the creditors were willing to agree to this proposal; others opposed it. The creditors were against the recalling of comprisings, etc., used against the Earl's cautioners; and the Council were unanimously of opinion that this, besides being a breach of the law, would overthrow all trust, commerce and intercourse within the kingdom. An account of these their proceedings the Council communicated to the King in a letter, dated Holyroodhouse, 15th July 1624.[2]

The King, in his answer to the Privy Council, dated 28th of the same month, certified that it was his special pleasure that, as he wrote to them before concerning the escheats, they should not expede any confirmation or infeftment grounded upon any of the comprisings of divers of the lands of the Earl of Nithsdale and his creditors until they understood his further pleasure.[3]

Being credibly advertised that certain persons intended to take action against the Earl before the Privy Council, the King, in a letter to the Council, 9th December same year, required them to suspend all such proceedings during

[1] Original Royal Letter in the Mar Charter-chest.   [3] Original Royal Letter in the Mar Charter-chest.
[2] The Melrose Papers, vol. ii. p. 576.

the winter session, which, being already half past, could not do prejudice to any party.[1]

Previous to the Earl's coming up from Scotland to the Court, great complaints were made of the all but absolute power wielded in the State by the Earls of Mar and Melrose. The former, it was said, disposed of the King's revenue, and the other ruled in the Council and Session, each according to his pleasure. The Earl of Nithsdale, when Sir George Hay, Chancellor, complained to him on the subject, suggested that as the people of Ireland, when pressed by the extortion of the Officers of State, had, by petitioning the King, obtained a commission to be sent to Ireland to remedy their grievances, a similar commission might be obtained for Scotland were the King truly informed of its condition. Approving of the suggestion, the Chancellor brought about a meeting between the Earl of Nithsdale and the Earls of Morton, Roxburgh and Lauderdale in the Palace of Holyroodhouse. Encouraged by their promises of support, the Earl of Nithsdale now, when at Court, proposed and succeeded in obtaining the appointment of a commission. On the commission were the Earls of Mar and Melrose, but along with them were joined independent commissioners over whom they had no influence.

The death of King James the Sixth, which took place shortly after, drew the greater part of the Scottish nobility to the Court. The Earl of Nithsdale was then sick at Denmark House.[2] He was repeatedly visited by the Earls of Morton and Roxburgh, and he urged them, from respect to their King and country, to endeavour to promote its liberties. But to his recommendations they listened coldly.

After their return to Scotland, the first intelligence which he received was that they aspired to the exercise of unlimited power. He acquainted King Charles the First with their intentions, and humbly besought him not suddenly to follow their counsel till the Archbishop of St. Andrews and the Earl of Melrose, who had much knowledge and experience in regard to Scottish affairs, were consulted; and he was instructed by the King to write for them, with a promise that no conclusion would be come to without their advice. The

[1] The Melrose Papers, vol. ii. p. 4.

His name appears in the list of the nobility of Scotland who attended the funeral of King James the Sixth in May 1625.—The Melrose Papers, vol. ii. p. 589.

intrigues which followed on the part of Morton and Roxburgh to gain over to their side the Archbishop of St. Andrews and the Earls of Mar and Melrose we here pass over.[1]

The commission, formerly mentioned, having been sent down to Scotland, the Earl of Nithsdale was earnestly desired to follow them, and to aid them by his counsel. But at that time he went to Italy, and nothing was done in the business till his return.

When in Italy the Earl of Nithsdale visited Rome. He left Rome before the 10th of January 1625, as appears from a letter to him of that date by Mr. George Con, who was then in that city. Con writes that, immediately after his Lordship's departure, Lord Angus went to St. Peter's, where his Lordship was remembered, and from thence Con and others went to Lord Angus's lodgings, where the Earl of Nithsdale was remembered by all the party in the old fashion.[2] By the 3d of February that year, Con, as he writes to the Earl in a letter of that date, had received two letters, one of the 15th and another of the 17th of January, informing him of his honour's good health and prosperous voyage. " All thir pairts," he further says, " ar in armes, and ther hes bien sindries killit on the uayes since your honour did depairt, quhilk maketh me that I vill neuer be at rest until I heir of your honour's happie arryue to Paris."[3] Con, in another letter to him, dated Paris, 29th May 1625, acknowledges the receipt of the long-desired news of his honour's good health by Sir James Auchterlonie, by whose courtesy he had the honour to kiss Lord Carlisle's[4] hand, without any further discourse.[5]

The Earl of Nithsdale returned to Scotland before the 24th of August, same year, on which date a letter was written to him by Sir John Maxwell of Pollok, knight, and others his cautioners. They desired to know his Lordship's will as to the means they should take in regard to their distress as his cautioners, and what they might expect as to their relief. Not only were their lands apprised, but they were denounced his Majesty's rebels, and letters of caption were given out against them. They did not know how soon they might be apprehended. They requested his Majesty's interposition.[6]

---

[1] Intrigues among certain of the leading statesmen in Scotland in the end of the reign of James the Sixth and beginning of that of Charles the First. At Terregles.   [2] *Vide* vol. ii. p. 67.

[3] *Vide* vol. ii. pp. 68, 69.
[4] The Earl's son, Robert, who afterwards succeeded him as second Earl of Nithsdale.
[5] *Vide* vol. ii. p. 70.   [6] *Vide* vol. ii. p. 71.

In October 1625, a Convention of Estates was held for the consideration of a project of King Charles the First, of revoking grants which had been made by his father to his nobility and other favourites, or what they had usurped, of the tithes and benefices of the Roman Catholic Church forfeited to the Crown at the Reformation. The proposition was unpopular, and was rejected by nearly all the nobility and gentry, many of whom had shared in the plunder of Church property. Bishop Burnet gives a curious anecdote of what took place at the Convention. The instructions of the Earl of Nithsdale, as commissioner, were to exact an unconditional surrender; but the parties interested had previously conspired, and resolved that if he persisted in prosecuting the measure, " they would fall upon him and all his party in the old Scottish manner, and knock him on the head;" and so resolute was their purpose, that one of their number, Belhaven, who was blind, being seated beside the Earl of Dumfries, seized upon Nithsdale with one hand, and was prepared, had any commotion arisen, to plunge a dagger into his heart. Perceiving this determined opposition, Nithsdale disguised his instructions, and returned to London without accomplishing the object of his mission.[1]

The Earl of Nithsdale was a member of the Parliament which met at Edinburgh 1st November 1625.[2]

About the middle of that month he again left Scotland for England. We find him at the Court in London at the close of the month. A letter which he wrote to the Earl of Annandale is dated Hampton Court, 28th November that year. He states that he had received the Earl's letter of the 18th of that month, whereby he perceived that the humour of the Scottish leading men continued to oppose the King's instructions. He would leave them to answer for it when they came to Court. He thought that the Earl had already been upon his journey; he would therefore have him to make haste, that he might be at Court as soon as they. He was sorry that the Earl had put his hand to divers letters which had come to the Court from the Council, especially concerning the settling of the Council. He adds, " The soner yow be hear the better; yow mey be confidente that quhat conserns my

[1] Burnet's History of his Own Time, Imperial Edit., 1837, p. 11.

[2] The Acts of the Parliaments of Scotland, vol. v. p. 175.

selfe sall be noe dearer to me then what belongs to yow, ather in honour or wtherveyis."[1]

The Earl of Nithsdale was one of the members of a commission called " The Commission of the Council of War," appointed in July 1626, by King Charles the First.   This Commission, which consisted of persons of whose advice, from their knowledge and experience in military affairs, his Majesty might avail himself, was intrusted with full power to meet and determine what was most necessary for the instruction of the people in the use of arms, what places within the kingdom were best adapted for fortification, what martial constitutions and discipline were most suitable for his Majesty's armies by sea or land, and whatever else might concern the martial affairs of the kingdom.[2]

From the encouragement which he gave to the Roman Catholics in and about Dumfries, the Earl of Nithsdale became specially obnoxious to the Presbyterians.

At a meeting of the Privy Council in the autumn of the year 1626, all the ministers of Dumfries appeared before the Council and complained, in strong terms, of " the insolent behaviour of the Papists" in those parts, laying the blame of all the infection that was in the country upon his Lordship and Lord Herries.   " It is pitie," says Spottiswoode, Archbishop of St. Andrews, one of the Earl of Nithsdale's correspondents on State affairs, in a letter to him, dated Leith, 22d September that year, " zour Lordship wil not be movit to leave that vnhappie course quhich shal vndoe zour Lordship, and mak us al sory that love zow, and how much preiudice in the mean quhyl this wil bringe to his Majestie's service I cannot expresse."[3]

Spottiswoode exhorts him, as he loves his Majesty, the standing of his house, aye, and the safety of his soul, to take another course, and resolve at least to be a hearer of the Word, " for zour lordship not resorting to the church quhen zou wer last at Edinburgh hath gifen zour adversaries greater advantage than any thinge else."[4]

Charles the First, by a promise of subsidies, engaged the King of Denmark to take part in the war against the Emperor Ferdinand the Second. Ferdinand, by the imperial army under the command of Maximilian, Duke of Bavaria,

[1] The Melrose Papers, vol. ii. p. 594.   [3] *Vide* vol. ii. p. 77.
[2] Original Commission at Terregles.   [4] *Vide* vol. ii. p. 77.

had defeated Frederick, Elector of the Palatinate, the brother-in-law of the English monarch, near Prague, 19th November 1620, and had not only deprived him of the kingdom of Bohemia but of the Principality of the Palatinate. This explains the policy of King Charles the First. The Earl of Nithsdale was placed at the head of the enterprise of Charles to send forces into Denmark. He obtained from Christian the Fourth, King of Denmark, 28th February 1627, commission as General to raise a regiment of 3000 Scottish soldiers for the assistance of Christian and Lower Saxony.[1]

There were difficulties in raising the full number of forces intended to be sent to the King of Denmark. Divers persons, having small means of living at home, would willingly embark in that enterprise, provided they were protected from their creditors. King Charles therefore, in a letter to the Privy Council of Scotland, dated 29th April 1627, desired them to show favour to such persons, yet in such a way as not to give their creditors just cause of complaint.[2]

The Earl of Nithsdale, in a letter to Elizabeth Queen of Bohemia, daughter of King James the Sixth, and wife of Frederick, Elector of the Palatinate, requested that she would endeavour, according to her brother's command, to obtain for him in Holland a Sergeant-Major. Elizabeth, in her answer from the Hague, 22d May 1627, returned him many thanks for his letter, and especially for the testimony which he gave her by his actions of his affection. She could not get for him in Holland a Sergeant-Major, but she recommended one William Cunningham, who was her first page, and who had served in all the wars on behalf of her husband, the Elector, both on foot and horse, his last place having been that of a Lieutenant-Colonel under Count Mansfeldt. He spoke very good High Dutch, which she thought the Earl would have much need of.[3]

Some Scottish troops had landed in Denmark before 11th June 1627. This we learn from a letter of that date from Lieutenant-Colonel Alexander Seton to Robert Earl of Nithsdale, designated General of the Scots in the service of his Majesty King of Denmark, written from Butesenburgh. He informs the Earl that he had received his Lordship's letter, and had presented his Lordship's humble service to his Majesty, with an account of his Lordship's great trouble and expense in this undertaking. His Majesty wished the

---

[1] *Vide* vol. ii. p. 6.   [2] *Vide* vol. ii. pp. 7, 8.   [3] *Vide* vol. ii. p. 8.

arrival of his Lordship and the rest of the troops.   There was some discontent that the men sent out were not put in companies.   "Our army," the writer adds, "is in good case," but he hopes that it would be better when honoured with such a worthy head as his Lordship.[1]

More troops were to follow.   The regiments to be sent to Denmark not having been ready on the day appointed, which had expired on or before the 15th of July 1627, King Charles, in a letter to the Privy Council of Scotland, prorogued the time till the last day of August following.[2]

In raising men for the Earl of Nithsdale's undertaking, James, eighth Lord Ogilvy, afterwards Earl of Airlie, was especially energetic.   A considerable number of letters from Lord Ogilvy to the Earl are printed in volume second of this work, and they bear ample testimony to his indefatigable zeal, and also to his success in levying troops.

Meanwhile the Earl of Nithsdale and his sureties were exposed to the risk of prosecution on the part of his creditors, and in the event of his going abroad his sureties might be greatly distressed.   He therefore obtained from King Charles the First letters of protection for himself and his sureties, dated 11th May 1627, extending from that date to the 7th of March 1629.   The letters granted them full liberty of dwelling peaceably within the kingdom of Scotland, for transacting their lawful business, and of enjoying all their honours, privileges, and offices.   They also forbade all judges and officers of law, civil or criminal, to molest them, under the pain of incurring his Majesty's highest displeasure as despisers of his royal authority, and of being punished with all rigour in their bodies, lands, and goods, according to his royal pleasure.[3]

It was at first expected that the Earl would set out for Germany in July that year.   Sir George Hamilton, third son of Claud Lord Paisley, in a letter to him, dated 7th July, refers to the reports which he had heard of his Lordship's speedy departure.[4]   But from another letter to him, from the same correspondent, dated 20th August following, we learn that the Earl was then in Scotland, and that the rendezvous of his troops was to be on the 31st of that month.   The writer adds, "I am given to vnderstand that your Lordship will,

---

[1] *Vide* vol. ii. p. 79.

[2] *Vide* vol. ii. p. 10.

[3] Original Letters of Protection at Terregles.

[4] *Vide* vol. ii. p. 99.

after your owne departing, leave some one appoynted for bringing of more men after yow."[1]   The Earl was still in Scotland on 7th October thereafter, as appears from a letter to him from John, sixth Lord Herries, of that date, desiring him, before going out of the country, to receive his own charter-chest.[2]

Soon after, he appears to have gone to Germany.   The next time we meet with him in Scotland is on the 23d of February 1628.   He must therefore have been abroad between the two last-mentioned dates.   In the MS. account of the Herries family, it is said that he took 3000 men over to Germany to assist the King of Denmark in his wars, and that to defray the expense he obtained from the King the rents of Orkney for a time.   A considerable number of the men raised in Scotland for the assistance of the King of Denmark embarked at different times before the Earl of Nithsdale's departure for Germany, as we learn from his correspondence with Lord Ogilvy and others.

The enterprise however came to nothing, the King of Denmark having sustained only disaster and defeat in his encounters with the Imperial troops.

Towards the close of the year the Earl of Nithsdale received £4000 sterling for levying forces in Scotland for the service of the King of Denmark and for transporting them to that kingdom.   The Earl having expended even more than that sum on the undertaking, King Charles the First, in a letter to the Privy Council of Scotland, dated 27th November 1628, ordered them to discharge the Earl and Sir James Baillie, who had become surety for the employment of that money in these levies.[3]

In January 1627, King Charles the First appointed a commission for giving reasonable satisfaction and composition to such of his subjects as had right to erection of benefices, temporalities, feu-mails and kirk teinds, who should surrender them into the hands of his Majesty.   On 29th May that year this commission enacted that his Majesty and his successors should derive a constant rent out of the whole teinds of the kingdom, consisting of victual or silver.   On 29th June they further enacted that all superiorities of erections should be freely resigned into his Majesty's hands without any composition except for the feu-farms, feu-mails, and other constant rent of the said superiorities, the fixing of the amount of which being referred to the determination

[1] *Vide* vol. ii. p. 100.   [2] *Vide* vol. ii. p. 106.   [3] *Vide* vol. ii. p. 12.

of his Sacred Majesty.   In consequence of these enactments, Robert Earl of Nithsdale, on 23d February 1628, and other lords of erections, titulars, tacksmen and gentry, heritors of lands, surrendered, at Holyroodhouse, to his Majesty the right and title of superiority of all and sundry lands, baronies, mills, woods, fishings, towers, and manor-places belonging to the erections and temporalities of benefices to which they had or might pretend to have right of superiority at the date of the surrender, and which were held of them as lords of erection, reserving to them the feu-mails and feu-farms of their said superiorities until they received the payment, which should be ordained to be made to them for the same.

To make resignation into the hands of the King, or before the commissioners appointed for receiving resignations, they constituted Mr. William Elphinston, cupbearer to his Majesty, their procurator.[1]

In the year 1627, Charles the First, led by the counsels of the Duke of Buckingham, engaged in unprovoked hostilities against France.   The Duke, with a fleet of 100 sail and an army of 6000 or 7000 men, sailed from Portsmouth on the 27th of June that year on an expedition against France, and towards the end of July appeared before Rochelle for the assistance of the Protestants, but the inhabitants, not sufficiently certified of the design of the Duke, shut their gates against him.   Directing his course to the Isle of Rhee, he attacked it, but, ignorant of military and naval affairs, he was forced in November that year to return to England, having lost two-thirds of his land forces.   He was assassinated at Portsmouth on 23d August 1628.   Peace was afterwards concluded with France.

The Earl of Nithsdale was very earnest and persevering in his endeavours to promote a good understanding between the Courts of England and France. With this view he maintained a correspondence with the Cardinal Armand du Plessis de Richelieu, the Prime Minister of Louis the Thirteenth, and Marshal Tillieres.   The Marshal, writing to the Earl, 21st December, informed him that he had put his letter, which he had received from Sieur Watson, into the hands of the Cardinal de Richelieu, who had read it with attention, and who esteemed the Earl's person, acknowledged his merit, and was persuaded of his good intentions towards France.[2]   Cardinal de Richelieu, writing to the

---

[1] The Acts of the Parliaments of Scotland, vol. v. pp. 189-192.   [2] Vol. ii. p. 111.

Earl from Paris, 29th December same year, acknowledges the receipt of a letter which he had written to him, and, referring to the Earl's earnest desire for a friendly union between the two Crowns, assures him that he would be always glad to correspond with him about that matter, as in general in regard to all that should concern the public good.[1]

But the Earl's efforts to accomplish a peace between England and France were not at first wholly of a promising character. Of this he complains in a letter to Marshal Tillieres, dated King Street [London], 27th February 1629. "How carfullie," he writes, "I have folloued this matter may be witnessed by these I have had adoe with heer. That the success haith bene noe better the blame must lye wpon the Cardinall and such others as haith bene trusted on that syde, who sheuld nocht have maid me an actor if they had nocht intenditt to have bene satisfied with my first advyse, which I dar avoue sall be fond to have bene faithfullie bestoued."[2]

The negotiations lingered without coming speedily to a satisfactory conclusion. The Earl of Nithsdale strove hopefully to remove obstacles to an amicable result, but regretted the delay. Writing from Kingston, 14th October 1629, to Mr. Scott, in Holborn, London, he wisely judged that past mistakes must be forgotten, which the French ambassador, Edmonts, on whom he pronounces the encomium of being one of the most accomplished men that he ever spoke with, was willing to do, and the Treasurer had sworn that he should leave nothing undone that might settle love and friendship between his master and the King of France. He informed the French ambassador that he intended shortly to go home after he had brought him and the Treasurer together. The French ambassador, who would rather that the Earl had stayed, "inqueyered," says the Earl, "when I wald returne." "I ansuered, wpon direction from the Cardinall or aduertisment ather from him selfe, or from yow, I sheuld be reddie to doe all the service in my pouer, which I did acknolege my selfe tyed toe."[3] In a letter to Cardinal Richelieu, from London, 19th October, he commends the wisdom of the French ambassador and expresses himself hopefully of the treaty of peace.[4]

The Cardinal, in a letter to the Earl, dated De Remilly, en Sauoie, 29th

[1] Vol. ii. p. 112.
[2] Vol. ii. p. 113.
[3] Vol. ii. p. 116.
[4] Vol. ii. p. 118.

May 1630, reciprocates the Earl's fervent aspirations for peace between England and France. "Having seen by the letter which you have been pleased to write to me the desire which you have for the establishment of a perfect amity between the two Crowns, I cannot but praise your zeal in that respect, and assure you that I will always contribute to the utmost of my power to accomplish that end."[1]

But the Cardinal's conditions were considered by Charles the First and his Counsellors to be of such a character that they could not be entertained. The Earl, in a letter to the Cardinal, undated, but written about the year 1630, assumes the tone of disappointment, complaint, and remonstrance. "After conference with this bearer," he writes, "sent be yow, I did clearlie sie how much reconsiliation betuixt the King, my maister, and your King did import to Christendome at this present, and finding your ernest desyer tharof, . . . I was hartalie willing to have mett ather with your honour or Count de Tiliars, when I sheuld have been carefull to have advysed yow of the fittest way that, in my opinion, ane peace being offered be yow myght have been interteaned heer." The Earl blames him for having in some instances pressed matters that tended to the dishonour of the King of England in a manner which he could hardly have thought would have been done by a man of the Cardinal's worth. His master had in consequence been offended; nor would the Earl now go to France, as he had intended, in the hope that he should have had an opportunity of speaking freely, but with all respect, to the French King. He would have the Cardinal to make no delay, as the Spaniard was a powerful man,[2] and to send one over to England with warrant to inquire whether the King of England did not incline to peace. "The protestens in France must have contentment be my maister's means, according to the agrement maid when yow moved my maister to engege him selfe for your maister to tham. . . . Consider that the King my maister's friendship is much more stedable to yow then yours can be to him, for we can assuredlie harme yow bee sea, which yow can hardlie doe to us ather bee sea or land. Yow have the reputasion of a wyse prelatt, and I was a witnes yow war a speciall instrument that the

---

[1] Vol. ii. p. 121.

[2] One of the highest objects of the ambition of Richelieu, when he acquired ascendancy in the counsels of Louis the Thirteenth, was to humble the power of Austria and Spain, and to enlarge the territories of France, at the expense of Austria, by extending them to the Rhine.

dochter of France cam to this kingdome. Be now a good means of recon-siliation."[1]

But all difficulties were removed, and a peace was concluded between England and France. The Earl, in a subsequent letter to the Cardinal, not dated, but about 1630, says that matters had come to a conclusion which he had long wished for, and all possibility of hindrance quite removed, of which the bearer was directed to give the full assurance. " I must mack offer," he adds, " of my poor service as due to your Lordship, being the means by whom so much happines sall wndoutedlie cum to bothe our Kings."[2] A few other letters, which afterwards passed between the Earl and the Cardinal, printed in the second volume of this work, are chiefly of a complimentary character.[3]

Disturbances on the Borders still continued, and, as Justiciary in the middle shires, the Earl of Nithsdale had much disagreeable work to perform. He was constantly in danger of coming into hostile collision with the John-stons. He apprehended two Johnstons, Thomas and John, within his own bounds, and at the earnest desire of divers of his own tenants and others, whom they had wronged, he intended to keep them in custody till they were tried by an assize for theft, reset of theft, of fugitives and outlaws. The Privy Council, however, ordered that they should be set at liberty upon their finding caution to underly the law before the Commissioners of the middle shires. He accordingly dismissed them, and caused them to be summoned to compear before the Commissioners, who were to meet at Lanark on the 15th of April 1631. On that day he came to Lanark with two of the Commis-sioners, Lord Drumlanrig and Sir John Charteris of Hempisfield, and forty-five honest men who were to act as an assize, with a force of two hundred gentlemen. But the Johnstons did not make their appearance. It seemed to the Earl of Nithsdale as if the Privy Council believed that he was acting from malice. Accordingly, in a letter to the Council, without date, but writ-ten 18th April 1631, he expresses his hopes that the Lords of Council would not under such an idea be so prone hereafter to interrupt him in his laudable endeavours to punish theft and curb oppression. He would have them to reflect upon the dangers to which his poor tenants upon the Borders were exposed in their lives and goods, now that these fellows were let loose. He suggests

---

[1] Vol. ii. p. 122.   [2] Vol. ii. p. 123.   [3] Vol. ii. pp. 125, 126.

that the protectors of such culprits should, without delay, be ordered to exhibit them again before their Lordships, who, if they had doubts of his impartiality, should nominate others than himself to try them.

At the same time he sent back by the bearer the Commission of Justiciary within his own bounds, granted to him by their Lordships, as he had found from this instance that it stood him in so little stead.[1]

The Earl of Nithsdale was a member of the Parliament which met at Edinburgh, 18th June 1633.[2]

The Earl was one of the Commissioners of England and Scotland who were appointed by King Charles the First, 12th June 1636, for the punishment and prevention of the great enormities which were committed in extensive districts on the Borders both of Scotland and England.

This Commission was appointed in consequence of the heavy complaints made to the Government of the insecurity of life and property, by the inhabitants of the shires of Berwick, Roxburgh, Selkirk, Peebles, and Dumfries, of the stewartries of Kirkcudbright and Annandale, of the counties of Northumberland, Cumberland, and Westmoreland, and of the towns, villages, and parishes of Northame, called the Holy Island and Bedlingtoun, parcel of his Majesty's county Palatine of Durham. In these counties, stewartries, islands, villages, parishes, and towns, divers malefactors assembled both in public and private places, and went about by day and by night in armed bodies, disturbing the peace of both kingdoms by the perpetration of all kinds of enormities. They wickedly abused, maimed, and killed divers of his Majesty's subjects, robbed and despoiled others of their goods, took and imprisoned others, subjecting them in prison to extreme hunger and cold even unto death, in order to extort from them heavy fines for the redemption of their persons; burned houses and barns full of corn, and committed other deeds of violence. They threatened with death all who should in the courts of justice prosecute any of the offenders. The perpetrators of these outrages in Scotland or England, frequently passed from the one kingdom to the other, and often escaped with impunity. The Commissioners appointed for repressing them were invested each, and any two or more, of them, with power to pursue and arrest them, and his Majesty's Sheriffs, Stewards, Mayors, Bailies, Justices

---

[1] *Vide* vol. ii. p. 46. [2] The Acts of the Parliaments of Scotland, vol. v. pp. 8, 11.

of Peace, Provosts, and others, his ministers in Scotland and England, were ordered to assist the Commissioners with their whole power, when called to do so. Scotsmen thus apprehended were however to be brought to the jail of Scotland, and Englishmen to that of England. It was assigned to any three or more of the Commissioners to hold Courts as often as they judged needful, on such days, and at such times and places, as they should appoint for trying by an assize all such cases. Yet no Court was to be held unless one of the following noblemen was present as one of the quorum of the Commissioners of Scotland, viz., John Earl of Traquair, High Treasurer of Scotland, William Marquis of Douglas, Robert Earl of Nithsdale, Robert Earl of Roxburgh, and William Earl of Queensberry.[1]

In the year 1638, the Earl of Nithsdale repaired and fortified the Castle of Carlaverock, ornamenting it by numerous heraldic decorations, as already narrated in the description of that Castle.[2] It had been greatly damaged by Lord Sussex when in Scotland in the year 1570; and in the year 1607, such was its dilapidated condition that Camden describes it as " a weak house." But the first Earl of Nithsdale restored it to more than its former beauty and strength, that it might be adapted at once for a baronial residence and a stronghold.

In the civil war between Charles the First and his Scottish subjects, which began in the year 1638, the Earl of Nithsdale was an ardent and steady supporter of the King. Charles, having resolved to go in person to York about Easter, that he might be near Scotland, in order to his adopting such measures as in the circumstances of his affairs might be considered requisite, advertised the Earl in a letter from Whitehall, 18th January 1639, Scots style, of his purpose. He did this that either upon the Earl's stay there or upon his retiring to Scotland, he might take the best course he could to secure those whom he knew to be well affected to his Majesty's service, that they might do nothing that tended to the approbation of the Assembly at Glasgow in 1638, and to prepare them otherwise for his Majesty's service.[3] On receiving this letter the Earl convened all his friends, and took them bound to obey the King. On that account he was from time to time proceeded against as a malignant.[4]

[1] Original Commission at Terregles.
[2] Vide pp. 57, 58.
[3] Vol. ii. p. 14.

[4] Statement of the losses sustained by Robert Earl of Nithsdale on account of his adherence to King Charles I. At Terregles.

In the same month the Earl, on receiving another letter from the King, supplied the castles of Carlaverock and Thrieve with a considerable store of arms and ammunition, as well as with garrisons, the former with eighty men, and the latter with seventy.

The King having levied an army to invade Scotland, and having set up the Royal Standard at York, the Earl of Nithsdale and Lord Herries, with the most considerable of their friends, were, from the state of parties in Scotland—the Covenanters carrying all before them—forced to fly into England, where they lived at great cost until the pacification. These expenses, including those of the garrisons, amounted to £5000 sterling.[1] The King's army, numbering 12,000 men, horse and foot, advanced to the Birks of Berwick, a little above Berwick-on-Tweed, whilst the army of the Covenanters, amounting to between 26,000 and 30,000 horse and foot, under the command of General Leslie, encamped on Dunse-law. But a pacification was concluded between the King and the Covenanters at the Birks of Berwick, signed by the King and Commissioners on both sides, 19th June that year, and both armies returned without having shed a drop of blood.

The Earl of Nithsdale remained at Carlisle till after the pacification concluded between the King and his Scottish subjects. Upon the Earl's return to Scotland, several gentlemen of the name of Scott came, at his request, to the kirk of Carlaverock to receive their money.[2]

The pacification between King Charles and his Scottish subjects did not last long. Charles, in a letter to the Earl, from Whitehall, 27th March 1640, bids him look to himself, for by the 13th of the next month " ye will heare of a breache betwixt me and my Couenanting Rebelles." Of this the King had written to the Marquis of Douglas, but under condition of secrecy, which was likewise imposed on the Earl, who was only permitted to advertise Wintoun.[3]

The advice in this letter to the Earl to " look to himself" was opportune, and by a private order from the King he was commanded to garrison his castles. This he did without delay. That they might sustain a protracted siege, he furnished the Castles of Carlaverock and the Thrieve with a large quantity of arms and ammunition, and with a year's provisions, as well as

[1] Statement of the losses, etc.
[2] Notes in the history of Robert, first Earl of Nithsdale.—MS. at Terregles.   [3] Vol. ii. p. 15.

garrisoned them, the former with 200 soldiers and the latter with 100, every soldier having 8d. per day for pay; and he thus supported the garrison for six months.[1]

Informed of the preparations of the Earl of Nithsdale for making a formidable resistance, the Estates at Edinburgh sent a body of troops, under the command of Lieutenant-Colonel John Home, to besiege these castles. This was a detachment from the Scottish army; and while it proceeded on this mission, which was one of the first active operations in the civil war in Scotland between the King and his subjects, Leslie marched into England to join the forces of the English Parliament.

At an early period of the siege propositions were made by Colonel Home to the Earl of Nithsdale for a capitulation of the Castle of Carlaverock. In instructions relative to the capitulation of that castle, 14th July 1640, subscribed by the Earl, he desired that whatever proposals to that effect were made by the colonel should be made in writing, signed under his hand, and under the hand of some other of the officers; and he promised to act in a similar manner. The last instruction is in these terms:—"Thoght I acknoledge ne authoratie within this kingdome which doeth not proseed from our Soueraing, yet sall I deall as befitteth a good subiect and a trew Scotish man, whe sall be reddie to manteen the honour both of our King and cuntrie, als much as any subiect, se far as my mean power mey reach."[2]

The siege, however, continued, and the Earl of Nithsdale sustained, with much bravery, the assaults of the besiegers for thirteen weeks. Powerful batteries were brought to bear upon the Castles of Carlaverock and Thrieve by Colonel Home, and so vigorously was the siege conducted that the Earl was doubtful whether, unless speedy assistance was afforded, he would be able to hold out for any length of time.

King Charles was very desirous to grant him succour, and suggestions were made by the Earl's friends as to the best means of doing so. To attempt to relieve him by sea was not considered expedient. Relief by sea could be sent to him only from the Irish army at Carrickfergus, and there was to be taken into account the uncertainty of wind and weather, and the great diffi-

---

[1] Statement of the losses sustained by Robert Earl of Nithsdale, etc., at Terregles.

[2] Instructions, etc., at Terregles.

culty both of embarking and landing men, horses, ordnance, and victual on so sudden an emergency. The easiest and least expensive way would be by a brigade of 1000 horse, of whom a third part at least should be cuirassiers, in order to strike terror into the enemy, and the rest light horse. If so many good horse could not be spared, 600 horse at least, of which there might be two troops of cuirassiers, three companies of dragoons, and three companies of the best musketeers of the garrison of Carlisle, mounted upon palfreys, in all 1200, might be sent upon this service. The absence of so many of the garrison of Carlisle might be supplied from the trained bands of Cumberland and Westmoreland. Nor was it doubted but that, upon the recommendation of the King, the lieutenants of Cumberland, Northumberland and Westmoreland, many gentlemen and able-bodied men would hazard their persons for the relief of the Earl of Nithsdale, who was much beloved in all these counties. It was probable too that, upon their entering Scotland, they would be strengthened by the accession of divers of the country people, and especially of his Lordship's own tenants and followers.[1]

But such were the difficulties of affording assistance to the Earl so soon as his necessities required, that the King, when informed that favourable conditions were offered to him and his men upon their surrendering, permitted him, in a letter to him, dated York, 15th September 1640, to accept of the conditions offered. This letter relates to Carlaverock alone. In another letter, written on the same day, his Majesty, apprehensive that the Committee of Estates at Edinburgh would not agree to terms so favourable as those offered by Colonel Home, gave the Earl allowance to accept of such conditions as he could obtain, by which the lives and liberties of himself, his family, and those that were with him, might be preserved. This second letter authorizes the surrender of the royal Castle of Thrieve also. It was probably written with the object of removing a scruple on the part of the chivalrous Earl, who appears on all occasions to have well understood the point of honour.

[1] Information anent the relief of the siege of Carlaverock. At Terregles. From this document we learn that the Earl of Nithsdale and his lady were then in the Castle of Carlaverock. Spalding records that word came to Aberdeen on Tuesday, 11th August 1640, that the Earl of Nithsdale, standing to the King's opinion with coroner, Stewart and some brave soldiers manfully defended two strongholds, Lochmaben and Carlaverock, against the fearful assaults of one Captain Cochrane, accompanied with about 700 soldiers, and slew with shot sundry of the assailants.—[Memorials of the Troubles in Scotland and in England, vol. i. p. 316.]

Having obtained the King's permission to capitulate, the Earl of Niths-dale surrendered to Colonel Home the Castle of Carlaverock, after the articles of capitulation were signed by them at that Castle, on the 26th of September 1640.   In the circumstances his Lordship could not have expected better terms of capitulation.[1]

In the first article it was condescended on that there should be no other course taken with the Earl of Nithsdale, his friends and followers, in their religion, than with others of his and their profession ; and that he, his friends and followers, should not be further troubled in their persons, houses, estates, and goods, than according to the common course of the laws of the kingdom. It was further agreed that his Lordship's friends, followers and soldiers might depart with their arms and shot, with all their bag and baggage, trunks, and household stuff, belonging on their honour to his Lordship, and should have safe-conduct to Langholm or any other place within Nithsdale.   Whereas it was desired by his Lordship that goods intromittit with, belonging to his friends and followers, should be restored, it was agreed to that the course which should be taken with others of his and their condition should be taken with him and them.   Again his Lordship became bound that neither he himself nor his friends and followers should in any time coming take up arms, nor have intelligence with any in prejudice of the kingdom, upon their honour and credit.   His Lordship, his friends, and followers were besides to contribute and do everything incumbent on them, according to the general course of the kingdom.   Lastly, they were to deliver up the house and fortalice of Carlaverock to Lieutenant-Colonel Home, with the cannon and superplus of ammunition and other pro-vision, and to remove themselves out of that Castle, and this his Lordship obliged himself and his officers, whole garrison and followers, to perform upon his honour and credit, between the date hereof and the 29th of September 1640.[2]

The Castle of Carlaverock, like other baronial fortalices, was intended equally as a residence for the family, and for the accommodation of a garrison,

---

[1] The losses sustained by the besieged have not been recorded.   During the siege the Earl and his tenants' whole moveables of corn and chattels were plundered and destroyed by the besiegers.   These losses, with the expense of the garrisons, noticed be-fore, in the Castles Carlaverock and Thrieve for six months, are said to have amounted to £10,000 ster-ling.—Statement of the losses sustained by Robert Earl of Nithsdale, etc., at Terregles.

[2] Extract Articles of Capitulation of the Castle of Carlaverock, between Robert, first Earl of Niths-dale, and Lieutenant-Colonel Home. At Terregles. The Articles were registered in the Books of the Committee of Nithsdale, 1st October 1640.

by which, when attacked, it might be defended. An account of the household furniture of the castle at that period must be curious and interesting, as throwing light on the domestic condition of our baronial families in those days. We are fortunately supplied with minute particulars of the household furniture of that castle at the time when it was surrendered, in two inventories. The one is headed " A note of such things as were left in the house of Cearlawrok, at my Lords departure in the yeare of God 1640 ;" and is duly attested by witnesses. In the wine cellar there were four barrels of sack; and in another cellar three hogsheads of French wine. There were numerous beds and bedclothes, which, however, are not particularly described; many stools and chairs covered some with silver cloth and others with brown ; cupboards, a crucifix, two virginals, chests, carpets, window curtains, etc., the Earl's and his lady's portraits. In Lord Nithsdale's chamber were a bed furnished with damask, and a cupboard overlaid with gold lace, two chairs and three stools of damask, a carpet, and a chair covered with brown cloth, a clock, twenty-eight muskets, twenty-eight bandelires, two two-handed swords, and nine collars for dogs.[1] The other Inventory is in some respects still more minute, and gives us a more complete idea of the elegance of the furniture of the Castle of Carlaverock, and also of the value of the respective articles. It is an inventory of the household effects in that castle, intromitted with by Lieutenant-Colonel Home. He is said to have intromitted with five beds, two of silk and three of cloth, each supplied with five curtains, massive silk fringes of half-a-quarter deep, and a counterpane tester of the same stuff, all laid with braid, silk lace, and a small fringe about; with chairs and stools answerable, laid with lace and fringe ; with feather-bed and bolster, blankets and rug, pillars and bedsteads of timber answerable ; every bed with the furniture estimated at £110 sterling. The Colonel was also charged with having intromitted with ten lesser beds, of which four had cloth curtains and six had serge, each estimated at £15 sterling ; with twenty other beds for servants, each estimated at £7 sterling ; with forty carpets, estimated overhead at forty shillings sterling apiece ; with the furniture of a drawing-room of silver cloth, consisting of a couch-bed and great chair, six other chairs, and six stools, all garnished with silk and silver fringe, estimated at £100

[1] Original Inventory at Terregles.

sterling; with two dozen of chairs and stools, covered with red velvet and garnished with fringes of cramose silk and gilt nails, estimated at £60 sterling; and with five dozen of Turkey worked chairs and stools, each chair estimated at £15 sterling, and each stool at nine shillings sterling. Home is also said to have intromitted with a library of books which cost the Earl of Nithsdale £200 sterling. This may now seem to be a small sum expended upon a library, but it would be equal to more than £1000 in the present day. Home was also charged with having intromitted with two great trunks full of hollands sheets and pillowbers, or the coverings of pillows, Dornick and damask tablecloths, napkins and towels, to the number of forty pair of sheets or thereby, and twenty stand of napery or thereby, every pair of sheets consisting of seventeen ells of cloths, at six shillings sterling per ell, amounting to £5, 2s. per pair.[1]

The Castle of Thrieve, which was also surrendered to the Covenanters, was kept for them by a garrison under the command of Ensign Gibb. It was, however, judged by the Committee of the Stewartry of Kirkcudbright that as the Castle of Thrieve could serve no useful purpose it should be flighted or dismantled. They expressed their opinion on this point in a letter to the Committee of Estates, who sent to them a warrant for dismantling the Thrieve. Colonel Home, when at the Committee at Edinburgh, being informed of this, sent instructions to Ensign Gibb, dated Dumfries, 17th October 1640, to the effect that if the Committee of Galloway desired him to quit the castle in order to their proceeding to flight it, he should come out with his garrison on seeing the warrant signed, under the hands of two or three of them, and taking a copy thereof, but otherwise he was to remain and inform Home by letter shortly.[2]

The Committee of the Stewartry of Kirkcudbright, at their meeting held at the house of Thrieve on the 19th of the same month, having received the warrant of the Committee of Estates for the flighting of the House of Thrieve, ordained that it should be flighted by the Laird of Balmaghe. The slate roof of the house and the battlements were to be taken down, with the lofting, doors and windows; the whole ironwork was to be taken out; and the vault was to be

---

[1] Original Inventory at Terregles.
[2] Minute Book of War Committee of the Stewartry of Kirkcudbright, pp. 67, 68.

stopped.   The Laird of Balmaghe was also empowered to dispose of the timber, stones and ironwork, for the use of the public, his necessary expenses being deducted, and, during the flighting, to put six musketeers and a sergeant into the house, to be entertained at the public expense.[1]

The Earl of Nithsdale was now desirous to embark in the service of King Louis the Thirteenth of France, who, under the administration of Cardinal de Richelieu, was everywhere victorious over Spain and Austria, the humiliation of which was the favourite aim of that sagacious statesman.   The French King, in a letter to the Earl of Nithsdale, written from St. Germain-en-Laye, 23d March 1641, expresses the satisfaction he had in knowing by the Earl's letter presented to him by Lord Maxwell,[2] his brother, the Earl's affection towards the French Crown, and his desire to be employed in the French service.   " As to this that you have offered to bring here soldiers for my service," says the French monarch, " the Secretary Montereul, my agent on that side, will inform you more particularly of my intentions."[3]

Whether the Earl of Nithsdale went to France or not is uncertain.   When the Parliament which sat down on 15th July 1641 called absents from the Parliament, both those who were in Scotland and those who were out of the kingdom that had been summoned to appear before it, the Earl of Nithsdale was among those out of the kingdom who had been summoned at the Market Cross of Edinburgh and Pier of Leith upon sixty days' warning, to appear under the pain of forfeiture.[4]   He may, however, have been in England.

The Earl returned to Scotland before the close of the year.

From the extent of his lands, lordships and baronies, the Earl of Nithsdale possessed in his courts of barony or of regality the extensive judicial powers with which these courts were invested.   The judicial proceedings of one of these courts is notable, from its having been made the ground of a criminal process against the bailie-depute nineteen years after the court had been held.

This was the trial of John Maxwell of Bromeholme, who was the Earl of Nithsdale's bailie-depute of Eskdale, Ewisdale, Wauchopdale, etc.,[5] at the Jus-

[1] Minute Book, etc., p. 66.

[2] The Earl's brother was at this time in France.

[3] *Vide* vol. ii. p. 18.

[4] Spalding's Memorials of the Troubles in Scotland and in England, vol. ii. pp. 56, 57.

[5] He was sworn and admitted to this post of bailie-depute at a court held at Langholm, on 7th February 1622, by Robert Earl of Nithsdale and James Maxwell of Kirkconnell, his Lordship's brother and bailie.   John Maxwell of Bromeholme was brother to Archibald Maxwell of Cowhill.

ticiary Court held at Edinburgh on the 9th of April 1641, at the instance of James Robertoun, the King's Justiciary Depute.   The indictment charged him with putting violent hands on the persons of Rosie Baittie, relict of Hector Irving in Auchincaven, and William Irving her son, his Majesty's peaceable subjects, breaking open the doors of her dwelling in Auchincaven, taking her and her said son violently forth thereof under night, binding them with cords, and carrying them as prisoners to the Water of Ewes, near to the place of Langholm, and cruelly drowning them therein in January 1624.   It was urged that he had no power or commission to that effect, and that no trial had preceded, nor had any doom or sentence been passed upon them, nor had they been impeached of any crime before any judge ordinary either criminal or civil.

The pursuers were Margaret Irving, daughter to Rosie Baittie, and sister to William Irving, her son ; Daniel Irving, brother-in-law to Rosie Baittie, and uncle to William Irving, her son ; and Sir Thomas Hope of Craighall, knight-baronet, his Majesty's advocate for his Highness's interest.

The prolocutors in defence were Mr. James Baird and Mr. Thomas Nicolson, advocates.

It was pleaded on behalf of the pannel by his prolocutors that he could not be tried by an assize for the alleged crime, as whatever had been done by him in that matter had been done according to law.   Rosie Baittie and William Irving, her son, had been both apprehended for certain thefts, and were tried for them by an assize before John Maxwell of Bromeholme, as judge and bailie of the lordship of Eskdale, etc., in a fenced court held by him at the Langholm, on the 22d of November 1623 ; and they were duly and orderly convicted of these crimes.   Upon their conviction the sentence of death was pronounced upon them, and executed.   For verification of this criminal process led and deduced against them, an extract minute from the court books of the lordship of Eskdale, etc., by the Clerk of Court, under his subscription manual, was produced.   The minute bore that at the barony and bailie court of the lordship of Eskdale, etc., held at the place and date already mentioned, by John Maxwell of Bromeholme, bailie of the lordship, etc., Rosie Baittie or Irving, relict of Hector Irving, and William Irving, her son, were indicted and tried by an assize for various thefts said to have been committed by them—for stealing seven sheep from Margaret Irving in Carnwith, from the lands of Car, in the month of September then last bypast; four sheep from Christopher Armstrong in Stabholme, from the said lands in the said month of September then last bypast; four sheep from John Caver, Woodhouseleys, from the lands of Woodhouseleys, on 19th November then current; and for common theft, receipt of theft, infang, outfang and pykrie.[1] The assize unanimously found and declared that the pannels were guilty of the crimes for which they were indicted, with the exception that William Irving was declared to be innocent of the charge of stealing four sheep from Christopher Armstrong. John Maxwell, bailie, therefore ordained the pannels to be taken to that part of the water of Ewes called the Green, and there to be drowned within the said water; whereupon the dempster gave doom.

The Lord Advocate, after the production and reading of the said rolement of court, asked instruments thereupon, and declared the same to be null, *ipso jure*, inasmuch as it was the rolement only of a baron court, which in the kingdom of Scotland had not power to sit or judge any thief unless he had been taken with the fang[2] and red hand. Nor was the Earl of Nithsdale's infeftment produced, and even if it had, it bore only for infang and outfang theft. If the crime were infang, even the sheriff, who was superior to a judge in a baron court, could not proceed without a fang, and that upon fifteen days' warning. Nor could the pannels have been taken out of their house without citation, and this rolement of court produced by the pannel bore no citation at all. Again, the act of court did not meet the dittay which was founded upon the violent taking of the persons murdered from their own house, and that in the month of January 1624. In duply for the pannel it was offered to be proven instantly by witnesses at the bar that the persons drowned were truly taken with red hand, with all the fangs libelled in the said rolement of court, at least one or other of them. It was answered by the Lord Advocate that no probation could be received but what was verified by the rolement of the court itself. The Justice continued the case and his interlocutor to the 23d of June next, and ordained the pannel to find caution for his

---

[1] Pykrie—rapine, petty theft, pilfering.—Jamieson.

[2] Taken with the fang, that is, with the stolen goods.—Skene. With the fang, *i.e.*, having in possession. For, as Skene observes, it is equivalent to "hand-haveand, and back-bearand."—Jamieson.

re-entry and compearance on that day [in the Town-Hall] of Edinburgh, under the pain of 1000 merks. John Maxwell, younger of Cowhill, became his cautioner.[1] The further proceedings do not appear.

After the Earl of Nithsdale left Carlaverock, he appeared on the English side. But he gave no support in arms to the King at this time, though he and his necessitous soldiers were forced to remain with the King until they could be transported to France, being, from the nature of their parole, useless as soldiers within the kingdom. The Committee of Estates, on receiving intelligence of his movements, ordered that the Castle of Carlaverock should be demolished, that the Earl's goods should be taken possession of, and that the rents of his estates should be uplifted for their use. These orders were duly executed. The ancient Castle of Carlaverock now ceased to be either a place of strength or a baronial residence, and it has never since been restored.

The Earl of Nithsdale now complained that Lieutenant-Colonel Home, in this and in other respects, had violated the conditions upon which the Castle of Carlaverock was surrendered. He alleged that, besides the written conditions of capitulation, Colonel Home had promised, upon his oath, that the Earl's house and moveables should not be injured, that his goods should be protected from pillage till he should send for them, and that his brother's house of Kirkconnell, and his own house of Langholm, should be delivered to him the first night after his removal from Carlaverock. Yet Colonel Home, he affirmed, had defaced the Castle of Carlaverock, broken down its doors, windows, etc., so that £40,000 would not repair the damage; had also taken out the whole inside plenishing, and had uplifted the Earl's rents and driven away his goods.

On 16th November 1641, a complaint and supplication was presented by the Earl to the King and the Estates of Parliament. He complained of the non-fulfilment of some of the conditions upon which he had surrendered to Lieutenant-Colonel Home the Castle of Carlaverock, and of the intrusion of several persons, without any order or warrant, into a portion of his estate. From the engrossment of the Parliament with more important affairs, he prayed his Majesty and the Parliament to appoint a committee to hear both

---

[1] Extract Criminal Process at Terregles.

the petitioner and such as he complained upon, and to decide therein as they should judge to be equitable.[1]   The petition was remitted to his Majesty.[2]

Colonel Home, in defence, answered that he had acted by order of the Committee of Estates and the General, and that in obedience to their instructions he had consulted with the Council of War at Nithsdale.   It was by their instructions that the Castle of Carlaverock was dismantled, and that the goods then taken and driven away from it were delivered by the Colonel's officers and soldiers to Andrew Stewart, the commissioner appointed by the Committee of Estates, to whom he was, upon his obtaining from him a receipt, to deliver them.   As to the four articles of capitulation, Colonel Home offered to prove that they had been fulfilled.   He urged that his Lordship's friends and followers had gone out of the castle with their arms, shot, bag and baggage, trunks and household stuff, and everything belonging to him and them, upon their honour and credit.   He affirmed that he furnished to him and them for transportation of their moveables more than eight score horses, of which thirty went away unloaded.   For the safe-conduct of the garrison he appointed Captain Arnot, with an ensign, two sergeants, and twenty-five musketeers, to conduct the Earl to the house of Langholm, which was all that he desired. He denied that, besides the articles of capitulation, he had promised upon his oath that he would restore the castle and moveables left by him, and keep it from pillage till the return of himself or of some one in his name.   He pleaded that that was more than he could do, being a servant of the public, who could not transgress his commission.   He denied that on his receiving the castle he had defaced and demolished it.   He offered to prove that within an hour after it had been surrendered to him, having inspected it and its works, and having given it in charge to one of his captains and a company of six score men, he retired with his regiment to Dumfries ; nor did he remove from that town and return to the castle till he received orders from the Committee of Estates for its demolition.   What was done in that way was done by warrant

---

[1] In a statement of the losses sustained by the Earl of Nithsdale, etc., it is said that the besiegers, immediately after the Earl had embraced conditions from them, plundered the houses of Carlaverock, Dumfries, College, and Thrieve, carried away the whole furniture thereof, and dismantled and razed these houses, all in violation of the terms of the capitulation, causing to the Earl a loss of more than £15,000 sterling.

[2] The Acts of the Parliaments of Scotland, vol. v. p. 487.

of the Committee, and most justly, since it was well known that the Earl of Nithsdale, his officers and soldiers, were on the English side carrying arms, contrary to the condition of the capitulation.

To these answers of Colonel Home the Earl of Nithsdale replied. In regard to the imputation that he and his soldiers broke the capitulation by conducting soldiers to the English side, he asserted that Colonel Home, by not delivering to him his houses of Kirkconnell and Langholm, as he had promised, forced him to make his retreat into England. He maintained that he did not, and never should show his face against his native country; but not having his house,[1] in terms of the capitulation, which might have led him to stay at home, he left Scotland, and his men would not stay behind him. By doing this he had been put to great expense; and he had resolved to send the poor handful of people that were with him immediately to France, as the King's warrant for their transportation thither under his royal hand and seal would testify; which, if necessary, he was ready to produce.[2]

The Earl of Nithsdale was charged with having been implicated in a plot with the Earl of Antrim, a powerful Irish Roman Catholic nobleman, for sending Irish forces to the support of Charles the First against the Parliament of England. This plot was discovered from divers letters, instructions, and papers, which were found on the person of the Earl of Antrim, when, in May 1643, in returning from Queen Henrietta, at York, where he had been a long time, to Ulster, in furtherance of his schemes on behalf of King Charles, he was made a prisoner by General-Major Munro in the county of Down. The principal passages in these letters from the Earl of Nithsdale to the Earl of Antrim, while at York, that were found in the last-mentioned Earl's pocket, may here be quoted.

In one of them, dated Carlisle, 2d May 1643, the Earl of Nithsdale thus writes to his Lordship :—" Materis ar fallin out quyte contrarie to my expectatioun, so as I suld not advise yow to mak suche haist of your journey as we resolved. I haue sent this berar of purpois, who is the man I send to Mon-

---

[1] On 22d October 1641, the King represented to the Estates of Parliament that he had abstained from giving permission to the Earl of Nithsdale to repair to his own house in Scotland, upon misinformation that he was forfeited; but the Earl not having been forfeited his Majesty desired the advice of Parliament. The Parliament thought that his Majesty might permit the Earl to repair to his own residences within the kingdom of Scotland. —The Acts of the Parliaments of Scotland, vol. v. p. 440.

[2] Replies by Lord Nithsdale *contra* Lieutenant-Colonel Home's Answers. At Terregles.

troiss, who will particularlie schow yow how materis go, and how great folly it war to look for any assistans from Scotland. Good Schir Ritcherd Grahame, and a number of roundheidis in these pairtis, vpone your servantis cuming post, haue spred report that yow and I ar vpone ane plot to bring forces from Ireland to tak in this country, in so muche, as I haue bene forsit to afferme the contrary with othes, as I micht justlie doe. . . . He wilbe at York within two or thrie dayes; he will schift it af vpone the puritanes of this country, whereof he is the heid; bot, vpone my word, your lordschip is littill beholding vnto him, to my knouledge."

In another of these letters to the Earl of Antrim the Earl of Nithsdale writes :—" I haue daylie expected these dayes past to haue wryte, whiche yow desyred, from the pairtie yow know. Hammiltoun, I doe fear, haue done bad offices to the King since his returne. My Lord, I am veray confident Mont-'rose will not flinsche from the King what he professed at Yorke. I think muche I haue hard nothing from my Lord of Aboyne; bot befoir I sall sie yow, I luke with confidenss to give yow ane better account how materis ar resolued in Scotland." In a postscript he adds :—" My Lord, blame not your servand, who hath bene so long heir. I wold not suffer him till pairt till I had sum griter assureans (from the Erll of Montroiss, and the rest who ar for the K.) then as yit, and till my seruandis returne, I can give."

In a third letter to the Earl of Antrim, dated Carlisle, 8th May 1643, the Earl of Nithsdale says :—" It suld haue bein a blemish vpone me if I had not treulie givin yow notice how materis go. I am not altogidder disperat of Montrose ; but say he were changed, I am in good hope yow sall not lack well-affected subiectis in Scotland to prosecute that poynt we resolued on. Ane thing I think strange, that the ammvnition granted to your lordschip and Aboyne sould be stopped. My lord, without this, neither can the Marques of Huntly doe seruice, nor can your freindes in the iles and hielandis be vsefull for yow. So do your best to haue it quikly sent away, and be confident yow sall haue assistans, though it must tak a longer tyme, of the quhilk I sall give your lordschip notice."[1]

It is worthy of notice that the Earl of Nithsdale writes in this letter as if doubtful of the steadfastness of the loyalty of Montrose to the King. At this

---

[1] Spalding's Memorials of the Troubles in Scotland and in England, vol. ii. pp. 245, 246.

time tempting offers, it would appear, were made to Montrose should he return to the side of the Covenanters.[1] This might leave room for uncertainty as to the course which he might adopt ; but he did not change.

The strong mordacious terms in which the Committee of Estates describe the Earl of Antrim's conspiracy we here subjoin, as illustrating the bitterness of feeling engendered in times of intestine commotion :—

"A trecherouss and damnabill plot of the Irish, English, and Scottish papistis is begvn to be discovered by the vnexpected apprehending of the Erll of Antrim cvming from York, where he had keipit his meitinges and correspondence by letteris with certane popish lordis his confederatis, and amongst otheris, with the Erll of Niddisdaill and Vicount of Oboyne ; there devlish designes and devyses ar cum to licht, and brocht to our knouledge, pairtlie by letteris from Ireland, schewing the depositioun and confessioun of a servand of the Erll of Antrims, and pairtlie by letteris whiche were found in the Erll his owne pocketis, all sent to them from Ireland. His seruand, who wes hangit at Cragfergus, the   day of May, deponed (as the letteris beare) before and at the tyme of his deathe, that the designe wes to reconceill the Inglish and Irish in Ireland, that thay, by there joynt pouer, haveing expelled the Scottis, the Irish forces there might be sent aganist the Parliament of England, to deall with sum fit instrument there, by all there strenth to surprise the Iyllis and the Hielandis, and to depopulate and waste so muche of this kingdome as there pouer could extend vnto, being assured of the like dealling in the north by the papistis and there assistans there ; and to haue a magazine at Carleill for 20,000 men, to fall in with all hostilitie vpone the south pairtis of this kingdome. The letteris sent from Nithisdaill and Oboyne, all writtin and subscrivit be there handis to the Erll of Antrim, and found with him, althogh in some thingis covertlie written, do cary this muche expreslie, that for furtherans of the designe and poynt resolved on, there wes assistans assured from the Iles, and from the north and south of Scotland ; that ammvnitioun and armes, without whiche they think there seruice vseles, were appointed to be sent vnto the north and other pairtis of this kingdom ; and that popish officiares were commandit, and had wndertaken to goe into Scotland, of whiche we ar informed, sum ar alreddie gone to the north."[2]

This paper was published at the market cross of Edinburgh, and at other crosses needful. To defeat the conspiracy, it was resolved by the Lords of the Privy Council of Scotland to proceed criminally against the Earl of Nithsdale and the Viscount of Aboyne, who were summoned at their dwelling-places, and at market crosses, to compear before the Lords of Council, under the pain of treason, at the meeting of the Committee of Estates, to be held on 22d June 1643. To this summons the Earl of Nithsdale and the Viscount of Aboyne did not yield obedience, maintaining their innocence, and alleging

---

[1] Napier's Montrose, vol. ii. pp. 209-211.
[2] Spalding's Memorials of the Troubles in Scotland and in England, vol. ii. pp. 248, 249.

that this was a forged draft intended to cause them compear that they might be warded, fined, or otherwise punished as the then ruling powers in Scotland pleased.[1]

For their non-compearance, they were declared to be forfeited, and denounced as traitors, and the sentence pronounced upon them was proclaimed at the cross of Edinburgh.   By this action, which was done without the warrant, consent, or authority of the King, they were forced to leave Scotland, and fled to the King for safety.[2]   The Earl of Montrose and Lord Ogilvy also fled from Scotland to the King.[3]   The letters of the Earl of Nithsdale to the Earl of Antrim, already quoted, having been brought under the consideration of the Convention of Estates, the Convention, on 28th June 1643, ordained that a letter should be written and sent to his Majesty, acquainting him with the depositions of the Earl of Antrim and his servants ; and with the letters written by Nithsdale and Aboyne to the Earl of Antrim.   They also ordained that a copy of these depositions should be delivered to Mr. Welden, that he might acquaint the Parliament therewith.[4]

The Earl of Antrim, before the end of this year, succeeded in effecting his escape, and fled to the King at Oxford, with whom, in co-operation with Montrose, he concerted measures for resisting the Covenanters.

In the year 1643, the Earl of Nithsdale was sequestrated, and his whole rents intromitted with by the Estates of Scotland from that year till 1647, which, estimated at £3000 sterling per annum, amounted during that period to £9000 sterling.[5]

In March 1644, the Earl of Nithsdale, with the Earls of Crawfurd, Montrose, Traquair, and Kinnoul, the Viscount of Aboyne, and Lord Ogilvy, gave in to the King and both Houses of Parliament, assembled at Oxford, a remonstrance and declaration of their judgment concerning the proceedings of the Convention of Estates in Scotland, especially expressing their detestation of the Covenant, and pledging themselves to suppress his Majesty's rebellious subjects.   In this document it is said—

" That it may be sein how much wee loth and abhor the samen, and ar

---

[1] Spalding's Memorials of the Troubles in Scotland and in England, vol. ii. p. 250.

[2] Ibid. vol. ii. p. 271.

[3] Ibid. vol. ii. p. 275.

[4] The Acts of the Parliaments of Scotland, vol. vi. p. 7.

[5] Statement of Losses sustained by Robert Earl of Nithsdale, etc., at Terregles.

resolved never to averr any thing that haue issued from them as ane act of ony lauchfull or warrantabill judicatorie : wee doe thairfoir, for oure selffis (and in name of all his Maiesteis faithfull subiectis in Scotland, that haue ane hatred and detestatioun of the saidis traittouris conventioun, with all that haue follouit thairvpone), vtterlie renunce and disclame the said pretendit meiting, as presumptuous and illegall, and called for no other end bot seditioun and rebellioun in that kingdome, with all committees, generall and particular, flowing from the samen, and all actis, ordinances, and decrees maid and givin thairin ; and especiallie that act concerning the traitterous and damnable cove-nant drawin wp and takin betuixt thame and the rebellis heir, whiche we most hartelie detest, and sall neuer enter thairin by force, persuasioun, or ony vther respect whatsumeuer ; as also all actis and orderis authorising the leavieing of armes, wnder cullour quhairof the present rebellious army that is gatherit to-gidder, whiche we esteim ane act of heighe tressoun, and hold oure selfis oblegit, be virtue of oure allegiance and act of pacificatioun, to oppose and withstand. Like as, we faithfullie promeiss, vpone oure honor, everie one of ws, to leave no meinis vnattempted to suppress the saidis rebellis now in armes aganist his Maiestie and his croun of England. . . . Oure desire is, that the honorable memberis of both housis heir convenit sould joyne with ws in a request to his Maiestie, that what Scottis man so euer sall refuse to set his hand to this decla-ratioun subscrivit by ws, may not be permitted to leive wnder his Maiesteis protectioun, bot be cheassed from amongis his Maiesteis lauchfull subiectis as partaker, in affectioun at the leist, with the odious rebellioun of both the kingdomes."[1]

About the same time George Marquis of Huntly collected forces against the Committee of Estates, for the reasons stated in his declaration, dated 16th March 1644. He relied on receiving the assistance of sundry noblemen in the north and south, and he also had assurance of the coming of the Earl of Nithsdale, with the Earls of Montrose, Crawford, Kinnoul, the Viscount Aboyne, Lord Ogilvy, and others, with forces from England.[2] It was calcu-lated that the army expected from England with the last-mentioned Earls would give the forces of the Committee of Estates in the south enough to do, and prevent their going to the north.[3]

[1] Spalding's Memorials, etc., vol. ii. pp. 327, 328.   [2] *Ibid.* vol. ii. p. 333.   [3] *Ibid.* vol. ii. p. 337.

In April 1644, the Earl of Nithsdale, with the Earls of Crawford, Traquair, Kinnoul, Carnwath, the Viscount Aboyne, and Lord Ogilvy, came with a company of horse and foot to Dumfries, but hastily returned to Carlisle.[1]

From the part which he took in opposition to the Covenant, the Earl of Nithsdale was, like many others, not only forfeited by the Estates of the Kingdom,[2] but rendered himself obnoxious to the Church. By order of the General Assembly in 1644, he was excommunicated along with the Earl of Montrose, the Earl of Crawford, the Viscount of Aboyne, Lord Herries and Lord Ogilvy, through all the kirks of Edinburgh, for serving the King against the Estates of the Kingdom, and public intimation of the sentence was ordered to be made on Sabbath in all the churches of Scotland. On Sunday, 23d June, William Strathauchin made intimation of the sentence from the pulpit of Old Aberdeen.[3]

The Earl of Nithsdale was in exile from the year 1639 till his death, except during the interval from the treaty between the King and the Scots, at the Birks of Berwick, 19th June 1639, and the breaking out of the civil war anew early in the year 1640 ; and the interval from the treaty at York in the autumn of the year 1640, till the King kept a Parliament himself at Edinburgh in August 1641, and went away, as was alleged, discontented. The Earl did not return to Scotland after the surrender of the Castle of Carlaverock till he came on the 15th of April 1644 with the Earl of Montrose to Dumfries, where Montrose endeavoured to raise the royal standard.[4] But Montrose was so powerfully opposed by the forces of the Covenanters that he fell back upon Carlisle, and the Earl of Nithsdale accompanied him.[5]

In the year 1645, Montrose having returned from Dunkeld to the North, there came to him beyond Dee Lord Gordon out of Auchindoun, M'Donald and his company. Also there came to him in April that year the Lord of Aboyne, the Master of Napier, Laird of Delgatie, the Laird of Keir, younger, who, with the Earl of Nithsdale and Lord Herries, had successfully broken out of Carlisle with about twenty-eight horse through David Leslie's army.[6]

Thereafter the Earl of Nithsdale retreated from Dumfries to England in the end of the year 1645.

---

[1] Spalding's Memorials, vol. ii. p. 350.
[2] Ibid. vol. ii. p. 430.   [3] Ibid. vol. ii. p. 381.
[4] Napier's Montrose, vol. ii. p. 242.
[5] Napier's Montrose, vol. ii. p. 251.
[6] Spalding's Memorials, etc., vol. ii. p. 469; Napier's Montrose, vol. ii. p. 402.

In the beginning of the year 1646, when Charles the First constituted the Secretary of State, Lord Digby, General of all the forces raised, or to be raised, for the King on the other side of Trent, the Earl of Nithsdale was among those who accompanied Digby on his march, at the head of fifteen hundred horse, to Doncaster.   But this expedition soon ended in disaster, Lord Digby having been routed at Sherborne, in Yorkshire, by a Parliamentary troop, with the loss of his baggage, in which was his cabinet of papers, that were published by the Parliament.   At Skipton the most of his scattered troops came together again, and Digby marched with them through Cumberland and Westmoreland to Dumfries.[1]

At Kaynglas in Cumberland the Earl of Nithsdale got a vessel and escaped to the Isle of Man, where he stayed till his death, which took place in the month of May in the same year (1646).   His body was interred in the Isle of Man.[2]

Robert, first Earl of Nithsdale, married, about the year 1620, Elizabeth, daughter of Sir Francis Beaumont.   According to Bishop Burnet, she was niece of the Duke of Buckingham.   By her he had issue a son, Robert, who succeeded him as second Earl of Nithsdale, and two daughters, Lady Elizabeth and Lady Jean Maxwell.   The former of these ladies was baptized at Dumfries on 23d October 1621, and she died there in September 1623, when the plague raged in that town.   She was buried in the kirk of Dumfries on the 7th of that month.[3]   The second daughter, Lady Jean Maxwell, died at Dumfries in the month of September 1649, and was buried there on the 28th of that month.[4]

Dame Elizabeth Beaumont, Countess of Nithsdale, who survived her husband, was subject to the censure of the Church as being a Roman Catholic. On 22d April 1647, intimation was ordered to be made, by the Synod of Dumfries, from all the pulpits within the bounds, that the sentence of excommunication had been passed upon the Countess, and also upon John Lord Herries, Dame Elizabeth Maxwell, Lady Herries, Dame Elizabeth Maxwell, elder of Kirkconnell, and about thirty others; and all persons were forbidden to reset them or resort to them, without the license of the Presbytery or the Kirk judicatories, under pain of ecclesiastical censures.[5]   In the Dumfries

[1] Clarendon's History of the Rebellion, Oxford, 1712, vol. ii. part ii. pp. 717, 718.

[2] Notes in the History of Robert, first Earl of

Nithsdale.   Family History.   MSS. at Terregles.

[3] Dumfries Parish Records.   [4] Ibid.

[5] Records of Synod of Dumfries.

Session Records is the following entry, 3d February 1659 :—" Capt. Ed. Maxwell delate for dishaunting the ordinances and that he is suspect of Popery—instance his inviting Lady Nithsdale and Lady Semple, both excommunicat for Popery, to a publick feast. Confesses that he invited the Lady Semple, but knew not that she was excommunicat ; and that Lady Nithsdale came to visit his wife in her seickness. He was ordained to consider the Confession of Faith, and be ready to declair what professioun he was of."[1]

Dame Elizabeth Beaumont, Countess of Nithsdale, by a charter made by way of contract between her and Robert Maxwell, fiar of Portrack, dated 8th September 1652, let to him, by way of half-manner tack and assignation, the mains of Carlaverock, with the equal half of the salmon-fishing belonging to the place of Carlaverock, used and wont, as it was possessed and uplifted by the last tenant thereof, named Dickson. The fishing is otherwise described as " the said salmon fishing in the water of Nith." The lease contained various stipulations, which were to be fulfilled by the tenant. Letters at the instance of the Countess of Nithsdale having been raised against him, he was commanded by the Commissioners of Administration of Justice to the people in Scotland, in the name of Richard, Lord Protector of the Commonwealth of England, Scotland, and Ireland, 1st February 1659, to observe these conditions.[2]

After having survived her husband for a quarter of a century, Elizabeth Countess of Nithsdale died in the year 1671.

[1] Presbytery Records.   [2] Original Charge at Terregles.

XX. ROBERT, SECOND EARL OF NITHSDALE,

"The Philosopher."

1646-1667.

Robert, second Earl of Nithsdale, who succeeded his father in May 1646, was born on the 1st, and baptized on the 21st of September 1620.[1]

Like his father, he was a steadfast supporter of the interests of King Charles the First in opposition to the Parliament of England and the Committee of Estates in Scotland. During the civil war he assisted the Royal forces in England. On the 12th of October 1644, when General Leslie took the town of Newcastle by storm, and many prisoners, both English and Scotch, Lord Maxwell was among the number. The English prisoners were sent to London to be judged by the Parliament according to the English law. The Scotch prisoners, who included the Earl of Crawford, the commander, Lord Reay, and Lord Ogilvy, who had been taken elsewhere, were sent to Edinburgh, and warded, in order to abide their trial, conformably to the laws of Scotland. They were brought to Edinburgh on the 7th of November by the Water Gate of the Canongate. They were not warded in the Castle, in which nobles were wont to be incarcerated, but in the Tolbooth.[2]

The Earl of Crawford was compelled to come up the Canongate, bareheaded, as a traitor. Lord Maxwell continued a prisoner in the Tolbooth of Edinburgh till after the defeat of the Covenanters at the battle of Kilsyth, on 15th August 1645, by Montrose, when, upon the submission of the town of Edinburgh to Montrose, he and the other prisoners in the Tolbooth were liberated. The triumphs of Montrose were, however, brief. His complete defeat at Philiphaugh by the Earl of Leven, on 12th September following, destroyed for the time all prospect of the restoration of the monarchy.[3]

By the articles of Westminster, entered into in July 1646, Lord Nithsdale was one of the Royalists whom it was proposed to except from a pardon, but Charles the First rejected the proposal.

An Act of Parliament was passed on the 3d of February 1647, in favour

[1] MS. Family History ; Dumfries Parish Records.
[2] Spalding's Memorials, etc., vol. ii. p. 430.
[3] Napier's Montrose, vol. ii. pp. 441, 452, 472.

of Robert Earl of Nithsdale, restoring him against his father's forfeiture. He was infefted as heir to his father in the lands and baronies of Maxwell, Carlaverock, Tinwald, and others, on the 9th and 12th of February 1649.[1]

From the great losses which he and his father had sustained in the service of King Charles the First, during the civil war, he found it necessary to sell part of the family inheritance. On 4th May 1649, it was arranged between him and his friends of his own name, that the Mearns should be sold for £20,000, over and above the sums due to Sir George Maxwell of Pollok. If that sum could not be got for the Mearns, these friends were to raise the money otherwise, and the Earl was to intimate to the Earl of Buccleuch that his necessities were not so great as to cause him to sell the Langholm. He also gave his noble word that he would do nothing as to the Langholm, or as to any of his other lands, without the advice of his friends. The agreement was left in the keeping of the Countess of Nithsdale, his mother.[2]

In an agreement, dated 3d August 1649, between the Earl and his mother, and their friends, after referring to a minute formerly subscribed by these friends, whereby they were to have advanced by the 1st of that month to the Earl £20,000 out of the price of the barony of Mearns, which he gave them power to sell, it was agreed, as, owing to the troubles, money was not easy to be obtained, to extend the time to the 30th September next. If at that time the money was not forthcoming, the Earl was to be left to do as he chose, and his friends were to be free from their obligation.[3] The lands and barony of Mearns were sold to Sir George Maxwell of Pollok, and by him they were sold, about the year 1660, to Sir Archibald Stewart of Blackhall. The barony of Mearns has descended to Sir Archibald's representative, Sir Michael Shaw Stewart, Baronet.

A transaction which the Earl of Nithsdale had with the famous minister, Mr. Robert Blair, minister at St. Andrews, may here be noticed. On 2d October 1649, he obtained from Mr. Blair a charter of the seven merk lands of Collunachtre, and twenty shilling lands of Auchinlec, in the parish of Riddicke, now Rerwick, stewartry of Kirkcudbright and shire of Wigton.[4]

The connexion of the house of Maxwell with Nithsdale, from which their

---

[1] Original Instrument of Sasine at Terregles.
[2] Original Agreement, *ibid.*
[3] Orginal Agreement at Terregles.
[4] Original Charter, *ibid.*

title of Earl of Nithsdale is derived, has been before noticed. One of the important privileges which they had in this part of the country was the fishings of the river Nith.

This Earl and his predecessors were entitled to a third part of all salmon and other fishes, taken at the foot of the river Nith, foreanent the lands and barony of Carlaverock, to be uplifted from the parishioners of Kilbean, and all other fishers upon that river.

A summons was raised at the instance of Elizabeth Beaumont, Countess of Nithsdale, conjunct fiar, or at the least liferenter, and Robert Earl of Nithsdale, her son, proprietor of the lands and barony of Carlaverock, and fishing thereof at the foot of the water of Nith, against certain persons, not named, dated 4th July 1653. The summons mentions that the complainers and their predecessors had been in possession of these fishings for divers ages without interruption.

The parties were summoned to compear before the Commissioners for the Administration of Justice to the people in Scotland, at Edinburgh, or where they should happen to be at the time, to hear themselves decerned to pay to the pursuers the third of all salmon and other fishes that had been taken by them, or by any others at their direction, for their behoof in time bypast, at the foot of the said water, foreanent the complainer's lands.[1]

At the Parliament which met 28th March 1651, the Earl of Nithsdale was appointed by his Majesty, with consent of the Estates of Parliament, one of the Colonels in the shire of Wigton and stewartry of Kirkcudbright.[2]

This Earl's house in Dumfries having become unfit for his residence, he purposed to have it in some suitable degree repaired. On 17th September 1659, he appointed John Maxwell of Cowhill and Robert Maxwell of Carnsalloch, or any one of them, to ascertain from masons, wrights, glaziers, slaters and plumbers, what would be the cost of repairing his house in Dumfries, and the garden dykes with necessary office-houses, rendering the same fit for him to live in. They ascertained that the expenses would extend at least to £3000 Scots money, and some whom they consulted estimated that the cost would extend to £5000.[3]

[1] Original Summons at Terregles.
[2] The Acts of the Parliaments of Scotland, vol. vi. p. 594.   [3] Original Report at Terregles.

After the restoration of King Charles the Second, on 29th May 1660, the Earl of Nithsdale was advised by his friends to go up to the Court at London, as he had enemies there who would be sufficiently forward in doing what they could against him. Robert Maxwell of Tinwald, in a letter to him, dated 22d July 1660, writes, "My lord, your freindes thinkes strange yow goe not to Court, and advyses yow to repair thither with the first convenience, for your lordship wantes not vnfreindes to speik of yow ther, als weil as they doe of vthers."[1] This correspondent in the same letter informs him of the promptitude with which the Government of the restored monarch were proceeding against such as had been conspicuous in supporting the English Parliament or Commonwealth and the Committee of Estates in Scotland during the late troubles. A commission had come down from Court for the apprehension of Warriston, Chieslie and the Provost of Edinburgh, of whom the two last were kept close prisoners in the Castle, whilst great search was made for Warriston. Middleton, who was the greatest man with his Majesty of any Scotsman, was expected to be his Majesty's Commissioner to the Parliament of Scotland, Glencairn to be Chancellor, Crawford to be Treasurer, Newburgh to be Secretary, and Sir Archibald Primrose to be Clerk Register. It is added in a postscript that Lord Argyll, Antrome, Heselrig, Sir Henry Vane and Thomas Scott were committed to the Tower, all of whom, it was thought, would suffer; that it was reported, though there was no certainty for it as yet, that Loudon, Southesk, Roxburgh, Lothian, Tweeddale, Wemyss and Sir Daniel Carmichael were apprehended, and were to be brought down to abide their trial, and that Argyll was shipped and was to be down this week, and to be conveyed from the foot of the Canongate on a hurrellbarrow, with his face backward, bareheaded, till he came to the Tolbooth, where he was to remain till he got his sentence.[2] In prospect of the meeting of the Parliament of Scotland, it was resolved to issue letters to particular gentlemen in every shire for convening the shire to elect their Commissioners to the Parliament; and his Lordship was advised, if no letters should come, to convene the stewartry of Kirkcudbright, and elect and give commission to a member who was free from complying, meddling

[1] Vol. ii. p. 147.

[2] The Marquis of Argyll landed at Leith 20th December 1660, and next day he walked up the High Street of Edinburgh, covered, betwixt two of the bailies to the Castle, where he continued till his trial.—Wodrow's History, vol. i. p. 131.

with, or having office under the English, or who was not connected with the remonstrators, but would be obsequious to his Majesty's desires, as none other would be admitted to this Parliament.[1]

In a letter to Commissary William Ross, dated 20th August 1660, the Earl denies that he was ambitious of obtaining preferment in the public service, as by some had been asserted. "Trewly," he says, "yow haue euer known my opinion in reference to publick imployments, how auers I ame from it. And althogh I could get a burthen of testificats from the clargie for my conformitie, and youre owne knowledge thereof, yet I will desire no such thing for cleareing of my self heerein, since it doth stop me from nothing to which I haue any minde at this time." Yet as he himself, his father and his friends, had sustained great losses in the service of King Charles the Second and his father, he was desirous that he should be included among those sufferers to whom some compensation might be made. "Because I finde," he writes, "that most, if not all, the nobilitie and gentrie haue gott promiss of satisfaction for theire losses both in oure King's and his father's time, as myself haue sien ounder some of theire hands ; my self and my friends haueing been so greate losers hitherto in that seruice, I should desire to be included amongst these other sufferers, wherein I can say, and make it evidently appeare, there is not one familie in Scotland hath suffered greater losses, nor hath remaned more constant to his Majestie and his royal father then those who depend on me, whereof thogh many hath losed theire lifes and rowind their estates, yet not one can be found to haue born arms in the contrare, which I think few can say bot myself."[2] In the close of the letter he expresses his intention immediately after receiving an answer from Ross of going to London.[3]

Ross, in a letter to him, written from Westminster, 15th September, says, in reference to his coming to London :—" I dowt not but diuerss of my former hath satisfied your Lordship that my Lord Dwk of Albamarll, and al the rest of your freands, aggree that it is conueniant your Lordship hast hither. I haue spok for your lodging to be at Mr. Sidnam's, hard by Chearincross, whar the Ladie Dirltown liued. I hop your Lordship wil mind to bring with yow what further desyrs the Lords of Hariss and Kirkcudbright hath, and let sertificats be to ueriefie thair particular sufferings."[4]

[1] Vol. ii. pp. 146, 147. [2] Vol. ii. p. 150. [3] Vol. ii. p. 151. [4] Vol. ii. p. 153.

A special object of the Earl's journey to London was to press on his Majesty the claims of his family for compensation. In a memorandum, dated 22d September 1660, to be used by him for this purpose when in London, among other losses suggested to be dwelt on was the loss of Langholm, and spending, by the King's command, on the keeping of Carlaverock Castle, the money which should have been used to redeem the Langholm estate. There was, besides, the destruction of the "haill moveables and plenishing" of his houses of Carlaverock, Castle of Dumfries, College of Lincluden, and Castle of Thrieve. These losses and expenses, with his rents uplifted during the disturbances, would amount to more than £40,000 sterling.[1]

This Earl presented a petition to King Charles the Second, praying for some reparation. The petition is as follows :—

To the King's most excellent Majestie, the humble petition of Robert Earle of Nithisdale,

Sheweth,—That youre Majestie's petitioner's late father, upon seuerall letters and orders from youre Majestie's Royal father, of euer blessed memory, hereto annexed, did tuo seuerall times garrison his hous of Carlaurock and Traue, haueing aboue 300 men therein ounder pay for eleuen months, besids vast expences for arms and munition, which hee manteende untill his Majestie ordered the deliuerie thereof ; in which time the sayds garrisons were not only beleguered, but the wholl corns, chattels, and other moueable goods belonging to your petitioner's father and his tenents wer wholly plundered and disposed of by the besiegers, who, contrary to the capitulation, after the surrander of the sayds garrisons, did plounder youre petitioner's houses of Carlaurock, Drumfries, Colledge, and Trave, not leaueing any thing therein, and did dismantle and rase the forsayds houses, and immediately thereafter sequestred and intrometted with the petitioner's father's wholl rents, and forfaited and banished him self, who dyed in exile for his loyaltie to youre most glorious father ; which seruices and sufferings (particularly) expressed in the annexed, doth in real expence and loss extend to 39,000 lib. sterling, whereby youre petitioner is made incapable to subsist.

May it therefor please your Majestie, upon consideration of the premisses, to grante your petitioner some reparation of his sayd expenses and losses, whereby his familie may be agane restored to theire former condicion, which will not only apeare in it self ane act of justice, but incorrage your petitioner, his familie, and interest (as formerly), to venture theire lives and fortouns upon all occasions in your Majestie's seruice. And your Majestie's petitioner shall euer pray, etc.

This petition was accompanied with a statement of the Earl's father's losses for his adherence to King Charles the First. This statement was arranged under six heads. The first four, which relate exclusively to the Earl's father's services and sufferings, have been already noticed in the life of that Earl, and are generally referred to in the petition now given. The last two may here be

---

[1] Original Memorandum at Terregles.

quoted as relating to this Earl's as well as to his father's losses in the service of his Sovereign :—

" 5. In anno [16]43 the Earle was sequestrated, and his wholl rents intrometted with by the Estates of Scotland, from the yeare 1643 till 1647, at 3000 lib. sterling per annum, which in the sayde time amounts to 9000.   At which time the present Earle was necessitated to repurchase his estate from the Parliament of Scotland, by which burthens thus contracted by the late Earle for aduancing his Majestie's seruice, and by the present Earle for repurchassing the estate from the Parliament, the estate is almost totaly rowined, the most considerable parte thereof being possessed by persons that aduanced the moonies expended in his Majestie's seruice.

" 6. Besides all which losses and expences the Earle him self was forfeited and banished the kingdome and died in exile, all which shall be instructed to haue been suffered by the Earle him self for his loyaltie to his Majestie.   Besides that the Lord Herries, the Lairds of Cowhill, Gribton, Orcherton, Carnselloch, Killilong, Portract, and many others, considerable gentlemen of the Earl's name and familie are totaly rowined in their Estates, and some of them executed at the Cross of Edinburgh for theire loyaltie ; notwithstanding of all which sufferings, the present Earle and his friends did not omitt to serue his Majestie when his armies wer in being, either in England or Scotland ; by which seruice and sufferings susteened by that familie the present Earle and his friends are rendered uncapable to subsist, without his Majestie be graciously pleased to prouide some speedie remedie : the afforsaide expenses and losses susteaned by the Earle extends to thrittie nine thousand lib. sterling, besids the usere since the expending thereof."[1]

With the view of obtaining some reparation for the Earl and his father's sufferings in the service of King Charles the Second and his father, the Countess Dowager of Nithsdale, the Earl's mother, corresponded with Sir William Compton, third son of Spencer, second Earl of Northampton.   Writing to her, 5th November 1660, in answer to one of her letters, Sir William does not hold out to her much encouragement : " I wish it lay in my power to serue your Ladyship and my Lord in a more efectual manner than reall expressions, for no person liueing should be more reddy to giue testimony thereof than I should. The persecutions and great sufferings that has atended your family since the first begining of the unhapie differences, can not but be taken notice of. Though the present coniuncture presents not yet any redres, what is delaied I hope will not be forgot. 'Tis many persons condition heere at present, waitie reasons moouing his Majestie to reward som whose sufferings haue bin little upon his acount, whilest others that haue ventured all must rest satisfied, the same zeale and loyalty that has led them into so many hasourds, afording them patience to be satisfied with his Majestie's proceedings, it tending to his settle-

---

[1] Original Statement of Losses, etc., at Terregles.

ment. I haue writt thus much to informe your Ladyship, that you may not be discouraged if my Lord receives no present advantage or recompence for his sufferings."[1]

In compliance with the advice of his friends, the Earl of Nithsdale went to London, and after staying there for a short time he returned to Scotland. George Maxwell of Munches, in a letter to him when he was in England, dated Iylle, 12th November 1660, thus writes:—"Your honor wald doe weill to haist home to proveyd for the Parlament, and to get some good horse. Iff yow get not ane better, I sall giue yow Archibald Stewartis, for I have bocht him."[2]

On the Earl's return to Scotland, he attended the first Parliament of King Charles the Second, which was opened at Edinburgh, 1st January 1661. At that Parliament his Majesty's Commissioner was John Earl of Middleton.[3]

By that Parliament the Earl of Nithsdale was appointed, 29th March, one of the Commissioners for the shire of Dumfries, and burghs within it, for regulating and uplifting the excise or taxes laid on numerous articles, in order to raise the sum of £40,000 sterling, yearly, during his Majesty's lifetime, granted by an Act of Parliament, dated the 22d of that month, towards the support of such forces as his Majesty should think fit to raise and keep up within this kingdom, or otherwise, towards the defraying of the necessary expenses of his Government, according to his royal pleasure.

The Earl of Nithsdale attended the Parliament till its close. His mother, writing to him when he was in Edinburgh, 22d May 1661, says, "Though I desire to see yow, I will not advise yow to leave the Parliament till yow see the conclution."[4]

Meanwhile the Earl's correspondent, Sir William Compton, informs him of what was doing in England. Writing to him, 3d June 1661, he says, "Since my last, the Parliament pased a vote for burning the Couenant by the hand of the hangman. Som were troubled at it here, but not many. Wee are now upon a bill for repealeing the Act by which the Bishops were excluded from siting in Parliament." He adds, "Wee haue reports here that the Marques of Arguile aserted the Couenant and his owne inosensie much at his death.

[1] Vol. ii. p. 154.

[2] *Ibid.* vol. ii. p. 156.

[3] The Acts of the Parliaments of Scotland, vol. vii. p. 3.

[4] Vol. ii. p. 158.

They were well coupeled, and equaly to be esteemed, for his inosensie, I beleue, had the greatest share in promoteing the eeules the other braught us into."[1]

Another of Lord Nithsdale's correspondents, Jean Maxwell of Kirkconnell, writing to him, 7th October 1662, on a more familiar subject, thanks his Lordship for a present of fishes, which was the meat she loved best. "We have all feasted upon them this night." She adds, "Receive your stotte, together with ane salter, for I heard yow say that yow stoode in neid of one; tho' it be little worth, it will serve your Lordship for the present, and when ye have occassion ye may buy ane better."[2]

The Earl was present as a member at the second session of the first Parliament of King Charles the Second, which met at Edinburgh 8th May 1662;[3] and at the third session, which was begun on 18th June 1663.[4] He was also a member of the Parliament held 2d August 1665. At this Parliament, John Earl of Rothes was his Majesty's High Commissioner.[5] The Earl of Nithsdale also appears on the roll of the Convention of Estates held 9th January 1667.[6]

A litigation took place between Robert, second Earl of Nithsdale, and Mary Countess of Buccleuch, concerning the barony of Langholm in the county of Dumfries. At last an agreement was made between the Earl and the curators for the Duke of Buccleuch and Monmouth, dated 30th June 1665, whereby the Earl agreed to dispone for £5000 sterling to the Duke and the family of Buccleuch the barony of Langholm irredeemably.[7] The money was not, however, paid for many years after.[8]

This Earl was commonly designated "the Philosopher." Among other pursuits he was said to have been addicted to the study of astrology. It was reported that the Earl had cast the horoscope of Charles the Second, and predicted his restoration to the throne of his ancestors when his prospects were far from encouraging. James Earl of Northampton refers to this in a letter to him, dated 21st August 1660:—"I thought these happy dais would haue brought your Lordship into southerne parts to haue participated your joies you foretold would happen by your speculation on your northern stars."[9] But

---

[1] Vol. ii. p. 158.   [2] Ibid. vol. ii. p. 159.

[3] The Acts of the Parliaments of Scotland, vol. vii. p. 368.

[4] Ibid. vol. vii. p. 446.

[5] Ibid. vol. vii. p. 526.

[6] The Acts of the Parliaments of Scotland, vol. vii. p. 536.

[7] Original Agreement at Terregles.

[8] Vide Memoir of John, third Earl of Nithsdale.

[9] Vol. ii. p. 151.

in a letter to Commissary William Ross, 20th August 1660, the Earl of Nithsdale denies that he had ever attempted to do any such thing, and calls the reports in circulation to that effect " aspersions."[1]

Robert, second Earl of Nithsdale, died in the Isle of Carlaverock, on Saturday, 5th October 1667, and his body was buried in the kirk of Carlaverock.[2] A discharge by John Tailzeor, wright in Dumfries, for the price of the late Earl of Nithsdale's coffin, is dated 13th January 1669.[3] Having died unmarried, this Earl was succeeded by his kinsman and nearest male heir, John Maxwell, seventh Lord Herries.

[1] Vol. ii. p. 150.

[2] This is stated in a Decreet, dated 7th November 1685, in the printed Inventory of Nithsdale Muniments, p. 318, No. 99.—MS. Family History; also Letter from Mr. William Maxwell, of Kirkconnell, Advocate, 27th June 1682, at Terregles.

[3] Original Discharge at Terregles.

SIGNATURE AND SEAL OF ROBERT SECOND EARL OF NITHSDALE.

XX. JOHN, THIRD EARL OF NITHSDALE.

ELIZABETH GORDON (OF LOCHINVAR), HIS COUNTESS.

1667-1677.

JOHN LORD HERRIES, who succeeded his cousin, Robert, second Earl of Nithsdale, as third Earl of Nithsdale, in the year 1667, was the son of John, sixth Lord Herries, by his wife, Elizabeth Maxwell, daughter of John, seventh Lord Maxwell, created Earl of Morton.

When Master of Herries he married, in the year 1626, Elizabeth Gordon, daughter of Sir Robert Gordon of Lochinvar, knight. Their marriage-contract is dated 19th August that year. Lord Herries, his father, in contemplation of the marriage, became bound to infeft the Master and his heirs heritably in all lands, lordships, baronies, offices, patronages, etc., belonging to his lordship, under reservation of his liferent of the whole, and of Elizabeth Gordon's liferent of the lands of Kirkgunzeon, which were warranted to her to be worth 4000 merks yearly; and as Dame Elizabeth Maxwell, Lady Herries, then stood infefted in liferent in the lands of Kirkgunzeon, Lord Herries became bound, in the event of the Master of Herries predeceasing his parents and Elizabeth Gordon, to infeft the latter, during her lifetime, in the lands of Hoddum, Tunnergarth, Littill Huttoun, and Lockerbie, which were warranted to be worth 4000 merks *per annum*. Sir Robert Gordon became bound to pay 20,000 merks of tocher with his daughter Elizabeth. Among the witnesses to the contract were Robert Earl of Nithsdale and George Earl of Wintoun,[1] who was a relation by marriage.

The estates of John Master of Herries became considerably burdened by the provision made out of them for his seven younger brothers. His father, in the marriage-contract now mentioned, while making over to the Master the fee of his estates, reserved power to make provision for his younger children. Being diseased and sickly, and believing that he would not long survive, he directed, in the beginning of the year 1627, that his second son, James, should receive 5000 merks; his third son, William, 4000 merks;

[1] Copy Minute of Contract at Terregles.

his fourth son, Alexander, 3000 merks ; and his four other sons, Robert, Edward, Frederick, and Michael, 8000 merks equally among them. Accordingly, John Master of Herries became bound, 15th February that year, to execute a bond over his estates in favour of his brothers for these sums.

John Master of Herries, on the death of his father, which took place about the month of May 1631, succeeded to the Herries estates and titles.

A precept from the Chancery of King Charles the First, dated at Edinburgh, 5th November 1631, was directed to the steward of Kirkcudbright and his deputies, for infefting John, then Lord Herries, as heir of his father, John Lord Herries, in the lands and baronies, etc., anciently erected into the barony of Herries, of which the principal messuage was Terregles. The lands are said to have been in non-entry for one term or thereby. The new heir was infefted in the lands and barony of Herries on the 8th of the same month of November.[1]

On 26th December 1632, John Lord Herries became bound to infeft his spouse, Lady Elizabeth Gordon, in the tower and manor-place of Terregles, and others, during the lifetime of Elizabeth Maxwell, Lady Herries, elder, his mother. The reason for this transaction was that as by his marriage-contract it was agreed that Lady Elizabeth Gordon should be infefted for her lifetime in the mansion-place of Kirkgunzeon, and so much of the barony of Kirkgunzeon as would amount to 4000 merks of yearly rent, and as Elizabeth Maxwell, Lady Herries, his mother, was also infefted in liferent in these lands, the stipulated amount could not be obtained from them.[2]

During the civil war Lord Herries suffered heavy losses for his loyalty to King Charles the First. In the year 1639, when that monarch, deeply incensed at the proceedings of the Glasgow Assembly of 1638, levied an army to invade Scotland, setting up the royal standard at York, the Scots, receiving intelligence of the action of the monarch, levied an army, which came near the Border, encamped on Dunse-law, the royal army lying at the Birks of Berwick, a little above Berwick-on-Tweed. At this time the Covenanters seized the Castle of Edinburgh, and sent 2000 or 3000 men into Nithsdale, under the command of Sir Robert Monro and Pitscottie, to suppress the Earl of Nithsdale, Lord Herries, and their friends, as being Non-Covenanters. Upon this

[1] Original Precept and Instrument of Sasine at Terregles.   [2] Original Bond at Terregles.

Lord Herries fled to Carlisle, where he and his whole family remained, and did not return till the pacification at the Birks of Berwick-on-Tweed, which was signed by the King and Commissioners on both sides on 19th June 1639.[1] They then returned to Scotland. They had been absent three months, and during that time their expenses amounted to 5000 merks.

During Lord Herries's absence the soldiers, under the command of Monro and Pitscottie, broke open the gates of his house of Terregles, and having entered into a room in which the best of the furniture of his house lay, they carried away as much as they could, with some of his plate, to the value in all of 5000 merks.

To fortify the Castle of Carlaverock, which his chief held out against the Committee of Estates, and to arm the soldiers for defence, Lord Herries furnished to that castle two pieces of brass ordnance, the one about 1000 lb. weight and the other about 400, and two pieces of iron cannon, the one a four-pounder and the other a two, with their whole furniture; twenty double muskets, forty carabines, and two hundred pikes, all which were taken by Lieutenant-Colonel Home. At the same time, to defend the Castle of Thrieve when besieged he sent twenty double muskets.

In April 1644, when the Earl of Callendar and his army came first to Dumfries, Lord Herries's house of Terregles was quartered in by the Laird of Lamyngtoun and twenty gentlemen in his company, with their horses, and twenty-four soldiers, who entertained themselves for three weeks with the provision which Lord Herries had left in his house.[2]

In the year 1644, Lord Herries, for serving the King, was excommunicated by the Church, like his chief, the Earl of Nithsdale, and, by the orders of the General Assembly, the sentence was intimated in all the kirks of Edinburgh, and it was ordained to be intimated in all the churches in Scotland. It was announced by Mr. Strathauchin, minister of Old Aberdeen, from his pulpit, on Sabbath, 23d June, that year, after the forenoon service.[3]

About the middle of the month of April 1644, when the Earl of Montrose, having taken possession of the town of Dumfries, endeavoured to raise the royal

[1] Balfour's Annals, vol. ii. pp. 327, 328.

[2] The Parliamentary Report has—"The Laird of Lamyngtoun wes quartered in the Lord Herreis house of Tarregles, with threttie horse, the space of tuentie three dayes, and tuentie four foot for eight dayes, vpon frie quarters."

[3] Spalding's Memorials, etc., vol. ii. p. 381.

standard, Lord Herries was one of those noblemen who joined him.   For this demonstration of malignancy his life and estates were forfeited by the Committee of Estates,[1] and by their command his whole rent was uplifted in the years 1644 and 1645, extending to the sum of 70,000 merks.   From the beginning of September 1644, to the 13th of September 1645, Montrose's career in Scotland was one of uninterrupted triumph over the Covenanters, but at the last-mentioned date he was completely routed at Philiphaugh.   During that period Lord Herries lived in banishment, and his lady and children were thrust out of his house, without any allowance being afforded to her except the promise of 2000 merks, which were never paid.   In these two years his expenses abroad, and those of his lady and family at home, amounted to 20,000 merks.

After Carlisle was surrendered, in the year 1645, when the King's army came down from Wales, Lord Herries, who was with the King at Doncaster—from which the King was forced to retire—and sick, was taken a prisoner by Major Lilburne, who despoiled him of his clothes, and took from him £100 sterling of gold, extending to 3000 merks.   He was released in the course of a month by David Leslie.   Thereafter he was robbed upon the Borders, and his horse, baggage, and moneys were taken from him.

In the year 1647 a fine of £10,000 Scots was imposed upon him by the Committee of Estates, and this sum he was forced to pay before he was suffered to enjoy his estate.   He paid it to Lord Kirkcudbright's regiment.   This, with the annual rent thereof, estimated for some years after, amounted to 27,000 merks.[2]

In the year 1649 the Committee of War of the stewartry of Kirkcudbright, forced Lord Herries, on account of his disaffectedness, as they termed it, to put out horse and foot, and raised out of his estate nine months' maintenance, amounting in all to the sum of £2520.

By the Committee of Estates the sum of 15,000 merks was voted to be paid out of his forfeited estates to Lord Kirkcudbright's regiment, for the good service which they had rendered at Pil . . . ch [? Philiphaugh].   In that regiment James Agnew, brother of Andrew Agnew, apparent of Lochnaw, was colonel, and John M'Dougall major.   After the death of Colonel James Agnew, his brother Andrew, as his executor, and John M'Dougall, presented a petition to

[1] Spalding's Memorials, etc., vol. ii. p. 430.
[2] Account of the losses of John Lord Herries for his loyalty to King Charles the First.   At Terregles.

Parliamentary Report of his losses in Acts of the Parliaments of Scotland, vol. vii. p. 345.

the Lords Commissioners of Parliament, craving warrant to summon before the House Lord Herries and Archibald M'Kie, quarter-master of the said regiment, to answer for non-payment to the complainers of their respective proportion of the above sum.   The petition is undated, but on it is indorsed a warrant by the Committee of Estates, dated at Edinburgh, 26th February 1649, to warn the said parties to compear before the House, or a Committee thereof, on 3d April following, to answer to the complaint; and also an execution of the warrant.[1]

Of that sum the proportion due to Lieutenant-Colonel James Agnew for the arrears which the Committee of Estates owed him was 3750 merks.

On 10th August 1649 the Committee of Estates found that the money was justly due to Andrew Agnew; and Sir Robert Adair, at Glenluce, 19th October that year, gave full power to George Campbell, his captain-lieutenant, to pass to the lands of Lord Herries, with a competent number of his horse, and to remain there, taking free quarters from his lordship and his tenants, till payment was made of the foresaid sum, or till a sufficient discharge was produced to him, under the hand of Andrew Agnew or others concerned. The greater part of the money was paid shortly after by Lord Herries, who obtained a discharge, dated at Dumfries, 8th November that year, from George Campbell, for the sum of 2400 merks, which his Lordship paid to him on behalf of Andrew Agnew of Lochnaw.

In the year 1651, before the King's army marched over the Borders to Worcester, Captain Crackinthorpe and his whole troop lay twenty days in Lord Herries's house upon free quarters.   Immediately thereafter Major Bethell came with his troop and lay fourteen days at Lord Herries's house.   On the same day that he removed, Captain Hallard came with his troop of 140 horse and lay for three days.   After his removal Lieutenant Carter, with 90 horse, took quarters for fifteen days.   Thereafter Captain Wayne took quarters with a troop of 80 dragoons for ten days.[2]

In the course of the same year the Master of Herries and others had a sharp skirmish with one Major Scott and fourteen score horse, whom they appear to have routed near the Castle of Glencairn.   Robert Maxwell of Tinwald was killed there, and the Master was wounded in the arm by a shot.[3]

[1] Original Petition at Terregles.

[2] Account of the losses of John Lord Herries, ut supra.   Parliamentary Report of his losses in Acts of Parliaments of Scotland, vol. vii. p. 345.

[3] Sibbald's MS., Advocates' Library.

Lord Herries's estate was burdened with heavy debts. Great sums were ordained to be paid out of it in fines. His whole rent had been uplifted for the public use for three years, and a great part of it was also liferented. Under such circumstances his pecuniary difficulties must have been great. He therefore presented a petition to the Committee of Estates praying for some relief. In compliance with his petition, the Committee of Estates, to relieve him of a part of his fines, assigned to him what was not accounted for by the Commissaries in their intromissions with his rents. Forced by his necessities to have recourse again to the Committee of Estates, he presented to them another petition, dated 29th February 1648, in which he humbly prayed that the Committee would assign to him the bond by which they had bound his mother to make yearly payment of £600 to the public, out of the readiest of her liferent income derived from the petitioner's estate. This would be a means of subsistence to himself and his family, and would preserve them from ruin. The Committee having considered the petition, and also a report of a sub-committee upon it, assigned to him their right to the bond, the first year of the grant from his mother's liferents to begin for the crop 1647.[1]

From memoranda, written after the Restoration,[2] as to certain legal matters between John Lord Herries and Alice Maxwell, daughter of James Maxwell, his Lordship's uncle, it would appear that the mother of Alice, an Englishwoman, had used her influence with the English to send a troop of horse to Terregles in the late troubles, and to compel Lord Herries to enter into certain obligations which he considered unjust.[3]

He was also imprisoned at the instance of Alice Maxwell for an alleged debt. This appears from a petition, undated, but before the year 1659, which he presented to the Commissioners for Administration of Justice to the people of Scotland, complaining that he had been incarcerated for nearly nine months in the Tolbooth of Edinburgh, at the instance of Alice Maxwell, for an alleged debt, and craving that his case might be heard and that he might be set at liberty.

Lord Herries was a member of the first Parliament of King Charles the Second, which met at Edinburgh, 1st January 1661.[4]

---

[1] Extract Act at Terregles.
[2] Dated 9th June 1665.
[3] Original Memoranda at Terregles.
[4] The Acts of the Parliaments of Scotland, vol. vii. p. 4.

To this Parliament he presented a petition, dated 22d May 1661, humbly praying that they would appoint some of their number to cognosce upon his sufferings, for his loyalty and obedience to the King in his person, means, and estate, upon every revolution since the year 1638, and to make report, that thereafter they might be recorded in the books of Parliament. The Marquis of Montrose, the Earl of Roxburgh, the Lord President of the Session, the Lord Carden, the Provost of Edinburgh, and John Bell, Provost of Glasgow, or any four of them, were appointed to try the petitioner's losses, and to report to the Parliament.[1] A report of the losses of Lord Herries was presented and read in Parliament, 12th July 1661, by this Committee. His losses were estimated to amount to the sum of £77,322, 12s. Scots, besides the insupportable burden of cess and quarterings, to which he was liable with the rest of the kingdom during the late unhappy troubles.

Lord Herries also presented to the Parliament a petition, craving that Sir Andrew Agnew of Lochnaw should be ordered to repay him 3750 merks, unjustly taken by him in virtue of a decreet of the Committee of Estates in 1649, with interest, and to make compensation for other injuries. On the 5th of September 1662, the Lords of the Articles remitted the petition to the Earls of Dumfries and Galloway, who were to speak with the parties, and report to next meeting.[2]

Lord Herries was a member of the Convention of Estates, held at Edinburgh 2d August 1665.[3]

On the death of Robert, second Earl of Nithsdale, 5th October 1667, Lord Herries became third Earl of Nithsdale.

By an ordinance of the Privy Council of Scotland, it was forbidden to transport horses out of the kingdom of Ireland to Scotland under pain of confiscation. Notwithstanding this prohibition, sundry persons brought twenty-four horses out of the kingdom of Ireland within the stewartry of Kirkcudbright. The Earl of Nithsdale, steward of that stewartrie, having permitted them to carry these horses along with them, and to make use of them to their best advantage, they bound themselves, by a bond dated 29th May 1668, to procure from the Lords of his Majesty's Treasury a sufficient

---

[1] The Acts of the Parliaments of Scotland, vol. vii. p. 345. [2] Original Petition at Terregles. [3] The Acts of the Parliaments of Scotland, vol. vii. p. 527.

acquittance for their bringing over horses from Ireland, contrary to the public laws of the kingdom.[1]

A special part of the policy of the Government of Charles the Second was to put down conventicles held by the ejected ministers, which it was alleged not only fomented and nourished separation and schism, but tended to sedition and the disturbance of the public peace. To suppress these meetings in the shire of Wigton and the stewartry of Kirkcudbright, the Lords of the Privy Council of Scotland addressed a letter, dated at Edinburgh, 4th March 1669, to John Earl of Nithsdale, or to his son, Robert Lord Maxwell, as being commissioners of the militia of the said shire and stewartry. The Earl and his son were to communicate the letter to the rest of the commissioners of the militia of the shire and stewartry.

The letter required them to inform themselves as to any conventicles that had been kept since the 1st of November last, or that should be kept thereafter, and to call before them the ministers who had preached at them, or the heritors or substantial tenants who had been present, or whose children had been baptized by persons not authorized by the Church since that date, and to take caution of them, should they be found guilty, for their appearance before the Council whenever they should be called. Should any of them, on being called before his Lordship and the rest of the commissioners, not compear, or compearing, refuse to give caution, the commissioners, with the advice and concurrence of the captain, lieutenant, or cornets of the troops of the said shire and stewartry, were to seize upon such persons, and send them to the Council by a party of the militia, along with the proofs of their guilt.

The Lords of Council ordained that the said commissioners should give an account of their diligence to the Council against the 6th of April next.[2]

On 6th April 1670, John Earl of Nithsdale, Lord Maxwell and Herries, was retoured at Edinburgh, as heir of Robert Earl of Nithsdale (father of the deceased Robert Earl of Nithsdale), grandson of the deceased Robert Lord Maxwell, who was brother-german of John Lord Herries, great grandfather of the said noble Earl, John, now Earl of Nithsdale, Lord Maxwell and Herries, in the lands and barony of Carlaverock and Locherwood, the lands of Springkel, Naeton and Logane, in the stewartry of Annandale, with the office of steward

---

[1] Original Bond at Terregles.   [2] Vol. ii. pp. 55, 56.

of the stewartry of Kirkcudbright, the lands of Carnsalloch, Durousquhen, and superiority of the £5 lands of old extent in the territory of the burgh of Dumfries; the lands of Balmacruichie in the shire of Perth, with many other lands in the shire of Roxburgh and stewartry of Kirkcudbright, all united into the lordship and barony of Maxwell; the lands and barony of Tynewall, etc., and the lands of Munreith, in the shire of Wigton; the lands of Duncow, the lands of Keir, with the salmon-fishings in the water of Nith, the lands of Bardannoches, Kirkbryde, etc., within the barony of Holywood; the lands of Kirkconnell in the parish of Kirkconnell and stewartry of Annandale, and many other lands in the stewartries of Annandale and Kirkcudbright, and shires of Roxburgh and Wigton, all united into the earldom of Nithsdale.[1]

On 14th May following, John Earl of Nithsdale was, on a precept of sasine by King Charles the Second, infefted in the said earldom of Nithsdale.[2]

John Earl of Nithsdale was heritable steward of the stewartry of Kirkcudbright. His Lordship's depute having, in the discharge of the duties of this office, tried and condemned John Allan in Glensoan, a common and notorious thief, for several thefts, Allan raised an advocation before his Majesty's justice on the ground that neither Lord Herries, nor any steward in Scotland, had power to judge theft upon citation, but only as barons might do, when the person tried had been taken "red hand." The case was called before the Lord Justice-Clerk and Mr. William Murray, depute to his Majesty's Justice-General. Lord Herries answered that, being his Majesty's immediate officer within the stewartry of Kirkcudbright, which was his Majesty's property, as were all other stewartries in the kingdom, he had sufficient authority to judge theft upon citation as well as red hand. He offered to prove that, in all time past, the stewards of Kirkcudbright and all other stewards were wont so to do, nor was it ever heard that the steward of his Majesty's proper lands had no more power than a baron. The Justice-Clerk and depute, however, sustained Allan's argument, repelled the answer, and discharged Lord Herries and his deputes from judging the same. To this judgment Lord Herries objected, affirming that it involved the utter ruin and overthrow of his jurisdiction and of that of all stewards and sheriffs, whose interest and jurisdiction were hereby brought in question. He accordingly presented a petition, un-

---

[1] Original Retour at Terregles.   [2] Original Instrument of Sasine at Terregles.

dated, but indorsed 1670, to the Estates of Parliament, craving the reduction of the interlocutor.[1]

John Earl of Nithsdale attended the second session of the second Parliament of King Charles the Second, held at Edinburgh, 22d July 1670.[2]

This Earl received a commission from the Lords of the Privy Council, dated 27th July 1671, appointing him, in execution of the sixteenth Act of his Majesty's second Parliament, overseer for the repairing of highways and bridges within the stewartry of Kirkcudbright. The commission invested him with power to convene the justices of peace and commissioners of excise of the stewartry, at such diets and places as he should think fit, for putting the Act of Parliament in execution, and to impose fines on the absents. It also empowered him personally, or by a substitute, to visit the places where the highways needed to be changed, to design and form them, to be careful that they were of the required breadth, to cause all tenants, cottars, and their servants, work six days for each year, to inflict fines on such as refused or neglected to do their duty, to cause dykes or ditches to be made by the sides of the highways, and to punish those who should break and abuse them by ploughing or laying stones or rubbish upon them, the fines to be employed in repairing the highways of the stewartry.[3]

John Earl of Nithsdale, in a letter to James Duke of Buccleuch, dated 10th August 1671, complained that the sum of £5000, for which the barony of Langholm had been purchased from his predecessor, Robert, second Earl of Nithsdale, for the Duke of Buccleuch, had not been paid. The Duke in his reply to the Earl, in September following, pleaded that it was not long since he came of age and was in a legal capacity to meddle with any part of his estate in Scotland in his own name, and therefore had not yet had time to inquire into the transactions of his curators during his minority. He found by the agreement, made in June 1665, that his curators were to pay £5000 by three equal payments, but not till he had obtained a good and perfect title to that estate. Whether the non-performance of the condition was the reason why the money had not been paid he knew not, but he would require his commissioners to give his lordship all just satisfaction.[4]

[1] Original Petition at Terregles.
[2] The Acts of the Parliaments of Scotland, vol. viii. p. 3.
[3] Original Commission at Terregles.
[4] Vol. ii. p. 159.

The Earl subscribed a declaration as to the unlawfulness of subjects entering into leagues and covenants, dated at Houpheid, 7th May, the year not given, but before the year 1677. The other subscribers were Robert Lord Maxwell, John Maxwell of Breckandsyde, William Griersoune of Bargatoune, and Alexander Maxwell. They declared that they judged it unlawful for subjects, upon pretence of reformation or any other pretence whatsoever, to enter into leagues and covenants, or to take up arms against the King or those commissioned by him, and that all those gatherings, convocations, protestations, and erection and keeping of Council Tables, that were used in the late troubles, were unlawful and seditious. They further declared that the oaths, of which one was called The National Covenant, as sworn and explained in the year 1638 and thereafter, and the other, The Solemn League and Covenant, were unlawful oaths, and were taken by and imposed on the subjects of this kingdom, contrary to its fundamental laws and liberties, and that there lay no obligation on them or any of the subjects from the said oaths, to make any alteration of the government either in Church or State, as then established.[1]

In a gift by King Charles the Second, under the Privy Seal, at Edinburgh, 19th February 1675, to Sir David Dunbar of Baldoon, knight-baronet, of the non-entries, mails, and duties of the earldom of Nithsdale, for the time that they had been in non-entry, the mails and duties of that earldom are said to have been in non-entry since the decease of Robert Earl of Nithsdale, in the Isle of Man, in May 1646. In this gift there was excepted the barony of Langholm, belonging to the Duke and Duchess of Buccleuch, and acquired by them or their predecessors, by wadset or otherwise, from the Earls of Nithsdale.[2]

In the Library of the Faculty of Advocates, there is preserved a manuscript, which bears on the title-page to be " An Abridgement of the Regne of Queen Marie, faithfully copied from the Abridgement of the Scotish History by Lord Herreis, whose MSS. lays in the Scots Colledge of Douay, in Flanders." On the other side of the page the transcriber has given what appears to have been the title of the original work from which his copy was made, as follows : " An Abridgement of the Scotishe historie, from the first foundation untill our tyms, collected with great integritie—Beginning first with a breefe description of all the Ils belonging to the Croune of Scotland.

[1] Original Declaration.   [2] Original Gift at Terregles.

Signed Herreis, 1656." After this title he has written, "What follows is copied verbatim from the original manuscript of Lord Herreis, beginning by the regne of Q. Marie, pagina 310 of the MSS., and ends pagina 436. The Queen's death is related, page 501. And Lord Herreis continues his abridgement down till the year 1631. The whole MSS. is of 624 pages."

The original MS. probably perished, with many others belonging to the Scots College at Douay, during the first French Revolution. The copy which is preserved in Edinburgh was printed for the Abbotsford Club in 1836, under the title, "Historical Memoirs of the Reign of Queen Mary of Scots, and a portion of the Reign of King James the Sixth, by Lord Herries."

The author appears to have had access to important historical authorities; but, unfortunately, his transcriber has curtailed various portions of his narrative on the ground of the author's prolixity,—in some cases "cutting short his labour of transcription by a flourish of his pen, and an etc., etc." Had he been more conscientious in transcribing details we might have been better able to judge of the author's sources of information, and it may be also of his identity.

Tradition has attributed the original work to John Lord Herries, afterwards third Earl of Nithsdale; and Abercromby in his Martial Achievements of the Scots Nation, published in 1715, names him as the author of it. But Father James Hudson, who was born in the year 1665, and was a contemporary of the third Earl of Nithsdale, thus describes the Manuscript History in a letter to Lady Nithsdale, written on the 25th of June 1743 :[1]—"My freind brought me also a large manuscript book with this title : History of Scotland by my lord Herreis, which would make a large quarto as big as the whole Bible. I begun to peruse it, but was forc'd to give it over. For it is all writ in that hand which was used in Scotland 150 years ago, and therefor would require one of our writers in Edinburgh to read and copy it. A great pity that it should thus ly unprinted. But alas! This would require both one that could read and understand the old manuscript, and also one that could turn it into good English."[2]

---

[1] Father Hudson was a correspondent of Lady Nithsdale during her exile, and several of his letters are printed in the second volume. A notice of this Father is given at p. 174 of that volume.

[2] Original Letter at Everingham Park.

If Father Hudson was right in the date which he assigned to the writing, the History, if written by a Lord Herries, must have been by one of this Lord's predecessors, but in the absence of the original manuscript, nothing satisfactory can now be determined as to the real author. It is much to be regretted that a work, the author of which must have had great knowledge of the History of Scotland, should now only be known by the meagre abstract of it which is preserved in the Library of the Faculty of Advocates.

A good many letters which the Earl wrote to his Countess in the course of his life, particularly in the years 1655 and 1656, and in which he goes into detail about many minor matters, have been preserved at Terregles. But these it has not been considered necessary to print.

After enjoying the title and estates of Herries for thirty-five years, and afterwards the earldom of Nithsdale and the Maxwell estates for eleven years, John, third Earl of Nithsdale, died between the months of February and June 1677. He had by his Countess, Elizabeth Gordon, three sons :—

1. Robert, who succeeded him as fourth Earl of Nithsdale.

2. John Maxwell. Under the designation of second lawful son to John Lord Herries, he was an attesting witness to a bond by his father, dated 20th July 1653.[1] He married Elizabeth, daughter and heiress of William Glendoning of Gelston, in the stewartry of Kirkcudbright. Of that marriage the only issue was a daughter, Elizabeth Maxwell, who succeeded her uncle, William of Kelton. John Maxwell died between the 1st of January and 17th July 1658, when Elizabeth Glendoning is charged for mournings for his burial.[2] Elizabeth Maxwell married Robert Maxwell of Kirkhouse. By a disposition, dated 8th April 1685, and registered in the Books of Council and Session on the 24th of August of the same year, they assigned to William Earl of Nithsdale and Lady Mary Maxwell, his sister, all lands belonging to Elizabeth Maxwell. Elizabeth Glendoning married, secondly (contract dated 26th April 1659), Thomas, third son of Robert Maxwell of Orchardton, and had issue, in 1692, seven children.[3]

[1] Printed Inventory of the Nithsdale Muniments, etc. Edinburgh, 1865, p. 288, No. 639.

[2] *Ibid.* p. 292, No. 658, p. 293, No. 664, and p. 318, No. 9.

[3] Records of Sheriff-Court at Kirkcudbright.

3. William Maxwell of Kelton and Buittle, in the stewartry of Kirkcudbright. A letter from him to Robert, first Earl of Nithsdale, is
printed in the Second Volume of this Work. The writer complains of the severity used towards him at the date of the letter
in 1641. He married, contract dated 30th June 1674, Agnes
Gordon, eldest lawful daughter of Alexander Viscount Kenmure,[1]
died in 1684, without issue, and was succeeded by his niece,
Elizabeth Maxwell, daughter of his brother John. Agnes Gordon,
"Lady Kelton," survived her husband, and married, secondly,
John Lindsay of Wauchope.[2]

[1] Original Marriage Contract at Kenmure.

[2] John Earl of Nithsdale had also a natural son, John Maxwell, who is so designated in a Suspension dated 11th September 1657.—[Inventory of the Nithsdale Muniments, etc. Edinburgh, 1865, p. 291, No. 657.]

SEAL OF JOHN LORD HERRIES, AFTERWARDS THIRD EARL OF NITHSDALE, 1656.

SIGNATURE OF JOHN, THIRD EARL OF NITHSDALE, 1668.

XXI. ROBERT, FOURTH EARL OF NITHSDALE.

LADY LUCIE DOUGLAS, HIS COUNTESS.

1677-1683.

ROBERT MAXWELL, eldest son and heir of John, third Earl of Nithsdale, was born about the close of the year 1627, or the beginning of the year 1628. When little more than three years of age, he became Master of Herries, on his father's succeeding to the estates and titles of the barony of Herries.

Under the designation of Robert Master of Herries, he obtained from King Charles the Second a commission, dated Whitehall, 1st January 1667, appointing him a lieutenant in the Earl of Annandale's troop of horse in Lieutenant-General Drummond's regiment. It is superscribed by the King, and subscribed by the Earl of Lauderdale as Secretary of State.[1]

In the same year his father became third Earl of Nithsdale, and his eldest son was thereafter known as Lord Maxwell. Two years thereafter, Lord Maxwell married Lady Lucie Douglas, youngest daughter of William Marquis of Douglas and Dame Mary Gordon, Marchioness of Douglas. Their marriage contract is dated at Edinburgh and Terregles, 6th and 25th March 1669. In the contract John Earl of Nithsdale became bound to infeft Robert Lord Maxwell, his eldest son and apparent heir, and Lady Lucie Douglas, his spouse, in conjunct fee, and the heirs-male of their bodies, whom failing, Lord Maxwell's nearest heirs-male and assignees, in the lands and barony of Kirkgunzeon, the castle, patronage of the church, etc., thereof, under reservation of the granter's own liferent of that patronage and of the superiority of the said barony, and excluding Lady Lucie Douglas therefrom in the event of her surviving her said husband. These lands, exclusive of the patronage and superiority, were warranted to be worth 4000 merks yearly. Failing heirs-male of the marriage, the Earl became bound to pay to the heirs-female certain sums specified.

---

[1] Original Commission at Terregles.

William Duke of Hamilton paid to Robert Lord Maxwell, in name of tocher, with his sister, Lady Lucie Douglas, the sum of 9000 merks.[1]

During the reign of King Charles the Second, as well as during that of his brother King James the Seventh, the condition of Scotland was very unsettled and unhappy. The enforcement of ecclesiastical conformity by civil penalties was unfortunately the policy of the Government, and this gave rise to oppressions which provoked to insurrection. In the year 1666 a party of the Nonconformists took up arms. They were defeated 28th November that year at Pentland hills, and many of them were forfeited in their lives and fortunes and declared to be fugitives. These measures, however, only stimulated them to more fearless and determined resistance. Conventicles were more frequent, and ultimately preaching in the fields became not uncommon. An Act was passed by the Parliament in 1670, prohibiting house conventicles under severe penalties, and making it a capital crime to preach at field conventicles, or to convocate the people to such meetings. The Act empowered and commanded sheriffs, stewards of stewartries, lords of regalities and their deputies to call before them and to try all such persons, and to give effect to the Act in its various provisions.

For the repression of conventicles, the heritors of the county and the magistrates of the burgh of Dumfries were required, by a letter addressed by the Privy Council to the Commissioners of Excise for that county, on the 20th of March 1672, to raise forty-one men as their proportion of 1000 who were to be levied in the kingdom for his Majesty's service. A committee, with Lord Maxwell as its president, was appointed to give effect to the Council's orders. The committee reported that the burgh of Dumfries would have to "outreik" and provide two men, and also "the twentieth part of a third man," for assisting the burghs of Annan, Sanquhar, and Lochmaben, who with this assistance were to raise that third man. The remaining thirty-eight soldiers were to be provided by the county.[2]

A commission was given by the Lords of the Committee for Church Affairs, appointed by the Privy Council, to Robert Lord Maxwell for apprehending such of those who were forfeited or declared to be fugitives for their

[1] Original Contract at Terregles.
[2] Minutes of the Commissioners, quoted in Mr. M'Dowall's History of Dumfries, p. 474.

accession to the late rebellion as might be found in the stewartry of Kirkcud-bright, and to do his utmost for the suppression and prevention of conventicles in those bounds. The commission is as follows :—

Edinburgh, the tuenty fyft day of July 1673.

The Lords of the Committie appointed by the Lord Commissioner his Grace and Lords of his Majestie's Privy Councill for church affaires, being informed that diverse persons who were forfault or declared fugitives for being in the rebellion in the year 1666 doe haunt and resort within the Stewartrie of Kirkcudburgh, are resett therein by severall persons, and that late have keeped numerous conventicles, and committed severall other disorders, Doe, conform to the power granted to them, give full power, authority and commission to Robert Lord Maxwell to passe, persew, take and apprehend the persons vnderwrytten, viz., Welsh of Cornlie, Welsh of Scarr, George Rome of Beoch, and Thomas Lennox of Pluntoun, and furthwith to send them in prisoners to the Tolbuith of Edinburgh : As also to search for, seize and apprehend any other persons haunting in the said Stewartrie who were forfaulted or declared fugitives for being in the said rebellion, and to secure them in the nixt convenient prisons vntill they be brought to justice : And farder, the saides lordes doe hereby authorise and requyre the said Lord Maxwell to vse his outmost indevoures and power for suppressing and preventing of conventicles in these boundes, and for that effect to call and persew all persons therein who are guilty of keeping of conventicles, and to putt the lawes in vigorous execution against them, alse weill heretors as others : And for the better execution hereof the saids lordes doe impower the said Lord Maxwell, from tyme to tyme, as he shall judge necessary, to call together the militia troup in the said Stewartrie vnder his command, or such part thereof as he shall think necessar, who are hereby commanded to obey such orders as they shall receaue from him ; and ordaines all magistratts of burghes and justices of peace to be aiding and assisting to him herein, as they shall be requyred, and generally all and sundry other thinges necessar to doe and perform for the better execution of this commission.

St. Andrews.	ROTHES, Cancell :	JA: DALRYMPLE.
	HAMILTON.	CH: MAITLAND.
	TWEEDDALE.	A. PRIMEROSE.
	DUNDONALD.	JO: NISBET.[1]

Some money and jewels having been stolen from the Marchioness of Douglas, Lord Maxwell succeeded in recovering them from the thief by whom they had been stolen. On returning them he obtained a receipt, dated 29th July 1675, from William Duke of Hamilton, as factor for his brother, Lord James Douglas. These articles included a jewel, two seal rings, three small rings, "five jacobus, three whole carolus, and two half-carolus," a double rose-noble, two Spanish pieces, one double and two single ducats, three five-merk pieces, two five-shilling sterling pieces, and a two-merk-and-a-half piece. Acknowledgment is also made of the receipt from Lord Maxwell of a ticket

[1] Original Commission at Terregles.

for six guineas and fifteen merk-pieces, payable to the said Lord James upon demand,—these being a part of the gold recovered from the thief.[1]

A commission, dated 13th February 1677, was again given by the Privy Council to Lord Maxwell, for the suppression of conventicles. It invested him with full power to apprehend outed ministers or preachers who kept conventicles, or substantial persons who had been present at them, in any place within the shires of Dumfries and Wigton and stewartry of Kirkcudbright. It also empowered him to disperse or apprehend them by force of arms, in case of resistance, conform to the Acts of Parliament and Council; and to imprison them in the nearest convenient prison until his Majesty's Privy Council were acquainted with their names and gave orders concerning them. The Privy Council at the same time recommended to Sir William Sharp to give commission to Lord Maxwell to uplift the fine of 5000 merks Scots imposed upon the parish of Dunscore for the robbery of the minister thereof; to put the letters of horning and caption raised against the parishioners in execution; and to pay to the cash-keeper out of the first and readiest of his intromissions £1000 Scots, which were appointed to be paid as damages to that minister.[2]

On the resignation of his father, John Earl of Nithsdale, Robert Lord Maxwell obtained a charter, dated 16th February 1677, from King Charles the Second, of the lands, lordships, baronies, mills, woods, fishings, offices, tithes, patronages of benefices and chapels, and superiorities, belonging to the earldom of Nithsdale, as particularly described in his father's retour as heir to Robert Earl of Nithsdale, to be held of the Crown in feu and heritage for ever, for the payments therein mentioned.[3]

As Lord Maxwell he gave a precept, dated at Edinburgh, 23d February 1677, directing the Duke and Duchess of Monmouth to pay to Sir Thomas Wallace of Craigie, knight-baronet, Lord Justice-Clerk, 4000 merks, with the annual rent due to him out of the amount owing by them to his father, John Earl of Nithsdale and himself, as specified in a minute of agreement between the said Duke and Duchess.[4]

On 29th June same year, under the designation of Robert Earl of Nithsdale, his father being then dead, he was infefted in the lands and baronies, etc.,

---

[1] Original Receipt at Terregles.
[2] Extract Commission from Records of Privy Council, ibid.
[3] Original Charter of Resignation at Terregles.
[4] Original Precept, ibid.

belonging to the earldom of Nithsdale, at the Castle of Carlaverock, the principal messuage of the earldom.[1]

As Steward of Kirkcudbright this Earl had accounts to settle in the Exchequer. This he had not got done by reason of the death of George Maxwell of Munches, Steward-depute, and of Thomas Bontin, one of the under clerks, in whose hands there were left by Munches some receipts and discharges not yet recovered. Being under a charge of horning to come and outred the Exchequer accounts, he was very desirous to do it, but could not without protection of the Lord Commissioner and the Lords of His Majesty's Treasury and Exchequer from captions and acts of wardening that were against him for civil debts. He therefore presented a petition to them, praying to be allowed some competent time to come and obey the Exchequer's charge, and that all personal execution against him at the instance of creditors and others should in the meantime be discharged. The Lords granted at Edinburgh, 14th June 1678, protection to the petitioner until the 15th day of August next to come.[2]

He was a member of the Convention of Estates held at Edinburgh, 26th June 1678.[3]

He obtained from King Charles the Second, under the Privy Seal, a grant of a pension of £200 sterling *per annum*, dated at Whitehall, 28th September same year.[4]

Reference is made by Colonel John Grahame of Claverhouse in one of his letters to the apprehension of a minister by the Earl of Nithsdale :—" There is here [in Dumfries] in prison a minister [who] was taken above a year agoe by my Lord Nidsdelle, and by the well affected magistrats of this [town], has had the liberty of an open prison ; and mor conventicles has been keept by him there, than has been in any on house of the kingdom. This is a great abuse ; and if the magistrats be not punished, at least the man ought not to be suffered any longer here, for that prison is more frequented than the kirk."[5]

In the year 1679 the Covenanters again took up arms against the Government. To suppress them the Government were energetic in raising

[1] Original Instrument of Sasine at Terregles.
[2] Original Petition, *ibid.*
[3] The Acts of the Parliaments of Scotland, vol. viii. p. 213.
[4] Original Grant at Terregles.
[5] Letters of John Grahame of Claverhouse, Viscount of Dundee, printed for the Bannatyne Club, 1826, p. 19.

forces. The Earl of Nithsdale received instructions on 6th June that year to call together the whole gentlemen, heritors and freeholders in the shire of Wigton and stewartry of Kirkcudbright, with as many servants and followers as they could bring out on horse with arms, and to march straight to Edinburgh.[1] Other noblemen received similar instructions.

The Covenanters were defeated at the battle of Bothwell Bridge, fought on the 22d of June that year.

This was followed by a vigorous prosecution of all who were known to have been in the rebellion, or who were assisters or resetters of the rebels, before the Court of Justiciary. Among the papers preserved at Terregles is a " Memorandum to the Earl of Nithsdale of the heritors and wadsetters within the stewartry and shire of Galloway, that lifted arms at the late rebellion," with lists of witnesses against rebels in Dumfries and Kirkcudbright and shire of Wigton.

In a Memorandum to libel those who were at the late rebellion, or who advised, reset, or assisted by furnishing horse and arms to the rebels, it is said that William Welsh of Scar was in the rebellion, or at least furnished a horse for "outreiking" James Welsh, his brother, who rode with the Galloway party upon the said horse the length of Dumfries about six miles, and that the said William and James Welsh had often since reset and harboured the deceased Mr. John Welsh, a notorious traitor and others, for which they ought to be forfeited. These Memoranda appear to have been sent to the Earl of Nithsdale.

A Commission, dated 26th March 1680, was granted by the Lords of the Committee of the Privy Council for public affairs, to him and the Laird of Broughton, giving them, or any one of them, full power to apprehend any persons who, as they were informed, could be witnesses against any of those landed men in the shire of Wigton or stewartry of Kirkcudbright, who were in the rebellion ; to examine them and take their declaration in writing, but not upon oath. The Earl of Nithsdale and the Laird of Broughton were to send in the examinations of these witnesses to the King's Advocate or solicitor with all diligence, to take sufficient caution of such of the witnesses as could find it for their appearance before the justices, and to imprison such as could not find caution until they were sent to Edinburgh to bear witness. This Commission is subscribed by the Earl of Murray, Sir George M'Kenzie, and three other Councillors.[2]

---

[1] Wodrow's History. vol. iii. p. 84.   [2] Original Commission at Terregles.

At Terregles, 20th October 1681, the Earl made a disposition in favour of William Lord Maxwell, his only lawful son, and his heirs-male and assignees, heritably and irredeemably, of the office of steward of the stewartry of Kirkcudbright, under reservation of the Earl's liferent.[1]

In carrying out the policy of the Government against the Nonconformists, John Graham of Claverhouse, afterwards Viscount Dundee, was a conspicuous actor. He obtained a commission, dated 31st January 1682, to be sheriff of Wigton. In this capacity he was to call before him and his deputes and to punish such as were guilty of the ecclesiastical disorders of withdrawing from their parish churches, attending conventicles and resetting rebels in that shire, in the shire of Dumfries and in the stewartries of Kirkcudbright and Annandale.[2]

To assist Claverhouse in this enterprise, the Earl of Nithsdale supplied to him or his depute a memorandum, which is here subjoined :—

MEMORANDUM from the EARLE OF NITHISDAILL to the LAIRD OF CLAIVERHOUSE or his depute.

First. That he wold be pleased either to call a court himselfe, as sheriff of Wigtoun, or cause his deput ; and cite in the possessors of any lands belonging to Eiri-olland, and particularlie the mill and milltoun ; as also the possessors of the mains of Eiri-olland ; as also the lands of Chang, the yearlie rent of it, and what wedsets is wpon it ; as also to cite in witnesses what other lands is in present in possessione of Sir William Maxwell of Monrith, which formarlie belonged to Eiri-olland : As also to take inspection of the lands of Cullwhasin and Baccaskin, of which lands Alexander Hunter was heritor before Bodwell brigg :[3] as also to take inspection of the twa parts of Litle Eiries, belonging to Andrew Martin : As also the lands of Drumbuy, to witt, wha possesseth them as tennants, and wha claims them in heritage for the present : And that the Sheriff or his deput wold be pleased to do this effectuallie, with there awne convenience : and return ane answer to the Earle of Nithisdaill, togidder with the depositions of the witnesses, signed be the judge and the deponents.

And to remember to cite in Dewarton what lands he is in possessione of or his breether, if he have any, and of whom he had the lands from, and how long they have bein in his possessione.

.To remember Captain Jhon M'Culloch to be on of the wittnesses in all particularis above specified.

---

[1] Original Disposition at Terregles.

[2] Wodrow's History, vol. iii. p. 370.

[3] Wodrow records, on the authority of written accounts from Galloway, that Alexander Hunter of Colquhasben, in the parish of Old Luce, in Galloway, who had been at Bothwell, was forfeited, and that his estate was given to the Countess of Nithsdale, and that she and hers possessed it till the year 1689.

He adds, that the lands of another neighbouring heritor, Alexander Hay of Ardwallen, who was forfeited for being at Bothwell Bridge, were given to the family of Nithsdale, and that a great many other forfeited estates of Presbyterian gentlemen in that country were gifted to that family.—Wodrow's History, vol. iii. p. 181.

Be pleased also, either your selfe, or cause som of your constituts, to convein   .   .   .
Rome, old Lady Holme, and her eldest son, for resett of ministers and feild conventicles ; and if possible to find her guiltie of fyneing.

Item, to secure the persones contiened in this list who arre alreadie citted as witnesses untill they giue band, ilk ane of them, under such a penaltie as yow think fit, that they shall appeare before the justice generall, justice clerck, or lords of justiciarie, att Edinburgh, the eleventh of December next, in obedience to the citatione giuen them, to beare witnes in the summons of treasone raised at the instance of his majestie's aduocat against severall persons in the shire and stewartrie of Galloway.[1]

In place of the pension of £200 per annum granted to the Earl by King Charles the Second, his Majesty gave orders, in a letter to the Lords Commissioners of his Treasury for Scotland, dated 29th April 1682, that a royal grant should be made to him of as much land out of the estates of the rebels within the shire of Wigton and stewartry of Kirkcudbright as would yield a free yearly rent of 4000 merks Scots, besides the payment of such portion of his annual rent as was then in arrears.

The letter is in the following terms :—

CHARLES R.

Right trusty and right welebeloved cousins and councellours, and right trusty and well beloved councellours, wee greet yow well. Whereas some years agoe wee were graciously pleased to grant unto our right trusty and well beloved cousine, Robert Earle of Nithisdale, a yearly pension of 200 lb. sterline money, whereof (as wee are informed) there is a considerable arrear as yet due to him : and wee, now, out of our farther bounty and Royall favour towards the said Earle, being resolved, in liew and place of the said pension, to grant unto him heretably so much land of the estates of rebells within the shyre of Wigtoun and Stewartrie of Kirkcudbright, whither already forfeited and not disposed of, or hitherto concealed, as in yearly rent will amount to the sum of four thousand merks Scots money, free of all burdens : It is our will and pleasure, and wee doe hereby authorize and requyre you, in the first place to pay, or cause to be payed unto him furthwith, so much as remaines in arrears of his said pension, and that, after your takeing first cognition and tryall of the yearly extent and value of the saids lands, you send up a signature containing our grant thereof in his favours, not exceeding the said sum of four thousand merks of yearly rent, free of all burdens, to be signed by us here ; or yourselves to grant a valide right and security thereof unto him by vertue of the commission formerly granted by us unto yow, for the sale and disposall of all forfeited estates as his lawyers shall advyse and desyre as fittest for his security. In the meantyme it is our expresse pleasure that his said yearly pension of two hundred pound sterline be punctually paied in time comeing, untill he shall be legally and effectually secured in the saids lands, after which wee doe hereby ordaine the said gift of pension to termine and be voyd. For all which this shall be your warrant, and so wee bid yow heartily

---

[1] Original Memorandum at Terregles.

farewell. Given at our Court at Windsor Castle the 29th day of Aprile 1682, and of our reigne the 34th year. By his Majestie's command,

MORRAY.

Direct to The Lords Commissioners
  of His Majestie's Thesaurarie.

[Bot] by the 11 Article of his Majestie's additionall Instructions to the Treasurer or Treasurer Depute, dated 14th June 1684, they are enjoyned as followes :—

You are to cause the Countes of Nithisdale rest satisfied with her pension or (at her option) to take herselfe to the gift of forfeiturs, granted by us to that familie, seeing wee are resolved not to allow both.[1]

Robert, fourth Earl of Nithsdale, executed his last will and testament at Terregles, on 7th August 1682. In it he appointed tutors to his two children, William and Mary, and ordained that his Countess should have the custody and education of his two children during her widowhood and their minority. The document is as follows :—

WE, Robert Earle of Nithsdaill, Lord Maxuell, Herries, Eskdaill, and Cairlyll, etc., being seik in bodie but perfyte in memorie, blissed be God! Doe make our lettir will and testament as follows :—Imprimis, We recommend our soull to God, hopeing to be saved by the merits of Jesus Chryst, our blissed Saviour and Redeemer, and ordeans our bodie to be honorablie buried, in Christiane maner, in our buriall place of Terreglis : Item, We nominat ane michtie and potent prince, William Duik of Hamiltoune, and, in caice of his deceas, [James] Earle of Arran and William Marques of Quenisberry, and, in caice of his deceis, James Lord Drumlangrig, his eldest sone, [John] Lord Carmichaell and Dame Lucie Douglas our countes, or any tuo of them, to be tutors to our childrein, William and Marie, and, in caice of the foirnamed persons non-acceptance, we nominat our said countess to be sole tutrix to them, and the foirnamed persones and [James] Marques of Douglas, [John] Marques of Atholl, Sir Robert Maxuell of Orcheardstoun, John Maxuell of Breckansyde, James Maxuell of Kirkconnell, Robert Maxuell of Carneselloche, to be assisters, advysers and ovirsiers to our said countes in the said office of tutorie ; and we ordeane our said countes to have the custody and educatione of our saids tuo childrein dureing hir widouity and ther minority ; and that our charter-chist be lykuayes keiped by hir dureing her widouitie : In witnes quhairof (written be John Gibsone, notar in Drumfreis) we have subscrivit thir presentis att Terreglis the sevint day of August j^m vi^c ffourscoir tua yeris, befoir thir witnesses, Allexander Herries, callit of Glaisters, and William Lindsay our servitors, and the said John Gibsone.

Alexander Herreis, witnes.   NITHSDAILL.[2]
William Lindsay, witnes.
J. Gibson, witnes.

Robert, fourth Earl of Nithsdale, died at Edinburgh, before 23d March 1683. On 2d April that year, one hundred merks were paid for the Earl's corpse

[1] Old copy of Warrant among Privy Council Warrants, etc., relative to Scotland, 1663-1684, in Queensberry volume MS. at Drumlanrig.   [2] Original Will at Terregles.

lying in the Abbey church at Holyrood.[1] His body was afterwards in-terred in the burial-place of the family at Terregles. There is amongst the papers at Terregles an account of the expenses of the funeral of the Earl. The account includes a charge—" For the barrell to put his bowells in."

He had by his Countess, Lady Lucie Douglas, an only son, William, born in the year 1676, who succeeded him as fifth Earl of Nithsdale, and two daughters, Anne, who died young and unmarried, and Mary, who became the wife of Charles, fourth Earl of Traquair. In a bond of provision, dated 20th June 1678, by the Earl in favour of Lady Mary, she is called his only daughter.[2]

The marriage of Mary with that Earl took place on Tuesday, 9th January 1694. Their marriage-contract is dated at the Canongate on the same day. Lucie Countess of Nithsdale thereby consented and took burden upon her for her daughter. The witnesses to the contract were William Earl of Nithsdale, James Maxwell of Kirkconnell, and William Alves, writer in Edinburgh.[3] William, third Duke of Hamilton, in a letter to Mary Countess of Traquair, dated London, 30th January 1693-4, congratulates her on her marriage, since it was to so worthy a man as he heard the Earl of Traquair was, though he had not the honour of his acquaintance.[4] To her mother as well as to her other relations this marriage must have been a source of great satisfaction.

This was not the first connexion between the Nithsdale and Traquair families. The Earl of Traquair's grandmother, on the mother's side, was Elizabeth Maxwell, daughter of William, sixth Lord Herries.

The Earl and Countess of Traquair had a large family of seventeen children, four sons and thirteen daughters. She had twice female twins. The sons were—

1. Charles, who was born on Wednesday 31st March 1697, and became fifth Earl of Traquair. He died in May 1764.[5] An engraving of his portrait has been made for this work from the original portrait at Traquair.

2. William, who was born on Sunday, 27th February 1698, and died, un-married, before 1764, when his younger brother succeeded the elder.

3. John, who was born on Friday, the 3d of February 1699, and

---

[1] Original Receipt at Terregles.
[2] Original Bond, *ibid.*
[3] Original Contract, *ibid.*
[4] Vol. ii. p. 161.
[5] Annual Register.

who succeeded his brother Charles as sixth Earl of Traquair in 1764. An engraving of his portrait is given in this work from the original portrait at Traquair.

4. Robert, who was born on Thursday, 9th February 1710.

The daughters were—

1. Lucie, who was born 18th February 1695. Elizabeth Howard, Duchess of Gordon, in a letter to Mary Countess of Traquair, dated 9th March that year, says, "I was extreamly glad to heare of your ladyship's hapy deliuery, and since of your recouery ; wishing you much joy of this litle lady, and that a young Lord may follow at the yeare's end."[1] In the second volume of this work are a number of interesting letters from this daughter to her mother from Paris, whither Lucie and her sister Anne had been sent, in the autumn of the year 1713, for their education in a conventual establishment in the French metropolis.[2] Lady Lucie died, unmarried, at Edinburgh on 12th April 1768.

2. Anne, who was born on Friday 6th March 1696, and died at Edinburgh on 5th April 1755.

3. Elizabeth, who was born on Monday, 12th February 1700. She probably died young, before the year 1706, when another daughter received the same name.

4. Winifred, who was born on Saturday, 7th June 1701.

5. Mary, who was born on Tuesday, 11th August 1702. She married John Drummond, styled Duke of Perth, who joined the standard of Prince Charles Edward in September 1745, and distinguished himself in almost every battle fought during that insurrection. Mary Duchess of Perth died without issue, at Edinburgh, on 4th February 1773.

6 and 7. Isabell and Jean (twins), who were born on Friday, 7th May 1703.

8. Catherine, who was born on Sunday, 4th March 1705. She married her cousin, William Lord Maxwell, son of William, fifth Earl of Nithsdale.

---

[1] Vol. ii. p. 163.   [2] Vol. ii. pp. 176, 181-186. 191-198.

9. Elizabeth second of the name, who was born on Monday, 5th August 1706.

10. Henrietta, who was born on Monday, 15th September 1707.

11 and 12. Barbara and Margaret (twins), who were born on Friday, 3d September 1708. On them the celebrated physician, Dr. Archibald Pitcairne, wrote Latin verses, "In Barbaram et Margaritam Caroli Stuarti Comitis de Traquair filias gemellas."

> Tertia Septembris vos orbi misit ovanti,
>   Et te, Cromwelli, dire tyranne ! Stygi.
> Quam gratum errorem matri patrique creatis,
>   Quam cupidos dabitis, quam timidosque procos.

Lady Barbara died unmarried at Edinburgh on 15th November 1794. Lady Margaret predeceased her, also unmarried, at Edinburgh, on 4th April 1791.

13. Louisa, who was born on Saturday, 27th October 1711.[1]

Dr. Archibald Pitcairne was the physician of the Traquair family. A number of medical prescriptions, written by him chiefly to Mary Countess of Traquair between the years 1697 and 1711, two years before his death, are preserved, along with a few letters from him,[2] among the family papers at Traquair. Some of the remedies prescribed are of a curious character. One of his letters to her we here give entire :—

Edinburgh, 7th January 1711.

MADAM,—I have thought most seriouslie about your Ladyship's question, and am convinced there is no sort of reason or ground to think the children have deriv'd their trouble from any fault in your Ladyship. Since your health is at present perfectlie good, I beg yow may continow it by being merrie and cheerful, making some travel in good weather, and beleiving still that the world shall grow better.

I have seen Dr. Stevenson and Dr. Balfour for preventing fits in children. Order a Betonie-plaister for their head as they were new-borne. I'm sure it did no harme.

I send the Earl a new-year's gift. There is always something got by plundring churches.—I am, your Ladyships most obedient and sincere humble servant,

A. PITCAIRNE.

To the Right Honourable the Countess of Traquair.[3]

Charles, fourth Earl of Traquair, died at Traquair on 13th June 1741, in the eighty-second year of his age.

---

[1] List of her children, by Mary Countess of Traquair, among Traquair Writs.

[2] One of his letters is printed in the Second Volume.   [3] Original Letter at Terregles.

In a letter from Lord John Drummond, afterwards styled Duke of Perth, to Thomas Drummond of Logiealmond, dated 8th August 1741, his Lordship refers in very favourable terms to his late father-in-law. Lord John makes his acknowledgments for the kind concern taken by his correspondent in the loss which Lady John Drummond had sustained in the death of her father. Lord John adds :—

Though it was foreseen by all of us a great while before it happened, and expected sooner than it did happen by the physicians who attended him, yet it gave a general concern to all who were acquainted with him, whether personally or by his caracter, and could not but be most afflicting to all his family and nearest relations. The notions people are prepossessed of in relation to merit, that it is immortal, and should never dye, makes us apt to think that such as are possessed of a most distinguished merit should be so too, and the shock to nature is greater when death snatches them from us, as their virtues and the lovelyness of their temper are more knowen and grow more familiar to us. He was religious without hypocrasie, generous without profusion, friendly without show or dissimulation, a most affectionate and loving husband, a kind father, and a good master, and a man of the strictest honour and loyalty in regard to his king and country. These qualitys, and a great many more, will ever make his memory dear to us, and to all honest men to whom now or hereafter they shall be make knowen.[1]

Mary Countess of Traquair survived her husband for eighteen years, having died at Edinburgh on Saturday, 22d September 1759, in the eighty-eighth year of her age. The following was the inscription on her tomb-stone :—

A

MONUMENTAL INSCRIPTION

SACRED TO THE MEMORY

OF

LADY MARY MAXWELL

COUNTESS DOWAGER OF TRAQUAIR

WHOSE DISTINGUISHED WORTH

COMMANDED THE ESTEEM OF

ALL WHO HAD THE HAPPINESS

OF

HER ACQUAINTANCE .

BEING FIRMLY GROUNDED IN THE FAITH

OF WHAT SHE THOUGHT

THE ONLY TRUE RELIGION

HER WHOLE BEHAVIOUR

WAS

---

[1] The Red Book of Grandtully, by Wm. Fraser, 1868, vol. ii. p. 348.

A BRIGHT EXAMPLE

OF THE SACRED PRECEPTS

OF

CHRISTIANITY .

SHE WAS

SINCERE AND WARM IN HER DEVOTION

EXTENSIVE AND UNAFFECTED IN HER BENEFICENCE

PIOUS WITHOUT ENTHUSIASM

CHARITABLE WITHOUT OSTENTATION

MEEK WITHOUT WEAKNESS

SHE DISCHARGED HER DUTY IN EVERY PERIOD

OF LIFE

WITH BECOMING INTEGRITY .

SHE WAS

AN OBEDIENT CHILD

A LOVING WIFE

AN AFFECTIONATE MOTHER

AN UNDISSEMBLING FRIEND

AND

(WHAT WAS GREATER THAN ALL)

SHE WAS

FORGIVING TO HER ENEMIES.

IT PLEASED

ALMIGHTY GOD

TO REMOVE HER FROM OUR VALE OF TEARS

ON SATURDAY, SEPTEMBER 22D 1759

IN THE EIGHTY-EIGHTH YEAR OF HER AGE

WHEN THIS

VENERABLE SAINT

FULL OF HOLINESS AS OF DAYS

CALMLY RESIGNED HER BREATH .

MARK THE PERFECT AND BEHOLD THE UPRIGHT

FOR THEIR LATTER END IS PEACE .

R.I.P.

Portraits of Charles Earl and Mary Countess of Traquair, are preserved at Traquair, and engravings have been made of them for this work.

After the death of Robert, fourth Earl of Nithsdale, Lady Lucie Douglas,

Countess-Dowager of Nithsdale, obtained from King Charles the Second a grant, dated 23d March 1683, of a yearly pension of £200 sterling, for the better maintenance of herself and her son, the fifth Earl, and her daughter, Lady Mary Maxwell, during his Majesty's pleasure only. The grant narrates the grounds upon which it was made. These were the low condition of the family of Nithsdale, the great burdens that lay on the estate, chiefly by sequestrations and forfeitures in the beginning and during the course of the late troubles, for the constant adherence of the Earl of Nithsdale to his Majesty's interest, and the ill-provided state of the Countess, who had the burden of the maintenance and education of William, now Earl of Nithsdale, his son, and Lady Mary Maxwell, his sister.[1]

The Countess-Dowager of Nithsdale subscribed a declaration at Terregles, 30th April 1683, as to the unlawfulness of subjects, upon pretence of reformation or other pretences whatsoever, entering into leagues and covenants, or rising up in arms against the King or those commissioned by him. It is precisely the same as that subscribed by John, third Earl of Nithsdale, in the year 1677.[2]

Lucie Countess of Nithsdale made intimation at Edinburgh, 5th April 1684, to William Duke of Hamilton, her brother, as nearest of kin on the mother's side to William Earl of Nithsdale, her son, a minor, for whom she was tutrix-testamentar, to attend at the opening and inventorying of the charter-chest of the late Earl, at Terregles, on 15th June 1684.[3]

After the accession of King James the Seventh to the throne on the death of King Charles the Second, William Earl of Nithsdale and his mother, Lucie Countess of Nithsdale, presented a petition to his Majesty, praying for the continuance of the pension of £200 which had been granted to his father, the late Earl, by King Charles the Second, and for a grant to them of 4000 merks of yearly rent out of the forfeited estates of the rebels. The petition is as follows :—

PETITION to his MOST SACRED MAJESTIE for the EARLE OF NITHISDAILL, 1685.

To his Most Sacred Majestie, the Supplication of William Earle of Nithisdaill and Lucie Countess of Nithisdaill, his mother,

Most humblie Sheweth,—That your Majestie's Royall brother, of ever blessed memorie, having taken to his consideration the great sufferings and losses sustained by our familie for their constant loyaltie and adherence to his and his father's interest during the rebellion and usurpation, from the year 1638 to his own happie return and restauration, He was graciouslie pleased, in the

[1] Original Grant at Terregles.　　[2] Vide p. 393.　　[3] Original Instrument of Intimation at Terregles.

year [1678], to grant to the late Earle of Nithisdaill, my father, ane yearlie pension of two hundreth pound sterline, and whereof there was unpayed to him the soume of five hundreth pound sterling, or thereby, at Whitsunday 1682, when the method of his Majestie's Exchequer in Scotland was altered and changed, and whereof no part is yet payed : And the same being represented to his Majestie, he was graciouslie pleased, by an other letter, dated 29 day of Aprill 1682, direct to the Lords of Exchequer for the time, to ordain the payment of the said bygone arriers to be made to my said deceast father ; and ordaining them to dispone to him als much of the rebells forfaulted, or to be forfaulted their estates within the shire of Wigtoun and stewartrie of Kirkcudbright, as would amount to four thousand merks of yearly rent, free of all burding : And after my father's deceass his late Sacred Majestie was graciously pleased to continue the forsaid pension with my mother for alimenting of me during his own royall pleasure allenarlie : And now, seeing that the late Earle of Nithisdaill, my father, in whose favour the forsaids pensions and letters were granted, is now deceased, and that, by his late Majestie's decease, the former pension granted to my said father is become extinct, and that by the great losses and sufferings of the family of Nithisdaill upon the accompt of their constant loyaltie, as said is, the estate of Nithisdaill is become so weak and overburdened that it is in present hazard of being totallie ruined and extinct, unless supported by your Sacred Majestie's Royall bounty and goodness.

> May it therefore please your Sacred Majestie to have compassion upon an ancient family, who was never attainted with the least act of disloyalty, and who is onlie become under such distress and burdings by the oppression and unjustice of traitors and rebells for their constant adherence to your Majestie's royall predecessors ; and to prevent their utter ruine, to recomend to the Lord High Treasurer of Scotland, etc, to dispon to me als much of the forfaulted rebells' estates as will extend to the soume of four thousand merks of yearlie rent, conform to your Majestie's royall brother's grant ; and to ordain him to make payment to me and my mother of the bygone arriers of my father's pension of two hundreth pound sterling yearly, preceiding Whitsunday 1682 : And that your Sacred Majestie would be graciously pleased to continue the said pension of two hundreth pound sterling with me, and ordaine the same to be payed to my mother towards mine and my sister's aliment and education in time coming, during your Majestie's pleasure, conform to his late Majestie's gifts and letters under his royall hand, respective forsaid. And for the welfare of your Sacred Majestie and royall successors your petitioner shall ever pray.[1]

In compliance with this petition a grant was made to the Countess of Nithsdale, by King James, of a yearly pension of £200, for the maintenance of herself and her children, dated at Whitehall, 23d October 1685.[2]

The Countess in her widowhood spent much of her time at Terregles and Edinburgh as well as in visiting her daughter at Traquair. She skilfully managed not only the household affairs at Terregles, but other money and property transactions, doing all in her power to retrieve the fortunes of the

[1] Duplicate Petition at Terregles.   [2] Original Grant at Terregles.

family, and to liquidate the debt and encumbrances with which the estate was burdened.

The Countess died, between three and four o'clock, on the morning of the 8th of January 1713. A particular account of her last illness is given by Father Hudson, who resided with the Earl of Nithsdale, in a letter to her daughter, Mary Countess of Traquair, dated 17th January 1713. " Her Ladyship," he writes, " commanded me (in case it should please God to call her hence in this sickness,) to send her Ladyship's blessing to your Ladyship, my Lord, and all her grandchildren at Traquair. . . . I take this occasion to condole with your Ladyship for the great losse undergone by being depriv'd of a most tender and affectionat mother, but, at the same time, hope that your Ladyship's comfort will soon follow, by the assureance many eye-witnesses here, and I especially, can give of the happy circumstances that attended a most pious and Christian death." [Vol. ii. pp. 174, 175.]

SEALS OF ROBERT MASTER OF HERRIES, AFTERWARDS FOURTH EARL OF NITHSDALE. 1656.

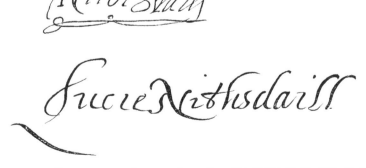

SIGNATURES OF ROBERT, FOURTH EARL, AND LUCIE COUNTESS OF NITHSDALE, 1682 AND 1688.

XXII. WILLIAM, FIFTH AND LAST EARL OF NITHSDALE.

LADY WINIFRED HERBERT, HIS COUNTESS.

1683-1744.

THIS Earl was born in the year 1676, and was about seven years of age when he succeeded his father as Earl of Nithsdale.

During his minority his father disponed to Sir Robert Grierson of Lag, knight, the office of steward of the stewartry of Kirkcudbright, "ay, and whill he be fourtein years of age." Sir Robert held the office only for the promotion of his Majesty's service, and granted a backbond, about the year 1685, disponing to Lady Mary Maxwell the whole lardner mart, and half of the benefit and profit of the office, the other half being reserved for the payment of deputies who performed the duties of the office.[1]

The Earl's curators were his mother, the Countess of Nithsdale, John Maxwell of Breckonsyde and Samuel Maxwell of Newlaw. The last was steward-depute of the stewartry of Kirkcudbright, under Sir Robert Grierson of Lag. By an agreement between Lady Lucie Douglas, Countess Dowager of Nithsdale, tutrix to William Earl of Nithsdale, her son, and Samuel Maxwell of Newlaw, dated at Edinburgh, 2d January 1686, the latter was continued in the office of steward-depute till 1689, for which he bound himself to pay to the Countess yearly 300 merks Scots, and to warrant and collect for her behoof the lardner marts.[2]

By the influence of his friends, this Earl, when only a boy, obtained the lands of sundry proprietors in the shire of Wigton and stewartry of Kirkcudbright, who were forfeited for their accession to the rebellion of Bothwell Bridge. In a draft signature by King James the Seventh, undated, but indorsed 1686, directions are given that a charter should be expede under the Great Seal in favour of this Earl of the lands of Francis Hay of Arioland, Alexander M'Kie of Drumbuy, Alexander Hunter of Cullwhassen, Andrew Martin of Little Airres, Henry M'Culloch of Barholm, John Bell of Whitsyd, James

---

[1] Copy of Backbond at Terregles.   [2] Original Agreement at Terregles.

Welsh of Little Cloudane, John Welsh of Cornlie, Mr. Samuel Arnot [of Braiko] . . . Fullertoun of Over Sennick, Alexander Halyday of Meifield, Mr. Thomas Verner, John Brown (Newtoun), Robert M'Clellan of Barmackgetchan, John M'Naught (Drumhumfra), Gordon of Barharrow, Crichton (Belhassie).[1]

The rental of the rebels' lands was given in to the Commissioners of the Treasury[2] by Samuel Maxwell of Newlaw and George Maxwell of Munches, acting under a commission granted to them by the Commissioners of his Majesty's Treasury in April 1686. The lands and their proprietors are specially mentioned. The list of proprietors, except that Gordon of Barharrow is not included, corresponds with that in the above draft signature, and the gross rental amounted to £2612, 19s. Scots.

Before the gift of these forfeited lands was formally made to William Earl of Nithsdale, his mother, as his tutrix, entered into a contract with Sir William Maxwell of Monreith, dated at Dumfries, 26th September 1687, in which it was agreed that as soon as the gift which the King had promised to the Earl of certain rebels' lands in Galloway was passed, part of them should be disponed to Sir William.[3] But the grant by the Crown did not make the Earl's possession of the forfeited lands quite secure, and a change of Government might have entirely deprived him of them. As it was, such obstructions were put in the way by the Government of the day that the proposed sale could not be carried out. To obviate the difficulties thus raised, William Earl of Nithsdale, and his mother as his tutrix, presented a petition to the Lords of Council and Session, praying that they might be permitted to sell the parts of the forfeited estates granted to them at a price not under eight years' purchase, and that the Lords should declare the rights and disposition which they might grant to the buyers to be as good and valid securities as if a special decreet of vendition had been obtained for each parcel of the land sold.[4] But on 23d February 1688 the Lords refused the prayer of the petition.

At Dumfries, 26th May 1696, William Earl of Nithsdale was retoured as

[1] Draft Signature at Terregles.

[2] A copy attested by Thomas Moncreiffe, clerk to the Commissioners of the Treasury, at Edinburgh, 16th September 1686, is preserved among the Muniments at Terregles.

[3] Original Contract, *ibid.*

[4] Original Petition, *ibid.*

heir to his father Robert, Earl of Nithsdale, in the lands and baronies of Maxwell, Carlaverock and others specified ;[1] and he was infefted therein on 2d September following.[2]

At Terregles, 14th September same year, he made a disposition, with consent of his curators, of the office of steward of the stewartry of Kirkcudbright, with all the emoluments of the office, to Sir John Maxwell of Pollok, knight and baronet.[3]

He claimed to be retoured heir-male and of tailzie of Robert Earl of Nithsdale, commonly called "The Philosopher," in the lands and baronies of Langholm, Castlemilk, and many others, in the shire of Dumfries.[4]   On 7th April 1698, the Earl also obtained letters under the Great Seal, by King William the Third, for infefting him as heir to Robert Earl of Nithsdale, commonly called "The Philosopher."[5]

The Earl for the most part resided with his mother at Terregles from the year 1695 until 1699, about which time he went to Paris, probably to pay homage to his exiled sovereign at St. Germain, though his motive may have been of a different character, as in the spring of the year 1699 he became the accepted suitor for the hand of Lady Winifred Herbert, fifth and youngest daughter of the then deceased William, third Marquis of Powis.   Their marriage-contract is dated at Paris, 2d March that year.   They bind themselves to solemnize the holy bond of matrimony betwixt the date of the contract and Easter following.   William Earl of Nithsdale engaged to infeft Lady Winifred in liferent during her lifetime after his decease, in case she should survive him, in 9900 merks Scots yearly, to be uplifted from all his lands, particularly from the baronies of Terregles, Kirkgunzeon, Lochruton, and Ur, the barony of Kirkpatrick in the stewartry of Kirkcudbright, and the barony of Duncow and Keir in the shire of Nithsdale.   The contract was written by David Murray, servitor to Mr. Alexander Stevenson of Chesters, banker in Paris.   The witnesses were the Right Honourable Earl of Kinnoul, Sir George Maxwell of Orchardton, Baronet, William Grierson, younger of Lag, Mr. Alexander Stevenson

---

[1] Original Retour at Terregles.
[2] Original Instrument of Sasine, *ibid.*
[3] Original Disposition, *ibid.*

[4] Original Claim, undated, at Terregles.
[5] Original Royal Letters, *ibid.*

of Chesters, banker, and Mr. Gideon Murray of the parish of Sulpice, gentleman.[1] In implement of this contract, William Earl of Nithsdale granted a bond of corroboration, dated at Terregles, 9th August 1699, for infefting Lady Winifred in the above annual rent; and she was infefted therein at the castles of Terregles and Carlaverock on the same day.[2] He also granted a charter, dated at Terregles, 5th April 1701, in her favour, of that annual rent, to be held of the granter blench.[3]

From no letters preserved at Traquair nor from any documents extant at Terregles does it appear where the young couple spent the year after their marriage. But that they were settled and living at Terregles in October 1700 is evident from different vouchers and accounts still existing in the charter-room. Among these is the bill of a blacksmith, which is here given, not only as proving that Lord and Lady Nithsdale were residing at Terregles in 1700, but also as showing the number of horses which they kept.

Count of Smithwork wrought be Walter Howall, smith, To the Earl of Nithsdale.

1700. 12 October, Six sett of new shoes to six of the coatch horses,	.	07 04 00
14 October, four removes to the dragon horses,	.	.	00 04 00
15 October, four new shoes to the young coatch horse,	.	.	01 04 00
27 October, four removes to the Mountigne horse,	.	.	00 04 00
— November, four newe shoes to the bay gelding,	.	.	00 16 00
— Four newe shoes to the little whyte naig,	.	.	00 16 00
etc., etc.			
1701. 4 January, seven sets of new shoes to the seven coatch horses,	.	08 08 00
etc., etc.			

In this bill are items also for shoes to "the whyte padd, the gray naig, and little ponnie." The account, which is carried down to 7th May 1701, amounts in all to the sum of £62, 4s., and at the end is an order to pay, signed by the Earl of "Nithsdaill."[4]

The Earl of Nithsdale, being a member of the Church of Rome, was exposed to annoyance from some of those zealous Presbyterians, who thought that, to carry out the statutes against Roman Catholics, they were entitled to transgress all the other laws of the realm. Upon the 24th December 1703,

[1] Contemporary Copy Contract at Terregles.
[2] Original Bond and Instrument of Sasine, *ibid.*
[3] Original Charter at Terregles.
[4] Original Account, *ibid.*

the ministers of Irongray and Torthorall, and several other ministers, assembled a number of fanatics, and attacked the house of Terregles, under pretence of searching for priests and Jesuits.

Their proceedings are well described in the Information which was lodged against them on behalf of Lord Nithsdale. This document sets forth and argues the heinous character of their crime from the following considerations :—1st. The invasion and assault was made upon the Earl's dwelling-house, which is a kind of sanctuary, and which the law says in many places ought to be *cuique tutissimum refugium et receptaculum*, a breach whereof was reckoned by the ancients *crimen gravissimum*, and next to sacrilege. 2d. The crime was committed under cloud of night, when people are in more hazard of mischievous attempts and less able to provide for their own safety. 3d. The actors were armed with guns, swords, and other mortal weapons, and consisted of above five or six score, which amounted to an unwarrantable convocation of the lieges. 4th. The door of the smith's forge was first forced up, and with the iron hammers and engines brought from thence they broke open the outer and inner gate, with horrid and frightful noise and beating. 5th. They violently entered the house, searched all the rooms, and caused break up the door of the Earl's closet, where his writs and evidents lay, the key whereof was then in Edinburgh with himself. 6th. It was a further aggravation of the foresaid violent proceedings that they were done in the Earl's absence and while the Countess was indisposed and confined to her bed-chamber, and in such a dreadful and hostile manner that her life was in imminent danger. 7th. The rabble and convocation were raised, armed, and assisted in perpetrating the foresaid barbarity and violence by Mr. James Guthrie, Mr. John M'Murdie, minister at Torthoral, Mr. John Henderson, minister at Kirkmahoe, and Mr. Alexander Robison, minister at Tinwald, whose lawless and arbitrary carriage, so unlike and opposite to the spirit of the Gospel, aggravated the crime to a vast degree.

Criminal letters were raised by the Earl of Nithsdale before the Justiciary Court against Mr. James Guthrie, minister of Irongray, and others who were ringleaders in these outrageous proceedings. They were summoned to compear before the Lord Justice-Clerk and Commissioners of Justiciary within the Criminal Court-house of Edinburgh, the 7th day of February next to come, to underly the law for the crimes libelled, which being found proven by the verdict of an assize before the Lords Commissioners of Justiciary, they and each of them ought not only to be decerned in the sum of 5000 merks Scots of damages to the complainer, but also punished in their persons and goods to the example and terror of others to commit the like in time coming.

Mr. James Guthrie and others raised letters of exculpation against the Earl of Nithsdale.   In these, after referring to the criminal letters raised against them by the Earl, they state that they had several relevant defences against the libel, and also competent objections against the assizers and witnesses in the list given them, whereof they would be heavily prejudged unless they obtained warrant and diligence for citing witnesses for proving these defences and objections.   A draft of these letters of exculpation, with a list of six witnesses to be adduced on their behalf, was delivered to the Earl on 31st January 1704 by a sheriff-officer.

Criminal letters, dated at Edinburgh 28th January 1704, were raised at the instance of Mr. James Guthrie, minister at Irongray, and others, against the Earl of Nithsdale and Maxwell of Kirkconnell.   These letters begin with an enumeration of the laws and Acts of Parliament against the hearing of mass and concealing thereof, and the resetting of Jesuits, seminary priests, and trafficking Papists, as crimes of a high nature.   They then proceed to complain that the Earl of Nithsdale and Maxwell of Kirkconnell, being professed Papists, had upon the 17th, 18th, 19th, 20th, or one or other of the rest of the days of the month of March, or on the 1st, 2d, 3d, or one or other of the days of the months of May, June, July, August, September, October, November, December 1703 years, or on the 1st, 2d, or 3d, or any other of the days of the month of January 1704, heard mass, and were present thereat in the Earl of Nithsdale's house of Terregles, or in the house of Kirkconnell, and did conceal the same ; as also that upon one or other of the days of the months of the years above specified, they did reset and entertain within the house of Terregles or Kirkconnell, or in one or other of the said houses, three nights together, or three nights at several times, or at least did, one time or other, upon the days of the months above specified, reset and entertain Jesuits, priests, and trafficking Papists, and particularly   Innes,   Murray,   Maxwell, or one or other of them, who were notourly known and commonly reputed to be priests and trafficking Papists. Of these crimes of hearing mass and being present thereat and concealing the same, and of resetting and entertaining Jesuits, priests, and trafficking Papists, and other crimes above mentioned, the said Earl of Nithsdale and Maxwell of Kirkconnell are charged with being actors art and part, which being found proven by an assize, they ought to be punished in their persons and goods conformably to the laws and Acts of Parliament referred to, and other pains of law to the terror of others to commit the like thereafter.

By these criminal letters the Earl of Nithsdale was charged to find sufficient caution acted in the Books of Adjournal, that he should compear before the Lord Justice-Clerk and Commissioners of Justiciary, within the Tolbooth or criminal house of Edinburgh, upon the 21st day of February next to come, to underly the law for the crimes libelled in the said letters, under the pain of rebellion. Then follow the names of the assize who were to sit in judgment on the Earl of Nithsdale, consisting of many of the nobility, and a list of numerous witnesses who were to be adduced against him.

It was alleged by Mr. Guthrie and others in their defence that the Act of Parliament, 1700, for preventing the growth of Popery, warranted all the lieges, and encouraged them, by a reward of 500 merks, to apprehend and seize the persons of trafficking priests and Jesuits, and that Guthrie, M'Murdie and their associates, being informed that such men were reset in the Earl of Nithsdale's house, who was a professed Papist, thought themselves obliged to repair thither and make search. If their zeal against superstition and idolatry moved them a little to exceed, it was excusable : to find it criminal were to encourage, in opposition to the laws of the land, priests and Popery, which too much abounded in that country.

It was answered by the Earl of Nithsdale—1st, That the allegation that there were priests and Jesuits in the house of Terregles was groundless and calumnious. 2d, That to encourage persons, by a reward of 500 merks, to apprehend trafficking priests and Jesuits mentioned in the Act of Parliament 1700, did not authorize a tumultuary rabble to invade houses, much less to convocate great numbers of armed men to break up gates and doors, and violently to enter houses under cloud of night. 3d, That when persons were declared rebels, fugitives, and intercommuned even for crimes of high treason, whereby it was left free and lawful to any of the lieges to seize them, yet dwelling-houses, in which they were suspected to lurk, were not to be assaulted without warrant from the Government, at least from a magistrate. 4*th*, That if men's houses were to be exposed to the violent attacks of arbitrary armed rabbles, this would dissolve the very cement of society, and no subject could be safe under the protection of law and government.   5*th*, That the justice and wisdom of Parliament in legislating, and of magistrates in the execution of the law, were the security of the people, and for arbitrary rabbles to break up dwelling-houses under pretext of security from criminals, without authority, in the night-time, was what the law and government of the nation could not countenance, and of which the certain consequence would be to afford an opportunity to all the scum of the kingdom to murder, assault, and plunder at their pleasure.   6*th*, That the danger and pernicious effects of such a proceeding were obvious, and further evinced from the consideration that when a house was attacked and gates broken open, under cloud of night, without authority, those within, by the laws of God and man, were justified *vim vi repellere*—to use fire-arms, and to kill in their own defence ; which of itself was sufficient to repel the argument from the Statute 1700, and to demonstrate its absurdity.

In the Justiciary Court held at Edinburgh, 7th February 1704, the process at the instance of the Earl of Nithsdale and her Majesty's Advocate against Mr. James Guthrie, minister of Irongray, and the other defenders, was continued till Monday the 14th instant at nine o'clock forenoon.   The assizers and witnesses were ordained to attend, each under the pain of 200 merks, and the pannels to renew their caution for their appearance at that diet.   The diet against the absent assizers was also continued till the 3d day of March next.

On 14th February, the Lords further continued the diet against Mr. Guthrie and others till Monday the 21st, and ordained all the assizers and witnesses to attend, each under the pain of 300 merks, and the pannels to renew their caution.

Meanwhile endeavours having been made to compromise the case, this was successfully accomplished, as we learn from a minute of the Court of Justiciary, 21st February 1704, to the effect that the Lords Commissioners of Justiciary deserted the diet at the Earl of Nithsdale's instance, with his concurrence, against Mr. James Guthrie, minister of Irongray, and the other defenders ; as also that the diet of the other criminal action, at the instance of Mr. James Guthrie and the other pursuers, against the Earl of Nithsdale and Maxwell of Kirkconnell, was deserted *simpliciter*.[1]

William Earl of Nithsdale was denuded of the office of heritable steward-principal of the stewartry of Kirkcudbright, which was conferred on James Duke of Queensberry.

At Terregles, 20th September 1705, the Earl subscribed a declaration acknowledging that the commission by which that Duke, as heritable steward-principal of the said stewartry, appointed William Young of Auchenskeoch in 1705 to be steward-depute thereof, was granted " at our desire, by our advice," as were all former similar commissions by the Duke since he had obtained the stewardship.[2]

Even before the death of Queen Anne, many families in Scotland had resolved to attempt the restoration of the exiled Stuarts to the British throne ; but, alive to the dangers of the adventure, most of them adopted measures to secure their patrimonial estates in the event of failure.

With this view some noblemen, in the year 1712, executed entails in favour of their eldest sons. William Earl of Nithsdale, by a disposition of tailzie dated 28th November that year, disponed to his only son, William Lord Maxwell, by his Countess Winifred, and the other heirs of tailzie therein mentioned, the lands and earldom of Nithsdale and lordship of Terregles, etc., with the dignities and titles of Earl of Nithsdale, Lord Maxwell, Herries, Eskdale, and Carlyle, reserving his own liferent and that of Lady Winifred Herbert, his spouse, the power also to dispone or to encumber the estate for debts already contracted, and to the extent of £3000 sterling more, as well as to provide his other children with such portions as he should think fit.[3] This arrangement was fortunate for the family, as it secured to them the estates when the Earl was forfeited for his share in the rebellion of 1715.

This Earl, who was never provident of money, contracted heavy debts, and his creditors became clamorous for payment. He was willing to restrict

[1] Justiciary Records.

[2] Original Declaration at Terregles.

[3] Extract Registered Deed of Entail at Terregles, registered in the Books of Council and Session, 15th April 1718.

himself to the sum of £500 yearly till they were paid, the rest of his rents to be appropriated to the liquidation of his debts. Maxwell of Munches and Charles Earl of Traquair, though with considerable reluctance, consented to become his trustees, whose business it was to see that the annual rents were rightly applied. The Earl of Traquair only consented from the consideration that this, as Maxwell of Munches asserted, was the only way to prevent the Earl of Nithsdale from contracting new debts, and conserving what remained of the estate ; but at the same time he said that if any of the creditors asked their principal sums he would never become bound to pay them. Munches so far satisfied him that they became joint trustees. Lord Traquair afterwards received a letter from Munches, desiring him, in his character as trustee, to become surety for a debt of £4000, but he declined to involve himself in such an engagement.[1]

The proceedings of the Courts of Barony frequently gave rise to heavy complaints of oppression, which there is little doubt were often well founded. In the year 1715 William Makmyn, smith in Auchencairn, in the parish of Redwick, presented a humble representation to the Earl of Nithsdale, complaining against Robert Maxwell of Hazlefield, his Lordship's bailie of the barony of Dundrennan, and praying for redress. He complains that the said Robert Maxwell was, without cause, prejudiced against him, vowing to do him mischief, if in the compass of his power. He had the strongest reasons for suspicion that the said bailie instigated his neighbours to pursue him on groundless and vexatious clamours, that he might pronounce sentences against him to his oppression and ruin. He, in particular, complains that the bailie had instigated Thomas Maxwell of Coull, factor to Sir George Maxwell of Orchardton, who, with one David Cairns, brother to John Cairns of Torr (who was under sentence of exile and banishment by the Lords of Justiciary, in their circuit at Dumfries about three years previous, for rioting and duelling, and other offences of which he was convicted), had the year past unjustly framed libels and indictments against him for his alleged cutting and rooting out timber, and cutting and taking away broom out of Orchyardtown and Torr's grounds, and who, in the course of their vexatious proceedings against him, had held courts for the most part every week in every part of the parish

[1] Vide vol. ii. pp. 203-209.

on purpose to harass and ruin him, in which courts the said David Cairns, who had avowed malice and revenge against him, was both his procurator-fiscal and clerk. They gave sentences against him, notwithstanding all the relevant defences offered by his procurators.

Makmyn further complains that they suborned some wicked persons to rifle his house in the night, and to threaten to burn him and his children; that they had made three several assaults on his house in the night-time, within the past fourteen days; that they came into his forge, took away his smith's hammers and tongs, and cut his smith's bellows, rendering them useless; and that they went into his garden and plucked up all his onions, kail, and herbs, whereby, and by the threatenings of further ruin, he was in great hazard of his life, and his family of starvation.

He had been advised to go to Edinburgh and apply to the Lord Justice-Clerk and Lords Commissioners for redress. But considering that Hazlefield, who, he had reason to believe, was the spring of all his troubles, was the Earl of Nithsdale's bailie, and accountable to him, he thought it advisable to seek redress in the first place from his Lordship.

He therefore humbly prayed his Lordship to put a stop to Hazlefield's career in the said processes, and that they be remitted (as in law they ought to be) to the steward-depute, who should proceed against him according to justice, and thus save him from ruin.[1]

In the year 1715 an attempt was made, under the leadership of the Earl of Mar, to recover the British throne for the son of James the Seventh. On 26th August that year, at a pretended hunting match, the standard of the Chevalier of St. George, who assumed the title of James the Eighth, was planted at Braemar, in presence of a large gathering of Jacobite Highland and Lowland chieftains. At another gathering of these chieftains at Braemar, with 2000 men, on 6th September, the Chevalier was proclaimed King of Scotland, England, France and Ireland. They marched to Dunkeld, where they were largely re-inforced by the Marquis of Tullibardine and others; and, mustering 8000 men, they advanced to Perth, which they took without resistance. Meanwhile William Earl of Nithsdale and William sixth Viscount of Kenmure, hastened to assist the English Jacobite insurgents

[1] Original Representation at Terregles.

under Forster and Derwentwater, and joined them on 19th October.[1] The Earl of Nithsdale, from his position and from the devotion of his family to the House of Stewart, would have been placed at the head of the insurrection in the north of Scotland had he not been a Roman Catholic. Under the circumstances, it was deemed expedient to assign in preference the chief command to Lord Kenmure, who was a Protestant, and a nobleman of undoubted courage, although deficient in military skill and experience.

According to Rae, only a few of the tenants of the Earl of Nithsdale joined with him in the rebellion, whilst many of them enrolled themselves as volunteers on the side of King George the First. "As my Lord Nithsdale's tenants in Carlaverock," says that historian, "so likewise his other tenants in Troqueer, Terregles and Kirkgunzeon, with those of the Viscount of Kenmure and Earl of Carnwath, were in arms at Dumfries, and manifested a great deal of zeal against the rebellion ; nor were there any with these noblemen in the Rebellion but two or three domestic servants with each. And this I thought just to make known to the candid reader, to wipe off a calumny cast upon these honest people by a late historian [Patten], who was also a rebel, who, speaking of the chiefs of Scotland, and what men they could raise, says, 'The Earl of Nithsdale 300 men, with their chief, against the Government ; the Earl of Carnwath 300 men, most with their chief, against the Government, and in the Rebellion,' and the same he affirms of the Viscount Kenmure."[2]

But whatever was the number under the command of Kenmure, great confidence was placed in their bravery by their own party, as is expressed in the Jacobite song, " Kenmure's on and awa, Willie."

> Kenmure's on and awa, Willie,
>   Kenmure's on and awa ;
> And Kenmure's lord is the bravest lord
>   That ever Galloway saw.
> Success to Kenmure's band, Willie,
>   Success to Kenmure's band ;
> There's no' a heart that fears a Whig
>   E'er rides by Kenmure's hand.
>
> O, Kenmure's lads are men, Willie,
>   O, Kenmure's lads are men ;

---

[1] Salmon's Chronological Historian.   [2] Rae's History of the Rebellion, p. 257.

> Their hearts and swords are metal true,
>   And that their foes shall ken.
> They 'll live and die wi' fame, Willie,
>   They 'll live and die wi' fame ;
> And soon wi' sound of victory
>   May Kenmure's lads come hame.[1]

But these poetical predictions were not realized. The insurrection was speedily crushed. The Earl of Nithsdale, with Lord Kenmure and other Scottish Lords, the Earl of Derwentwater, Mr. Forster and the English insurgents advanced to Preston in Lancashire. In a Highland Jacobite song, entitled "The Jacobite Muster-Roll," written, not, as Allan Cunningham seems to conjecture, in reference to the Earl of Mar's march to Sheriffmuir, but in reference to this march into England, the name of the Earl of Nithsdale is signalized among others :—-

> Wigton 's coming, Nithsdale 's coming,
> Carnwath 's coming, Kenmure 's coming,
> Derwentwater and Forster 's coming,
> Withrington and Nairn 's coming—
>   Little wat ye wha 's coming—
>   Blythe Cowhill and a's coming.[2]

The insurgents took Preston. But, invested on all sides by the Royal troops under the command of General Wills, they were forced to surrender at discretion, simply on condition that Wills would prevent his soldiers from putting them to the sword, until he should receive further orders. This was on the 14th of November. Nearly 1500 were made prisoners, among whom was the Earl of Nithsdale.[3]

The following song, entitled "Lament for Lord Maxwell," was written on the capture of the Earl of Nithsdale at Preston. The minstrel is an aged warrior of eighty years, whose mournful strains bespeak his intense and undying affection to the representative of the House of Nithsdale :—-

> Green Nithsdale, make moan for thy leaf 's in the fa',
> The lealest of thy warriors are drapping awa' ;
> The rose in thy bonnet, that flourished sae and shone,
> Has lost its white hue, and is faded and gone !

[1] Allan Cunningham's Songs of Scotland, vol. iii. p. 180.

[2] Ibid. vol. iii. p. 206.

[3] Patten's History of the Rebellion, pp. 120-123, 132 ; Rae's History of the Rebellion, 321, 322.

Our matrons may sigh, our hoary men may wail,—
He 's gone, and gone for ever, the Lord of Nithisdale !
But those that smile sweetest may have sadness ere lang,
And some may mix sorrow with their merry merry sang.

Full loud was the merriment among our ladies a',
They sang in the parlour, and danced in the ha'—
O Jamie 's coming hame again to chase the Whigs awa' :
But they cannot wipe the tears now so fast as they fa'.
Our Lady dow do nought now but wipe aye her een—
Her heart 's like to burst the gold-lace of her gown ;
Men silent gaze upon her, and minstrels make a wail—
O dool for our brave warrior, the Lord of Nithisdale !

Wae to thee proud Preston !—to hissing and to hate
I give thee : may wailings be frequent at thy gate !
Now eighty summer shoots of the forest I have seen,
To the saddle-lapps in blude i' the battle I hae been,
But I never ken'd o' dool till I ken'd it yestreen.
O that I were laid where the sods are growing green !—
I tint half mysel' when my gude lord I did tine—
He 's a drop of dearest blood in this auld heart of mine.

By the bud of the leaf, by the rising of the flower,—
By the sang of the birds, where some stream tottles o'er,
I 'll wander awa there, and big a wee bit bower,
To hap my gray head frae the drap and the shower ;
And there I 'll sit and moan till I sink into the grave,
For Nithsdale's bonnie Lord—ay the bravest of the brave !—
O that I lay but with him in sorrow and in pine,
And the steel that harms his gentle neck wad do as much for mine !!¹

Six of the prisoners were shot. The noblemen and principal officers were
sent to London. Lady Cowper,² wife of Sir William Cowper, Lord High
Chancellor of Great Britain, who was appointed Lord High Steward of Great
Britain for the trial of the rebel Lords, gives in her diary some interesting
particulars of the bringing of them into London. — " The 5th [December 1715].
I went into waiting. The Princess was extremely kind to me. The coming of
the Pretender into Scotland began to be talked of, though it did not happen so

¹ The Songs of Scotland, by Allan Cunningham, vol. iii. p. 186.

² Lady Cowper was Mary, daughter of John Clavering, of Chopwell, in the county of Durham.

soon as was expected. This week the prisoners were brought to town from Preston. They came in with their arms tied, and their horses (whose bridles were taken off) led each by a soldier. The mob insulted them terribly, carrying a warming-pan [1] before them, and saying a thousand barbarous things, which some of the prisoners returned with spirit. The chief of my father's family was amongst them. He is above seventy years old. A desperate fortune had drove him from home in hopes to have repaired it. I did not see them come into town, nor let any of my children do so. I thought it would be an insulting of the relations I had here; though almost everybody went to see them." [2]

After being led pinioned through some of the principal streets, by way of triumph, the prisoners were committed prisoners, some to the Tower and others to Newgate, the Fleet, and Marshalsea. [3] The Earl of Nithsdale, like the other lords, was sent to the Tower, and he was confined in an apartment of the house of the Lieutenant of the Tower.

It was resolved by King George the First and his Government to make an example of the chief of the prisoners. The victims selected were James Earl of Derwentwater, William Lord Widdrington, William Earl of Nithsdale, Robert Earl of Carnwath, William Viscount Kenmure, and William Lord Nairn. On Monday, 9th January, it was moved in the House of Commons, by Mr. Lechmere, that these Lords should be proceeded against by way of impeachment. He supported his motion in a lengthened speech. "In justice to the King," he said, "as well as to the people, we ought to take this into our own hands, and not to intrust the prosecution of it with anybody but ourselves. Everybody knows to what hazards prosecutions in the ordinary course of justice are liable, though they are never so well concerted by those whose business it is to carry them on, but how sure soever the success may be in a case so notorious as this, yet it is

---

[1] The allusion is to an invented story, circulated in London at the time of the birth of the Pretender, that he was a spurious infant brought in a warming-pan into the bed-room of Queen Mary of Modena at the time of her alleged confinement. The story is minutely told by Bishop Burnet in his History of his Own Time.

[2] Lady Cowper's Diary, pages 61, 62.

[3] "9 December, 1715.—The principal prisoners taken at Preston were brought to London. They were pinioned at Barnet, and so led through the city."—Salmon's Chronological Historian, 3rd edition; London, 1747, vol. ii. p. 56.

obvious to everybody of what different weight and influence the prosecutions of Parliament are from those in the ordinary forms."

The motion was carried. The House resolved to impeach the rebel Lords; and on the same night the articles of impeachment were laid before the House of Lords. On the following day the impeached Lords were brought to the bar of that House, charged with the articles, and ordered to give in their answer by the 16th. They were allowed to have counsel and any other persons whom they should name to assist them in their defence. The time for giving in their answers was afterwards extended to the 19th, when they respectively pleaded guilty. The 9th of February was the day appointed for passing sentence upon them.

In the articles of impeachment they were charged with having, in or about the months of September, October or November 1715, and at divers other times, and in divers places within this kingdom, traitorously confederated and conspired with many other evil-disposed persons, to raise within the counties of Teviotdale, Northumberland, Cumberland, and the county Palatine of Lancaster, and elsewhere within this kingdom, a most cruel and bloody war against his Majesty, in order to depose and murder him, and deprive him of his royal state, crown and dignity. They were further charged with having, during their march and invasion, traitorously caused the Pretender to be proclaimed King of these realms; with having traitorously seized and possessed themselves of the town of Preston, in the county Palatine of Lancaster, and with having, then and there, fought against his Majesty's forces.

Of all these treasons and crimes the knights, citizens, and burgesses in Parliament assembled did, in the name of themselves and of all the Commons of Great Britain, impeach the said Lords.

On 19th January 1716, the culprit Earls were brought, each in succession, to the bar of the House of Lords by the Gentleman Usher of the Black Rod, in order to their giving in their respective answers to the articles of impeachment. When brought each knelt, and the Lord Chancellor, Cowper, as Lord High Steward on that occasion, demanded if they were ready to give in their answers, to which they answered in the affirmative. Advised by their friends, they pleaded guilty. A denial of their guilt, which would have been a denial of the King's rights, would, they were told, only incense him still more against them and cut off all hope of pardon, whilst a confession of guilt might mollify his resentment and incline him to the side of clemency. But if they trusted to this, the event proved that they were leaning on a broken reed.

The answer of William Earl of Nithsdale to the articles of impeachment was as follows :—

" It is with the utmost confusion the said Earl appears at your Lordships' Bar, under the weight of an impeachment by the Commons of Great Britain, for high treason. He humbly begs leave, in extenuation of his crime, to assure your Lordships that he was always a zealous assertor of the liberties of his country, and never engaged in forming or carrying on any design to subvert the ancient established Government and the good laws of this kingdom ; but being summoned by those intrusted with the administration of the Government in Scotland to appear at Edinburgh, and being assured if he went thither he should be made close prisoner, he did not obey the summons ; but in all humble manner applied for their indulgence in dispensing with his being committed to gaol, offering to give any bail for his peaceable and quiet behaviour ; which being refused, and being at that time in so ill a state of health that a confinement in Edinburgh Castle would have endangered his life, he was forced to abscond, and kept private till several of the persons mentioned in the said impeachment, with many other of his neighbours, appeared in arms, very near the place where the said Earl lay concealed ; and then he inconsiderately and unfortunately (with four of his domestics, and no other person whatsoever) joined them, and proceeded in their company to the places mentioned in the said articles of impeachment, but he knew nothing of the intended insurrection till they were actually in arms. The said Earl is deeply sensible of his great offence, and, not affecting delay, nor being willing to give your Lordships or the Honourable House of Commons any unnecessary trouble, he does, with a sorrow equal to his crime, confess that he is guilty of the treason in the said articles of impeachment contained, and throws himself at his Majesty's feet, imploring his royal mercy. And to incline his Majesty thereto, and induce your Lordships to recommend him as an object thereof, he begs leave to inform your Lordships that when he and the rest that were with him at Preston had engaged in a battle, a cessation of arms being agreed to, they had intimations from his Majesty's officers that if they submitted they might expect the King's mercy ; and history abounding with instances of conditions stipulated by Generals even with Rebels, and afterwards agreed to and confirmed by their Sovereigns, they were prevailed on by such encouragement, together with the consideration of his Majesty's known clemency, to surrender themselves prisoners, whereby the lives of great numbers of his Majesty's good subjects were saved, which by an obstinate resistance would inevitably have been destroyed. And therefore he most humbly begs your Lordships will be pleased to represent his case to his Majesty in the most favourable manner, not doubting but by your Lordships' powerful intercession he shall find that as he performed the duty of a good Christian in concurring to prevent the effusion of blood, so he acted the part of a wise man in relying upon a mercy so extensive as that of his Majesty ; and he presumes, when the honourable House of Commons are apprized of the nature of his case, they will not interpose to prevent him from having a share in the benefit of that mercy.   NITHSDAILL."[1]

On 9th February the prisoners were brought to the bar in the court erected in Westminster Hall. The procession is minutely described by Lady Cowper in her diary :—" February 9th, the day of the trials. My Lord was named High Steward by the King, to his vexation and mine ; but it could not be helped, and so we must submit, though we both heartily wished it had been Lord Nottingham. The form of the attendance was this from hence. The servants had all new liveries ; ten footmen, four coaches with two horses and one with six ; eighteen gentlemen out of livery, and Garter at Arms and Usher of the Black Rod in the same coach ; Garter carrying the wand. I was told it was customary to make fine liveries upon this occasion, but had them al plain. I think it very wrong to make a parade upon so dismal an occasion as that of putting to death one's fellow-creatures ; nor could I go to the trial to see them receive their sentences, having a relation among them, Lord Widdrington. The Prince was there, and came home much touched with compassion. What pity it is that such cruelties should be necessary !"[2]

The articles of impeachment were first read to the prisoners at the bar, and then the answers given in by them on 19th January. Next, the Lord

<hr>

[1] State Trials, vol. vi. pp. 1-10.   [2] P. 72.

High Steward, addressing the prisoners, said, "My Lords that are prisoners at the bar, I am to acquaint your Lordships that upon any occasion which shall be offered you to speak for yourselves, you are to direct your speech to the Lords in general, and so is any other person that shall have occasion to speak to this Court." Then, naming the prisoners, he added, "You stand impeached of High Treason by the Commons of Great Britain in Parliament assembled, which treason is contained in the articles that have been lately read; to this you have severally pleaded guilty, and are thereby convicted. What say you, James Earl of Derwentwater, why judgment should not pass upon you according to law?"

The Lord High Steward having asked William Earl of Nithsdale what his Lordship had to say for himself why judgment should not pass upon him according to law, the Earl said,—" My Lords, I have confessed myself guilty, relying on his Majesty's mercy; and I beg leave to assure your Lordships I was never privy to any plot or design against his Majesty's person or Government, and was unprovided with any necessaries for such a purpose; but rashly and inconsiderately, with only four of my servants, joined those who appeared in arms in my neighbourhood, and was one of the last who went unto them. At Preston, my Lords, his Majesty's Generals gave great hopes and encouragement to believe that surrendering to his Majesty's mercy was the ready way to obtain it, with repeated assurances that his Majesty was a prince of the greatest clemency. Upon those hopes and assurances I submitted myself, and still entirely depend on his Majesty's goodness, earnestly beseeching your Lordships and the Honourable House of Commons to intercede with his Majesty on my behalf. And I solemnly promise your Lordships I shall, during the remainder of my life, pay the utmost duty and gratitude to his most gracious Majesty, and the highest veneration and respect to your Lordships and the Honourable House of Commons."

The Lord High Steward then asked his Lordship, who was indistinctly heard, whether he had pleaded anything in arrest of judgment. The Earl answered that he had not.[1]

Having put similar questions to the other Lords, which were similarly answered, the Lord High Steward commenced his address to the prisoners.

[1] State Trials, vol. vi. p. 13.

"James Earl of Derwentwater, William Lord Widdrington, William Earl of Nithsdale, Robert Earl of Carnwath, William Viscount Kenmure, William Lord Nairn, you stand impeached by the Commons of Great Britain in Parliament assembled of high treason, in traitorously imagining and compassing the death of his most Sacred Majesty, and in conspiring for that end to levy a bloody and destructive war against his Majesty, in order to depose and murder him, and in levying war accordingly, and proclaiming a Pretender to his crown to be King of these realms; which impeachment is as much a course of proceeding, according to the common law, as any other whatsoever. If you had been indicted, the indictment must have been removed and brought before the House of Lords (the Parliament sitting). In that case you had, it is true, been accused only by the Grand Jury of one county; in the present the whole body of the Commons of Great Britain by their representatives are your accusers."

He then animadverted upon their pleas in mitigation of their offences. These, he argued, could not be admitted as an extenuation of their guilt. He made one admission as to the temptation which the Earl of Nithsdale, and others who professed the religion of the Church of Rome, had to engage in this treason, namely, that success on their part must for ever have established in this kingdom the religion which they professed.

Having concluded his address to the prisoners, the Lord High Steward proceeded to pronounce upon them their sentence.

"And now, my Lords, nothing remains but that I pronounce upon you (and sorry I am that it falls to my lot to do it) that terrible sentence of the law, which must be the same that is usually given against the meanest offender in the like kind. The most ignominious and painful parts of it are usually remitted by the grace of the Crown to persons of your quality; but the law in this case being deaf to all distinctions of persons, requires I should pronounce, and accordingly it is adjudged by this Court, that you, James Earl of Derwentwater, William Lord Widdrington, William Earl of Nithsdale, Robert Earl of Carnwath, William Viscount Kenmure and William Lord Nairn, and every one of you, return to the prison of the Tower, from whence you came; from thence you must be drawn to the place of execution; when you come there you must be hanged by the neck, but not till you be dead, for you must be cut down alive, then your bowels must be taken out and burnt before your faces ; then your heads must be severed from your bodies, and your bodies divided each into four quarters, and these must be at the King's disposal. And God Almighty be merciful to your souls ! "[1]

On 18th February the writs for the execution of the six condemned Lords in the Tower were delivered to the lieutenant, and the sheriffs of London and Middlesex.[2]

After the sentence was passed upon the prisoners, great interest was made in order to obtain for them the exercise of the royal clemency.   On 22d February they petitioned both Houses of Parliament to intercede with the King on their behalf.   The House of Lords carried a vote, by a majority of four, to present a petition to the King, praying him to " reprieve such of them as should deserve his mercy."   The King replied, that " on this and all other occasions he would do what he judged most consistent with the dignity of his crown and the welfare of his people."   The House of Commons, though many members were inclined to mercy, to avoid importunity, adjourned till after the day appointed for the execution.[3]   It was resolved by the Government that four of the prisoners, Lords Widdrington, Nithsdale, Carnwath and Nairn, should be reprieved.   It has been usually stated by historians that the Earl of Nithsdale was placed beyond the pale of the royal mercy.   But it would appear from Lady Cowper's Diary that he too was reprieved,[4] although he and his devoted wife little expected such a favour while she laboured so successfully in effecting his escape.   " February 23 [1716]. We sat up till past two," writes Lady Cowper, " to do a pleasing office, which was to reprieve four of the Lords in the Tower, though the Earl of Nithsdale had made his escape ; but it was not then known, and so he was reprieved with the rest."[5]   The King, Walpole and Chancellor Cowper were firm in their determination that Lord Derwentwater and Viscount Kenmure should suffer the penalty of death.   It was ordered that these Lords should be executed on 24th February.[6]

[1] State Trials, fol. London, 1730, vol. vi. pp. 14-16.
[2] Salmon's Chronological Historian, vol. ii. p. 59.
[3] Ibid. vol. ii. p. 59.
[4] " 24th July 1717, Lords Carnwath, Widdring-ton, and Nairn were released out of the Tower."
—Salmon's Chronological Historian.
[5] Lady Cowper's Diary, p. 85.
[6] State Trials, vol. vi. p. 16.

Not expecting any leniency from the Government, the Earl of Nithsdale, in prospect of his suffering death, wrote as follows with his own hand
what he intended as his dying speech :—

" Being in a short time to appear at the tribunal of the sovereign Judge of
the living and the dead, with whom I have endeavoured to make my peace,
and from whom I hope for mercy, I think myself obliged to publish my
sentiments to the world. This I owe to God, to my neighbour and to myself.
I declare, therefore, in the first place, that I die as by God's grace I have
alway lived, a true and dutiful son of the Holy Catholic Apostolic Roman
Church. Secondly, I declare that I drew my sword merely out of the motives
of justice and piety, to assert the undoubted and hereditary right of that Prince,
whom I then believed, and still believe, to be my only liege lord, and lawful
sovereign, James the Eighth of Scotland and Third of England, and to deliver
my native country from the oppression and misery under which it groans If
I fall a victim to so good and glorious a cause, it is what many of my ancestors have done, who generally shed their blood for the defence of their king
and country. As to any design on the life of him who now possesses the
throne (and by whose orders I am now put to death), I take heaven and earth
to witness, that I never formed or was privy to, any such thing. So far was I
from such a resolution, that I could not look upon it without detestation and
horror. I say the same of any attempt against the ancient constitution of
these realms, either in Church or State. Thirdly, As to my pleading guilty, I
declare that I only intended to acknowledge that I had taken and appeared
in arms, for the motives above specified ; if in my answer to the articles of
impeachment, or any other writ, I made use of the word crime, I only meant
an offence against the present Government, and not any real crime. However, I acknowledge and I am heartily sorry for my weakness for making
use of that expression, and crave God mercy and pardon of those whom I
have scandalized or offended by it. Fourthly, and Lastly, I declare that in
imitation of my Lord and Saviour Jesus Christ, and in obedience to His
most just command, I heartily and sincerely forgive all my enemies, not only
those who did or wished me any harm, but those also who are most accessory
to my death, and thirst most after my blood, earnestly desiring that, by the

effusion of the same, the wrath of God justly incensed against these nations may be pacified.   " WILLIAM EARL OF NITHSDAILL."[1]

The Earl of Nithsdale also wrote from the Tower a letter expressing his submission to his fate, to his brother-in-law, Charles Earl of Traquair, and his own sister Lady Mary Maxwell, Countess of Traquair, dated 22d February, only two days before the day fixed for his execution, at which time he seems to have had no hope of either a pardon or a reprieve, and to have been ignorant of the scheme which his devoted wife had formed, or was forming, in order to effect his escape.   The letter is as follows :—

" MY DEAREST BROTHER AND SISTER,—I most willingly make use of some of the most precious moments of my life to give you the last assurances of my tenderness towards your persons, and off my gratitude for your manifold favours, and espesialy for your generosity towards me in these my hard circumstances. . . . I allso most humbly thank you for your unparalelled goodness towards my dearest wife and children, whom I most ernestly recommend to you, as what is most dear to me after my own soul.   You have been informed, by my orders, of what has passed here relating to me, and what my dearest wife has done for me, so all I shall say is, that there cannot be enough said to her praise.   Everybody admires her, everybody applaudes her, and extolles her for the proofs she has given me of her love.   So I beg of you, dearest brother and sister, that whatever love and affection you bear to me, you would transfer it unto her as most worthy of it. . . .   As to myself, I thank allmighty God for it, I am entirely resigned to His most holly will, and humbly adore his Prouidence."[2]

The night before the day fixed for his execution, Lord Nithsdale escaped from the Tower by the contrivance of his wife.[3]   The story of his escape is given in the memoir of Lady Nithsdale.

Early on the morning of the 24th of February the scaffold on Tower Hill

[1] Copy MS. at Traquair. Two copies of the Earl's intended dying speech, written in his own hand, and briefer, are preserved among the Traquair MSS. The copy in the text is said to be from a paper written by his own hand in the Tower of London, the day before he was to have been beheaded.

[2] Vol. ii. pp. 221, 222.

[3] It is hardly necessary here to notice that Smollett was so ignorant of this fact that in his History of England he says that the Earl of Nithsdale " made his escape in woman's apparel, furnished and conveyed to him by his *own mother*."—Vol. ii. p. 228, edit. Edin. 1791.

was surrounded with the guards, and a little before ten o'clock the Earl of Derwentwater and the Lord Viscount Kenmure were carried in a hackney coach from the Tower to the Transport Office on Tower Hill, where there was a room hung with black for their reception, and there was a passage or gallery railed in, which led from thence to the scaffold, which was also covered with black. The Earl of Derwentwater was first led to the scaffold. From assurances his friends had given him of his life, he was under some surprise on being brought to execution. Lord Kenmure seemed well prepared for the fatal axe. He made no formal speech, but died with fortitude, avowing that he remained loyal to the House of Stuart to the last, and testifying his sorrow for having pleaded guilty.[1]

"The Earl of Derwentwater," says Allan Cunningham, "was a young and brave and generous nobleman, and his fate was vehemently lamented in the north of England." The Aurora Borealis shone remarkably vivid on the evening of the day of his execution, and is still known in the north by the name of "Lord Derwentwater's lights."[2]

Among other mournful ditties on these tragedies is "Lord Derwentwater's Good Night," a touching and beautiful song,—

> And fare thee well, my bonnie gray steed,
>   That carried me ay sae free,
> I wish I had been asleep in my bed,
>   The last time I mounted thee :
> The warning bell now bids me cease,
>   My trouble's nearly o'er ;
> Yon sun now rising from the sea
>   Shall rise on me no more.[3]

The escape of the Earl of Nithsdale by the skill and intrepidity of his Countess created a deep sensation at the Court in London, and throughout the kingdom. It excited the resentment of the King against him and his Countess, while it delighted all the Earl's Jacobite friends, and even many of those who were sincerely attached to the House of Hanover, but who deprecated severe measures as unnecessary in the treatment of the Jacobite leaders. On this event Lady Cowper has the following entry in her Diary :—

[1] Salmon's Chronological Historian, vol. ii. p. 59.
[2] Allan Cunningham's Songs of Scotland, vol. iii. p. 194.   [3] Ibid. p. 194.

" February 24th. It is confirmed that Lord Nithsdale is escaped. I hope
he 'll get clear off. I never was better pleased at anything in my life, and I
believe everybody is the same." [1]

In a rude song of welcome of the period, entitled, " What news to me,
Cummer ? " the Earl's escape is thus commemorated :—

> " Now what news to me, cummer,—
>   Now what news to me ?"
> " Enough o' news," quo' the cummer,
>   " The best that God can gie."
> " Has the Duke hanged himsel', cummer,—
>   Has the Duke hanged himsel',
> Or taken frae the other Willie
>   The hottest nook o' hell ?"
>
> " The Duke 's hale and fier, carle,—
>   The blacker be his fa' !
> But our gude Lord of Nithsdale,
>   He 's won frae 'mang them a'."
> " Now bring me my bonnet, cummer,—
>   Bring me my shoon ;
> I 'll gang and meet the gude Nithsdale,
>   As he comes to the toun."
>
> " Alake the day !" quo' the cummer,—
>   " Alake the day," quo' she ;
> " He 's fled awa' to bonnie France,
>   Wi' nought but ae pennie !"
> " We 'll sell a' our corn, cummer,—
>   We 'll sell a' our bear ;
> And we 'll send to our ain lord,
>   A' our sett gear.
>
> " Make the piper blaw, cummer, —
>   Make the piper blaw ;
> And let the lads and lasses both
>   Their souple shanks shaw.
> We 'll a' be glad, cummer,—
>   We 'll a' be glad ;
> And play ' The Stuarts back again,'
>   To make the Whigs mad." [2]

---

[1] P. 87.   [2] Allan Cunningham's Songs of Scotland, vol. iii. p. 189.

Having made his escape from the Tower, the Earl was secreted in different places in London for some time. He was then conveyed, disguised in a livery coat, by a servant of the Venetian ambassador to Dover, whither that servant, whose name was Mr. Michell, had been ordered to go with a coach and six horses to bring the ambassador's brother to London. At Dover, Michell hired a small vessel, in which the Earl was carried to Calais. The voyage was accomplished so speedily that the master of the vessel remarked that they could not have sailed faster had they been fleeing for their lives. He did not know that he had a passenger in that condition. Michell might have returned to London unsuspected, but at the Earl's desire he went along with him, and he afterwards obtained a place in the service of the Chevalier.

After his arrival in Paris the Earl was seized with an illness so severe that his life was despaired of, but he happily recovered. His nephew, Charles Lord Linton, in a letter to his mother, Mary Countess of Traquair, dated [Paris] 25th March 1716, writes,—" My unckle, after haveing been dispair'd of by all, is now perfectly recover'd. He came to town yesterday, and stays at present in the same lodgeing with us ; he doth not design to stay long here, but has a mind to go [to] some place elsewhere more wholesome to breath in, for fear he should relapse into his late sickness."[1]

The Earl, in a letter to his brother-in-law, Charles Earl of Traquair, dated Paris, 24th April same year, after thanking him for his goodness, says,—" I have seen severall times your two sons, but allvayes with a new satisfaction. I ever looked on them as very hopfull youths, and with joy find that they not only answer, but surpasse the expectation I had conceved of them. I intend this afternoon to take leve of them, being to part hence the morow for the south."[2]

Charles Lord Linton, in a letter to his mother, dated [Paris] 6th May 1716, gives other particulars concerning the Earl of Nithsdale :—" I, as soon as my unckle arrived, reckoning that he wou'd be somewhat low in his pocket, offer'd him any little thing that I cou'd command, not doubting but that my father and you wou'd allow it. He said that he did not stand in need of any then. However, before he went away, he asked of me two hundred livers, which I immediately gave him. All the time he stayed here, he keept his

---

[1] Vol. ii. p. 235.   [2] Vol. ii. p. 236.

health perfectly well, tho' we were somewhat apprehensive at the beginning of the effects that a new air might produce upon his health. He went frequently to see Mrs. Arther,[1] who was extreamly kind to him, and furnished him with money. What hasten'd his going away was an invitation of Mrs. Arther's son[2] to him in very obligeing termes. He showed me the letter, which was endeed full of kind expressions. Amongst the rest there is one that I can not omitt setting down here, to witt,—'As long,' saith he, ' as I have a loafe of bread in the world, assure your selfe you shall allways have a share of it.' My unckle parted from this about ten days [ago] in good health, so that before this time is at his journey's end."[3]

On his way to Rome to join the Chevalier, which was in July 1716, the Earl suffered shipwreck, and his life was with difficulty saved. Lady Niths-dale, in a letter to Mary Countess of Traquair, dated La Flèche, 10th June [1717] writes : "I must lett you know that your friend and mine [the Earl of Nithsdale] is well, at least was so the last time I was so happy to heare from him. He has had another great preservation, being six dayes in so greate a danger at sea, that all the seamen left of working, and left themselves to the mercy of the weaves, and was at last cast into Antibe, from whence they coasted it to Lighorn. However, he is now safe with his master, and both of them in good health."[4]

The Earl did not find the service of the Chevalier so agreeable as he had expected. Writing to Lady Nithsdale from Rome, he dwells chiefly upon the inconveniences of living there, and tells her that it was his fixed resolution to leave his master.[5] In her letters to him she endeavoured to dis-suade him from his purpose of leaving the Chevalier ; and his sister Mary, Countess of Traquair, a lady of great amiableness of character, who did much to relieve him in his pecuniary difficulties, and who was affectionately attached to Countess Winifred, whose side she took in the differences that arose between Winifred and the Earl, entreated him not to leave the service of the Chevalier. Countess Winifred, writing to her, 14th November [1717], returns her most humble thanks for the letter she had written to her brother, "which," says

---

[1] Mary of Modena, Queen of James the Seventh.
[2] The Chevalier, James the Eighth.
[3] Vol. ii. p. 237.
[4] Vol. ii. p. 257.
[5] Vol. ii. pp. 259, 260.

she," I doe not question, but [it] will fix him in his resolution of staying where it certainly is so much more for his advantage to be."[1]

The Earl went to take leave of the Chevalier, but the Chevalier evinced the utmost reluctance to part with him, there being, he said, so few about him. He told him that he would probably be married before winter, and expressed a strong desire that the Earl should be in his family.[2] This encouraged the Earl to remain in his service ; and in prospect of the Chevalier's marriage, he earnestly besought his Countess to leave Paris, where she was with Mary of Modena, Queen of King James the Seventh, and come to Rome, where he believed she would obtain an honourable place in the Chevalier's establishment.[3]

The Earl was never a good manager of money. When at home, he was often in pecuniary difficulties. When abroad, deriving nothing from his estates, which were forfeited, and having only a small pension allowed him by the Chevalier, he was constantly in urgent need of relief. To his sister Mary, Countess of Traquair, he was much indebted for assistance, as well as to the Earl of Traquair, who devoted much of his time and attention to assisting the Earl of Nithsdale, as he afterwards did his son, in the management and settlement of their affairs. In a letter to her, dated 13th September 1719, he says,—" I hope you will not think me so ungreat for all the favours I have receved from your dear Lord and you as to neglect my returning you my most humble thanks for your so kind answering my last bill, especialy when you had nothing in your hands of mine, and at a time when I know you would be streaten'd on account of your childrien."[4]

In another letter to her, dated 12th November 1720, he begs her to intercede with her husband to procure him a bill's being answered for £50.[5] On this occasion, as on many others, she sent him the needed supply.[6]

In March 1722, he wrote to her several letters, again asking from her pecuniary help. His request was enforced by a letter to his sister from Lady Nithsdale. They wished her speedily to advance to them £150, to satisfy their creditors for debt contracted, and, for repayment, to sell their furniture, which had been taken to Traquair.[7]

---

[1] Vol. ii. p. 265.   [3] Vol. ii. p. 276.   [5] Vol. ii. p. 317.   [7] Vol. ii. pp. 329-332.
[2] Vol. ii. p. 276.   [4] Vol. ii. p. 298.   [6] Vol. ii. p. 324.

The money solicited was again sent by the Countess of Traquair, as appears from a letter to her, 21st July that year, from Lady Nithsdale, who in it expressed the hope that the impossibility of expecting another favour of this kind would keep the Earl from again falling into the like circumstances. "If not," she adds, "it is not my fault ; all my comfort is, that neither me nor his children has contributed to it, since they have never coast him a farthing since [they were] of this side of the sea. Nor have I had a six-pence, not only out of his pention, but even of all the money he has heretofore received, or now does from you ; which I say not by way of complaint, for I desire it not, but only wish he could make himselfe easy with it, and I would be most happy."[1]

In a letter to the same friend, dated 22d September [1722], Lady Niths-dale says,—" As to the furniture, I was very sincere in desiring your parting with it, and never expected to look vpon that as having any more clame to it, but flater myselfe, that you will not be a looser by what you have sent by my desire. As to other bills, I know nothing of them but what I doe from yourselfe, for this is the only [one] I medled in, and had not I seen my husband in the condition he was, should never have consented to part with the only thing I had left ; I may safely call it so, as much as a wife can, since it was not a farthing of his money that bought it, tho' at the same time [I] have had noe share of the money [that] was sent."[2]

The Earl was desirous that some expedient might be fallen upon to procure him £100 a year, which he said would make him easy. He and Lady Nithsdale, though the Chevalier was as liberal to them as to any of their com-panions, could not live with decency at Rome upon the pensions allowed to them, and it would be necessary for them either to remove to a place in which they could live at less expense, or to receive some regular supplies from Scotland. Both of them were unwilling to remove elsewhere, as in that case, according to the proverb, " out of sight out of mind," all that they had hitherto suffered in the interests of the Chevalier would be forgotten, and their present allowance would be diminished if not altogether withheld at the earliest opportunity. He suggested that this might be procured out of his estate in Scotland. Countess Winifred broke the proposal in a letter to Mary Countess of Traquair,

[1] Vol. ii. pp. 344, 345.   [2] Vol. ii. p. 347.

22d March 1723. Her letter was followed by another from the Earl to his sister, dated 14th April.[1] But this plan does not appear to have succeeded. His sister, in a letter to him, dated Edinburgh, January 1724, writes :—" I have sent you enclosed a schem of the state of your affairs, to show you that my husband has had no management of your son's estate, but that it has been still in the Government's hands since you left it till the 9th of November last, on which day your liferent was bought (to a great advantage, as everybody thinks) in behalf of the creditors."[2] In that letter she severely blames him for having drawn a bill upon her husband for £100 sterling.[3]

Writing to his sister-in-law, Viscountess Montague,[4] from Rome, 13th June 1724, he says :—" I hope you will not thinke that my so seldom writing proceeds from the want of gratitude for the many and great obligations I owe you on my son's account."[5]

After this the Earl lived twenty years. During that period there is nothing important in his life to record. He continued to live at Rome, still hoping that the exiled Stuart family might be restored to the throne of their ancestors.

Charles Edward, the eldest son of the Chevalier of St. George, inflamed with the ambition of re-acquiring the British throne, was waiting for a propitious opportunity of making an effort for that purpose, in which he was encouraged by the Jacobites both in England and Scotland. The attempt was not made till the year 1745.[6] The Earl of Nithsdale did not live to witness this last enterprise on behalf of the exiled Stuarts. He died at Rome, 20th March 1744.

Lady Nithsdale survived her husband for five years, having died at Rome in 1749. By her he had three sons and two daughters. Lucie, Robert, and George died young. William Lord Maxwell, the only surviving son of the marriage, inherited the Nithsdale and Herries estates on the death of his father, but the Nithsdale peerage was never restored.

The surviving daughter, Lady Anne Maxwell, became the wife of John

[1] Vol. ii. pp. 349-351.

[2] Vol. ii. p. 355.   [3] Vol. ii. p. 354.

[4] Viscountess Montague was Lady Mary Herbert, eldest daughter of William, first Marquis of Powis, and sister-german of Winifred Countess of Nithsdale. She married, first, Richard, son of Carril, Viscount Molineux, in Ireland ; secondly, Francis Viscount Montague ; and, thirdly, Sir George Maxwell, Baronet, of Orchardton, in the Stewartry of Kirkcudbright.

[5] Vol. ii. p. 355.

[6] The Chevalier himself was still living. He died at Rome, on 30th December 1765, in the 78th year of his age.—Annual Register.

fourth Lord Bellew, of the kingdom of Ireland, who was born in the year 1702, and took his seat in Parliament on 7th September 1725. Their marriage was celebrated at Lucca, 13th September 1731.[1] Lord Bellew's proposal to marry Lady Anne, which was made through an intermediary, having been accepted by her father, Lord Bellew, in a letter to the Earl from Liège, 27th April 1731, expresses his obligations and satisfaction :—" I propose," he says, " to be entirely happy in the possession of the Lady, who has so fine a character with all those that know her. . . . No consideration shall hinder me from going to Rome, if you shall judge it proper." The Earl dispensed with his going to Rome in the meantime. Lord Bellew, in another letter to him from Liège, 14th June, same year, writes :—" I was honour'd with the receipt of your Lordship's letter, and this is to return you, in the most sincere and respectfull manner possible, my thanks for the honour you have done me in accepting of the proposals made by me for to marry the Lady Anne Maxwell, your Lordship's daughter. I am much oblig'd to you, my Lord, for your consideration of the present situation of my affairs, and not insisting on my immediate going to Rome."[2]

On the day of their marriage, John Lord Bellew, in an agreement between them, agreed and consented that all his children, both male and female, by Lady Anne Maxwell, his future spouse, should be entirely left to her care, to be educated and brought up as to her it should seem meet. Should either her or his death take place during their minority, his pleasure was that all the children, the fruits of the marriage, should be left to the care and tuition of her father and mother, or either of them, or in the event of failure of both, to any other person or persons whom she should appoint.

Lady Bellew had a son, Edward, born 3d April 1735, who died in September following, and was buried at Hendon ; and a daughter, Mary Frances, born in Italy in 1733, and married, 1st January 1772, to the Honourable Count Taafe, second son of Viscount Taafe.[3] Lady Bellew died of a fever in London, 3d May 1735, and was buried at Hendon Church in Middlesex. In the obituary of the *Caledonian Mercury* for 1st September 1735, is the following :—"Yesterday died the daughter of the Lord Bellew, of whom her mother, daughter of the late Earl of Nithsdale, died in childbed four months ago."

[1] Vol. ii. p. 362.   [2] Vol. ii. pp. 360, 361.   [3] Annual Register.

WILLIAM FIFTH EARL OF NITHSDALE

(ATTAINTED)

There is at Terregles a half-length oil portrait of Lady Bellew. An engraving of the portrait has been made for the present work.

Lord Bellew married, secondly, in 1737, Mary, only daughter to Maurice Fitzgerald of Castle Ishen, in the county of Cork, widow of Justin, the fifth Earl of Fingal, and upon her death, 19th March 1741, thirdly, in 1749, Lady Henrietta Lee, fourth daughter to George Henry Earl of Lichfield. By both these ladies he had issue. He died 18th August 1770.

A portrait of William Earl of Nithsdale has been engraved for the present work from the original painting at Terregles.

SEAL OF WILLIAM, FIFTH EARL OF NITHSDALE.

SIGNATURE OF WILLIAM, FIFTH EARL OF NITHSDALE.

LADY WINIFRED HERBERT, COUNTESS OF NITHSDALE,
1699-1749.

LADY WINIFRED[1] HERBERT, Countess of William, fifth Earl of Nithsdale, as already stated, was the fifth and youngest daughter of William Herbert, first Marquis of Powis, by his spouse, Lady Elizabeth Somerset, daughter of Edward Marquis of Worcester. The Marquis of Powis allied himself with King James the Second after his abdication in 1688, when he was created Duke of Powis and Marquis of Montgomerie. These titles were not legalized, although by courtesy the Marquis and his wife were usually styled Duke and Duchess of Powis by their friends. The Duke was appointed Steward and Lord Chamberlain to the household of the exiled King.

The family of Herbert trace their descent from Henry Fitzherbert, Chamberlain to Henry the First, King of England, who reigned between the years 1100 and 1135. His descendants were raised to the peerage as Earls of Pembroke and Montgomerie, Earls of Powis, Earl of Torrington, etc. Henry Herbert, second Earl Pembroke of a new creation, was a distinguished statesman. His third Countess was Mary, daughter of Sir Henry Sydney, Knight of the Garter : she was a lady of great distinction, and died in 1621. Their elder son was William, third Earl of Pembroke, K.G. Sir Philip Sydney dedicated to Lady Pembroke his Arcadia. The inscription on her monument in Salisbury Cathedral is well known :—

> Underneath this marble herse,
> Lies the subject of all verse,
> Sydney's sister, Pembroke's mother ;
> Death, ere thou hast slain another,
> Wise, and fair, and good as she,
> Time shall throw a dart at thee.

Like her family, Lady Nithsdale was devoted to the Roman Catholic religion, and she was loyal to the House of Stuart, not only as being the legitimate descendants of an ancient race of Kings, but also as avowed adherents of the religion which she professed. Her sister, Lady Lucy Herbert, with

[1] This Christian name was used in the Herbert family at an early period. The eighth daughter of Sir Edward Herbert and Mary Stanley was named Winifred.

whom her own history is associated, was the Abbess of the English Augustine Nuns at Bruges, in France.[1]

From the little to be gleaned from the family letters, and the numerous household accounts still preserved at Terregles, it would appear that from the time of their marriage in 1699 until the year 1715 the Earl and Countess of Nithsdale almost constantly resided at Terregles, with the exception of occasional visits to Edinburgh. The embarrassed state of the Earl's affairs prevented him from living so much away from home as he might otherwise have done. The Dowager Countess of Nithsdale, Lady Lucie Douglas, up to the time of her death in 1713, appears to have resided chiefly at Terregles, and in the management of household affairs she relieved her daughter-in-law, Lady Nithsdale, who seems to have suffered much from ill health, and who, if we may judge from her portrait, must have been of a very delicate frame. Charles Earl of Traquair, in a letter to his Countess, Lady Mary Maxwell, from Edinburgh, 17th February 1704, makes an allusion to Lady Nithsdale as being unwell :—" My Dearest,—I thought to have been out this day, but the Doctor will not allow me so soon. Wherefor, knowing how uneasie you would be, I think it better for you to come here to morrow, for your sister, my Lady Nithsdaill, is very ill, and would gladly see you. Be not allarmed my D[ear] Hart, for it's only what I wrot in my last that ails me. Your Brother's coachman will meet you at Athelstone : so adieu till meeting, my Dear life."[2]

In the insurrection on behalf of the royal family of Stuart, in the year 1715, Lady Nithsdale shared in the sympathies of other Jacobite ladies who were vehement in their zeal in behalf of the exiles, and transported by flattering visions of the return of ancient royalty to Scotland, in the splendours of which they expected to participate. In the Jacobite song, of which the Earl of Nithsdale is the hero, entitled "Lament for Lord Maxwell," formerly given, the exultation of the Countess of Nithsdale and other Jacobite ladies at the landing of the Chevalier in Scotland, their dejection upon his defeat at Preston, and the capture of their husbands and friends, are described.

[1] Of the other three sisters of Lady Nithsdale, two married into Scotch families. Lady Mary, the eldest sister, married, as her third husband, Sir Robert Maxwell of Orchardton. Lady Frances, the second sister, became Countess of Seaforth. An engraving has been made for this work, of the original portrait of Lady Lucy Herbert at Terregles.

[2] Original Letter at Traquair.

Whilst her husband was absent in the army of the Chevalier, the Countess of Nithsdale was residing at Terregles with her children.   Intelligence speedily reached her of the disastrous fate of the insurgent army at Preston in Lancashire, of the capture of the Earl of Nithsdale with many other noblemen, and of his being on his way with the other captured lords to the Tower of London.   She received from him a letter, dated Middlewatch, 27th November 1715.   He was in good health, but his money had fallen short.   He desired her to get somebody to meet him with a supply at Barnet or St. Albans, whither he expected to be on the 10th of the following month.   He and the others, he believed, would be made close prisoners.   As he would be without anybody to do him any service, he pressed her, as he had done in a previous letter, to come to London to him.   Aware that a traitor's death was the doom awaiting him, she resolved to start without delay for London, to do her utmost to assist him, and, if possible, to save his life.   From the delicacy of her frame, she seemed to be ill fitted to bear anxiety and fatigue, and to enact the heroic part by which she was about to distinguish herself.   But her nobility of character, and fertility of resource, inspired her with a fortitude that rose superior to hardships, dangers, or difficulties.

In preparing for the journey, she dismissed all her servants but the grieve and the dairy woman, and engaged the gardener's wife to keep fires from time to time in the mansion-house of Terregles.   Mr. Maxwell of Carruchan, a friend and near relation of the family, promised to oversee the grieve, who was to do nothing without his orders.   In a letter to Charles Earl of Traquair, dated Terregles, 9th December 1715, Lady Nithsdale, in stating these particulars, says,—"I beg your Lordship will excuse my distracted letter, but my head is so full of thoughts, and my heart of trouble, that I am vncapable of any thing."   She sent her daughter, Lady Anne Maxwell, a child, to her husband's sister, Mary Countess of Traquair, by whom she was affectionately welcomed and tenderly cared for.   Before setting out, pondering the prospective interests of her son as she did the present welfare of her husband, Lady Nithsdale gave a signal proof of the foresight for which she was conspicuous.   Should the Earl be condemned and forfeited in his life and estates, was nothing to be done to save her son from beggary?

She believed that something might be done. The Earl had made a disposition of his estates to his only son, Lord Maxwell, in the year 1712, before the rebellion, reserving to himself only the liferent. There was then the hope that, should the Earl be forfeited in his estates, it might with good reason be urged that only his liferent could be forfeited, as this was all that he possessed at the time he joined in the rebellion. Hence the importance of preserving safe all the family papers. All these papers were in her possession. How then was she to secure them? She knew nobody to whom she could intrust them. Her house, in which they were deposited, was constantly liable to be searched, and they were accordingly there especially unsafe. She therefore resolved, as the only thing practicable in the circumstances, to bury them in the garden at Terregles, which she did, and none but herself and the gardener[1] knew anything of the matter. She and the gardener, when it was dark, dug a hole in a secluded corner of the garden into which they placed the writs, carefully covered so as to exclude from them as much as possible the damp, and threw back the earth in such a manner that all trace of what was done was lost. The wisdom of this precaution was soon manifest : the house was often searched after she went away.

At this time Lady Nithsdale was much indebted for supplies of money to William Alves, the law agent of the family in Edinburgh. He had been in the strictest habits of friendship with the Earl, by whom he was highly esteemed, and to whom he had rendered assistance in many of his earlier difficulties.

The expenses of the armament for the insurrection and the defeat at Preston having exhausted the most of his funds, as well as those of his friends, who might have rendered him assistance, and money being still necessary for the Earl's support, Mr. Alves advanced to the Countess the sum of £50 to assist her in her journey to London. But meeting with some disappointments her Ladyship was detained so long in the country that neither the money which she had, nor what Mr. Alves had advanced to her, was sufficient to serve her

---

[1] It is probably to the death of this gardener that allusion is made by Lady Nithsdale in a letter to the Countess of Traquair, dated 4th February [1721]. *Vide* vol. ii. p. 322. Though the gardens at Terregles are much altered since Lady Nithsdale left them, yet some old beech hedges and a broad green terrace still remain much the same as then. It is supposed that it was at the end of the grass terrace that she, with the help of this confidential gardener, buried the family papers.

purpose. Knowing this, and at the same time the difficulty of procuring a supply, Mr. Alves, by a letter to her, allowed her to draw on him for other £50, as she should require. Occupied with the preparation for her journey, she did not acknowledge the receipt of this letter till her arrival at Newcastle.

The nearest road to London lay through Lancaster and Lichfield; but the country in that direction being much disturbed, she purposed to cross the Borders and travel to Newcastle, then to York.

The season was unfavourable. It was winter, and the severest that had almost been ever remembered in the country. A heavy snow storm had stopped the coaches and the public posts, rendering it necessary for Lady Nithsdale to travel the most of the way on horseback. In proof of the severity of that winter, it may be stated that several post-boys and others were frozen to death, and that the snow lay a yard deep in many places. The Thames was frozen over, and all manner of diversions took place upon the ice.[1]

Attended by a faithful groom and Cecilia Evans, a Welsh woman who had been her maid at the time of her marriage, and in whom she had the greatest confidence, the Countess, starting on her journey, first rode to Newcastle. In a letter written from that town to her sister-in-law, Mary Countess of Traquair, 15th December [1715], she writes:—"This, according to my promis, is to lett you know that I am safe thus far, but have got no places,[2] so am forced to goe on horseback to York, where I have as litle hopes to get any, but met a gentleman that will be there a night sooner than I can, and will secure any that is to be had, if not hire horses for me to London, which long journey on horse back I wish I may be able to vndergo without stoping. I am sure nothing shall be wanting that I am able to doe to loos noe time in waiting on my Lord, whatever fatigue it coasts me." She adds, " I am much oblig'd to Mr. Lindsay for his care off me, and solicitude about my daughter's journey, which I hope arrived in good health. To any but yourself I ought to make an excuse for the trouble I give you in her, but I am too well convinced that she is wellcome to make an appologie."[3]

---

[1] Salmon's Chronological Historian, under date 31st December 1715, vol. ii. pp. 56, 57.

[2] Meaning seats in the stage-coach, often a matter of difficulty in the days of the old mode of travelling by stage-coaches.

[3] Vol. ii. p. 214.

From the town of Newcastle Lady Nithsdale also wrote to Commissary Alves the following letter, which has been before alluded to :—

Newcastle, 15th December [1715].

Sir,—I had not time before I left my own house to thank you for your kind offer, which at this time is most unexpressibly obliging ; and after having heartily thanked you for it, must accept it, and desire to know in what terms you would have my promise of repaying it worded. I am got thus far, and have found no places. How the letter has miscarryed I know not ; but the Master of the coach protests that he returned the answer, which if I had had would have spared me fifty miles' riding, since I am very little nearer than I was at my own House. However I must have patience, and go for York to-morrow, where I have as little hopes to get any ; but, if I do not, intend to hyre horses and go quit through. As soon as I can speak with my Lord, will send you word what he desires in order to your doing diligence, which I suppose he will be for, when he hears how things stand. However, since I am so near seeing of him, and that there is no such immediat heast, I will speak to him, which is all from her who shall always esteem herself much obliged to you for your kindness, and is your humble servant,   W. Nithsdaill.

To Commissary Alves, at his house in the Covenant Close.

I hope your wife is well to whom I desire to be remembered.[1]

Not getting seats in the coach, the Countess of Nithsdale and Mrs. Evans were forced to travel on horseback from Newcastle to York. This journey they accomplished in safety. At York, Lady Nithsdale was able to procure in the York coach only one seat, which she occupied herself, hiring a horse for Mrs. Evans.

A heavy fall of snow and other accidents prevented the coach from proceeding farther than Grantham, which was sixteen miles from Stamford. Impatient of delay, the Countess again hired horses, purposing to make the rest of the journey to London on horseback, on roads in many places almost blocked up with drifted snow in which her horses sank up to the girths. For one day she was compelled to stop.[2] In a letter to Lady Traquair, written from Stamford, 25th December, she says, " I must confess such a journey I beleeve was scarce ever made, considering the weather, by a woman. But an earnest desire compasses a greate deale, with God's help ; and I may say that

---

[1] Old copy Letter at Terregles.

[2] This account of Lady Nithsdale's journey to London is taken from the letters written by her at the time to her sister-in-law, the Countess of Traquair. In some slight particulars it differs from the briefer notices which she gives of that journey in her letter narrating the escape of the Earl. But as that letter was written two years after the event, such small discrepancies were to be expected ; and the account in the letters, written at the time when she made the journey, must evidently be regarded as the most exact.

the delays and stops I have unavoidably met with to my more speedy perform-ance of it, has been by far the greatest dificulty I have had, tho' if I had known what I was to have gone through, I should have doubted whether I was able to have done it.   However, if I meet my dear Lord well, and am so hapy as to be able to serve him, I shall think all my trouble well repay'd."   She adds, "I thinke myself most fortunate in having comply'd with your kind desire of leaving my litle girle with you.   Had I had her with me she would have been in her grave by this time with the excessive cold. . . . I have had the benefit of the coach from York but two dayes and a half."[1]

The following notice, still preserved at the Black Swan Hotel in York, will throw light on Lady Nithsdale's journey to London; for, though it is dated a few years previous to it, the accommodation afforded by the coach was not much improved, nor its speed much accelerated :—

YORK, FOUR DAYS, STAGE COACH.

Begins on Friday, the 12th of April 1706.   All that are desirous to pass from London to York, or from York to London, or any other place on that road,—Let them repair to the Black Swan in Holbourn in London, and to the Black Swan in Coney Street, York; at both which places they may be received in a Stage Coach every Monday, Wednesday, and Friday, which per-forms the whole journey in four days (if God permits); and sets forth at five in the morning, and returns from York to Stamford in two days, and from Stamford by Huntington to London in two days more, and the like stages on their return.

Allowing each passenger 14 lbs. weight, and all above, 3d. a pound.   Performed by

> Benjamin Kingston.
> Henry Harrisson.
> Walter Bayne.

Also this gives notice that Newcastle Stage-Coach sets out from York every Monday and Friday, and from Newcastle every Monday and Friday.

After a good many days, Lady Nithsdale got safe to London without any accident whatever.   It ought to be specially noticed that in detailing in her letters to her sister-in-law the stages of this memorable and arduous journey, she does not utter one word of complaint, every consideration about herself being forgotten in the one object that engrossed her thoughts—her anxiety to assist and comfort the Earl in his imprisonment, and to use every means in her power to save him from the scaffold.

Immediately on her arrival in the English metropolis, she went personally

[1] Vol. ii. p. 215.

to all those in power, and solicited their friendly offices. They did not deceive her; they plainly told her that though perhaps some of the prisoners might be pardoned, her husband would certainly not be one of the number. They did not freely tell her the cause of this difference, but she shrewdly guessed it. "A Catholick, vpon the Borders," she says, "and one who had a great follow - ing, and whos family had ever vpon all occasions stuck to the royal family, and the only suport the Catholicks had amongst that Whigish part of the countrey, would be well out of the way."[1]

At this time Lady Nithsdale wrote the following letter to Mr. Alves :—

London, January the 19th, [1716.]

SIR,—I have been in such a condition on my Lord's account that I hope you will excuse me for being so long without acknowledging and thanking you for the fifty pound you were so kind as to send me. My Lord's affairs, and that of the rest of his unfortunate companions, looks with such a dismal face that it is no wonder that I have nothing in my head but what regards his present circumstances, otherways I would have made many an excuse for my neglect so long in owning the favour you did me. I beg you annew to use diligence at Carlaverock. I need say nothing in particular of my Lord, for the public prints will give an account. He is I hear well, and I am, your assured friend and servant,   W. N.[2]

To Commissary Alves.

The next thing for Lady Nithsdale to do was to gain admission to the Tower to see the Earl. She was allowed to see him on certain conditions.

The great anxiety and fatigue which she had undergone brought upon her, soon after her arrival in London, a severe illness, which confined her to bed. Having recovered, she wrote the following letter to Commissary Alves, in relation to her pecuniary affairs, which were such as to cause her great anxiety :—

London, February the 2d [1716].

SIR,—I have been very ill for sometime, so that I could not possibly think much less write, which is the occasion that you have not again heard from me after my acknowledgement of your late favour of the money which my Lord, as well as myself, is most sensible of his obliga- tion to you for, but beggs you will add that of not requiring the 100 pound of John Simerall, which he took from him out of the Carguninon rent when he left the country. I should be glad to know what you have done as to your diligence on Carlaverock, and whither you have received any thing, for my Lord is at a very great expence in the Tower, and I am forced to stay out on account of doeing for him, which makes the expence greater, so altogether I know not which hand to turn me for money, being sent word from home that every thing he has is arrested,

---

[1] Vol. ii. p. 223.   [2] Old copy Letter at Terregles.

so all my hopes of the smallest supply is from some part of what you have done diligence on in Carlaverock. I beg your answer as soon as possible, which will extremly oblige your assured friend to serve you,   W. NITHSDAILL.

My service to your wife. Direct for me at Mrs. Mills' in Bute Street, near St. James Square. Directed on the back to Commissary Alves.[1]

She wrote also a letter to Lady Traquair, dated 4th February, in which she says,—"All the comfort I had in it [my sickness] was that, all the while I lay ill, had I been otherwise, nothing could be done for my Lord, during that time, nor can yett, till after next Thursday, when 'tis suposed sentance will be past against them. God Almighty help vs, and send vs success after. I am in such a distresed way, that I can say nothing of what fills my heart with gratitude, your extrordinary kindness to my litle girle, the greatness of which, Mary sends me word, is beyond expression. May God Almighty repay what is not in my power on that account, but hope you will be so just as to beleeve, that tho' my tongue and pen falls short of expressing what I feel in return of your kindness to her, yet that and your other favours are so deeply engraven in my heart, that the remembrance shall never be bloted out but with my last breath."[2]

From the postscript to this letter we learn that, in all her anxiety for her husband, Lady Nithsdale did not forget his unfortunate fellow prisoners : "I forgott [to] tell you," she writes, "that just before I fell sick, I was at the prison, and saw Kerkhouse, who was very well. I call'd for Wells, but something or other hinder'd him from coming just than, and I was forced to goe without doing it, but the others told me he was well."[3]   It was then, as it still is, a common custom to call individuals by the name of their property. In Rae's History of the Rebellion, among the prisoners taken at Preston are mentioned one Andrew Cassie of Kirkhouse and W. Scott of Walls, who are probably the two individuals alluded to by Lady Nithsdale.

On 19th January 1716, the Earl of Nithsdale and the other five Lords were brought to the bar of the House of Lords to give in their answers to the articles of impeachment. They pleaded guilty. They also pled in extenuation their submission to the General of the Royalist army at Preston, in order to avoid the effusion of blood, and implored his Majesty's clemency. But all availed not.

[1] Old copy Letter at Terregles.   [2] Vol. ii. p. 217.   [3] Vol. ii. p. 218.

They were sentenced, on 9th February, to die the death of traitors. The proceedings at the trial have already been fully stated in the memoir of the Earl.

After sentence of death had been pronounced on the Earl he still hoped that the King, were a petition presented to him, would relent. Lady Nithsdale did not share in his hopes; but to satisfy him, she promised to get one drawn up, and to make an effort to present it, notwithstanding the precautions which the King had taken to prevent any from obtaining access to him on behalf of the condemned Lords. On Monday 13th February, dressed in a black manteau and petticoat, as if in mourning, and accompanied by Mrs. Morgan—a lady to be afterwards more particularly noticed in connexion with the Earl's escape from the Tower,—who was to point out to her the King, whom she did not know, and another lady, she went into a public room between the King's apartment and the drawing-room, into which she knew that he was to enter. They knew that he must pass the whole length of the room, and accordingly she and her attendants took their place at the middle of the three windows in it, that she might have time to address him. As he passed she knelt down and presented the petition, telling him in French that she was the unhappy Countess of Nithsdale. The King paid no heed to her. She seized the skirt of his coat, and held fast, pathetically appealing in French to his mercy, and was thus dragged by him upon her knees almost from the middle of the public-room to the drawing-room door. One of the King's body-guard, putting his arms around her waist, pulled her back, and another disengaged the skirt of the King's coat from her hand. The unhappy Countess was left almost fainting on the floor, with her rejected petition beside her. It was taken up by one of the pitying bystanders, and fortunately given to Lord Dorset, who was the Lord of the Bed-Chamber then in waiting.[1] Lord Dorset was well acquainted with Mrs. Morgan, and under her influence and that of the Duke of Montrose,[2] Lady Nithsdale's warm and steadfast friend, he managed to have the petition read more than once to the King, whose rude treatment of Lady Nithsdale was much talked of. The King of England, it was said, never used to refuse a petition from

[1] Lionel Cranfield Sackville, seventh Earl and first Duke of Dorset, K.G. He died in the year 1765.

[2] James Graham, fourth Marquis and first Duke of Montrose. He married Lady Christian Carnegie, daughter of David, third Earl of Northesk. He died 7th January 1741-2.

the hands of the poorest woman, and it was a gratuitous and an unheard of brutality, to treat as he did a person of her quality. The King, far from relenting, was much embittered against the Countess by the freedom with which his conduct was censured on this occasion ; and afterwards, when all the ladies whose Lords had been concerned in the insurrection put in claims for their jointures, Lady Nithsdale's being among the number, he went so far as to say that she did not deserve, and should not obtain, hers.   She was accordingly excepted, and he would never listen to anything said in her favour.

In reference to the petition she had endeavoured to present to the King, Lady Nithsdale, in a letter written on Saturday the 18th of February 1716 to her sister-in-law, the Countess of Traquair, writes :—" What effect it will have I know not, but I am sure I have left nothing vndone that was in my power, and this night am going in to him, where, if I am not permited to stay in the night time, shall take a chamber hard by, and goe in to him every morning, and stay all day, for till there is some alteration more in his circumstances, nothing can be done. But for feare I should be confin'd not to goe out, if there be any thing can be done hereafter, am resolved to ly out if they doe not promis to lett me out when I please.   But whether I am to lye out, or in, shall take care he shall not be imposed on, as hitherto he has been, being forced to trust to their buying every thing he wanted for diet or other necessarys."[1]   From this letter it seems that Lady Nithsdale was already devising means for the Earl's escape.

On that day (18th) a warrant for the execution of the Earl of Nithsdale, and the other five Lords, was signed, and the day appointed for their execution was the Friday following (the 24th).[2]

To save the life of her husband was the thought uppermost in Lady Nithsdale's mind, and to effect this she omitted nothing that ingenuity could devise or execute. Honourable testimony is borne to her indefatigable efforts in a letter by the Rev. J. Scott to Lady Traquair, dated 21st February 1716 :—" I must needs doe my Lady the justice of assuring your Ladyship that she has left no stone unturn'd, that she has omitted nothing that could be expected from the most loving wife upon earth, her

[1] Vol. ii. p. 218.   [2] Vol. ii. p. 219.

tenderness for her dear Lord supporting and strengthening her to perform what nobody would have thought her able to undergoe.   Mistriss Evans having already given an account of what she did last week att the Palace,[1] I shall only add that she did it in so lively a manner that the whole Court was moved to a tender compassion.   The whole town applauds her, and extolles her to the skyes for it, and many who thirst after the blood of the others, wish my Lord Nithisdaill may be spared to his Lady."   He adds, "This day" (Tuesday, 21st February) "she attended the House of Peers, accompanied by the Dutchesses of Montmoth, Hamilton, and Montrose, the Lady Orkney, and severall others ; but the Duke of Richemond, who ought to have presented her petition, would not doe it ; but his Grace gave his word of honor that he would present it to-morrow morning.   So she intends to petition both Houses of Parliament to-morrow.   All the Scots nobility, except one Duke, have shew'd great concern and kindness to my Lord and Lady, but the Duke of Montrose has distinguished himself above all the rest.   His Grace is to give this night to the King a petition for a reprieve, signed by the four Scots Lords who are prisoners."[2]

These Lords were the Earls of Nithsdale and Carnwath, Viscount Kenmure and Lord Nairn.   Speaking of the petition, Lady Cowper says in her Diary :—"February 21 [1716].—The Ladies of the condemned Lords brought their petition to the House of Lords to solicit the King for a reprieve. The Duke of St. Albans was the man chosen to deliver it, but the Prince advised him not to do so without the King's leave.   The Archbishop of Canterbury opposes the Court strenuously in the rejecting the petition."[3]

Hopeless of the extension of the royal clemency to the Earl, Lady Nithsdale formed the design of effecting his escape.   He was confined in the house of Colonel D'Oyly, lieutenant-depute of the Tower, in a small room which looked out on Water Lane, the ramparts, and the wharf, and was sixty feet from the ground floor.   The way from the room was through the Council Chamber, and the passages and stairs of D'Oyly's house.   The door was guarded by a sentinel, the floor by two, the passages and stairs by several, and the outer door by two.   How was it possible, then, for the Earl to escape ?

[1] The letter of Mrs. Evans here referred to is unfortunately lost.
[2] Vol. ii. p. 220.   [3] Lady Cowper's Diary, p. 80.

But what would have been judged impracticable to less energetic minds did not seem to be so to Lady Nithsdale.

After visiting the Earl, and discovering that the rules of the prison were not enforced so rigidly as they might have been ; that the wives and children of the keepers had ready access to the place, and were often there, she had sagacity enough to discover that, by nice management, his escape was by no means hopeless.   Her plan was to dress him in female attire, and personally to conduct him through the sentries, as if he had been a female friend who had come with her to the prison to pay a farewell visit to the Earl.   Her purpose she confided at first to none but her attached and faithful servant, Mrs. Evans.   Her chief difficulty lay in persuading the Earl to take advantage of the means she had planned for his escape.   He could not help smiling at an idea apparently so preposterous.   It would have seemed to him a more likely means of escape to force his way with sword in hand through the guards.

She immediately proceeded to concert her measures.   After the Earl's condemnation she was refused access to him, except on condition that she would stay with him in prison.   This she declined to do, on the plea that her health could not stand such confinement ; the true reason being that this would have defeated her plan for saving the life of the Earl.   She was, however, frequently admitted to see him, and, with other friends, was permitted, during the last week, to go and take leave of the condemned Lords.   In making these visits she conciliated the guards by giving them money.   By the help of Mrs. Evans she provided all that was necessary for the Earl's disguise.

On Wednesday, 22d February, two days before that fixed for the execution, a general petition was presented to the House of Lords, praying them to intercede with the King to pardon the prisoners.   Lady Nithsdale, and the other ladies of the prisoners, had expected that it would have been presented on the day before, but the Duke of St. Albans,[1] notwithstanding his promise to the Countess of Derwentwater,[2] had neglected to present it.

There was, however, still another day before the fatal day, and he pro-

[1] Charles Beauclerk, first Duke of St. Albans, K.G., son of King Charles the Second, by Eleanor Gwyn.

[2] Anna Maria, eldest daughter of Sir John Webbe of Oldstock and of Hythrop, in the county of Gloucester, Baronet.   Her husband was James Ratcliff, third Earl of Derwentwater.

mised not to fail again. Lady Nithsdale, to prevent a second disappointment, engaged the Duke of Montrose, thus securing, as far as she could, the presentation of the petition by the one or the other. Attended by a numerous train of most of the ladies of quality then in town, she proceeded to the lobby of the House of Lords to solicit the favour of the Lords as they went in. She was treated with civility by them all, and the petition was favourably responded to, chiefly through a speech delivered by Lord Pembroke,[1] who, though he begged her not to come near him, sent her word that he would do his utmost on behalf of the prisoners. It was disputed whether the King had power to pardon prisoners whom the Parliament had accused; but it was carried by the House of Lords that the King had this power, and they agreed, in terms of the petition, to intercede with him for mercy to the condemned Lords. One of the Lords, however, explained that their intercession would be only for such of the prisoners as deserved it, and not in general. This extinguished in Lady Nithsdale all hope of the Earl's obtaining a pardon. She knew what this meant. Those only would be considered deserving of mercy who would give information as to all who had embarked in the insurrection. The Earl of Nithsdale, she knew, would never purchase life at such a price, nor did she desire that he should. Yet, to further her design, she took advantage of the resolution adopted by the House of Lords to petition the King in behalf of the condemned Lords in general. Hastening to the Tower, and putting on a joyous air, she went up to the guards at each station and told them that she brought them good news. There was now, she said, no fear of the prisoners, as the motion that the Lords should intercede with the King on their behalf had passed. The sentries, by believing that the prisoners would be pardoned, would, she judged, be less vigilant. To keep them in good humour, she gave them some money, and bade them drink the health of the King and the Peers; but she was not profuse in her gifts, to prevent suspicion of her having some design on foot.

This was on Wednesday, two days before the time fixed for the Earl's execution. The intercession of the Lords on behalf of the prisoners was only partially successful. Four of the condemned were reprieved, to be afterwards

---

[1] Thomas Herbert, eighth Earl of Pembroke and fifth Earl of Montgomerie, K.G., of whose family Lady Nithsdale's was a branch. He died 22d January 1732-3.

pardoned—Lords Widdrington, Nithsdale, Carnwath, and Nairn ;[1] but on the other two, Lord Derwentwater and Lord Kenmure, the law was left to take effect.   Busy with the preparations for the Earl's escape, Lady Nithsdale did not visit him until the afternoon of the following day (Thursday).   When about to go and see him, she made known her design to Mrs. Mills, with whom she lodged, and prayed her immediately to go with her, as it was a part of her plan that, in coming out of prison, the Earl might pass for her, for she was as tall as he was, and, being with child, would be about the same size. Lady Nithsdale had also communicated her purpose to Mrs. Morgan, and requested this lady, who was tall and slender, to put under her own riding-hood another which Lady Nithsdale had provided to put on Mrs. Mills, who was to give her own to the Earl, which fitted him well.

These two ladies, ready to do Lady Nithsdale any service of friendship in their power, at once consented to act each her part.   All three went into the coach, and, not to give them leisure to think of the consequences, her ladyship continued without ceasing to talk with them.   On arriving at the Tower, she first brought in Mrs. Morgan—for she could take in with her only one at a time—who brought in the clothes which Mrs. Mills was to exchange for her own.   Mrs. Morgan having left the clothes, Lady Nithsdale quickly conducted her out again, going with her partly down-stairs, saying to her at parting, " Pray do me the kindness to send my maid to me that I may be dressed, else I shall be too late with my petition."   Then she took into the room Mrs. Mills, who, as instructed by her, came in with her handkerchief at her face as if in tears for her friend, the Earl, who was about to suffer death. The Earl was to go out in the same manner, the more effectually to conceal him from the guards.   Mrs. Mills's eyebrows were somewhat yellow, and the Earl's were thick and black, but Lady Nithsdale, by a little paint and ringlets of the same coloured hair which she had brought with her, remedied this. There was no time to shave his long beard ; but she had got some white paint to cover it and the rest of his face, and some red paint for his cheeks.   The guards, who, from the little money which she had given them the night before, were in good humour, allowed her to go in and out with the two ladies ; and,

[1] The Earl of Nithsdale's escape from the Tower, a new crime, which greatly excited the resentment of the King, prevented his obtaining, as the other three Lords did, a royal pardon.

believing that a pardon would be granted to the prisoners, they were not so watchful as they would otherwise have been. Mrs. Mills having exchanged her dress, Lady Nithsdale conducted her out of the Earl's room, addressing her as they passed through the other room, in which were nine persons, the guards' wives and daughters, "Pray, Mrs. Catherine, look for my woman, who has apparently forgotten the petition which I am to give in, and bid her make haste to come to me." The sentinels at the door opened it immediately. Having seen out Mrs. Mills, who did not go out as she had come in, with a handkerchief on her eyes as if weeping, Lady Nithsdale returned to the Earl, and, having got him quite ready, now she thought was the time for action. It was growing very dark, and, afraid lest the keepers should bring in the candles, which would have defeated her pains, she, without longer delay, came out of the room leading by the hand the Earl, who was clothed in the attire of Mrs. Mills,[1] and held a handkerchief about his eyes as if in tears, which served to conceal his face. To prevent suspicion, she spoke to him in a plaintive tone, complaining that Mrs. Evans, by her long delay, had ruined her ; and, addressing him as " dear Mrs. Betty," she said, " Run and bring her with you for God's sake ; you know my lodgings, and if ever you made haste in your life do it now, for I am almost distracted with this disappointment."

The guard, who had not been minutely observant of the coming in and departure of the ladies, without the least suspicion quickly opened the door. Lady Nithsdale went down-stairs with the Earl, still conjuring him as "dear Mrs. Betty" to make haste. Having got him out of the door, she stepped behind him, lest the sentinel might have discovered something in his gait to cause suspicion. At the foot of the stairs she found Mrs. Evans, who conducted the Earl with great presence of mind to a house near Drury Lane, that belonged to a friend of her own, in whom she could confide. Mrs. Mills having procured for him another place to stay in, the Earl was taken to it. This was a house just before the Court of Guards, occupied by a poor woman, who had one little room up a small pair of stairs, in which was a small bed.

[1] " From the woman's cloak and hood," says Allan Cunningham, " in which the Earl was disguised, the Jacobites of the north formed a new token of cognisance—all the ladies who favoured the Stuarts wore ' Nithsdales,' till fashion got the better of political love." He adds, " I wish the royal clemency had extended to the ancient and noble name of Maxwell, when other names were restored to their honours."—Songs of Scotland, vol. iii. p. 188.

Thus was the romantic adventure of Lady Nithsdale successful by the kind assistance of two ladies, without whose help it might have failed.

Lady Nithsdale had made a show of sending the lady—who was the Earl —on a message. It was therefore necessary for her to return to his room and to appear to be perplexed and in anguish as before. This she did, calling forth the compassion of all about the place. On reaching the Earl's chamber, her presence of mind and contrivance never forsaking her, she affected to speak to him, and to answer as if he had spoken to her, imitated his voice, and walked up and down the room as if they had been walking and talking together, till she thought that he had time enough to be out of reach. Then opening the door to depart, she went half out, and holding it in her hand, that those without might hear, she took a solemn and an affectionate leave of his Lordship for that night, complained of the delay of Mrs. Evans in coming to her, said that she behoved to go herself in search of her, and promised that, if the Tower was open, she would yet see him that night, but that otherwise she would see him in the morning, when she hoped to have good news to tell him. Before shutting the door, to prevent its being opened on the outside, she drew into the inside a little string that lifted a wooden latch, and then, to shut the door surely, shut it with a flap. In passing she told the Earl's valet de chambre, who knew nothing of the matter, that his Lordship, as he was at prayers, did not wish the candles to be brought till he called for them. So she went down-stairs. Getting into one of the hackney coaches, that were waiting in the place, Lady Nithsdale went to her own lodgings, where she had left Mr. Mackenzie to stay for the petition that was to have been given in if her adventure failed, and told him that there was now no need for presenting the petition, as his Lordship was out of the Tower, and she hoped out of the hands of the Government. She then ordered a chair and went to Anne, Duchess of Buccleuch, who, as the widow of the unfortunate Duke of Monmouth, who had suffered for treason, could sympathize with the agony of Lady Nithsdale under similar circumstances. The Duchess had promised to go along with her when she went to give in her petition. She did not go up to the Duchess, who had company, but left her thankful acknowledgments to her for her promised favour, and desired her not to trouble herself further, as it was thought that a general petition in the name of all would be sufficient.

Having left the residence of the Duchess of Buccleuch, Lady Nithsdale went in a chair to another sympathizing Duchess, her Grace the Duchess of Montrose, who was Lady Christian Carnegie, daughter of David, third Earl of Northesk.

The Duchess of Montrose, afraid lest their meeting together might open the sluices of Lady Nithsdale's anguish, instructed her servants, if the Countess of Nithsdale came to see her, to say that the Duchess was not at home. By some mistake the servants brought Lady Nithsdale into the Duchess's room. When the Duchess came into the chamber, the Countess smiled, and ran to her in a transport of joy. The Duchess started, and, ignorant of the Earl of Nithsdale's escape, thought Lady Nithsdale's head, from her apparent ecstasy, was turned through anguish, till she learned from her own lips her successful enterprise.

The Duchess of Montrose besought her, as King George the First was mightily incensed at her for the petition which she had ventured to present to him, to betake herself to a place of safety, and said that she would go to the Court and see how the news of the Earl's escape was received. She did so. The King stormed terribly. "He was betrayed," he exclaimed, "for such an event could not have happened without connivance." To prevent a similar mishap, he immediately despatched two messengers to the Tower, to see that the other prisoners were well guarded. But when he had time to reflect, taking a cooler view of the case, he said that "for a man in my Lord's situation, it was the very best thing he could have done."

Having left the Duchess of Montrose, Lady Nithsdale went to the house which had previously been found for her by Mrs. Evans, who, as she had promised, soon after came thither, and informed her of the hiding-place of the Earl, and, as narrated before, of what had happened to him after his escape. Referring to the little room up a small pair of stairs, and to "a poor little bed" in it, Lady Nithsdale says,—"Into this bed we were forced to goe imediatly, for feare they should heare more walking than vsual. She left vs a botle of wine and some bread, and Mrs. Mills brought vs some more the next day in her pocket, but other thing we gott not from Thu[r]sday evening to Saturday evening, that Mrs. Mills came when it was dark, and cary'd my Lord to the Venetian Embaçador's, who knew nothing of the matter."[1] One of the

---

[1] Vol. ii. p. 229.

ambassador's servants, named Mr. Michell, kept the Earl in his own room till Wednesday; and then conveyed him to France as already described.

The Countess went to a trustworthy friend's house in Drury Lane, where she lay quiet till tidings reached her of the Earl's safe arrival on the other side of the water. It was believed that she had gone with him. The Government therefore did not search for her.

In a letter to the Duchess of Buccleuch, she begged the Duchess to endeavour to obtain for her permission to go in safety about her business. The Government refused. There were repeated discussions about the way in which she was to be treated. It was proposed to apprehend her. The Solicitor-General,[1] a man whom she had never seen and of whom she knew nothing, would have her to be leniently dealt with. He said that, since she so far deferred to the Government as to hide herself, it would be cruelty to search for her. It was therefore resolved not to make any particular search for her, and to arrest her only in the event of her openly appearing either in the kingdom of England or in that of Scotland.

Having remained for some time concealed in London, the danger of her being apprehended rendering any open appearance on her part imprudent and dangerous, she resolved to undertake a journey to Scotland on horseback.

Reference has been already made to her burying at Terregles the family writs before starting for London. These writs, if left to lie long in the earth, might have been injured or destroyed by damp, and thus the title-deeds to the estates of the families of Maxwell and Herries might have perished, to the irreparable detriment of her son. It was no doubt dangerous for her to travel from London to Scotland,—not, indeed, from the obstruction of bad roads and ill weather, as when she went to London, but from the risk of her being seized and imprisoned. She had, however, perilled her life for the father; and now she resolved to run a second hazard for the son. She purchased three horses for the journey, and, attended by Mrs. Evans and a trusty valet, who had accompanied her from Scotland to London, she set out on horseback direct for Traquair, lodging, to preserve her *incognito*, in all the small inns where she

---

[1] Sir John Fortescue-Aland was appointed to the office of Solicitor-General of England on 16th December 1715. He was afterwards, in 1746, created a Peer of Ireland, with the title of Baron Fortescue of Credan.

would not be known, as she was in the best inns on both roads. She arrived in safety at Traquair about the end of the month of April or the beginning of the month of May, and to her great joy found her beloved daughter Anne, as well as her other relatives, in health and comfort. At this place she felt secure, as the Lord Lieutenant of the county, who was her husband's friend, would not search for her without first giving her a private warning to get out of the way. She rested at Traquair for two days without any fear, but made it pass as if she had come to Scotland with the leave of the Government. She, however, sent no notice to those in her house of Terregles, lest it might reach the magistrates of Dumfries.

Proceeding to Terregles, she found that her arrival in Scotland was then unknown. She did not, however, now conceal it, but endeavoured to convey the impression that she had got permission from the Government to return to Scotland. To strengthen this belief, she sent word of her arrival to all her neighbours, and intimated the pleasure she would have in seeing them. Meanwhile she did not delay to excavate the buried family writs, which she found, though the winter had been severe, perfectly safe, and as dry as if they had been by the fireside, which could hardly have happened had they lain long in the earth ; and she immediately sent them to Traquair, thus accomplishing the work for which she had come to Scotland.

She again returned to Traquair, where she remained for several weeks. This appears from various letters which she wrote in the month of May from Traquair to Major Maxwell at Terregles. Early in that month she wrote from Traquair to him about the selling of what was her own property, and procuring money. In a letter to him, 6th May, she says, " I heare there is some trees a cutting down. I supose it is none neare the howse, for those my Lord would be angrie at, but should be glad if any others could bring me money. But I fancy it is only for reparation of tenants' houses we are oblig'd to repair." [1] In another letter to him, written from Traquair, 18th May, she says, " I beg you to take all the care you can about selling my things as soon as possible, and as many as you can, for I find my stay here must be very short, and I shall be much straitened for money." Various articles of furniture she wished to be sent to Traquair and others to

[1] Vol. ii. p. 239.

be sold. " The cabinet in my closet get sold, if it can be, tables and stands, and anything that can yeild money. Lett great care be taken of the horses, because I shall want them soon, and the stables well shut, that they may not be seased. The three boles of malt in William M'William's hands I desire I may get money for also ; and, in short, any thing I can get it by."[1]

In a third letter to Major Maxwell at Terregles, written from Traquair, 22d May, she would have him sell the grass upon the meadows, if he could, and three bolls of malt, and send the money as soon as possible. Some horses and cows, and other things she wished to be sold. If there could be got a strong horse that would carry double, and had an easy trot, she would be glad to buy it ; for being advanced in pregnancy she was afraid of riding single on account of the pommel.[2] Writing again to him from Traquair, 28th May, she complains that the cows had gone off at the sale for much less than she expected, but she did not blame him for that, as people had taken advantage of the necessity she was in of parting with them.[3] A female correspondent, writing to her from Terregles, 15th June, informs her that the sale of her effects was nearly finished, notwithstanding the warning her friends had got not to meddle with rebels' goods. But they answered that her Ladyship was no rebel, and that the goods were hers.[4]

How long Lady Nithsdale remained at this time at Traquair before starting again for London is not quite certain. What at length hastened her departure was the purpose of the magistrates of Dumfries, who doubted whether she had obtained leave from the Government to return to Scotland, to wait upon her, and see whether she could produce a safe-conduct. Intelligence of their purpose reaching her, she prepared without delay for her journey. On the following morning, by break of day, she set out on horseback, with the same company that had attended her to Scotland.[5] Travelling, as before, on by-ways, and resting at by-inns, she arrived safely in London. She was there in the beginning of July. A letter which she wrote to Lady Traquair,

---

[1] Vol. ii. p. 240.   [2] Vol. ii. p. 241.
[3] Ibid. p. 242.   [4] Ibid. p. 244.

[5] From Lady Nithsdale's letters to Major Maxwell, now quoted, it appears that she remained longer in Scotland, and at Traquair, than is implied in her letter to her sister, Lady Lucie Herbert. She evidently stayed at Terregles only a few days, and then returned to Traquair, where she was at the beginning of May, and throughout that month as well as during a part of June. She probably went direct for London from Traquair, not from Terregles, as seems to be mistakenly stated in her letter to her sister.

informing her of her safe arrival, is dated London, 3d June [1] [July]. In that letter she informs her that on her arrival in London she found two letters from the Earl of Nithsdale, in answer to those which she had written to him, pressing her to hasten to come over to him at Paris, and to bring over with her their dear little daughter; the one dated 1st June, in which he said that he had written to her five weeks ago from Paris, urging her to come over, and the other dated the 10th of June.[2]

On her arrival in London she learned that it was the common talk that she was in Scotland, and was there appearing openly, notwithstanding the prohibition. "She has done me," said the King, "more mischief than any woman in Christendom," and he gave orders that she should be searched for. She lay quiet till the commotion had subsided. By an eminent lawyer, whom she consulted, she was instructed that in matters of treason so rigorous was the law that in a case like hers a wife's head would have to answer for her husband's, though in all other cases a wife could not be pursued for effecting her husband's escape; and that the King was so incensed against her in consequence of the unpopularity he had acquired by reason of the rudeness with which he had treated her when she offered to present to him the petition formerly mentioned, that, were she arrested, her life would be in danger. The lawyer therefore, and all her friends, advised her to leave England.[3] About a fortnight after she embarked for France, and the trials, fatigues, and risks which it had been her fate hitherto to undergo were only to be repeated under other forms.

On 19th July, she writes from London to Mary Countess of Traquair,

---

[1] The date of June in this letter is evidently incorrect. She had written to Major Maxwell from Traquair on 28th May, and it was impossible for her to go on horseback from Traquair to London in four or five days, especially when she was advanced in pregnancy. Besides, she refers to a letter from her husband, written on 10th June, waiting for her on her arrival in London.

[2] Vol. ii. p. 245.

[3] The authority for the story of the escape of the Earl is Lady Nithsdale's own account, in a letter by her to her sister, Lady Lucie Herbert, Abbess of the English Augustine Nuns at Bruges. It is without date, but was probably written from the "Royal Palais de Rome, April 16th 1718;" the date given in a copy of the letter made for William Maxwell of Nithsdale, her son. *Vide* vol. ii. pp. 222-234. Her account of the escape of the Earl, in a manner resembles that of Madame de Lavalette's rescue of her husband from the Conciergerie at Paris in 1815. The particulars of the Earl's escape are narrated by Lady Nithsdale in a style of unvarnished natural simplicity, without the smallest attempt at elegant or sensational writing, or even at gaining the sympathy of the reader. Yet such is the effect, that most readers will peruse her ingenuous narrative with interest, and even with emotion — sympathizing with her anxieties when her plan was executing, and with her joy when it resulted in triumph.

probably the last letter which she wrote previous to her sailing for the Continent, that she was just going on board a ship.[1]   She set sail on that night,[2] which was Thursday, at twelve o'clock, intending to go to Bruges.   On leaving London she was in good health.   But after embarking she was afflicted with sea-sickness, and the vomiting brought upon her a miscarriage.   So severe was her illness, that when about three miles from Bruges, she was landed, on the first Sunday after she set sail, at three o'clock in the afternoon, at Sluce, which is a little beyond Ostend.   To have proceeded farther would have endangered her life.   Her maid, Mrs. Evans, under the assumed name of Powell, who assisted and shared in all her troubles, fatigues, and dangers, and who, till her death, remained with her as her faithful friend and attached attendant, in a letter to Mary Countess of Traquair, dated Sluce [Helvoitsluys], 28th June [July], old style, says : "I have been in many dangerous illness with her, but never like this. . . . Some of her danger is abated since come on shore, which must have ended her had she been longer on sea, because the vomiting continually stress'd her. . . . We shall stay here till she is past danger, for we can't goe to Bruges from hence by water, but wagons or coach, and the jolting wou'd quite ruine her yet."[3]

A few days after her arrival at Bruges, Lady Nithsdale, in a letter to her sister-in-law, Mary Countess of Traquair, dated from that place, 22d August [1716], says, "I was carry'd out of the ship in a sad condition, and it is not many days since I gott hether, for I thought it not possible to move sooner.   However, I am now on the recovering hand, God be praysed."[4]

She was with the Earl at Lille on 16th October following.[5]   Having left Lille, she went to her old mistress, Mary of Modena, Queen of King James the Seventh, who received her kindly, but was not in a position to take her back into her service.   She endeavoured to get from her a letter to her son, recommending him to take the Earl into his service, but his affairs also were

[1] Vol. ii. p. 247.

[2] Ibid. p. 249.

[3] Vol. ii. p. 247.   This letter of Mrs. Evans is the only one written by her preserved among the papers at Traquair, though she no doubt wrote several letters to Lady Traquair.   Many bundles of papers at Traquair were so completely destroyed with damp and want of care that it was impos- sible to decipher them, or gain the least insight into their purport.   Many of Mrs. Evans' letters as well as Lady Nithsdale's were, perhaps, contained in these bundles.   One letter from Mrs. Evans at Terregles, on household matters, is much tattered, but the signature is entire.

[4] Vol. ii. p. 249.

[5] Ibid. p. 251.

not in a condition to admit of his increasing his establishment, which, as he was about to undertake a journey, he would rather diminish.   These resources failing her, she made efforts to get a pension.   She succeeded in obtaining for herself 100 livres per month, and for the Earl 200 livres, sums insufficient for their maintenance, the more especially as the Earl was improvident in money matters.

"Let me doe what I will," says she, in animadverting on his money-spending habits, in a letter from Paris, 29th February [1717], to Mary Countess of Traquair, "he cannot be brought to submit to live according to what he has.   And when I indeavered to persuad him to keep in compass, he atributed my advice to my gruging him every thing, which stop't my mouth ; since I am sure that I would not grudge my heart's blood, if it could doe him any service. . . . As long as I had any thing it went.   After all was gone, I was forced to take forty pounds sterling that I had put out of our litle girles to bring us hether. . . . I had, a litle after our meeting at Lile, in-deaver'd to persuad him to goe back to his master, upon the notice he received that 50 livers a month was taken of his pension, but that I did not dare persist in, for he seem'd to imagine that I had a mind to be rid of him, which one would have thought could scarce come into his mind. . . . When I per-suaded him at Lile, I was in hopes soon to follow him ; but now God knows when I shall see him. . . . He was to be at Lions last Tusday, and I cannot hope to heare from him till I am arrived at La Flesh, for I go from hence to morrow morning, at seven o'clock."   They stayed at Lille till they spent all, and then went to Paris, at which the preceding letter is dated.[1]   Shortly after, Lady Nithsdale's letters are written at La Flèche, from which place two of her letters are dated, the one 28th of March, and the other 10th of June [1717].[2]

At La Flèche Lady Nithsdale, 3d May 1717, appointed Mr. Alexander Ferguson of Isle, and Mr. John Alves, advocate, her factors and com-missioners, giving them full power and warrant in her name and behalf, to subscribe and give in to the Commissioners appointed by Act of Parlia-ment for inquiring into the forfeited estates in Scotland, her claims to her jointure settled upon the estate of Nithsdale, to which she had right by

[1] Vol. ii. pp. 252, 253.   [2] Vol. ii. pp. 254, 257.

contract of marriage, with power to them to do everything thereanent that she could do herself.[1]

But this appointment was probably disregarded.   While the ladies of the other attainted Lords got their jointures, the virtuous and heroic Lady Niths-dale was cruelly denied the same boon.

Whilst the Earl went to join the Chevalier at Rome, Lady Nithsdale remained in France.   At Rome the Earl's hopes were excited, partly by pro-mises made by the Chevalier, and partly by his own imagination.   On informing him that he was about to be married, the Chevalier expressed himself as very desirous to have the Earl in his family.   This encouraged the Earl's expectations, and he entreated Lady Nithsdale, who was in Paris with the ex-Queen Mary of Modena, to come to Rome, in the full hope that she too would obtain an honourable place in the Chevalier's household.   " As for your journey hether," he writes, " the sooner you thinke of it the better ; therefore it is your interest to manage it with your Mistris and other freinds, so as to be ready on a call, for you cannot imagine what prejudice a delaye may doe in such a matter ; for first come first served, they say ; and were you here I am confident my Master would refuse you nothing you could in reason aske, for he speakes of you with affection, and I am sure you would gaine on him every day ; so I thinke you ought to write to my brother and sister Tra-quair to see if they can help you any thing towards your journey, which I hope they will doe on the score of the furniture they have in their hands, and that it may one day or other tend to their advantage."

Lady Nithsdale, in a letter to Mary Countess of Traquair, dated 28th June [1718], earnestly begs from her pecuniary help to enable her to go to Rome to join her husband, sending her the above extract from one of his letters ; the more especially as she had just lost by death her mistress, Mary of Modena, who, had she been alive, would from her private purse have given her the money necessary for accomplishing the journey.[2]

The Earl of Nithsdale's suggestion of borrowing money from his sister on his furniture, which had been sent to Traquair, offended her and her husband,

[1] Original Commission at Terregles.

[2] Vol. ii. pp. 276, 277.—Mary of Modena died at St. Germain-en-Laye, 7th May 1718, in the sixtieth year of her age, and the thirtieth of her exile, having survived her husband, King James the Seventh, sixteen years and eight months.

the Earl of Traquair, who had taken the furniture, not because they needed it, but simply to secure it.   Lady Nithsdale makes an apology to the Countess in a letter to her, dated Paris, 6th August [1718].[1]

The Chevalier invited Lady Nithsdale to come to join her husband at Rome.   To defray the expenses of the journey she obtained a little money, and a gentleman, whom she was to maintain, having been ordered to go along with her, her allowance was somewhat augmented, though still insufficient.[2] She was to begin her journey on the 9th of September.   In a letter to Father Hudson, from Lyons, 12th September, she says,—" I am got thus far on my journey safe : I shall write again to you from Turin."[3]

At Rome Lady Nithsdale experienced only disappointment and mortification.

In a letter to Mary Countess of Traquair, dated 3d January [1719 ?], she says,—" I have still difer'd writing to you since I came to this place, hopeing to hav some agreeable newse to make a letter wellcome, that had so far to goe, but we still are in the same situation, and live vpon hopes, and, indeed, without hopes heart would break, but I can say noe more.   But they tell vs that a short time will give vs what we have been so long expecting."[4]   But the frequent blighting of her hopes in the past did not encourage her to look for much in the future.   Her letters abound with complaints of pecuniary pressure.   She could not get the Earl to regulate his expenditure in correspondence with his means.   In contracting debt his manner was to promise to make payment at a certain time, but then failing, he was thus kept as he had been at home, in constant difficulties.[5]   " All my comfort is," she writes, "that I have had noe share in this misfortune, for he has never been the man that has offer'd me one farthing of all the money he has taken vp, and as yet all is spent, but how is a ridle to me." " To the end," she again says, " that he might not make me the pretence [of his scarcity of money], as he ever did, I doe not touch a peney of what he has, but leave it all to him to mentain him and his man, which is all he has, and live vpon what is allow'd me, which is just the same sum ; and I am forced to

[1] Vol. ii. p. 279.
[2] Lady Nithsdale's letter to Father James Hudson in Galloway, written in August and September 1718.   Vol. ii. p. 282
[3] Vol. ii. p. 282.
[4] Ibid. p. 285.
[5] Ibid. pp. 286, 303, 325.

keep four instead of his one ; to wit, a boy, to whom I must give a livery, my woman, and the child's maid; for tho' the child is with my sister she only gives her meat, drink, and lodging, and cloths, but I am forced to pay Mary's wages, and provide the child in masters, that coasts me alone 36 livres a month."[1]

Lady Nithsdale had enemies in the Court of the Chevalier, or cold friends, who attended chiefly to their own interests.   In the same letter to the Countess of Traquair she complains of being kept at as great a distance from the Chevalier as could well be, and of the industry used to let her, if possible, have none of his ear.

He was going to a house that his family could scarce fill, and yet she could not obtain a place under his roof.   " But that," she says, " and many other things must be lookt over ; at least we shall have bread by being near him, and I have the hapiness once againe to be with my deare husband, that I love above my life . . . We do not keep house, but pay so much a meal, and our servants at board wages ; and I pay what adition to his lodgings I occasion, which is only a room for Evans."[2]

In 1719 the Chevalier married Clementina Sobieski (born 17th July 1702), fourth daughter of James Louis Sobieski, Prince of Poland.

The marriage having been negotiated, the Princess Clementina and her mother, after some adventures, arrived in safety at Bologna on 2d May 1719. They did not find the Chevalier, who was then in Spain.   But the Honourable James Murray, second son of David, fifth Viscount Stormont, who was despatched by the Chevalier, arrived from Madrid on the 8th of May to act as proxy for James in the ceremony of marriage, and next day the marriage by proxy took place.   Cardinal Ongo pronounced the benediction.   Clementina remained at Bologna for four months, when, on James's return from Spain, they were married in person at Monte Frasconi in September 1719 by the Pope.

For the purpose of having their letters safely conveyed to Scotland, Lord and Lady Nithsdale generally used assumed names.   The Earl adopted the names of " William Brown" and " William Sinclair," while the Countess usually

---

[1] Vol. ii. pp. 285, 286.   She complains similarly in a letter to the Countess of Traquair, dated 2d July [1722], vol. ii. pp. 342, 343.   [2] Vol. ii. p. 287.

assumed the names of " W. Joanes," and occasionally that of " W. Johnston." Lady Traquair was generally addressed by letter as " Mrs. Young."

The correspondence between the exiled family of Nithsdale and their near relations at Traquair was chiefly conducted by Lady Nithsdale and Lady Traquair. Lord Nithsdale was an indifferent correspondent, the writing of letters being a trouble to him: his son, Lord Maxwell, was also, like his father, a careless correspondent.

Lady Nithsdale's letters are numerous, and are written in a frank and friendly spirit. Being about the Court of the Prince (James the Third) and his Princess, her letters contain many notices of the royal exiles.

Lady Nithsdale announces to her sister-in-law the arrival at Rome, on the 16th May 1719, of the Princess Clementina of Poland, as the wife of James the Third. Lady Nithsdale went to meet the Princess, whom she describes as very charming, obliging, and well-bred. She said that the King, whom she always styles " Our Master," must be extremely happy with her, and so would all those who had the good fortune to have any dependence upon her. Her personal appearance is described as being very pretty. She had good eyes, a fine skin, was well shaped for her height, but was not tall, although she might still be so, as she was only seventeen, and looked even younger.[1]

In another letter, written in the autumn of the same year, Lady Nithsdale informs Lady Traquair that the Prince and Princess were both very well and very fond of one another. The prospects of a diminished Court during the winter were not cheering to Lady Nithsdale, who appears to have received some disagreeable treatment from the courtiers during the temporary absence of the royal family. Lord Nithsdale wished the Countess to retire from the Court, but, for the good of her children and family, she resolved to brave the difficulties she experienced. Between the Court officials and her husband's expensive habits Lady Nithsdale's situation was far from being enviable. She continued to wear mourning clothes, being unable from the want of money to purchase more suitable apparel.

In the spring of the following year there happened an auspicious event, which not only gladdened the hearts of the royal family, but was a source of joy to their adherents. This was the fact that the Princess was with child,

[1] Vol. ii. p. 294.

the tidings of which Lady Nithsdale joyfully announces to her sister-in-law in a letter, dated 20th March 1720.[1] Yet even this event caused annoyance to Lady Nithsdale. She was not informed of the circumstance by the Princess, who had confided it to the Honourable Mrs. Hay, daughter of Lord Stormont, and the wife of the Honourable John Hay, who was Secretary to the Prince, and created Earl of Inverness. Lady Nithsdale thought this a slight, and was offended. Mrs. Hay, she writes, had no experience " of that kind," though " I have had occasion to be better versed in those things, having been so long maried and had so many children."[2]

The state of the Princess appears to have been intentionally concealed from Lady Nithsdale. When the Princess was indisposed, which she frequently was, after the reports of her pregnancy, Lady Nithsdale attended thrice daily to inquire for her. She was not informed of the real cause of the indisposition, but was told by the Princess and others that it was nothing but a cold, although they knew differently.

This neglect towards Lady Nithsdale, in addition to what she had already experienced, led her to believe that, when the royal infant was born, the charge of it would not be committed to her. If such was the intention, she resolved to retire from the Court, as to stay longer there could be of no advantage to herself or her family, whilst she would escape the disrespect and mortifications to which she was constantly exposed.

In the letter just quoted, Lady Nithsdale alludes to her having been long married, and to the many children she had had. As the names of only four children are known, two who survived, and two who died young, it may be inferred that several other children, whose names have not been ascertained, owing probably to their having died in infancy, had been borne by her during the twenty years of her marriage, previous to the date of that letter.

In the summer of the same year Lady Nithsdale, in writing to her sister-in-law, recurs to the subject of her position at the Court: she had entered it in the firm belief that her being about the Prince and Princess might be beneficial to her family and children. Had she had nobody but herself, she affirms, with chafed feelings which she could not repress, that she would rather eat a crust in quiet, than be liable to daily slights and mortifications.

[1] Vol. ii. p. 307.   [2] *Ibid.* ii. p. 308.

To prevent the retort, in the event of her not being appointed to the charge of the royal child looked for, that she had not applied for the post, Lady Nithsdale addressed to the Prince a special letter wishing to know if she might hope that the "young Lord or Lady, when it pleased God to send it," would be committed to her care. She was unwilling to boast of being as skilful as any in the bringing up of young children ; but "it can't," she says, " be thought but that I must have some insight in it after having been near twenty years amongst them." She would yield to none in the zeal and care for them if confided to her. It was the honour, and not interest, that she coveted, as she was aware that her pension could not be augmented.

The Prince replied graciously to Lady Nithsdale. He admitted in flattering terms that she had all the necessary qualities ; but he did not intend to appoint either governess or under-governess, as the Princess, having but little to do, would herself look to the expected infant.

In the same letter Lady Nithsdale gives the reasons which induced her to continue in the service of the exiled royal family. Although not an agreeable or profitable employment, she considered it to be her duty to remain in that position for the sake of her family, who, in case any favourable turn of affairs should restore the Prince to the throne of his ancestors, could not be overlooked, as they would probably be if they retired from the royal service.

In a letter to her sister-in-law, dated 4th February 1721, Lady Nithsdale, after referring to a previous letter in which she had intimated the birth of a prince, mentions that he was very well and a fine child, and that his father was very fond of him.[1] She again returns to reasons for remaining in the service of the royal family. Were it not for the good of her own family she would herself have preferred a more private position. But she adds, we live for others in this world, and not for ourselves. Duty must be preferred ; and no part of that would she omit, whilst she would leave the rest to God.

In the same letter she adverts to her pecuniary straits, and her difficulty in providing suitable apparel for herself in attending on the Princess Clementina. She mentions, as a secret between herself and her sister-in-law, that she had the happiness to receive one handsome suit from the Pope, which was procured for her through the kindness of a cardinal.

[1] Vol. ii. p. 321.

The young Prince now became a constant topic in the correspondence of Lady Nithsdale, and full details as to his teething, weaning, and the other incidents of babyhood, may be found in her letters.[1]

In 1725 she was able to announce the birth of another Prince, afterwards Cardinal York, born on the 6th of March, a few minutes before eleven o'clock in the forenoon.

Lady Nithsdale's faithful and devoted maid, Mrs. Evans, under the designation of Cecil Evans, daughter of the deceased Captain Roger Evans, received from William Earl of Nithsdale a bond, dated at Rome 16th February, new style, 1723, by which he bound himself and his heirs to pay to her the sum of £200 sterling, with the ordinary annual rent of that principal sum from the date of the bond, so long as it should remain unpaid. This was to be in full satisfaction to her of all wages and salaries, or any other thing whatsoever which she could demand from him for whatever cause bygone. The following is the high testimony to her merits borne by the Earl in the preamble to the bond:—
" Whereas Cecil Evans, daughter of the deceased Captain Roger Evans, has for these good many years, with the greatest care, faithfulness, and affection, attended on the Countess of Nithsdale, my spouse, and also in a great measure I myself owe my life, under God, to her, she being chiefly instrumental in my making my escape out of the Tower of London, and since that time she has followed my and my said spouse's fate in foreign countries with the same care and concern, during which time her yearly salary and wages has run on unpay'd, and I being resolved, in lieu of bygone salaries and wages, and as a token of my gratitude and regard for her, to grant her this obligation, do

---

[1] The earliest indication of Prince Charles is in a letter from his father dated, Rome, April 29, 1720, in which he says,—" You will, I am sure, be glad to know that the Queen is with child, and in perfect good health, as well as myself."—[Original Holograph Letter at Blair-Drummond.] " Queen " Clementina bore to the Chevalier, 6th March 1725, a second son, Henry Benedict Marie Clement, named Duke of York, and made a Cardinal in the year 1747, under the title of Cardinal York. The Chevalier and Clementina did not live harmoniously together. She betook herself to the convent of St. Cecilia, and remained there till 1727, when she left and travelled to rejoin him at Bologna. On arriv- ing there she found that he had left for Avignon, in consequence of intelligence received of the death of George the First at Osnabrück. The Chevalier only rejoined her at Bologna in January 1728. She died at Rome on the 18th of January 1735, aged thirty-five years, and was buried with great pomp at St. Peter's. The Chevalier survived her for thirty years, having died in the year 1765, leaving issue by her his two sons. The eldest, Charles Edward Stuart, having died without issue, was succeeded in his pretensions and titles by his only brother Henry, Cardinal York, and as he died unmarried, the line of King James the Seventh wholly terminated in him.

therefore,"[1] etc. The bond bears to be written by James Edgar, son of David Edgar of Keithock, and he is one of the attesting witnesses to the signature of the Earl at Rome, along with Colin Erskine, son of Sir Alexander Erskine of Cambo, Lyon-King-of-Arms of Scotland. James Edgar was for many years private secretary to the titular King James the Eighth. Annexed to the bond there is a holograph ratification of it by William Lord Maxwell, dated at Bologna, 12th February 1727.

Ten years after the date of that bond, Cecilia Evans executed an assignation, whereby she assigned £50 sterling to Mistress Mary Bellew, daughter of of John Lord Bellew and Ann Lady Bellew, whom failing, to Ann Lady Bellew; and the remaining £150 sterling to Mary Lindsay, attending Anne Lady Bellew, out of which she was thereby enjoined, and by her acceptance thereof promised, to pay £30 sterling to a relation of Cecilia Evans, whom she had named to her, and given directions by word of mouth as to the payment of it; and as William Earl of Nithsdale was to pay all the debts she should happen to be owing at the time of her decease, and to be at the expenses of her funeral, masses for her soul, and other charities, she gave and assigned to him the whole annual-rent of the aforesaid principal sum that should happen to be due by virtue of the bond above mentioned at the time of her decease; and she also discharged him of all bygone wages and other claims and demands she had or might have upon him on any account whatsoever.[2] This assignation was executed at Rome, on the 7th of May 1733; and it is attested by Mr. John Stewart, uncle to the Earl of Bute, James Edgar, brother to Alexander Edgar of Keithock, and George Abernethie, son of the late Alexander Abernethie of Claymyres.

The money which Lady Nithsdale had received from Mr. William Alves to enable her to travel to London in the year 1715, and also to stay there till the Earl's escape, remained unpaid. Mr. Alves having died in September 1722, his son John, who assumed the management of his affairs, wrote a letter to the Countess of Nithsdale in the year 1729, informing her of his father's death, and requesting that she would give him an order for the repayment of the money which she had borrowed. To this letter she wrote the following answer from Rome, in which she expresses her grateful sense of

[1] Original Bond at Terregles.   [2] Original Assignation at Terregles.

the favour which had been done to her by his father, but, at the same time, her surprise that this money had not been recovered from the estate of Nithsdale :—

January 5th, 1730.

SIR,—The contents of your letter, received by the last post, was no small surprize to me, imagining that what money was advanced to me by your father was paid by an assignment he had upon the estate for all the debts was due to him, not doubting but mine was comprehended in them, and my son assured me that all your father's claims was now intirely satisfyed, but will be sure to write to him about it, and will send you word as soon as I receive his answer, and be assured that tho' justice did not oblige me to it, I have so much gratitude for the memory of one that was so obliging as to advance me money at such a time, not to do all things in my power to shew my regard to his son,—I am, Sir, your humble servant,

W. NITHSDAILL.

To Mr. John Alves, to the care of William Veatch, Writer to the Signet.[1]

The money being still unpaid, either John or Andrew Alves, sons of Mr. Alves, wrote a letter to the Countess, with the view of obtaining a settlement of the account. Their history of the transaction was to the effect that, upon her Ladyship's return to Scotland, in the summer of the year 1716, Mr. Alves waited on her at Traquair, where she granted him her obligation for the £100 she had got, and for £50 more in a letter of credit, then given her upon Mr. William Steuart, secretary to the Duke of Queensberry, as a friend, for a very important piece of service, in view for the Earl of Nithsdale's behoof. The obligation was in these terms :—" I, Winifred Countess of Nithsdale, grants me to have received from William Alves, Writer to the Signet, the sum of Fifty Pounds sterling, which with Fifty Pounds sterling contained in a bill drawn by me upon him, and a letter of credit given me this day on Mr. William Steuart, secretary to the Duke of Queensberry and Dover, for £50 sterling, which, when I receive, makes in haill the sum of £150 sterling ; which I promise to pay to the said William Alves with my conveniency. In witness whereof I have written and subscribed these presents at Traquair, the fifth day of June 1716.   WINIFRED NITHSDALE."

Lady Nithsdale made the following reply to the letter of Mr. Alves :—

May 15th 1738.

SIR,—I received from Doctor Wright the notes you sent to my Lord and me, about the money I received from your father. The fifty pound I am positively sure I had from his own hand, when or on what account I cannot be so positive, whether to go up to my Lord when in the

[1] Copy Letter at Terregles.

Tower, or to return back when I came to secure the papers that were underground ; but the date you mention must be a mistake, since I was gone from Traquair before that time,[1] but neither the mistake of date or place ought to be a stop to a just debt such as that is, and therefor if it is not found to have been comprehended in his other claims of which he is cleared, my Lord and I will do what is in our power to induce my son to pay it at the soonest.   As to the bill which you say I drew upon him for other Fifty, and that I was to receive from Mr. William Stewart, Secretary to the Duke of Queensberry and Dover, I remember nothing of the matter, so that Hundred pound must require their respective notes from me to witness it ; if I remembered them, as I do the fifty above mentioned, I would not desire them, for justice would be a sufficient motive, but not doing it I cannot desire my son to pay it without, but hope Mr. Veitch, who knew all the affair, as you told me, will supply.   I have wrote to him about it this very post, and have desired him to inform my son that it may also be payed if found due, and not cleared as before mentioned ; and have wrote to my son also in the strongest terms to desire him to pay what is found due at the soonest, you being in such straits, which could I relieve I would not want justice as a motive ; my own inclination would be a sufficient prompt to induce me to it, as being son to a father that had the affairs of the family so long in his hands.—I am, your humble servant,

W. NITHSDAILL.

The marriage of her son, William Lord Maxwell, with his cousin, Lady Catherine Stuart, daughter of the Earl of Traquair, and her steadfast friend and constant correspondent, who has been so often mentioned, and the marriage of her daughter, Lady Anne Maxwell, at Lucca, 13th September 1731, to John, fourth Lord Bellew, an Irish nobleman, afforded Lady Nithsdale much satisfaction.   Informing Lady Traquair of both these marriages, at which the Earl, but not herself, was present, in a letter to her from [Rome], 2d October that year,[2] she says, as to the character of Lord Bellew : "He has a sufficient estate, and the best character from every one that speakes of him that I have heard, which he has not bely'd in his generous setlements vpon her, far beyond what her small portion could require, and your brother sends me word he is extreamly fond of her, so I hope she will be happy."[3]   In another letter to the same correspondent, dated 30th January 1732, she writes : "The character you have heard of your neice, I supose, has been given by freinds,

[1] The accuracy of this statement of Lady Niths- dale is doubtful.   From the preceding narrative there is reason to think that she was at Traquair on 5th June, the date of receipt.

[2] This is the first letter that now exists from Lady Nithsdale to the Countess of Traquair, since that dated 7th March [1725], formerly quoted.   It is hardly to be supposed that the correspondence

between them should have so suddenly ceased, without any apparent cause.   Lady Nithsdale's letters to her sister-in-law between these years may have formed part of the many bundles of papers in the Traquair Charter-chest, which were found in so decayed a condition that it was impossible to ascertain their purport.

[3] Vol. ii. p. 362.

but, thanke God, she had the good fortune to be prety well spoaken of, and I hope she will make a good wife ; and Lord B[ellew] seems by reputation to have all the qualitys to make a wife happy, and is very fond of her. It would alwise be very natural for me to wish it, but I must confess I am the more solicitous about it, because she has had noe hand in the choise, but obay'd her parants, which I hope God will reward with a true hapiness between them."[1]

The latest of Lady Nithsdale's letters which has been preserved, is written to Lady Traquair, and is dated 29th January 1739.[2] Previous to that date there is no letter of hers to Lady Traquair extant after 10th December 1732.[3] There is thus a blank of nearly seven years in her correspondence with her sister-in-law. It is not probable that during that period all communication between them had ceased, though it may have been kept up with less regularity than formerly. Many of Lady Nithsdale's letters may have perished in the damp which was allowed to injure many of the papers at Traquair, where Lady Nithsdale's letters to the Countess of Traquair were deposited. There is, however, reason to believe, from the tremulousness of her handwriting in her signature, as appended to certain documents a few years posterior, that, from the infirmities of age, she found it difficult to maintain her correspondence with her former vigour.

After the death of the Earl in the year 1744, Lady Nithsdale was induced, though not without difficulty, to accept of a yearly annuity of £200 from her son, Lord Maxwell, who then inherited the estates, and purposed to apply £100 of that sum to the extinction of the debts of the deceased Earl, which, it would appear, would by this means be extinguished at the end of three years. This we learn from the following letter to Lord Maxwell from Mr. Alexander Smith, afterwards Vicar-Apostolic of the lowland district of Scotland, who styles him the Earl of Nithsdale, the son and heir of the deceased Earl of Nithsdale, for whom he acted :—

MY LORD,—It is with great pleasure I have now the honour to inform your Lordship of the good success of our negotiations, which I understand by a letter I have from Mr. Grant our agent, dated 6th April, N.S., whereof I shall here set down the most material part in Mr. Grant's own words : " In consequence of what you write concerning a certain good lady, I have not only

[1] Vol. ii. p. 363.   [2] Vol. ii. p. 369.   [3] Vol. ii. p. 366.

spoke to her myself, but have got some persons of great weight to address her on the same subject. She has at last, with much difficulty and by force of strong persuasions, acquiesced to what her son proposes, and accepts of the £200 he promises to remit her yearly, with this express condition, that, in case she should die before her late husband's debts are entirely pay'd, he should oblige himself to continue the said remittance after her death, till such time as they are utterly extinguish'd. This is not to be call'd a hard condition, for as she intends to apply one hundred pounds to this end, if she lives but this year, and two more, these debts will be all extinguish'd—I mean what are real debts. As for the legacies he left, she do's not trouble her head about them, but leaves them entirely to her son's discretion and generosity, and if he is so straitned as you represent, he needs not be in any great embarras about them." . . .

Thus far Mr. Grant, who, it seems, do's not so much notice ordinary formalities as the method your Lordship proposed at first, of giving the money here immediately (which I mention'd to him as an evident proof to convince the good old lady of her son's sincere inclination and exact readiness to satisfy her Ladyship so far as he was able), whereas the more natural way was to get a bill from my Lady, which might ever serve for a discharge, and we shall afterwards follow that method at present in acknowledging the receipt of the £100 ; we shall engage to procure a proper discharge.

Altho' perhaps ther wou'd not be a strict obligation in rigour of justice, yet I'm confident your Lordship wou'd have the goodness to pay your father's lawful debts, and therefore will the more readily comply with your mother's earnest demand. . . . I have the honour to be, with all regard, my Lord, your Lordship's most obedient humble servant,

AL. SMITH.

Edinburgh, 1st June 1745.
The Right Honourable the Earle of Nithesdale, at Terregles.[1]

The debts of the deceased Earl of Nithsdale were paid during the course of the year in which this letter was written. This we learn from a letter of Mr. Alexander Smith to Mr. Robison at Terregles, factor to William Lord Maxwell, styled Earl of Nithsdale, dated Edinburgh, 26th September 1745 : " I still resolv'd to write in answer to your last, but something or other interven'd, and meanwhile we got word from the good old Lady together with a bill; but our confusions here have even hindered me to notify that, tho' it came a good while ago. The bill is for £100 and ten shillings sterling. At the same time Mr. Grant writes to inform my Lord that, as his father's debts are now quite extinguish'd, his lady mother will have no occasion for more than one hundred pounds sterling *per annum* from him henceforth. She is now quite easy and happy, that she is free of what was a great and heavy burthen upon her. Please let his Lordship know so much."[2]

Various bills and receipts for money, dated at Rome and signed by

[1] Original Letter at Terregles.   [2] Original Letter at Terregles.

Lady Nithsdale, or by another hand in her name, are preserved at Terregles. The latest receipt is for 400 Roman crowns, or £100 sterling, dated at Rome, 7th March 1747. The signature of "Win. Nidsdale" was intended to pass for her signature; but it does not appear to have been adhibited by herself. Indeed, by that time she was probably incapable of writing even her own name. Nearly two years previously she was able to write only part of her name. One of the bills referred to is drawn by Lady Nithsdale on Messrs. Andrew Drummond and Company, bankers, London, for £100 sterling. It is dated at Rome, 18th June 1745, and the signature appended appears to be holograph of Lady Nithsdale, of which a facsimile is annexed, showing the great change that had come over her handwriting.

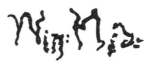

Another bill was drawn by her upon her son, whom she styles "The Right Honourable The Earl of Nidsdale at Terregles." It is dated at Rome, 30th June 1745, and is more indistinctly subscribed by Lady Nithsdale than the previous bill, indicating her inability to complete her signature, as is evident from the following facsimile :

In her youth, and for many years, her handwriting, of which several specimens are given in facsimile in the second volume, was very distinct. But now, after a life of great anxieties, which had told severely on her delicate frame, she was but the wreck of her former self. The few remaining years of her life were spent at Rome, where she died about the month of May 1749, after surviving her husband for five years.[1]

They both died at Rome, and were probably interred there. When the

---

[1] Among the entries of deaths between the 25th of May and the 11th of June 1749, there occurs in the Scots Magazine for that year, the following notice of the death of Lady Nithsdale : "Lately at Rome, the Countess Dowager of Nithsdale." Vol. xi. p. 253.

LADY WINIFRED HERBERT,
DAUGHTER OF THE MARQUIS OF POWIS,
COUNTESS OF WILLIAM FIFTH EARL OF NITHSDALE.

late Mr. Marmaduke Maxwell of Terregles was staying in Rome in the year 1870, he made inquiries for any monument or grave of these two ancestors; but after much inquiry he was unable to find any trace of the last resting place of either the Earl or his Countess.[1]

Of the early years of Lady Nithsdale before her marriage in 1699 little is known. The date of her birth has not been ascertained from any register. If she was about twenty years of age at the time of her marriage, she would be seventy at her death. Of her later years, after her husband's death in 1744, to her own death in 1749, few particulars can now be ascertained.

The devotion of Lady Nithsdale to her unfortunate husband, her disinterested character, and her exemplary virtues as a wife and a mother, have commanded the veneration of her descendants, who, justly proud of such an ancestor, never mention her name but with the utmost honour, gratitude, and affection. Nor is this admiration confined to them : a character so self-sacrificing and so exalted must command the respect of all who read the story of her chequered and romantic life.

One of the family treasures at Terregles is a portrait of Lady Nithsdale, taken when she was in the bloom of youth. The face is oval, with a broad and high forehead. The expression betokens much sweetness of disposition, in combination with great shrewdness and force of character, such as, under the impulse of wifely tenderness and affection, could contrive and execute the noble deed of heroism with which her name in history is associated.[2]

[1] Letter, Mr. Marmaduke Maxwell to William Fraser, dated Terregles, 12th July 1870.

[2] The story of Lady Nithsdale's life was made the subject of a romance by Lady Dacre, under the title of " Tales of the Peerage and the Peasantry," 2 vols. 8vo. London : Richard Bentley, 1835.

DESCENDANTS OF THE LAST EARL OF NITHSDALE.

1744-1872.

It will be sufficient to notice very briefly those who have held the Maxwell and Herries estates from the time of Lady Nithsdale down to the present time.

William Lord Maxwell, only son of the fifth and forfeited Earl of Niths-dale, came into possession of these estates on the death of his father, in the year 1744. In the hope of securing the estates to the family, in the event of an unsuccessful rising in favour of the Stuart family, the Earl of Nithsdale, on 28th November 1712, made an entail of his estates to his son and a variety of heirs, with the reservation of his own liferent.

After much litigation in the Court of Session and the House of Lords, it was finally decided by the latter tribunal, on 21st January 1723, that the deed of entail made by the Earl was valid, and that he only forfeited his life interest in his estates. On his death, in 1744, his son succeeded to them, although he had during his father's life been practically in possession of the estates, as the life interest of his father was purchased from the Government for his behoof. He possessed them for upwards of thirty years, having survived till the year 1776.

During that period he was by his friends commonly styled Earl of Niths-dale, out of courtesy, as the only son of the late Earl, and the successor to his landed estates. His wife, too, took the style of Countess of Nithsdale, which was usually accorded to her, although her strictly legal style was Lady Catherine Maxwell of Nithsdale.

In the year after Lord Maxwell's succession to the Nithsdale estates, there occurred the second great insurrection on behalf of the Stuarts. This was evidently a great trial to him. Was he now to follow the fatal example of his father, and rush into the new rebellion, with the risk of forfeiting his life and estates? or were the misfortunes of the father in 1715 to operate as a warning to the son in 1745? Lord Maxwell evidently halted between two opinions. His feelings as a true Jacobite were in favour of the success of the rising; but his good sense foretold a failure, and he deprecated being a desperado. His friend and neighbour, Mr. Craik of Arbigland, urgently advised him not to go out. His correspondence with Mr. Craik, at the commencement of the insurrection, shows how much Lord Maxwell sympathized with it, and he appears to have taken some active steps in support of it, for Mr. Craik writes to him, in the year 1746, that he had endangered his estate, and rendered himself liable to be apprehended.[1] But he must have withdrawn in time, for the Government, which was more inclined to leniency than in 1715, took no proceedings against him or his estates.

During his long possession of the Nithsdale estates, Lord Maxwell appears to have led a quiet and retired life. The business connected with the estates was chiefly managed by his commissioners, two of whom were John Maxwell of Terraughty and George Maxwell of Munches. Lord Maxwell's mother, in her correspondence with Lady Traquair, endeavoured to excuse his neglect of writing to his aunt by saying that he had his father's fault of being an indifferent correspondent, being indolent in using his pen. This charge of negligence as a correspondent against Lord Maxwell is confirmed by a subsequent letter from his own wife, in which she regrets his not writing to his aunt on an interesting occasion. His wife calls him her "Lazy Lord," who writes to nobody.[2] There is little to record of his personal history.

Of the early life of Lord Maxwell some traces occur in the correspondence in the Second Volume. He was educated in a college for a considerable period. This is stated in a letter from Lady Nithsdale to her sister-in-law, Lady Traquair, dated 9th September 1721, when it was proposed that Lord Maxwell should be sent to Scotland by his parents to attend to his own affairs. His presence in Scotland, it had been hinted, might be suspected as connected with political affairs, or with intrigues on behalf of the exiled royal family of Stuart: but in reference to any such suspicions Lord Maxwell's parents hoped that he had not been trained up so long in a college without being well grounded in the principles of religion. In the autumn of the same year Lord Maxwell visited his aunt at Traquair. While residing there with his cousins,

[1] Vol. ii. pp. 376, 382.   [2] Vol. ii. p. 395.

WILLIAM MAXWELL OF NITHSDALE,
COMMONLY CALLED EARL OF NITHSDALE.

LADY CATHERINE STEWART
WIFE OF WILLIAM MAXWELL OF NITHSDALE.

an attachment appears to have been formed between him and Lady Catherine Stuart, which ultimately led to their marriage. She was the fourth daughter of Charles, fourth Earl of Traquair, by his Countess, Lady Mary Maxwell. His mother, in a letter to the Lady Traquair, dated [Rome] 2d October 1731, referring to this marriage, says, that her son, writing to his father, informed him that they were to be married on his birth-day, the 27th of June.[1]

Lady Catherine Stuart is probably the lady referred to in a letter of the Marchioness of Stafford, when she writes : " I remember hearing the late Lady Stafford talk of visiting a Lady Nithsdale at Harrowgate, who was very deaf, and who, I suppose, was one of the Traquair family, and who Lady Alva remembered seeing on horseback, in the fashion of the times, with a three-cornered hat and flowing wig."[2]

Several of Lady Catherine Stuart's letters, after her marriage with Lord Maxwell, are printed in the collection of letters in the Second Volume. In a letter written from Terregles, 26th December 1745, she alludes to the recent visit of Prince Charles to Dumfries, where he slept one night on his return from his unfortunate expedition into England. The house in which the Prince slept is now used as the Commercial Hotel ; and the room which he occupied remains in the same state as when he used it. In that letter Lady Catherine Stuart warmly sympathizes with the rising ; but it bears strong evidence that the country around her was unfavourable. So uncomfortable was her position at Terregles, that she earnestly begs her mother, Lady Traquair, to give her shelter for a time at Traquair.[3] By the state of affairs, her husband, Lord Maxwell, was much disconcerted, and this did not add to the comfort of his wife. She was again at Terregles in May of the following year, when her husband was indisposed, complaining heavily of pain in his stomach.[4]

Other letters of Lady Catherine Stuart are printed in the Second Volume, and while these sheets were passing through the press, another letter, written by her Ladyship, not included in that volume, was forwarded to the Author. It is entirely holograph of Lady Catherine ; and as it contains several notices of her husband, herself, and their daughter " Winny " and her education, with other family affairs, it may here be appropriately introduced :—

[1] Vol. ii. p. 361.
[2] Vol. ii. p. 402.
[3] Vol. ii. p. 384.
[4] Vol. ii. p. 386.

Bath, the 17th March 1752.

Sir,—I had the favour of yours, above a fortnight ago, which I would have answer'd sooner, but I was waiting till I should hear from my Lord, which I now have done, and has wrote to him since, but am sorry to find he is at present troubled with a lowness of spirits, tho' I would fain hope it's only owing to his late illness, which, thank God, I did not know till it was over, or it would have given me great concern. I have had no word from Winny this several weeks past, but am glad to find that you think she's improving, by her letter to her papa. Her governess, endeed, writes me very agreeable accounts of her, so I flatter my self that the money bestow'd on her will not be misspent. It was always my oppinion that some hundred pounds on her education was much better employ'd than adding it to her fortune ; but as I am too old for improvement, I fear my Lord and you will be grudeging what is spent on me. However, I must still beg the favour of you to send me some money, as soon's possible, for as I borrowed some before I got the sixty pound, I had it to repay ; for, thank God, I have very good credit, and tho', I think, I live as sparingly as I well cane, without being reckon'd scrub, yet am quite sensible my expences must run pretty high. But I hope this shall be the last year of my life that I put the estate to any exterordinair charge on my own account.

Bath is a charming sweet place, and I agreed extreamly with the waters, but has not been quite so well since Lent. I wish with all my heart my Lord were here, I am perswaded it would do him good, but I fear he will not take my advice. I thank you for giving me the newes of our countrey, and pray let me know in your nixt if you have finished your bargain with Sir Thomas, and if your new house is begun, and likewise let me know if ther's any alterations about Terregles since I left it. I would gladly have had our old room fitted up for a drawing room, but since my Lord will not have it done, I must submit ; and I hope you have paid off some of the accompts that was owing. I had almost forgot to tell you that I got lately a letter from Mrs. Reid, the miller's widow, telling me that she's in hasard of being put out of her possession, unless I interpose, so if she behaves right, I beg you'll be her friend, and do something for her, as you know the reason why she has so many enemys, and I also desire you'll be so good as to take notice of poor Ketty Lawson, if alive, and give her some small help from me. I am sorry for Mrs. Maxwell of Lawston's situation, and I wrote to my Lord about her ; his lowness of spirits gives me great uneasyness, and I beg you'll be often with him and devert him as much as possible, and pray let him know nothing of his affairs that cane vexe him, for I know he cannot bear that when he's ill ; and as I suppose Mr. Hay will now be soon with you, pray make my compliments to him, and tell him the same, and I shall be glad to hear that our rents are coming well in, and I again beg you'll remember to send me some money as quick as ever you cane, for quietly, and betwixt you and me, I have been living this three weeks past on what is borrowed. I desired my Lord in my last letter to send me some cash, but as this is the case, if you think he orders too little, you may add twenty pound without leting him know, for I would not have him geting the least thing to trouble him at present. So burn this, but be sure to offer my kind compliments to my good friend Munches and his family, for I don't want any body else should know of this. . . . I heartily wish you all manner of happiness, and am, Sir, your sincere friend and humble servant,

CATHERINE NITHSDALE.[1]

To Mr. McCartney [of Halketleaths].

[1] Original Letter with Mr. Maxwell of Breoch.

Lady Catherine Stuart died at Paris on 16th June 1765. Her death is thus mentioned in a letter written by the family solicitor in Edinburgh to her son-in-law, Mr. Constable of Everingham :—" Altho' I imagine by this time you have got the melancholly accounts of good Lady Nithsdale's death on the 16th, which only came to me late last night by a letter from Mr. Robert Grant of the 18th, I could not omitt expressing the sincere grief which Mrs. Syme and I feel on this melancholly occasion, and the sympathy we have for your lady and you. . . . My Lord Nithsdale's loss is irreparable. Mankind in general must lament the good and kind Lady Nithsdale."[1]

Her husband survived her Ladyship for eleven years. Of their marriage there was issue—two daughters, Mary, called Lady Mary Maxwell. In the Second Volume there is a letter printed which was written by this young lady to her grandmother, Lady Traquair, and dated at York, 17th November 1743.[2] Mary was then in her eleventh year. She died at Terregles, on the 21st of December 1747, in her fifteenth year, unmarried. Her father, on the occasion of the death of his eldest daughter, " Lady Mary Maxwell," ordered five guineas to be paid to the Kirk-session of Terregles, for the use of the poor of the parish.[3]

The younger daughter of William Lord Maxwell was named after her grandmother, Winifred. On the death of her father, at London, on 2d August 1776,[4] she succeeded to him as being his only surviving child and heir in the Maxwell and Herries estates, commonly called the Nithsdale estates.

Winifred Maxwell of Nithsdale, or, as she was commonly styled, " Lady Winifred," was educated in France, and in after years she retained many of the habits which she had acquired in that country. While in her twenty-third year she married William Haggerston Constable of Everingham, in the county of York, Esquire, second son of Sir Carnaby Haggerston of Haggerston Castle, in the county of Northumberland. He was heir of his maternal grand-uncle, Sir Marmaduke Constable of Everingham Park,

---

[1] Vol. ii. p. 395. Portraits of Lord Maxwell and his wife are at Terregles. Engravings of them are given in this work.

[2] Vol. ii. p. 373.

[3] Original Receipt, dated 17th March 1748, at Terregles.

[4] The date of his death is recorded in the Special Retour by which his daughter was served heir to him. The Retour was expede on 23d December 1766. Extract Retour at Terregles.

in the county of York, Baronet, and thus adopted the name of Constable as holding the estate of Everingham. This match was very gratifying to Lady Winifred's mother, Lady Catherine Maxwell, who wrote in very favourable terms of his good sense, his polite manners, and his attachment to the Roman Catholic religion, his only fault in the eyes of the young lady whom he had come to Terregles to woo, being at first "his prodigious size," whilst she was of low stature and slender in form. Lady Catherine Stuart, Lady Nithsdale, in a letter to Mary Countess of Traquair, dated 29th May [1758], thus writes: "I dout not but your Ladyshipe has heard by this time that there is a fine English squire at Terregles, so would guess his errand. He is second son to the late Sir Carnaby Haggerston, but is called Constable, as his grand-uncle, Sir Marmaduke of that name, left him his heir to a handsome estate. He has made proposals to Winny, so I thought it my duty to acquaint your Ladyship of it. He has been here now this twelve days, and he seems to be a very sensible, well bred, pretty gentleman, and a good Roman Catholic, so hopes to have your Ladyship's approbation to the match. She was much startled at first at his prodigious size, but now I think she seems to have got over that fault, which, indeed, is the only one cane be found to his appearance, but that's certain, he's amongst the tallest men I ever saw, so your Ladyship may judge what sort of a figure they will make together, but that is not an essential matter as to happiness." She adds, "My Lord seems very well pleased with the young squire, but as ther's no termes mention'd yet, it's hard to know how they may agree."[1]

The courtship lasted from May to October 1758, on the 16th of which month the formal contract for the marriage of the fine English squire and Lady Winifred was made at Terregles, and the marriage was celebrated there on the following day.[2] By the contract, to which William Maxwell of Niths-dale was a party, it was provided that the Nithsdale estates, failing sons to be born to him, should be inherited by his daughter, whose husband should be bound to assume and wear the titles and sirname of Maxwell and proper arms of the two families of Maxwell and Herries.[3] After his marriage,

[1] Vol. ii. pp. 394, 395.
[2] In the announcement of the marriage both the lady and her father are styled as if no forfeiture had taken place. He is called "the Earl of Niths-dale," and she is styled "Lady Winifred Maxwell, his Lordship's only daughter."—[The Scots Maga-zine, vol. xx. p. 553.]
[3] Original Contract at Terregles. There is also a

the husband of Winifred adopted the sirname of Maxwell before that of Constable.

On the death of her father, William Maxwell of Nithsdale, Lady Winifred was served heir to him by a special retour, dated 23d December 1776, in the Nithsdale estates, including the baronies of Carlaverock and Terregles.

When the Poet Burns, who was then resident in Dumfries-shire, heard that the present Mansion House of Terregles was to be built for the permanent residence of Lady Winifred and her husband, he wrote the following song, entitled—

NITHSDALE'S WELCOME HAME.

The noble Maxwells and their powers
  Are coming o'er the Border,
And they'll gae bigg Terregles towers,
  And set them a' in order.
And they declare Terregles fair
  For their abode they choose it ;
There's no a heart in a' the land
  But's lighter at the news o't.

Though stars in skies may disappear,
  And angry tempests gather,
The happy hour may soon be near
  That brings us pleasant weather :
The weary night o' care and grief
  May hae a joyful morrow ;
So dawning day has brought relief,
  Fareweel our night o' sorrow ! [1]

From his Jacobitism, Burns was strongly attracted to the families of rank in Dumfries-shire whose ancestors had suffered for their loyalty to the exiled Stuarts. This as well as the noble character of Lady Winifred, whose grand-father William last Earl of Nithsdale had forfeited his titles and narrowly escaped the scaffold, made the Poet desirous of obtaining an introduction to her. Failing to obtain the desired introduction in the way and time that he expected, Burns addressed to her the following characteristic letter in which he claims with her common Jacobite sympathies :—

list of the furnishings made to "Lady Winnie" on her marriage.

[1] Chambers's Life and Works of Robert Burns, vol. iii. p. 241.

"Ellisland, 16th December 1789.

"MY LADY,—In vain have I from day to day expected to hear from Mrs. Young, as she promised me at Dalswinton that she would do me the honour to introduce me at Tinwald;[1] and it was impossible, not from your Ladyship's accessibility, but from my own feelings, that I could go alone. Lately, indeed Mr. Maxwell of Carruchan, in his usual goodness, offered to accompany me, when an unlucky indisposition on my part hindered my embracing the opportunity. To court the notice or the tables of the great, except where I sometimes have had a little matter to ask of them, or more often the pleasanter task of witnessing my gratitude to them, is what I never have done, and I trust never shall do. But with your Ladyship I have the honour to be connected by one of the strongest and most endearing ties in the whole moral world. Common sufferers in a cause where even to be unfortunate is glorious —the cause of heroic loyalty! Though my fathers had not illustrious honours, and vast properties to hazard in the contest, though they left their humble cottages only to add so many units more to the unnoted crowd that followed their leaders, yet what they could they did, and what they had they lost : with unshaken firmness and unconcealed political attachments, they shook hands with ruin for what they esteemed the cause of their King and their country. This language and the enclosed verses[2] are for your Ladyship's eye alone. Poets are not very famous for their prudence; but as I can do nothing for a cause which is now nearly no more, I do not wish to hurt myself. I have the honour to be, my Lady,

"Your Ladyship's obliged and obedient humble servant,

"ROB^T. BURNS."[3]

On the Jacobitism expressed in this letter Sir Walter Scott, in sending it to Mr. Lockhart, remarks : —"You will see that he plays high Jacobite, and on that account it is curious; though I imagine his Jacobitism, like my own, belonged to the fancy rather than the reason."[4]

This communication appears to have opened friendly relations between Lady Winifred and the poet, as in the course of little more than a twelve-

[1] Tinwald House was the temporary residence of Lady Winifred and Mr. Maxwell Constable, while the present Mansion House of Terregles was being built.

[2] Those addressed to Mr. William Tytler.

[3] Chambers's Life and Works of Robert Burns, vol. iii. p. 94.

[4] Ibid. vol. iii. p. 87.

month afterwards, when Burns was suffering from a fractured arm, her Ladyship sent him as a present a snuff-box, the lid of which was ornamented by an elegant miniature of Queen Mary.[1] Burns, in thankful acknowledgment of the gift, wrote to the donor the following letter :—

" Ellisland, 11th April 1791.

"My Lady,—Nothing less than the unlucky accident of having lately broken my right arm could have prevented me, the moment I received your Ladyship's elegant present by Mrs. Miller, from returning you my warmest and most grateful acknowledgments. I assure your Ladyship I shall set it apart—the symbols of religion shall only be more sacred. In the moment of poetic composition, the box shall be my inspiring genius. When I would breathe the comprehensive wish of benevolence for the happiness of others, I shall recollect your Ladyship ; when I would interest my fancy in the distresses incident to humanity, I shall remember the unfortunate Mary.

" Robᵀ. Burns." [2]

Marmaduke, the eldest son and heir of the marriage of Lady Winifred and Mr. Maxwell Constable, was born at London on 2d January 1760. Mr. J. Norris of London, in a letter to Mr. James Morison, factor, at Terregles, dated on the 8th of that month, thus alludes to the happy event :—"I dare say you would be glade to see my lady[3] and Lady Winny with the young squire. You are, no doubt, informed her Ladyship was brought to bed last Wednesday of a fine lusty boy, as big at its first appearance in the world as a child of three months old ; it would appear it will be of the Haggerston kind."[4]

The factor in his answer, dated 14th January 1760, describes the rejoicings on the Nithsdale and Herries estates on the birth of the heir. " I shall proceed to tell you what great rejoicings we had upon the most agreeable accounts of Lady Winny's safe delivery of a son. First, I had a great bonfire on the top of the White Hill, when all his Lordship's tenants

---

[1] The miniature of Queen Mary on the box was unhappily injured many years ago, when one of Burns's sons, who took it with him to India, was leaping on board a vessel.

[2] Chambers's Life and Works of Robert Burns, vol. iii. p. 184.

[3] This refers to Lady Catherine Maxwell, titular Countess of Nithsdale.

[4] Original Letter at Terregles. The Scots Magazine, vol. xxii. p. 50.

of the parish mett and drunk three or four proper healths. They brought all their guns along with them, and at every health they gave a platoon. There was another upon the top of Lawston Hill, where his Lordship's tenants of Kirkgunzeon, Lochrutton and Urr, mett and observed the same rules. There was one on the Corbelly Hill, another at Duncow, and one in Carlaverock. In a word, his Lordship's tenants of every parish assembled at the same hour in their different districts, and honest Mark M'Coon had the whole front of his house illuminated, a bonfire opposite to his house, and a bowl of punch upon the Cross.   Joy, indeed, appeared in every countenance.   There were upwards of 200 people and 40 guns assembled at each bonfire, and I prepared something to drink the healths. This account I hope wont be disagreeable to his Lordship, as it was the only mark of regard his Lordship's tenants and me could show." [1]

The marriage of Lady Winifred with Mr. Maxwell Constable subsisted for thirty-nine years. He died on Tuesday, 20th June 1797, and his remains were interred in the family burying-place called the " queer," in the church of Terregles on the Tuesday following. By his last will and testament, dated 1st July 1794, he appointed Edward Haggerston of Ellingham, of Northumberland, and John Maxwell of Terraughty in Scotland, his sole executors and trustees.[2]

During the time that "Lady Winifred" possessed the Nithsdale and Herries estates, which was about a quarter of a century, she resided chiefly at Terregles, where she dispensed a very generous and almost unbounded hospitality.   She seldom sat down to dinner without a company of between twenty and thirty friends and neighbours. Terregles in her day was a kind of open house, where friends and neighbours frequently came and stayed without any formal previous arrangement. Such hospitality became costly, and Lady Winifred found it necessary to sell the barony of Duncow, the lands of Newlands, Craigley, Deanstown, and other portions of the estates.

By William Haggerston Maxwell Constable, Lady Winifred had, besides her eldest son already mentioned, two sons and four daughters, whose names are given in the Genealogical Table of the family printed in this Volume. She

[1] Copy answer at Terregles.
[2] This is stated in a Deed of Factory by the above-named trustees in favour of George Maxwell of Carruchan, dated 30th June 1797.   At Terregles.

survived her husband little more than four years, and died rather unexpectedly, at Terregles, on 13th July 1801, in the sixty-sixth year of her age. Her remains were interred in the family burying-place in the church of Terregles on the 23d of that month. An engraving is given in this work of the portrait of "Lady Winifred" from the original at Terregles.

Mr. Marmaduke Constable Maxwell was served heir to his mother, on 23d September 1801, in the Nithsdale and Herries estates, including the baronies of Carlaverock and Terregles; and he was also appointed the executor of the personal estate of his mother, under the burden of special legacies to several old friends. In consequence of his frequent residence out of the kingdom he found it necessary to intrust the chief management of the Scotch estates to commissioners, who were John Maxwell of Terraughty and George Maxwell of Carruchan.

Mr. Constable Maxwell married, in the year 1800, Theresa Apolonia, daughter of Edmund Wakeman, Esquire of Beckford, in the county of Worcester. Of that marriage there were five sons and three daughters, whose names will be found entered in the Genealogical Pedigree of the family, printed in this Volume.

Allusion is made to his marriage by John Maxwell of Terraughty, in a letter to Charles Earl of Traquair, dated 22d December 1800 :—" M. C. Maxwell, Esquire of Everingham," he writes, " has taken to himself a wife, and Lady Winifred is so pleased, has given up a large part of the jointure due from his English estate, and has presented Mr. Stanley with £600 on his marriage, so they seem all very happy."[1]

Mr. Marmaduke Constable Maxwell executed a disposition and deed of entail, dated 16th May 1814, for the settlement of his estates of Nithsdale and others. The deed narrates that upon his death these estates and his estates of Everingham and others in England would, if not otherwise settled, descend to his eldest son. He, however, resolved, for certain weighty causes, that his whole estates in Scotland should not be possessed by the same person, in case he should leave more sons than one, as he considered his estates in Scotland and England to be fully adequate to the maintenance, in a suitable manner, of two separate families. Leaving then his eldest son to succeed to

[1] Vol. ii. p. 399.

WINIFRED MAXWELL OF NITHSDALE
(STYLED LADY)
WIFE OF WILLIAM HAGGERSTON CONSTABLE OF EVERINGHAM PARK.

the estate of Everingham in England and to that of Nithsdale in Scotland, he disponed, under certain conditions and reservations, to himself in liferent, and to Marmaduke Constable Maxwell, his second son, in fee, and to the heirs-male of his body, whom failing, to his other sons successively in the order of their seniority and the heirs-male of their bodies ; whom failing, to the other heirs therein mentioned, the lands and baronies of Terregles and Kirkgunzeon and others.[1]

After possessing the Nithsdale estates for about eighteen years, Mr. Marmaduke Constable Maxwell suddenly died at Abbeville, in France, on his way to Paris, on the 30th of June 1819.   Lady Lucy Stuart, in a letter to her brother, Charles Earl of Traquair, dated 9th July of that year, writes : " I am truly grieved to have the painful task to inform you of the very sudden death of our truly valuable cousin, Mr. Constable Maxwell.   He was on his road to Paris, where he was going to amuse his eldest daughter, in company with his brother, Mr. Middleton, and at Abbeville an apoplectic fit carried him off in a short hour.   His loss will be severely felt by many ; to me it is a real one ; he was on all occasions ready to oblige me.   His poor wife is under the hospitable roof of Sutton Place, in a state of affliction, which my pen cannot give you any idea of." [2]

Mr. Marmaduke Constable Maxwell was succeeded in his English estate of Everingham, and in his Scotch estate of Nithsdale, by his eldest son, William Constable Maxwell, now Lord Herries.

An Act of Parliament was passed, in the year 1848, in favour of William Constable Maxwell, Esquire, and all the other descendants of the body of William Earl of Nithsdale, restoring them against the forfeiture of the Earl. In virtue of this Act, Mr. Constable Maxwell claimed the dignity of Lord Herries, as having been vested in the said Earl William, and descendible to his heirs of line, of whom Mr. Constable Maxwell was the representative ; and, by the Act, he and the other descendants of the Earl were fully and honourably restored in blood, that they might be enabled to prefer their claims and adduce evidence of and establish their right to all honours, dignities, and titles thereunto belonging, to which they would have been

[1] Extract Entail at Terregles.

[2] Vol. ii. p. 400. It is remarkable that his son, the late Honourable Marmaduke Constable Max-well, should also have died suddenly at Calais, in France, while passing through that country, on 16th July 1872.

entitled as heirs of the body of the said William Earl of Nithsdale, had the said sentence of forfeiture never been passed upon him. This statute having received the royal assent, Mr. Constable Maxwell presented a petition to her Majesty, praying that she would be graciously pleased to adjudge and declare that he was entitled to the honour and dignity of Lord Herries of Terregles. This petition was referred by her Majesty to the consideration of the House of Lords. The claim of Mr. Constable Maxwell was opposed by the late William Maxwell of Carruchan, as the heir-male of the family of Nithsdale, on the ground that the peerage of Herries held by the forfeited Earl was a male dignity. After a protracted contest before the Committee for Privileges, the Committee reported, on 2d June 1858, that Mr. Constable Maxwell had made out his claim, and in virtue of that decision he became the tenth LORD HERRIES OF TERREGLES.

William Lord Herries was born on 25th August 1804, and married, on 12th November 1835, Marcia, eldest daughter of the Honourable Sir Edward Marmaduke Vavasour, Baronet, of Hazelwood, in the county of York. Sir Edward was formerly the Honourable Edward-Marmaduke Stourton, second son of Charles Philip, sixteenth Lord Stourton, by Mary, his wife, co-heiress of Marmaduke Baron Langdale. Lord and Lady Herries have had issue Marmaduke Master of Herries, born 4th October 1837, and six other sons and nine daughters, whose names are all entered in the Genealogical Table of the family, printed in the present Volume.

ARMORIAL BEARINGS.

Shield : Quarterly, 1st argent, an eagle, displayed, with two heads, sable, beaked and membered, gules, surmounted of an escutcheon of the first, charged with a saltire of the second, and surcharged in the centre with a hedgehog, or, for NITHSDALE ; 2d quarterly, 1st and 4th argent, a saltire sable ; 2d and 3d argent, three hedgehogs, sable, for HERRIES ; 3d quarterly, gules and vair, over all a bend, or, for CONSTABLE ; 4th azure, on a bend cotised, argent, three billets sable for HAGGERSTON.

Crest : A stag's head with ten tynes, or.

Supporters : Two savages or wild men wreathed about the loins, and holding clubs, proper.

Motto : Dominus dedit.

Maxwell lord maxwell

Hereis lord of ferreghs :-

FROM THE "BOOKE AND REGISTER OF ARMES DONE BY SIR DAVID LINDESAY
OF THE MONTH LYONE KING OF ARMES" A.D. 1542.

P.P. 36 & 41.

IN THE LIBRARY OF THE FACULTY OF ADVOCATES, EDINBURGH.

JOHN, FOURTH LORD HERRIES OF TERREGLES.

AGNES HERRIES, HIS WIFE.

1512-1582.

SIR JOHN MAXWELL of Terregles, Lord Herries, was the second son of Robert, fifth Lord Maxwell, and of his spouse Janet Douglas, daughter of Sir William Douglas of Drumlanrig ; and it will be seen that by his public services he fully sustained the character of the two distinguished families of Maxwell and Douglas, from whom he derived his descent. He was born about the year 1512, and was educated in Sweet Heart Abbey, or as it was also called New Abbey,[1] to distinguish it from Dundrennan, which was called the Old Abbey. Sweet Heart Abbey was a monastic institution situated in a valley of surpassing beauty, immediately below the high mountain of Criffel in the stewartry of Kirkcudbright, and about seven miles south from Dumfries. Its monks were of the Cistercian order. It was founded by Devorgilla, daughter of Allan Lord of Galloway, grand-daughter to David Earl of Huntingdon (brother of King William the Lion), and wife to John Baliol of Castle Bernard. Here her husband, who died in 1260, was buried, and his heart having been embalmed, was at the desire of Devorgilla enclosed in an enamelled ivory " cophyn, lokyt, and bwndyn wyth syluer brycht," and deposited within the walls of the church near the high altar.[2]

Such is the origin of Sweet Heart Abbey, which when entire must have been a beautiful building : even now its ruins form a striking feature in the landscape. For this establishment as his *alma mater*, Lord Herries ever retained a strong affection, of which, as we shall afterwards see, he gave signal proof.

He was tutor to two of his nephews, who, as minors, successively inherited the estates and titles of the house of Maxwell, and being to them, and also for a time to his own brother, presumptive heir, he was often desig-

[1] The fact that Lord Herries was educated at New Abbey is stated in a gift by Mr. Gilbert Brown, the Abbot, to Lord Herries, of the Isle of Loch-kindelocht, 27th August 1577. [At Terregles.]

[2] Wyntown's Orygynale Cronykil of Scotland, vol. ii. pp. 68-70 ; Edition 1795.

nated Master of Maxwell. He thus had the management of the Maxwell estates, with all the offices attached to them. He was also at an early age put in possession of a great part of the Herries estates by his marriage, and thus possessed such power in the south-western parts of Scotland, as rendered it important to any party to secure his assistance. This may be regarded as the key to the position which he occupied. It explains the influence which he acquired in the State, the part which he acted in political affairs, and the mark which he has left on the history of his country.

When in 1545 his father Robert, fifth Lord Maxwell, and his elder brother Robert, Master of Maxwell, were prisoners in England, the future Lord Herries held the Castle of Lochmaben, of which the English were very desirous to get possession. His father professed to be willing to deliver it up, but would not undertake that it should be surrendered unless he was allowed to go personally for that purpose. The English, doubtful of the sincerity of his professions, refused permission, and his son showed that although young he had considerable force of character, by refusing to place the castle, with which he had been intrusted, into the hands of the enemies of his country.[1]

The Master of Maxwell married, in 1547, Agnes Herries, eldest daughter of William, third Lord Herries, of whose large estates, as he died without male issue, his three daughters Agnes, Catherine, and Jean, were co-heiresses. Agnes thus brought to the Master of Maxwell her third share of the Herries estates, with the mansion-house of Terregles. After he was knighted, and before he became Lord Herries, he is known in history as Sir John Maxwell of Terregles, knight.

Sir John afterwards acquired from Catherine and Jean Herries, the two younger sisters of Agnes Herries, the two shares of the Herries estates which were inherited by them as co heiresses of their father. The whole Herries property was thus ultimately consolidated in John Lord Herries.

The circumstances connected with the marriage of John, Master of Maxwell, with the heiress of Herries were peculiar, and some of them of a tragic character. He was even then conspicuous as a young man of ability, and it was his power as a border chief, rendering his opposition formidable and his support important, that gained him the youthful heiress.

[1] *Vide* pp. 203-205.

In the year 1547, he was employed on behalf of Matthew Earl of Lennox in negotiating with the Earl of Angus, the father-in-law of the Earl of Lennox, and some other friends, who were willing to assist Lennox in recovering by force his estate in Scotland on condition that he would quit the English interest for that of Scotland. At this time the Master of Maxwell was seeking in marriage the heiress of Herries, then under the protection of the Earl of Arran, Governor of Scotland, who intended to marry her to his own son, Lord John Hamilton. The Master of Maxwell, indignant at the Governor for crossing him in his suit, brought Lennox's business to such a point that 2000 horse were appointed and in readiness to meet the Earl of Lennox and Lord Wharton, Lieutenant for England, at Dumfries. He delivered to Lord Wharton certain young gentlemen as pledges. But things took a different turn. To gain the Master of Maxwell, the Governor offered to him the heiress of Herries if he would abandon this invasion and fall back with his cavalry. This offer was accepted. When, therefore, Lennox came to Dumfries he found no troops there for his assistance. To reconnoitre the district he sent out 600 horse, and the whole country being then in arms and divided into different parties, they happened to encounter 700 horse commanded by the Laird of Drumlanrig, by whom at first they were nearly worsted ; but recovering, they vanquished and put to flight Drumlanrig, many of whose men were taken prisoners. Drumlanrig himself escaped through the swiftness of his horse. The Master of Maxwell, with his followers and friends, was also upon the field, and he escaped, but was in great danger of his life, for sundry spears were broken upon him in his flight. The Earl of Lennox, discovering this unscrupulous violation of the articles of agreement, and that the whole country was in opposition, after resting some days at Dumfries, advised Lord Wharton to retreat into England, which he did, and by the orders of the English Council he hanged at Carlisle the Master of Maxwell's pledges. Among the executed were the warden of the Greyfriars in Dumfries, and the vicar of Carlaverock.[1]

[1] Historical Memoirs of the Reign of Mary Queen of Scots, etc., printed for the Abbotsford Club, 1836, pp. 22, 23. The account of these foray encounters as given in Holinshed's History (vol. v. p. 556, London, 1808, 4to) is not materially different from that of the Historical Memoirs. The spring of action assigned by the latter authority to Lord Herries in these transactions is wholly unnoticed by Holinshed.

Such was the tragic wooing of the border heiress of the House of Herries.

The Herries estates were of large extent. Besides the baronies of Terregles and Kirkgunzeon, and the half of the barony of Ur in the stewartry of Kirkcudbright, they included the lands of Moffatdale and Avendale, Locarbie, Hutoun, Tolnagarth, Hoddam, Ecclefechane, Nether Wormonbie, Schelis, the barony of Mortoun Woods, in the stewartry of Annandale and shire of Dumfries, also the barony of Myretoun, in the shire of Wigton, with the fishing of Heresker in the water of Solway, the barony of Bernwell and Symontoun, the lands of Fewrule and others.[1]

Previous to this arrangement of the marriage, several gifts of the Herries estates had been made by Queen Mary and the Regent Arran in favour of the second son of the latter, John Hamilton, Commendator of Arbroath. Although he relinquished, in the circumstances now related, the marriage of the eldest co-heiress, John Hamilton still held the gift of the ward and marriage of the other two co-heiresses, and kept a firm hold of the estates of Herries. Such was the nature of wardholdings, that he appears to have been all but sole proprietor of them. For many years John Hamilton and his father received large sums from Sir John Maxwell; and even as late as the year 1566, nearly twenty years after the marriage of Sir John and Agnes Herries, a contract was entered into between him and John Hamilton, whereby Sir John became bound to pay to Hamilton £1000, and also to convey to him the lands of Barnewell, part of the lordship of Herries. Sir John Maxwell also thereby became bound to promote, with all his influence, a marriage between his nephew, John Lord Maxwell and Jane Fleming, granddaughter to the Duke of Chatelherault, the father of John Hamilton, and also to take part with the Duke and his friends in all time coming.[2]

The reasons contained in the grant which was made by John Hamilton, with consent of his father and the Lords of Privy Council, to Sir John Maxwell, of the marriage of Agnes Herries, are entitled to special notice. It was made on the ground that through his manifold labours, Sir John Maxwell not only had drawn a great part of the inhabitants of the west borders

---

[1] Charter by Queen Mary to John Master of Maxwell and Agnes Herries, his spouse, 1st February 1549-50, at Terregles.   [2] Original Contract at Terregles.

from the assurance of the English, the old enemies of Scotland, to the obedience of " our Sovereign Lady, and the granter's father, her tutor, and governor of her realm," and recovered from the English the houses of Torthorwell and Cokpule, and divers other strengths in which the English lay, to the subjection of the country, but had also expelled the English from those parts of the kingdom, by which means he had done good service to the Queen and the granter's father, and had also paid to the granter's father, his tutor, in his name, divers great sums of money and profits for his advantage.[1]

As John, Master of Maxwell, and Agnes Herries were related to each other in the third degree of affinity, they ought, according to the laws of the Roman Catholic Church, to have obtained a Papal dispensation previous to their marriage to render it valid. This they had neglected to obtain. They therefore presented a petition to the Papal Court at Rome, praying for absolution and the grace of dispensation. This was granted on the 26th of May 1555.

The following is a translation of the Dispensation from the original Latin :—

Amice, by Divine Compassion Cardinal Priest by the title of Saint Angelus, to the beloved in Christ—John Maxwell, layman, and Agnes Herries, woman, man and wife, in the Diocese of Glasgow, greeting in the Lord. The purport of a petition lately brought before us on your behalf contained that heretofore you (both or one of you not being in ignorance that you were related to one another in the third degree of affinity) did in fact by words effectual publicly contract matrimony together, and did consummate the same, issue being begotten thereof: But whereas, as the same petition went on to say, you may not be able to remain in such matrimony, yet if a divorce should pass between you, grievous scandal might probably arise therefrom, you have caused humble supplication to be made that you may be provided, in respect of these things, by the Apostolic See, with the benefit of due absolution and the grace of timely dispensation. We, therefore, inclining to your supplications in this behalf, by the authority of our Lord the Pope, the care of whose Penitentiary we discharge, and by his special and express command to us, given in this matter by word of mouth, Do, by the tenor of these presents, entirely absolve and free you and each of you from the general sentence of excommunication, and from all other ecclesiastical sentences, censures, and pains which you or either of you, because of the premises, have or hath incurred by the crime of incest and such like excesses ; and we do mercifully hold you dispensed, so that, notwithstanding the like impediment of the third degree of affinity, you can and may be able freely and lawfully anew to contract matrimony between you by words effectual and publicly, and to solemnize the same in the face of the Church, and afterwards to remain therein, so always that you, Agnes, were not forced into this by any one ;

1 Original Gift, dated 19th March 1547-8, at Terregles.

Decreeing that the issue begotten, if any there be, and to be begotten thereafter to be legitimate, notwithstanding the premises and the Apostolical and general or special constitutions and ordinances passed in provincial and synodal councils, and other things whatsoever to the contrary. And we will that you shall be bound altogether to fulfil the penance therefor to be enjoined you by the confessor whom each of you shall deem fit to choose for the premises, and to either of you surviving the other the same penance shall perpetually remain without hope of wedlock.

Given at Rome, at Saint Peter's, under the seal of the Office of the Penitentiary, on the 7th day before the Kalends of June (26th May), in the first year of the Pontificate of the Lord Pope Paul the Fourth. [1555.]   A. GAILLART.[1]

F. BRAMOLINUS.

After the death of his brother Robert, sixth Lord Maxwell, in September 1552, Sir John Maxwell was appointed Warden of the West Marches, but so great were the difficulties which he met with in the execution of this office that at this time he did not long retain it. The state of the office was brought under the consideration of the Privy Council, 28th August 1553. Having respect to the common weal of the realm, and to the great expenses sustained by John, Master of Maxwell, Warden of the West Marches, since the decease of Robert Lord Maxwell, his brother, in that office, the Council offered to him the office with £500 yearly during the Queen's minority, and other reward, either by benefit or other casualty at the Queen's pleasure, as well as satisfaction to him by the punishment of late offenders. Yet he declined to continue to hold the office, or to come into the country in its then distracted state, until the offenders to the authority and to him were punished, or until he was supported with a power sufficient to punish them.[2]

He therefore demitted the office, which was conferred on Sir James Douglas of Drumlanrig, knight. The Queen and Lords of Council, 29th August 1553, specially give the reasons of the demission of Sir John Maxwell. They mention, with commendation, the old service rendered by him and his predecessors in the office of wardenry upon the West Marches. They next state that he had fallen under deadly feud with divers clans of that territory, through which he could not serve so effectively as before. Then, considering that his uncle, Sir James Douglas of Drumlanrig, knight, was a most tender kinsman to the house of Maxwell, and most qualified to serve as Warden, they, in the meantime, nominated Sir

---

[1] Original Dispensation at Terregles.
[2] Regist. Secreti Concilii Acta, March 1550—   January 1553, fol. 73. MS. H.M. General Register House, Edinburgh.

James to that office, and required John Master of Maxwell to assist him in advancing the Queen's authority in the exercise of the office, to which he readily consented. To enable Sir James to perform the duties of warden, and to be as near the borders as possible, the Council required John Master of Maxwell to lend to him the Castle of Lochmaben during the time of his office of Wardenry, which he consented to do.[1] On 30th August, Sir James Douglas was formally appointed warden.[2]

James, fourth Earl of Bothwell, Admiral of Scotland, having with some French troops in October 1559, waylaid John Cockburn of Ormiston in East Lothian, and robbed him of £1000 sterling in French crowns, and 200 crowns for his own use, which he had received from Queen Elizabeth's Commissioners at Berwick for the Lords of the Congregation, the Master of Maxwell, with the Earl of Arran and Lord James Stewart, started with some horse on 31st October to apprehend the robber, but he escaped to his castle of Creichtoun or Morhame with the money. As he refused to make restitution, his house was despoiled, but in it nothing of any great importance was found, except his evidents and certain clothing.[3]

Sir John Maxwell brought intelligence to the Lords of the Congregation at Glasgow, from the Duke of Norfolk, Earl Marshal of England, and Lieutenant in its northern counties, of Queen Elizabeth's resolution to interpose in behalf of the Scottish Protestants. The Master of Maxwell was one of the Commissioners appointed by the Lords of the Congregation to meet with the Duke of Norfolk for negotiating a treaty between Scotland and England. The other Commissioners were Lord James Stewart, afterwards Earl of Murray, Lord Ruthven, William Maitland of Lethington, younger, Secretary, John Wishart of Pittarow, and Mr. Henry Balnaves of Halhill. They all went to Berwick by sea, except the Master of Maxwell.[4]

At Berwick, 27th February 1559-60, the Scottish Commissioners and the Duke of Norfolk subscribed their names and affixed their seals to the treaty between England and Scotland.[5]

The Master of Maxwell and others[6] signed a letter to Queen Elizabeth,

[1] Regist. Secreti Concilii Acta, March 1550--January 1553, fol. 74.

[2] Ibid. fol. 75.

[3] Knox's History, vol. i. pp. 454-456, 459.

[4] Keith's History, p. 117.

[5] Knox's Works, vol. ii. p. 45.

[6] The others who signed were the Duke of Chatelherault, the Earls of Arran, Huntly, Argyll,

dated Camp before Leith, 28th April 1560, in which they say that they had heard the Bishop of Valence, the French Ambassador, at length, in compliance with her wish, but found so little surety in the Queen Dowager's offers, that they had been forced to end all communication with him ; and they return thanks for her Majesty's liberal support and favourable help in their cause, for which they could render no other recompense but the assurance of their service to her Majesty.[1]

William Maitland, in a letter to Cecil, written also from the camp before Leith, on the 25th of the following month (May), speaks of the hope of being joined by the remaining neutrals, and of the affection of the Earl of Morton and Master of Maxwell to her Highness's service.[2]

He was present at a convention, held on 15th January 1560-1, to hear the report of Sir James Sandilands of Calder, who had been despatched to France with the Acts of the former Convention, to obtain, if possible, the signature of Queen Mary and her husband to them, but who brought no answer, except intelligence of the death of King Francis the Second, which took place on 5th December 1560. Other nobles present were James Duke of Chatelherault and his sons, the Earls of Argyll, Morton, Rothes, Crawford, Marshall, Glencairn, Cassillis, and Lord Somerville.[3]

As Warden of the West Marches of Scotland, Sir John Maxwell repeatedly complained against Lord Dacre, Warden of the West Marches of England opposite, for the want of the redress of some border grievances. He did this in a letter to Mr. Randolph, the English ambassador, written from Dumfries, 7th October 1560, and begged that he would communicate the complaint to Sir William Cecil.[4] In a letter to Cecil from Edinburgh, 31st January 1560-1, Sir John complained that Lord Dacre refused to exchange a Scotch felon who had been the principal slayer, or causer of the slaughter of eleven Englishmen, for an Englishman who recently slew a man within the city of Carlisle.[5]

Glencairn, Rothes, John, brother of the Earl of Menteith, Lord James Stewart, Lords Ruthven, Boyd, Ogilvy, and Ochiltree.

[1] Calendar of State Papers, *ut supra*, vol. i. p. 146, No. 48.

[2] *Ibid.* vol. i. p. 151, No. 94.

[3] Knox's History, vol. ii. pp. 120-124, 138. Historical Memoirs of the Reign of Mary Queen of Scots, etc., p. 52.

[4] Calendar of State Papers, *ut supra*, vol. i. p. 164, No. 37, I.

[5] *Ibid*, vol. i. p. 168, No. 12.

These differences still continuing, the Privy Council of England wrote a letter, 13th July 1561, to the Duke of Chatelherault and others, the Privy Council of Scotland, concerning the matters in dispute between Lord Dacre and the Master of Maxwell, and certain disorders alleged to have been committed by the Grahams. The letter is signed by Lord Keeper Bacon and eleven others.[1]

For the settlement of these contentions, an indenture was made between Lord Dacre, Warden of the English West Marches, and Sir John Maxwell, knight, Warden of the Scottish West Marches, at Carlisle, 22d August that year, relating to various points which were to be observed by the Lords Wardens and subjects of the West Marches of both realms.[2]

The Master of Maxwell subsequently continuing to complain against Lord Dacre, Queen Mary, in a letter to Queen Elizabeth, from Holyrood, 5th January 1563, requests her consideration of these complaints.[3]

In a letter to Queen Elizabeth, written from Carlisle, 22d August 1561, John, Master of Maxwell, refers to his meeting with her Commissioners at Carlisle for the redress of sundry offences committed by some of her subjects, and to the favourable disposition of the Commissioners. At the same time he professes gratitude for her Majesty's assistance in delivering Scotland from the French and otherwise assisting them, and desires that amity between the two kingdoms may continue.[4]

The Lords of the Congregation having intended to send Commissioners to London to thank Queen Elizabeth for her assistance, Randolph, her ambassador, recommended that the Master of Maxwell should be one of the number. In a letter to Sir William Cecil from Edinburgh, 15th August 1560, he thus writes :—" Of those that shall be sent into England . . . I wolde that the Master of Maxwell, who laborethe to be Lord Heres, might be one."[5] Afterwards writing from Dumfries, 31st March 1562, to Sir William Cecil, Sir John offers his services, if there be anything due to his countrymen that lies in his power.[6]

---

[1] Calendar of State Papers, *ut supra*, vol. i. p. 172, No. 49.

[2] Keith's History, Edinburgh, fol. 1734, Appendix, p. 95.

[3] Calendar of State Papers, vol. i. p. 186, No. 2.

[4] Calendar of State Papers, vol. i. p. 173, No. 59.

[5] Knox's Works, vol. vi. pp. 113, 115.

[6] Calendar of State Papers, vol. i. p. 179, No. 36.

On 4th September 1561, at the palace of Queen Mary near Edinburgh, in presence of the Queen, the Master of Maxwell was invested with the office of Warden of the West Marches until her Majesty's next returning towards Edinburgh, or her palace foresaid.[1]

Sir John Maxwell and Sir John Ballenden entered into a convention with English Commissioners at Dumfries, 23d September 1563, for the redressing of mutual trespasses on the contiguous districts.[2]

When, in the middle of December 1563, Knox was called before Queen Mary and her Council between six and seven o'clock in the evening, the Queen sat in the Chair of State, "haifing twa faithfull supportis, the Maister of Maxwell upoun the ane tor (arm), and Secretour Lethingtoun on the uther tor of the chyre ; quhairupoun thay waittit dillegentlie all time of that accusatioun, sumtymes the one occupying hir ear, sumtymes the uther. . . Knox standing at the uther end of the tabill bair-heided."[3]

To the Master of Maxwell and the other courtiers the refusal of Knox to yield to the wishes of Queen Mary on the head of religion, was very embarrassing. They were loud in their complaints about Knox's prayers for the Queen, and the doctrine he taught touching her estate and obedience to her authority. What to his view was duty in these matters, was to theirs rudeness and disloyalty. For this reason they did not appear on the first day of the meeting of the General Assembly, held at Edinburgh on 25th June 1564, to which a great part of the Protestant nobility convened.

The others, besides the Master of Maxwell, who absented themselves, were the Duke of Chatelherault, the Earls of Argyll, Murray, Morton, Glencairn, Marischal, Rothes, Secretary Lethington, the Justice-Clerk, the Clerk-Register, and the Laird of Pittarow, Comptroller. The Assembly appointed certain of the brethren humbly to request them to come and assist them with their presence and counsel, intimating at the same time that if they intended to desert them it were better that this should be known then than afterwards.[4] The Master of Maxwell and the other courtiers at first were not a little offended at this apparent suspicion of their defection, yet they joined the Assembly on the next day. But withdrawing they entered the Inner Council

[1] Regist. Secreti Concilii Acta, September 1561—   [3] Knox's History, vol. ii. p. 404.
March 1563.   [4] Ibid. vol. ii. p. 423.
[2] Nicholson's Border Laws, pp. 84-103.

House, and after a brief consultation sent a messenger to request a conference with the superintendents and others of the ministers. This was granted by the Assembly, on the understanding that nothing should be concluded without the knowledge and advice of the Assembly. The private conference took place. The complaint of the courtiers was principally against Knox, whom they craved to moderate himself in praying for the Queen, and in the doctrine which he propounded regarding her estate and obedience to her authority. Knox defended himself with his usual boldness and fluency of speech. " Gif I war in the Quenis Majestie's place," said the Master of Maxwell, " I wald nocht suffer sick thingis as I heir." [1]

Impatient of the protracted debate between Knox and Secretary Lethington, the Master of Maxwell, on whom the Secretary leaned, said, " I am almoist werie: I wald that sum uther wald ressoun in the chief heid, quhilk is nocht tuychit." Then the Earl of Morton, Chancellor, commanded Mr. George Hay to argue against Knox on the question of the obedience due to magistrates, which he did ; but Lethington again took up and chiefly maintained the argument. [2]

In his efforts to restore and maintain peace on the Borders, Sir John Maxwell acted with characteristic energy. A convention or agreement for the accomplishment of that object on the borders of both nations was settled and sealed by Commissioners appointed by both Queens. On the part of Scotland it was sealed by Sir John Maxwell of Terregles and Sir Thomas Bellenden, Justice-Clerk ; and on the part of England, by Sir Henry Scrope, Warden of the West Marches, Sir John Forrester, Warden of the Middle Marches, Sir Thomas Gargraif, Vice-President of the Queen's Council in the North, and John Rookbie, Doctor of Law, also one of the said Council, at Carlisle and at Dumfries, on 11th and 23d September 1563. [3]

In the discharge of the duties of his office as Warden of the West Marches, Sir John Maxwell, however, met with many difficulties. Not only did the commons and yeomen within his wardenry fail to accompany him as Warden on the days of truce, but the barons and landed proprietors were equally remiss, and thus was the Queen's service neglected and the Warden obstructed in the discharge of his duty.

[1] Knox's History, vol. ii. p. 428.　　[2] *Ibid.* vol. ii. p. 434.　　[3] Keith's History, p. 244.

Sir John complained. The Queen therefore, with the advice of the Lords of her Secret Council, at Edinburgh, 12th December 1564, ordained letters to be directed to officers of her sheriffs in that part, charging them to pass to the market crosses of Dumfries, Kirkcudbright, Wigton, and all other places needful within the bounds of the wardenry, and there, by open proclamation, in her Highness's name and by her authority, to command all and sundry earls, lords, barons, freeholders, gentlemen, and substantial yeomen, dwelling within the bounds of the wardenry, to meet and accompany the Warden all days of truce, or other tryst or convention which he should appoint, either by open proclamation, warden officer, or missive writings, for keeping the country in peace and stanching theft. This they were commanded to do under the penalty—for each baron ten pounds, for each landed man five pounds, and for each substantial yeoman fifty shillings, for each fault, to be taken up, to the advantage of the common service, by the person whom the Queen should appoint.[1]

In the discord which arose between Queen Mary and many of her nobles, the Master of Maxwell associated himself with the Duke of Chatelherault and the Earls of Argyll, Murray, and Rothes,[2] who were opposed to her and Darnley and Lennox. He laboured by all means, as Knox testifies, to obtain redress for the Protestant Lords, though without success, and entertained them most honourably in Dumfries. He thus incurred the resentment of the Queen, and was summoned to appear before her and her husband, as the other Protestant Lords had been. He received from her and the King a letter, dated Edinburgh, 23d August 1565, requesting him to meet them at Stirling on the Monday following, at night. They had heard, as the letter states, that he had received intelligence from the rebels.[3] He was also commanded by the Queen to deliver up the castle of Lochmaben, which he had in keeping for her. He obeyed not. Yet he was not put to the horn as the rest had been. It was while the malcontent Lords were at Dumfries that they united in sending a letter, dated from that place 10th September 1565, to Queen Elizabeth, informing her of Queen Mary's proceedings against them, by which the troops they required for their protection had been cut off from them ; and they request

[1] Regist. Secreti Concilii Acta, March 1563—June 1567.   [2] Calendar of State Papers, *ut supra*, vol. i. p. 216, Nos. 6, 8.   [3] *Ibid.* vol. i. p. 217, No. 19.

her aid in defence of their religion, lives and heritages. The letter is sub-scribed by the Duke of Chatelherault, the Earls of Murray, Glencairn, and Rothes, Lord Ochiltree, Master of Maxwell, and Laird of Drumlanrig.[1] They addressed a letter, of the same date, to Sir William Cecil, soliciting the aid of England.[2]

At Dumfries, on 1st October same year, Sir John Maxwell, Warden of the West Marches, Sir William Kirkcaldy of Grange, and others, witnessed a receipt by James Stewart, Earl of Murray, for £1000, received from the Earl of Bedford, to be employed by the nobility of Scotland for the maintenance of the true religion and the Scottish commonwealth.[3]

The Master of Maxwell, who in matters of this kind was vacillating, was not inclined to carry opposition to Queen Mary so far as many of the Protestant Lords would have done ; and soon after he deserted the Protestant Lords and joined her adherents.

On 8th October, the Queen and King marched from Edinburgh to Dumfries with all their forces.

Three days after the King and Queen had arrived at that town, the con-federate Lords, on hearing of their approach, sent Sir John Maxwell to meet them, who advanced towards the Queen as if to intercede for the Lords. They had made choice of him as the one who was most likely to be well received ; for although he affected to belong to the confederate party, he had not hitherto been in action against the King and Queen. But whether he was sent in reality to treat for an accommodation, or merely to gain time and to discover the designs of the other side, is doubtful. It is certain, how-ever, that he made his own peace with the Queen, and returning to Dumfries, plainly told the disaffected Lords that he could not help them, and advised them to flee into England, and wait for a more propitious time. He promised to follow and join his forces with theirs as soon as he could set his affairs in order.[4]

The confederate Lords, following this advice, gave place to the King and Queen, who committed the charge of the country to the Master of Max-well, and returned to Edinburgh.[5]

[1] Calendar of State Papers, *ut supra*, vol. i. p. 19, No. 40.

[2] State Papers, Scotland, Elizabeth, in State Paper Office, London, vol. ii. No. 39.

[3] Calendar of State Papers, vol. ii. p. 836.

[4] Calderwood's History, vol. ii. pp. 292-94.

[5] Historical Memoirs of the Reign of Mary Queen of Scots, etc., p. 72.

The Master of Maxwell had been conducted to the King and Queen by the Earl of Bothwell, and divers other nobles. He submitted to the Queen, though he had entertained the rebel Lords in the most friendly manner, subscribed their letters, and spoke as strongly against their enemies as any of themselves. The Earls of Atholl and Huntly, in whom, with Bothwell, Queen Mary chiefly confided, became his sureties. All past offences were forgiven him on his promising that he should be henceforth a faithful and an obedient subject. On the following day the Queen's army, numbering about 18,000 men, was dispersed. The King and Queen went to Lochmaben, where the Master of Maxwell gave a banquet, after which they marched to Tweeddale, next to Peebles, and then to Edinburgh.[1] The Earl of Bedford, in a letter to Sir William Cecil, dated Carlisle, 14th October 1565, says,—"The Queen of Scots is still at Dumfries. The Master of Maxwell has repaired to her, and his lands, goods and offices have been restored to him. The Lords and the rest go to Newcastle, to remain there, as Berwick is not a fit place for them to abide at."[2] Queen Mary seems ever after to have reposed with entire confidence in the Master of Maxwell. He professed to have a strong desire to bring her and her rebellious subjects to a good understanding. Thomas Randolph, in a letter to Sir William Cecil, from Edinburgh, 31st October same year, informs her of the Master of Maxwell's endeavours for a reconciliation, and of the possibility of such an event.[3] But some of Queen Elizabeth's counsellors, as the Earl of Bedford, regarded him, and with reason, as a man who was not to be depended on.[4]

Having been appointed Warden of the West Marches of Scotland, Sir John accepted the office upon certain conditions, to which their Majesties, with advice of the Privy Council, 8th November 1565, agreed. These were to the following effect :—

Should any person or persons privately or openly accuse and delate Sir John of any offence committed by him against their Highnesses, or wrong done by him in the execution of his office of Warden or otherwise, the accuser and delater was to be required to give his complaint in writing, and credit was not

[1] Knox's History, vol. ii. p. 512.
[2] Calendar of State Papers, *ut supra*, vol. ii. p. 829.
[3] Calendar of State Papers, vol. i. p. 223, No. 78.
[4] *Ibid.* vol. ii. p. 828.

to be given thereto until Sir John was heard in self-defence ; yet if after trial the report should be found to be true, punishment was to follow according to the nature of the fault.   Again, as the country was at that time distracted, their Majesties condescended to send forty or fifty soldiers to the West Border to assist in restoring and maintaining tranquillity, and to with-stand England in the event of its invading Scotland, the number to be diminished or augmented according as war or peace should happen between their Majesties and England.   Farther, as Sir John during his tenure of the office of Warden had, in the execution of justice on malefactors, fallen under the deadly feud of the principal clans and broken men of the West Marches, their Majesties, at whose command he had notwithstanding accepted the burden of that office, to encourage him boldly to advance their authority and service, regardless of such deadly feud, willed, and on the word of princes faithfully promised, that if, during the time of his exercise of the office of Warden, he should be slain or die, his wife and eldest son should have the ward of all his lands and heritable possessions, which by his decease should fall into the hands of the Crown, with the marriage of his son and heir for the time, and disponed the same ward and marriage to Sir John's wife and eldest son, to be used by them as lawfully in all respects as the heirs of freeholders slain at the battle of Pinkie enjoyed their wards and marriages by the Act made at Monktownhall shortly before that battle.[1]

Soon after Queen Mary and Darnley made a public declaration of their confidence in Sir John Maxwell.   As he had formerly acted with the Lords of the Congregation, certain articles were presented to the King and Queen, charging him with high treason and other crimes.   Their Majesties caused these charges to be investigated in their presence by the Lords of Secret Council, and the result was that they found them to be untrue.

Their Majesties, therefore, made a Declaration attesting Sir John's inno-cence of these charges and his faithful services, dated Holyroodhouse, 1st January 1565-6.   The nature of the charges and the grounds of his vindication may be learned from this Declaration.

First, it was alleged that, having gone to England, he had sworn himself an Englishman, and had compelled sundry of their Majesties' subjects to do the

---

[1] Regist. Secreti Concilii Acta, March 1563—June 1567.

like.   In his defence their Majesties answered that they knew perfectly that although after the loss of the unhappy battle of Pinkie, when many of their subjects, both inland and on the borders, had been compelled to take assurance with England, Sir John with his father and brother, and the most of their friends and servants having been made prisoners, had done this, yet by his assurance he never offended any of their Majesties' good subjects, nor did he ever constrain any to follow his example, as was unjustly alleged.   Their Majesties had therefore long since granted remission to him as they had done to all others their good subjects.   It was further said that he had made his escape from the Castle of Edinburgh.   Their Majesties replied that they understood from his offers that he was willing to abide the laws and to submit to punishment in body or goods as the cause might deserve, and that for this also they had granted him remission.   He had been further accused of having lately accompanied in Dumfries a number of their Majesties' subjects, who were rebels, and had passed with them into England.   Their Majesties answered that, having understood that he never intended to remain with these rebels, that he would not take part with England nor pass with them into that kingdom, and that he was never of their counsel nor privy to any offences with which they were chargeable before their coming to Dumfries, they had on his humbly beseeching their princely clemency, again granted him remission. It was alleged that through him, and from his avarice, their Majesties' subjects in these parts of the realm had been for many years past plundered, slain, and oppressed by England and the thieves ; and also that he had received six thousands merk to assist them, and a purse of ryallis and gold from England to bribe him to discover the secrets of their Majesties' Council to the English Government.   Their Majesties answered that they well knew that, on the contrary, he had been and was their true servant and a good justiciar, and that in their service he had taken great pains for many years past by executing the laws upon many notable offenders, and defending loyal subjects from the very enormities and oppressions which were laid to his charge.   Nor had he received the money alleged, nor had he discovered their Majesties' secrets to the English Government.   Their Majesties' will, therefore, was that he should be reputed as their trusty servant and counsellor in all times coming.   This declaration they commanded to be inserted in the Books of Council *ad per-*

petuam rei memoriam, and a copy of it to be given to him under their hand and signet.[1]

In the plot which was formed for the assassination of David Rizzio, French secretary to Queen Mary, by Darnley, Morton, Ruthven, Lindsay, and Secretary Maitland, the Master of Maxwell was earnestly pressed by Maitland to take part ;[2] but he was not to be persuaded. The murder of Rizzio was perpetrated in the Palace of Holyrood House, on Saturday, 9th March 1565-6, in the presence of Queen Mary, with whom Rizzio was at supper, in company with the Countess of Argyll and some other friends. The punishment of a murder committed in the royal palace, by which the Queen had been so intensely horrified, now occupied her earnest counsels, and she consulted with the Master of Maxwell and others as to the most effectual means of bringing the perpetrators to justice.[3]

In testimony of their confidence in Sir John Maxwell, King Henry and Queen Mary granted a charter under the Great Seal, dated 8th May 1566, to him and Agnes Herries, his spouse, in conjunct-fee, and to the longer liver of them, and the lawful heirs-male of their bodies, of the lands and barony of Terregles and Kirkgunzeon, and of the lands of the half of the barony of Ur, all which belonged to Sir John Maxwell and Agnes Herries, his spouse, heritably, and which they resigned into the hands of the King and Queen.

The speciality of this charter is that the holding of these lands and baronies was changed from ward and relief to free blench. They were to be held of the Crown for payment of one penny Scots yearly, in name of blench farm, if asked only. The reasons for this favour, as stated in the preamble, are worthy of being recorded. Their Majesties granted it, as the narrative of the charter bears in the original Latin, in consideration of the good, faithful and gratuitous services of their faithful cousin and counsellor, John Maxwell of Terregles, knight, Warden of the West Marches of the kingdom, towards England, in the exercise of the offices of Warden and Justiciar for the space of twenty-two years or thereby past ; by whom, with vast solicitude and sustained effort, and by the execution of justice upon a great number of perverse men, chief

[1] Regist. Secreti Concilii Acta, March 1563—June 1567.

[2] Calderwood's History, vol. ii. p. 311.

[3] Knox's History, vol. ii. p. 524.

factions, and malefactors dwelling in the said West Marches, who formerly could be restrained by no means from theft, slaughter, and depredation, the country was reduced to due and lawful obedience ; for which service rendered, and justice administered, the said John remained under the mortal hatred of a great number of factious and perverse men within the said bounds ; and in that service he had spent a great part of his life, and had incurred great expense.[1]

On 17th of the same month of May, Sir John Maxwell and Agnes Herries, his spouse, were, on a precept in terms of the Crown charter, infefted in the said lands, etc.[2]　The charter was ratified by Parliament on 19th April 1567, previous to which date Sir John Maxwell had become Lord Herries.

Queen Elizabeth also bore testimony to the efficiency with which Sir John Maxwell performed the duties of his office as Warden of the West Marches of Scotland.　In a letter to Queen Mary from Woodstock, 25th August 1566, she writes that she understood from Lord Scrope, Warden of the West Marches of England, that whereas he was answerable to the Master of Maxwell for the west parts under the said Master's rule, matters were in such sort that the subjects on both the parts had in no instance to complain.[3]

Sir John Maxwell became Lord Herries in the end of the year 1566.　In April of the following year he received from the Lyon King of Arms a patent of armorial bearings, which are the Maxwell and Herries arms quarterly.　The Patent is as follows, with an engraving of the coat-of-arms as "depaintit :"—

"Twill all and sindrie quhome it efferis quhais knawlege thir presentis salcum Greting in God evirlesting,—We, Schir Robert Forman of Luthrie, knicht, Lyoun King of Armes, with oure brithir herauldis of the realme of Scotland, being requirit be the richt honorable Johnne Lord Maxwell of Hereiss to assigne and gif vnto him sick armes in mettaill and culloure as maist deulie suld appertene to him and his posteritie as become ws of oure office to do : Quhairfore we, having respect to thais thingis that appertenit, hes assignit and assignis to him, quarterlie, the first and thrid, siluer, ane saulter,[4]

[1] Original Charter at Terregles.

[2] Memorandum of Sasine at Terregles.

[3] Regist. Secreti Concilii Acta, May 1559—March 1567.

[4] This blazon does not accord with the arms as "depaintit" on the patent, which show the Maxwell arms in the first and fourth quarters, and the Herries arms in the second and third.—[Original Patent at Terregles.]

sable, with ane Lambeaw of thre feitt, gulis ; secund and ferde, siluer, thre
hurtcheonis, sable, with the beraris of the scheild helme, Tymmerall and Detoun,
as heir vnder is depaintit, quhilk he and his posteritie may lefullie beir without re-
proche : Quhilk we testifie be thir presentis, subscriuit be Marchemont hairauld,
oure clerk of Office, quhairvnto oure seile of office is appensit.   At Edinburgh,
the secund day of Aprile, the zeir of God ane thousand fyve hundreth thre
score sevin zeiris."   " ADAME McCULLOCHT, Marchemont hairauld,
                                Clerk of the Office of Armes of Scotland."

    When Queen Mary, after the murder of Darnley, was compelled, by the
resentment of her subjects, who charged her with complicity in the deed,
to bring Bothwell to trial, John Lord Herries was one of the assize held

on him before the Court of Justiciary at Edinburgh, 12th April 1567.[1]   But
so dexterous were the arrangements for the trial that the acquittal of Bothwell
was certain.   The Earl of Lennox, who was summoned as a pursuer, had only
ten free days allowed him in the summons, whereas, according to the law,
he ought to have had forty ; and he was commanded to come to Edinburgh
with none but his domestic servants in his train—a retinue so small that
under the circumstances he considered it unsafe for him to appear in
the capital.   The accusers were the Queen's two advocates, who acted
in the accusation as they were instructed.   The Court having met, Robert
Cunningham, procurator for the Earl of Lennox, appeared, and protested
that nothing that was done that day should be prejudicial to his client,
inasmuch as the procedure of the Court was contrary to the laws and
practice of the kingdom, and as the party accused was allowed to be
attended by so numerous a body of friends and forces as to render it dangerous personally for the accuser to pursue, nor could the Justice-General, who
was the Earl of Argyll, be free impartially to administer justice.   This protestation was repelled, and the Court proceeded.   Most of the assize were
Bothwell's particular friends.   Their verdict was that there was no cause to
condemn the Earl of Bothwell according to the dittay, advantage having been
taken of a misstatement in it which accused him of the murder of the King on
the 9th, whereas the crime was committed on the 10th.   At the same time
the assize declared that should any hereafter accuse Bothwell conformably to
law, they would be free from all danger or damage on that account.[2]

   It is said that Lord Herries besought Queen Mary on his knees not to
marry Bothwell ; a step which, he assured her, would injure her reputation
and expose her to the reproach and resentment of her subjects.[3] He was,
however, induced or constrained, with others of the nobility, to sign a paper
recommending the Earl of Bothwell as a fit husband for her, and was one
of the witnesses to the contract of marriage between them, dated Edinburgh,
14th May 1567,[4] the day before the marriage.

[1] Keith's History, p. 377.

[2] Knox's History, vol. ii. p. 552.   Historical Memoirs of the Reign of Mary Queen of Scots, pp. 86, 87.

[3] The authority for this statement is Sir James Melville, who says that Lord Herries came ex-

pressly to Edinburgh to implore her not to marry Bothwell (Keith's History, p. 386). Its truth is confirmed by a letter of Lord Scrope, to be after- wards quoted.

[4] Register of Deeds in the Court of Session, vol. ix. p. 86, February 13th, 1566—July 12th, 1569.

Whilst Queen Mary's marriage with Bothwell exasperated all classes of her subjects, and whilst an association for the protection of the young Prince and for punishing the murder of the late King was formed at Stirling, consisting of the principal nobility, even of many who, from the dread of Bothwell's exorbitant power, had been constrained to recommend him as a husband to Mary, Lord Herries continued steadfast in his attachment and loyalty to her. He was one of the nobles who subscribed at Dumbarton, in July 1567, a bond for supporting her against the confederate insurgent Lords.[1]

The army of the confederate Lords met the forces of Queen Mary and Bothwell on the 15th of that month at Carberry hill,[2] about six miles east of Edinburgh. Queen Mary's troops were irresolute and unwilling to fight ; and, after a conference with Kirkcaldy of Grange, she surrendered herself to the confederate Lords, who conducted her to Edinburgh, and thence sent her under a guard on the following day to the Castle of Lochleven.

Earnest to obtain the liberty of his sovereign, Lord Herries corresponded on that subject with Sir Nicholas Throkmorton, who, as Queen Elizabeth's ambassador, arrived in Edinburgh in July 1567, with instructions to declare her Majesty's sentiments to the Queen of Scots in regard to the murder of Darnley, her inconsiderate marriage with the Earl of Bothwell, the misunderstanding between her and her nobility, and to make an offer about the custody of the Prince, whom she wished to be brought up in England.[3] Sir Nicholas on his arrival at Edinburgh was refused audience of the Queen of Scots, but he learned that she was determined not to prosecute the murder, nor to abandon the Earl of Bothwell, and that a divorce was intended by the Lords.[4] In his despatches to Queen Elizabeth and Cecil, he repeatedly informs them of the general confusion in Scotland, the perilous situation of the Queen of Scots, the purpose of the Lords to dethrone her, and to crown the Prince, her son ;[5] and his apprehension that the tragedy would end in the Queen's person after the coronation, as it began in the persons of Rizzio and Darnley.[6] He was instructed by Queen Elizabeth to warn the Lords of the consequences of

[1] Keith's History, p. 436.

[2] Carberry hill is the property of Lord Elphinstone, and is situated to the east of his lordship's residence of Carberry Tower. To commemorate the battle, his lordship has erected a large stone on the summit of the hill, having engraved thereon an antique Crown, and the Monogram M.R.

[3] Calendar of State Papers—Scotland, 1509-1603, vol. i. p. 250, No. 81 ; p. 251, No. 18.

[4] Ibid. vol. i. p. 252, No. 19.

[5] Ibid. vol. i. p. 253, Nos. 24, 28, 32.

[6] Ibid. vol. i. p. 254, No. 37.

their proceedings, which were contrary both to Scripture and to law, and commanded not to attend the coronation of the Prince,[1] which took place on 29th July 1567, after a renunciation of the Crown in his favour had been extorted from his mother at Lochleven Castle.[2]

The opinion formed of the character of Lord Herries by Throkmorton is characteristic : it is laudatory of his abilities, but in other respects not complimentary. Throkmorton seems to have thought that even a statesman so shrewd as Sir William Cecil might be outwitted by his Lordship's dexterity in the arts of policy. Writing to Cecil, 20th August 1567, Throkmorton says :—

" The Lord Herryes ys the connynge horseleache and the wysest of the wholle faction; but as the Quene of Scotland sayethe of hym, there ys no bodye can be sure of hym; he takethe pleasure to beare all the worlde in hande ; we have good occasyon to be well ware of hym. Sir, yow remember how he handled us when he delyvered Dunfryse, Carlaverocke, and the Harmytage into our handes. He made us beleave all should be ours to the Fyrthe; and when wee trusted hym best, how he helped to chase us awaye, I am sure you have not forgotten. Heere amongst hys owne countreymen he ys noted to be the moost cautelous man of hys natyon. It may lyke you to remember, he suffred hys owne hostages, the hostages of the Lard of Loughanver and Garles, hys nexte neyghboures and frendes to be hanged for promesse broken by hym. Thys muche I speake of hym, because he ys the lykelyest and moost dangerous man to inchaunte yow."[3]

While Throkmorton was thus depicting in dark colours the character of Lord Herries, his Lordship, from his zeal in Queen Mary's service, and calculating on Throkmorton's goodwill towards her, wrote to him a letter, dated " Off Dumfries, 23d August 1567," soliciting Queen Elizabeth's interposition, and expressing his readiness to serve him in whatever he would command him for the relief of Queen Mary, who was still straitly confined in Lochleven.[4]

Throkmorton, in his reply to Lord Herries, dated at Edinburgh, 24th August 1567, informed him that he had received instructions from his Sovereign to endeavour, by all kinds of persuasions, and even by strong

[1] Calendar of State Papers, *ut supra*, vol. i. p. 254, No. 39.

[2] Knox's History, vol. ii. pp. 565, 566.

[3] Quoted in Historical Memoirs of the Reign of Mary Queen of Scots, printed for the Abbotsford Club, Prefatory Notice, p. x.

[4] British Museum, Ayscough, 4126, No. 67.

representations, to prevail upon the Scottish Lords to desist from their severe and disloyal treatment of their Queen ; but that it seemed to him that all efforts in this way were to no purpose.

It is notable that although Throkmorton abused Lord Herries behind his back, he was fair and flattering to him in his correspondence, addressing him, as he repeatedly does in this letter, " your good lordship."[1]

The Earl of Murray assumed the Regency 22d August 1567.   Lord Herries, as we learn from a letter of Lord Scrope to Throkmorton from Carlisle, on the 25th of that month, was summoned to Edinburgh by the Earl of Murray, but refused to have any conference with him and his party so long as they retained their Queen in captivity ; he also refused to give up any of his offices.   In another letter from Lord Scrope to the same correspondent, 2d September, mention is made that a herald, on his arrival at Glasgow on Sunday to proclaim the Earl of Murray's regency, was not permitted to make the proclamation.   Lord Herries gave orders forbidding it, and commanded the herald to depart out of his rule.   Letters had arrived from the Bishop of St. Andrews and Abbot of Arbroath, praying Lord Herries to be at Glasgow on the 3d of September to meet the Earls of Argyll and Huntly, with others, to consult for the pacifying of the existing troubles.[2]   At Edinburgh, on 8th October 1567, in presence of the Regent and Secret Council, Michael Lord Carlyle, John Gordon of Lochinvar, Thomas M'Lellan of Bomby, Thomas M'Culloch of Cardoness, Roger Kirkpatrick of Closeburn, William Kirkpatrick of Kirkmichael and Thomas Kirkpatrick of Alisland, renounced a bond subscribed by them to George Earl of Huntly and John Lord Herries, and acknowledged the lawful coronation of the King.[4]   On 14th October, Lord Herries, notwithstanding his former opposition, came to Edinburgh and acknowledged the authority of the King and Regent.   Mr. James Melville, in a letter to Throkmorton from Edinburgh, 18th October, says that Lord Herries was minded to the present weal and quietness of the state.[5]

Having become reconciled to the Regent, Lord Herries was present at the Parliament held in December 1567.   In this Parliament, on the 29th of

[1] British Museum, Ayscough, 4126, No. 69.
[2] Calendar of State Papers, Scotland, 1509—1603, vol. ii. p. 845.
[3] Calderwood's History, vol. ii. p. 387.
[4] Minutes of Evidence, Herries Peerage, p. 226.
[5] Calendar of State Papers, vol. ii. p. 846.

that month, he joined with the Earls of Huntly and Argyll in a protestation, each for himself, that no fault should be imputed to them, or
any of them, for any thing they had done since the 10th of June last,
although they had not acted as it became them. The Regent, in presence
of the Parliament, declared that he forgave them for the past, as well as
all other lieges of the realm who would in future assist the King and his
Regent and their adherents in the conduct of public affairs, and in the
punishment of the murderer of the King. This declaration made by the
Regent was thereafter sanctioned by the Parliament.[1]   By this Parliament
Mary's resignation of the crown was ratified ; the King's authority and Murray's
regency confirmed ; and the imprisonment of the Queen pronounced lawful.
Mary's letters to Bothwell were produced, and she was declared to have
been accessory to the murder of Darnley. All the Acts of Parliament of the
year 1560 in favour of the Protestant religion were ratified.

At this Parliament Lord Herries delivered a remarkable speech in the
name of the Duke of Chatelherault, and other nobles of Queen Mary's party,
who had been reconciled to the Regent and were at the Parliament, urging
with great solemnity the importance of the union of the whole realm. He
eulogized the nobles who, from the beginning, had adopted measures for the
punishment of the Earl of Bothwell, and defended them in imprisoning in
Lochleven the Queen, whose inordinate affection to that wicked man was such
that she could not be persuaded to leave him. He declared that he, and
those in whose names he spoke, would hazard their lives and lands for maintaining the cause in which these nobles had embarked ; and that if the
Queen herself were in Scotland with 20,000 men, this would not alter their
purpose. He hoped that the remaining noblemen of their party, Huntly,
Argyll, and others who had not yet acknowledged the King's authority, would
do so ; and he would earnestly endeavour to persuade them to submission.
If they remained obstinate, the Duke and he, with their friends, would
join with the Regent in correcting them. "So plausible an oration," says
a contemporary reporter, "and more advantageous for our party, none
of ourselves could have made. He did not forget to term my lord Regent
by the name of Regent (there was no mention at all of the Earl of Murray),

---

[1] Anderson's Collections, vol. iv. part ii. p. 153.

and to call him grace at every word when his speeches were directed to him, accompanying all his words with low courtesies after his manner."[1] There seems no reason to doubt the accuracy of this report of Lord Herries's speech. Such a sudden change of sides as was then made by himself, the Duke of Chatelherault, and others of the Queen's party with whom he acted, was not uncommon in those times. But common though this shifting policy then was, it is not without surprise that we find that Lord Herries and others of the Queen's adherents who were present at this Parliament, and who had so openly avowed their adherence to the King's government, entered into a bond before the close of the month in which that Parliament was held, pledging themselves to do their utmost to effect the liberation of the Queen from Lochleven, for which they would hazard their lives, and to restore her to her authority ; as well as to concur for the punishment of the murder of Darnley, and to preserve the person of the Prince. The bond we here give entire :—

For as much as considering the Queen's Majesty our Sovereigne, to be detained at present in Lochlevin in captivity, wherefore the most part of her Majesty's lieges cannot have free access to her Highness, and seeing it becomes us of dewty to seek her liberty and freedome, We Earles, Lordes, and Barons vnderscribing, promise faithfully to vse the vtmost of our endeavors by all reasonable meanes to procure her Majestie's freedom and liberty vpon such honest conditions as may stand with her Majesty's honor, the common weal of the whole realm, and security of the whole nobility, who at present have her Majestie in keeping, whereby this our native realm may be governed, ruled, and guided by her Majestie, and her nobilitie, for the common quietness, the administration of justice and weal of the country; and in case the noblemen who at present [have] her Majesty in their hands, refusse to set her at liberty, vpon such reasonable conditions as said is—in that case, we shall employ ourselves, our kindred, friends, servants, and partakers, our bodies, and lives to set her Highnes at liberty as said is, and also to concur to the punishment of the murther of the King, her Majestie's husband, and for sure preservation of the person of the Prince, as we shall answer to God, and on our honour and credit ; and to the effect shall concur every one with other at our most power ; and if any shall set vpon vs, or any of vs, for the doeing as aforesaid—in that case, we promise faithfully to espouse one another's interest, under the pain of perjury and infamy, as we shall answer to God. In witness whereof we have subscribed these presents at Hamiltone, the 25th of December 1567.

St. Andrews.	Fleeming.
Argyle.	Herries.
Huntly.	Stirling.
Galloway.	Killwonning.
Ross.	W. Hamilton of Sanquhar, Knt.[2]

[1] Robertson's History of Scotland, Appendix No. xxiv.

[2] Ayscough, 3199, No. 78. The spelling of the names of the subscribers is here given as in a copy of the Bond, although several of the names appear to be modernized, and "Stirling" is probably a mistake for Skirling.

On Sunday 2d May 1568, Queen Mary effected her escape from Loch-leven, rode with all speed to Niddry Castle,[1] the seat of Lord Seton in west Lothian, and next morning travelled with the same haste to Hamilton. Thither repaired to her Lord Herries and many other nobles, barons, and gentlemen, who, with their friends and attendants, soon formed a strong army.

A bond, dated 8th May 1568, for the defence of her person and authority, was entered into, and subscribed by nine Earls, nine Bishops, and eighteen Lords, amongst whom were Lord Herries and many gentlemen, including several who, at the last Parliament, had openly submitted to the King's authority.[2]

There followed the battle of Langside, in Renfrewshire, fought on 13th May that year, when Queen Mary was defeated, and her prospects for ever blighted. Her forces were 6000 men, and the Regent's were scarcely 4000. The bad fortune which so often attended the unhappy Queen was again con-spicuous, as was subsequently the final arbitrament of her cause. Before leaving Hamilton she granted a commission to the Earl of Argyll as Lieu-tenant-General of all her forces ;[3] but the Earl, on the march from Hamilton to Langside, having been suddenly seized with severe indisposition, was un-able to lead her forces, and the want of their general no doubt materially contributed to the disaster which ensued.

Eight days before the battle, Queen Mary, still at Hamilton, wrote to Sir John Maxwell of Pollok a short, but anxious letter, calling upon him to join her forces,[4] as she trusted in his constancy. The loyal Laird of Pollok re-sponded to the royal command. He assisted his chiefs, Lord Maxwell and Lord Herries, in the battle of Langside, but without avail.

Lord Herries had the command of Queen Mary's horse, who were almost all borderers, dependants, and tenants of Lord Maxwell, his nephew, then a minor.[5]

---

[1] Niddry Castle is now a ruin on the north side of the Edinburgh and Glasgow Railway, in the parish and county of Linlithgow. Niddry was the property of the Seton family in the time of William the Lion, who granted a charter to Philip de Seton, of the lands of Seton, Winton, and Winchburgh, of which last Niddry Castle was the chief messuage. Niddry is the property of the Earl of Hopetoun, whose second title is Lord Niddry.

[2] Keith's History, p. 475.

[3] Original Commission in Argyll Charter-chest.

[4] Memoirs of the Maxwells of Pollok, vol. ii. p. 1. A facsimile of the letter is also given there.

[5] Calderwood's History, vol. ii. p. 414 ; Keith's History, pp. 472, 476, 480.

Of Queen Mary's troops 300 were slain, and many were made prisoners, who were carried to the Castle of Edinburgh. On the Regent's side only one man was killed, but many were hurt, among whom was Andrew Lord Ochiltree, whom Lord Herries is said to have cut on the neck.[1]

The Queen stood on Cathcart hill, about a mile from the battle, to witness it; and, on the flight of her army, she was escorted from the field by Lords Herries, Fleming and Livingston.[2] Accompanied by them, she rode all night without halting till she came to Sanquhar. Thence she continued her flight to Terregles, the residence of Lord Herries, where she rested several days. At first she attempted to take the road for Dumbarton, in which impregnable fortress she expected to find personal safety; but the passages being held by her enemies, she was advised by Lord Herries to go into Galloway, where in the meantime she would be secure, and whence she might easily pass into England by sea or by land, or find a passage to France. She was accordingly conducted by Lord Herries to his own house at Terregles.

It may be noted in passing that the remains of the bed occupied by Queen Mary during her stay at Terregles on this occasion still exist at Terregles. They consist of a wooden scroll about eight feet in length and one foot in breadth, a flat cloth canopy, which must have been supported by a timber frame, and a head-piece six feet long and five broad, which had hung from the roof inside down to the pillow. The materials of the bed are a serge tick stuffed with wool, which still has its original white and fresh appearance, and covered with satin, now no longer white as it once was, richly embroidered with flowers in needle-work.

It may also be noted that various articles that belonged to Queen Mary are still carefully preserved by the present Lord Herries. One of these is a Prayer Book beautifully engrossed on very fine vellum, and exquisitely illuminated. It bears the date of 1544, two years after the birth of Mary. Other interesting relics of Queen Mary, also belonging to Lord Herries, are the leading-strings of King James the Sixth. These consist of two separate strings and a belt for the body. The two strings are of red silk.

[1] Historical Memoirs of the Reign of Mary Queen of Scots, etc., printed for the Abbotsford Club, p. 103.

[2] Calendar of State Papers, Scotland 1509—1603, vol. i. p. 262, No. 21.

On both sides of one of the strings are beautifully worked, in letters of gold about an inch long, the letters being reversed on the different sides, the words :—

𝕬𝖓𝖌𝖊𝖑𝖎𝖘 · 𝖘𝖛𝖎𝖘 · 𝕯𝖊𝖛𝖘 · 𝖒𝖆𝖓𝖉𝖆𝖛𝖎𝖙 · 𝖉𝖊 · 𝖙𝖊 ·

On both sides of the other string are similarly worked the words :—

𝖀𝖙 · 𝖈𝖚𝖘𝖙𝖔𝖉𝖎𝖆𝖓𝖙 · 𝖙𝖊 · 𝖎𝖓 · 𝖔𝖒𝖓𝖎𝖇𝖛𝖘 · 𝖛𝖎𝖎𝖘 · 𝖙𝖛𝖎𝖘 ·

The strings are ornamented with a worked border of flowers, fruit, etc. The belt for the body is still more richly wrought, with small crowns in the bottom. The whole is understood to have been the work of Queen Mary. These articles are supposed to have been left by her at Terregles, or given to Lord Herries. After she was sent by Queen Elizabeth to Bolton Castle, she applied to the Regent Murray for her wardrobe. While at Bolton she granted, on 15th October 1568, an acknowledgment of having received from her beloved servitour, Robert Melville, all her jewels, etc., which she had caused to be delivered to him, when she was in Lochleven. The Queen thereby declared that he had behaved as a faithful servant, to her satisfaction.[1]

To return to our narrative : From Terregles she went to Dundrennan Abbey, near Kirkcudbright, sixty miles from the field of Langside, whence she could retire by sea into England or France.

Whilst at Terregles she held a consultation with her friends. So gloomy were her prospects in Scotland, that she regarded her person as in the utmost danger. What course was she now to pursue ? was the question that pressed itself upon the attention of herself and her friends. Were she to return to France, how could she bear the mortification of appearing as a fugitive in a country where before she had been honoured with every mark of royal dignity ? and what sympathy could she expect from the French Queen-mother ? Averse therefore to take this course, she expressed her resolution to retire into England, and to throw herself on the protection of Queen Elizabeth. To her taking this imprudent step, which she had ever after cause to regret, Lord Herries was much opposed. He besought her even on his knees not to commit herself to the English Queen, on whose generosity, he assured her, she could not confide for safety. From a letter written by Lord Herries in French, relative to the

---

[1] Original Receipt, signed by Queen Mary, at Melville House.

events of this time, we translate an extract :—" Before her Majesty departed from Scotland, I promised to her, on pain of losing my head, and all that I have in the world, that she should remain securely in the country where she was, for the space of forty days, and after, according to her good pleasure, that she might take the way of France or of Dumbarton ; for then there were no enemies nearer than sixty miles," etc.[1]   He could not however prevail on his affrighted Sovereign to follow his advice.

By her command he wrote a letter, 15th May 1568, to Lowther, Deputy-Governor of Carlisle, inquiring whether, if she should seek refuge in England, she might come safely to Carlisle.   Lowther immediately answered in doubtful terms, saying that Lord Scrope, Governor of Carlisle, and Warden of the Marches there, was then in London ; that he had no authority to promise anything, but that he would send by post to know her Majesty's pleasure ; and that, in the meantime, if the Queen of Scots was under the necessity of crossing the Borders, he would receive and protect her at Carlisle, if she came there, till Queen Elizabeth's pleasure might be further known.   But so great was Queen Mary's sense of danger that, before this answer could be received, she embarked at a small creek in the Solway Firth, near Dundrennan, in Galloway, in a fisher's boat with about twenty attendants, and landed on the evening of Sunday, 16th May, at Workington, in Cumberland.[2]   On the following day she came to Cockermouth.   On the 18th of May she was carried by Lord Scrope to Carlisle Castle, where he resided.   Accompanied by sixteen persons she was conducted thither by Captain Read, with fifty soldiers.

At her request Lord Herries, of the aid of whose counsels she was specially desirous, had embarked with her, and while she was at Carlisle he posted at the end of the month of May, by her orders, to London, carrying letters from her to Queen Elizabeth, in which she expressed the hard condition to which she had been reduced by her rebellious subjects, and her strong desire to be admitted to a personal interview with Elizabeth.   He bore also letters which had been sent to her some time before by Queen Elizabeth, with a diamond ring which had been presented to her by the English Queen " in token of a sure friendship, which by her letters she desired her to keep, that

---

[1] Teulet, vol. ii. p. 234.   [2] Keith's History, pp. 481, 482.

if she should happen to fall in distress, the sight of that ring should be an infallible tye for Elizabeth to assist her with all her power."[1]

When at Carlisle, Queen Mary was visited by Lord Scrope, warden of the West Marches on the English side, and Sir Francis Knollys, Queen Elizabeth's vice-chamberlain, who had been despatched to her by the English Queen with letters professing the utmost sympathy and affection for Mary.

Meanwhile, Lord Herries was on his way to the Court, accompanied by Lord Fleming. Queen Mary, in a letter from Carlisle, 28th May 1568, to Queen Elizabeth, says :—" I have despatched my Lord Herries, my faithfull and well-beloved subject, to inform you at length of all those things, and others as to which I have learned by Scrope and Knollys that you are in doubt, supplicating you to credit him as myself." In the beginning of this letter she writes :—" I am sorry that the haste in which I wrote my last letter made me omit, as I perceive by yours, the principal thing which moved me to write to you, and, what is more, the principal cause of my coming into this your kingdom : which is, that, having this long time been a prisoner, and, as I had already written to you, treated unjustly both by the deeds and false reports of my rebellious subjects, I desired especially to come in person to make my complaint to you, as well on account of proximity of blood, similitude of estate, and professed friendship, as to vindicate myself to you from such calumnies as they have dared to prefer against my honour."[2] Queen Mary having thus offered to submit her cause to Elizabeth, the English Queen became the arbiter between the Queen of the Scots and her subjects.

In a letter to Cecil, 29th May, Queen Mary recommends Lord Herries, the bearer, whom she had commanded fully to make known to him her condition.[3]

Queen Mary's demand to be admitted to a personal interview with Queen Elizabeth was declined. It was urged that to grant this while she was criminated as the murderer of her husband, would expose Elizabeth's character to reproach ; but it was promised that, on the establishment of her innocence, she should obtain a reception becoming her royal dignity.

On these matters, Lord Scrope and Sir Francis Knollys in a letter to Queen Elizabeth from Carlisle, 29th May, thus write :—" We arryved here

---

[1] Historical Memoirs of the Reign of Mary Queen of Scots, p. 104.

[2] Labanoff, tom. ii. pp. 80, 81.

[3] *Ibid.* p. 84.

at Karlell yesterdaye at 6 of the klocke afternoone; and by the waye my Lord Harrys mett us six mylles from this towne, and after he had discoursed of the lamentable estate of the Quene of Scotts, hys mystres, inveying motche agaynst the treasonable crueltie of hir enemyes, and also saying as motche as he cowlde for the innocencye of hys mystres towching the murder of hir husband, the which, he sayd, wold be easelye proved, if the Quene, hys mystres, myght be heard to speyk for her selfe in your Hyghnes presence; and affyrming, that he trusted your Hyghnes wolde eyther gyve hir ayde, to the chastenyng of hir subjects, for her releeffe and comforte, or els that your Hyghnes wold gyve her leave to pass throw your countrye into France, to seke releeffe otherwais : Whereunto we answered, that your Hyghnes could in no wyse lyke her sekying ayde in France, therby to bring French men into Scotland ; and we dowted whether your Hyghnes could thynke it mete to receave hyr so honorablye into your presence, as your desyrous affectyon, and good wyll towards her dyd wyshe, untyll your Hyghnes myght be well instructed and satisfied by probable reasons, that she was cleare and innocent of the sayd morder, by some sotche wyse man as he, that myght set forthe the same manyfestlye : Whereupon, and throghe other conferrences private with me the Lord Scrope, he semed to determyne to ryde towardes your Hyghnes, for that intent, within a day or twayne, which was the thyng that we specyally sought for."[1]

In instructions to Lord Fleming, whom Queen Mary had appointed her ambassador at the French Court, to negotiate in regard to her affairs, dated Carlisle, 30th May 1568, mention is made that when the result of the mission of Lord Herries and Lord Fleming to the Court of England to treat in regard to the promises which Queen Elizabeth had made to assist Queen Mary against Murray and the other rebels, was ascertained, Lord Fleming was to go to France to communicate the conclusions to the French King.[2]

Separate instructions were also given at the same time by Queen Mary to Lord Fleming, authorizing him, among other things, to pray the Cardinal of Lorraine to write to Lord Herries, thanking him for the good services which he had rendered and continued to render to her who had nothing in her necessity

[1] Goodall's Mary Queen of Scots, vol. ii. pp. 69, 70.
[2] Labanoff, tom. ii. p. 86.

but what he had supplied, and with which he commonly provided her.   It was therefore her earnest desire that he might be acknowledged in some honourable way.   Should Lords Herries and Fleming, by the command of the Queen and for her service, borrow money at London to assist in relieving her affairs, it was in the hope that there might be sent to her from France, by the Cardinal and others there intrusted with her affairs, what should repay the money thus borrowed, at the term promised.[1]

Queen Mary was the all-engrossing subject at the English Court.   Queen Elizabeth, in a letter to the Earl of Murray, 8th June 1568, concerning the Scottish Queen and Lord Herries's embassy, thus writes :—" As the Quene of Scots, our good sister, is lately come into our realme, as we are well assured you knowe, with the causes of her arrivall in the partes where she now is, and that she hath sent to us the Lord Herrys with credit to report unto us her estate ; and to descover her whole late troubles and great injuries done to her by her subjects."[2]

Finding that Queen Elizabeth was so little disposed to make any concessions in favour of Queen Mary, Lord Herries regretted that he had been sent on such an errand.   Alexander Clark, in a letter to Sir William Cecil from Scrooby, 2d June, mentions that Lords Herries and Fleming were offended at being brought to Court.[3]   Lord Herries, therefore, in a letter to one of the English statesmen, 12th June 1568, requests that he may have leave to return to Carlisle, and that Lord Fleming may have licence to go to France ; if not, that they and other noblemen, to the number of one hundred, may be allowed to pass and repass from Scotland during the abode of their sovereign in England.[4]

At the same time, so offended was Queen Mary at Elizabeth for having purposed to appoint English commissioners to hear both parties, and for having desired the Regent Murray to appoint commissioners to appear before them to vindicate his conduct towards his Sovereign, that she retracted, in a letter to Queen Elizabeth, 13th June 1568, the offer she had made to submit her cause to her, refusing to reply to the accusations of her subjects, who were not her equals, though willing to vindicate herself in the presence of Elizabeth.

[1] Labanoff, tom. ii. pp. 92, 93.
[2] Goodall's Mary Queen of Scots, vol. ii. p. 73.
[3] Calendar of State Papers, vol. i. p. 213, No. 34.
[4] Ibid. vol. ii. p. 855, No. 19.

Towards the close of the month of June, Lord Herries intended to visit France. Queen Mary, in a letter to Queen Elizabeth from Carlisle, prays her to grant him a passport. "My Lord Herries," she writes, "will tell you more at length what treatment and how little favour I receive. I would supplicate you to give your passport to him favourably, and to give him good countenance, that it may be known that you approve of the service which he has done me in delivering me. He goes to pass his time in France, in order to learn the language, and to be acknowledged and recompensed in part by the King, my good brother, and my uncles, by their commandment, on account of the desire which they have to know him who has done a service which is so agreeable to them, and I have wished to give him leave, since I have no need here for many of my good servants. He only asks to be allowed to go, for he has no affair, except his own pleasure, at least for me." [1]

It appears that Queen Elizabeth did not at this time grant a passport to Lord Herries to go to France, as, in writing to Queen Mary from Greenwich, 30th June, and giving her reasons for having refused to grant permission to Lord Fleming to go to France, she refers to the detention of Lord Herries at the English Court whilst Lord Fleming was to return to Scotland.[2] With this detention of Lord Herries Queen Mary was dissatisfied. In a letter to Queen Elizabeth from Carlisle, 5th July, she says:—"I beseech you to return to me my Lord Herries, for I cannot be without him, having none of my council here, and also to suffer me, if it please you, without further delay to depart hence, whithersoever it be out of this country." [3]

On the 7th of the same month, in a letter to Archibald fifth Earl of Argyll, after thanking him for his great constancy towards her, Queen Mary writes :—" My Lord Herreis hes writtin to my Lord of Murraye expresly that hie vse na forder extremitie aganis zow our fauouraris and trew subiectis." [4]

After the victory gained at Langside on 13th May, the Regent Murray made a military progress in June. Various castles, including Hoddom, Lochmaben, and Annand, were spared on hope of obedience which was promised ;

[1] Labanoff, tom. ii. p. 124.
[2] Calendar of State Papers, *ut supra*, vol. ii. p. 855, No. 24.

[3] Robertson's History of Scotland, Appendix, No. xxv ; Labanoff, tom. ii. p. 133.
[4] Letters to the Argyll Family, p. 6.

while others, as the castles of Skirling and Kenmure, were razed, for an example. The castle of Terregles was spared for a singular reason. " The Lord Herreis' hous of Terreglis the Regent gave full orders to throw it doune. But the Laird of Drumlangrig, whoe was the Lord Herreis' uncle, and much in favour with the Regent, told that the Lord Herreis wold take it for a favour if he wold ease him of [his] pains, for he was resolved to throw it doune himselfe, and build it in another place. The Regent sware he scorned to be a barrow-man to his old walls. And so it was safe."[1] On an old Plan of the estate of Terregles there is a sketch of the ancient house of Terregles as it existed pre-vious to its removal for the erection of the present mansion. An engraving of the old house is here subjoined.

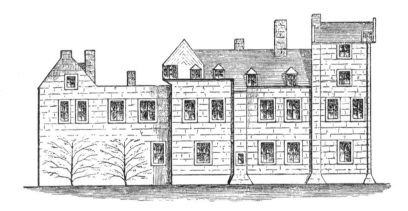

Another effect of the Regent's victory at Langside was that Lord Herries was deprived of the wardenship of the West Marches, which was granted to Douglas of Drumlanrig, a supporter of the Regent's government, who con-tinued to hold that office for five years.

On 13th July, Queen Mary was carried from Carlisle, by the orders of Queen Elizabeth's Privy Council, to Bolton Castle, the property of Lord Scrope, situated on the borders of Yorkshire,[2] where it would be more difficult to maintain correspondence with her friends in Scotland than at Carlisle.

At the Court of Queen Elizabeth Lord Herries had repeated audiences of her Majesty. She told him that it was her pleasure that French soldiers

[1] Historical Memoirs, ut supra, p. 106.   [2] Calderwood's History, vol. ii. p. 428.

ANCIENT OAK DOOR AT TERREGLES.

BEARING THE INITIALS OF WILLIAM LORD HERRIES. 1601.

should not be received in Scotland, and that none of her subjects in England should be troubled by any of Queen Mary's party. If this expression of her will was not disregarded, she would do her utmost, according to her former resolution and declaration, to reconcile Queen Mary to her honour and advantage with her subjects. She would therefore have Lord Herries and his Sovereign's friends to beware not to give her occasion to alter her good intentions towards them. Lord Herries often told her that if she would restore Queen Mary to her crown, and assist in the subjugation of her rebellious subjects, she need have no apprehension of Frenchmen coming into Scotland. Queen Mary would seek the help neither of Frenchmen nor of any other foreigners, but only that of the Queen of England, if she would give it speedily ; but otherwise she and her friends would be forced to seek assistance from France or Spain, or wherever it might be obtained. He frequently showed Queen Elizabeth that things were driving on to the ruin of his Sovereign and her obedient subjects, on whom sentences of forfeiture were daily passed. Her adversaries spent all her patrimony and revenues, destroyed kirks and policies under their usurped authority ; old men, priests that never bore arms, wives and children, in numerous instances, were cruelly murdered ; women were ravished, and burning and spoliation by thieves were quite common. He denied, though the contrary had been affirmed, that any attempt was intended against England by any of Queen Mary's friends, such an allegation having been invented, like many other things, to incite the resentment of the Queen of England.[1]

Towards the end of July, Lord Herries went from the English Court to Queen Mary to Bolton Castle, to give her an account of his embassy to the Court of England, of Elizabeth's professions of friendship for her, and other particulars. Sir Francis Knollys, in a letter to Sir William Cecil from Bolton Castle, 25th July 1568, mentions the arrival of Lord Herries. In a letter to Cecil from Bolton, 28th July, Lord Herries informs him of Queen Mary's acceptance of Queen Elizabeth's professions towards her, and of her request to be allowed to return to Scotland ; of the answer which he (Herries) received from Queen Elizabeth and himself (Cecil) on the subject ; and of other pro-

[1] These facts are communicated in a letter from Lord Herries to Lord Scrope and Sir Francis Knollys, dated Dumfries, 17th August 1568. Papers in British Museum, Ayscough, 3199, No. 28.

positions made to him in England in regard to the Queen's resumption of her government, with the Queen's answer to them.[1]

With Lord Herries's account of his negotiations at the Court of England Queen Mary was gratified. In a letter to Queen Elizabeth from Bolton, 29th July, she expresses her satisfaction, from what Lord Herries had reported to her, that Elizabeth's good disposition had begun to appear, which relieved her from the necessity of writing to her as hitherto in the unpleasant style of complaint.[2]

Lord Herries, in presence of Lord Scrope, Sir Francis Knollys, and Queen Mary at the Castle of Bolton in the same month, repeated the message which he had received from Queen Elizabeth to Queen Mary. Queen Elizabeth, he said, commanded him to say to her that if she would commit her cause to be heard by her order—not to make her judge over her, but rather to commit herself to her as her dear cousin and friend for advice and counsel, she would surely restore her to her throne and regal dignity. First, she would send for the noblemen of Scotland that were her adversaries, to ask them before such English noblemen as Queen Mary herself should approve of, to explain why they had deposed their Sovereign from her government. If they could produce some reason for their so doing, which she thought they could not, she would restore Queen Mary to her regal power, on condition that these her Lords and subjects should continue in the honours, states, and dignities pertaining to them. But should they be unable to adduce any reason of their doings, she would absolutely restore her by force, if necessary, provided Queen Mary would renounce her claim to the Crown of England during the lifetime of Queen Elizabeth and of the issue of her body, quit the league with France, abandon the Mass in Scotland, and adopt the English Common Prayer-Book. This message, which Lord Herries brought from the Queen of England, he repeated seven or eight times to Queen Mary, in the hearing of Lord Scrope and Sir Francis Knollys. At first Queen Mary seemed to hesitate in yielding to what was proposed, but upon further conference with Lord Herries, she said that she would thankfully submit her cause to her Highness accordingly.[3]

[1] Calendar of State Papers, vol. ii. p. 856, Nos. 28, 29.

[2] Labanoff, tom. ii. p. 143.

[3] The Book of Common Order used by the Protestants of Scotland, both before and after the establishment of the Reformation, was the "Order of Geneva."

Touching Queen Mary's receiving of the English Common Prayer-Book, Sir Francis Knollys said to Lord Herries that if thereby he meant to condemn the form and order of Common Prayer then used in Scotland,[1] as well as in divers well reformed churches in Germany, Switzerland, France, and Savoy, and if withal he would reject and annihilate the Confession of Faith, acknowledged in Scotland by Parliament, because there is no such Confession of Faith acknowledged in England ; or, if he meant to expel all the learned preachers of Scotland, should they not receive and wear cornered caps and typpets, with surplices and copes, which they have left since their first receiving of the Gospel into that realm ; then, however he meant to further religion by that means he might so fight for the shadow and image of religion that he might bring the body and truth in danger.[2] Lord Herries answered that in cities and towns where learned preachers remained, he would willingly allow the form and order of Common Prayer and preaching then used in Scotland to be retained, but in the country, where learned men were lacking, it would be better that the form of Common Prayer used in England should be introduced. In this Sir Francis Knollys quite agreed with him.

Sir Francis, in his conferences with Lord Herries, complained of the increase of Queen Mary's retinue, of the baser sort, at the expense of Queen Elizabeth. This Lord Herries did not approve ; he acknowledged that Queen Elizabeth had found the same fault ; he had endeavoured to obtain an abatement of this ground of complaint ; and he requested to know what number Sir Francis thought would be sufficient. Sir Francis judged that thirty men and six gentlewomen were enough to remain at the charges of Queen Elizabeth. He trusted that although Queen Mary was reluctant to put away any, yet she would be willing to maintain the overplus at her own expense in the town.

Sir Francis mentions that Lord Herries had departed from Bolton Castle on the 28th July, and adds, " My Lord Herrys myslyketh, not in words, that she [Queen Mary] shold be brydled in her regiment by assistance of noblemen of hyr realme, in consideration of hyr rashness and foule mariage with the Erle of Bodwell, whom he wold have persequted to death."[3]

---

[1] Letter from Sir Francis Knollys to Secretary Cecil, 28th July 1568, in Anderson's Collections, vol. iv. part i. p. 109.

[2] Anderson's Collections, vol. iv. part i. pp. 110, 111.

[3] *Ibid.* vol. iv. part i. pp. 112, 113.

A Parliament having been proclaimed by the Regent Murray to be held at Edinburgh on the 16th of August 1568, for the forfeiture of Queen Mary's adherents, it was resolved to prevent its meeting by force; and a proclamation, dated The Largs, 28th July, was issued by Archibald, fifth Earl of Argyll, her Lieutenant, commanding all persons between sixteen and sixty years of age to be in readiness, "boding fear of war," by the 10th of August, to assist in opposing the enemies of their sovereign.[1] But Queen Elizabeth having insisted on Queen Mary's friends not attacking the Lords who supported the King's authority, and being desirous to reconcile her and her subjects without bloodshed, Lord Herries by the orders of Queen Mary sent to the Earls of Huntly and Argyll, her Lieutenants and others, instructing them that it was the will of the Queen of England, and the command of his own sovereign, that they should desist from pursuing any of the other party. "Which," says he in a letter to Lord Scrope and Sir Francis Knollys after his return to Scotland, formerly quoted, dated "off Dumfries, 17th August 1568," "I doubt not but they will obey."

With the view of obstructing the meeting of the Regent's Parliament the Earl of Argyll required Lord Herries to come to Glasgow, declaring that his Lordship's balling, as Argyll termed it, was the cause of the stay of his whole army. Lord Herries replied that he could not come through the country to Glasgow without some great purpose, in consequence of the distance, which to some of his folk was more than sixty miles by land, and for the most part through their enemies. He would have been at the head of Douglas Water on the 16th of that month at night; but when pressing to be there, he received on the 15th letters from his sovereign, as Argyll and other Lords had done, commanding him not to invade any of her adversaries. He accordingly desisted from his purpose. He hoped therefore that Argyll would pardon him.[2]

Queen Mary was desirous to convey to the English Court the intelligence that she and her adherents had stayed her faithful subjects from pursuing the other party, in compliance with the wishes of Queen Elizabeth, as soon

---

[1] Calendar of State Papers, *ut supra*, vol. i. p. 264, No. 50.

[2] Letters to the Argyll Family, p. 7. These facts

Lord Herries communicated to the Earl of Argyll in a letter from Dumfries, 19th August 1568.

as she had received Elizabeth's assurance in writing. She wrote to that effect in a letter to Sir William Cecil, from Bolton, 16th August 1568 ; adding, that considering the premisses, Lord Herries, before the receipt of Queen Elizabeth's assurance, could not have taken upon him to stay the rest of his Sovereign's nobility from defending their persons, friends, honour, land, and goods ; and that on this account he ought to be excused.[1]

The Parliament, as appointed, was held at Edinburgh on the 16th of August, notwithstanding the strong desire expressed by Queen Elizabeth to Regent Murray that it should be put off. Sentence of forfeiture was passed upon the chief of Queen Mary's adherents, including fifteen Hamiltons and Lord Herries. But the sentence was delayed in regard to Lord Herries and others of them, in deference to Queen Elizabeth.[2]

It had been reported to Queen Elizabeth that, since his return to Scotland from the Court of England, Lord Herries had caused some of his countrymen to commit depredations upon the frontiers of England, and that he intended that Queen Mary's friends should take up arms against her disobedient subjects. In a letter he besought her Majesty not to give credit to such false reports.

He informs her, in a letter from Dumfries, 19th August, that as soon as she had expressed to him her strong desire that the pretended Parliament should not be held, he despatched to the Earl of Murray a messenger with a letter and instructions to that effect. Murray, having heard at length the messenger's instructions, would not open Lord Herries's letter because his Lordship did not style him Regent. "And," says he, "as I shew your Majestie I think never to style him swa nor obey him with that style." He sent to Murray another messenger four or five days before the intended meeting of Parliament with a letter of like import, intimating that Queen Elizabeth was opposed to its meeting, and desired that all hostility on both sides should cease, whilst he offered on behalf of Queen Mary's adherents, that they should not molest the other party, but live quietly, as Queen Elizabeth had commanded, provided Murray would similarly engage on behalf of his party. This letter he sent subscribed and unclosed, but without any address on the back that he might not mis-style him. Lord Herries's messenger, on being

[1] Labanoff, tom. ii. p. 158.
[2] Calendar of State Papers, Scotland, 1509—1603, vol. i. p. 266, Nos. 62, 64.

heard at length by Murray and the Earl of Morton, got no answer. From " this warnying that I had given thame of your Majestie's mynd and offer for my maistres part it may appear I was not myndit to move discord. . . . That I have bene causer or actor or counsellour in ony manner of way to truble your Majestie's subjectis or yett the fortherer of ony trubles in this countre sen my cuming from your Hienes, I vterlie deny."

He presses Queen Elizabeth to bring the question between Queen Mary and her rebellious subjects, which had been referred to her by both parties, to a speedy decision,—otherwise his sovereign would be forced to seek assistance from some other Christian prince,—urging the near relationship of Queen Mary to her, and especially Queen Elizabeth's promise of love, friendship, and assistance, which was the occasion of Queen Mary's coming into England.[1]

In a letter to Lord Scrope, dated Dumfries, 21st August 1568, Lord Herries, after giving him intelligence of Murray's proceedings in his pretended Parliament, and of the forfeiture of some of the Queen's adherents, expresses his astonishment at these transactions, remembering the faithful promise so often made to him by the Queen of England.[2]

Queen Mary, in a letter to Queen Elizabeth from Bolton, 23d August, refers to the account given in letters from Lord Herries of the troublesome estate of things in Scotland.[3]

In a letter on 27th of the same month to the Earl of Argyll, she informs him of her receipt, by her servant, James Borthwick, of two writings from Queen Elizabeth, written with her own hand. These she had caused to be translated into Scots, of the which she had sent copies to Lord Herries and the Bishop of St. Andrews, who would acquaint the Earl therewith, and it might be considered what favourable effect this might have upon Queen Mary's interests, for she communicated to the Earl Queen Elizabeth's assurance as she had received it.[4]

In another letter to the Earl of Argyll from Bolton, 31st August, she heartily thanks him for the great fervency, goodwill, and forwardness he had

[1] The facts in the preceding paragraphs are stated in a letter from Lord Herries to Queen Elizabeth, from Dumfries, 19th August 1568, in British Museum, Ayscough, 3199, No. 33.

[2] Calendar of State Papers, *ut supra*, vol. ii. p. 857, Nos. 40, 41.

[3] Labanoff, tom. ii. p. 160.

[4] *Ibid.* tom. ii. p. 167 ; Argyll Letters, p. 9.

shown in the last assembly of her adherents, as she understood from his communication to her.   The Earl's dissolution of the assembly, and the staying of
further proceedings, she had caused to be done from a good intention, in compliance with a letter from Queen Elizabeth, a copy of which she sent him.
Lord Herries had advertised her that the Earl and the rest of her nobility
were much displeased with him on that account.   She prays the Earl not to
blame Lord Herries, as he had done nothing but by her express commandment.   He was far more blamed by the other party, as being wholly the
occasion of the enormities perpetrated on the Borders, and of other tumults in
the country.[1]

In a letter to Lord Scrope and Sir Francis Knollys, 3d September 1568,
Lord Herries again dwells upon the promises which had been made by Queen
Elizabeth to Queen Mary.   " Our sovereign," he writes, " havand her Majesty's
promise be writing, of luff, friendship, and assistance, gif need had so requirit,
enterit that realm upon the 16th day of May ;   sen that time the Queen's
Majesty has commanded me diverse times to declare she would accept her
cause, and do for her, and to put her in peaceable possession of this realme ;
and when I required of her Majesty, in my maistress' name, that her Highness would either do for her (as her special trust was she wold) according to
her former promises, or otherwise give her counsal, wold not consent (as I
show her grace I fand diverse repugnant), then that she would permit her to
pass in France, or to some other prince, to seek support, or failing hereof
(quhilk was aganis all reason), that she would permit her to return to her
awin countrie in sic semple manner as she came out of it."[2]

The Regent Murray having taken possession of several of Lord Herries's
houses, and the West Marches being much disturbed, Lord Herries, in a letter
to him, dated at Dumfries, 1st September 1568, requests to know if the obedient
subjects of his Sovereign would be molested by the other party in their return
from England ; entreats him to reform the disorders in those parts, and to
put some good man into the wardenry thereof ; and begs that certain houses
which had been taken from him during his absence in England might be
restored to him.[3]

[1] Labanoff, tom. ii. p. 169 ; Argyll Letters, p.
10.
[2] Robertson's History of Scotland, App. No. xxvii.
[3] Calendar of State Papers, vol. i. p. 266.

The Regent, in his reply to him from Edinburgh, 11th September, accuses him as being the cause of all the disorders in his parts, and justifies himself for taking certain houses from him.[1] At the same time Lord Scrope and Sir Francis Knollys complain of Lord Herries. In a letter to him of the same date as the preceding, they reprove him for the intemperate style of his letter and the threats contained in it of bringing in the French unless her Majesty did for him what he wished.[2]

Queen Mary having submitted her cause to Queen Elizabeth, the English Queen purposed that Commissioners from the Regent and Queen Mary should respectively state their case before her Commissioners at York. The Regent, though with some hesitation, consented to this course, and appointed as his Commissioners James Douglas Earl of Morton, Patrick Lord Lindsay, William Maitland of Lethington, Secretary, Adam Bishop of Orkney, Robert Commendator of Dunfermline, Mr. James Macgill of Rankeillour, Mr. Henry Balnaves and Mr. George Buchanan.[3] They went to England on 27th September, accompanied by the Regent and an hundred horse. Queen Mary's Commissioners were John Bishop of Ross, William Lord Livingston, Robert Lord Boyd, John Lord Herries, Gavin Commendator of Kilwinning, Sir John Gordon of Lochinvar, and Sir James Cockburn of Skraling.[4] Their Commission is dated at Bolton, 29th September 1568.[5] Queen Elizabeth's Commissioners were Thomas Duke of Norfolk, Earl Marshal of England, Thomas Earl of Sussex, Viscount of Fitzwalter, Lord Egremont and Bornewell, President of the Council of the North, and Sir Ralph Sadler, Knight.

As Queen Mary's Commissioner on this occasion, Lord Herries is allowed to have performed his duty with ability and fidelity.

The purport of the articles and instructions given by Queen Mary, of the date mentioned, to these her Commissioners to be treated at the conference to be held in the city of York, the last day of September instant, or any other

---

[1] Calendar of State Papers, vol. i. p. 267, No. 75.

[2] *Ibid.* vol. ii. p. 858, No. 51.

[3] Their Commission is dated at Edinburgh, 18th September 1568.—(Goodall's Mary Queen of Scots, vol. ii. p. 119.) For the conference at York, George Buchanan received a new dress of black velvet, the expense of which, £72, 17s. 6d., was defrayed by the Government. Henry Balnaves, a Lord of Session, and John Wood, Regent Murray's secretary and also a Lord of Session, were similarly supplied with still more expensive suits of black velvet.—(Treasurer's Book.)

[4] Calderwood's History, vol. ii. pp. 429, 430.

[5] Goodall's Mary Queen of Scots, vol. ii. p. 118.

day or days, place or places, within the realm of England, in presence of the Queen of England, or of her Commissioners, is here subjoined.

First, at their meeting at York, they were to declare to the Duke of Norfolk, Earl of Sussex, and Sir Ralph Sadler, Commissioners for the Queen of England, that they had come there in the name of the Queen of Scots, with the advice of her faithful subjects, sufficiently authorized, to the conference appointed by the Queen of England and her.   The cause of this meeting, which was by reason that at her first coming within the realm of England she had sent her trusty and faithful counsellor Lord Herries, to her dearest sister the Queen of England, desiring her in the most friendly manner to consider the estate of the Queen of Scots, and how grievous it was, not only to that Queen, but to all other princes, that subjects at their pleasure, should be suffered so far to forget their natural and dutiful obedience as to put hands on their sovereign and native prince, which the Earls of Murray, Mortoun, and sundry others their adherents, had done, against her person, doing what they could not only to deprive her of her authority and the government of her realm, but also intrometting with and despoiling her strengths, disponing and wasting her jewels, moveables, and whole patrimony, oppressing her faithful subjects by slaughter, imprisoning their persons, rifling their goods, and casting down their houses and fortalices.   Having most sure confidence in her good sister and most tender cousin, the Queen of England, by reason of proximity of blood, and divers promises of kindness before expressed, the familiar writings and messages that had passed between them, she desired effectually to receive from her Majesty support, whereby she might be reponed in the authority and government of her own realm of Scotland, of which she was native and just princess and Queen, and might cause her disobedient subjects to acknowledge their offences and their unnatural treatment of her, render her strengths, restore her jewels and moveables, and desist from usurping her authority in time coming within her realm.   To these her desires she received most friendly and loving answers and writings, by Lord Herries, from the Queen of England, who of her goodness promised by her own forces to support her, and to repone her in her own realm, and earnestly desired her to desist from asking assistance from the King of Spain or any other prince, a desire which Queen Mary had obeyed, putting her whole confidence next to God in her Grace's promises.

The instructions further bear that, before entering on any conference, Queen Mary's Commissioners were to protest that although she was contented that the causes in dispute between her and her disobedient subjects should be considered and settled by the Queen of England, or her Commissioners authorized for that purpose, in preference to all others, she did not thereby intend in any wise to acknowledge herself to be subject to any judge on earth, inasmuch as she was a free princess, having an Imperial Crown given her by God, and no other superior ; and therefore that neither she nor her posterity should be in any wise prejudged thereby.

Her Commissioners were further to show in her name to the Duke of Norfolk and the other Lords Commissioners of the Queen of England, that James, Earl of Morton, John, Earl of Mar, Alexander, Earl of Glencairn, the Lords Home, Lindsay, Ruthven, Sempill, Cathcart, Ochiltree, with others their assistants, had assembled in arms a great part of Queen Mary's subjects, declaring by their proclamations that it was for her relief that they beset her in her way between her Castles of Dunbar and Edinburgh, and that they took her prisoner, confined her in Lochleven Castle, and afterwards intrometted with her cuinzie-house, pressing-irons, gold and silver, cuinzeit and uncuinzeit, passed to the Castle of Stirling, and crowned her son the prince, then only thirteen months old.   James, Earl of Murray, assumed the name of Regent, usurping thereby the supreme authority of her realm, in the name of that infant, intrometted with the whole strengths of her realm, jewels, munition, and patrimony of her Crown ; and when it pleased God of his great mercy to deliver her from that strait thraldom in which she was detained eleven months so hardly that none of her true subjects could have free access to speak with her, she made open declaration and solemn oath in Hamilton that her former writings in prison were extorted against her will from fear of her life.

Her Commissioners, as soon as anything should be answered by her disobedient subjects to the complaints foresaid, were to desire the same to be given in writing that they might advise thereon with herself before giving an answer.

If they were pressed for an answer, and if any allegation should be made which appeared to amount to a charge that she was implicated in her husband's death, they were, under the protestation foresaid, to say that she lamented more deeply the tragedy of her husband's death than any of her subjects could do, and had they suffered her to use her authority unmolested, she would have punished the perpetrators, even as she was yet willing to punish them, as law and justice required.

Her Commissioners were to affirm in her name that she had neither knowledge of, nor was art and part in that crime, nor did any of her subjects declare to her, before her being taken and imprisoned, that those were the principal authors and committers thereof who were afterwards so accused. Her Commissioners were further, if it was alleged that her marriage with the Earl of Bothwell was a presumption against her, to answer that she never agreed to marry him until the greater part of the nobility had acquitted him by an assize, and until that acquittal was ratified in parliament, nor until they had given their consent to her marriage with him and had solicited and persuaded her thereto, as their handwriting would testify.[1]

The first day of the session of Queen Elizabeth's Commissioners at York was the 4th of October 1568. The earlier meetings were occupied in the production by the several parties of their commissions and the taking an oath of fidelity.

At the session of the third day, being the 6th of the same month, Queen Mary's Commissioners, being required by Queen Elizabeth's Commissioners to take an oath of fidelity, took it after making some difficulties, especially Lord Herries, who was willing to promise by oath to say nothing but what was just and true, but not all that he knew to be true, in this matter.[2]

On the 7th, Queen Mary's Commissioners solemnly protested that whilst their Sovereign was willing to have the differences between her and her disobedient subjects considered and settled by the Queen of England, or her Commissioners, they did not intend that their Sovereign, who was a free Princess, to whom the Imperial Crown was given by God, should acknowledge subjection to any Prince on earth.[3]

After this protestation was given in, and a protestation made by Queen Elizabeth's Commissioners, that they did not and would not allow the protest

[1] Labanoff, tom. ii. pp. 195-210.

[2] The meaning of Lord Herries seems to have been, that, in the hope of some reconciliation between Queen Mary and her subjects being effected, he was willing to decline charging Murray, Morton, and others of their party as the murderers of Lord Darnley.—Goodall's Queen Mary, vol. ii. pp. 108-112, 116, 125.

[3] Goodall's Mary Queen of Scots, vol. ii. p. 124.

of the Commissioners of the Queen of Scots to be in any wise prejudicial to the right, title, and interest which the Crown of England claimed as superiors over the realm of Scotland, Lord Herries began to discourse on the beginnings of the troubles in Scotland, how the Queen's evil and disobedient subjects began to take arms against her, committed her to prison, deposed her from her royal seat, with many other circumstances relating thereto, and then descended to other particulars, such as injuries done to himself and others of the Queen's true subjects, as he termed them.[1]

On the 8th of October, Queen Mary's Commissioners gave in to the English Commissioners a complaint against Murray and his party, charging him with assuming, under the name of Regent, the supreme authority in the name of the infant Prince. To this complaint an answer was given in by Murray and his party on Monday 10th October.[2]

To these proceedings the Duke of Norfolk, Earl of Sussex, and Sir Ralph Sadler refer in a letter to Queen Elizabeth, from York, 9th October 1568.[3] Sir Francis Knollys, writing to Sir William Cecil from York on the same day, says that Herries and Lethington were desirous to settle matters without the extremity of odious accusations.[4]

On Saturday, 16th October, Queen Mary's Commissioners gave in to the English Commissioners a reply to the answer of the Earl of Murray and his adherents.[5]

Uncertain how to proceed in the matter, Queen Elizabeth, in a letter to the Duke of Norfolk and her other Commissioners at York, 16th October, desired that Sir Ralph Sadler, Lethington, and James M'Gill, Lord Herries and the Abbot of Kilwinning, might come up to the Court to deliberate upon the case ; and she gave instructions as to their coming.[6] The resolution to which, with the advice of her ministers, she came, was that the Commissioners for both parties should each send two of their number to London, to her Majesty, within eight days, and that the conference at York should cease till the return of the Commissioners.

[1] Letter of Norfolk, Sussex, and Sadler from York, 9th Oct. 1568, to Queen Elizabeth.—Goodall's Mary Queen of Scots, vol. ii. p. 135.

[2] Goodall's Mary Queen of Scots, vol. ii. pp. 128, 139, 144.

[3] Calendar of State Papers, *ut supra*, vol. ii. p. 860, No. 8.

[4] *Ibid.* vol. ii. p. 860, No. 11.

[5] Goodall, vol. ii. p. 162.

[6] Calendar of State Papers, vol. ii. p. 861, No. 18 ; Goodall's Queen Mary, vol. ii. p. 171.

... rest consigne ... great zele beir. ... our ...... to schaw zow
that at this conference ... borne in ... betuix ... commissioneris and
thais of the Quene of England ... ... wabbellis ... borne hard and ...
... to thair advantage bot rather by dishonour and gud advancement
of ... In the meane tyme ... send ... to send
... of ... lordis ... him ... ...
... haue ... ... The bischope of ...
... ... and the abbot of ... At ... returning ...
to haue ... gud resolutioun And as ... of the furtherance ...
... mak zow participant of the same Not doubting that ze will continewe
in ... gud mynd ... ... Referring the rest to ... most ...
Committis zow to ye protectioun of god almychtie Off Bolton the xvi day
of october 1568.

Your gud frend

Marie R

This resolution of the English Queen having been intimated on 19th October to Lord Herries and his fellow Commissioners, they went, on the 20th, from York to Bolton. On Thursday 21st they had a personal interview with Queen Mary ; and, in compliance with Queen Elizabeth's desire, John Bishop of Ross and Lord Herries received a commission from their Sovereign to go to London on her behalf.[1] The following is the letter of credence to the Bishop of Ross and Lord Herries, dated Bolton, 22d October 1568, which she addressed to Queen Elizabeth :—

Right high, right excellent, and mighty Princess, our dearest good sister and cousin, after our most hearty commendations : It is well known to you [that by the] inobedience of certain our subjects against us, and we being most assured of your tender love and aid, was moved to come in this your realm to lament our [griefs] and have your support, having good experience of the great care and solicitude taken by you for our honour and cause ; wherethrough ye have addettit us unto [you.] . . . We have, as ye thought good, caused certain of [our] council repair at York to the Lords, your Commissioners, and having declared unto them in our behalf a part of the wrongs which we have sustained, [and] upon their invented answer, gave a true declaration which we believe are come in your hands. We understand it is your pleasure, a part of them shall repair to you, whereof we are right glad, assuring ourselves it is now in the hands of the world, where we most desired. And since ye, good sister, know our cause best, we doubt not to receive presently good end thereof, wherethrough we may be perpetually addettit unto you. And for satisfying our desire in our [cause] if further declaration shall need, we have sent our trusty counsellors, the Bishop of Ross, and my Lord Herries to await upon your pleasure and commandment. . . .[2]

Queen Mary, in a letter to a supporter of her interest, includes the Abbot of Kilwinning as one of her Commissioners. The letter is as follows :—

Traist cousigne,—We greit zow veill : The present heirof salbe to schaw zow that at this conference hes bene in York, betuix our Commissioneris and thais of the Quene of Ingland, quhair our rebbellis hes bene hard and found nathing to thair advantage, bot rather to thair dishonour and gud advancement of our desyres. In the meane tyme our said sister hes desyrit ws to send sum of our Lordis towartis hir, as in lyk maner wilbe thair of the saidis rebellis. Quhairfoir we haif send vp our traist counsalouris, the Bischop of Ross, my Lord Hereis, and the Abbot of Kilwynning, at quhais returning we luik to haif ane gud resolutioune : And as we ar aduertisit of the furtherance thairof sall mak zow participant of the samyn : nocht doubting that ze will contenew in zour gud mynd towart ws. Referring the rest to our nixt aduertisment, committis zow to the protectioune of God Almychtie. Off Bowtoun, the xxiiii of October, 1568.

Zour gud frind,
MARIE R.[3]

From this letter it appears that Queen Mary was gratified with the

---

[1] Goodall's Queen Mary, vol. ii. p. 175.
[2] Labanoff, tom. ii. pp. 224-226.
[3] Original Letter at Marchmont. The address is wanting. A facsimile of the letter is here given.

proceedings at York, so far as they had hitherto gone. This is easily explained. The Regent Murray had studiously avoided accusing Queen Mary of being accessory to the murder of her husband ; and this was to suppress that which would have afforded the best justification of his proceedings against her.

The two Commissioners sent to London by the Earl of Murray, were William Maitland of Lethington, younger, and Mr. James MacGill of Rankeillor.

Lord Herries and the Bishop of Ross appeared before Queen Elizabeth and some of her nobility, in her great chamber of presence, at Hampton Court, on 31st October. After long communing she said, that she would declare the reason of her sending for them by some of her council, who should confer with them. On Monday 1st November she made a similar reply to Lethington and Mr. James MacGill.[1]

Queen Elizabeth, that Queen Mary's cause should be investigated nearer the court, where the English Commissioners might have an easy opportunity of conferring with their Sovereign, and of obtaining her advice in all their proceedings, desired that Queen Mary's Commissioners should obtain a new commission, similar to what they had got for the conference at York. A new commission was granted. To Lord Herries and the Bishop of Ross were joined Lord Boyd and the Commendator of Kilwinning.[2]

The commission is dated Bolton, 22d November 1568 ; it states that the conferences at York were appointed only for making a pacification betwixt Queen Mary and her rebellious subjects, and restoring her to her realm, authority and government, and that she being head of her subjects, it would be unsuitable for her to accuse them in presence of a foreign Sovereign, and much more to be accused by them, who were the offenders. Her Commissioners were to declare to Queen Elizabeth that by her advice Queen Mary consented to grant pardon to her rebellious subjects, provided this was not prejudicial to her estate and crown. She ordered them to break the conferences if it was intended to proceed upon any other basis.[3]

In a letter to her Commissioners of the same date, she writes :—" And ye my Lord Herries, we pray you in all things foresaid to employ yourself, and

---

[1] Calderwood's History, vol. ii. 447.   [2] Goodall's Queen Mary, vol. ii. 18.   [3] Labanoff, tom. ii. 229.

follow our intention with such dexterity as you can very well use ; and to add hereto, as ye shall think necessary, following the knowledge which ye have of the premisses."[1]

Lord Herries and the Bishop of Ross, having learned that Westminster was the place fixed upon for the conference, went to Hampton Court, and said to the Queen, that it might be prejudicial for their Sovereign to enter Westminster, a place of judicature for causes both criminal and civil. They also desired that, as the Earl of Murray and others, his adherents, had been admitted to an interview with Queen Elizabeth, Queen Mary should also be similarly admitted, that she might vindicate her innocence. The place, said Queen Elizabeth, should be a chamber, in which a court of judicature had never yet been held. But she declined to admit into her presence the Queen of Scots, until her cause was tried and concluded.[2]

On the 25th of November, Lord Herries, Robert Lord Boyd, John Bishop of Ross, and Gavin, Commendator of Kilwinning, appeared at Westminster, in the outer chamber, beside the House of Parliament, before Queen Elizabeth's Commissioners. The Commission of the English Commissioners having been produced and read, Queen Mary's Commissioners expressed their readiness to produce theirs, but before entering into conference, they had to protest that they did not enter a judicial place, nor were to proceed in any respect in a judicial form, or before any judge or judges, but as Commissioners of a free Princess, in form of treaty only, with the Commissioners of the Queen of England. They presented the protestation subscribed with their hands, and at their request it was read and admitted. The English Commissioners protested that they did not mean to proceed judicially as judges, or in a judicial place, but simply according to their commission.[3]

The English Commissioners having given their oath of fidelity, Queen Mary's Commissioners also gave theirs under protestation, as at York, after which they presented the complaint and reply given in at York. The Regent Murray and his colleagues also took the oath of fidelity. On Friday, 26th November, Murray and his colleagues gave in an eke to the answer which they had presented at York. In their former answer they had suppressed the

[1] Labanoff, tom. ii. p. 236.
[2] Calderwood's History, vol. ii. p. 448.
[3] Calderwood's History, vol. ii. pp. 449, 450 ; Goodall's Queen Mary, vol. ii. pp. 193, 196.

chief grounds upon which their whole proceedings were founded.   They were now compelled, they say, for their justification, to declare that as the Earl of Bothwell was the chief executor of the murder of the late King Henry, so the Queen was privy to it, counselled, devised, persuaded, and commanded it, and was the protector of the murderer by stopping inquisition and punishment according to the laws of the kingdom.   Since their marriage, she and Bothwell had begun to exercise a cruel tyranny in the whole commonwealth, and intended to treat the innocent Prince, their sovereign lord, as they had done his father, thereby to transfer the crown from the right line to a bloody murderer.

In reference to this eke, the Regent and his adherents at the same time presented a protestation.   When pressed, they said, by English and French ambassadors to give the reason or reasons of their detaining their Queen in Lochleven Castle, their only answer, from devotion and affection towards her, had been that her excessive affection towards Bothwell, the chief author and executor of the murder, rendered this necessary, as it was impossible, so long as she was at liberty, to punish him.   But the suppression of the chief cause of their proceedings against their Queen—that she was accessory to the murder—brought into doubt the justice of their cause.   If now they accused her of so odious a crime, they protested that they had no delight in seeing their Queen dishonoured ; that they did not do so willingly, but were compelled for their just defence.[1]

At the meeting on the 29th of November, this eke of the Regent Murray and his colleagues was shown to Queen Mary's Commissioners.   Upon receiving a true copy, they withdrew into another chamber, whence, after remaining for some time, they returned and expressed their surprise that the other party, on the greater number of whom their Sovereign had conferred so many benefits, should have boldly committed to writing such accusations against her.   The matter, they said, from its great weight, would require from them further deliberation.   What they had then said was not to be regarded as their answer.[2]

At the meeting on the 1st of December, Lord Herries, at the request of the Bishop of Ross, having obtained from the English Commissioners liberty to

[1] Calderwood's History, vol. ii. pp. 451, 455 ; Goodall's Queen Mary, vol. ii. p. 206.
[2] Goodall's Queen Mary, vol. ii. p. 209.

speak, vehemently inveighed against the Regent and his party as the slanderers of his mistress, as the contrivers of the slaughter of Darnley, in which they had got the Earl of Bothwell to become their confederate. He accused them of having plotted the death of their Queen, after having murdered her secretary in her presence, because she intended to revoke the patrimony of the Crown bestowed on some of them ; and he affirmed that it was not the punishment of the murderers of her husband which moved them to this proud rebellion, but the ambition to usurp her supreme authority, and the avaricious desire to gain possession of her great wealth.[1] The following is the speech :—

My Lords, We are hertely sorry to here that thes our countrymen should intende to colour their most unjust, ingrate, and shamefull doings, as to the worlde is patent, against their native Sovereigne, liege lady and maistres, that haithe ben so beneficiall to them ; her Grace hathe made the gratest of them, of meane men in their owne calling, erles and lords ; and now without any evill deserving of her Grace's part to any of them in dede or wourde, to be thuswise recompensed with calumpnious and false invented brutes, slandered in so grate a matier to her reproache, whereof they themselves, that now pretende herewith to excuse there open treasons, were the first inventors, wryters with their owne hands of that devilish bande, the conspiracie of the slaughter of that innocent yong gentleman, Henry Stewart,[2] late spouse to our Sovereign, and presented to their wicked confederate James, erl Bothaile, as was made manifest before ten thousand people at thexecucion of certen the principall offenders in Edinburgh ; but seeing they can get no other excuse to this their treasonable usurpacion and manifest wrongs—yea, such usurpacion and wrongs as never hath ben sene the lyke subiects to have done before, for the first and best of them hathe not in Parliament the first vote of eightene of that realme. No, no, my lords, this is not the cause whie they have put their hands in their Sovereign, the anoynted of God, most often by his woorde expressly prohibited ; a mateir to other Princes right daungerous, and worthie to be forsene ; for if this in them be tollerate, what Prince lyveth upon the face of the yerth, that ambicious subiects may not invent som slaunder in their lyving to com to their supreme auctoryte. Because your wisdomes understandeth well how farre their doings passt the bounds of subiects permitted in the holie and sacred scriptures, and loyall duetie to their native princes in humane lawes, we will not speke thereof. Onely will we playnly declare the very truth and cause of their usurpacion. The Quenes Highnes, our and their native Sovereign, being of herself (as welle is known), a liberall princesse, gave them in her youth, for their unshamefast begging, without other their worthie deservinge, the twoo parts of the patrymonye perteyning to the crown of Scotland. And when her Grace came to farther yeres, and more perfite understanding, seing that her successours, kings of that realme, might not mayntene their estate upon the third parte, albeit her Grace might for the time, having so grate dowerie of France, and other casualities not proper to the crowne ; for their evill deservings, and most proude contempcion, procuring her slaunder so far as in them was, sleing her secretarie (*David Rizzio, an Italian*) in her Grace's presence, caused her use the priviledge of the lawes, alwaies granted to the kings of that realme of before, made revocacion before her full

---

[1] Goodall's Queen Mary, vol. ii. p. 211. [2] Lord Darnley murdered 18th Feb. 1567.

age of twenty-five yeres. They understanding right well this to be a way, when it pleased her Grace and her successours by the lawes, to take from them the lyvyngs before given them, and thus wise well deserved, when they had herein advised with their machiveles doctrine, seing her soonne an infant not a yere olde, coulde fynde no better way then to cut of their sovereigne liege lady, which, if it had not ben the Quenes Majestie of this realme her grate diligence, without doubt had ben donne, for that they understode they might long possess their   , or that infant had witte or power to displace them : and in the meane tyme gatte gret ryches, under the colour of a pretended auctoryte. That it was not the punyshment of that slaughter that moved them to this prowde rebellion, but the usurping of their Sovereigne's supreme auctorytee, and to possesse themselfs with her grete ryches and her trew subiects, we will boldly avow, and constantly do affirme the same, as by the sequele doth and shall playnly appear. This shalbe knowne the cause and grounde of their mynde to the Quenes Majestie of this realme, the Kings of France, Spayne, and all other Prynces. And as the Quenes Majestie (Elizabeth) hath wrytten and sayed, her Highnes neither could nor wolde be iudge in this cause, considering the Quenes Grace, our mistres, and her progenitors, have benn free pryncesses. Neither yet wold her Highnes permitte them to com to her presence that thus had used their native Sovereigne. So can we not doubt, but your right honorable lordships, reporting this to her Majestie, we shall fynde her of that good mynde and disposicion to our sovereigne, her Majestie's owne bloode, that upon the affirmed promise of frendship and assistence bytween them, of her free option and voluntary will, is com into this realme to her Majestie, seing her Highnes help that her Grace may enjoye her owne given her of God, which otherwise hath at all tymes found, and we of reason can require. Howbeit, our Sovereign had not tyme to have advise with her estates,   her cause, nor   herein to   with the Quenes Majestie. But, in very simple manner, put herself in her Majestie's handes upon the promisses, trusting only in her Majestie's honour, which ever hath ben found to others of farre meaner degree, that in such manner have sought in this country. And, at her Highnes commandement and promes of assistance, hath lefte the seking of ayde of any other prynces, having no other but her Majestie's high honour to appeale her cause unto. And that ye, my lords, of the noble auncyent worthie blood of this realme, ar convenit to here and understand this cause ; and that your honours shall report the same to your Sovereign, is our grete comforte to have good answer, which we humbly require.[1]

Whilst Queen Mary was now accused, by the Regent, in the most direct and explicit terms, of the murder of Darnley, her Commissioners not only indignantly repelled the imputation, but threw back the charge, denouncing the Regent himself as the real murderer. They demanded that their Sovereign should have access to the presence of Elizabeth, her nobility, and ambassadors of foreign countries, for the declaration of her innocence.[2] Lord Herries and Queen Mary's other Commissioners went to Hampton Court, and presented a supplication to Queen Elizabeth to that effect. Queen Elizabeth's answer was unfavourable. She could not admit Queen Mary into her presence so long as

---

[1] Sadler's State Papers, vol. ii. pp. 334-337. [2] Goodall's Queen Mary, vol. ii. p. 217.

she lay under the imputation of a crime so atrocious. Queen Mary's Commissioners declared that they would neither receive nor answer the accusations of her accusers until she was first admitted into the presence of Queen Elizabeth, a matter as to which they had received special instructions. Queen Elizabeth told them that she would receive probation upon the eke given in by the Regent and his party.[1]

Lord Herries and the other Commissioners of Queen Mary, in presence of the English Commissioners at Westminster, on 6th December, requested that till Queen Mary was heard all conference should be stayed, and her rebellious subjects refused a hearing of their pretended probation ; and they protested that if this was not yielded, their mistress's honour, person, crown, or estate should not be prejudged by whatever should be done. In that case they discharged the present conference in obedience to their Sovereign's command.[2]

On 9th December, two of Queen Mary's Commissioners, the Bishop of Ross and Lord Boyd, presented before the English Commissioners the petition, protestation, and discharge of the conference on behalf of Queen Mary.[3]

On 16th December, Lord Herries and Queen Mary's other Commissioners came to Hampton Court, as desired by Queen Elizabeth, when, in answer to their supplication, she expressed herself as unable to discover how Queen Mary could more readily procure her own condemnation than by refusing to make answer.[4]

Queen Mary's Commissioners still urged that their Sovereign should be admitted into the presence of the English Queen. They also prayed that their mistress, if Elizabeth would not assist in restoring her to her throne, might be allowed to pass into Scotland, or at least into France, craving at the same time their passports to Scotland. Queen Elizabeth granted them a passport to Bolton to report her answer to Queen Mary ; but she would not allow them to depart to Scotland. Lord Boyd and the Bishop of Ross prepared to leave London ; but she desired Lord Herries and the Bishop of Ross to return to Hampton Court on 23d December. Lord Boyd departed from London on the 22d with Elizabeth's answer to Mary.[5]

[1] Calderwood's History, vol. ii. p. 456 ; Goodall's Queen Mary, vol. ii. pp. 221, 222.

[2] Calderwood's History, vol. ii. p. 456 ; Goodall, vol. ii. p. 227.

[3] Goodall, vol. ii. pp. 238, 240 ; Anderson's Collections, vol. iv. part ii. pp. 157, 161.

[4] Calderwood's History, vol. ii. pp. 457-460.

[5] Ibid. vol. ii. pp. 457, 460.

Meanwhile, as a sort of interlude in the history of these conferences, Lord Herries, from his persistency in not only asserting the innocence of Queen Mary, but in imputing to Murray's party the crime of which they accused her, was challenged by Patrick Lord Lindsay of the Byres. The challenge is in these terms :—

" Lord Herries, I am informit that ze have spokin and affirmit that my Lord Regentis Grace, and his cumpanie here present, wer giltie of the abhominabill murthour of umquhile the King, our Soverane lordis fader. Gif ze have swa spokin, ze have said untrewlie, and thairin have leyit in zour throte, quhilk I will mantene, God-willing, aganis zou, as becomis me of honour and dewtie : And heirupon I desire zour answer. Subscrivit with my hand, at Kingston, the 22nd day of December 1568. PATRICK LYNDSAY."

Lord Herries, in his answer, denied that he had ever impeached Lord Lindsay with that crime, and chivalrously offered to fight the guilty traitors. In his reply, dated London, 22d December, carried by John Hamilton of Broomhill, after quoting the terms of Lord Lindsay's letter, he adds :—" In respect they have accusit the Quenis Majestie, mine and your native Soverane, of that foul crime, far by the dewtie that guid subjectis aucht, or ever has bene sene to have done to thair native Soverane, I have said 'Thair is of that cumpanie, present with the Erle of Murray, giltie of that abhominabill tressoun, in the foirknawledge and consent thairto.' That ze wer privie to it, Lord Lyndsay, I know nocht : And gif ze will say that I have speciallie spokin of zow, ze lied in your throte ; and that I will defend, as of my honour and dewtie becumis me : Bot let aucht of the principallis, that is of thame subscryve the like writing ze have send to me, and I shall point thame furth, and fight with sum of the tratouris thairin : For metest it is that tratouris sould pay for thair awin tressoun."

Lord Herries having been desired by the Earl of Leicester to come to Court on the day on which he received and replied to the above challenge, he answered the Earl, sending him at the same time a copy of the challenge and of his reply to it :—

" Pleis it zour richt honorabill lordship be adverteisit, ane servant of the Bishop of Ross has shawin me, zour Lordship desyrit me to cum to the Court

thys day ; and the occasioun thairof was, upon sum inoportune suit of the
Erle of Murray's."

"My Lord,

"I am reddy, at the Quenis Majestie of this realme's commandement, or
upon zour lordships desyre, to cum quhair ze will command me, and that
with my hartlie gude will.   For the Erle of Murray, swa lang as he misknawis
his dewtie to his native Soverane, I will nether for his inoportunes nor plesour
travell.   Bot, for my awin trewth and dewtie, gif it be to answer to sic writingis
as first I red befoir zour honouris at Westminster, the Quenis Majestie's
Commissionaris, and efter presentit unto hir Hienes, I advow thame, and with
the grace of Almightie God, shall leif na part unprowin, that trewth and
honour requiris ; quhairof I haif sent zour lordship heirwith ane copie ; as
alswa ane letter I ressavit this day of the Lord Lyndsay, with my answer to
it.   Gif neid sall require my awin presence to advow the samin, it will pleis
zour Lordship to adverteis this my servand, and I sall nocht faill to be thair
at the hour appointit be zour Lordship, gif God sall spair my lyif : To quhais
protectioun I hartelie commit zour honorabill Lordship.

"Off London the xxii. day of December 1568, be your Lordship's to
command at my power lefullie, with my humbill service,

" HERYS."[1]

On 24th December Lord Herries and the Bishop of Ross went to Hampton
Court and had a conference with the Duke of Norfolk, the Marquis of
Northampton, the Earl of Leicester, Lord Howard, the Lord Chamberlain, and
Cecil, Secretary, who had been appointed by the Queen for that purpose.
Being inquired at by the Duke of Norfolk whether they intended to accuse the
Regent and his party of the murder of Darnley, Lord Herries and the Bishop
of Ross replied that they had received that day written instructions to that
effect from their Mistress, dated Bolton, 19th December.[2]

These instructions, which are addressed to the Bishop of Ross, Lord
Herries, and the Abbot of Kilwinning, are a protestation against the false
accusations circulated by the agents of Murray and by Murray himself against
Queen Mary.   They contain an "answer to the eik that was presented by the

---

[1] Goodall's Queen Mary, vol. ii. pp. 271-273.
[2] Calderwood's History, vol. ii. p. 461 ; Goodall, vol. ii. pp. 280, 285-288.

Earl of Murray and his adherents," dated Bolton, 19th December 1568. The answer begins with charging the Earl of Murray and his adherents, her rebellious subjects, with having, to colour their horrible crimes committed against their Sovereign, declared in their eik, "that as the Earl of Bothwell has been the principal executor of the murder committed on the person of the late Henry Stewart our husband, so we knew, counselled, devised, persuaded, and commanded the said murder," whereby they have falsely and traitorously lied, imputing to her maliciously the crime of which they themselves were the authors, inventors, doers, and some of them the proper executors.[1]

On the 25th of December, Lord Herries, the Bishop of Ross, and the Abbot of Kilwinning, in the presence of Queen Elizabeth and her Council, at Hampton Court, produced Queen Mary's written instructions which had been despatched to them.[2]

Queen Mary in a letter sent to the Bishop of Ross, Lord Herries, and the Abbot of Kilwinning, dated Bolton, 2d January 1568-9, writes,—" We understand the bravadis that the Erle of Murray and his complices have maid, feeling thameselfis simplie tuitchit be sum of zou, to have been culpabill of that quhilk falselie thay pretendit to impute unto us ; and alswa the answer quhilk ze have maid to our guid sister the Quene, conform to our lettres ; of the quhilk thay have pleinzeit. Quhairin not onlie we appreive zour proceidingis, bot alswa prayis zou to continew in our name. For sithens it hath pleisit God to deliver us from thair powar and cruel handis, we have bene informit, and understandis anouch daylie, be letteris and reportis, to mak our guid sister knaw, that thay are tratouris, first inventaris, conspiratouris, and sum of thame executouris of the murthour of the King, our husband ; with uther crimes little less horribill and execrabill than the said murthour, quhairof I am deliberat to gif zou sic instructiounis schortlie that may mak the samin mair manifest, as occasioun servis."[3]

At Hampton Court, on 7th January 1568-9, the Bishop of Ross, Lord Herries, and the Abbot of Kilwinning, in presence of Queen Elizabeth and her Council, declared that they had presently received instructions from the

---

[1] Labanoff, tom. ii. p. 257.
[2] Calderwood's History, vol. ii. pp. 461-465.   [3] Labanoff, tom. ii. p. 262.

Queen of Scots, their sovereign, commanding them anew to signify to the Queen of England that she would accuse Murray and his adherents as principal authors, inventors, and executors of that deed for which she was falsely accused by them, and therefore desired the writings produced by them, or copies thereof, to be delivered to them, that their mistress might fully answer them. Queen Mary's Commissioners, that Queen Elizabeth might the better understand the mind of their sovereign, produced a letter which they had received from her, dated Bolton, 2d January 1568-9, expressing her approval of their proceedings, and praying them to make her good sister understand that the Earl of Murray and his accomplices were traitors, first inventors, conspirators, and some of them executors of the murder of the King, her husband.[1]

Having heard this letter read, Queen Elizabeth proposed that some arrangement should be made between the Queen of Scots and her subjects, and that she should demit the crown and government in favour of her son the Prince, without prejudice of its returning to her in the event of his death.

Our sovereign, said the Bishop of Ross, would be willing to have an appointment with her subjects, notwithstanding their great offences committed against her, but she will never agree to demit her crown.[2]

At Hampton Court, on Sunday 9th January, Queen Mary's Commissioners, the Bishop of Ross, Lord Herries and the Abbot of Kilwinning, in presence of Queen Elizabeth's Council again declared that the Queen, their Mistress, would never consent to demit her crown.[3]

On the 11th of January, at Hampton Court, in presence of Queen Elizabeth's Council, compeared Queen Mary's Commissioners and James Earl of Murray and his colleagues. Sir William Cecil in name of the Council declared that the Earl of Murray, Morton, and their adherents, had obtained licence from Queen Elizabeth to return to Scotland, and as they were accused of being participant in the murder of Lord Darnley, and as the Earl of Murray desired to be confronted with Queen Mary's Commissioners, he wished to know from the Bishop of Ross, Lord Herries and the Abbot of Kilwinning, whether or not they would accuse them of that crime in their Mistress's name, or in their own names.

All and each of them answered, that they had received special command

---

[1] Goodall, vol. ii. pp. 297, 298. [2] *Ibid.* vol. ii. p. 300. [3] *Ibid.* pp. 303, 304.

from Queen Mary, by her letters under her signet and handwriting at several times, which had been shown to the Queen of England and her Council, commanding them to accuse the Earl of Murray and others, his adherents, as being the principal authors, inventors, doers, and some of them proper executors of that murder. They had already given in their accusation in writing to Queen Elizabeth and her Council, and had offered also to defend the innocence of their Mistress, provided they received copies of the writings given in publicly or privately against her. Being required whether they themselves would accuse the Earl of Murray in special, or any of his adherents, they answered that whenever the Queen their Mistress accused them in particular, they would therein discharge their duty ; but at present they would neither acquit nor condemn them further than the Queen their Mistress had commanded them.[1]

At Hampton Court, 12th January, the Earl of Murray and his adherents, appearing in the presence of Queen Elizabeth, obtained licence to depart to Scotland.[2]

At Hampton Court, 13th January, the Bishop of Ross, Lord Herries and the Abbot of Kilwinning, having, as desired, appeared before Queen Elizabeth and her Council, Sir William Cecil declared to them in her and her Council's name, that she would not refuse to the Queen of Scots the doubles of all the writings produced against her, provided she got a special writing under Queen Mary's signet with her own hand, promising that she would answer to these writings, and to what was laid to her charge without exception. Should Queen Mary succeed in proving her innocence, she might expect from Queen Elizabeth such support and aid as her necessities required, and as became one Princess to render to another. Should she fail in vindicating herself, she was to look for no support or aid from Queen Elizabeth.

The reply of the Bishop of Ross, Lord Herries, and the Abbot of Kilwinning was precise. The Earl of Murray and his adherents, they said, who had been publicly accused by them in Queen Mary's name before the Queen of England and her Council, were licensed by Queen Elizabeth to depart into Scotland without having heard the defence of her innocence, and without the trial of their guilt. It did not, therefore, appear meet that Queen Mary should

---

[1] Goodall, vol. ii. pp. 307-309.   [2] Ibid. vol. ii. p. 309.

make any further answer, unless her said rebels were stopped within the realm of England until the trial was ended. If Murray and his adherents were suffered to depart, they prayed that it might be also lawful to the Queen their sovereign and to them to depart into Scotland.

"Your Mistress," said Sir William Cecil, "cannot, for divers reasons, be suffered to depart; but the Council will move Queen Elizabeth to give licence to her Commissioners to depart into Scotland."[1]

Thus the conference ended without any definite conclusion. Neither Queen Mary nor Queen Elizabeth, as is evident from their delays and evasions, desired, for different reasons, to make any progress in the investigation of the questions that were raised.

Both the Commissioners of the Regent and those of Queen Mary were dismissed by the English Queen, with a declaration that nothing had been found to impeach the honour of the Regent or his dutiful conduct towards his sovereign, and that nothing had been produced to cause her to form an unfavourable opinion of the actions of the Queen of Scots. She would not, therefore, interfere with the affairs of Scotland. But she, notwithstanding, supported the party of the Regent, who, having taken leave of her, was honourably conducted from sheriff to sheriff with strong guards till he came to Berwick. Thence he proceeded to Edinburgh, into which he entered in a kind of triumph on 2d February.[2]

The Duke of Norfolk having projected a marriage between himself and Queen Mary, it had been resolved by the Court of England to remove her from Bolton Castle—Lord Scrope, its owner, being brother-in-law to the Duke of Norfolk—to the Castle of Tutbury, on the Dove, in Staffordshire, which belonged to the Earl of Shrewsbury, to whose keeping she was committed.

The Bishop of Ross and Lord Herries, in a letter to Queen Mary, dated Kingston, 4th November 1568, had informed her that they had heard from Cecil and Sir Ralph Sadler that Lord Scrope and the Lord Vice-Chamberlain had communicated a report to the Court that the Abbot of Arbroath had taken up 300 horsemen to convey her from Bolton.[3] They answered that such sayings were invented by their adversaries.

[1] Goodall, vol. ii. pp. 310-312.
[2] Historical Memoirs of the Reign of Mary Queen of Scots, etc., p. 113.
[3] State Papers, in State Paper Office, London, vol. ii. No. 41, I.

Queen Mary and her attendants removed from Bolton Castle on 26th January, and arrived at the Castle of Tutbury on 3d February 1568-9 ; a removal with which she was far from being satisfied. Queen Elizabeth in a letter to her, 3d February, referred to her discontent at being removed from Bolton ; begged her to quiet herself ; and assured her that if she ministered no impediment to herself, all care should be taken of her cause. She sent back the Bishop of Ross and Lord Herries, whom she commended.[1]

So satisfied was Queen Mary with the diligence and fidelity of her Commissioners that, on 9th February, she granted a ratification of their proceedings in the following terms :—

" Marie, be the grace of God Quene of Scottis and Dovarier of Fraunce : Forsamekle as we apointit our traist cousignis, counsalouris and freindis, Johnne Bischope of Ross, Williame Lorde Levingston, Robert Lord Boyde, Johnne Lord Herys, Gawyne Commendatar of Kilvynnyng, Johnne Gordon of Lochinvar, knycht, James Cockburne of Skirling, knycht, Oure Commissioneris to treate for ws and for our effaris with our derrest sister the Quene of Ingland, or hir Commissioneris, at the citie of Yoorke, or in onie vther place within the realme of Ingland quhair it plesit hir to apoynt, We, haveing pervsed thair proceedingis and vnderstanding thair faythfull mynde and trew seruice thairintill, dois verie weill allow thairof, quhilk we make notifit be thir presentis : Gevin vnder our signett and subscriuit with our hand, at Tutberrye, the nynt day of Februar the zeir of God I^m v^c thre scoir aucht zeiris, and our regnne the tuentie sevint zeir."[2]

In similar good spirits, Queen Mary, in a letter to Queen Elizabeth from Tutbury, 10th February 1568-9, thus writes :—" Madam, my good sister, I have heard by the Bishop of Ross and my Lord Herries, the good affection

[1] Calendar of State Papers, *ut supra*, vol. ii. p. 870, No. 36.

[2] Original Ratification among Boyd Papers at Kilmarnock, printed in Miscellany of the Abbotsford Club, vol. i. p. 21.

with which you have proceeded with them in all my affairs ; a thing not less comfortable than I had hoped from your good disposition ; especially having learned by them that it was your good pleasure that I should be treated with the honourable respects and gracious entertainment which I have received since I arrived at Bolton, from Master Knollys and my Lord Scrope, of whom I cannot do less than testify to you their diligence and great desire to accomplish your commandments."[1]

On 17th February, the Duke of Chatelherault, (the next heir to the Crown of Scotland after King James the Sixth,) who had resided for some years in France, and who had been despatched by that Court to Scotland with the view of strengthening the interests of Queen Mary, arrived in Edinburgh from England. He had been detained for some months by Queen Elizabeth under various pretexts, but at last he was allowed by her to depart for Scotland.

Lord Herries and the Abbot of Kilwinning, who supported the claims of the Duke to the Regency in opposition to the Regent Murray, accompanied him to Scotland. Intelligence of the presence in Scotland of a rival, who might prove more or less dangerous, stimulated the vigilance of Murray. In a letter to Cecil from Stirling, 25th of that month, having mentioned the arrival of the Duke with Lord Herries, and their refusal to redress the wrongs committed by them, he insists upon the immediate necessity of taking up arms against them.[2]

The Duke of Chatelherault had obtained from Queen Mary a commission constituting him lieutenant-general of the kingdom, and on his arrival in Scotland he assembled his friends, proclaimed his commission, forbade obedience to be given to Murray, and ordered that no one but himself should be acknowledged as Regent. Supported by Lord Herries and others, he also raised an army for the maintenance of her interests in opposition to Murray. With his accustomed promptitude, Murray collected money, levied troops of horse, and held a rendezvous at Glasgow. At this opposition the Duke, who found that his friends wavered and that the people in general complained, becoming alarmed, was willing to come to terms with the Regent, who, in order to break this new combination, was disposed to grant favourable conditions.[3]

[1] Labanoff, tom. ii. p. 298.
[2] Calendar of State Papers, Scotland, 1509-1603, vol. i. p. 269, No. 12.
[3] Historical Memoirs of the Reign of Mary Queen of Scots, p. 113.

Meanwhile Queen Mary, doubtful how matters might go, implored the sympathy of Queen Elizabeth. In a letter to Sir William Cecil from Tutbury, 13th March 1568-9, she mentions having received a copy of a proclamation made by her rebels, and a letter from Lord Herries, advertising her of things which she was unable to credit, as being contrary to the promises which had been made to her. She could not refrain from freely writing about it to the Queen her good sister, as being a thing which touched her so sensibly in conscience and honour that she could no longer dissemble her complaint, which she had charged the bearer to communicate to Cecil.[1]

With the view of accommodating matters, a meeting took place at Glasgow, 13th March 1568-9, between the Regent Murray and the nobility who adhered to him on the one part, and the Earl of Cassilis, Lord Herries, etc., and the Abbot of Kilwinning, in the name of the Duke of Chatelherault and other nobles, his adherents, on the other part. But the articles proposed at this meeting by the Earl of Murray were not agreed upon.[2]

Matters were, however, tending towards a peaceful settlement between the conflicting parties. William Maitland, in a letter to Sir William Cecil from Edinburgh, 22d March, after mentioning an interview between Lord Herries, the Duke, Regent Murray, and others, informs him that there was a chance of a union among them.[3]

An agreement between the Duke of Chatelherault, as representing Queen Mary's party, and the Regent, was ultimately arrived at, though much to the regret of some of Queen Mary's friends.[4] The Duke agreed to surrender all pretensions as lieutenant-general for the Queen, and to acknowledge the authority of King James. The Regent, on the other hand, became bound that he would get the sentence of forfeiture pronounced on Queen Mary's friends rescinded, their estates restored, and a convention called, to be held at Edinburgh on the 14th of April, for effecting a reconciliation.

Still Queen Mary appears to have confided in the loyal attachment of Lord Herries. The Earl of Shrewsbury, in a letter to Sir William Cecil, dated Tutbury, 8th April 1569, speaks of her faith in him.[5]

[1] Labanoff, tom. ii. p. 304.
[2] Calendar of State Papers, *ut supra*, vol. i. p. 270, No. 17.
[3] *Ibid.* vol. i. p. 270, No. 18.

[4] Calendar of State Papers, Scotland, 1509-1603, vol. ii. p. 873, No. 69.
[5] *Ibid.* vol. ii. p. 874, No. 70.

After the conclusion of the treaty, the Duke, the Earl of Cassillis, and Lord Herries went to Stirling to visit the young King, and were there magnificently entertained by the Regent and his friends. Lord Herries and the Duke of Chatelherault were present at the convention, with many other lords, besides barons and gentlemen. The Duke of Chatelherault showed a disposition to recede from the performance of what he had promised. When required to take oath by the Regent, he desired a respite until the 10th of May, intending during the interval to advise with the rest of the Queen's party. Upon this the Regent imprisoned him in the Castle of Edinburgh, and with him Lord Herries, whom he wholly blamed for putting new thoughts into the Duke's head.[1] They lay prisoners in the Castle till after the assassination of the Regent Murray at Linlithgow, when they were set at liberty.[2]

Queen Mary's history of these transactions is given in a letter to Monsieur de la Mothe Fénélon from Wingfield, 18th April 1569. "By letters which I have received from Scotland," she writes, "since the departure of the Bishop of Ross, I have learned how things have passed there, that is, how the Duke of Chatelherault and others that were still in my obedience, finding themselves destitute of all succour, and pressed by my rebels, who had had leisure to prepare themselves before he was permitted to depart from this country, who moreover were strengthened by money from this side to raise and maintain soldiers, and besides openly assisted with English foot and horse by Lord Hudson, governor of Berwick, have been constrained to yield to what the Queen of England said to the Duke of Chatelherault at his departure, that if he did not acknowledge the authority of my son . . . . he need not expect to receive support or favour from her, but that, on the contrary, she would hurt him to the utmost of her ability. Under these circumstances, the Duke and Lord Herries intrusted their persons to the Earl of Murray, who ordered them to be imprisoned in the castle of Edinburgh, where they now are, in order to force them to agree to some articles which he proposes to them, besides their said submission. They complain, supplicating me to employ my friends, with protestation that what they have done was for the purpose of reserving themselves, that they might afterwards be

[1] Historical Memoirs of the Reign of Mary Queen of Scots, p. 114.
[2] Calderwood's History, vol. ii. p. 558.

able to do me service, and not be wholly ruined, seeing the Queen of England banded with my rebels; and if to save their lives and to get out of prison they may perhaps yield to another thing, they supplicate me to think (whatever the security which my said rebels may extort) that it will last no longer than they shall be able to have succour : which I pray you to make the King, my good brother, and the Queen, my good mother, to understand."[1]

Lord Herries in a letter to Queen Elizabeth, dated Edinburgh Castle, 5th July 1569, defends his conduct generally, explains his interview with the Earl of Murray, denies that he had ever spoken ill of his sovereign or dealt falsely or doubly in her cause, and assures her Majesty that he is not, as reported, kept in ward by his own consent. In a letter to Sir William Cecil, forwarding a copy of the preceding letter, he assures him that the accusations brought against him were untrue.[2] In a letter to Murray without date, but indorsed as sent to Murray 24th July 1569, he gives various particulars in regard to the circumstances connected with his imprisonment. He had, he says, come on the 11th of March last to his Grace in Glasgow upon his Grace's written assurance that he would be allowed to come and depart at his pleasure. Having prayed on 16th April that his subscription to certain articles might be delayed till the coming of certain noblemen of Queen Mary's party, he was, after having supped in the Regent's own chamber, conveyed by the Regent's and Council's orders to the castle of Edinburgh by Lords Lindsay and Ruthven. He complains of injuries and spoil committed on his tenantry, and begs to be released.[3] In this letter he states that in striving for the commonweal of his native country he had sustained great travels and expenses and received dangerous wounds in his body.

Yet the Regent writes favourably of Lord Herries. In a letter to Cecil [October] 1569 he speaks of the " good words of Lord Herries ;"[4] and the Bishop of Ross, as if aware of the friendship between Lord Herries and Murray, requests the former in a letter to him from London, 23rd October 1569, to intercede with the Earl of Murray for the payment of the men of Carlisle of certain moneys borrowed from them by the Queen of Scots.[5]

[1] Labanoff, tom. ii. p. 322.

[2] State Papers in State Paper Office, London, Scotland, Elizabeth, vol. xvi. Nos. 31, 32.

[3] State Papers, Scotland, Elizabeth, vol. xvi. No. 39.

[4] Calendar of State Papers, ut supra, vol. i. p. 274, No. 71.

[5] Ibid. vol. ii. p. 881, No. 46.

What Lord Herries and others of Queen Mary's party were desirous to effect was some arrangement by which she might be admitted to at least some part of the regal power.   He signed along with the Duke of Chatelherault, the Earls of Huntly, Erroll, Argyll, Athole, Lords Home, Maitland, and twenty others, a letter dated Edinburgh, 16th April 1570, to Queen Elizabeth, in which they beg her Majesty to quench the heat that had begun amongst them; appeal to her sense of Christian charity whether, requiring water at her hands to repress a flame, she could bring oil, tinder, or other materials to increase and nourish it?   The cause of their troubles was the two titles of the mother and son to the Crown of Scotland, and they suggest that her Majesty may put an end to the difficulties by entering into honourable conditions with their Queen.[1]

Lord Herries was too loyal and active in the service of Queen Mary for Kirkcaldy of Grange, Governor of the Castle of Edinburgh to detain him a prisoner in the Castle longer than circumstances compelled him.   Not long after the assassination of Murray he was set at liberty.   Kirkcaldy in a letter to Thomas Randolph, from the Castle, 16th April 1570, mentions the good meaning of Lord Herries, and gives the reasons for his liberation.[2]

Lord Herries and the Duke of Chatelherault forthwith assembled with other Lords, adherents of Queen Mary, at Niddry-Seton, for consultation, and, as they there agreed, collected their friends and adherents, and held a convention about the middle of April at Linlithgow, whence they marched to Edinburgh, where they were strengthened by the powerful support of Kirkcaldy of Grange, Governor of the Castle.   They were, however, thrown into consternation on hearing that Queen Elizabeth had sent English forces to the borders; and leaving Edinburgh, they returned to Linlithgow, and thence went to Glasgow, where they dispersed.

Lord Herries was suspected by the English Government of being connected with the insurrection raised by Leonard Dacre in the year 1570 and 1571 against Queen Elizabeth.

Thomas Earl of Sussex, and Sir Ralph Sadler, in a letter to Queen Elizabeth from Durham, 21st January 1570, inform her that they had

[1] Calendar of State Papers, *ut supra*, vol. i. p. 281.   [2] Calendar of State Papers, *ut supra*, vol. i. p. 282, No. 55, I.

received intelligence that Lord Grange wrote to Fernihurst that if the Regent should attempt anything against him and Buccleuch, for receiving the rebels on the frontiers, he would deliver the Duke, Lord Herries, and all others in his charge ; and that Sir John Forster declared that the whole Borders of Scotland were prepared for defence of the rebels, and looked for the assistance of Leonard Dacre.[1]

Lord Scrope, in a letter to Sir William Cecil, from Carlisle, 18th February same year, writes that Leonard Dacre, under colour of defending his tenants of Gillesland, was levying forces, as he supposed, against the English Government; that Dacre had that day assembled upwards of 3000 men, English and Scottish ; that he had joined to him, under assurance, the Lords Hume, Cessford, Buccleuch, and other Lords of Teviotdale, who had willed him to keep his house ; that they in person with their men would come to his relief ; and that he also looked for the friends and forces of Lord Herries and Maxwell.[2]

How far Lord Herries was involved with Lord Dacre in that insurrection is uncertain.   But the Earl of Sussex in a letter to Lord Herries, written from Warkworth, 15th August 1570, charges him with conspiring with Leonard Dacre and others, her Majesty's rebels.   " I am sory," he writes, " that your lordship, whom I haue allwayes taken to haue bene a good instrument to contynew the amity betwene the realmes of England and Scotland, hath gevin me iust cawse to alter that opinion, not onely for that ye haue kept and maintayned, and permitted to be kept and maintayned, Leonard Dacres, Edward Dacres, Richard Dacres, Egremont Radclif, and others within your rule, being, as your lordship manifestly knoweth, notoriowse rebellis and manifest conspiratouris against the Queen my Soueraigne, and in leavyeing of armes against her Majestie, violent disturbers of the common peace and quiet of this realme, but also for that ye haue both secretly had conferences with them by your owne speche, and by your messingers."   Sussex then requires his Lordship to deliver up these rebels to Lord Scrope, Warden of Queen Elizabeth's West Marches.   " In the doing wherof," he adds, " I shall take your Lordship as a wellwiller to the Queen my Soueraigne, and a good frende to the contynewance of the amity betwene bothe realmes.   And if your Lordship shall refuse to make present delivery of

---

[1] Calendar of State Papers, Domestic Series, Elizabeth, Addenda, 1566-1579, p. 202, No. 37.

[2] Ibid. p. 237, No. 97, p. 239, No. 102. I. p. 249, No. 2.   Vide pp. 225, 226 of this volume.

them, I must take you as an evill willer to the Queen my Soueraigne, and an enemy to the good quiet of bothe realmes and the contynewance of amity betwene them, wherof I wold be very sory."[1]

Sussex's letter to Lord Herries appears to have induced him to act with caution. In a letter to Queen Elizabeth from Warkworth, 10th September 1570, Sussex informs her of the promise of Lord Herries not to receive her Majesty's rebels, and of the good effects of his chastisement. He encloses a letter to him from Lord Herries, date not given, but about September of the same year, in which Lord Herries explains his conduct in receiving the Queen of England's rebels, and in signing a request for aid from France; expresses his devotion towards the Queen of England, next to his own Queen, and promises to abide by her Majesty's appointment towards her.[2]

The election of Matthew Earl of Lennox to be Regent on 12th July 1570, was not favourable to the cause of Queen Mary in Scotland.

In this year Lord Herries in Galloway and Nithsdale, and the Laird of Johnston in Annandale, effectively resisted Lord Scrope, who had come with an army into Annandale and penetrated even to Dumfries. They were in the field with all the horse they could raise, and the country people were commanded to drive all their goods to the moors, and themselves to go out of the way. Fearing distress in his army, Lord Scrope retired to Carlisle with the loss of many men, cut off by skirmishing parties. In his retreat he threw down the castle of Dumfries, a house of Lord Maxwell's; blew up with powder the castle of Hoddom, belonging to Lord Herries, and the castle of Annan belonging to the Queen, but in the keeping of Lord Herries.[3]

In a letter to the Commissioners of Queen Mary in England, dated Terregles, 22d March 1571, Lord Herries details the ill state of Scotland and the violent measures pursued by the Earl of Lennox against all the adherents of the Queen of Scots.

The Earl of Lennox came to Ayr declaring that he would destroy the Earl of Cassillis and his whole bounds, for avoiding of which that Earl was constrained to enter himself in ward in Stirling. Lennox and his faction,

---

[1] State Papers in State Paper Office, London, vol. xix. No. 10.

[2] Calendar of State Papers, *ut supra*, vol. i. p. 302, Nos. 27. I.

[3] Historical Memoirs of the Reign of Mary Queen of Scots, p. 127.

with aid as was thought from England and promises of further help, might well move Carrick and Eglinton to obey them. He also sent proclamations charging Galloway above Cree to come and obey him, declaring that otherwise they should be punished with fire and sword.[1]

Lord Herries was a member of the parliament held in the name of Queen Mary in the Tolbooth of Edinburgh 12th June 1571.[2]

In the plot of the Duke of Norfolk in favour of Queen Mary, discovered by Queen Elizabeth's government in August that year, Lord Herries was implicated. A sum of money was sent to him by the Duke for distribution among Queen Mary's adherents in Scotland. But a person not in the secret, who was employed to carry the money to the Borders, suspecting from the weight that it was gold, not silver, as he had been made to believe, carried it directly to the Privy Council, and this led to the discovery of the conspiracy by the Government. The Duke, his domestics, and such as were privy to the design, were arrested. Norfolk was tried, found guilty, and executed.[3]

Lord Herries joined in the endeavours made by the Regent Mar (who on the assassination of Lennox, 14th September 1571, was elevated to the regency), Randolph, the English Ambassador, Sir William Drury, the Marshal of Berwick, and others, to accommodate matters. Sir William Drury and Mr. Randolph, in a letter to Lord Hunsdon, dated Leith, 10th April 1572, mention that Lord Herries and Maxwell were about to submit.[4]

Meanwhile Kirkcaldy of Grange continued to hold the castle of Edinburgh for Queen Mary in opposition to the Regent, expecting foreign assistance. Articles proposed by Mar to Queen Mary's party in the castle of Edinburgh for pacification of the troubles of Scotland, dated 30th March 1572, were delivered to Queen Elizabeth's ambassadors, Sir William Drury and Thomas Randolph.[5] These articles Kirkcaldy refused to accept.

On the death of the Regent Mar, which took place on 28th October 1572, the Earl of Morton was appointed to the regency. Efforts were still made to compose the differences between the two parties.

Lord Herries submitted to the King's government on the conclusion of

---

[1] State Papers—Mary Queen of Scots, in State Paper Office, vol. 6, No. 21.

[2] Calendar of State Papers *ut supra*, vol. i. p. 317, No. 76. *Vide* also p. 227 of this volume.

[3] Anderson's Collections, vol. iii. pp. 169-231.

[4] Calendar of State Papers, vol. i. p. 345, No. 70.

[5] *Ibid.* vol. i. pp. 341, 343, Nos. 36, 51. II.

the treaty of peace at Perth, 23d February 1572-3, between the Regent Morton, representing the King's party, and Chatelherault and Huntly acting for the Queen's party, under the mediation of Henry Killigrew, Queen Elizabeth's Ambassador. In terms of this treaty both parties were to declare their approbation of the reformed religion as then established in Scotland, to submit to the King's government and acknowledge Morton's authority as Regent : the sentence of forfeiture passed against Queen Mary's friends was to be repealed, and indemnity granted for all crimes committed by them since 15th June 1567, and the treaty was to be ratified by parliament.[1] Kirkcaldy of Grange was the most resolute in refusing to submit. Lord Herries requested Queen Elizabeth's statesmen to parley with those in the castle.[2]

Having received supplies of troops and artillery from Queen Elizabeth, the Regent besieged the castle of Edinburgh. Kirkcaldy, though he made a brave defence, was forced by a mutiny among his garrison to capitulate on 28th May 1573.[3] He was hanged at the Cross of Edinburgh. Thus was the civil war in Scotland brought to a termination.

The Earl of Morton's rapacity and oppressions having become intolerable, Lord Herries combined with other nobles in a plot to deprive him of the office of Regent. King James having been advised by a Council of nobles, held 4th March 1578, to deprive Morton, and himself to assume the government, though he was then only in the twelfth year of his age, Lord Herries was sent along with Lord Glammis, Chancellor, to Morton, then resident in Dalkeith, to require him to resign the regency, the castle of Edinburgh, Holyrood-house, and the coin house, with the jewels which it contained. Morton accompanied Lord Herries and Lord Glammis to Edinburgh, and was present there when, on 12th March, it was proclaimed that the King had assumed the government, and when Morton resigned to him the authority of Regent. Lord Herries was one of the Council of twelve who were then chosen.[4]

Lord Herries was present, as one of the Commissioners from the Council, at the General Assembly which met at Edinburgh, 24th April, of which Mr. Andrew Melville was Moderator.[5]

[1] Robertson's Hist. of Scot., Appendix, No. xxxix.
[2] Killigrew to Lord Burghley, from Edinburgh, 5th May 1573, in Calendar of State Papers, vol. i. p. 375, No. 38.
[3] Calendar of State Papers, vol. ii. p. 848.
[4] Calderwood's History, vol. iii. p. 397. Vide p. 234 of this Volume.
[5] Calderwood's History, vol. iii. p. 399.

In the beginning of July Lord Herries, Athole, Montrose, Lindsay, Ogilvy, Maxwell and others convened in Edinburgh, with the design, as was supposed, of preventing the meeting of the Parliament which was then to be held. The Parliament met 10th July, in the Tolbooth of Edinburgh, and continued till the 25th July, when, by command of the King, it was transferred to the castle of Stirling. Lord Herries and the other Lords resolved not to attend the Parliament in Stirling, since the Earl of Morton had both the King and Castle in keeping, alleging that being held in a place of strength, where it might be dangerous for the members freely to express their opinions, it could not be a free Parliament.[1]

The Borders, in which disturbances were constantly occurring, had always been a source of much anxiety to the government, and how to maintain them in tranquillity was a question constantly pressing itself upon its attention. Lord Herries had long held the office of Warden of the West Marches, and from his experience as well as from his eminent reputation for wisdom, his opinion and advice were asked by the government. He gave in to the Privy Council, on 23d January 1578-9, a document which was then read containing a historical view, full of valuable information concerning the condition of the West Marches, and his judgment as to the most effective means of maintaining order within them, and as to the duties incumbent on the Warden and Justiciary of those parts.[2]

With several of his recommendations Lord Herries's nephew John, eighth Lord Maxwell, was much dissatisfied, and he prepared an answer expressed in warm, sometimes acrimonious, terms to his uncle's discourse.[3] The answer was read in audience of the council, at the castle of Stirling, 22d January.

On the same day the wardenship of the West Marches was conferred on Lord Herries and accepted by him, much to the displeasure of his nephew, who had offered to serve in that office.[4] His commission under the great seal is dated at Stirling Castle, 24th January. It includes in the West Marches, of which he was Warden and also Justiciary, Eskdale, Euisdale, Wachopdale, Annandale, Nithsdale and Galloway. The commission proceeds on the resignation of John Lord Maxwell.[5]

[1] Calderwood's History, vol. iii. p. 410. Vide p. 235 of this Volume.

[2] This document is too long to be inserted in this place, but it is printed in the Appendix of Charters, etc.

[3] Vide pp. 239, 240 of this Volume.

[4] Vide p. 243 of this Volume.

[5] Original Commission at Terregles.

The keeping of the Castle of Lochmaben was also committed to Lord Herries.[1] So diligently did he execute the office of Warden that Queen Elizabeth in a letter to him from Westminster, 15th April 1579, thanks him for his zeal in the administration of justice, and in repressing and punishing the disorders of those who sought to disturb the amity between the two kingdoms.[2]

He closely associated himself with Esme Stewart, Lord d'Aubigny, who having arrived in Scotland, 8th September 1579, became a favourite of King James the Sixth, and was soon after created Earl and Duke of Lennox. When the Duke proclaimed a Chamberlain Court to be held 27th August 1582, he purposed to bring to Edinburgh Lord Herries and others of his friends with their forces to occupy the town and keep it in awe. Lord Herries and others came to the town. But the designs of the Duke of Lennox were defeated by the raid of Ruthven, 22d August that year, when the King was invited or taken against his will by the Earls of Mar, Gowrie, and others to Ruthven Castle, the Earl of Arran and the Duke of Lennox being excluded from his presence.[3]

On the 1st of September Lord Herries and two others were sent by the Duke of Lennox to the King, but all private conference was denied them. Lords Herries and Newbattle were also sent to the King to endeavour to effect a reconciliation between the Duke and his opponents, but they, too, were denied a private conference. They returned with the answer that the Duke must depart from Scotland within fourteen days; that he must remain at Dalkeith or Aberdour accompanied only with forty persons, till his departure; and that the Castle of Dumbarton must be immediately surrendered.[4]

Lord Herries was often deputed by the Duke to assure the King that he was prepared to compear before the estates of the kingdom, and to be judged on all the accusations brought against him by the Earls of Mar and Gowrie and their confederates.[5] But from the unpopularity of the Duke, his lordship's efforts were in vain.

He was also appointed by the Duke to offer to the ministers of Edinburgh to mediate between the Duke and them.[6] But here also he found that the Duke's adversaries were not to be conciliated.

---

[1] Vide p. 244 of this Volume.
[2] Calendar of State Papers, vol. i. p. 398, No. 60.
[3] Calderwood's History, vol. iii. pp. 635, 637, 643. Vide p. 255 of this Volume.
[4] Calderwood's History, vol. iii. pp. 646, 647.
[5] Ibid. vol. iii. p. 667.
[6] Ibid. vol. iii. p. 668.

Lord Herries built the house of Hoddomstains in Annandale, and the watchtower of repentance to be a beacon, the house of Kirkgunzeon in Galloway, and Mosstroops Tower in Terregles. He also caused the warden dykes of Dumfries to be cast for the safety of the town against the thieves of Annandale, and the dykes of Annan for a like purpose.

In the manuscript account of the family of Herries,[1] Lord Herries is said to have caused the Abbeys of Dundrennan and New Abbey to be pulled down. This however was not the fact. On the contrary, though commanded by the Lords of the congregation to demolish New Abbey, he declined to do so. This we learn from a gift which he obtained from Mr. Gilbert Brown, Abbot, dated at the Abbey of Sweetheart, 27th August 1577, of the "Yle of Lochkindelocht, with all the fowlis that sall abyde and big thair," and the fishing of the said Loch, reserving the kirk and kirkyard to the parish to which it appertains. In this gift it is particularly stated that it was made in consideration of the service done to the said Abbey by his lordship, when as Warden of the West Marches and "Generale Justice of this cuntre," he refused to obey the order of the Lords of the congregation to demolish their kirk and place of New Abbey "quhair he was maist part brocht vp in his youth," when the other Abbeys in the kingdom were suppressed.[2]

If a few instances of vacillation occur in Lord Herries's support of Queen Mary, these appear to have arisen from the overawing power of the other

[1] MS. History of the Herries Family at Terregles.

[2] Original Gift at Terregles.

As a memorial of Lord Herries, notice may be taken of an old manuscript volume of Acts of the Parliaments of Scotland, now in the library of Kirkconnell, which bears on the first leaf the following inscription, showing that it was originally the property of Lord Herries :—

"Johnne Lord Herreis with my hand the zeir off God ane thousand fyve hundreth fourscoir and ane zeir. So be it; amen. In nomine Domini nostri Jesu Christi crucifixi furca qui me redemit suo precioso sanguine, ipse me regat benedicat custodiat, confirmat in omni bono opere hodie et quotidie, et post hanc miseram vitam perducat me in vitam eternam.

"Look upon me, O my Lord, gef I have done any thyng that is nocht rycht in the eies of thy mercie, for Jesus Chryst thy dere sones."

This inscription is apparently a copy by a young scribe, perhaps one of Lord Herries's children, of what had been written by himself on a fly-leaf which does not now exist. The volume embraces Acts of Parliament in the reigns of King James the First, Second, Third, Fourth, and Fifth, with the Acts made by James Duke of Chatelherault, Governor of the kingdom, and the Queen Dowager Regent. It begins with the Acts of the Parliament held at Edinburgh 26th May 1424, and closes with ordinances for the Steward Court of Annandale made by advice of the barons of the West Wardenry, commanded to be observed by the Queen and Privy Council, 6th January 1562. The volume, which consists of about 400 pages folio, is written in a very distinct hand of the sixteenth century, very like the handwriting with which the records of the Privy Council are engrossed in the reign of Queen Mary. The running titles of the pages, and the headings of the chapters, are in red ink, of a very brilliant colour.

IN THE CHURCH OF TERREGLES.

ARMORIAL BEARINGS OF AGNES LADY HERRIES
ON THE CHURCH OF TERREGLES.

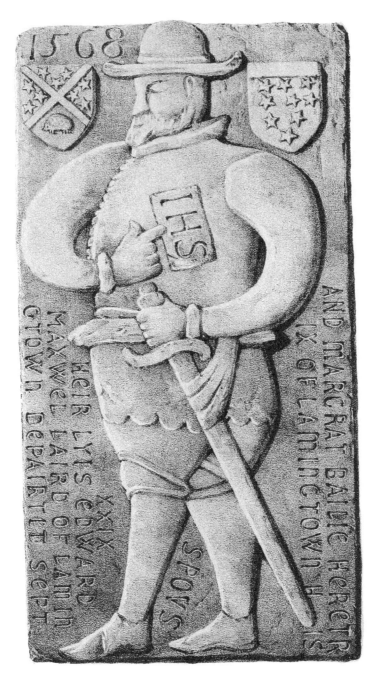

TOMBSTONE OF EDWARD MAXWELL OR BAILLIE OF LAMINGTON
IN THE CHURCH OF TERREGLES.

party for the time. There is no reason to believe that in heart he ever declined from loyalty to that Queen. Lord Herries, Lord Boyd and the Bishop of Ross compiled a book entitled " The defence of the honour of the Queen of Scots." [1]

Lord Herries made his will at Terregles on 26th May 1582. It appoints his wife and his eldest son to be his executors, and the Laird of Lochinvar, his son-in-law, to be oversman. It minutely specifies what his wife and each of his children were to receive at his death. It is printed in volume second of this work.

Lord Herries died suddenly in Edinburgh on Sunday, 20th January 1582-3, in the afternoon, when going to an upper chamber in William Fowler's lodging in the time of sermon to see the boys bicker. He said before dinner that he durst not trust himself to go to the afternoon's preaching, because he found himself weak. Leaning to a wall, he fell down by little and little, saying to a woman that followed, " Hold me, for I am not weale." [2]

He was interred in the choir of the church of Terregles, which he had built as a place of sepulture for himself and his family. No monument exists there to his memory ; but two monuments to two of his sons—Sir Robert Maxwell of Spottes, and Edward Maxwell of Lamington—still exist, of which drawings are given in this work. [3]

Of the marriage of John Lord Herries and Agnes Lady Herries there was issue four sons and seven daughters, whose names are entered in the pedigree of the family at the end of this volume.

Agnes Lady Herries survived her husband ten years, having died on the 14th of March 1593. On the previous day, at Terregles, she made her will, in which she nominated as her executors her sons, William Lord Herries, Sir Robert Maxwell of Spottes and Edward Maxwell of Lamington. She ordained her body to be buried beside her husband. She bequeathed to her sons, daughters, and grandchildren special legacies of silver plate and valuable wearing apparel, including gold ornaments, etc. She besought her bairns, as they would deserve her blessing, to agree among themselves and to pay her debts thankfully, and the fees of her servants, which she wished to be doubled, as

---

[1] An examination of Alexander Hervey of Aberdeen, 14th April 1570, respecting his knowledge of that book, is in Calendar of State Papers *ut*

supra, vol. ii. p. 888, No. 30.
[2] Calderwood's History, vol. viii. p. 232.
[3] MS. Account of the Herries Family at Terregles.

they would answer to the High Judge on the latter day. She also ordained
that there should be dealt the day of her burial twenty pounds of money and
six bolls of meal. The will is printed at length in the Minutes of Evidence
which was adduced in the claim of the present Lord Herries for the Peerage
of Herries, p. 61.

WILLIAM, FIFTH LORD HERRIES, 1582-1603.
JOHN, SIXTH LORD HERRIES, 1603-1631.
JOHN, SEVENTH LORD HERRIES, 1631-1667.

OF the two generations of Lords Herries after the fourth Lord, whose Memoir has now been given, it is unnecessary to say much. William Maxwell, his eldest son, succeeded his father as fifth Lord Herries in 1582, and died on 10th October 1603. By his marriage with Katharine Ker, sister of Mark Ker, first Earl of Lothian, there were five sons and four daughters, whose names are stated in the pedigree of the Maxwells Lords Herries, printed at the end of this volume.

John Maxwell, the eldest son of William, fifth Lord Herries, succeeded his father as sixth Lord Herries in 1603, and died in 1631. By his marriage with Lady Elizabeth Maxwell, daughter of John Maxwell, Earl of Morton, he had eight sons and one daughter, whose names are also entered in the pedigree of the Maxwells Lords Herries.

As has been seen in a previous part of this work, John, the seventh Lord Herries, who was the eldest son of the sixth Lord, succeeded as third Earl of Nithsdale on the death of his kinsman, Robert, second Earl of Nithsdale, without issue in 1667. To the memoirs already given of that Earl, whose descendants continued the line of the Earls of Nithsdale, the reader is here referred.[1]

[1] *Vide supra*, p. 383, *et seq.*

SEAL AND SIGNATURE OF WILLIAM MAXWELL, FIFTH LORD HERRIES.

JOHN MAXWELL OF TERRAUGHTY AND MUNCHES.

1720-1814.

JOHN MAXWELL, the subject of this notice, was the second son of John Maxwell of Breckonside and Terraughty. He was a great-great-grandson of John, sixth Lord Herries.[1] He was born at Buittle Castle, in the parish of Buittle and stewartry of Kirkcudbright, on 7th February, old style, 1720. The place of his birth is notable as having been one of the residences of the ancient Lords of Galloway, and latterly of John Balliol, some time King of Scotland, whose mother, Devorgilla, was the heiress of the Lords of Galloway. It was while residing at Buittle Castle, or, as it is called in the deed " Botle," in the year 1282, that she executed the charter of the foundation of Balliol College, Oxford, which is still preserved in the library of that renowned seat of learning.[2]

At the death of his father, which took place 12th May 1724, John Maxwell was not four years of age, and being a younger son, he did not succeed to the estates of Breckonside and Terraughty, which were inherited by his eldest brother William, by his father's first marriage. He was, however, entitled on that event, by the contract of marriage between his father and mother, dated 21st April 1719, as heir of that marriage, to 8000 merks, subject to his mother's liferent. But owing to the embarrassment of the affairs of his brother William, who, in 1736, sold the lands of Breckonside to William Veitch, Writer to the Signet, and whose lands of Terraughty, about the same time, were adjudged from him, and subsequently became the property of John M'George of Meikle Cocklick, John Maxwell never received the 8000 merks to which he was entitled, and was ultimately obliged to accept of 5000 merks as full payment. Upon the interest of this money his mother, by her wise management, brought up her family respectably and gave them a good education.

On his father's death, his mother having left the house of Buittle, where

---

[1] He was great-grandson of the grandson of the celebrated Lord Herries. "One cannot learn," says Mr. Robert Chambers, "without a pleasing kind of surprise that a relation in the fifth [it should be sixth] degree of one who was Warden of the West Marches in 1545, should have lived to the close of the French Revolution wars, which was the case of Mr. Maxwell, for he died in January 1814."—Chambers's Life and Works of Robert Burns, vol. iii. p. 205.

[2] Facsimiles of the National MSS. of Scotland, 1870, Part II. No. IV.

she then resided, went to reside in the village of Kirkpatrick Durham. Here he passed his early days. In order to make provision for himself, he was afterwards, according to the custom of the time, in the case of younger sons of families even of rank, apprenticed to the trade of a joiner in the neighbouring town of Dumfries—a business which he afterwards carried on successfully on his own account. His history, during a long life of nearly a century, was very remarkable, and in some respects romantic.

Having received a good education and being well qualified for the transaction of business, he was not only successful in his occupation of a joiner, but soon elevated his position. He was appointed one of the chamberlains of the Duke of Queensberry, and for fifteen years had the sole management of his extensive estates in Dumfriesshire, during which period he resided at Drumlanrig. He was also for a long period intrusted with the superintendence of the whole of the Nithsdale and Herries estates by successive owners. He was much consulted by proprietors in the shire of Dumfries and stewartry of Kirkcudbright in reference to the acquisition and management of their estates. It was on his opinion and by his advice that Mr. Oswald of Auchencruive purchased his extensive estates in the stewartry of Kirkcudbright, which, as well as his estates in Ayrshire, were for many years under the management of Mr. Maxwell. He took an active part in the public affairs of the county, and was one of the principal promoters of the new bridge over the Nith at Dumfries, to the superintendence of which he devoted much of his time. In all his employments he showed great capacity and acted with the strictest regard to integrity. Beginning as a small tradesman, he prospered so well as ultimately to possess landed estates rented at upwards of £5000 per annum.

Mr. Maxwell married Agnes Hannay, eldest daughter of Mr. William Hannay in Dumfries.

By the death of his wife's uncle, Mr. Alexander Mein, writer in Dumfries, there fell to Mr. Maxwell by her succession a considerable sum of money, which with the fruits of his own industry enabled him to purchase the property of Portrack, in the parish of Holywood. In 1754 he purchased from John M'George of Meikle Cocklick the estate of Terraughty, from which, on his advancing to old age, he was commonly called "Old Terraughty;" and he afterwards acquired several other properties.

After having borne to him nine children, his wife, Agnes Hannay, died on the 13th of September 1756. On this occasion he received an affectionate letter of condolence from his mother, who was Elizabeth Maxwell, eldest daughter of James Maxwell of Arkland. She was then residing with her daughter Elizabeth, wife of the Rev. Mr. Robert McMorine, minister of Kirkpatrick Durham. The letter is as follows :—

My DEIR SON,—Your childrine heir is very wiell. I expeked to have sien you heir the last weik and was very unisie in my mind, firine you were sike. Mr. Couterd of Aremine was heir yesterday, and he told me that you was weill. My deire son, I know, from experins, the griefs and cers of your mind. It is owr dutty to submite to the will of provdince, and be content with the will of God, that can do nothing wrong. This life is short and unserton, and so is owr injoyments, and we ought to pleais owr afexions on God and hevenly things and rest on him, as owr alone happiness, who can make all to work togeither for good to them that love him, and dow all that we can to preper for that rest that is preapred for the pepell of God, and then all sorow and sighine shall be at ene end. Yow have reson to belise God for the mercys yow have, and its wrong for you to break your heart or hellth. It was the will of God to remuve your deir wife by death, and its apointed for all. Belised are the dide that day in the Lord ; they rest from there labure. My deir son, may it plise God to inebell you to behave so as yow may not ofend him who meid yow, and be content with all his wise providences who cane make up all our wants. Our blised Lord seys its throw much trebellesion we have heir ; but he tells ws in him we shall have pise, and he hes promised to kipe them in perfit pice whos mind is steyed on him ; and if we fent in the day of adverccy owr strenth is small. Dow what you can for your chilldrin, and ther is no more requrd. I intreat you send me word how you are and the childrine. I will be gleed to sie you when its convenent for you, and give my compliments to your mother and sister.[1] My son and doughter ofers ther compliments to yow and your childrine gives there humbell dutty to you, and there grandmother and antt. My deir son, may the Allmight God, for Crist Jusus seke, teak cer of yow, preserve from every evell thing and give yow helth and every thing nidfull for yow. May it plis God to blis you and yours with spirituall and hevenly blisings.—I rest, my deir son, your afexnet mother,   ELIZABETH MAXWEL.

Kirkpaterik Mance, September 29th, 1756.
    To John Maxwell of Traghtie in Drumfrice.[2]

After the death of William Maxwell of Nithsdale, only son of the last Earl of Nithsdale, in 1776, John Maxwell, on the 4th of June 1778, expeded a service as heir-male to Robert, fourth Earl of Nithsdale.

A gentleman who occupied so prominent a position as John Maxwell of Terraughty, naturally attracted the attention of the poet Burns, who was then

---

[1] His mother-in-law and sister-in-law.   [2] Original Letter at Munches.

To Terraughty on his Birth Day

Health to the Maxwels' Vetran Chief
Health ay unsoura'd by care or grief
Inspir'd I turn Fates Sybil leaf
              This natal Morn
I see thy life is stuff o' prief
              Scarce quite half worn

This day thou meets Threescore eleven
And I can tell that bounteous Heaven
(The second sight ye ken is given ~~to~~
              To ilk a Poet)
On thee a tack o' seven-times-seven
              Will yet Bestow it

If envious Buckies view wi' sorrow
Thy lengthen'd days on this blest morrow
May Desolation's lang-teeth'd Harrow
              Nine miles an hour
Rake them like Sodom & Gomorroh
              In Brunstane Stour

But for thy Frien's and they are mony
Baeth Honest men & lasses bonie
May Couthie fortune kind and cannie
              An Social Glee,
Wi' mornings blythe and eenings funny

Farewell auld Birkie Lord be near ye
              Bless them & thee
And then the Deel he dare na steer ye
Your friens ay love, your faes ay fear ye
              For me Shame fa me
If niest my heart I dinna wear ye
              While Burns they ca me

connected with Dumfriesshire. On the birthday of Mr. Maxwell, in the year 1791, when he had reached the seventy-first year of his age, Burns addressed to him the following lines :—

"TO TERRAUGHTY ON HIS BIRTHDAY.

" Health to the Maxwel's vet'ran Chief !
Health, ay unscour'd by Care or grief :
Inspir'd, I turn Fate's sybil leaf
         This natal morn.
I see thy life is stuff o' prief,
         Scarse quite half worn.

This day thou meets Threescore eleven,
And I can tell that bounteous Heaven
(The second-sight, ye ken, is given
         To ilka Poet),
On thee a tack o' seven times seven
         Will yet Bestow it.

If envious Buckies view wi' sorrow
Thy lengthen'd days on this blest morrow,
May Desolation's lang-teeth'd Harrow,
         Nine miles an hour,
Rake them like Sodom and Gomorrah,
         In Brunstane Stour !

But for thy Frien's, and they are mony,
Baith Honest men and lasses bonnie,
May Couthie fortune, kind and cannie,
         An' Social Glee,
Wi' mornings blythe and e'enings funny,
         Bless them and thee.

Farewell, auld Birkie ! Lord be near ye,
And then the Deel he darena steer ye :
Your frien's ay love, your faes ay fear ye ;
         For me, shame fa' me,
If niest my heart I dinna wear ye
         While Burns they ca' me." [1]

[1] Facsimile from the Original in this work. It is now in the possession of Mr. John Taylor Johnston, President of the Central Railroad Company of New Jersey, 119, Liberty Street, New York. It differs in a few unimportant particulars from the commonly printed copies of this poem.

On subsequent occasions, Burns introduces the name of Mr. Maxwell in several of his poems.   Under the name of "Jockie," he refers to him in the muster of electors assembled at Kirkcudbright to elect a Member of Parliament in 1795 for that stewartry, the representation of which was successfully contested by Mr. Heron, the Whig candidate, in opposition to Mr. Gordon of Balmaghie, the Government candidate.

> " For there frae the Niddisdale borders,
>   The Maxwells will gather in droves,
> Tough Jockie, staunch Geordie,[1] and Welwood,[2]
>   That griens for the fishes and the loaves."[3]

John Maxwell of Terraughty had married, secondly, in 1770, Miss Agnes Maxwell, eldest daughter of William Maxwell of Munches and Dinwoodie.   On the death of her brother, George Maxwell, on 8th September 1793, from the effects of a fall from his horse two days before,[4] she succeeded to the estates of Munches and Dinwoodie ; and as she conveyed them to her husband by a deed of settlement, he became proprietor of these estates on her death, in 1809, at the advanced age of ninety years.

During Mr. Maxwell of Terraughty's lifetime, which extended over nearly a century, great improvements took place in the cultivation of the soil, the manners of the people, their means of living, and their wealth.   A letter which he wrote to W. M. Herries, Esq. of Spottes, a few years before his death, illustrating the state of society and of agriculture in the stewartry of Kirkcudbright and in Nithsdale, during the first half of the eighteenth century, is so valuable and interesting that we here insert it entire.

Munshes, February 8, 1811.

DEAR SIR,—The last time that Mr. Young of Youngfield was here he signified to me, as you had previously done, that John Christian Curwen of Workington Hall, Esq., had mentioned that he was very desirous of knowing the state of agriculture in the stewartry of Kirkcudbright and in Nithsdale as far back as my remembrance goes.

I was born at Buittle, in this parish, which in old times was the fortress and residence of John Baliol, on the 7th day of February, old style, 1720, and do distinctly remember several cir-

---

[1] George Maxwell of Carruchan.
[2] Mr. Welwood Maxwell.
[3] Chambers's Life and Works of Robert Burns, vol. iv. p. 143.
[4] Memorandum concerning his death in Munshes Papers.

cumstances that happened in the year 1723 and 1724. Of these particulars, [one is] the falling of the bridge of Buittle, which was built by John Frew in 1722, and fell in the succeeding summer, while I was in Buittle garden, seeing my father's servants gathering nettles. That same year many of the proprietors enclosed their grounds, to stock them with black cattle, and by that means turned out a vast number of tenants at the term of Whitsunday 1723, whereby numbers of them became destitute, and in consequence rose in a mob, when, with pitchforks, gavellocks, and spades, they levelled the park-dikes of Barncailzie and Munshes, at Dalbeattie, which I saw with my own eyes. The mob passed by Dalbeattie and Buittle, and did the same on the estates of Netherlaw, Dunrod, etc., and the laird of Murdoch, then proprietor of Kilwhaneday, who turned out sixteen families at that term. The proprietors rose, with the servants and dependants, to quell this mob, but were not of sufficient force to do it, and were obliged to send for two troops of dragoons from Edinburgh, who, upon their appearing, the mob dispersed. After that warrants were granted for apprehending many of the tenants and persons concerned in the said mob. Several of them were tried ; those who had any funds were fined, some were banished to the plantations, whilst others were imprisoned, and it brought great distress upon this part of the country. At that period justice was not very properly administered, for a respectable man, of the name of M·Clacherty, who lived in Balmaghie parish, was concerned in the mob, and, on his being brought to trial, one of the justices admired a handsome Galloway which he rode, and the justice told him if he would give him the Galloway he would effect his acquittal, which he accordingly did. This misfortune, with what happened to the Mississippi Company in the year 1720, did most generally distress this quarter of the kingdom. It is not pleasant to represent the wretched state of individuals, as times then went in Scotland. The tenants in general lived very meanly, on kail, groats, milk, graddon ground in querns turned by the hand, and the grain dried in a pot, together with a crook ewe now and then about Martinmas. They were clothed very plainly, and their habitations were most uncomfortable. Their general wear was of cloth, made of waulked plaiding, black and white wool mixed, very coarse, and the cloth rarely dyed. Their hose were made of white plaiding cloth sewed together, with single-soled shoes, and a black or blue bonnet,—none having hats but the lairds, who thought themselves very well dressed for going to church on Sunday, with a black kelt-coat of their wife's making. It is not proper for me here to narrate the distress and poverty, that were felt in the country during these times, which continued till about the year 1735. In 1725, potatoes were first introduced into this stewartry by William Hyland, from Ireland, who carried them on horses' backs to Edinburgh, where he sold them by pounds and ounces. During these times, when potatoes were not generally raised in the country, there was, for the most part, a great scarcity of food, bordering on famine, for, in the stewartry of Kirkcudbright and county of Dumfries, there was not as much victual produced as was necessary for supplying the inhabitants, and the chief part of what was required for that purpose, was brought from the sand-beds of Esk in tumbling cars, on the Wednesdays, to Dumfries ; and when the waters were high, by reason of spates, and there being no bridges, so that these cars could not come with the meal, I have seen the tradesmen's wives in the streets of Dumfries crying because there was none to be got. At that period there was only one baker in Dumfries, and he made bawbee baps of coarse flour, chiefly bran, which he occasionally carried in creels to the fairs of Urr and Kirkpatrick. The produce of the country in general was grey corn, and you might have travelled from Dumfries to Kirkcudbright, which is twenty-seven miles, without seeing any other grain, except in a gentleman's croft, which in general produced bear or big, for one-third part, another third in white oats, and the remaining third in grey oats. At that period there was no wheat raised in the country ; what was used was brought from Teviot, and it was believed that the soil would not produce wheat. In the year 1735 there was no mill in the country for grinding that sort of grain, and the first flour-mill that was constructed in these bounds was built by old Heron, at Cloudon, in the parish of Irongray, some years after that date.

In these times cattle were also very low. I remember of being present at the Bridge-end of Dumfries, in 1736, when Anthony M'Kie of Netherlaw sold five score of five-year old Galloway cattle, in good condition, to an Englishman, at £2, 12s. 6d. each ; and old Robert Halliday, who was tenant of a great part of the Preston estate, told me that he reckoned he could graze his cattle on his farm for 2s. 6d. a head, that is to say, that his rent corresponded to that sum.

At this period few of the proprietors gave themselves any concern anent the articles of husbandry, their chief one being about black-cattle. William Craik, Esq. of Arbigland's father died in 1735, and his son was a man of uncommon accomplishments, who, in his younger days, employed his time in grazing of cattle and studying the shapes of the best kinds,—his father having given him the farm of Maxwelltown to live upon. The estate of Arbigland was then in its natural state, very much covered with whins and broom, and yielding little rent, being only about 3000 merks a year. That young gentleman was among the first that undertook to improve the soil ; and the practice of husbandry which he pursued, together with the care and trouble which he took in ameliorating his farm, was very great. Some of it he brought to such perfection, by clearing off all weeds and stones, and pulverized it so completely, that I, on walking over the surface, sunk as if I had trodden on new fallen snow.

The estate of Arbigland was bought by his grandfather, in 1722, from the Earl of Southesk, for 22,000 merks.

In 1735 there were only two carts for hire in the town of Dumfries, and one belonging to a private gentleman.

About the year 1737 and 1738 there was almost no lime used for building in Dumfries except a little shell-lime, made of cockle-shells, burned at Colvend, and brought to Dumfries in bags, a distance of twenty miles ; and, in 1740, when Provost Bell built his house, the under storey was built with clay and the upper storeys with lime, brought from Whitehaven in dry-ware casks. There was then no lime used for improving the land. In 1749 I had day labourers at 6d. per day, and the best masons at 1s. This was at the building of Mollance House,—the walls of which cost £49 sterling.

If you think that anything mentioned here can be of any use or entertainment to Mr. Curwen, I give you full leave to make the same known, with my best respects ; and I am,

Dear Sir,

Yours sincerely,

JOHN MAXWELL.

To W. M. Herries, Esq. of Spottes.[1]

---

[1] New Statistical Account of Scotland, Parish of Buittle, vol. iv. p. 206.

It may be mentioned as a proof of the great rise in the value of land during the lifetime of John Maxwell of Terraughty, that the estate of Terraughty, which cost him £886 sterling, was, at the time of his death, considered worth £500 a year ; that the small farm of Halmyre, for which he paid £80, was, when he purchased it, let for £3, 6s. 8d., that he lived to let it in lease at £80 per annum, and that it was sold soon after his death by his trustees for £2000.

John Maxwell of Terraughty died in January 1814, aged nearly ninety-four years.

Mr. Andrew Carruthers, afterwards Roman Catholic Bishop in Edinburgh, wrote from Munches, at the request of the family, a letter intimating the death to the Earl of Traquair in the following terms :—

Munches, 25th January 1814.

My Lord,—Our aged and respected friend, Mr. Maxwell of Terraughtie and Munches, died here this morning, having nearly completed his ninety-fourth year. His memory and other mental faculties had scarcely suffered any decay, and he continued to the end to transact the greatest part of the business of his estates, to enjoy the society of his friends, and to take a lively interest in all public events, as well as in his own private affairs. The immediate cause of his death appeared to be a pulmonic affection, occasioned by the severity of the weather. I should not omit here to add, that he was exceedingly gratified with Lord Linton's late visit, and had frequently since expressed his high regard for his Lordship and the family of Traquair. I write this note at the express desire of the family here ; and remain,

With much sincere regard,

My Lord,

Your Lordship's very obedient servant,

ANDREW CARRUTHERS.

Right Honourable Earl of Traquair, Peebles.[1]

The Earl of Traquair's answer to this letter is as follows :—

February 14.

My dear Sir,—I am much oblidged to the family of Terraughty for their attention in notefy-ing to me the death of my much respected friend, old Mr. Maxwell, and I sincerely condole with them for their loss in Mr. Maxwell's death. I am glad to hear he enjoyed his mental faculties to the last, and that my son's visit was so acceptable to him. I imagine Doctor Maxwell will pro-

[1] Original Letter, with copy Answer annexed, at Terregles.

bably not quit Terraughty, as I understand he has done a great deal there in improving the place ; and as he likes society, the neighbourhood of Dumfries will no doubt be a great inducement to remain where he is.

I beg my kind compliments to Miss Maxwell and the rest of the family, in which I am joined by my son.

By his first wife, Agnes Hannay, Mr. Maxwell of Terraughty had three sons and six daughters. Their names and the dates of their birth, as recorded in the Munches family Bible, in the handwriting of their father, are all stated in the Pedigree of the Maxwells of Terraughty, printed in this volume. By his second wife, the heiress of Munches, he had no children.

Alexander Herries Maxwell, the eldest son of John Maxwell of Terraughty, succeeded his father in January 1814, but survived him only for a short time, having died 28th June 1815, without surviving issue. The next heir-male was George Maxwell of Carruchan, whose descendants are traced in the Pedigree of the Carruchan Branch of the Maxwell family, No. V., p. 589, *infra.*

John Maxwell

SIGNATURE OF JOHN MAXWELL OF TERRAUGHTY, 1800.

Dumfries, 23d July, 1796.

Sir,

Robert Burns, my Father, died on Thursday morning last, and is to be interred in the church yard here, on Monday next at one o'clock afternoon. Your attendance at the funeral is requested by,

Sir,

Your most humble Servant,

Robert Burns.

PEDIGREES

OF

THE EARLS OF NITHSDALE,

LORDS MAXWELL AND HERRIES,

AND OF

CADET BRANCHES OF THE

MAXWELL FAMILY.

I.—THE EARLS OF NITHSDALE AND LORDS MAXWELL.

I.—UNDWIN, father of Maccus, c. 1070, p. 1.

II.—MACCUS, who gave name to the Barony of Maccuswell or Maxwell, near Kelso, and to the lands and parish of Maxtoun, both in the county of Roxburgh : also to the Family of Maxwell. Died c. 1150, pp. 1-17.

III.—HERBERT DE MACCUSWELL, Sheriff of Teviotdale. 1150-1200, pp. 17, 21.

LIULPHUS, c. 1172. Had a daughter, Cecilia, and a son, Uchtred, p. 18.

EDMUND DE MACCUSWELL, c. 1152, p. 19.

ROBERT, of Lessuden, 1200, p. 19.

IV. 1.—SIR JOHN DE MACCUSWELL, also Sheriff of Teviotdale and Chamberlain of Scotland. He was the first Maxwell of Carlaverock. 1200-1241, s.p., p. 27.

ROBERT, c. 1210, s.p., p. 26.

IV. 2.—AYMER DE MAXWELL, fourth Lord of Maxwell, second of Carlaverock, and Chamberlain of Scotland. He married Mary of Mearns, and acquired the Barony of Mearns, in the county of Renfrew. 1241-1266, pp. 26, 64.

V.—SIR HERBERT DE MAXWELL of Maxwell, Carlaverock, and Mearns. He also acquired, in 1296, from John of Pencaitland, the lands of Pencaitland, in the county of Haddington, 1266-c. 1298. Swore fealty to Edward I. 1296. He first used the saltire as his armorial bearing, p. 81.

EDWARD MAXWELL, 1248, s.p., p. 80.

SIR JOHN MAXWELL, ancestor of the Maxwells of Pollok, as shown in the *Pollok Book*. P. 80.

ALEXANDER, c. 1300, p. 80.

VI.—JOHN OF MAXWELL, sixth Lord of Maxwell. He swore fealty to Edward I. in 1296, p. 92.

VII. 1.—SIR EUSTACE MAXWELL, seventh of Maxwell, Carlaverock, Mearns, etc. 1312-1342, p. 94.

VII. 2.—SIR JOHN DE MAXWELL, eighth Lord of Maxwell. Was taken prisoner at the battle of Durham on 17th October 1346. 1342-1347, p. 106.

VIII. 1.—HERBERT DE MAXWELL of Carlaverock. 1347-1354. Died without issue, p. 110.

VIII. 2.—SIR JOHN MAXWELL, Knight, of Maxwell, Carlaverock, Mearns, and Libberton. 1353 or 4-1373. He had by his wife, Christian Erskine, (?) a son, Robert, who succeeded him, p. 112.

IX.—SIR ROBERT DE MAXWELL of Maxwell, Carlaverock, etc. 1373-1409. He rebuilt Carlaverock Castle, pp. 119, 120.

X.—SIR HERBERT MAXWELL of Carlaverock. 1409-1420. Appointed Steward of Annandale in 1409. Married Katherine, daughter of John Stewart, Lord of Dalswinton, in 1386, p. 121.

AYMER, p. 120.

XI.—SIR HERBERT MAXWELL of Maxwell, Carlaverock, etc. 1420-1453. Was served heir of his father on 16th October 1421. CREATED LORD MAXWELL c. 1440. He married, first, a daughter of Herbert Herries of Terregles ; and secondly, Katherine, daughter of Sir William Seton of Seton. He died before 14th February 1453-4, p. 125.

AYMER DE MAXWELL, called brother of Herbert in January 1424-5. Ancestor of the Maxwells of Kirkconnell. *Vide* Pedigree of them, p. 600.

MARGARET, not in text, p. 124, married Sir John de Montgomerie of Eagleshame, in the county of Renfrew.

XII.—ROBERT, second Lord Maxwell. 1453-1485. Served heir of his father, 14th February 1453-4. He married Janet Forrester of Corstorphine. Died 1486, p. 140.

SIR EDWARD, ancestor of the Maxwells of Monreith, p. 138. *Vide* Pedigree, p. 597.

GEORGE, ancestor of Maxwells of Carnsalloch, county of Dumfries, p. 139.

DAVID, p. 139.

ADAM, ancestor of Maxwells of Southbar, p. 139.

JOHN and WILLIAM. p. 139.

GAVIN, p. 139.

KATHERINE, by first wife. p. 138. JANET and MARIOT, by second wife, p. 139.

XIII.—JOHN Master of Maxwell, called third Lord Maxwell, his father having resigned in his favour the fee of the baronies of Maxwell and Carlaverock, and the lands of Mearns, on 14th February 1477-8. Was Steward of Annandale. He married Janet Creichton, daughter of George Earl of Caithness. Was killed at the battle of Kirtle in Annandale, on 22d July 1484, thus predeceasing his father, p. 152.

THOMAS, who married Agnes Maxwell, heiress of Kirkconnell, p. 151. *Vide* Pedigree, p. 600.

DAVID. ROBERT. AYMER. p. 151.

CHRISTIAN, a daughter, p. 151.

a

THE EARLS OF NITHSDALE AND LORDS MAXWELL,—*continued.*

a

JOHN, fourth Lord [Max]well, 1486-1513. [?] married Agnes, [dau]ghter of Sir Alex[and]er Stewart of Gar[lies.] He fell at the [batt]le of Flodden, 9th [Sept]ember 1513, p. [594.]	ROBERT, ancestor of the Maxwells of Cowhill, Dinwiddie, Killylung, Broomholm, Drumpark, and Glenarm, p. 155. *Vide* Pedigree, p. 594.	JAMES, ancestor of the Maxwells of Cavens, p. 155.	HOMER, ancestor of the Maxwells of Portrack, p. 155.	JOHN, Abbot of Holywood, county of Dumfries. No issue, p. 155.	THOMAS, ancestor of the Maxwells of Gleneslin, parish of Dunscore and county of Dumfries, p. 155.	WILLIAM. GEORGE, of Barnton, county of Edinburgh, pp. 155, 156.	JANET, who married William, son and heir of John Lord Carlile ; and CHRISTIAN, p. 156.

[R]OBERT, fifth Lord Maxwell. [15]46. Was Warden of the [wester]n Marches. Made a prisoner [by the] English at Solway Moss in [15]42, and carried to the Tower of [Londo]n. Allowed to return to [Scotla]nd in October 1545. He [marrie]d, first, Janet Douglas of [Dr]umlanrig, by whom he had two [sons] and one daughter ; and [second]ly, Agnes Stewart, daughter [of Jam]es Earl of Buchan. Died [?] July 1546, p. 173.	HERBERT, ancestor of the Maxwells of Clowden, in the stewartry of Kirkcudbright, p. 168.	JOHN, Abbot of Dundrennan. EDWARD, p. 168, p. 171.	HENRY, who was made a prisoner by the Scots at Solway Moss, and sent to the Tower of London in 1542, p. 171.	MARY, married Sir James Johnston of Johnston, county of Dumfries, p. 172.	AGNES, married Robert Charteris of Amisfield, county of Dumfries, p. 172.	ELIZABETH, married Jardine of Applegirth, county of Dumfries, p. 172.	KATHERINE, married John Glendonyng of that Ilk, in the county of Dumfries, p. 172.

—ROBERT, sixth Lord Maxwell. 1546-1552. Married [Bea]trix Douglas, second daughter of James, third Earl of [Mor]ton, about July 1530. Commissioner to treat with England, [?] May 1551. Died 14th September 1552. P. 210.	XVI. 2.—SIR JOHN MAXWELL of Terregles, fourth LORD HERRIES. *Vide* Pedigree, p. 586.	MARGARET, married, 1st, Archibald Douglas, sixth Earl of Angus ; 2d, Sir William Baillie of Lamington, in the county of Lanark, and had a son, James Baillie, who predeceased his father, and a daughter, Margaret, who married her cousin, Edward Maxwell, p. 208.

[?]—ROBERT, seventh Lord Maxwell. [?] died in his fourth year. 1552-1553. [2]22.	XVII. 2.—JOHN, eighth Lord Maxwell. 1554-1593. Warden of the West Marches. Served heir to his father, 24th May 1569. Married Elizabeth, daughter of David Earl of Angus, in 1572. Created *Earl of Morton* 29th October 1581. Killed by the Johnstons at Dryfe Sands, near Lockerbie, 7th December 1593, p. 223. Issue, three sons and four daughters. His widow died in 1637.

[?]I.—JOHN, ninth Lord Maxwell, [?] Earl of Morton. 1593-1613. Served [heir to] his father in 1601. Married Mar[garet,] daughter of John Marquis of Hamilton.— Killed Sir James Johnstone, 6th [?] 1608, for which he was beheaded [in M]ay 1613, *s.p.* Buried at Newbattle [?], p. 300.	XVIII. 2.—ROBERT MAXWELL of Carlaverock, was restored, and became tenth Lord Maxwell and third Earl of Morton. Created *Earl of Nithsdale*, 29th August 1620. Married Elizabeth Beaumont. Issue, one son and two daughters. Died in May 1646, pp. 296, 325.	JAMES of Springkell, *Master of Maxwell.* He died without male issue before 5th October 1667, when his nephew's titles and estates passed to John, seventh Lord Herries. He had an only daughter, Jean, p. 296.	ELIZABETH, Lady Herries. MARGARET, Lady Craigie. JEAN, who died unmarried.	AGNES, Lady Penzerie, pp. 296, 297. She died at London, in 1655. Her brother James was her executor as nearest of kin. [Extract at Terregles.]

[XI]X. 1.—ROBERT, second Earl of Nithsdale, eleventh Lord Maxwell, " The Philosopher." Was excommunicated in 1644 by the General Assembly, and taken prisoner at Newcastle the same year. Died, unmarried, 5th October 1667. On the death of this Earl, the male line of Robert, sixth Lord Maxwell, became extinct. He was succeeded by his cousin, John, seventh Lord Herries, great-grandson of Sir John Maxwell, fourth Lord Herries, p. 373. *Vide* Pedigree of the Earls of Nithsdale and the Lords Herries.	LADY ELIZABETH MAXWELL, p. 371.	LADY JEAN MAXWELL, p. 371.

II.—THE EARLS OF NITHSDALE AND LORDS HERRIES.

XVI. 2.—Sir John Maxwell of Terregles, Knight, second son of Robert, fifth Lord Maxwell, and Janet Douglas. He married, in 1547, Agn Herries, eldest daughter of William, third Lord Herries. Sir John became fourth Lord Herries in 1566. Died 20th January 1582. P. 49 —*Vide* Pedigree of the Herries Family.

XVII.—William Maxwell, succeeded his father as fifth Lord Herries on 20th January 1582. Married Katharine Ker, sister of Mark, first Earl of Lothian. He died 10th October 1603. P. 571.	Sir Robert of Spotts.—*Vide* Pedigree of *Orchardton*. Edward of Lamington.—*Vide* Pedigree of *Lamington*.	John of Newlaw. Issue. James, "lawful son," 1567.	Elizabeth, Lady Lochinvar. Margaret, first Countess of Lothian.	Agnes, Lady Amisfield. Mary, Lady Yester.	Sarah, Lady Johnst Grizel, Lady Bomb Nicolas, Lady

XVIII.—John Maxwell, sixth Lord Herries, succeeded his father in 1603. He married Elizabeth, daughter of John, eighth Lord Maxwell. He died in 1631. Issue, eight sons and a daughter.—P. 571.	Sir William of Gribton. Died before 17th October 1628, when his son John was served heir to him. John had a son, James Maxwell of Gribton, living on 30th November 1697.	Sir Robert of Sweetheart. s.p.	Edward. James.	Elizabeth, Lady Urchell. 1609.	Marg Lady

XIX.—John Maxwell, seventh Lord Herries, succeeded his cousin as third Earl of Nithsdale and twelfth Lord Maxwell in 1667. He married Elizabeth, eldest daughter of Sir Robert Gordon of Lochinvar. He died between February and June 1677. P. 383.

James Maxwell of Breconside.—*Vide* Pedigree of Breconside, etc., p. 587.

Robert of Barnbachel, a Captain in France, died without issue.—[MS. at Terregles.]

Captain Edward Maxwell of Lawston. Married, before November 1665, Margaret, daughter of William Glen, litster, burgess of Dumfries. Issue, three sons—John, the eldest, and William, the youngest, died without issue—and two daughters, Anne and Marie. The latter married Thomas Irving of Gribton.

Frederick Maxwell of Lawston, second son. Was heir to his eldest brother. Married, on 1st January 1702, Jean Murray, sister to Laird of Conheath.— [Lawston Titles, etc.]

Frederick. William, a Captain in France, died without issue.—[MS. at Terregles.] Alexander.

Michael. He was killed at Cumlongan, by a bowl going wrong out of his companion's hand. It hit him in the breast, and he died instantly.

Eliza Count Wir Had

Edward Maxwell, eldest son. Was, with his brothers and sisters, infeft. on 20th August 1729, in an annual rent out of Lawston and house in Brigend of Dumfries. He died, without issue, before 1754.—[Lawston Titles at Terregles.]

Frederick Maxwell of Lawston. Had two sons.

Marg Eliza

Charles Maxwell of Lawston, eldest son. Got a charter from Lady Winifred Maxwell, on 18th October 1779, of one-third part of Lawston. Left no issue.

Frederick Maxwell of Milnhead. Was bred a joiner. Succeeded George Maxwell of Carruch factor on Nithsdale estates. Was left Milnhead by Miss Agnes Brown, who executed a deed of conveying these lands first to him and his heirs, and then, failing such, to Henry C. Maxwe present proprietor, who succeeded to them on his death in March 1823, without issue. Bein *last of his line*, he left such lands as he had himself acquired and could dispose of, to the nephew of his wife, the present Sir Robert Gordon, Bart. of Letterfourie, then only the secon his brother, Sir William, being alive. Frederick Maxwell's wife was Agnes, sister of William donwyn of Parton.

XX.—Robert Maxwell, fourth Earl of Nithsdale, thirteenth Lord Maxwell, eighth Lord Herries. Married Lucie, eighth daughter of William, first Marquis of Douglas. Died in March 1696. P. 397.	John Maxwell of Gelston. Died in 1658. No male issue, but an only daughter, Elizabeth, who succeeded her uncle William. She married, in 1674, Robert Maxwell of Kirkhouse. P. 395.	William Maxwell of l and Buittle. Died 1685. No issue. P.

XXI.—William Maxwell, fifth Earl of Nithsdale, fourteenth Lord Maxwell, and ninth Lord Herries, was attainted in 1716, and died at Rome in 1744. He married, in 1699, Lady Winifred Herbert, youngest daughter of William, first Marquis of Powis. The Countess of Nithsdale died at Rome in 1749. P. 414.

Mary, Countess of Traq

XXII.—William Maxwell of Nithsdale, commonly called Lord Maxwell. He married his cousin, Lady Catharine Stuart, fourth daughter Charles, fourth Earl of Traquair. She died in 1765, survived by her husband, who died in 1776, leaving an only surviving daughter. P. 48

XXIII.—Winifred Maxwell of Nithsdale. Married, on 17th October 1758, William Haggerston Constable of Everingham Park, in the coun of York. Issue, three sons and four daughters. He died on 20th June 1797. She died on 13th July 1801. P. 488.

a

THE EARLS OF NITHSDALE AND LORDS HERRIES—*continued.*

a

KE CONSTABLE MAXWELL ...sdale and Everingham Born 2d January 1760. 1802, Theresa Apolonia, ... of Edmund Wakeman ...ford. Died 30th June	WILLIAM, born 25th December 1760, who assumed the surname and arms of Middleton. Issue.	CHARLES, born 25th March 1764, who assumed the sur-name and arms of Stanley. Had issue.	CATHERINE, born 7th January 1762.	MARY-ANN, born 18th July 1766, married John Webb Weston, of Sutton Place.	TERESA, born 18th August 1768.	CLEMENTINA, born 29th December 1774.

CONSTABLE MAX-Nithsdale, born 25th 1804. Was, on 2d 858, found by the f Lords entitled to inal Barony of Her- is now TENTH LORD s. Married, 12th er 1835, Marcia, of the Hon. Sir Marmaduke Vava- d has had issue.	MARMADUKE of Ter-regles, born 1st January 1806. Married, in 1836, Mary, daughter of the Rev. Anthony Marsden of Gar-grave. Died on 16th July 1872.	PETER, born 7th February 1807. Married, in 1834, Helena-Mary, daughter of John-Peter-Bruno Bowden. He died on . Issue, five sons and three daughters. The elder son, Frederick Henry Constable Maxwell, is now of Terregles; the second is Alfred; the third, Robert; the fourth, Edward; and the fifth, Wilfred. The daughters are Helena; Agatha-Mary, married Edward Pilkington; and Alice-Clare.	HENRY, born 28th December 1809. Married, 23d July 1840, Julia, daugh-ter of Peter Middleton, and has had ten children— all living, except one.	JOSEPH, a member of the Society of Jesus, born 1811. Died at Dalkeith in 1869.	MARY, married the Hon. Charles Langdale. Died 1857.	THERESA, married the Hon. Charles Everard-Clifford.

RMADUKE, ...aster of ...ries, born ... October 1837.	WILLIAM, born 24th April 1841.	JOSEPH. Officer, Rifle Brigade, born 16th January 1847.	BERNARD, born 3d April 1848.	WALTER, born 13th August 1849.	JOHN, born 5th July 1855.	PETER, born 4th July 1857. Died 11th November 1869.	MARCIA. MARY AGNES, a Nun. ELEONORA-MARY, a Nun. EMILY-JOSEPHINE, a Nun. GWENDALINE, a Nun. — WINEFREDE. TERESA. EVERILDA. MARY-ANN.

III.—THE FAMILY OF HERRIES, LORDS HERRIES OF TERREGLES, IN THE STEWARTRY OF KIRKCUDBRIGHT.

WILLIAM DE HERIZ, witnessed a Donation by Henry Prince of Scotland to the Monastery of Wederhall and Holmcultram, in England, *circa* 1150.

NIGEL DE HERIZ, witnessed, along with his brother Thomas, a Donation to the Monastery of Kelso *tempore* King William the Lion, *circa* 1200.

WILLIAM DE HERIZ, witnessed a Donation to the Monastery of Kelso, *circa* 1190.

THOMAS DE HERIZ, witnessed, along with his brother Nigel, a Donation to the Monastery of Kelso, *circa* 1200.

HENRY DE HERIZ, was appointed by King Alexander the Second Keeper of his royal forests. As "Forestarius regis" he witnessed a Charter by that King, *circa* 1240. He had two sons,

SIR WILLIAM DE HERIZ, Knight. He granted a charter to Sir William of Karlyle, Knight, and the Lady Margaret, his spouse (sister of King Robert the Bruce), of an acre of land, held of the Lord of Annandale, in the tenement of Keynpatrick. No date. *Circa* 1296.—[Original at Drumlanrig.] He swore fealty to King Edward the First of England for his lands in Dumfriesshire, in 1296. William de Heriz and Robert de Tilliol held Lochmaben Castle for King Edward in 1301.—[Stevenson's Historical Documents, vol. ii. p. 432.]

GILBERT DE HERIZ, who witnessed a Donation to the Monastery of Newbattle, in 1266.

ROBERT DE HERRIS. In an original Charter by King Robert the Bruce he is designated Dominus de Nithsdale, 1323. Supposed to have been the father of

SIR JOHN HERRIES, first of Terregles. On the resignation of Thomas Earl of Mar, he received from King David Bruce a Charter erecting Terregles into a Barony, etc., 17th October 1364.

SIR JOHN HERRIES, second of Terregles, witnessed a Charter by King Robert III. in 1393. He had a safe-conduct to England in 1405.

SIR HERBERT HERRIES, third of Terregles, one of the hostages for the ransom of King James the First, 1423.

SIR JOHN HERRIES of Annandale. Hanged by Douglas.

JOHN HERRIES, fourth of Terregles. Found to be *non compos mentis*, 1458-1478.

HERBERT. He obtained a Crown grant of Curatory of his brother John, 24th January 1458.

WILLIAM, Rector of Kirkpatrick Irongray, 1453.

ROBERT of Kirkpatrick Irongray, 1463.

DAUGHTER, married Sir Herbert Maxwell of Carlaverock.

SIR DAVID HERRIES, fifth of Terregles, married Margaret Crichton of Sanquhar, 1477. He had a son, George, ancestor of the Herries' of Terraughty.

SIR HERBERT HERRIES, sixth of Terregles. He was, by King James the Fourth, created Lord Herries of Terregles, *circa* 1489. He married, 1st, Marion Carlyle of Torthorwald, who was living in 1482; 2dly, Mariot Cuningham. Issue, four sons,

ROBERT, second Lord Herries of Terregles. He married Lady Janet Douglas, daughter of Archibald, fifth Earl of Angus. Killed at Flodden, 1513.

MUNGO. JOHN. Both died *s.p.*

ROGER of Maidenpaup, tutor-at-law to William Lord Herries, 1517.

WILLIAM, third Lord Herries of Terregles, married Catherine, daughter of James Kennedy of Blairquhan, 1513-1543. Issue, three daughters,

ARCHIBALD HERRIES of Maidenpaup, 1561. His grandson, William Herries, sold Maidenpaup in 1629.

MARGARET, married Gilbert Maclellan, ancestor of Lord Kirkcudbright.

AGNES HERRIES, married Sir John Maxwell, second son of Robert, fifth Lord Maxwell.—*Vide* Pedigree No. II. p. 584, for continuation.

CATHERINE HERRIES, married Alexander Stewart of Garlies, ancestor of the Earl of Galloway, 1550.

JEAN HERRIES, married Sir James Cockburn of Skirling, 1550.

SEAL OF ARCHIBALD HERRIES OF MAIDENPAUP, HEIR-MALE OF THE LORDS HERRIES IN 1561.

IV.—THE MAXWELLS OF BRECONSIDE IN THE PARISH OF KIRKGUNZEON, AND TERRAUGHTY IN THE PARISH OF TROQUEER, IN THE STEWARTRY OF KIRKCUDBRIGHT.

JAMES MAXWELL of Breconside of Kirkgunzeon, second son of John, sixth Lord Herries, from whom he had a Bond of Provision, dated 10th October 1627. He married Margaret, daughter of Vans of Barnbarroch, relict of Sir John Gordon of Lochinvar. Issue, two sons. He died after 22d June 1649. There is a tradition that Margaret Vans had by her two husbands twenty-nine children.

JOHN MAXWELL, second of Breconside and of Terraughty. Succeeded his father after 22d June 1649. He died before 3d May 1718, unmarried. Succeeded by his nephew,

ALEXANDER, of Park of Dalbeattie and Terraughty. Married, 1st, Margaret, youngest daughter of Alexander Maxwell of Conheath and Terraughty, by whom he had six sons and two daughters. 2dly, Janet, daughter of John Irving, Provost of Dumfries. Issue by her at his death was " eight small infants." One son and five daughters survived. He died on 10th October 1701.

JOHN MAXWELL, third of Breconside and of Terraughty. Married, 1st, Helen Murray, his cousin-german, by their mothers, by whom he had one son ; 2dly, in April 1719, Elizabeth, eldest daughter of James Maxwell of Arkland, by whom he had one son and two daughters. He died on 12th May 1724, and was buried in the middle of the quire of Buittle Church. He was survived by his second wife, who died in 1766.

GEORGE, joiner or cabinet-maker, London. He died there in January or February 1748, unmarried. JAMES, and three other sons, all died in infancy.

WILLIAM, of Carruchan. *Vide* Pedigree of Carruchan, p. 589.

JAMES, born and died in 1691.

HERBERT, born in 1698. History unknown.

ALEXANDER, an upholsterer in London. Born 1696. Died in London. History not known.

CHARLES, upholsterer in London, born at Terraughty, 28th July 1700. Married Miss MacBrair, by whom he had two sons and a daughter, Margaret, who died at London on 22d April 1758.

CATHERINE (of first marriage). She married Robert Neilson of Barncailzie. She died at Edinburgh on 18th November 1758. ELIZABETH. She died young. LUCY. Born 1693. Died 1764. MARGARET. Died young. MARY. Died young. RACHEL. Living in 1758.

WINIFRED. On 11th February 1783, she made a settlement in favour of her nieces, Ann and Marian Maxwells (of Carruchan). Winifred died at Dumfries on 5th August 1787.

WILLIAM MAXWELL, fourth of Breconside and of Terraughty. Was in left in Terraughty as heir to his father, 1st Dec. 1735. He married Janet MacCartney, and had no male issue, but a daughter, Helen, who married William Burgess of Kirkland of Urr, and their descendants are believed to exist. William Maxwell sold Breconside in 1736. He died in March 1756.

JOHN MAXWELL of Portrack, Terraughty, Munches, and Dinwoodie, born at Buittle, 7th February 1720. He purchased Terraughty in 1754. Married, 1st, in 1741, Agnes, daughter of William Hannay, Dumfries. She died on 13th September 1755. Issue, three sons and six daughters ; 2dly, in February 1770, Agnes Maxwell, who, in 1793, succeeded her brother, George Maxwell, in Munches. She died in 1809, aged 90 years, without issue. She conveyed Munches and Dinwoodie to her husband, who, on 22d July 1813, executed an entail of them in favour of his children by his first marriage. On the death of William Maxwell of Nithsdale, only son of the last Earl of Nithsdale, John Maxwell became the heir-male of the Maxwell family ; and he was served heir-male of Robert, the fourth Earl, on 4th June 1778. He died at Munches on 25th January 1814, aged 94 years.

ELIZABETH, born 27th October 1721. Married the Rev. Robert Macmorine, minister of Kirkpatrick-Durham. Had a large family. She died about the year 1800.

MARGARET, born 5th November 1723. She died 11th April 1742, unmarried.

CHARLES MAXWELL, in Fleet Street, London, 1758. Married, 1st, Deitraid, and had two daughters : Mrs. Turnbull, in America, and Mrs. Williams, in England ; 2dly, Douglas of the family of Kelhead, by whom he had two sons, Charles and William, who died in the Army. Charles was Governor of St. Kitts.

WILLIAM, was a merchant in Bristol, and afterwards went to New York, and had descendants.

ROBERT, went to Grenada, West Indies, and married, 1st, by whom he had an only daughter and child, who died in Dumfries. He married, 2dly, and had Homer Maxwell and other children. Homer died unmarried.

ALEXANDER HERRIES MAXWELL of Munches and Terraughty, born 28th January 1744. He married, 1st, Charlotte, third daughter of James Douglas, physician in Carlisle, son of Sir William Douglas of Kelhead ; and 2d, in 1783, Marion, eldest daughter of William Gordon of Greenlaw, relict of William Kirkpatrick of Raeberry. By the first marriage he had an only daughter, Charlotte, who died young. There was no issue of the second marriage. He died at Terraughty, on 28th June 1815, and was succeeded in Munches, Dinwoodie, and Terraughty by his niece, Clementina.

WILLIAM, born 14th February 1746. He was for some time tenant of the farm of East Blackshaw, in Carlaverock. Married Janet, daughter of John Syme, W.S., Edinburgh. Issue, three sons and two daughters. He predeceased his father on 25th February 1789. His wife survived him till 1810.

JOHN, born 21st August 1747. Died on 1753, in his sixth year.

ELIZABETH, married John Harley, surgeon in Dumfries. Their descendants are now Maxwells of Portrack.
AGNES, born 15th July 1749. Married Rev. John Robertson, minister of Kirkconnell, Dumfriesshire, and had issue.
JEAN, born 18th December 1750. Married William Hyslop of Lochend, and had issue.
HELEN, born 2d February 1752, died in infancy.
CATHERINE, born 5th April 1754. Married Wellwood Maxwell of Barncleuch. Issue, *vide* Barncleuch Pedigree.
MARGARET, born 15th August 1755. Died 1849, unmarried.

A

PEDIGREE OF THE MAXWELLS OF BRECONSIDE AND TERRAUGHTY,—*continued.*

A

JOHN MAXWELL, born 30th January 1780. A Lieutenant in the Army. Died, unmarried, in 1810.	GEORGE, born 2d November 1785. Died, unmarried, in India, in 1810.	ALEXANDER, born 20th April 1788. A midshipman in the Navy, who died at sea, unmarried.	CLEMENTINA, born 31st March 1782. Married, in 1813, John Herries Maxwell of Barncleuch, who died in 1843. Issue, two sons and one daughter. She succeeded to Munches, Dinwoodie, and Terraughty on the death of her uncle, Alexander, on 28th June 1815. She died on 23d May 1858.	AGNES, born 27th May 1784. Died 13th May 1869, unmarried.

WELLWOOD HERRIES MAXWELL, born 15th October 1817, succeeded to Munches and Terraughty on the death of his mother in 1858. Was elected M.P. for the Stewartry of Kirkcudbright in 1868. Married, in 1844, Jane-Home, eldest daughter of Sir William Jardine of Applegarth, Baronet, and has had issue, five sons and six daughters.	JOHN, died in infancy, 12th May 1814.	JANET, married, in 1839, William Maxwell of Carruchan, heir-male of the Earls of Nithsdale. Died 9th January 1842, without issue.

JOHN, born 3d October 1846. Died 5th December 1856.	WILLIAM-JARDINE, born 4th March 1852.	WELLWOOD, born 28th December 1857.	ALEXANDER, born 26th June 1860.	HUGH, born 12th May 1862.	JESSIE JANE, married Charles George Hood Kinnear, Esq. Issue.	CATHERINE, born 20th May 1848. Died 13th December 1856.	CLEMENTINA, born 6th June 1850.	AGNES, born 1st April 1854.	MARGARET, born 6th February 1856.	CATHERINE HELEN, born 17th October 1864.

ARMORIAL BEARINGS matriculated on 28th April 1868, by WELLWOOD HERRIES MAXWELL of Munches, etc., in the Lyon Court of Scotland.

Shield : Quarterly, 1st and 4th grand quarters, argent, an eagle displayed, with two heads sable, beaked and membered gules, bearing on his breast an escutcheon of the first, charged with a saltire of the second, surcharged with an urcheon or, for MAXWELL ; 2nd grand quarter, argent, three urcheons sable, for HERRIES ; 3rd grand quarter, counter quartered first and fourth, argent, a saltire sable, on a bordure of the second eight lozenges of the first, for MAXWELL of BARNCLEUCH ; 2nd and 3rd, argent, a saltire invecked sable, between two pellets, in flank, on a chief gules, three cushions, or, for JOHNSTONE of CLAUCHRIE.

Crest : A stag lodged in front of a holly tree, proper.

Motto : REVIRESCO.

V.—THE MAXWELLS OF CARRUCHAN, IN THE PARISH OF TROQUEER AND STEWARTRY OF KIRKCUDBRIGHT.

CAPTAIN WILLIAM MAXWELL of Carruchan, eldest son of the second marriage of Alexander Maxwell of Park and Terraughty [who was a grandson of John, sixth Lord Herries], and Janet, daughter of John Irvine, Provost of Dumfries, born in 1689. He was with Prince Charles Edward at the battle of Culloden in 1745. He was afterwards a prisoner in Carlisle Castle, from which he made his escape. Married, 1st, Barbara, youngest daughter of George Maxwell of Munches, by whom he had an only child, Anna. 2dly, Agnes Maxwell of Carruchan, who died in January 1771, and by her he had one son and two daughters. Died 16th May 1772, aged 83 years.

GEORGE MAXWELL of Carruchan, born 1738. He married, on 9th April 1771, Henrietta Carruthers, by whom he had three sons. She survived him. On the death of Alexander Herries Maxwell of Terraughty on 28th June 1815, he became the heir-male of the Maxwell family; and but for the attainder of the fifth Earl, he would have been EARL OF NITHSDALE, LORD MAXWELL, etc. He died on 20th November 1822, aged 84. He had three sons.

ANNA (only child of the first marriage), died at an advanced age, in 1820, unmarried.

MARION MAXWELL. AGNES MAXWELL. They received a Bond of Provision from their brother on 16th September 1777, and in 1800 Ann made a Will in favour of Marion, her half sister.

WILLIAM, who was born on 16th February 1773, and was Paymaster of the 8th Dragoons, and died in 1800, without issue.

JAMES, born 16th June 1775. who died in Jamaica in 1800, without issue.

GEORGE MAXWELL, younger of Carruchan, Lieutenant-Colonel of the Galloway Militia. He married (Contract dated 4th June 1804) Jane, eldest daughter of John Clark of Drummore. He predeceased his father in 1821, in France, leaving four sons.

GEORGE WALTER MAXWELL, eldest son, born 17th March 1805. On the death of his grandfather, on 20th November 1822, he succeeded to Carruchan, and obtained a Crown charter, dated 5th July 1823. He was heir-male of the family of Maxwell, and would have been Earl of Nithsdale and Lord Maxwell but for the attainder of the fifth Earl. He was drowned while bathing in the river Nith, on 4th August (September, in service) 1827, unmarried.

JOHN, born 10th May 1806. Died at sea, on his way to India, as a Cadet in the East India Company's Service, on 24th June 1824, unmarried.

WILLIAM MAXWELL of Carruchan, was born in May 1807. On the death of his eldest brother, George, became heir-male of the Maxwell family. As such he claimed the titles of Earl of Nithsdale, Lords Maxwell, Herries, etc. He married, 1st, Janet, only daughter of John and Clementina Maxwell of Munches, s.p.; 2dly, Mary, only daughter of Dr. John Clark of Speddoch, who is now of Carruchan. Mr. Maxwell of Carruchan died on 21st May 1863, s.p.

ALEXANDER, born 19th May 1808. He died in 1834, unmarried.

JANE. CHRISTIANA MAXWELL. Died in 1861, unmarried.

Other children died young, unmarried.

ARMORIAL BEARINGS OF THE LATE WILLIAM MAXWELL OF CARRUCHAN, ESQUIRE.

Shield : Argent, a double-headed eagle displayed, sable, beaked and membered gules, surmounted of an escutcheon of the first, charged with a saltire of the second, and surcharged in the centre with a hedgehog, or.

Supporters : Two stags proper.

Crest : A stag lodged before a holly bush, both proper.

Motto : REVIRESCO.

Letters-patent from the Earl of Kinnoull, Lord Lyon, to the said William Maxwell, as heir-male of Robert, fourth Earl of Nithsdale, dated 15th day of March 1848.—[Original Patent at Carruchan.]

VI.—THE MAXWELLS OF ORCHARDTON, IN THE PARISH OF BUITTLE AND STEWARTRY OF KIRKCUDBRIGHT.

I.—SIR ROBERT MAXWELL of Spottis, second son of John, fourth Lord Herries, and Agnes, Lady Herries, was ancestor of the Maxwells of Orchardton. By a Contract between Lords Maxwell and Herries, dated 21st February 1573, he acquired the eleven merk land of Spottis and others; and he received from his brother, Sir William Maxwell of Aven, Master of Herries, the lands of Netherlaw, in Rerwick, in which he and his wife were infefted on 27th April 1577. On 2d January 1584, he and his spouse were infefted in the lands of Nether Linkings; and on 25th May 1590 he acquired the lands of King's Grange or Little Spottis, in parish of Urr. On 3d August 1593 he acquired the lands of West Netherlaw and others, and before his father's death, in 1582, he had taken Orchardton in wadset. He married, before 27th April 1577, 1st, Elizabeth Gordon, Lady Gelston; and 2dly, Sara, sister of Sir James Johnston, his brother-in-law. He was present when Sir James was killed by Lord Maxwell in 1608, and gave evidence at the trial. He died before 31st October 1615. He and Elizabeth Gordon, his first wife, were interred in the family burying-place at Terregles. The monument erected there to their memory is represented in this Work. By his first wife he had

II.—SIR ROBERT MAXWELL of Spottis and Orchardton, first Baronet. He was retoured heir to his father in the lands of Spottis and others on 31st October 1615. He was created a Baronet in 1663. He had three sons. He died before 20th October 1681.

III.—SIR ROBERT MAXWELL of Orchardton, second Baronet. On 20th October 1681 he was retoured heir to his father in the lands of Orchardton and others; and on 28th February 1682 he was retoured heir to him in the lands of St. Mary's Isle and others. He married, 1st, Janet, daughter of John Gordon of Rusco; and, on 14th October 1654, a post-nuptial contract was made, settling the estates on him and her. The name of his second wife, by whom he had no issue, has not been ascertained. He married, 3dly, Margaret, daughter of Henry Maxwell, grandson of the Dean of Armagh, of the family of Lord Farnham, s.p. He died, 24th January 1693. By the first marriage he had

THOMAS MAXWELL of Gelston, parish of Kelton. He married, in 1659, Elizabeth Glendinning, heiress of Gelston, and widow of John Maxwell of Gelston, through whom he obtained that estate. He died circa 1704, leaving a son.

HUGH MAXWELL of Cuil, in parish of Buittle.

IV.—SIR GEORGE MAXWELL of Orchardton, third Baronet. He was retoured heir to his father in the lands of Orchardton, in the parish of Buittle, 21st November 1699. He married Mary, Viscountess Dowager Montague, s.p. He died in 1719.

ELIZABETH, married James Butler of Stockton, and had a son, James, who died, s.p., before 1760.

V.—ROBERT MAXWELL of Gelston, afterwards, in 1719, Sir Robert Maxwell, fourth Baronet of Orchardton. He was served heir-male to his uncle, Sir Robert, on 6th June 1727. He married, 1st, about the year 1680, Barbara, daughter of George Maxwell of Munches; and, 2dly, in 1697, Ann, daughter of Lindsay of Wauchope. The issue of the first marriage was three sons, and the issue of the second, two sons and one daughter. He died in 1729.

THOMAS MAXWELL of Cuil. He died, s.p., 1719. "The Laird of Cool's Ghost" was the subject of a small chap-book.

VI.—SIR GEORGE MAXWELL of Orchardton, fifth Baronet, married, 1st, about 1715, Margaret Blacklock, and had a son, Thomas. Sir George Maxwell married, 2dly, in 1725, his cousin, Margaret, youngest daughter of Francis Maxwell of Breoch, and had an only son. He died in January 1747.

WILLIAM. JAMES. Both died s.p.

MUNGO MAXWELL. By arrangement on his father's second marriage, he succeeded to Orchardton, which he resigned to his eldest half-brother, and he retained Glenshinnoch and Potterland. Married Mary, daughter of Cairns of Barnbarroch, and had

ROBERT MAXWELL of Blackbelly, married Elizabeth, daughter of Robert Maxwell of Hazlefield, and had

ELIZABETH, born in June 1701, and died on 3d October 1779.—[Tombstone, Newabbey churchyard.] Married Rev. William Irving, minister, Newabbey.

A   B   C

THE MAXWELLS OF ORCHARDTON— *continued.*

	A			B			C	

VII.—SIR THOMAS MAX-WELL, sixth Baronet. He was served heir to his grandfather, Sir Robert, on 12th January 1740, as Protestant heir-male. He married Henrietta, daughter of Samuel Broun of Mollance, by Margaret MacClellan, eldest daughter of James Lord Kirkcudbright, but had no issue. He died on 3d February 1761. — [Buittle Records.]

BARBARA, married, in 1738, John MacWilliam, in Breoch. Issue, several sons and daughters.— [Buittle Records.]

ROBERT, of second marriage, died at Douay College about 1740.

VIII.—SIR ROBERT MAX-WELL of Orchardton, seventh Baronet, who was educated at Douay. He was at the battle of Culloden with Prince Charles. Was taken prisoner to Dumfries. Married Miss M'Lellan, who died in March 1772, and was buried at Buittle. Sir Robert sold Orchardton. He died suddenly, on 21st September 1786. —[Letter from Sir Alexander Gordon of that date.] Since then the Baronetcy has been dormant. There is an interesting Memoir of Sir Robert in the *Scots Magazine* for July 1787, vol. xlix. p. 319.

ANN. BARBARA. HENRIETTA. ELIZABETH. AGNES.

ROBERT MAXWELL of Black-belly, who married Elizabeth Henry, in the parish of Kelton, and had two sons.

WILLIAM. MUNGO. ANN. Of whom nothing is known.

WILLIAM, the eldest son, who was born at Kelton, 21st May 1755; enlisted in 1795 as a gunner in the 4th Battalion of the Royal Artillery. He was in Quebec with his regiment in 1806. He was the heir-male to the Ordchardton Baronetcy in 1786.

ROBERT MAXWELL. He lived in Bridgend of Dumfries (now Maxwellton) in 1805.

VII.—THE MAXWELLS OF NEWLAW IN THE PARISH OF RERWICK, AND OF BREOCH IN THE PARISH OF BUITTLE.

EDWARD MAXWELL of Lamington, third son of John Lord Herries and Agnes Lady Herries, born *circa* 1555. Appointed Commendator of Dundrennan before 28th January 1567-68. Was one of the chief leaders in the raid to Stirling of 1585. Sat in the special session of Parliament then called. Married his cousin, Margaret, daughter and heiress of Sir William Baillie of Lamington and his wife, Margaret Maxwell, sister of John Lord Herries. Issue, four sons. Died 29th September 1598.

SIR WILLIAM MAXWELL, took the surname of Baillie. Served heir to his father in the lands of Lamington, etc., on 26th March 1607. Knighted by King James VI. Married Elizabeth, daughter of Henry Stewart of Craighall. Issue, two sons and two daughters. The sons were

JOHN MAXWELL of Newlaw, second son. On 2d August 1592, King James VI. granted a charter to Edward Maxwell of Lamington, Margaret Baillie, his spouse, in liferent, and John Maxwell, their second son, of lands of Newlaw and Monkismure, etc.

JAMES MAXWELL of Balmangan. Royal Charter on 4th February 1597, to Margaret Baillie, Lady Lamington, in liferent, and to his son, James Maxwell, his heirs, etc., of lands of Balmangan.

EDWARD MAXWELL. [Herries Muniments, No. 363.]

SIR WILLIAM BAILLIE of Lamington, served heir to his father on 6th September 1615. Married Grizel, daughter of Sir Claud Hamilton of Ellieston.

JAMES BAILLIE of Watsonhead, supposed to be extinct.

SAMUEL MAXWELL of Newlaw, succeeded his father in lands of Newlaw. Was one of the tutors of William, fifth Earl of Nithsdale. Married, 1st, a daughter of Samuel Broun of Mollance ; 2dly, Mary Maxwell, relict of Captain Robert Maxwell of Hazlefield.

SUSANNA MAXWELL, married, 1st, John Maxwell, younger of Barfill, 1635; and, 2dly, Robert M'Lellan of Gatta, before 25th February 1652.

SIR SAMUEL BAILLIE of Lamington, married Margaret, daughter of John Lord Belhaven. Predeceased his father. Issue, a son and a daughter, Margaret, married to James Semple of Cathcart.

WILLIAM MAXWELL, younger of Newlaw, eldest son of first marriage. Infefted in lands of Castlecrevie on 28th Aug. 1693. Predeceased his father. Married Elizabeth, daughter of Alexander Viscount Kenmure.

SAMUEL MAXWELL, second son of first marriage. Died without issue.

EDWARD MAXWELL of Nether Riddick, eldest son of second marriage, infefted under disposition by his father, in five merk lands of Nether Riddick and five merk lands of Airds, on 18th August 1690. Married Grizell Grierson. Died before 21st January 1708.

ALEXANDER MAXWELL of Balmangan, in parish of Rerwick, called also of Newlaw (by his friends), second son of second marriage. Infefted, under Disposition by his father, in lands of Balmangan, on 18th August 1690. Married, 1st, in 1703, Barbara, daughter and heir-portioner of Francis Maxwell of Breoch ; 2dly, a lady (name unknown), by whom he had also a large family. Died *circa* 1766.

LUCIE MAXWELL daughter of sec marriage, infe by her father i annual-rent £1000 Scots ou lands of Neth Riddick and Ai but redeemable 18th August 16

SIR WILLIAM BAILLIE of Lamington, succeeded his grandfather. Married, 1st, Marjory, daughter of John, first Lord Bargeny, by whom he had a son, William, who died in his 17th year ; 2dly, Lady Henrietta Lindsay, daughter of William Earl of Crawford, and had issue two daughters.

MARGARET, married Sir James Carmichael of Bonington.

ALEXANDER MAXWELL of Newlaw, succeeded his grandfather. On 18th January 1704, Robert Maxwell of Hazlefield obtained decreet against him as only lawful son of William Maxwell, younger of Newlaw, deceased, and oye and heir to the deceased Samuel Maxwell of Newlaw, for certain sums of money. Was divested of his estate of Newlaw before his death, about 1747, unmarried.

JEAN MAXWELL, married John Maxwell of Carswada.

MARY MAXWELL.

ROBERT MAXWELL of Breoch, eldest of first marriage, born 1704. Infefted by Precept of Chancery 24th March 1744, in lands of Breoch upon 31st March 1744. Was a sea captain. In the year 1747 he and his father took part in a litigation for reducing the adjudication under which the estate of Newlaw was sold. Married, in 1770, Elizabeth Burnie, niece of Francis Caven, farmer, Castlegower. Died 12th May 1780.

FRANCIS MAXWELL, second son of first marriage. Hatter in London.

CHARLES MAXWELL, third son of first marriage.

MARY MAX daughter o marriage, n William Ha in Auchen and died at in 178

GEORGE MAXWELL, Master Mariner.

ELIZABETH MAXWELL, died at Halketleaths, and buried 6th July 1773.

A

B

THE MAXWELLS OF NEWLAW AND BREOCH—*continued.*

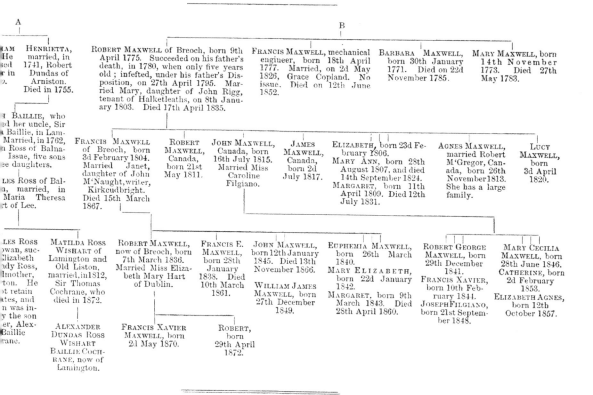

ARMORIAL BEARINGS.

Shield: Quarterly, 1st and 4th argent a saltier sable between 9 mullets, gules 3, 3, and 3, and a hurcheon of the second in base, for Maxwell of Newlaw ; 2nd and 3rd, the same between a crescent in chief and a mullet in base, gules, for Maxwell of Breoch.

Crest: A stag couchant before a holly bush.

Motto: REVIRESCO.

VIII.—THE MAXWELLS OF COWHILL, DRUMPARK, THREAVE, AND GRIBTON, IN THE COUNTY OF DUMFRIES.

ROBERT MAXWELL, second son of John, third Lord Maxwell, who died in 1484, was ancestor of the Maxwells of Cowhill, Drumpark, Threave, and Gribton.—[Charter of Whitestanes, 26th June 1486.] His wife is supposed to have been of the family of Maxwell of Aitkenhead, and his eldest son was

SIR JOHN MAXWELL of Cowhill, who married a daughter of Robert Herries of Terrauchtie.—[*Vide* Retour of Archibald Maxwell of Cowhill to Robert Herries, 11th May 1630.] He had

SIR ROBERT MAXWELL of Cowhill and Dinwiddie, married Elizabeth Maxwell, Lady Tinwald.—[Sasine in his favour as son and heir to John Maxwell of Cowhill, 11th July 1560.] He received a Crown charter of Meiklefield, Glengower, etc., 15th March 1566, which confirms three charters, dated in 1555, 1557, and 1559; and Crown charter of Dinwiddie, 13th January 1567. He died without issue.

ARCHIBALD MAXWELL of Cowhill, retoured heir to his brother, Sir Robert, on 29th August 1589 and 5th November 1590, in all his lands except Dinwoodie, which was settled by the charter, failing issue, on his brother, John Maxwell. His wife's name is not known, but he had three sons.

JOHN MAXWELL, married Joanna Dinwodie of Dinwodie.—[Crown charter in favour of Sir Robert Maxwell, 13th January 1567.]

GEORGE MAXWELL of Whitesta from whom descended the famil Maxwells of Killilung (now extir [*Vide* Decreet of Adjudicatior Implement by the Lords of Sess dated 11th August 1762, in action, William Lauder Max against John Maxwell of Bro holm, where pedigree is deducee

WILLIAM MAXWELL, no issue.

ARCHIBALD MAXWELL of Cowhill, retoured heir to his uncle, Sir Robert, on 25th January and 13th September 1608 and 25th January 1609, in all his lands except Dinwiddie, and was retoured heir-general to Robert Herries of Terraughtie, *abavi ex latere aviae*, 11th May 1630. He married Janet Vans, and had

JOHN MAXWELL of Broomholm. *Vide* Pedigree of *Broomholm*.

JOHN MAXWELL of Cowhill, concurred in the disposition to his brother Thomas in January 1647. He married Anna Elliot.—[Sasine 21st May 1689.] He had three daughters, but no sons.

THOMAS MAXWELL of Baltersan, married Helen   . He infeft in Baltersan, 29th January 1647, on Disposition from father, registered at Dumfries, 25th May 1719.

ELIZABETH MAXWELL, married Robert Eliot of Lariston.—[Particular Register, Sasine 8th Nov. 1689.]

JANET MAXWELL, married Dugald Maxwell, youngest son of Sir Patrick Maxwell of Newark.—[Gen. Reg. Sas., 14th Aug. 1667, Crown charter, 2d Dec. 1668.]

ESTHER MAXWELL, married Robert Maxwell of Killilung. Contract, 19th April 1682, registered in Books of Session, 16th June 1710.

JOHN MAXWELL of Baltersan, married, 1st, Agnes, daughter of Alexander Fergusson of Isle—[Particular Register, Sasine 29th October 1685]; and 2dly, Mary, daughter of John Maxwell of Milton, relict of Patrick M'Lellan of Collin.—[Sasine 30th July 1690.] By her he had no family, and he had no sons by the first wife.—[Disposition of Baltersan by John Maxwell, with consent of Mary Maxwell, his wife, to Robert Lauder, writer, Dumfries, dated 11th October 1708, registered at Dumfries, 25th May 1719.]

THOMAS MAXWELL of Crofts. [Sasine 6th Oct. 1681.] He married Janet Taylor [Sasine in her favour 6th Oct. 1681]. Infeft in Blairinnie on 29th Jan. 1694, and in Drumrash 28th Feb. 1716.

WILLIAM MAXWELL of Blairinnie. [Sasine 18th July 1684. Retour of Thomas Maxwell of Drumpark, as heir to his uncle William, 15th Jan. 1741.]

GEORGE MAXWELL of Fell, on disposition from his father, with consent of Thomas of Crofts, his brother. [Sasine 26th April 1692.] He afterwards acquired Glenarm.

JAN MAXW married Hamil younge Auchenr [Sasine Nov. 1

JANET, married Charles Murray of Barnhourie, who took the name of Maxwell of Cowhill.

DUGALD MAXWELL. [Crown charter in Cowhill 12th Feb. 1740.]

CHARLES MURRAY MAXWELL, married Miss Campbell of Skerrington.

MARGARET, who married Robert Maxwell of Portack.

LUCIE, who, in a disposition dated 9th Aug. 1710, recorded in Books of Session, 8th July 1713, styles herself youngest daughter, and one of three heirs-portioners of her father, Dugald Maxwell of Cowhill, and her grandfather, John Maxwell of Cowhill. On 9th June 1710, the three sisters were served heirs-portioners to their father.

SUSAN MAXW married Ferguss Halbi [Sasine April 1(

ELIZABETH MAXWELL, married Alexander Alves, contract dated 2d May 1704.—[Bond by her father, 27th March 1697, registered in Books of Session, 18th July 1698.]

ELLEN MAXWELL, married William Hamilton of Nether Corsock.—[Sasine 3d Oct. 1710.]

THOMAS MAXWELL, younger of Drumrash.--[Sasine 28th March 1720.] S heir to his father, Thomas, and to his uncle William, on 15th January He married, 1st, Agnes, eldest daughter of John Muirhead of Drumparl whom he had three sons; and, 2dly, Mary Rorison, by whom he ha family.—[Marriage contract dated 9th July 1742, recorded in Books of Ses with mutual settlement, 17th Nov. 1865.]

THOMAS MAXWELL of Drumpark, born 1st December 1720, served heir-general to his grandfather, John Muirhead of Drumpark, 18th May 1747. He married, Ellen, daughter of Francis Rogerson of Collin, contract dated 19th and 25th December 1744, recorded, with his "Testament," in Books of Session, 17th November 1865.

JOHN MAXWELL, born 20th July 1722.

ROBERT MAXWELL, copper merchant, Dum born 16th November 1726. He had daughters: Mrs. Peter Maxwell, Miss Maxwell, Mrs. Peyton, and Mrs. Nichol

THE MAXWELLS OF COWHILL, Etc.,—*continued.*

a

Row 1:

...MAS ...ELL ...park, ...ried ...ry ...ine.

HELEN MAXWELL, married William Litt in Fourmerkland, and had issue.

FRANCIS MAXWELL, writer and Town-clerk, Dumfries, married Ann, daughter of Archibald Malcolm, writer and Town-clerk, Dumfries. He had three sons and two daughters.

JOHN MAXWELL, merchant, Dumfries, married, 1st, on 8th February 1773, Dorothea Clark, and had issue, three sons and five daughters; viz., John, unmarried, born 29th October 1773; Helen, born 25th September 1774; Thomas, merchant, Dublin, unmarried, born 18th May 1776; Jean, born 8th March 1778; George, called Captain, unmarried, born 19th April 1780; Helen, born 6th February 1782; Euphemia, born 20th March 1784; Anna, born 1st March 1787, all of whom died without issue. He married, 2dly, Margaret Martin, by whom he had issue, one son and two daughters; viz., Dorothea (Mrs. Smith), born 2d October 1797; Margaret, born 29th April 1799; and William (died young, unmarried), born 26th July 1801.

ROBERT. ALEXANDER. Both died unmarried.

WILLIAM MAXWELL, merchant in Cork, died unmarried.

AGNES MAXWELL, married Kirkpatrick of Bogrie. Issue.

Row 2:

...s MAXWELL of Drum..., afterwards of Auch..uco, married Margaret, ..hter of John M'Vicar, ..hant, Dumfries. He ..Drumpark to his brother ..cis, and purchased ..enfranco. He died in .., leaving three sons and ..daughters.

FRANCIS MAXWELL of Drumpark, married, 1st, Charlotte Tomlinson, by whom he had one son and two daughters; and, 2dly, Catherine Lilias Adair Thomson, by whom he has one daughter.

ARCHIBALD MAXWELL of Threave, married Marion Boyd, second daughter of William Boyd of Marchhill.

FRANCIS MAXWELL of Gribton, married Margaret, eldest daughter of William Boyd of Marchhill.

ROBERT MAXWELL, merchant, Liverpool. Died unmarried.

CHRISTIAN MAXWELL, married Dr. Anthony Todd Thomson, of London University, and had issue, one son and two daughters; viz., Anna, who married John Morin of Allanton, and has issue; Catherine Lilias Adair, married Francis Maxwell of Drumpark, and has issue; Alexander, died unmarried.

HELEN MAXWELL, married John Swan. No issue.

Row 3:

...MAS ...ELL, ...hant, ...ool.— Note ...fra.] ...IN ...VELL, ...ied, ...872, ..t, third ..ter of E. A. ..hes, ..or of ..leniolen, ..vonshire. ..MES ..VELL.

MARGARET MAXWELL, married James Muter Turnbull, M.D., Liverpool. FRANCES MAXWELL.

THOMAS STEWART MAXWELL. Died unmarried.

JANE MAXWELL. Died unmarried. MARY MAXWELL. Married Alexander Fleming, M.D., Birmingham. AMY MAXWELL, of second marriage. Born 1854.

WILLIAM MAXWELL. FRANCIS MAXWELL. Both died unmarried.

ANNE MAXWELL. Married Samuel Sandbach of Handley, Co. Chester, and has issue. MARGARET MAXWELL. Married the Rev. Gilbert Sandbach, and has issue.

ROBERT MAXWELL. Married Maria Emma, daughter of John Pascoe Grenfell, Admiral in the Brazilian Navy, and has issue three sons and four daughters.

ARCHIBALD MAXWELL. Married Eliza, daughter of Robert Pacy, merchant, Rio de Janeiro, and has issue. THOMAS MAXWELL. Unmarried. JAMES MAXWELL. Married Ellen Elizabeth Johnson, who died 1867. No issue.

MARGARET MAXWELL. Married John Walker, Writer to the Signet, and has issue, three daughters— Margaret-Maxwell, Eleanor, and Eliza-Anne.

FRANCIS MAXWELL of Gribton. Married, 1st, Isabella Gertrude, daughter of Mark Sprot of Stewart of Southwick, by whom he had a daughter, Ethel; and 2ndly, Adelaide Louisa, daughter of Admiral James Hay of Belton, by whom he has one son, Francis, and two daughters, Mary-Hay and Adelaide Louisa.

ANNE MAXWELL. Unmarried. ELIZA MAXWELL. Died young.

NOTE A.—On 2d October 1865, The Lord Lyon of Scotland matriculated the arms of Thomas Maxwell as ninth of lineal descent from, and male representative of, Sir John Maxwell of Cowhill, viz. :—

Argent, a saltire sable, in base a holly leaf vert.

Crest: A stag, proper, attired of twelve tynes argent, lodged before a holly bush, also proper.

Motto above: REVIRESCO.

IX.—THE MAXWELLS OF BROOMHOLM,
PARISH OF LANGHOLM AND COUNTY OF DUMFRIES.

JOHN MAXWELL, first of Broomholm, was great-grandson of Robert Maxwell, second son of John, third Lord Maxwell, who died in 1484. Married Elizabeth Scott of Hartwood.—[Disposition of Arkinholm, 4th February 1628.] They had

JOHN MAXWELL, second of Broomholm, who married Jean Scott of Arkleton, contract dated 31st July 1640. They had

JOHN MAXWELL, third of Broomholm, who married Mary, daughter of William Maxwell of Springkell.—[Disposition, 2d September 1684.] Living 1723. They had

WILLIAM MAXWELL, fourth of Broomholm, who married Agnes Scott of Wool, marriage contract dated 2d July 1725. They had

PATRICK MAXWELL, second son, 1723.

JOHN MAXWELL, fifth of Broomholm, who married Wilhelmina Malcolm.—[Precept of Clare Constat. 13th August 1754.] Living 1796. They had a number of sons, who were in the service of the Hon. East India Company, and in commercial employments. Most of these sons predeceased their father, who died in 1806. Three sons who survived him were

GEORGE MAXWELL, sixth of Broomholm, Captain, R.N. He was served heir to his father in Broomholm, on 12th August 1806. He entailed Broomholm by entail, dated 28th April 1813, and relative nomination of heirs, 2d March 1825, and died, on 26th April 1833, without issue.

DAVID MAXWELL, seventh of Broomholm, second surviving son, Captain in the Dumfriesshire Militia: served heir of his brother, George, in Broomholm. Married Anne Park, and had issue—several sons and daughters. Died on 24th June 1835.

CHARLES MAXWELL, doctor of medicine. He married Jane Jardine, and had issue. He died in 1845. Of his children, only one daughter, Jane, now survives. His son,

DAVID MAXWELL, eldest son, and younger of Broomholm. Married, in 1817, Elizabeth, daughter of the Reverend John Laurie, minister of Ewes, and had issue—one son, George, and a daughter, Maria Anne. David Maxwell predeceased his father, on 6th January 1820.

CHARLES MAXWELL, junior, died in India, in the Hon. E. I. Co.'s medical service. He left one son,

GEORGE MAXWELL, eighth of Broomholm. Succeeded his grandfather in Broomholm in 1835. Married, in 1840, Charlotte, daughter of John William Ardiel, LL.D., of the Irish Bar. Issue, one son and two daughters.

MARIA ANNE MAXWELL.

MARLEY MAXWELL.

DAVID ARDIEL MAXWELL, younger of Broomholm.

ELIZABETH MAXWELL, born 1842.

CHARLOTTE DELIA MAXWELL, born 1843.

ARMORIAL BEARINGS: Quarterly 1st argent, on a saltire sable a crescent, or; 2nd argent, a lion rampant, azure, armed and langued, gules, for CRICHTON, EARL OF CAITHNESS; 3rd as the 2nd, and 4th as the 1st.

Crest: A hart at full speed, proper.

Motto above: VIRTUTEM SIC ET CULPAM.

Motto below the shield: PETO AC FUGIO.

As matriculated in the Lyon Court by John Maxwell of Broomholm, on 19th April 1759.

X.—THE MAXWELLS OF TINWALD IN THE COUNTY OF DUMFRIES,
AND OF MONREITH IN THE COUNTY OF WIGTON.

I.—SIR EDWARD MAXWELL, first of the Maxwells of Tinwald. He was the second son of Herbert, first Lord Maxwell; married Margaret Douglas, and had by her a son.—[History of the Maxwell Family, etc.]

II.—EDWARD MAXWELL of Tinwald. Edward Maxwell married, before 8th May 1455, Margaret, one of the four daughters and heirs-portioners of Henry Munduele of Tinwald; and on that date Margaret, as his wife, was infefted in the fourth part of the lands of Tinwald. Edward Maxwell afterwards acquired the remaining three-fourth parts of these lands—one on 18th January 1481, another on 1st November 1483, and also the other fourth part. On 18th January 1481 he acquired the lands of the barony of Monreith, on the resignation of Alexander Conynghame of Aikhead and Janet Knox, his spouse.—[Monreith Charter-chest.] By his wife, Margaret, he had a son.—[Printed Inventory of Maxwell Muniments, pp. 5, 8, Nos. 24 and 42.]

III.—HERBERT MAXWELL, younger of Tinwald. On 1st November 1483, Robert Boyd of Arneil renounced to Herbert and his father Edward all right which he had in the lands of Tinwald, the Temple lands of Dalgarnock, and others.—[Ibid. p. 8, No. 42.] Herbert predeceased his father before 3d November 1495. His wife's name has not been ascertained. He left two sons.

IV.—1. EDWARD MAXWELL of Tinwald, who succeeded his grandfather. In sasine of John Maxwell of Pollok, dated 3d November 1495, this Edward is described as grandson and heir-apparent of Edward Maxwell of Tinwald.—[Pollok Book, vol. i. p. 217.] He died before the year 1518, leaving a son.

IV.—2. WILLIAM MAXWELL, who was tutor to his nephew, Edward Maxwell of Tinwald. He is mentioned under this designation as one of the arbiters in a decreet of division of debateable lands between Carnsalloch and some lands belonging to the burgh of Dumfries, dated 12th January 1518.—[Decreet at Kenmure and in burgh of Dumfries.] He possessed the lands of Blairbuie, part of Monreith, and is hence styled William Maxwell of Blairbuie [Drumlanrig Inventory]; and on 30th May 1542 he received a charter of the Temple lands of Dalgarno [ibid.]. He had two sons.

V.—EDWARD, who succeeded him, and whose uncle, William, was tutor to him during his minority, in 1518. He died c. 1540, leaving two daughters.

V.—EDWARD, who in 1522 possessed the church lands of Tinwald, and married his cousin, Elizabeth Maxwell, eldest daughter of Edward Maxwell of Tinwald. He died before 1566.

MR. HERBERT MAXWELL. He also married his cousin, Margaret Maxwell, younger daughter of Edward Maxwell of Tinwald, in August 1541. They obtained a dispensation for their marriage, being related in the second and third degrees of consanguinity.—[Monreith Charter-chest.]

TINWALD LINE.

MONREITH LINE.

VI.—ELIZABETH MAXWELL, Lady Tinwald. She was infefted in the half of the lands of Tinwald on 29th October 1540, and in half of the lands of Monreith on 7th April 1541, and by arrangements afterwards made, she received as her portion the whole lands of Tinwald. She married, first, her cousin, Edward Maxwell, son of William Maxwell, tutor of Tinwald; and secondly, before 1566, Sir Robert Maxwell of Dinwoodie, without issue. By the former, she had three sons.

MARGARET MAXWELL, Lady Monreith, in parish of Kirkmaiden, now united to Glasserton. She was infefted in the half of Tinwald on 29th October 1540, and in half of Monreith on 7th April 1541. By a subsequent arrangement she received Monreith as her portion. She resigned Monreith into the hands of the Crown for new infeftment to Lord Maxwell.—[Monreith Charters.] She married, first, as above stated, her cousin, Mr. Herbert Maxwell; and secondly, George Maxwell, burgess of Dumfries. By her first husband she had one son, John. By her second husband she had Robert of Garrerie and Edward.

VII.—EDWARD MAXWELL of Tinwald. In 1546 his aunt, Margaret Maxwell, Lady Monreith, destined her lands to him, failing her son John of her first marriage. In the deed of settlement he is styled eldest son of Edward Maxwell of Tinwald. He had a son.

JAMES MAXWELL of Tinwald was served heir to Edward Maxwell of Tinwald, "abavi ex parte matris," and to Sir Edward Maxwell of Tinwald, "attavi ex parte matris," on 2d June 1630.—[Inquis. Gen. 1680 and 1681.] Married Agnes, one of three daughters and heirs-portioners of Robert Maxwell of Dinwoodie, and had a son.

HERBERT MAXWELL of Templand. He was also proprietor of Shaws of Tinwald, and Kilbean, and was frequently designated from these lands. He was chamberlain to Robert Earl of Nithsdale c. 1628. He married Sarah Kirkpatrick, and had a son.

JOHN MAXWELL of Monreith. He married Agnes MacCulloch, and had three sons—John, Robert, and Gavin. Died before 1605.—[Maxwell Muniments, No. 457.]

VIII.—WILLIAM MAXWELL of Tinwald. On 13th August 1589, as heir-apparent of Tinwald, he received a Crown-charter of Bracoch, and was infeft therein 25th September the same year. He married Nicholas, daughter of John Charteris of Amisfield.

ROBERT MAXWELL of Tinwald, who was served heir to his father on 26th November 1647. He married Elizabeth, daughter of Sir Robert Grierson of Lag, and had a son. He was killed in 1651.

JOHN MAXWELL of Templand, mentioned as such in a discharge to John Lord Herries, 12th May 1623. He married Jean Stirling of Friars Carse, and had

JOHN MAXWELL. On 20th October 1605 he was infefted as heir of John Maxwell, who was son and heir of Margaret Maxwell, Lady of Monreith. He died in January 1630. He married Catherine Maxwell of Garrain, and had

a   b   c   d

THE MAXWELLS OF TINWALD IN THE COUNTY OF DUMFRIES, AND
OF MONREITH IN THE COUNTY OF WIGTON--*continued.*

IX.—JAMES MAXWELL of Tinwald, who received from his brother Robert a charter of the lands of Breoch on 24th July 1623. He died before June 1630.

ROBERT MAXWELL received a Crown-charter of Breoch on 19th June 1623. He died before June 1630, when his grand-uncle, James, expede services to his ancestors.

ROBERT MAXWELL of Tinwald, who was served heir to his father on 26th May 1675. He married, 1st, Janet, daughter of Maxwell of Carnsalloch, by whom he had a child, who died young; and 2dly, Jean, daughter of Sir Robert Dalzell of Glenae, without issue, and was succeeded in Tinwald by his cousin, Francis Maxwell of Friars Carse.

HERBERT MAXWELL of Friars Carse. He got these lands from his mother in 1643. He had a son and a daughter.

JOHN MAXWELL, who received charters of certain lands, 29th September 1643.

WILLIAM MAXWELL, who, on 5th February 1630, was infefted as heir of his father. He married, in 1632, Margaret, daughter of John MacCulloch of Myreton. He died in 1670. He had two sons.

JOHN MAXWELL of Friars Carse. He married, in 1689, Catherine Herries of Mabie. He died in the Abbey, in March 1705.

ANNA MAXWELL, who married Mr. James Wilson, minister of Colvend.—[Retour, 10th November 1724.] Served heir to her brother John, of Carse, her father, Herbert, her grandfather, John, and great-grandfather, Herbert. She disponed Friars Carse to her nephew John, on 16th April 1737.

FRANCIS MAXWELL, succeeded his cousin, Robert Maxwell of Tinwald, and sold Tinwald in 1712. He died before 16th April 1737.

JOHN MAXWELL, younger son. His aunt Anna disponed to him the estate of Friars Carse on 16th April 1737. He and his aunt Anna, by disposition dated 22d July and 8th August 1737, disponed said estate to Robert Riddell, younger of Glenriddell.

JOHN MAXWELL, younger of Monreith. He was engaged in the rising at Pentland, for which he was outlawed. He acquired the superiority of Monreith from the Earl of Nithsdale; and he also obtained from the Protector a Charter of Erection of the Barony of Monreith. He married, in 1656, Margaret, daughter of Sir Andrew Agnew of Lochnaw. He died in Ireland in 1668.

X.—SIR WILLIAM MAXWELL of Monreith, created a Baronet of Nova Scotia on 8th January 1681. He acquired much property, including the lands and half barony of Mochrum Loch, and was hence designated William Maxwell of Loch until his succession to his nephew. He purchased Myreton in 1684. He obtained a reversal of the forfeiture passed against his brother, John, in favour of his nephew, William, who was then an infant, and at the same time he procured a tutory-dative to himself. He, with Sir Andrew Agnew of Lochnaw, represented Wigtonshire in the first Parliament of Charles the Second, 1667-1674. He married, first, in October 1668, Johanna, daughter of Patrick M'Dowall of Logan; and secondly, Elizabeth, daughter of Sir Thomas Hay of Park. He died in April 1709. He had three sons and five daughters.

MARY, married to Vans of Barnbarroch.

WILLIAM MAXWELL of Monreith, died a minor, 1671-2, unmarried.

AGNES, married Robert Gordon, younger of Shirmers: served heir of her grandfather, 2d June 1681.

WILLIAM, his eldest son, predeceased him, having been accidentally drowned in the Nith in May 1707.

XI.—SIR ALEXANDER, his second son, succeeded him as second Baronet. He was infefted in Monreith on 21st June 1711; was member for the Wigton District of Burghs in 1715; and he married, on 29th December 1711, Lady Jean Montgomerie, daughter of Alexander, ninth Earl of Eglinton. Died 23d May 1730.

JOHN, to whom he left Ardwell and Killassar. He married Mary MacGhie, and had a son, William, who succeeded him in these estates, and had seventeen children.

ISOBEL, married William Stewart of Castle-Stewart.

ELIZABETH, married Andrew Heron of Bargaly.

MARY, married Sir Thomas Hay of Park.

JOAN. AGNES. Both died unmarried.

XII.—SIR WILLIAM succeeded his father as third Baronet. He was of the military profession, and served some time in the army. He married Magdalene, daughter of Blair of Blair, and dying 22d August 1771, was succeeded by his son.

ALEXANDER, his second son, predeceased his father.

JAMES, third son, baptised 1st August 1724, was a major in the army. He married Elizabeth, daughter of William Maxwell of Ardwell. Issue —six sons and three daughters. The six sons were—(1.) Admiral Sir Murray Maxwell, K.C.B., father of the present Admiral John M.; (2.) Keith, Capt. R.N., died unmarried; (3.) John, Capt. R.N., died unmarried; (4.) Montgomerie, Col. 36th; (5.) Stewart, Major, Royal Artillery; (6.) Eglinton, of the East India Company's Naval Service.

MARGARET, married Carruthers of Dormont.

ELIZABETH, married Balfour of Powmill. **CATHERINE,** married William Booth.

SUSAN, married Captain Alexander Hay, younger of Park.

THE MAXWELLS OF MONREITH, IN THE COUNTY OF WIGTON—*continued.*

XIII.—SIR WILLIAM, fourth Baronet. He was Major of the West Lowland Fencibles. He married Katherine, daughter and heir of David Blair of Adamtoun, in Ayrshire. He sold Adamtoun, and re-purchased much of the old family estate sold by his father. He died in February 1812.

HAMILTON, was a distinguished officer in the army, and died unmarried in India in 1800.

DUNBAR, was an officer in the Royal Navy, and died unmarried in 1775.

CATHERINE, married, in 1767, John Fordyce of Aytoun, Berwickshire.

JANE, married Alexander, fourth Duke of Gordon.

EGLANTINE, married Sir Thomas Wallace of Craigie, Baronet.

XIV.—SIR WILLIAM, fifth Baronet, was born 5th March 1779. He was Colonel of the 26th Cameronians, served in the Peninsula, lost an arm, and was wounded in the side by a bullet at Corunna, and was wounded in the leg at the siege of Flushing. He married, 23d April 1803, Catherine, daughter of John Fordyce of Aytoun. He died, 22d August 1838.

ALEXANDER, Major, 23d Light Dragoons, predeceased his father, unmarried.

HAMILTON, Captain, 42d Highlanders, married, in 1813, Mary, daughter of Sir Robert Grierson of Lag. Issue—three sons, all married, and four daughters, all unmarried. He died 14th December 1850.

ANNE, married, in 1799, William Murray of Touchadam and Polmaise.

MADELINE, married James du Pre of Wilton Park, Bucks. Issue—three sons and eight daughters.

JANE, married, in 1802, John Maitland of Freugh, and had issue.

CHARLOTTE. MARY. SUSAN. All these three died unmarried.

XV.—SIR WILLIAM, sixth and present Baronet. He was born at Monreith on 2d October 1805. Adopted the military profession, was a captain in the army, and Lieutenant-Colonel Commandant of the Galloway Rifle Militia. He married, in 1833, Helenora, daughter of Sir Michael Shaw Stewart, fifth Baronet of Greenock and Blackhall, and has had five sons and five daughters.

EUSTACE, born 7th February 1819, of Royal Navy; died 1856, unmarried.

EDWARD-HERBERT, born 29th July, 1822, Colonel of the 88th Connaught Rangers, married Agnes, daughter of Admiral Hay of Belton.

CATHERINE ANN married Hugh Hathorn of Castlewigg, who predeceased her, s.p.

JANE ELIZABETH NORA, died, unmarried, 1846.

EGLANTINE AMABEL, died, unmarried, in 1830.

LOUISA CORNWALLIS, married, in 1833, Caledon George du Pre of Wilton Park, M.P. for Bucks.

CHARLOTTE QUEENSBERRY, married Fillippo Calandra de Rocolino.

GEORGINA GORDON, died, unmarried, in 1858.

XVI.—WILLIAM, died in infancy, 1834. WILLIAM, died in childhood, 1845. MICHAEL STEWART, died 1844.

HERBERT EUSTACE, born 8th January 1845, married, in 1869, Mary, elder daughter of Henry Fletcher Campbell of Boquhan, and has a son, William, born in 1869, and a daughter, Ann Christian, born in 1871.

EDWARD ADOLPHUS SEYMOUR, born 1849, died 1866.

CATHERINE SHAW STEWART.

ANNE MURRAY, married, in 1856, R. H. Johnston Stewart of Physgill.

ALLAN EGLANTINE.

ELEANORA LOUISA.

MARY, died in 1852.

ARMORIAL BEARINGS: Argent, an eagle with two heads, displayed, sable, beaked and membered, gules; on the breast, an escutcheon of the first, charged with a saltire of the second, surcharged in the centre with a hurcheon, or, all within a bordure gules.

Crest: An eagle, rising, proper; beaked and membered, gules.

Supporters: Two stags, proper.

Motto: REVIRESCO.

XI.—THE MAXWELLS OF KIRKCONNELL, IN THE PARISH OF TROQUEER, AND STEWARTRY OF KIRKCUDBRIGHT.

I.—AYMER DE MAXWELL, second son of Sir Herbert Maxwell of Maxwell and Carlaverock, was ancestor of the Maxwells of Kirkconnell. As lord of Kirkconnell he obtained a perambulation of the marches of Kirkconnell and the lands of Airdes.—[Instrument dated 11th July 1448.] He married, about the year 1430, Janet de Kirkconnell, the heiress of the ancient family of Kirkconnell. Aymer de Maxwell and Janet his wife received a Crown charter of resignation and confirmation of their lands of Kirkconnell, as they had belonged to the predecessors of Janet, dated 20th March 1456; and on 13th November 1461 he granted to George Nelson of Maidenpap a feu of part of the estate of Kelton. The date of the death of neither of them has been ascertained. They had a son.

II.—HERBERT MAXWELL of Kirkconnell, who possessed Auchenfad after his marriage and during his father's lifetime. It is not known whom he married, and the date of his death is also unknown. He had two sons.

III. — MAXWELL of Kirkconnell, whose Christian name has not been ascertained, and who predeceased his father. He had two daughters.

JOHN MAXWELL of Auchenfad, in 1461, who with his son, Herbert, were witnesses to the infeftment of Elizabeth Maxwell, the niece of John, on 5th November 1492.

IV.—ELISABETH MAXWELL, who succeeded her grandfather. On a precept from the Crown, directing sasine to be given her as heir of her grandfather, Herbert Maxwell of Kirkconnell and Kelton, she was infefted in the lands of Kelton, in the shire of Dumfries, on 5th November 1492. John Maxwell, her uncle, and Herbert Maxwell, son of John, were witnesses to her infeftment. She died without issue, and was succeeded by her nephew, Herbert.

AGNES, married Thomas Maxwell, second son of Robert, second Lord Maxwell, and had a son,

V.—HERBERT MAXWELL of Kirkconnell, who was, on precept from the Crown, infefted in the lands of Kirkconnell and Kelton, as heir of his aunt, Elisabeth, on 12th April 1495. He was at the affray between his chief, John Lord Maxwell, and Lord Crichton of Sanquhar, 30th July 1508, and he obtained a general remission from the Crown on 17th October 1508. The name of his first wife has not been ascertained, but by her he had four sons. He married, secondly, before 4th July 1517, Euphemia Lindsay, whose issue, if any, is unknown. He died in the end of the reign of King James the Fifth, and was succeeded by his grandson.

VI.—ROBERT MAXWELL of Auchenfad, eldest son of Herbert Maxwell of Kirkconnell, received from his father a charter of the lands of Kelton, 4th July 1517, and of Auchenfad on 16th August 1519. He married Janet Crichton, and predeceased his father, leaving two sons.

JOHN MAXWELL.

WILLIAM MAXWELL, who was in the household of Mary of Guise, and afterwards in a regiment of Scots men at arms in service of the French King. On 16th February 1557 he received a grant of Little Airds. He had a son.

EDWARD. An Edward Maxwell, formerly of Kirkconnell, had the liferent of that estate reserved to him in the Retour of John Maxwell, 8th July 1574 (infra).

VII.—HERBERT MAXWELL of Kirkconnell. On 28th December 1548 he was infefted in the lands of Kirkconnell and Kelton, as heir of his grandfather, Herbert; and on 22d January 1548-9 he received a charter of Auchenfad. On 2d May 1553, he granted to his brother, John, a liferent charter of Auchenfad. He married Janet Maxwell, and had one son and three daughters. He died before 1560, survived by his wife, who was living in 1574.

JOHN MAXWELL, tutor of Kirkconnell, during the minority of Bernard, his nephew. He was infefted in the lands of Kirkconnell and Kelton, according to the disposition mentioned, under his nephew, on 7th May 1571. His wife's name has not been ascertained. He died in August 1573.—[Confirmation of his will on 8th June 1583. Edin. Testaments.]

WILLIAM, who succeeded him in these lands, and had

JAMES MAXWELL, M.A., born in 1581, who wrote his autobiography and several works on religion and church history.

VIII.—BERNARD MAXWELL of Kirkconnell, succeeded his father in his minority. He was infefted in Kirkconnell on 21st April 1571, and in Kelton on the 30th of the same month. On 6th May 1571, he disponed the lands of Kirkconnell and Kelton to his uncle, John. He died on 16th March 1579.—[Edin. Testaments, 23d February 1580, vol. 8.]

AGNES.
CATHERINE. She was executor to her brother Bernard in 1579.
MARGARET. All living on 17th August 1567.

JOHN MAXWELL of Kirkconnell, who in his minority succeeded him. He was served heir-male to his father, on 8th July 1574, in the lands of Kirkconnell; and he was infefted therein on 8th October following. On 20th January 1589 he gave sasine of the lands of Kelton to Catherine and Nicholas, daughters and heirs of John Maxwell of Littlebar. He appears to have married a Murray of Cockpoole, and he had five sons. He died after 1st October 1614.

THOMAS MAXWELL, ancestor of the Maxwells of Barncleuch. Vide Pedigree of Barncleuch.

IX.—HERBERT MAXWELL of Kirkconnell, succeeded his father in the family estates, when he was one of the Equerries to King James VI., from whom he received a pension of £200 for life. On 29th June 1614, he received a grant of Little Airds, and on 28th August 1616 he received a charter of Kirkconnell and others. He died in October 1637, leaving

JOHN MAXWELL of Whitehill and Millhill, 1638, in parish of Troqueer, in wadset. Sir Richard Murray of Cockpoole is mentioned as his uncle in 1637.

JAMES, was a lawyer. THOMAS. Living in 1638.

ALEXANDER. Living 1642.

GEORGE. Living 1623.

X.—JOHN MAXWELL of Kirkconnell, was retoured heir to his father, Herbert, on 19th December 1638, in the lands of Kirkconnell, with salmon fishings in the water of Nith, etc., and he was infefted therein on 31st January 1639. He married, in 1642, Agnes, daughter of Stephen Laurie of Maxwelltown. Her tocher was the lands of Arbigland in wadset for 10,000 merks. He got into difficulties soon after his marriage, but the estate was preserved by the prudent management of his wife. He died in or before the year 1679, survived by his wife. They had

EDWARD. GEORGE. ROBERT.

BARBARA MAXWELL, Lady Mabie in 1623.

MARIA, contracted in marriage to Major Robert Scott of Haining in 1649.

HERBERT MAXWELL, an illegitimate son.

THE MAXWELLS OF KIRKCONNELL,—*continued*.

A

XI.—JAMES MAXWELL of Kirkconnell, succeeded his father about the year 1679. On 26th November 1688, Lady Maxwelltoun conveyed several mortgages or debts on the Kirkconnell estates, which she had acquired during his father's difficulties, and he himself afterwards cleared off others. In October 1686 his brother, Herbert Maxwell, a priest of the Society of Jesus, was appointed chaplain to John Earl of Melfort, secretary of King James VII., and about the same time this Laird was appointed one of the Receivers-General of Customs, his commission being dated 22d October 1688. He married, in 1672, Elizabeth, only daughter of Alexander Durham of Berwick, son of Sir John Durham of Duntarvie. He died in or before 28th August 1699, leaving

WILLIAM.
HERBERT.
STEPHEN, *s.p.*
Born 1656.
Died 10th August 1713.
"A man of rare prudence."

EUPHEMIA, married to the Laird of Conheath. MARION.

AGNES, married Edmund, eldest son of William Brown of Nunton.

XII.—JAMES MAXWELL of Kirkconnell, who was educated at Douay, was served heir-general to his father on 21st December 1699. He and the Earl of Nithsdale were cited to appear before the Justiciary Court in Edinburgh, on 2d February 1704, to answer for contravening the Acts of Parliament against hearing mass, and harbouring and concealing Jesuits and priests, etc. He died on 7th August 1705, *s.p.*, and was succeeded by his brother William.

WILLIAM MAXWELL of Kirkconnell was, like his brother James, whom he succeeded, educated at Douay, from which he returned in 1696. He was served heir to his brother James on 14th February 1706; and on 29th April following he married Janet, eldest daughter of George Maxwell of Carnsalloch. On 6th May 1708 he made a disposition of his estates, 1st, to himself; 2d, to his heirs-male; 3rd, to his heirs-female; 4th, to his second brother, Alexander, and his heirs-male, and others therein mentioned. He afterwards executed various other deeds, and died on 13th April 1746, and was buried at New Abbey. He had

ALEXANDER. STEPHEN AQUATIAS MAXWELL, *s.p.* He was born 1st June 1688, and died 28th November 1734.

AGNES. ELIZABETH, died Sept. 3, 1719.

XIII.—JAMES MAXWELL of Kirkconnell, commenced his studies at Douay College on 21st August 1721, and after concluding a course of Philosophy he returned to Scotland in 1728. He was infefted in the lands of Kirkconnell on 22d April 1734; and he received a Crown charter of the same on 26th January 1738. He took part in the insurrection of 1745, and became a confidential officer in the Prince's service. After the battle of Culloden he escaped to France, and resided there for several years, where he wrote a Narrative of the rebellion in 1745, printed for the Maitland Club in 1841. He returned to Scotland in 1750, and built, with bricks made on the property, the modern portion of the front of Kirkconnell house. The same year he sold Carnsalloch, and purchased Mabie. There is an oil portrait of this laird at Kirkconnell. He married, in 1758, Mary, youngest daughter of Thomas Riddell of Swinburne Castle, and died 23d July 1762, aged 54 years.

GEORGE, *s.p.*
WILLIAM.
ALBERT.

ELIZABETH, the eldest, married, before 1730, William Maxwell of Munches.

AGNES.
JANET.
MARY.
MARGARET.
MARION, married, in 1755, John Menzies of Pitfoddels, and had issue.

XIV.—JAMES MAXWELL of Kirkconnell, born in 1759. He went to Dinant College in 1770. Was served heir to his father on 16th November 1764, and by precept from the Crown was infefted in Kirkconnell on 19th April 1765. He married, 1st, Clementina Elizabeth Frances, only daughter of Simon Scrope, of Danby, Yorkshire. She died on 10th March 1815, *s.p.* He married, 2dly, Dorothy, daughter of William Witham, solicitor, Gray's Inn, London. The marriage-contract is dated 29th August 1817. There is an oil portrait of this laird, and also a miniature, at Kirkconnell. He died on 5th February 1827, and was buried in New Abbey. His only child and heiress is

WILLIAM, born 30th August 1760, with his brother Thomas, went to the New College of the Jesuits at Dinant, where they arrived on 3d September 1771. He was present in arms as one of the National Guard on 21st January 1793, when Louis XVI. was beheaded. He became one of the most eminent physicians in Scotland. He died at Edinburgh, on 13th October 1834.

THOMAS, who died 1st June 1792, aged 31 years, and was buried at New Abbey.

XV.—DOROTHY-MARY MAXWELL of Kirkconnell, who, on 27th July 1827, was served heir of tailzie and provision to her father, James Maxwell of Kirkconnell. On 17th April 1844 she married her cousin, Robert Shawe James Witham, now called Robert Maxwell Witham of Kirkconnell, eldest surviving son of William Witham of Gray's Inn, London, and has had issue, six sons and three daughters.

JAMES ROBERT, born 1st, died 5th May 1845.	JAMES-KIRKCONNELL. THOMAS. Twins, born on 4th Oct. 1848.	WILLIAM-HERBERT, born on 6th February 1851.	ROBERT-BERNARD, born on 8th August 1856.	AYMER RICHARD HENRY, born on 6th July 1861.	FRANCES-MARY.	JANET, died in infancy, in 1853.	DOROTHY-MAUD MARY.

ARMORIAL BEARINGS: Quarterly, 1st and 4th argent, an eagle displayed, sable, beaked and membered, gules; and on its breast an escutcheon of the first, charged with a saltire of the second, for MAXWELL: 2nd and 3rd azure, two crosiers in saltire adorsè, and in chief a mitre, or, for Kirkconnell of that Ilk.

Crest: A demi-eagle, proper.

Motto: SPERO MELIORA.

XII.—THE MAXWELLS OF BARNCLEUCH,
IN THE PARISH OF IRONGRAY AND STEWARTRY OF KIRKCUDBRIGHT.

THOMAS MAXWELL, a younger son of John Maxwell, who was tutor of Kirkconnell during the minority of his nephew, Bernard, was ancestor of the Maxwells of Barncleuch. In an Instrument of Sasine, dated 9th July 1606, he is styled "brother-german to John Maxwell of Kelton," a designation which can refer only to John Maxwell, eldest son of the tutor, who was served heir to him on 8th July 1574, and who died about 1619. Thomas Maxwell was a merchant burgess of Dumfries, and married, 1st, Agnes, daughter of James Rig, notary in Dumfries.—[Sasine 9th July 1606.] He married, 2dly, Isabel Corson, by whom he had

JOHN MAXWELL of Barncleuch, who was served heir to him on 6th January 1642. He married, contract dated 21st October 1637, Agnes Irving, who survived him, and married, 2dly, Robert Maxwell of Carnsalloch. John Maxwell and Agnes Irving had an only son,

JOHN MAXWELL of Barncleuch. He was served heir to his grandfather on 11th February 1665. He was nominated Provost of Dumfries in 1686. He married, on 15th June 1665, Margaret, daughter of John Irving of Friars Carse, Provost of Dumfries, and Elizabeth Crichton, his wife, who was a daughter of Sir Robert Crichton of Ryehill, brother of the Earl of Dumfries. On 28th September 1714, he was infeft in the lands of Friars Carse on Precept by John Laurie of Maxwell, who apprised these lands from John Irving. By Margaret Irving he had

| JOHN MAXWELL, first son, was born 13th August 1667. He died 3d October the same year. JOHN MAXWELL, second son, was born 31st July 1670, and died 25th December following. | JAMES MAXWELL, third son, was born 23d February 1673. He was served heir to his father, 10th November 1721. He married, 1st, Janet Carruthers, relict of Alexander Johnstone of Elshieshields, on 10th February 1704. She died 3d October 1707, and he married, 2dly, on 14th February 1716, Mary, eldest daughter of Dr. James Wellwood, and had by his first wife two sons, and by his second wife, four sons and eight daughters. He died in April 1748. | ROBERT, fourth son, was born 26th August 1679. He married, and had issue, in 1710. WILLIAM, fifth son, born 29th June 1681, died 30th September following. | JOHN, sixth son, born 22d August 1682. At Douay in 1709. WILLIAM, seventh son, was born 1st May 1685. In 1709, he was engaged to marry Anne Cardiff. ALEXANDER, eighth son, was born 27th December 1689, and died within three months. | AGNES, eldest daughter, was born 8th August 1666. ANNA-ELIZABETH, was born 30th December 1668. She married Colonel Rattray, a gentleman of the Bedchamber to King James VII. in France, and had issue. MARGARET, third daughter, was born 3d November 1671, and died 22d January 1673. | JANET, fourth daughter, was born 5th May 1674. MARIAN, fifth daughter, was born 17th May 1676. MARGARET, sixth daughter, died in 1679. | CHRISTIA[N] was born [4]th April 168[ ] She died April 178[ ] LUCIE, was bor[n] 7th Febru[ary] 1688, an[d] died 30t[h] March 16[ ] MARY, born 4th July 1691. |

| JOHN, first son, was born 7th June 1706, and died within six weeks. | JAMES, the second and only surviving son of the first marriage, was born on 25th September 1707, and succeeded his father in the family estates on 2d April 1748. He was served heir to him on 28th June following. On 8th March 1744, he and his father submitted all questions as to the possession of Friarscarse to the decision of James Ferguson, younger of Craigdarroch, and Captain William Maxwell of Carruchan, who decided that the Maxwells were bound to remove from the estate, and convey it to Mr. Riddell for £1500. He died unmarried, and was succeeded by his nephew, Wellwood Johnstone. | WELLWOOD, third son, was born 11th May 1721. On 6th October 1737, he was apprenticed to Thomas Gordon, surgeon, Dumfries. JOHN, fourth son, was born 16th July 1722. | CHARLES, fifth son, was born 30th January 1724. Living in 1742. WILLIAM, sixth son, was born 10th July 1727. | MARGARET, first daughter, born 26th October 1704. | BARBARA, second daughter, was born 21st November 1716. She married James Johnstone, brother to Thomas Johnstone of Clachrie, a cadet of the family of Westerhall, and had | ELIZABETH, third daughter, was born 11th December 1717. MARION, fourth daughter, was born 14th February 1719. She married George Wellburn, attorney in London. JANET, fifth daughter, was born 18th March 1720. | CHRISTIAN, six[th] daughter, was bo[rn] 28th February 17[ ] Died 23d May 17[ ] JANE, seventh daughter, was bo[rn] 4th October 172[ ] MARY, eighth daughter, was bo[rn] 15th April 173[ ] She married Ale[x]ander M'Goun [of] Smithstoun, with his consen[t] granted a discha[rge] to her brother James of Barn cleuch, 16th May 1720. |

| JAMES JOHN-STONE, born 27th March 1743. Died 2d February 1764. | JOHN JOHNSTONE, died at Dumfries, 30th December 1772.—[Letter from George Maxwell of Carruchan.] | WELLWOOD JOHNSTONE, who was educated as a surgeon, and practised, in 1772, in Calcutta. In terms of the settlements of his uncle, James Maxwell, he took the name of Maxwell, and became Wellwood Maxwell of Barncleuch. He married Catherine, daughter of John Maxwell of Terraughty. Of that marriage there was issue nine sons and four daughters. |

| JAMES, born 1780. Died 1782. Twin sons, born 1782. Died 1783. | JOHN, married his cousin, Clementina Maxwell of Munches, and had issue.— Vide separate Pedigrees of Munches and Terraughty. | WELLWOOD MAXWELL of the Grove, was born in 1785, and died in 1867. | ALEXANDER MAXWELL of Glengaber, was born in 1787, and died in 1867. | WILLIAM MAXWELL, merchant, Liverpool, was born in 1791. Alive 1873. | JAMES, born 1792. Died in November 1808. | GEORGE MAXWELL of Glenlee, born 1796. Died 1858. | AGNES, Mrs. Melville, born 1781. Died 1858. | MARY, Mrs. Hyslop, born 1789. Died 1840. | MARGARET, born 1790. Died 1798. | CATHERI[NE] Mrs. Da[ ] born 179[ ] Alive 1873. |

For the Armorial Bearings of Wellwood Herries Maxwell, Esq. of Barncleuch, *vide supra*, p. 588.

XIII.—THE MAXWELLS OF MUNCHES,

IN THE PARISH OF BUITTLE AND STEWARTRY OF KIRKCUDBRIGHT.

ALEXANDER MAXWELL of Logan, in the parish of Buittle. He was grandson of John Maxwell of Logan, who was a natural son of Robert, fifth Lord Maxwell. Alexander Maxwell had seven sons—Robert of Logan, John of Milton, Thomas of Carswadda, William of Mid-Kelton, George of Munches, Edward, and Alexander. He died about the year 1615.

GEORGE MAXWELL of Slognaw, in the parish of Kelton, the sixth son, acquired a wadset right to the lands of Munches on 3d May 1637, and was afterwards designated of Munches. He married, 1st, Margaret Macqueen—issue, a son, John; 2dly, contract dated 9th June 1655, Barbara, daughter of the then deceased James Maxwell of Tinwald and Agnes Maxwell, heiress of Dinwoodie, which estate was inherited by the descendants of this marriage. He had issue, a son and a daughter. He died in the end of 1683 or beginning of 1684.

WILLIAM MAXWELL of Mid-Kelton. He granted a disposition to his brother George, 24th August 1643.—[See also Commission in 1644.] He was a Protestant, and seems to have suffered death during the civil and religious contests of the times.—[See his Dying Declaration and his Testament, dated 29th July 1644.]

JOHN MAXWELL of Milton. He signed the Commission, 1644, and there are also letters from George Maxwell of Munches to his nephew, John of Milton, dated respectively 2d May and 26th November 1662, which prove these two Johns of Milton.

JOHN MAXWELL of Slognaw. Issue, two daughters. The elder married Francis Maxwell of Breoch, and the younger, Barbara, married Charles MacCartney of Halketleaths.

GEORGE MAXWELL, second of Munches, married, in October 1686, Agnes, second daughter of James Maxwell of Kirkblain. Of this marriage there were three sons and two daughters. He died 1728.

BARBARA MAXWELL, married, about the year 1680, Robert Maxwell of Gelston, afterwards Sir Robert Maxwell of Orchardton. Issue, three sons and two daughters.

WILLIAM MAXWELL, third of Munches. He was served heir-general to his father on 27th December 1728. He married, 1st, Agnes Brown of Bishopton, in 1721, and had by her two sons and three daughters. He married, 2dly, before 1730, Elizabeth, eldest daughter of William Maxwell of Kirkconnell, but by her he had no issue. He died at Munches, 6th January 1765, and was succeeded by

GEORGE. Living in 1700. Died young.

JAMES, the youngest son, was proprietor of Kirklebride and Kirkennan. He died in September 1755, s.p.

MARY, married, in 1727, Mr. James Brown, in Edinburgh. Of this marriage, it is said, there was a daughter, who married Gavin Brown of Bishopton, and had an only son, who was killed by a fall from his horse on his way from Dumfries to Milnhead.

BARBARA, married Captain William Maxwell, afterwards of Carruchan, eldest son, by a second marriage, of Alexander Maxwell of Terraughty, and left an only daughter.

ROBERT, died at Edinburgh, in the year 1747, vita patris, as is shown by an account of his deathbed and funeral expenses by Alexander Goldie, Writer to the Signet.

GEORGE MAXWELL, fourth of Munches, his only surviving son, who married, on 28th August 1776, Lucy, daughter of Sir Thomas Gage of Coldham, in the county of Suffolk, Baronet. Of this marriage there was no issue. He died at Fairgirth on Sunday, the 8th of September 1793, in consequence of a fall from his horse on the Friday preceding. He was succeeded by Agnes Maxwell, his only surviving sister.

AGNES MAXWELL of Munches, married, in February 1770 (as his second wife), John Maxwell of Terraughty. On the death of her brother, in September 1793, she succeeded to Munches. She expede, on 29th October 1793, a general service as heir to him. She died on 12th May 1809, aged 90 years, without issue. She previously conveyed Munches to her husband, and it is now inherited by Wellwood Herries Maxwell, Esq., M.P., eldest son of Mrs. Clementina Maxwell, the granddaughter of the said John Maxwell of Terraughty and Munches through his first wife.—[Vide Pedigree of the Maxwells of Terraughty and Munches.]

ANN was an Abbess in the Nunnery of York. She was alive in 1777, but died before 1809, s.p.

BETTY, the youngest daughter, died at Munches, unmarried, before 1809, s.p.

ANN MAXWELL, cousin and heir-at-law of Agnes Maxwell of Munches. Died in 1820 at a great age, s.p.

For the Armorial Bearings of Wellwood Herries Maxwell, Esq., now of Munches, vide supra, p. 588.

XIV.—THE MAXWELLS OF CARDONESS,
IN THE STEWARTRY OF KIRKCUDBRIGHT.

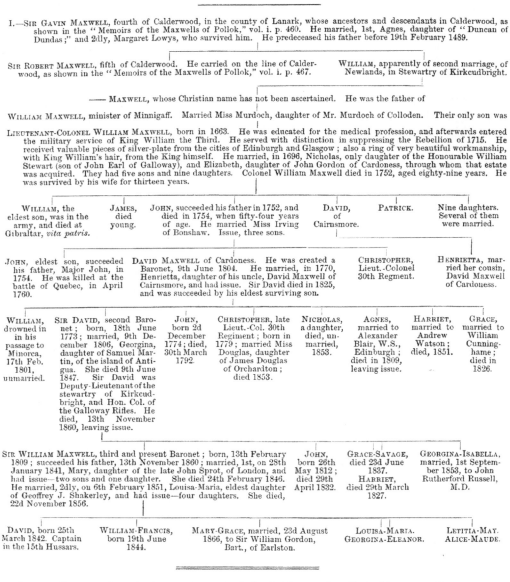

I.—Sir Gavin Maxwell, fourth of Calderwood, in the county of Lanark, whose ancestors and descendants in Calderwood, as shown in the "Memoirs of the Maxwells of Pollok," vol. i. p. 460. He married, 1st, Agnes, daughter of "Duncan of Dundas;" and 2dly, Margaret Lowys, who survived him. He predeceased his father before 19th February 1489.

Sir Robert Maxwell, fifth of Calderwood. He carried on the line of Calderwood, as shown in the "Memoirs of the Maxwells of Pollok," vol. i. p. 467.

William, apparently of second marriage, of Newlands, in Stewartry of Kirkcudbright.

—— Maxwell, whose Christian name has not been ascertained. He was the father of

William Maxwell, minister of Minnigaff. Married Miss Murdoch, daughter of Mr. Murdoch of Colloden. Their only son was

Lieutenant-Colonel William Maxwell, born in 1663. He was educated for the medical profession, and afterwards entered the military service of King William the Third. He served with distinction in suppressing the Rebellion of 1715. He received valuable pieces of silver-plate from the cities of Edinburgh and Glasgow; also a ring of very beautiful workmanship, with King William's hair, from the King himself. He married, in 1696, Nicholas, only daughter of the Honourable William Stewart (son of John Earl of Galloway), and Elizabeth, daughter of John Gordon of Cardoness, through whom that estate was acquired. They had five sons and nine daughters. Colonel William Maxwell died in 1752, aged eighty-nine years. He was survived by his wife for thirteen years.

| William, the eldest son, was in the army, and died at Gibraltar, vita patris. | James, died young. | John, succeeded his father in 1752, and died in 1754, when fifty-four years of age. He married Miss Irving of Bonshaw. Issue, three sons. | David, of Cairnsmore. | Patrick. | Nine daughters. Several of them were married. |

| John, eldest son, succeeded his father, Major John, in 1754. He was killed at the battle of Quebec, in April 1760. | David Maxwell of Cardoness. He was created a Baronet, 9th June 1804. He married, in 1770, Henrietta, daughter of his uncle, David Maxwell of Cairnsmore, and had issue. Sir David died in 1825, and was succeeded by his eldest surviving son. | Christopher, Lieut.-Colonel 30th Regiment. | Henrietta, married her cousin, David Maxwell of Cardoness. |

| William, drowned in in his passage to Minorca, 17th Feb. 1801, unmarried. | Sir David, second Baronet; born, 18th June 1773; married, 9th December 1806, Georgina, daughter of Samuel Martin, of the island of Antigua. She died 9th June 1847. Sir David was Deputy-Lieutenant of the stewartry of Kirkcudbright, and Hon. Col. of the Galloway Rifles. He died, 13th November 1860, leaving issue. | John, born 2d December 1774; died, 30th March 1792. | Christopher, late Lieut.-Col. 30th Regiment; born in 1779; married Miss Douglas, daughter of James Douglas of Orchardton; died 1853. | Nicholas, a daughter, died, unmarried, 1853. | Agnes, married to Alexander Blair, W.S., Edinburgh; died in 1809, leaving issue. | Harriet, married to Andrew Watson; died, 1851. | Grace, married to William Cunninghame; died in 1826. |

| Sir William Maxwell, third and present Baronet; born, 13th February 1809; succeeded his father, 13th November 1860; married, 1st, on 28th January 1841, Mary, daughter of the late John Sprot, of London, and had issue—two sons and one daughter. She died 24th February 1846. He married, 2dly, on 6th February 1851, Louisa-Maria, eldest daughter of Geoffrey J. Shakerley, and had issue—four daughters. She died, 22d November 1856. | John, born 26th May 1812; died 29th April 1832. | Grace-Savage, died 23d June 1837. Harriet, died 29th March 1827. | Georgina-Isabella, married, 1st September 1853, to John Rutherford Russell, M.D. |

| David, born 25th March 1842. Captain in the 15th Hussars. | William-Francis, born 19th June 1844. | Mary-Grace, married, 23d August 1866, to Sir William Gordon, Bart., of Earlston. | Louisa-Maria. Georgina-Eleanor. | Letitia-May. Alice-Maude. |

Armorial Bearings: Quarterly; 1st, argent, an eagle displayed with two heads, sable, for Maxwell of Nithsdale; 2d, azure, a gable-end of a Gothic church, with a cross at the top, and a Gothic leaded window, argent, as patron of Anworth; 3d, argent, a saltire sable within a bordure counter-compony of the second and first; 4th, argent, a bend, azure; the whole within a bordure, embattled, gules.

Supporters: A lion and a stag, proper.

Crest: A man's head, affrontée, within two laurel branches in orle, proper.

Motto: Think on.

THE TOMB OF MARGARET, COUNTESS OF DOUGLAS,
IN LINCLUDEN COLLEGE.

ARMORIAL STONES ON THE TOMB OF MARGARET COUNTESS OF DOUGLAS
IN LINCLUDEN COLLEGE.

alaide: de dieu

hic iacet dūa margareta:
regis: leonie: filia: quodā
comitissa de douglas:
dūa: galwidie: et: vallis
annandie

INSCRIPTION ON THE TOMB OF MARGARET COUNTESS OF DOUGLAS
IN LINCLUDEN COLLEGE.

ARMORIAL BEARINGS OF THE DOUGLAS FAMILY

IN LINCLUDEN COLLEGE.

ARMORIAL BEARINGS IN LINCLUDEN COLLEGE.

ARMORIAL STONES IN THE OUTSIDE WALLS,
OF LINCLUDEN COLLEGE.

ARMORIAL BEARINGS ON HILLS CASTLE.

ROYAL ARMS OF SCOTLAND.

2. MAXWELL OF HILLS.

SIR JOHN MAXWELL
LORD HERRIES.

4. EDWARD MAXWELL
AND AGNES MAXWELL.

5. EDWARD MAXWELL AND JANET CARSANE.

ARMORIAL STONE IN THE TOWER OF ISLE OF CARLAVEROCK, &c.

EDWARD MAXWELL OF ISLE AND HELEN DOUGLAS, 1622.

STONE ABOVE THE DOOR OF DRUMCOLTRAN.

Lightning Source UK Ltd.
Milton Keynes UK
UKOW06f0901271013

219880UK00009B/201/P

9 781845 301408